Microsoft® SQL Server™ 2005 Reporting Services Step by Step

Stacia Misner;
Hitachi Consulting

PUBLISHED BY
Microsoft Press
A Division of Microsoft Corporation
One Microsoft Way
Redmond, Washington 98052-6399

Library of Congress Control Number 2006921725

Printed and bound in the United States of America.

1 2 3 4 5 6 7 8 9 QWE 1 0 9 8 7 6

Distributed in Canada by H.B. Fenn and Company Ltd.

A CIP catalogue record for this book is available from the British Library.

Microsoft Press books are available through booksellers and distributors worldwide. For further information about international editions, contact your local Microsoft Corporation office or contact Microsoft Press International directly at fax (425) 936-7329. Visit our Web site at www.microsoft.com/mspress. Send comments to mspinput@microsoft.com.

Acquisitions Editor: Ben Ryan
Project Editor: Denise Bankaitis
Technical Editor: Robert Hogan
Copy Editor: William Evan Gelder
Indexer: John Lewis

Body Part No. X11-82270

Table of Contents

Part II Authoring Reports

Part III Managing the Report Server

Introduction

Microsoft Reporting Services is the component of Microsoft SQL Server 2005 that adds a server-based reporting solution to the Microsoft business intelligence framework. The goal of this book is to guide you through the installation of Reporting Services and through each stage of the reporting life cycle so that you can easily create, manage, and share reports in your organization. In support of this goal, step-by-step exercises are included to give you the opportunity to explore Reporting Services with confidence. When you complete these exercises, you'll be ready to tackle real-world reporting challenges!

To help you learn the many features of Reporting Services, this book is organized into five parts. Part I, "Getting Started with Reporting Services," explains how the components of Reporting Services fully support the reporting life cycle, shows you how to install these components, and provides you with a hands-on introduction to the reporting life cycle. Part II, "Authoring Reports," starts by showing you how to build simple reports, then gradually introduces advanced techniques to teach you how to use Reporting Services features to satisfy a variety of reporting requirements. Part III, "Managing the Report Server," covers all of the activities that you need to perform when managing the reporting environment. Part IV, "Delivering Reports," describes the many ways that you can use Reporting Services to provide reports to the user community. Part V, "Programming Reporting Services," introduces how to use Reporting Services as a development platform for custom applications that author, manage, or deliver reports.

Finding Your Best Starting Point

Although the range of topics addressed in this book is comprehensive, this book also caters to readers with varying skills who are involved in one or more stages of the reporting life cycle. Accordingly, you can choose to read only the chapters that apply to the stages of the reporting cycle for which you are responsible and skip the remaining chapters. To find the best place to start, use the following table.

If you are	Follow these steps
An information worker or analyst who develops reports	**1.** Install the sample files as described in "Installing and Using the Sample Files." **2.** Work through Part I to get an overview of Reporting Services and to install the product on your computer. **3.** Complete Part II to develop the necessary skills to author reports. **4.** Review the chapters that interest you in Part IV to understand how reports are accessed by users and how to use Report Builder as an alternative for report development.

If you are	Follow these steps
An administrator who maintains server resources	1. Install the sample files as described in "Installing and Using the Sample Files." 2. Complete Part I to understand the technologies used by Reporting Services and to install the product on your computer. 3. Complete Part III to learn how to manage and secure content on the server and how to configure and manage server components.
An information consumer who uses reports to make decisions	1. Install the sample files as described in "Installing and Using the Sample Files." 2. Complete Chapter 2 to install the product on your computer. 3. Work through Part IV to discover how to retrieve and save reports, how to subscribe to reports, and how to use Report Builder to develop your own reports.
A programmer who develops applications with reporting functionality	1. Install the sample files as described in "Installing and Using the Sample Files." 2. Work through Part I to get an overview of Reporting Services and install the product on your computer. 3. Skim Parts II–IV to understand the functionality that is included in Reporting Services. 4. Work through one or more chapters that interest you in Part V to explore specific areas of customization.

About the Companion CD-ROM

The CD that accompanies this book contains the sample files that you need to follow the step-by-step exercises throughout the book. For example, in Chapter 3, "Building Your First Report," you use a sample file that contains a SQL query so you don't have to type in the query yourself. In other chapters, you use Microsoft Visual Studio solution files that have reports or programs created for you as starting points in preparation for adding other features to the reports or programs. These sample files allow you to build on what you've learned rather than spend time setting up the prerequisites for an exercise.

System Requirements

To install Reporting Services and to use the samples provided on the companion CD, your computer configuration will need to meet the following requirements:

- Microsoft Windows 2000, Windows XP Professional, or Windows Server 2003 with the latest service pack installed.
- Microsoft SQL Server 2005, Developer or Enterprise Edition with any available service packs installed and using Windows or Mixed Mode authentication. Refer to the

Operating System Requirements listed at *http://msdn2.microsoft.com/en-us/library/ms143506(en-US,SQL.90).aspx* to determine which edition is compatible with your operating system.

- Microsoft Internet Explorer 6.0 SP1 or later.
- Microsoft Internet Information Services (IIS) 5.0 or later.

The step-by-step exercises in this book and the accompanying practice files were tested using Windows XP Professional and Microsoft SQL Server 2005 Developer Edition. If you're using another version of the operating system or a different edition of either application, you might notice some slight differences.

Installing and Using the Sample Files

The sample files require approximately 140 MB of disk space on your computer. To install and prepare the sample files for use with the exercises in this book, follow these steps:

1. Remove the CD-ROM from its package at the back of this book and insert it into your CD-ROM drive.

> **Note** If the presence of the CD-ROM is automatically detected and a Start window is displayed, you can skip to Step 4.

2. Click the Start button, click Run, and then type **D:\startcd** in the Open box, replacing the drive letter with the correct letter for your CD-ROM drive if necessary.
3. Click Install Sample Files to launch the Setup program, and then follow the directions on the screen.

   The sample files will be copied from the CD-ROM to your local hard drive. The default installation folder is C:\Documents and Settings\<username>\My Documents\Microsoft Press\rs2005sbs, where <username> is the login name you use to operate your computer. You can change this installation folder to a different location and reference the new location when working through the exercises. For each chapter that uses sample files, you will find a corresponding folder in the rs2005sbs folder. You'll be instructed where to find the appropriate sample files when an exercise requires the use of an existing file.

> **Tip** In the C:\Documents and Settings\<username>\My Documents\Microsoft Press\rs2005sbs\Answers folder, you will find a separate folder for each chapter in which you make changes to the sample files. The files in these folders are copies of these sample files when you complete a chapter. You can refer to these files if you want to preview the results of completing all exercises in a chapter.

4. Remove the CD-ROM from the drive when installation is complete.

Now that you've completed installation of the sample files, you need to follow some additional steps to prepare your computer to use these files. You start by setting up fictional user accounts and groups.

5. Click Start, right-click My Computer, and then click Manage.

> **Important** Do *not* create these accounts on a production server. It is recommended that you work through the exercises in this book on a test or development server. If you don't plan to perform the exercises in Chapter 10, "Managing Security," or Chapter 14, "Managing Subscriptions," you can skip to Step 18.

6. Expand Local Users and Groups, right-click the Users folder, and then click New User.
7. Type **EuropeDirector** in the User Name, Password, and Confirm Password boxes to create a new account, and then click Create.
8. Repeat the previous step to create the following accounts: **PacificDirector**, **NADirector**, and **SalesAnalyst**.
9. Click Close.
10. Right-click the Groups folder, and then click New Group.
11. Type **AWSalesDirector** in the Group Name box, and then click Add.
12. In the text box, type **EuropeDirector;PacificDirector;NADirector**.
13. Click OK to close all dialog boxes.
14. Right-click the Groups folder, and then click New Group.
15. Type **AWSalesAnalyst** in the Group Name box, and then click Add.
16. In the text box, type **SalesAnalyst**.
17. Click OK to close all dialog boxes.
18. Click Start, click Run, and then type **C:\Documents and Settings\<username>\My Documents\Microsoft Press\rs2005sbs\Setup\Restore\restore_databases.cmd** in the Open box.

    This step attaches the SQL Server databases that are the data sources for the reports that you will create and use throughout this book. It also creates the user logins and user tables that are used for demonstrating security and subscriptions.

19. Open SQL Server Management Studio, connect to Analysis Services, right-click the Databases folder, select Restore, type **rs2005sbs** in the Restore Database box, click Browse, type **C:\Documents and Settings\<username>\My Documents\Microsoft Press \rs2005sbs\Setup\Database** in the Selected Path box, type **rs2005sbs.abf** in the File Name box, and then click OK twice.

This step restores the database that is used to demonstrate how to use an Analysis Services database as a data source for a report.

You're now ready to get started!

Conventions and Features in This Book

To use your time effectively, be sure that you understand the stylistic conventions that are used throughout this book. The following list explains these conventions:

- Hands-on exercises for you to follow are presented as lists of numbered steps (1, 2, and so on).
- Text that you are to type appears in **bold** type.
- Properties that you need to set in Visual Studio or in Report Manager are sometimes displayed in a table as you work through steps.
- Pressing two keys at the same time is indicated by a plus sign between the two key names, such as Alt+Tab when you need to hold down the Alt key while pressing the Tab key.
- A note that is labeled as **Note** is used to give you more information about a specific topic.
- A note that is labeled as **Important** is used to point out information that can help you avoid a problem.
- A note that is labeled as **Tip** is used to convey advice that you might find useful when using Reporting Services.

Part I
Getting Started with Reporting Services

In this part:

The chapters in Part I provide a broad introduction to Microsoft SQL Server 2005 Reporting Services (Reporting Services). This chapter explains reporting and how Reporting Services supports this function. Chapter 2, "Installing Reporting Services," shows you how to install the components and explains the implication of decisions that you must make as you create your reporting environment. In Chapter 3, "Building Your First Report," you get your first hands-on experience with the reporting life cycle to prepare for examining Reporting Services components in greater detail throughout the remainder of this book.

Chapter 1

Understanding Reporting

After completing this chapter, you will be able to:

- Understand the purpose of enterprise and ad hoc reporting.
- Recognize the characteristics of a reporting platform.
- List the constituents of reporting user communities.
- Describe the stages of the reporting life cycle.
- List the features and components of Microsoft SQL Server 2005 Reporting Services.

In this chapter, you see what enterprise reporting and ad hoc reporting are all about, as well as how they differ from other types of reporting. You also review how different groups within your organization need to use or support reporting and how they participate in the reporting life cycle. With this foundation, you'll better understand how the various components of Reporting Services fully support the reporting needs of your organization.

Reporting Scenarios

Since you're reading this book, it's likely that you work for a company that needs to be able to share information. Whether your company is small or large, can you imagine what would happen if employees couldn't access the information they need to do their jobs? The decisions that each individual employee makes during the course of his daily tasks have a profound impact on successful business operations and rely on easy and regular access to information.

One way that a company commonly shares information is through enterprise reports. For the purposes of this book, an *enterprise report* is considered to be the presentation of information that is formally distributed to some or all individuals across an enterprise, or even to individuals outside the enterprise. This information can be presented in a variety of formats, for example, as a Microsoft Excel spreadsheet or a text document. It can also be delivered as a printed report or sent to a list of recipients as an e-mail attachment. Information can also be made available in a central location, such as on a Web page on a corporate intranet or embedded in a portal where users can access reports when needed.

Sometimes a company needs a less formal way of creating and sharing information, especially if business dynamics are changing rapidly and there's a need to provide quick access to current information to a small group. In this situation, it's less important to adhere to presentation standards, yet the quality of information must be consistent with traditional enterprise reports. These *ad hoc reports* tend to be simpler than enterprise reports in terms of data content and presentation features, and are usually based on standard nontechnical representations, or *models*, of underlying data sources. A business person should be able to create an ad hoc report without knowing how to write a relational query and without having to wait for technical assistance in order to pull together data to answer a new business question.

The diverse types of organizations that use reporting and the differences in their information needs make it difficult to compile a comprehensive list of all possible reporting scenarios. However, you can look at who is using the shared information to develop the following generalizations about reporting scenarios:

- *Internal reporting* is probably the most common enterprise reporting. This category of reporting involves the sharing of information within an organization across all levels of employees and usually involves standard departmental reports. For example, employees in the product warehouse might regularly receive detailed printed order reports every morning. Elsewhere in the company, managers might get a financial statement in an Excel workbook delivered as an e-mail attachment when the books are closed each month.
- *External reporting* can take many forms, but is defined as disseminating information to people outside an organization. This information might be printed and mailed, such as shareholder reports. Increasingly, companies are publishing annual reports as PDFs (Portable Document Format files) for interested parties. External reporting can even include the exchange of information between business systems, such as invoicing information sent to a customer's receivables system electronically.

You can also consider how the information is being accessed to develop the following additional generalizations:

- *Standard reporting* relies on a central storage location that can display a list of contents or a catalog of the available reports so users can find the reports they need. Usually, security is applied to report storage to control the reports that individual users can see. Reports might be organized in a proprietary reporting platform repository or some other type of document management system.
- *Ad hoc reporting* depends on the availability of a model that allows users to select which data elements should be included in a report, along with a designer tool that allows them to arrange the layout of these elements to produce a simple report. These reports might be saved to a central repository to share with others or they might be stored on the user's local hard drive for personal reference.
- *Embedded reporting* is the integration of reports into portals and in-house or third-party applications. For example, many companies are migrating to Web-based line-of-business applications for accounting and payroll functions. Instead of building reporting processes into these applications, these companies can leverage an extensible enterprise reporting platform to allow users to access information by using these applications.

These reporting scenarios have the following two characteristics in common:

- **Central storage** Reports or report models (for ad hoc reporting) are accessed from a central location. Reports might also be delivered directly to users from a central server. Many people need access to the same information, possibly in different formats. Often, access to information needs to be limited to those with a need to know.
- **Standardization** Enterprise reports conform to a standard design with a consistent layout, while ad hoc reports conform to a standard data model to ensure consistent results.

In addition, the proliferation of information that can (or should) be available to the average worker has led to increasingly more sophisticated requirements for an enterprise reporting solution. For example, users need to be able to do the following:

- Navigate easily within a large report.
- Move from one report to another while maintaining context.
- Access previous versions of a report to compare information at different points in time.
- View data consolidated from multiple sources into a single report.

An enterprise reporting solution also needs to satisfy administrative requirements. A reporting platform should have the following characteristics:

- Flexibility to store a single report from which multiple versions may be generated based on changeable parameters or user profiles.
- Ability to support a push-pull paradigm, in which users can seek out the information they need online or subscribe to information that is sent to them on a periodic basis.
- Capability to manage reports using a Web interface so that administrators can perform tasks without being tied to their desks.

Reporting User Communities

Many people within an organization are usually involved in some aspect of reporting. Typically, users are members of one or more of the following communities: information consumers, information explorers, and analysts.

Most users—typically 65–80 percent of the total user population—are information consumers. Information consumers usually view static and predefined reports. If they use printed reports, they might get them the old-fashioned way—someone does a batch print of hard copy reports, then sends it out or delivers it to each recipient's in-box. A more technically oriented environment might make a document repository available, providing the electronic equivalent of a file cabinet that information consumers can access at will. In some cases, information consumers need to receive reports on a recurring basis, such as a weekly update on key performance measurements. Some of these users might want to produce their own simpler reports when an existing report doesn't answer a particular question.

One of the many strengths of Reporting Services is its ability to provide easy access to a wide array of predefined reports, making information consumers a key audience served by Reporting Services. Although many people might prefer to view information online, they can still get printed reports or can get reports delivered via e-mail. In either case, reports can be processed on demand (where information is as current as the data in the source system) or on a scheduled basis (where information represents a specific point in time). For maximum flexibility, an information consumer can choose from a variety of formats that can be delivered to a range of devices. Finally, Reporting Services provides ad hoc reporting capabilities so information consumers can obtain quick answers as needed.

Information explorers typically constitute 15–25 percent of the user population. Like information consumers, they use predefined reports, but they also interact with reports. For example, information explorers commonly use filters to isolate segments of data. Information explorers might also interact with reports by starting with summary information and then moving to more granular levels of detail, whether drilling down to view details in the same report or drilling across to view related information in a separate report.

Interactive reports suitable for information explorers require more work to develop than static reports, but Reporting Services has a wide array of features to support the development of these reports. Parameters can be designed into a report to support filtering data at the source or in the report. An information explorer can change parameter values on demand, or an administrator can predefine specific parameters for different groups of information explorers. Reports can also include dynamic visibility to support drilling down or actions to support drilling across.

The smallest user community, typically representing 5–10 percent of users, includes analysts. This group possesses the skills to develop free-form reports that facilitate complex data analysis. Such reports are often in spreadsheet form; through them, analysts can enhance the data with sophisticated calculations, such as linear regressions and allocations. These reports can eventually be shared with information consumers and information explorers.

Out of the box, Reporting Services supports analytical needs by providing the ability to export a report to Excel. Conversely, an Excel workbook created by an analyst can be uploaded to Reporting Services as a resource to be shared with the rest of the user community. Also, because Reporting Services is an extensible architecture, a custom application or third-party plug-in can give analysts complete flexibility to develop free-form reports within the Reporting Services environment.

The Enterprise Reporting Life Cycle

The *enterprise reporting life cycle* is a three-stage process through which a report progresses from authoring to management to delivery. A reporting platform must not only serve the needs of each reporting community, but must also fully support each stage of the reporting life cycle. It should also provide the architecture, functionality, and utilities to support the activities of authoring, managing, and delivering reports. In other words, everything you need from the beginning to the end of the reporting process should be in one integrated product set. Reporting Services provides just that.

Authoring

The primary activities of the authoring stage include defining the data to be presented in a report, organizing the data into a structured layout, and applying formatting to enhance the report's appearance. For example, when executive management needs to monitor sales performance across product lines, a report author can create either an enterprise report or an ad hoc report to present sales data in a table layout. To facilitate analysis, however, the report author might use conditional formatting to highlight products for which performance exceeds defined performance goals or fails to meet these goals. This advanced formatting technique is an enterprise reporting activity.

To support authoring, Reporting Services provides a broad set of features to present data in structures, such as tables and charts, to group data within these structures, to allow calculations, and to add formatting. This reporting platform also facilitates access to a variety of organizational data sources, such as online transaction processing (OLTP) systems or data warehouses that store relational or online analytical processing (OLAP) data. Reporting Services allows an enterprise report author to easily combine data from multiple sources into a single report. All types of structured data are supported for enterprise reports—relational, hierarchical, and multidimensional data. To access data sources not explicitly supported by Reporting Services, custom data processing extensions can be added, which means the possibilities are endless.

In addition, Reporting Services allows the report author to design a report with consideration for its purpose. An ad hoc report author can add interactive sorting and apply filtering to a report, while an enterprise report author has access to a rich feature set that enables the development of both static and interactive reports for the full spectrum of the user community. For example, static enterprise reports, such as print-ready invoices for mailing, or interactive online reports, such as the presentation of key performance indicators accessible from the corporate portal, can be quickly and easily developed. Interactive reports that factor in how users need to explore and analyze data can also be designed. Parameters, dynamic visibility, and actions can be used individually or in combination to affect both the information visible in an enterprise report and the information's appearance.

Management

The management stage begins when a report or ad hoc reporting model is published to a server. This stage continues with the organization of the report or model with other content on the server and the performance of other administrative tasks, such as setting report properties, managing report execution, and applying security. Either a report author or an administrator is responsible for publishing a report to a centrally managed server. When the report is on the server, a report execution schedule can be established to update the report regularly, such as every Monday morning. In addition, security is applied to the report so that only certain users, perhaps executive management, can view the report.

Reporting Services provides mechanisms to publish reports and models to a central server through the authoring tool or through management tools. Once a report is online, security can be implemented to control access. Further, the execution of reports is configurable so that reports can be produced on demand or on a scheduled basis. Reporting Services includes all this functionality using a server infrastructure that can exist on a single server or be distributed across many servers or incorporated into a Web farm.

Access and Delivery

The access and delivery stage includes all activities related to the distribution of reports from a central repository, such as accessing reports online, rendering reports to various formats, saving and printing reports, and subscribing to reports. Some users, for instance, might choose to receive reports via e-mail as soon as these reports are executed each week or to receive a notification that a report is available for viewing online. Other users, by contrast, might prefer to view the reports online using the company intranet only as the need for information arises.

To support delivery, Reporting Services can produce reports using a variety of output formats which are referred to as rendering formats. A report can be made available through the intranet using a Web browser, or it can be sent embedded in an e-mail message or as an e-mail attachment in many formats, such as PDF or Excel. Reporting Services also provides flexible delivery mechanisms to support both push and pull distribution methods for internal and external users. Because Reporting Services is an extensible system, you can add rendering formats, different security frameworks, or alternative delivery options. In addition, the access or delivery of reports can be integrated into corporate applications.

Reporting Services Components

The requirements of a solid enterprise reporting solution are formidable, but Reporting Services meets this challenge with a set of integrated, multitiered components. Because Reporting Services is a Microsoft .NET-based platform that can use both a Web service and an application programming interface (API), it can be customized to fit within existing technical infrastructures. Furthermore, by separating components into discrete functional units, the Reporting Services architecture can be scaled to accommodate even the largest organization by distributing components across several servers. (You learn how to install these components in Chapter 2, "Installing Reporting Services.") Together, these components support the authoring, management, access, and delivery requirements of a reporting platform.

The Reporting Services architecture consists of three layers. The application layer includes two different client components for authoring–one to author enterprise reports, and the other to author ad hoc reports. The application layer also includes a client component for managing one or more Report Servers within a single server management interface, and a server component called Report Manager, which is installed on a Web server and used for report access and for some server management tasks. The server layer is the Report Server where all the processing and management of the reporting platform occurs. The data layer includes data providers to access data sources used in reports, as well as a pair of databases for the storage of reports and information used by Report Server. These components can be installed on a single server or distributed across several servers. The Reporting Services components are illustrated in the following figure:

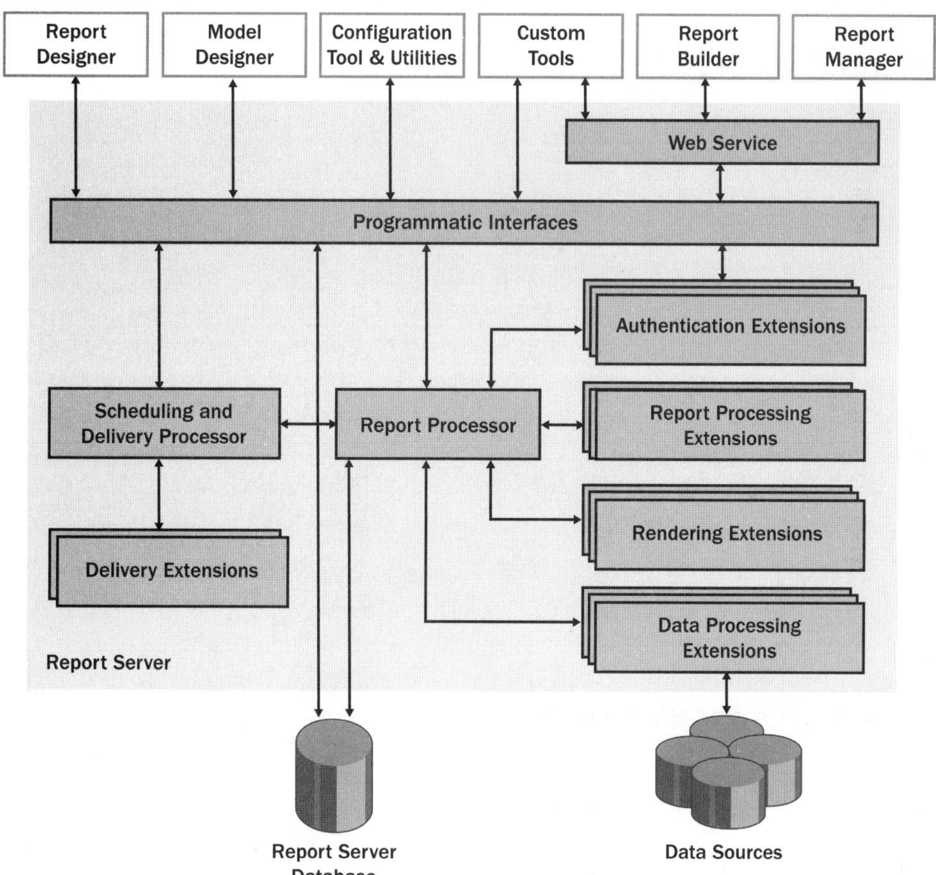

Authoring Components

When Reporting Services is installed, a client component called Report Designer is added as a set of templates to the Microsoft Visual Studio 2005 development environment. If you don't have this version of Visual Studio installed, installation of Reporting Services will also install the requisite components so you can use Report Designer.

The easiest way to build enterprise reports is to use the Report Designer templates. If you're a report author, you don't need to have programming skills to effectively use this tool. However, if you're already an experienced programmer, you can also take advantage of the programmatic interfaces to build a custom authoring tool.

Report Builder is a thin client application that installs on your computer when you first launch this application through Report Manager or by accessing its URL on the Report Server. Report Builder is used for ad hoc reporting and, like Report Designer, does not require programming skills to create useful reports. In fact, you don't even need to know how to write a query to access data, since the query is written for you based on the items you select from the report model, which is created using Model Designer, another client component that is added to the Visual Studio environment.

Report Designer

As an enterprise report author, you can use a graphical interface to build feature-rich reports using drag-and-drop techniques to create a query to retrieve data and to define the layout and appearance of data in the report. You can use ActiveX Data Objects (ADO) .NET-managed data providers to access many OLE DB and Open Database Connectivity (ODBC) data sources. If you need access to other data sources, you can build your own data providers. After defining a query to retrieve data from a selected data source, you use Report Designer to place data into one or more structures. You also use Report Designer to apply calculations to the data, as well as to access a complete set of features that support presentation options such as formatting and visibility. The result is a report definition in the form of an XML document using a nonproprietary schema known as Report Definition Language (RDL). You learn about Report Designer and Report Definition Language in Chapter 4, "Developing Basic Reports."

Report Designer also includes a preview version of the functionality used by the server to produce reports, so you can test a report before putting it on the server. That way, you can get an idea of how the users will see the report while you're still developing it. When you're ready to publish the report to the server, you use the Visual Studio build and deploy processes.

Report Builder

If you're an ad hoc report author, you employ a separate graphical interface to build simple reports by using drag-and-drop techniques to retrieve data from a single source and to define the layout and appearance of data in the report. Instead of defining a data source and building a query, as you do with Report Designer, you select a report model, which contains the data connection, metadata, and data relationships needed to produce and execute a query. In the current release of Report Builder, a report model can only access relational data in a SQL Server database. If you use the Standard, Enterprise, or Developer Edition, you can also access multidimensional data in an Analysis Services database. After selecting a report model, you select a table, matrix, or chart template, which becomes the structure into which you place data fields defined by the report model. You can also use Report Builder to add your own calculations, sort or filter data, and apply formatting, such as font colors or styles. You can view the report within Report Builder and, if you want to share it with other users of Reporting Services, you can publish the report to the server. You learn about Report Builder in Chapter 15, "Creating Reports with Report Builder."

Model Designer

The report model on which Report Builder depends is created using the Model Designer interface. You begin development of the report model by specifying a data source and specifying which tables and their relationships to use from that data source. Then you use a wizard to generate a report model, which will become the business description of the underlying data. You can make changes to the names of objects generated in the model, rearrange and organize these objects to simplify the users' navigation in the model, and remove unneeded objects. You learn about Report Builder in Chapter 8, "Building Report Models."

Programmatic Interface for Authoring

Using the Reporting Services API, application developers can build custom applications to create reports or add functionality to reports. In Chapter 16, "Report Authoring with Custom Development," you learn how to use custom code to extend the authoring capabilities of Reporting Services and how to generate RDL files programmatically.

Management Components

After you've installed Reporting Services, you can use the Reporting Services Configuration tool to set or modify configuration settings. The Report Manager is installed on a Web server and used for both management and for access and delivery tasks. Report management capabilities are also accessible in Microsoft SQL Server Management Studio. All of the tasks you can perform using Report Manager can also be performed within this management component if it's installed on your local computer. Additionally, Reporting Services provides command-line utilities for specific server management tasks. You also have the option to build your own Windows or Web-based management tools using the Reporting Services API.

Reporting Services Configuration Tool

The Reporting Services Configuration tool allows you to configure local or remote instances of Reporting Services. This tool is a client application you can employ to manage virtual directories used by the report server and Report Manager, define Windows accounts to run the Web and Windows services, create the report server database, manage encryption keys to protect report server data, and configure Simple Mail Transfer Protocol (SMTP) settings. Typically, you configure these settings once after installation, but as your reporting environment changes, you can use this tool to update the report server configuration.

Report Manager

Report Manager is a Web-based content management tool included with Reporting Services. Reporting Services separates administrative tasks into two main groups: content management and system management. If you're an administrator responsible for content management, you can use Report Manager to manage how reports are organized on the Report Server and how users interact with those reports. Content management using Report Manager is covered in more detail in Chapter 9, "Managing Content." As an administrator responsible for server resources and performance, you can use Report Manager to configure execution options (described in Chapter 9), to set security (described in Chapter 10, "Managing Security"), and to manage subscription and delivery options (described in Chapter 14, "Managing Subscriptions").

Microsoft SQL Server Management Studio

Microsoft SQL Server Management Studio is a new workstation component provided with Microsoft SQL Server 2005 as a single environment from which to administer any of the server components of SQL Server. This environment does not replace Report Manager, nor does it provide additional features. Instead, it gives you another way to perform the same activities. For example, you can manage content, configure security, and set options for report execution or subscriptions from the same management interface that you use to manage SQL Server or Analysis Services if you're responsible for administering these other server types. This interface can also be useful if you manage multiple report servers.

Command-Line Utilities

Reporting Services includes command-line utilities that allow you to manage a Report Server locally or from a remote location. The following command-line utilities are provided by Reporting Services for server administrators:

- **rsconfig** A connection management utility that can change the connection used by Report Server to connect to the ReportServer database.
- **rs** A script host that you can use to execute Microsoft Visual Basic .NET scripts for management tasks, such as publishing reports or copying data between ReportServer databases.
- **rskeymgmt** An encryption key management tool that you can use to back up encryption keys for future recovery of a database or to change encrypted data used by a Report Server.

You learn more about these utilities in Chapter 11, "Managing Server Components," except for the *rs* utility, which is discussed in Chapter 17, "Programming Report Server Management."

Programmatic Interface for Management

You can also use the Reporting Services API to perform server management activities, such as publishing or deleting reports. You can build your own application, or you can build Visual Basic .NET scripts to use in conjunction with the *rs* utility to perform administrative tasks on Report Server. You learn how to use the Reporting Services API for server management in Chapter 17.

Access and Delivery Components

The components of Reporting Services that are involved in the access and delivery of reports break down into two groups: client components and server components. You can choose to use the supplied client components or build your own client applications. However, you must use the core server components of Reporting Services, although you can use custom or third-party applications to extend the capabilities of the server components.

Report Manager

Report Manager is not just a management tool. The user community also uses Report Manager to access reports and subscribe to reports. You learn about general report access using Report Manager in Chapter 12, "Accessing Reports."

Processor Components

Report Server is the heart of Reporting Services. Although administrators interact with Report Server using the management components, the bulk of activity that occurs on Report Server is related to supporting the access and delivery of reports. Report Server runs as a Web service, allowing Report Manager, your own custom programs, and third-party applications to access server processes.

Report Server uses Microsoft Internet Information Services (IIS) to receive requests, and then activates the applicable subcomponents in response to the requests. There are two processor subcomponents of Report Server that act as command central to manage these requests and the corresponding output returned by the other subcomponents. The core processor, Report Processor, handles all requests related to the execution of reports and the production of the final output. To complete these requests, the Report Processor calls other subcomponents, referred to as *extensions*, to handle data processing, rendering, and security. The Scheduling and Delivery Processor responds to scheduled events and delivers reports. This processor uses delivery extensions to send reports to their destinations.

Report Processor The Report Processor is responsible for retrieving the report layout from the report definition and merging it with data returned from the query included in the report definition. At this point, the report is in an *intermediate format*. What happens next depends on the report request. If a user wants to see the report online, the intermediate format is passed to the appropriate rendering extension so the proper output format can be created, such as a Web page.

On the other hand, if the request is to generate a *report snapshot* (which is a report at a specific point in time), the intermediate format is stored in the ReportServer database. When a user requests the snapshot, the Report Processor retrieves the intermediate format, calls the rendering extension, and then sends the final format of the report to the user.

The Report Processor also manages requests for report models. These requests occur when a user browses a report model or runs a report in Report Builder, including drillthrough reports.

By separating the presentation processing from data retrieval and rendering, multiple users can view the same report at the same time, and each can change the viewing format. You learn more about execution options in Chapter 9.

Scheduling and Delivery Processor As its name implies, the Scheduling and Delivery Processor is responsible for running scheduled reports and for delivering reports to a location or a device on a scheduled basis. It uses SQL Server Agent to process schedules. When the applicable time arrives, SQL Server Agent sends instructions related to the schedule to the Scheduling and Delivery Processor. The report is rendered and passed to the delivery extension to send the report to specified recipients or a target location on a file share.

A report snapshot is an example of a scheduled report. The schedule information is specified by a user or administrator using Report Manager and stored in the ReportServer database. When the Scheduling and Delivery Processor finishes processing the snapshot, the intermediate format is stored in the ReportServer database. When a user wants to view the report, Report Server takes over by retrieving the intermediate format of the snapshot and calling the specified rendering extension to finalize the output. You learn more about scheduling reports in Chapter 9.

When users subscribe to reports, the desired delivery extension is selected and the time of delivery is specified. When the time comes to deliver a report, the Scheduling and Delivery Processor gets a rendered report and then passes the report to the applicable delivery extension. Delivery options for subscriptions are described in Chapter 14.

Server Extensions

Server extensions are used to perform specific functions. Reporting Services uses five different types of server extensions: authentication, data processing, report processing, rendering, and delivery. Over time, you can expect to see more extensions available for Reporting Services, whether developed by Microsoft or by other commercial software developers.

Authentication Extensions Authentication extensions are used to define the authorization model used by Reporting Services. Only one authentication extension is supplied, which supports Microsoft Windows and SQL Server security. You can, of course, create your own authentication extension to integrate Reporting Services with another security architecture.

Data Processing Extensions Data processing extensions are responsible for processing the query requests received from the Report Processor. The query request includes a data source, a query, and possibly, query parameters. The applicable data processing extension then opens a connection to the data source, returns a list of field names from the query, executes the query, and retrieves the query results, which are then returned to the Report Processor.

Reporting Services comes with six data processing extensions: SQL Server, Analysis Services, Oracle, OLE DB, ODBC, and XML. However, you can also use any ADO.NET data provider or build your own data processing extensions. You learn how to create a custom data processing extension in Chapter 16.

Report Processing Extensions Report processing extensions are used to process custom report items that may be embedded in a report. The Report Server already knows how to process standard report items, such as tables and text boxes, but if you add a custom report item—like a special gauge control or an embedded map from Microsoft MapPoint—then you need to provide an extension to handle the custom processing required by the new report item.

Rendering Extensions Rendering extensions are called by the Report Processor to take the data that was received from the data processing extension and merge that data with the report definition. The result is a finished report in a format specific to the device that will receive the report.

At the time of this writing, Reporting Services has the following rendering extensions: HTML, MHTML (MIME Encapsulation HTML), Excel, Acrobat PDF, CSV (comma separated values), and XML. As with other extension types, you can develop your own rendering extension to produce other output formats.

Delivery Extensions Reporting Services currently includes the following three delivery extensions:

- The e-mail delivery extension allows Reporting Services to embed a report in an e-mail message or send the report as an attachment. Alternatively, an e-mail notification can be sent that includes a link to the report. If the delivery is an e-mail notification, it can also be sent without the link to a pager, cellular phone, or any device that can receive a simple message.
- The file share delivery extension can be used to store reports in a centrally accessible location independent of the ReportServer database or as part of a report archive strategy.
- A null delivery provider is available for data-driven subscriptions to periodically load reports into the cache in advance of user viewing. This option is useful for reports that take a long time to execute.

You can also develop your own delivery extension to expand the delivery functionality of Reporting Services.

ReportServer Databases

Reporting Services centralizes report storage in two SQL Server databases. The ReportServer database stores information used to manage reports and resources, along with the reports themselves. In addition, this database is the storage location for security settings, encrypted data, data related to schedules and delivery, and information about extensions. The ReportServerTempDB database stores temporary data used for caching purposes. More information about these databases can be found in Chapter 11.

Programmatic Interface for Access and Delivery

You can use the Reporting Services API to create assemblies when you need to accommodate specialized security, data processing, rendering, or delivery scenarios. In Chapter 16, you learn how to build a custom data processing extension. The Reporting Services API also enables you to develop your own applications to allow users to view reports or to produce reports using different formats. You learn more about custom reporting in Chapter 18, "Building Custom Reporting Tools."

Chapter 1 Quick Reference

This term	Means this
Report	Information that is structured and formatted for print or online viewing.
Enterprise reporting	Sharing of information on a regular basis across a wide audience.
Ad hoc reporting	Reviewing, and possibly sharing, limited information with limited formatting requirements on an as-needed basis.
Enterprise reporting life cycle	The process of authoring, managing, and accessing reports.
Extensions	Subcomponents of Report Server used to provide specific functionality, such as data processing, rendering, report processing, authentication, and delivery.
Intermediate format	The result of merging data from a query with layout information from a report definition. The intermediate format is sent to a rendering extension to produce the final output, such as a Web page or an Excel file.
Report snapshot	A report that preserves a record of data at a point in time. A report snapshot is stored in the ReportServer database in its intermediate format and rendered only when a user requests the report.

Chapter 2

Installing Reporting Services

After completing this chapter, you will be able to:

- Select an edition and configuration of Reporting Services appropriate to your site.
- Prepare your technical infrastructure for a successful installation.
- Install Reporting Services.

In Chapter 1, "Understanding Reporting," you learned how the various components of Reporting Services combine to fully support enterprise reporting requirements. By understanding how each component functions and interacts with other components, you can better decide how to deploy Reporting Services in your organization. This chapter explains the available deployment options, reviews the prerequisites for installation, and walks you through an installation of Reporting Services.

Considering Deployment Options

To use Reporting Services to support the authoring, management, and delivery of reports, you need to install its components. But which components should you install–and where? Before you can start installing, you must understand how features compare across the five Reporting Services editions and how one or more servers can be configured to support Reporting Services. You also need to consider whether the existing naming conventions of your Web applications will influence the names that you assign to the virtual directories used by Report Server and Report Manager.

Choosing a Reporting Services Edition

Reporting Services is bundled with Microsoft SQL Server 2005, which is available in four separate editions (Express, Workgroup, Standard, and Enterprise). You can choose to implement any of the three corresponding Reporting Services editions for production–Workgroup Edition, Standard Edition, or Enterprise Edition. For development purposes, you can implement Developer Edition. Reporting Services is even available with SQL Server 2005 Express edition, which is useful for simple Web or client applications requiring basic reporting capabilities. If you're still evaluating Reporting Services, use the SQL Server 2005 Trial Software. You should understand the differences in features supported by each Reporting Services edition to make the proper selection. You can select from the following editions:

- **Workgroup Edition** Supports a single server configuration only. This edition does not support online analytical processing (OLAP) data sources, subscriptions, and many other features available in the Standard and Enterprise Editions. Rendering formats is limited to Excel, Portable Document Format (PDF), Image, remote graphics device interface (RGDI), Print, and Dynamic HTML (DHTML). Report Builder is supported using a SQL Server relational data source only. Use Workgroup Edition when you want an entry-level reporting solution for a branch office or departmental workgroup.
- **Standard Edition** Supports a single server configuration only. This edition does not support subscriptions that use a database query to set delivery options, known as *data-driven subscriptions*, and does not support scale-out deployment. Report Builder does not include the Infinite Clickthrough feature in this edition. Use Standard Edition when you have a limited number of users in a small-sized or medium-sized business.
- **Enterprise Edition** Supports a Web farm configuration that scales to satisfy high-volume reporting requirements and a large user population. Enterprise edition supports data-driven subscriptions as well as Infinite Clickthrough in Report Builder. This edition is required for deploying a large-scale reporting platform.
- **Developer Edition** Supports all features of Enterprise edition, but is licensed only for use in a development and test environment. If you're a developer who is building custom applications for Reporting Services, or if you need a separate environment for authoring reports or for viewing your reports on a test Report Server, use this edition.
- **Trial Software** Supports all features of the Enterprise edition, but expires after 180 days. You can use SQL Server 2005 Trial Software to explore all the features of Reporting Services before making a purchasing decision.

> **Note** When you decide to upgrade, you can simply install the Standard or Enterprise edition on the same server. You don't need to uninstall the Trial Software first. During the installation process, you're prompted for the name of the Report Server database. Just use the same database name that was created for use with the Evaluation edition, and you're all set!

Planning a Site Configuration

If you're using Express, Workgroup, or Standard editions, you must use the single server configuration for your Reporting Services deployment. You can use any of the other editions to deploy Reporting Services in a multiple server configuration. If you choose the multiple server configuration, remember that the Enterprise edition is the only edition licensed for production usage.

A single server deployment of Reporting Services requires only that you install Report Server and Report Manager on the same server. You have the option to install the Reporting Services databases on a local or remote SQL Server instance. However, the instance that you use must be either in the same domain or in a trusted domain. During the installation, when you select the SQL Server instance, you will also have an opportunity to supply a name for the main Reporting Services database. By default, the main database is named ReportServer and its companion database is named ReportServerTempDB. If you change the name of the main database, that name will be appended with TempDB to create a name for the companion database.

If you need a reporting platform that supports high availability or high volume, deploy Reporting Services in a multiple server configuration. In this configuration, multiple Report Servers run as a single virtual server with one set of Reporting Services databases supporting all Report Servers. This set of Reporting Services databases can be also be part of a SQL Server cluster, even if you don't cluster the Report Servers.

Note Reporting Services does not include tools to manage a Web farm, so you'll need to use Microsoft Application Center or third-party software to set one up and manage it. However, during installation of Reporting Services, you can add a Report Server to an existing Web farm.

Deciding Naming Conventions

In preparation for installation, you will need to consider the naming conventions that you will use for the Report Server and Report Manager virtual directories on the Web server. Users and administrators will access these virtual directories when they are using a browser to connect to Reporting Services. You can accept the default virtual directory names suggested during installation, or you can supply a different name if you prefer. If you decide to replace the default virtual directory names, use a virtual directory name that's 50 characters or fewer in length.

By default, the Report Server virtual directory is /ReportServer unless you're installing Report Server on a named instance, in which case the default virtual directory is /ReportServer$NamedInstance. For Report Manager, the default virtual directory is /Reports.

Preparing for Installation

Reporting Services has several prerequisites for installation. More specifically, each component of Reporting Services has certain software requirements that must be met for that component to be successfully installed. You need to understand how the operating system affects your installation options, what software must be installed prior to a Reporting Services installation, and how your technical environment needs to be configured.

Reviewing Operating System Requirements

The server and client components can be installed on any of the following operating systems: Microsoft Windows 2000 Server, Windows XP Professional, or Windows Server 2003. Of course, the latest service pack should be installed.

If you're using Windows Server 2003, you must configure the server as an Application Server for Microsoft Internet Information Services (IIS) and ASP.NET. To do so using Add Or Remove Programs in Control Panel, select the Application Server check box, and then click the Details button. Make sure that both the IIS and ASP.NET components are selected in the Application Server dialog box, click OK to close the dialog box, and then click Next to continue the update to the server configuration.

Reviewing Software Requirements

Regardless of whether you're using a single or multiple server configuration, you must install the server components, Report Server and Report Manager, on a Web server that is already running IIS 5.0 or later. It's possible to install these components on separate Web servers when using Enterprise Edition.

Each Web server on which you install Report Server or Report Manager must be configured to use the Microsoft .NET Framework version 2.0 or later. The Reporting Services installation process will automatically install and register ASP.NET in IIS if the .NET Framework is missing.

Reporting Services also requires a preexisting installation of SQL Server 2005. You must ensure that the latest service pack–if any–has been installed. The Reporting Services installation requires access to a SQL Server instance to create a ReportServer database that is used as a central repository for Reporting Services.

Note If you decide to install the server components on separate Web servers, you'll need to first install the ReportServer database independently to a SQL Server instance. You also need to install the ReportServer database first if you're using the Standard edition and separating the server components from the database components. After the ReportServer database is in place, you can install any of the other components in any order. You'll then need to specify the SQL Server instance hosting the ReportServer database during installation of the server components.

Reviewing Configuration Prerequisites

Additionally, the Setup process uses the IWAM_*computername* account to configure services on IIS. This account is enabled by default when IIS is installed, but is often disabled for security reasons. You'll need to make sure this account is enabled before starting the Reporting Services installation. You can disable the account again after the installation is complete.

During installation, virtual directories will be added in IIS to the Default Web Site. For the Reporting Services installation to successfully complete this task, the IP address of the Default Web Site must be set to the default value–(All Unassigned). In fact, the installation will fail if you have disabled the default site.

Note For installation of Reporting Services, you must enable the Default Web Site. If you choose not to use the default site site, it's still possible to move the virtual directories following the installation. You can use the Reporting Services Configuration Manager, which is discussed later in this chapter, to move these directories.

> **Note** Installation of Reporting Services will fail if you select the option to use Secure Sockets Layer (SSL) connections before the Web server is correctly configured for SSL. If necessary, you can bypass this step during installation and set up SSL on the Web server later. Then you'll need to set the *SecureConnectionLevel* value to 3 in the RSReportServer configuration file. Editing configuration files is discussed in Chapter 11, "Managing Server Components."

Creating Reporting Services Credentials

To install and run Reporting Services, you'll need to have one or more user accounts available to perform the following functions:

- **Log on to a SQL Server instance and install the Reporting Services databases** When you install Reporting Services, your account must be a member of the local system administrator's group. Your credentials are used by Setup for authentication on the SQL Server instance that will host the Reporting Services databases, ReportServer, and ReportServerTempDB. Your credentials are also used to install these databases to the SQL Server, so you'll need permissions to create and access databases.
- **Start the ReportServer service** This service primarily manages subscriptions and scheduled report executions. If you want to use either of these features, the service must be running. However, you can continue to use other Reporting Services features if this service is not running. During Reporting Services installation, you need to specify an account that will be used to start the ReportServer service. You can choose between a built-in account or a domain user account.

> **Important** If you're running Windows 2000 Server, Microsoft recommends that you use the Local System account, also known as the NT AUTHORITY/SYSTEM built-in account. Otherwise, you won't be able to use stored credentials or prompted credentials with external data sources. There are no similar restrictions if you're using Windows XP or Windows Server 2003. Any built-in account or domain user account can be used. (Using credentials with data sources is explained in Chapter 9, "Managing Content.")

- **Connect to the Reporting Services databases** The Report Server must be able to access the Reporting Services databases. You can create a dedicated user account for this purpose, either as a service account, a domain account, or a SQL Server login. During installation of Reporting Services, you must provide the credentials for this account. (If you choose to use a SQL Server login, this account will be created in the SQL Server instance if it doesn't already exist.) Setup will assign the account to the RSExecRole and public roles on the ReportServer, ReportServerTempDB, master, and msdb databases.

  If you choose to use a domain user account to connect to the Reporting Services databases, you must configure SQL Server Agent to use a user account in the same domain. The account used by SQL Server Agent does not need to be the same account used to connect to Reporting Services databases. Because schedules are created as SQL Server Agent jobs using the Report Server's domain account, SQL Server Agent needs permissions to access scheduled jobs owned by a domain account.

In this procedure, you'll add a service account that will be used for running the ReportServer service and for connecting to the Reporting Services databases.

Add a service account for Reporting Services

1. Open the Computer Management console.
2. Expand the *Local Users And Groups* node.
3. Right-click the Users folder and select New User.
4. Enter a user name: **ReportServer2005**.
5. Add a description: **Account used for running the SQL Server Reporting Services service**.
6. Provide a strong password.
7. Clear the User Must Change Password At Next Logon check box.
8. Select User Cannot Change Password.
9. Select Password Never Expires.

   The New User dialog box looks like this:

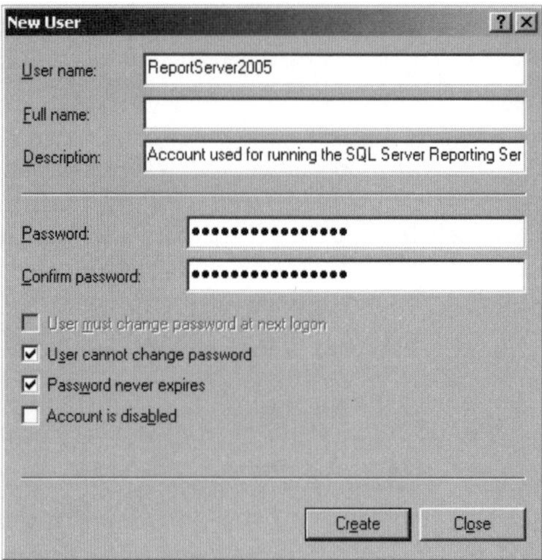

10. Click Create.
11. Click Close, and then close the Computer Management console.

Installing Reporting Services

You have the option to install Reporting Services using a setup wizard or by running a command-line executable. Setup can be launched from a CD, a local folder, or a file share that is specified using Universal Naming Convention (UNC) format. If you use the wizard, you select options on each page of the wizard to set property values for the installation. If you use the command-line executable, you can use command-line arguments or a template file to set property values. You must perform the installation locally, although you can choose which components to install if you're distributing components across several computers.

When using the setup wizard to install Reporting Services, you progress through a series of pages that are dependent on features you selected to install. If you install all components, you'll need to specify credentials for the ReportServer Windows service. When the setup wizard has finished with the installation, you'll need to use the Reporting Services Configuration Manager to complete the installation.

Launching Setup

The setup wizard steps you through the process of selecting components, providing credentials, and specifying other configuration settings needed to complete the Reporting Services installation. The pages of the wizard you see depend on the features that you choose to install.

Important If you plan to install Reporting Services on a Web server that is hosting Windows SharePoint Services, you'll need to perform several tasks after you install Reporting Services. These tasks include configuring SharePoint to avoid conflicts with Reporting Services, adding the session state module to SharePoint, and separating the application pools of each server in IIS. You can find detailed instructions at *http://msdn2.microsoft.com/en-us/library/ms159697.aspx*.

In this procedure, you'll launch the Reporting Services setup wizard.

Launch the setup wizard

1. Run Setup from the installation CD or a network share that contains the contents of the installation CD.

   When you run Setup, the first page that appears is the End User License Agreement.

2. After reviewing the agreement, select the I Accept The Licensing Terms And Conditions check box, and then click Next.

3. Review the required components on the Installing Prerequisites page, and then click Install.

The Installing Prerequisites portion of the installation may take several minutes. Click Next when installation of prerequisites is completed. On the SQL Server Installation Welcome page, click Next to start the System Configuration Check.

If the check is successful, then setup will continue. Otherwise, you'll need to stop and fix any listed problems. Click Next.

4. On the Registration Information page, type a Name and, optionally, a Company name, and then click Next.

   The Components To Install page is displayed:

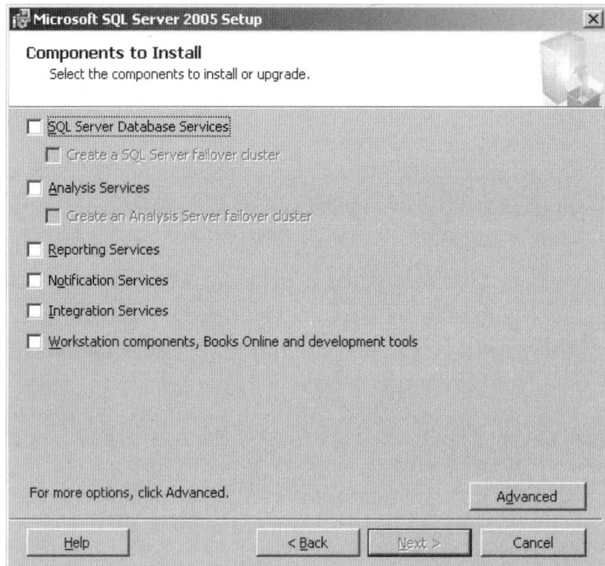

   Now you'll need to select the components you want to install.

Choosing the Components

Reporting Services includes several components that are installed on both client and server computers. These components include the Report Server, the Reporting Services databases, Report Manager, Report Designer, and several command prompt utilities for administrative tasks.

In this procedure, you'll add the Reporting Services Samples to the default selection of components to be installed.

Select components to install

1. Click the check box next to Reporting Services, and then click the check box next to Workstation Components, Books Online And Development Tools.

The dialog box now is shown here:

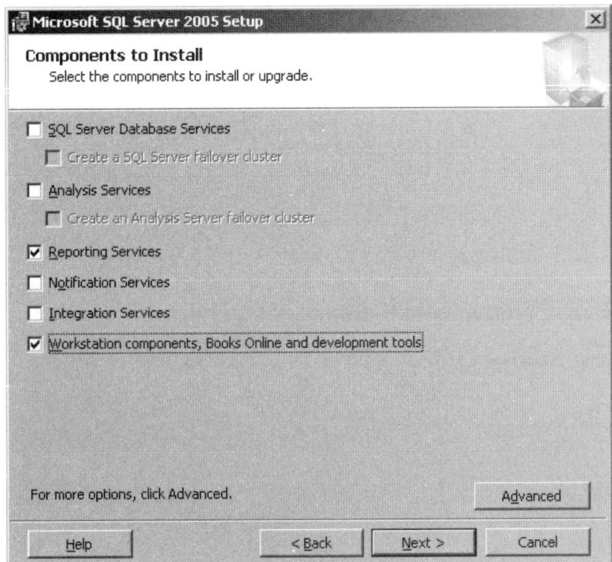

Note This book assumes that you have already installed SQL Server Database Services, Analysis Services, and Integration Services.

2. Click Advanced, click the plus sign next to Documentation, Samples, And Sample Databases, click the arrow next to Sample Databases, and select Entire Feature Will Be Installed On Local Hard Drive. Click the arrow next to Sample Code And Applications, and select Entire Feature Will Be Installed On Local Hard Drive.

Note You can skip this step if you don't want to use the samples that ship with SQL Server. You can always use Setup later to install the samples individually if you change your mind.

The Feature Selection page of the setup wizard is shown here:

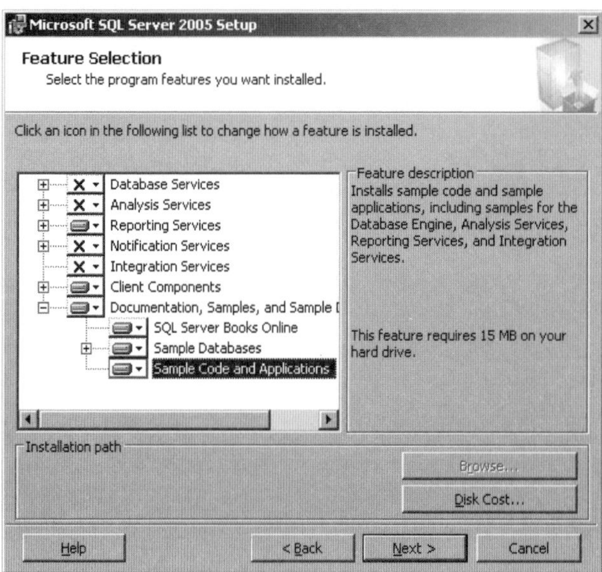

Notice that you can change the installation directory for some features. If you click a feature and the Browse button is unavailable, you're not allowed to change the location. Also, when you click a feature, the disk space required to install the selected feature is displayed. Use Disk Cost to see the total space required for all the features you selected to verify that you have enough space available in the specified installation locations.

3. Click Next.

   The Instance Name page of the setup wizard is shown here:

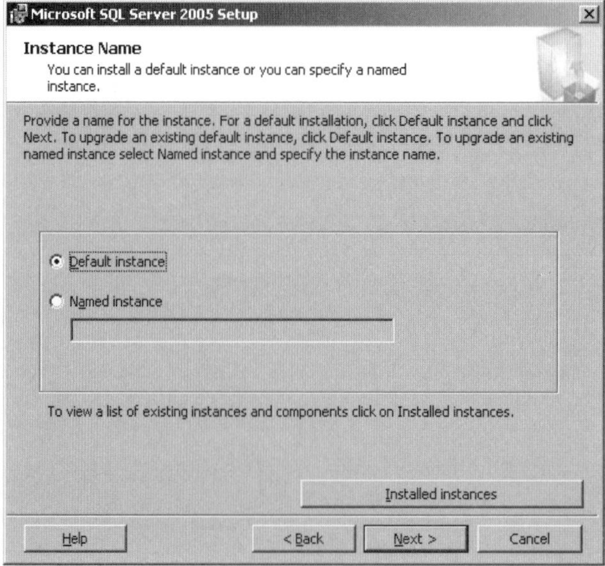

> **Note** This book assumes that you use the default instance. If you choose to create a named instance, you'll need to change server names and URL references accordingly when you perform the procedures throughout this book.

4. Click Next.

   The Existing Components page will list any components that you selected on the Feature Selection page. If you didn't choose any additional features, then this page will not be shown.

5. Click Next if required.

Selecting the Service Account

The SQL Server Reporting Services Windows service needs to run under a Local System or domain user account, as explained earlier in this chapter. If you're installing Reporting Services on Windows Server 2003, you can also choose to run the service using either the LocalService or NetworkService account. The options that you can choose from will depend on the operating system. You can also decide whether you want the service to automatically start when the server starts.

In this procedure, you'll assign the ReportServer2005 account as the service account for the Reporting Services Windows service.

Select a service account

1. On the Service Account page, click Use A Domain User Account.
2. Enter **ReportServer2005** as the user name, and then enter the account password that you created earlier and enter the domain name.

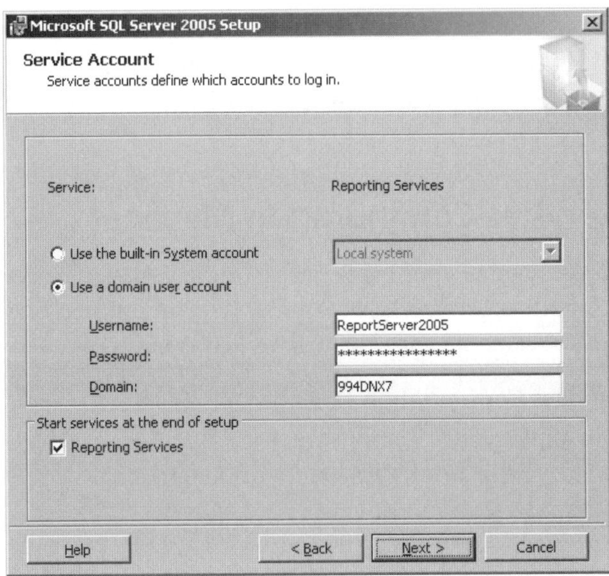

> **Note** If you need to change this account or its start options later, you can use the Services console.

3. Click Next.

   The Report Server Installation Options page of the setup wizard is shown here:

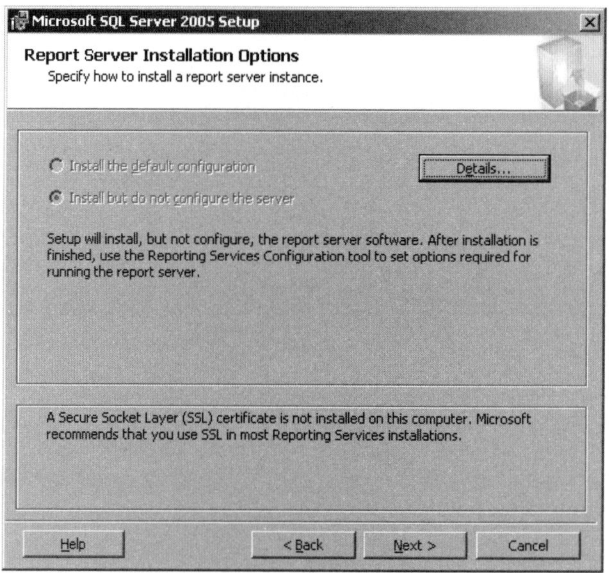

4. Click Next. On the Error and Usage Report Settings page, you can choose to send reports to Microsoft.
5. Click Next, and then click Install.
6. When setup is complete, click Next, and then click Finish. The Setup Progess dialog box will appear, detailing the progress of each component being installed.
7. Finally, the Completing Microsoft SQL Server 2005 Setup page will appear. Review the displayed information, and then click Finish.

Using the Reporting Services Configuration Manager

After installation, you must use the Reporting Services Configuration Manager to set properties for components of Reporting Services to work properly. The first step is to associate the Report Server with the SQL Server instance hosting the Reporting Services databases.

Start the Reporting Services Configuration Manager

1. Click Start, point to All Programs, point to Microsoft SQL Server 2005, point to Configuration Tools, and then click Reporting Services Configuration.

2. If you've installed Reporting Services to the local server using the default instance, you can click Connect in the Report Server Installation Instance Selection dialog box. Otherwise, change the Machine Name or Instance Name as necessary, and then click Connect.

   The Server Status page of the Reporting Services Configuration Manager looks like this:

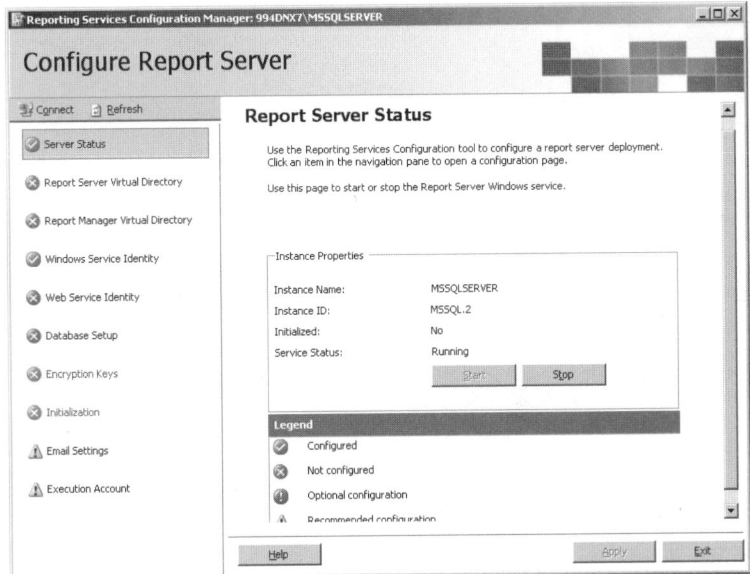

Here you can see that additional configuration is required for the virtual directories used by Reporting Services, the Web service identity, and the Database Setup. Additionally, the configuration settings for Email Settings and Execution Account are optional, but are recommended.

Configuring Virtual Directories

Virtual directories are used to access Report Server and Report Manager. These virtual directories are created on the Default Web Site in IIS. If your Web Server is dedicated to Reporting Services, you should redirect the home page to the Report Manager's home page, although this is not required. You can also secure data sent to browser or client applications with SSL encryption, but you must have an SSL certificate installed before starting the Reporting Services installation.

In this procedure, you'll specify names for the virtual directories assigned to Report Server and Report Manager.

Configure virtual directories

1. Click Report Server Virtual Directory in the left frame of the Reporting Services Configuration Manager, and then click New in the main frame.
2. Keep the default settings in the Create A New Virtual Directory dialog box.

Your screen looks like this:

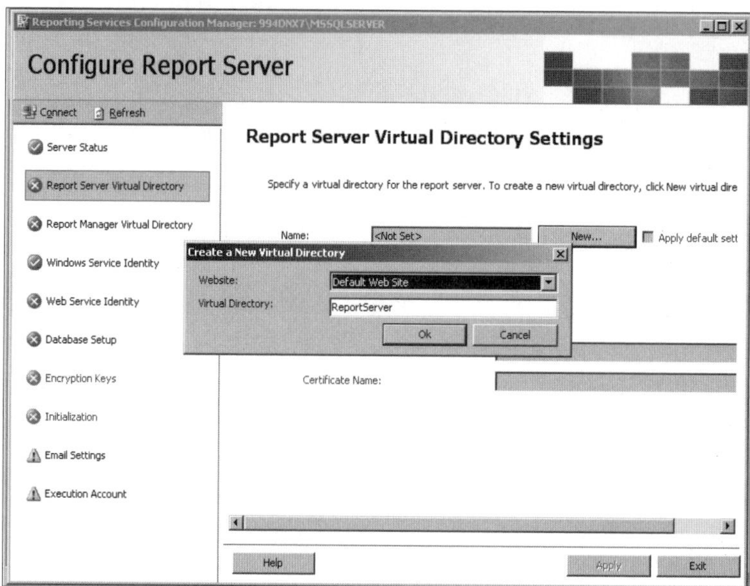

3. Click OK, click Report Manager Virtual Directory in the left frame, and then click New in the Create A New Virtual Directory dialog box to accept the default values.

   Your screen looks like this:

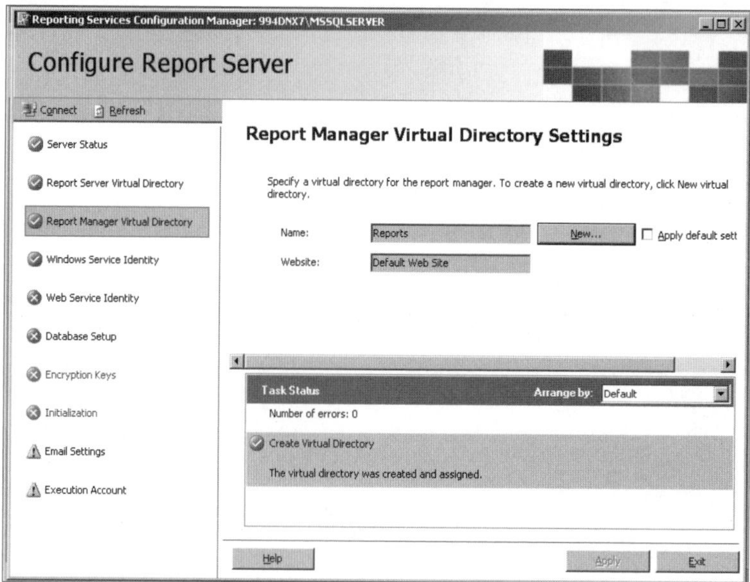

4. Click Web Service Identity in the left frame, and then click Apply in the main frame.

Your screen looks like this:

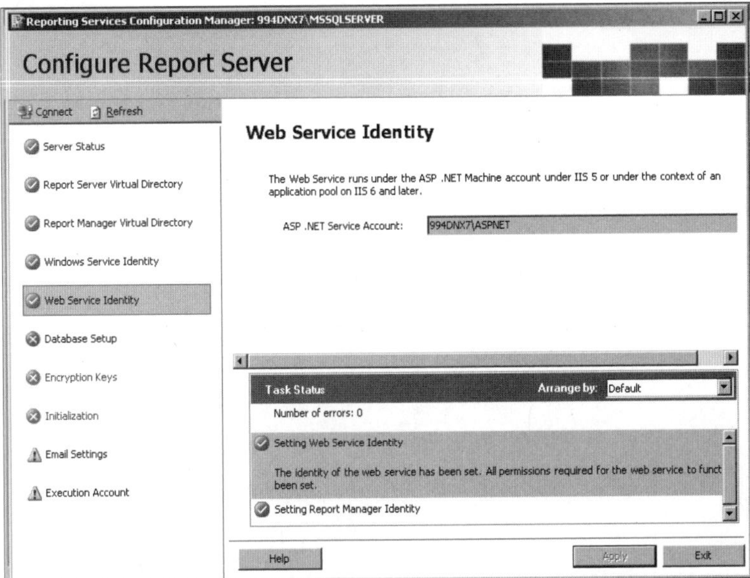

Specifying the Report Server Database

You need to select a local or remote SQL Server instance that will host the Reporting Services database. You can use an existing Report Server database or provide a unique name if you want to create a Report Server database. You also need to specify an account that Reporting Services will use to connect to this database at run time. The default account is the service account used to run the ReportServer Windows service, but you can also specify a domain user account or a SQL Server login to conform to existing security practices for your SQL Server instance.

In this procedure, you'll specify the SQL Server instance and the name of the database used by the Report Server.

Configure the Report Server database

1. Click Database Setup in the left frame, type **localhost** in the Server Name box, click Connect, and then click OK in the SQL Server Connection Dialog box to confirm the server and default credentials, Current User – Integrated Security.

2. Click New.

Your screen looks like this:

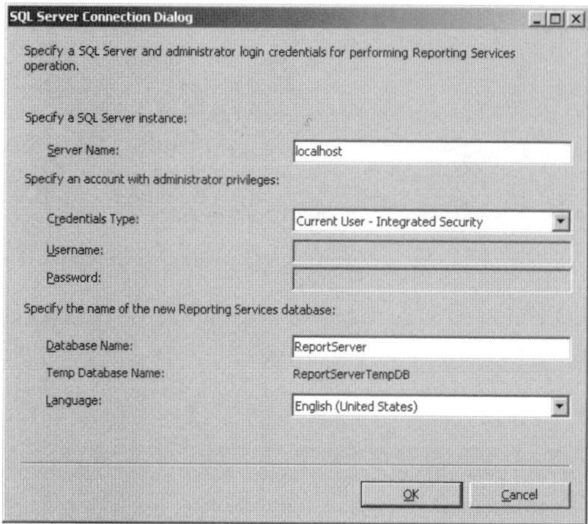

3. Click OK.

Your screen looks like this:

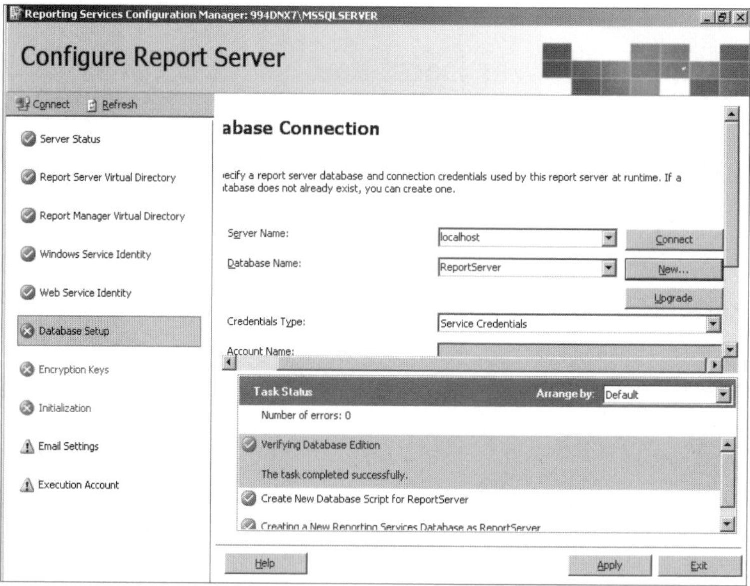

4. Click Apply, and then click OK to confirm the connection.

Specifying Report Delivery Options

If you'll be using e-mail delivery of subscriptions, you need to specify the name of the e-mail server that Reporting Services should use to send reports. You can also specify an e-mail account that will be added as the From address of the e-mail message. Specifying the report delivery options on this page is not required at this time because you can always edit Reporting Services configuration files later. However, by adding the information now, your Report Server will be ready for e-mail delivery as soon as installation is complete.

In this procedure, you'll specify e-mail delivery information for your Reporting Services installation. (You can skip this procedure if you don't want to perform the e-mail delivery procedures included in Chapter 14, "Managing Subscriptions.")

Configure e-mail delivery

1. In the Reporting Services Configuration Manager, click Email Settings in the left frame.
2. Type a Sender Address to be used as the sender for report deliveries: **postmaster @adventure-works.com**.
3. Enter an SMTP Server address: **localhost**.

> **Note** The procedures that you'll use later in this book to learn about e-mail delivery assume that you have Simple Mail Transfer Protocol (SMTP) on your local server if you follow this procedure as written. You can alternatively enter the server address of an existing SMTP server on your network or the SMTP gateway of your Exchange server if you prefer.

4. Click Apply.

   Your screen looks like this:

   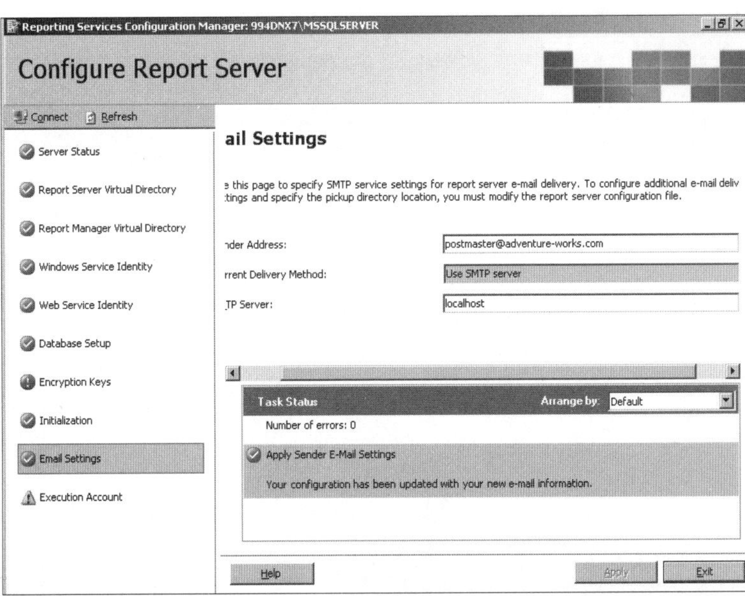

   The e-mail address that you enter doesn't need to be valid. This address becomes the default reply-to address. When you set up e-mail delivery for a report, you can override this default.

5. Click Exit.

Verifying the Installation

To verify that your installation of Reporting Services was successful, you should perform several tests. First, to test the Report Server, you can either check that the ReportServer service is running by using the Services console, or you can use your browser to navigate to the Report Server virtual directory, which by default is *http://servername/ReportServer*. To test Report Manager, use the application to add a new folder.

In this procedure, you'll confirm that the Report Server service is running and that Report Server and Report Manager are working.

Test Report Server and Report Manager

1. From the Administrative Tools program group, open the Services console and scroll to ReportServer to confirm that the service is running.

   The Services console looks similar to this:

   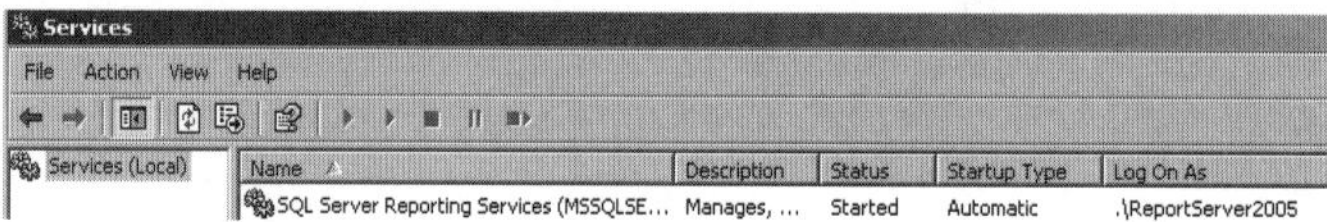

2. Open Microsoft Internet Explorer and type the server name and virtual directory name of Report Manager: ***http://localhost/Reports***.

   The Home page of Report Manager is displayed:

   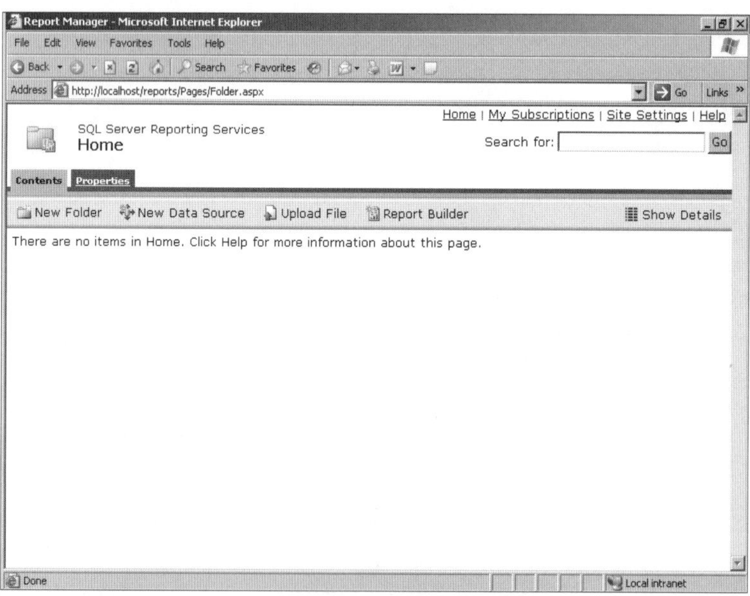

3. Click New Folder on the Report Manager toolbar.

   The New Folder page is displayed.

4. Type a name for the folder: **Adventure Works**.

Your screen looks like this:

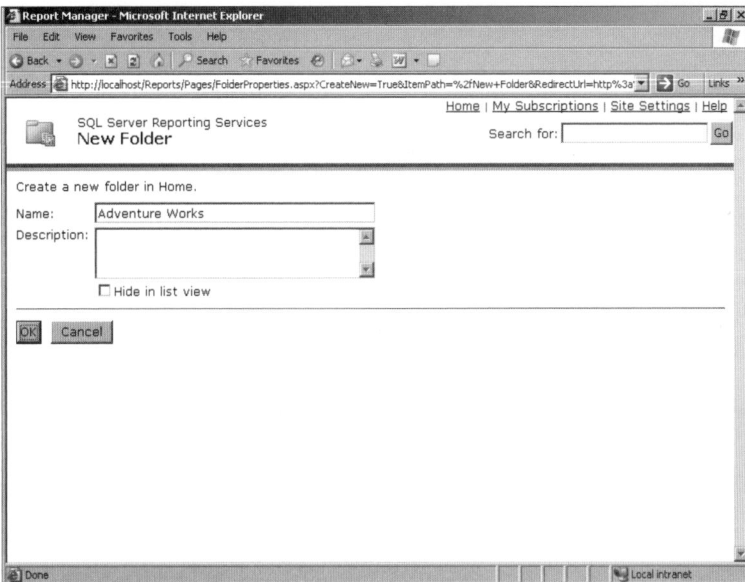

By creating a new folder, you are testing that the Report Manager is able to access the Report Server, which passes instructions to the ReportServer database.

5. Click OK.

   Your screen looks like this:

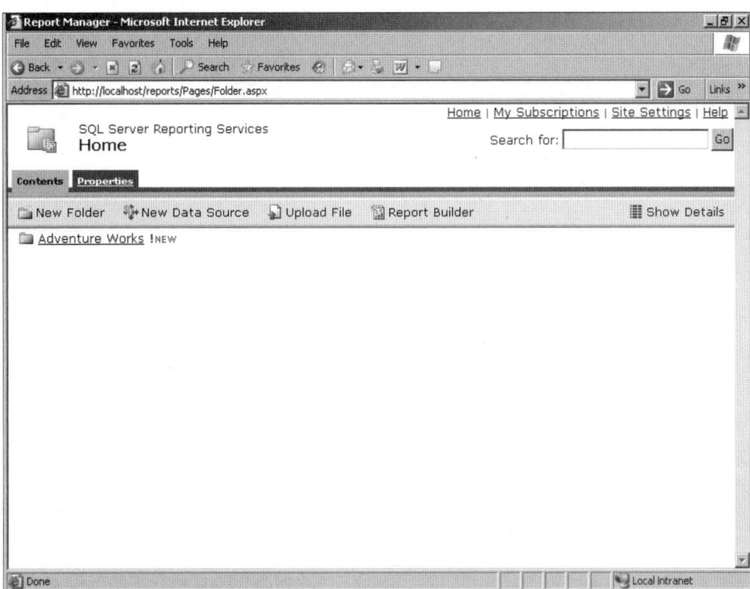

Your new folder is now ready for reports to be added. You'll add a report to this folder when you finish Chapter 3, "Building Your First Report."

Chapter 2 Quick Reference

To	Do this
Test features of Reporting Services before making a purchasing decision	Use the Evaluation edition in a single or multiple server deployment.
Use Reporting Services in a single server deployment	Use Standard edition for production and Developer edition for development and testing.
Use Reporting Services in a multiple server deployment	Use Enterprise edition for production and Developer edition for development and testing.
Prepare a server for installation of Report Server or Report Manager	Install IIS 5.0 or later on each server that will host either of these Reporting Services components. Additionally, install .NET Framework 2.0 or later and MDAC 2.6 or later.
Configure a computer for a Reporting Services installation	Enable the Distributed Transaction Coordinator service prior to running Setup.
Configure IIS in preparation for a Reporting Services installation	Enable the IWAM_*computername* account. Map the Default Web Site to (All Unassigned). Optionally, install an SSL certificate and associate the certificate with the Default Web Site.
Configure e-mail delivery	Install SMTP on the Web Server, or have the name of a SMTP or POP3 (Post Office Protocol version 3) server available on your network.
Establish Reporting Services credentials	Use the Local System account or a local system administration account that is a domain user (or LocalService or NetworkService for the service account, if running Windows Server 2003) to start the ReportServer Windows service. Use a service account, domain account, or SQL Server login for Report Server to use to connect to the Reporting Services databases.
Install Reporting Services	Double-click Setup.exe, found on the installation CD, to launch the setup wizard. *or* Run the *setup* command-line executable. Specify options using command-line arguments or a template file.

Chapter 3

Building Your First Report

After completing this chapter, you will be able to:

- Use the Report Designer wizards to create a simple tabular report.
- Publish a report solution.
- Use Report Manager to manage report properties.
- Use the HTML Viewer to access and export a report.

In Chapter 1, "Understanding Reporting," you learned about the three stages of the reporting life cycle: authoring, managing, and accessing reports. In Chapter 2, "Installing Reporting Services," you learned how to install and configure Reporting Services, so you should be ready to go exploring now. In this chapter, rather than review each component of Reporting Services in detail, you take a tour of it. You visit each stage of the reporting cycle as you build, manage, and review your first report, and you also learn about the key components of Reporting Services.

You start your tour by authoring a simple report using wizards in the Report Designer, which will enable you to set up and design the report. You also use the Report Designer to polish and publish your report. Then, you move on to the management stage and use Report Manager to update the report's description and execution properties. Finally, you wrap up your tour in the access stage by using Report Manager to explore the report online and to export it as a Microsoft Excel file. When finished, you wind up with a high-level understanding of the various components of Reporting Services and the way they work together to create a powerful reporting platform.

Authoring a Report

The process of authoring, or building, a report consists of several steps. The first step is to define a Reporting Services *data source*, which packages information about where the data to be used in your report is stored. To create a data source, you need to know which server hosts the data and which database or file stores the data, as well as have the credentials with permission to retrieve that data. Each report that you author must have at least one data source defined. Data sources are covered in more detail in Chapter 4, "Developing Basic Reports."

The second step in building a report is to create a *dataset* for the report. An important component of the dataset is a query, which requires that you know the language and syntax used to retrieve data. For example, if your report will use data from a Microsoft SQL Server database, you'll need to be able to create a Transact-SQL query (or know someone who can write it for you!). A dataset also includes a pointer to the data source and other information that's used when the query executes. When you use the Report Server Project Wizard, as you will in this chapter, you can define only one dataset, but you'll learn how to work with multiple datasets in a single report in Chapter 7, "Building Advanced Reports."

The third and final step in the construction of your report is the creation of a *report layout,* which is the design template used by Reporting Services to arrange and format the data. The report layout includes the structure, or *data region*, into which data is placed when the report is processed, such as a table or matrix. You can set properties for each section of a data region to define style properties, such as font, color, and format. Additionally, you can set these properties for report items, such as the report title in a textbox or the report background, which gives you enormous flexibility to control the look and feel of your report.

In this chapter, you use the Report Server Project Wizard and the Report Wizard to help you start and build a new report. You'll learn another way to begin a report in Chapter 4. These wizards, which are provided within the Report Designer, are handy tools that walk you through the three main steps of authoring a report.

Starting a New Report

When you start a new report using the Report Server Project Wizard, you are creating Microsoft Visual Studio containers to hold your report, a project, and a solution. You must name these containers and provide a storage location for them on your computer's hard drive or on a network file share.

In this procedure, you'll create a new report project called Adventure Works and specify a storage location for the project.

Start the Report Server Project Wizard

1. Start SQL Server Business Intelligence Development Studio.

   Notice the title of the application is Microsoft Visual Studio. SQL Server Business Intelligence Development Studio *is* Visual Studio. You are simply using a shortcut from the Microsoft SQL Server 2005 program group to access Visual Studio.

2. On the File menu, point to New, and then click Project.

   The New Project dialog box appears. Templates are organized by Project Type, represented as folders in this dialog box.

> **Note** If this is your first time working with Visual Studio, you might not be familiar with the way that items are organized in this environment. A report is placed inside of a project, which you can think of as a folder that organizes many reports into a collection. Because you're using the Report Server Project Wizard, you can work with only one project right now. However, you'll be adding reports to this project as you progress through this book. When you publish all reports in a project, they are automatically organized into the same folder on the Report Server.

3. Click Report Server Project Wizard.
4. Type a name for the project: **Adventure Works**.

   Notice that as you type, the text in the Solution Name box of the New Project dialog box changes to match the project name. You have the option of changing the solution name later if you change your mind.

> **Note** In the same way that a project is a container for a report, a solution is a container for one or more projects. Visual Studio lets you work with only one solution at a time, but you can access any project within the open solution.

5. Type a location for the project: **C:\Documents and Settings\<username>\My Documents\Microsoft Press\rs2005sbs\Workspace**.

> **Important** Be sure to replace the placeholder <username> with the name you use to log into your computer.

The New Project dialog box looks like this:

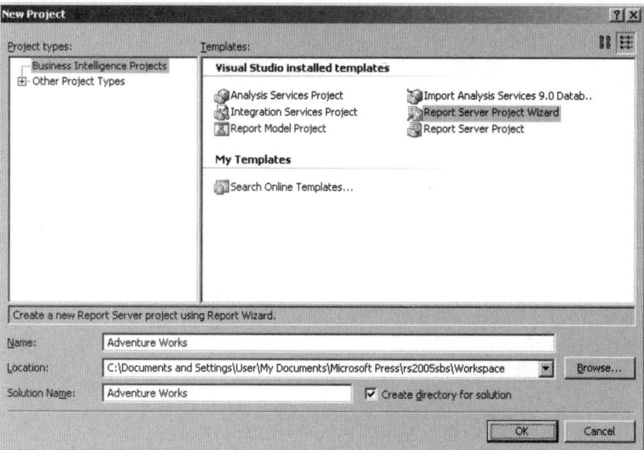

6. Click OK to continue.

   The Welcome page of the Report Wizard is displayed. Note that this wizard is different from the Report Server Project Wizard. The Report Server Project Wizard lets you create a solution, a project, and a report in one step, and then launches the Report Wizard. You can use the Report Wizard any time you want to add a report to an existing project using a wizard interface. (This is explained in more detail in Chapter 4.)

If you want to bypass this page of the Report Wizard in the future, you can select the check box here to disable the Welcome Page.

7. Click Next.

Connecting to a Data Source

The next step of the Report Wizard allows you to specify connection information. Here you identify the server and database hosting the data. If necessary, you can also supply credentials information to be used by Reporting Services for authentication when querying the database.

In this procedure, you'll create a data source that defines a connection to the rs2005sbsDW database in your SQL Server using Microsoft Windows authentication.

Select a data source

1. Type a name for the data source: **rs2005sbsDW**.
2. Select Microsoft SQL Server in the Type drop-down list, if necessary.

   The Select The Data Source page of the Report Wizard now looks like this:

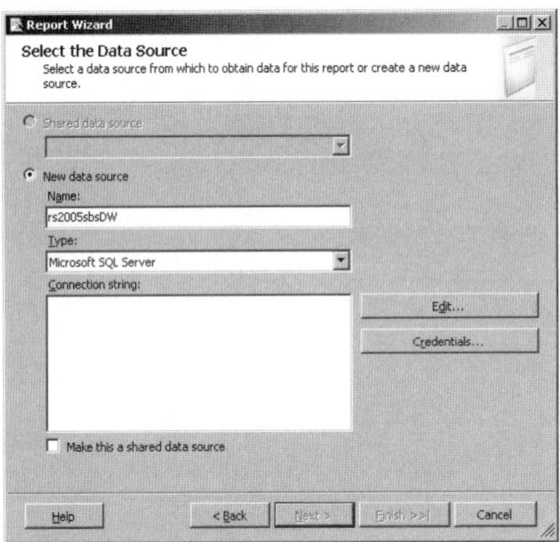

You can choose from seven connection types: Microsoft SQL Server, OLE DB, Microsoft SQL Server Analysis Services, Oracle, Open Database Connectivity (ODBC), XML, or Report Server Model. Once you select a connection type, you can type a connection string manually, or you can click Edit to use the Connection Properties dialog box to generate the connection string automatically. By default, the data source you create here will be available only to the current report, which allows you to manage its usage separately from other reports. You can select the Make This A Shared Data Source check box at the bottom of the dialog box to allow this data source to be shared with other reports, which simplifies the management of data sources in general.

3. Click Edit.

   The Connection Properties dialog box is displayed. Because you selected Microsoft SQL Server as the connection type on the Select The Data Source page of the Report Wizard, the data source defaults to Microsoft SQL Server (SqlClient).

4. Type **localhost** or the name of the SQL Server instance that you are using in the Server Name box.

> **Note** This book assumes that you have all Reporting Services components and SQL Server installed on one computer. In a real-world environment, there are advantages to using localhost instead of a SQL Server instance since you can easily reuse the data source when moving from development to production if everything is similarly contained in a single machine. However, if you maintain separate instances of SQL Server, this strategy will not be useful.

5. Click Use Windows Authentication.
6. Select or enter rs2005sbsDW in the Select Or Enter A Database Name drop-down list.

   The Connection Properties dialog box looks like this:

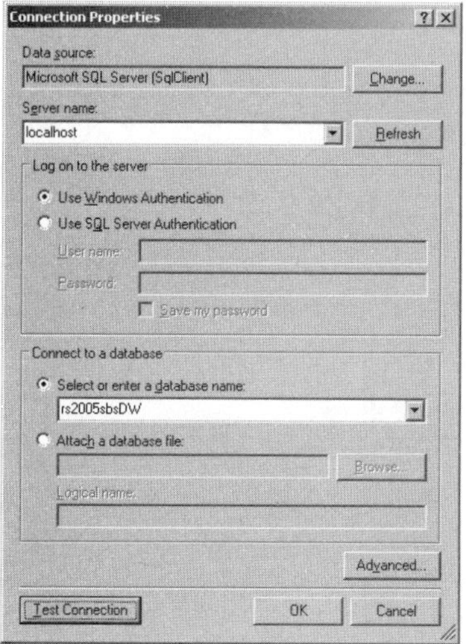

7. Click Test Connection to make sure you can connect to the rs2005sbsDW database, and then click OK to close the confirmation dialog box.
8. Click OK to close the Connection Properties dialog box.

The current page of the Report Wizard looks like this:

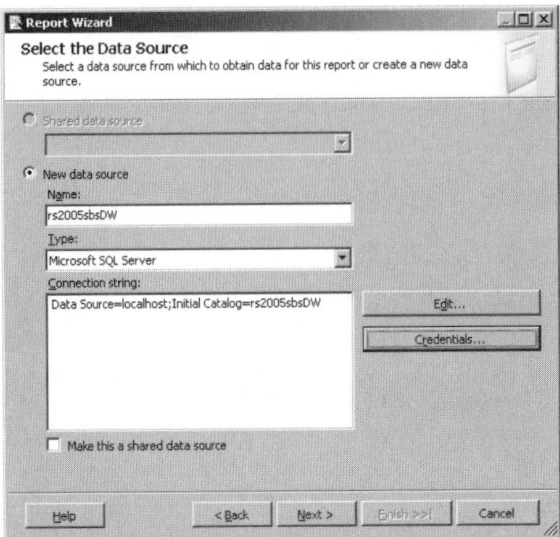

Notice the connection string generated for your SQL Server data source: `Data Source =localhost;Initial Catalog=rs2005sbsDW`. Remember that you can also type in a connection string for a data source, but it must use the syntax of the database to which Reporting Services will connect.

Now you have defined a data source that contains the information that Reporting Services needs to connect to the database it will use to retrieve data for your report. The data source includes a connection type, a connection string, and the credentials that will be used when the database is queried.

9. Click Credentials.

   The Data Source Credentials dialog box is displayed:

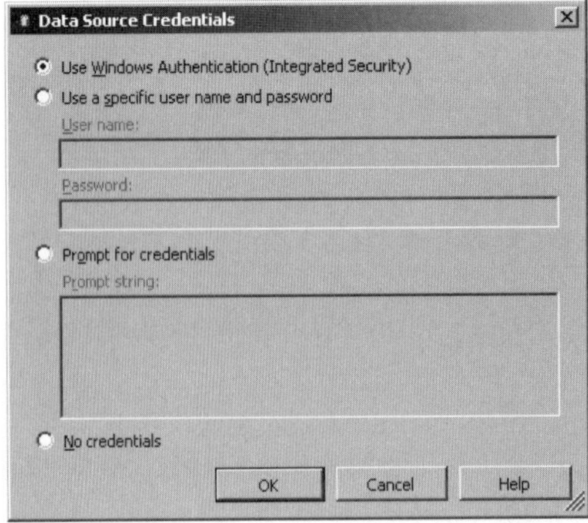

You can click the applicable option to override the authentication method you specified in the Connection Properties dialog box. Authentication methods include Windows Authentication, a single user's credentials, a prompt at run time for the user's credentials, or no credentials at all. (You'll learn more about credential management in Chapter 9, "Managing Content.")

10. Click Cancel.
11. Click Next.

Getting Data for the Report

In this next step of the Report Wizard, you design the query that will be displayed in the report. The query must conform to the relational database syntax you defined in the data source. You must get this query correct, or you won't be able to continue with this wizard.

In this procedure, you'll paste in a query that summarizes the Adventure Works sales for each employee by year, sales territory group, and sales territory country.

Design a query

1. Start Microsoft Notepad.
2. On the File menu, click Open.
3. Open the Sales Summary.txt file in the C:\Documents and Settings\<username>\My Documents\Microsoft Press\rs2005sbs\chap03 folder.
4. Copy the following query entirely:

```
SELECT
   SUM(FactResellerSales.SalesAmount) AS ActualSales,
   DimTime.CalendarYear,
   DimSalesTerritory.SalesTerritoryGroup,
   DimSalesTerritory.SalesTerritoryCountry,
   DimEmployee.FirstName + ' ' + DimEmployee.LastName AS Employee
FROM
   FactResellerSales
   INNER JOIN DimEmployee ON
         FactResellerSales.EmployeeKey = DimEmployee.EmployeeKey
   INNER JOIN DimTime ON
         FactResellerSales.OrderDateKey = DimTime.TimeKey
   INNER JOIN DimSalesTerritory ON
     FactResellerSales.SalesTerritoryKey = DimSalesTerritory.SalesTerritoryKey
AND
         DimEmployee.SalesTerritoryKey = DimSalesTerritory.SalesTerritoryKey
GROUP BY
   DimTime.CalendarYear,
   DimSalesTerritory.SalesTerritoryGroup,
   DimSalesTerritory.SalesTerritoryCountry,
   DimEmployee.FirstName + ' ' + DimEmployee.LastName
```

5. Paste the copied query into the Query String box on the Design The Query page of the Report Wizard.

   Now the current page of the Report Wizard looks like this:

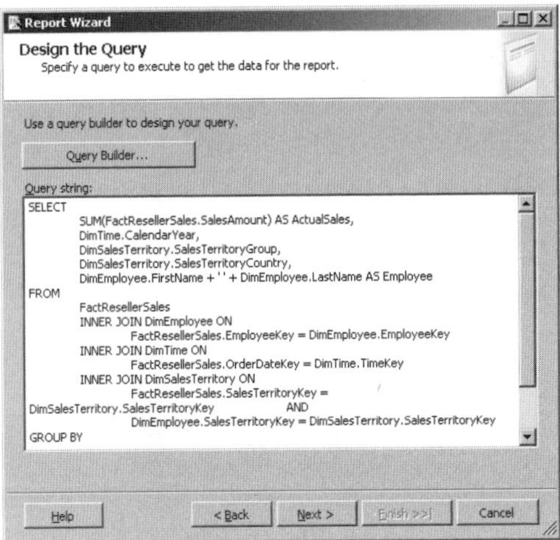

> **Note** Instead of typing or pasting in a query string, you can also click Query Builder to open the Query Builder to create a SELECT statement using a graphical interface. If you've used the Query Builder in SQL Server 2000 Enterprise Manager or the Query Designer in Microsoft SQL Server Management Studio for SQL Server 2005, you'll be in familiar territory. If you haven't used either of these applications, you can learn more about the Query Builder in Chapter 7.

   This query will be used to retrieve data from the defined data source for use in your report. The format of the query depends on the data source you selected. For this procedure, because you selected a Microsoft SQL Server data source, you use Transact-SQL to build your query.

   The query that you create is just one of several items stored in a dataset. As you learned earlier in this chapter, a dataset is a container for a pointer to the data source and the query you design. (You'll learn more about designing queries to create a dataset in Chapter 4.) In general, you can type a query directly into the Query String box, use the Query Builder button to open the Query Builder, or paste in a query that has been tested first in Query Analyzer or saved in a file.

6. Click Next.

   When you click Next, the query is validated against the data source. If there is any problem, such as an invalid column name, an error message will be displayed in the bottom section of the Design the Query page. You will not be able to continue past this page of the wizard until you correct the error.

Structuring Data in the Report

After defining the data source and the dataset, you're ready to move on to design considerations. Now you select a report type that defines how the data is structured in the report. In the wizard, you can choose between a tabular or a matrix report type only. You also arrange the data within the selected structure and finish the design by applying a style template. These steps make it easy to create a nice-looking report without a lot of effort, but you'll still have an opportunity to make adjustments to the layout and style before you publish the report.

In this procedure, you'll select the tabular report type for your report.

Choose a report type

Click Tabular.

1. The Report Wizard page looks like this:

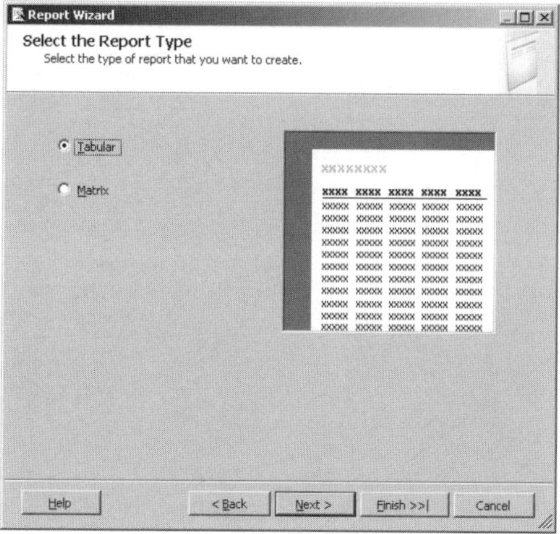

Notice that the Finish button is now enabled. You have, at this point, created a basic report that is ready for publishing. Now you can decide how you want to proceed. You could click Finish and make any desired modifications using the Report Designer. However, to find out everything you can do with this tool, you'll continue designing your report with the wizard.

The *report type* defines the structure, or data region, of the data that is returned by the query you design. The Report Wizard allows you to present this information as either a table or a matrix. (You do have more options, but the Report Wizard limits you to these two data regions, referred to as report types in the wizard.) The main difference between these two types of data regions is the number of columns. A table has a fixed number of columns, whereas a matrix has a variable number of columns that is determined by the query results. You'll find more information about these and other data regions in Chapter 6, "Organizing Data in Reports."

2. Click Next.

Placing Data in the Report Structure

In this step of the Report Wizard, you arrange the data within the report type that you selected. This process determines how data is grouped and the order in which it is displayed. You can think of grouped data as the vertical sections of a report (although groups can be displayed next to each other), and the data order as the sequence in which the data is presented in the same row—vertically for groups and horizontally for columns.

In this procedure, you'll arrange the five fields produced by the query to build a report that displays the ActualSales amount for each Employee as detail rows, in groups by SalesTerritoryGroup and SalesTerritoryCountry, with a page break for each CalendarYear.

Arrange data on the report

1. Click CalendarYear, and then click Page to place the *CalendarYear* field in the Page section of the Displayed Fields list.

   The Report Wizard looks like this:

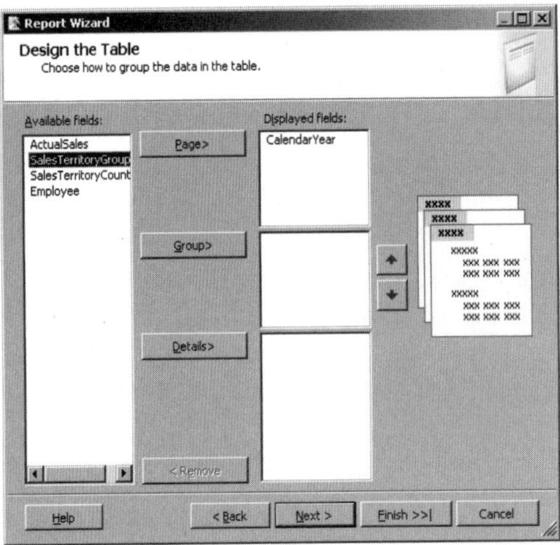

   When you place a field in a display section, the corresponding section in the sample table is highlighted to show you where the field will appear in your report. Each column of data returned by the query is linked, or mapped, to a report field that is displayed in the Available Fields list until assigned to a section of the data region. When assigned to a data region's section, the report fields appear in the Displayed Fields list. The section to which you assign the field determines whether you see detail rows, aggregated rows, or both types of rows in the report. Assignment of fields to data regions and the use of aggregations are discussed more thoroughly in Chapter 4 and Chapter 5, "Working with Expressions."

   Because you are using a tabular report type, you can assign fields to the page, group, or details section of the report. For example, a field assigned to the page section will not be included in the table in the report, but will instead be placed in a textbox positioned at the top-left corner of the report. Each distinct value for a page field creates a page break in the report. Fields added to the group section of the report are used to break the table into separate sections, which can include subtotals by section.

The table rows are built from the values for the fields assigned to the details section of the report. There is one table row for each row returned by the defined query. A numeric field in the details section is summed up into the subtotals if you select the option to include subtotals. You can decide later whether you want to hide the details in the report if you prefer to display just summary information.

Note If you choose a matrix report type, the field assignment is slightly different. The wizard still includes the page and details sections, but the group section is replaced by sections for columns and rows. You'll need to assign at least one field to each of these sections to build a matrix, which is also known as a crosstab. Matrix reports are covered in Chapter 6.

2. Click SalesTerritoryGroup, and then click Group to place the field in the Group section. Repeat for SalesTerritoryCountry. Alternatively, you can use the drag-and-drop feature to move a field from the list of available fields to the appropriate section.

   The order in which you add fields to each section determines the sequence in which the data is displayed in the report. The fields in the Group section will be displayed in order from top to bottom or from left to right, depending on the style template that you select in a later step in the wizard. Fields in the Details section will be displayed in columns in order from left to right.

3. Drag ActualSales to the Details section, which is the bottom section of the Displayed Fields list, and then drag Employee to the same section.

   The Design The Table page of the Report Wizard looks like this:

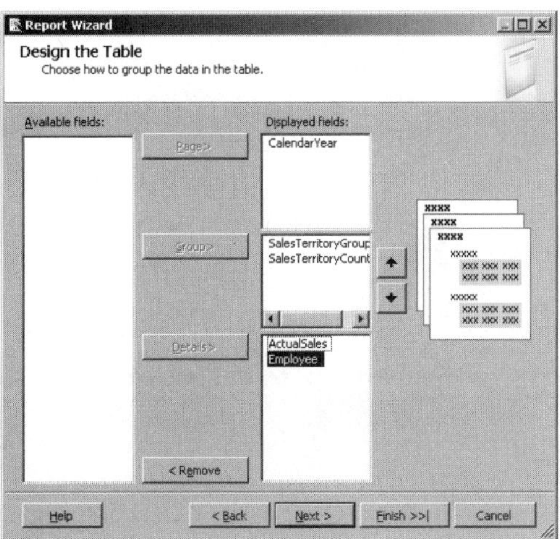

> **Tip** Even after the fields are placed into the Displayed Fields list, you can still rearrange them to affect their order in the respective sections.

If you had selected the Matrix option on the previous page, Select the Report Type, you would see the Design the Matrix page here instead of the Design The Table page.

4. Click Employee, and then click the Up button to move Employee above ActualSales. You can also drag and drop to rearrange fields within a data region.

   Now the page looks like this:

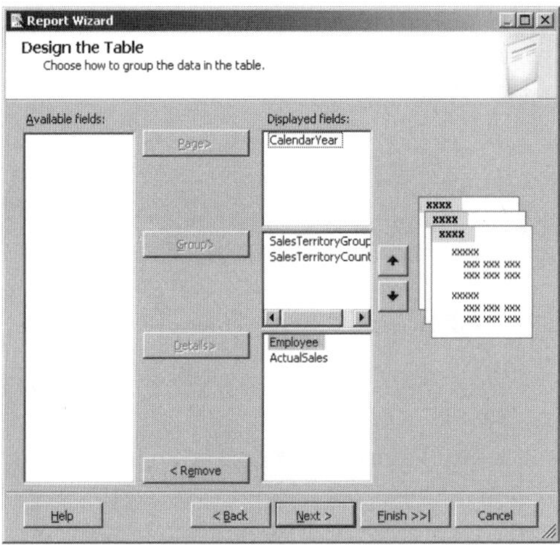

5. Click Next.

Applying a Style Template

In this step of the Report Wizard, you make your last design decision for your report. When you apply a style template, you define the look and feel of the report.

In this procedure, you'll define a block layout for the table, which includes group subtotals, and select the Bold style template.

Select a report style

1. Select Block.

> **Note** This page of the wizard will not be displayed if you selected a matrix report type.

Notice that the sample layout changes to give you a preview of the block layout. Here, you are choosing a layout style for the tabular report that controls the placement of detail rows relative to aggregated rows on the report. You can also choose to include subtotals or enable drilldown. The difference between the layout options will become clearer when you can actually view your report. At that time, you'll see examples of the other layout styles for comparison.

On this page of the Report Wizard, you must select either a stepped or block report layout style. In a stepped layout, each distinct group value is arranged on its own row and in its own column. The drilldown option (which displays hidden detail data) is available only for stepped layout. By contrast, the block layout is more compact–you place data in each column and start a new row only for additional detail rows within the same group or for a new group value.

2. Select the Include Subtotals check box to include subtotals in your report.
3. Click Next.
4. Click each table style to preview the style in the Choose The Table Style page.

   The assignment of a style template to a tabular or matrix report sets the overall color theme and font usage for the report.
5. Click Bold to set the style for your report.
6. Click Next.

Finishing the Report Wizard

You're almost finished building your report by using the wizard. You've defined where to find the data, what data to include in the report, and how the data will look in the report. All that remains is to specify a location on the Report Server that will be the ultimate destination of your report when it is published and to give your report a name. You also have an opportunity to review a summary of the selections that you made throughout the wizard and to proceed to a preview of your report.

In this procedure, you'll provide the URL for your local Report Server, specify the Adventure Works folder for deployment, and name your report. When you're finished with the wizard, you will be able to preview the report.

Set report and project properties

1. Confirm that the current page of the Report Wizard looks like this:

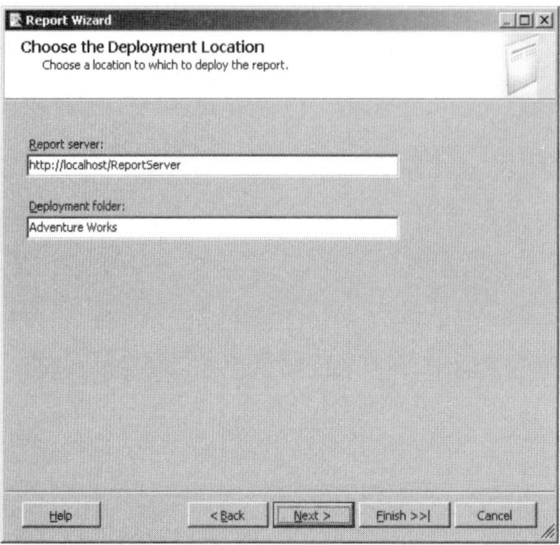

The deployment location is a URL for the Report Server that will host the report as well as the folder into which the report will be placed on the server. This step of the Report Wizard simply sets the project properties and does not actually *deploy*, or publish, the report to the Report Server. Notice that the default folder has the same name as your project. If this folder does not already exist, the folder will be created when you deploy the report. Otherwise, the report will be deployed to the existing folder.

> **Important** The server name will not be validated in this step. If you enter an incorrect server name, deployment fails. You can update the project properties in the Solution Explorer if this occurs. You'll learn how to do this in Chapter 9.

2. Click Next.
3. Type **Sales Summary** in the Report Name box.

> **Important** If you use the name of a report that has already been deployed to the Report Server, you will overwrite the published report during deployment of the report in Visual Studio—but only if you deploy the report to the same folder as the existing folder. There will be no warning message during deployment that you are about to overwrite an existing report, so be careful when assigning names and folder locations to reports.

4. Scroll through the information in the Report Summary box to review your selections.
5. Select the Preview Report check box to preview your report.

The final page of the Report Wizard now looks like this:

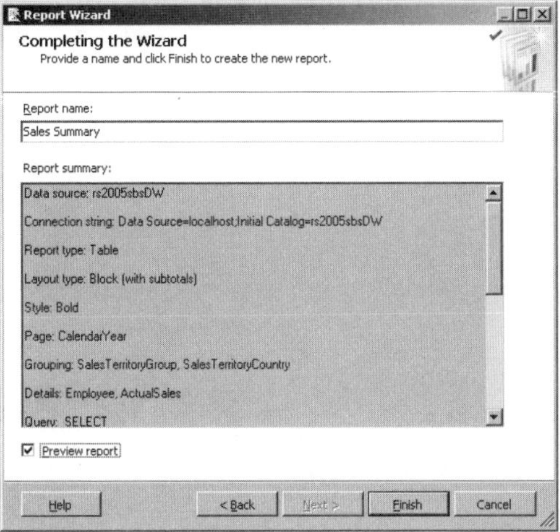

At the completion of the Report Wizard, you can immediately preview the report. Sometimes you might prefer to make some additional changes to the report before you display the preview. If you do not select the Preview Report check box, the Report Designer displays your report in layout mode. If the report is in layout mode, you can easily switch to preview mode by clicking the Preview tab in the Report Designer.

> **Tip** An important reason to preview the report is to check the size of the columns. The columns will all default to the same size and will probably not be wide enough for data. Also, you might need to adjust formatting for numeric values. You can fix these problems using the layout mode, and then review the fixes using the preview mode.

6. Click Finish.

Checking the Report Layout

When you finish designing your report, you need to preview it to check the layout and make some corrections to improve its appearance. You also need to make sure you get the data you expected and that the data is formatted correctly. When you finish making any necessary corrections, you wrap up this authoring stage of the reporting life cycle by publishing the report to the Report Server, where it can be accessed by the users.

In this procedure, you'll explore your report in preview mode so you can see the results of the selections you made in the Report Wizard.

Preview a report

1. If you selected the check box to preview the report on the last page of the Report Wizard, you will see your report in preview mode. If not, just click the Preview tab in the Report Designer.

   When you display a report in preview mode, the query is executed and the query results are stored in a dataset and assigned to fields. The report is then rendered according to the assignment of the fields to data regions that you specified as well as the layout and style that you selected. At this point, the report format and the report data are merged to produce the preview that you can see in the Report Designer. In preview mode, you can interact with the report just as if it were published to the server so you can test the results before making it available on the Report Server.

   Your screen now looks like this:

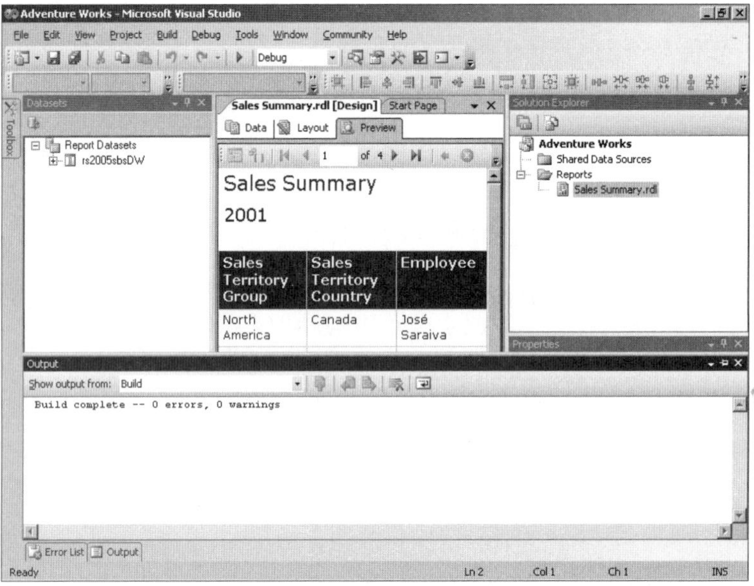

   Take a moment to review the layout of the data in the report. The *CalendarYear* field is displayed in the top-left corner. Just below the CalendarYear, you can see the column names in the table header with the details displayed in rows by groups. The first group is SalesTerritoryGroup, and the second group is SalesTerritoryCountry. Because these fields are defined as groups, their values are displayed only in the first row of details within that group. In the example, you can see actual sales amounts for employees in Canada which is grouped in North America. The row beneath these details is the group subtotal for Canada.

   Once you've closed the wizard, you can't return to it to make layout changes. Instead, you must create a new report, which you may find easier to do than making changes to the layout directly in the Report Designer. If you were to use the wizard to create a stepped report with subtotals (on the Choose The Table Layout page) using the same query, then the report would look like this:

Sales Summary (Stepped)

2001

Sales Territory Group	Sales Territory Country	Employee	Actual Sales
North America			9665054.34490999
	Canada		1817823.686814
		José Saraiva	1248852.64571
		Garrett Vargas	568971.041104
	United States		7847230.65809599
		Shu Ito	1068441.307732

Notice that North America is now in its own row, and its subtotal is included on the same row. Then Canada appears by itself on the next row, followed by the detail rows. This report style is longer than the block layout.

If you had instead used the wizard to create a report with a stepped layout with drill-down selected, the report—with North America and Canada expanded to show the detail rows—would look like this:

Sales Summary (Stepped - Drilldown)

2001

Sales Territory Group	Sales Territory Country	Employee	Actual Sales
⊟ North America			9665054.34490999
	⊟ Canada		1817823.686814
		José Saraiva	1248852.64571
		Garrett Vargas	568971.041104
	⊞ United States		7847230.65809599

With drilldown, the user can click the plus sign to expand the report and click the minus sign to collapse the report at will. By default, the report is completely collapsed when it is opened.

2. Scroll down to the bottom of the first page. Notice the group subtotal for United States. Beneath this group subtotal, you can see the group subtotal for SalesTerritoryGroup, which is the subtotal for Canada and the United States.

3. Click the Next Page button on the Preview toolbar to view the page for 2002.

   Since you assigned CalendarYear to the Page data region of the report, each page contains data for a separate year. You can use the page buttons on the Preview toolbar to navigate between pages, or you can type in the page number that you want to view as shown here:

   2 of 4

4. Scroll to the bottom of the second page to see the layout when there are multiple values for SalesTerritoryGroup, then scroll back to the top of the page.

5. If you can't see the full width of the report, scroll horizontally to see the Actual Sales column.

   The top of your report looks like this:

   2002

Sales Territory Group	Sales Territory Country	Employee	Actual Sales
Europe	France	Ranjit Varkey Chudukatil	1028496.74 5306
	Total		1028496.7 45306
	United Kingdom	José Saraiva	925011.839 071001
	Total		925011.83 9071001
Total			1953508.5 84377
North America	Canada	Jae Pak	3046514.64 750499
		José	1283648.26

   Notice that the text is wrapping in several columns: SalesTerritoryCountry, Employee, and ActualSales. If you are trying to fit many columns onto a printed page, you may need to use text wrapping to fit a table within the available horizontal space. However, for online viewing, you generally have more room available and you can minimize vertical scrolling for the user if you widen each column to accommodate the maximum expected string length. In addition, the format of the ActualSales values can be improved.

Correcting Report Layout Issues

Preview mode in Report Designer allows you to see where you need to clean up your report, but you need to switch to layout mode in order to fix the problems. In layout mode, you can adjust every property of every element in the report, giving you complete control over everything that you can see. You can easily switch back and forth to test the results of your changes to the report in layout mode.

In this procedure, you'll use layout mode to improve the appearance of the report and check the results by again previewing the report.

Fix column sizes and data formatting in the report layout

1. Click the Layout tab.

   The report is displayed in layout mode:

   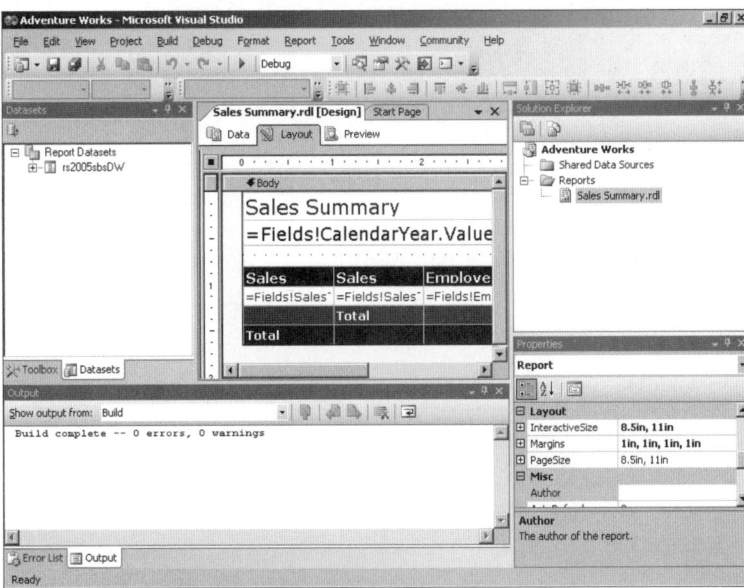

   Notice the rulers that appear both above and to the left of the report layout. You can use these rulers as a visual guide when making changes to the report, such as when resizing report items or positioning new report items.

2. Click any cell in the table to display the column and row handles.

   The table now looks like this:

   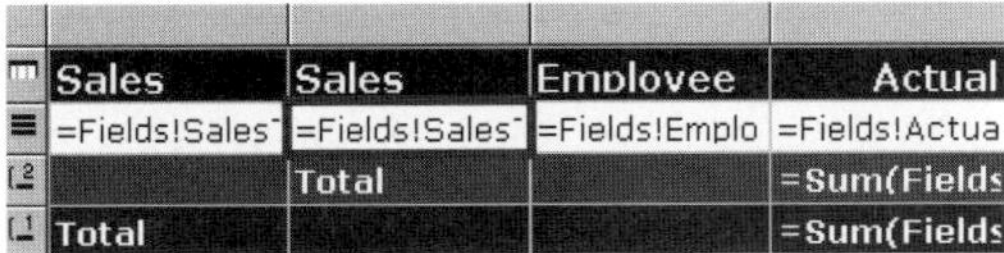

The column handles are the shaded cells that appear above the table, and the row handles are the shaded cells with icons that are shown to the left of the table. You use these handles to modify the table properties.

3. Position your cursor between the second and third column handles, and then click and drag to widen the second column, Sales Territory Country, to approximately 1.5 inches.

   Now the table looks like this:

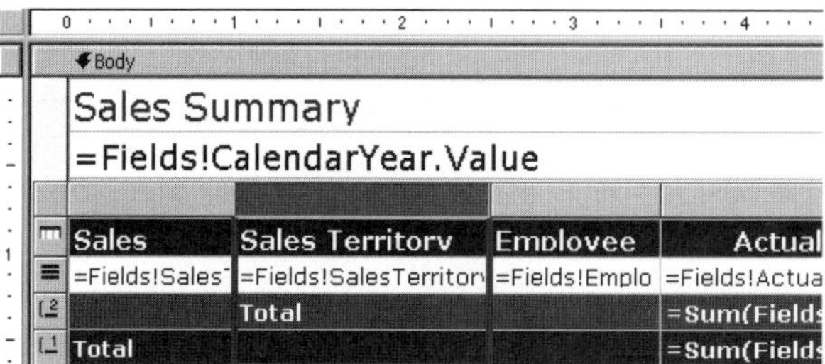

   You can drag the column only when the cursor is properly positioned and the cursor changes to a double-headed arrow. Making the column bigger eliminates the text wrapping problem, but it also requires you to have some idea of the maximum length of the data that could appear in that column.

4. Position the cursor between the third and fourth column handles, and then click and drag to widen the Employee column to approximately 1.75 inches.

5. Right-click the fourth column handle, above Actual Sales, to select the entire column, and then click Properties.

   The Properties window for the selected column, named TableColumn4, is displayed in Visual Studio:

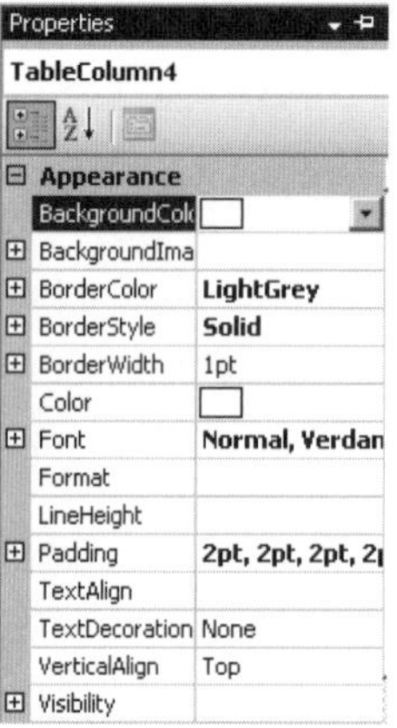

6. Scroll through the Properties window, if necessary, to find the *Format* property, and then type **C0** in the *Format* property field to format the field as currency with no decimal places.

> **Note** Use .NET formatting strings to control the data display. You can find more information about formatting numeric strings online at *http://msdn.microsoft.com/library/default.asp?url=/library/en-us/cpguide/html/cpconstandardnumericformatstrings.asp*. Information about formatting date strings is located at *http://msdn.microsoft.com/library/default.asp?url=/library/en-us/cpguide/html/cpconDateTimeFormatStrings.asp*.

Scroll to the bottom of the Properties window to find the *Width* property, and then type **1.25in** to resize this column.

You can provide a specific measurement for the *Width* property when you require more granular control over the size of a column.

Click the Preview tab to preview the modified report.

The newly formatted report is displayed:

Sales Summary

2001

Sales Territory Group	Sales Territory Country	Employee	Actual Sales
North America	Canada	José Saraiva	$1,248,853
		Garrett Vargas	$568,971
	Total		$1,817,824
	United States	Shu Ito	$1,068,441
		Linda Mitchell	$1,374,860
		Michael Blythe	$903,230

The text wrapping problem is solved, and the format of the Actual Sales column is improved. Your first report is ready for publishing!

Publishing a Report

Now you'll wrap up the authoring stage of the reporting life cycle by publishing the report to the Report Server, where it can be accessed by the user community.

In this procedure, you'll deploy a report solution that enables you to publish your report to your local Report Server.

Deploy a report solution

1. On the File menu, click Save All.
2. In the Solution Explorer window, right-click the Adventure Works project at the top of the tree, and then click Properties.

   The Adventure Works Property Pages dialog box is displayed. You can see the Target ReportFolder and TargetServerURL properties for which values were provided on the Choose The Deployment Location page of the Report Wizard.
3. Click Configuration Manager.
4. Verify that the Deploy check box is selected.

   The Configuration Manager dialog box looks like this:

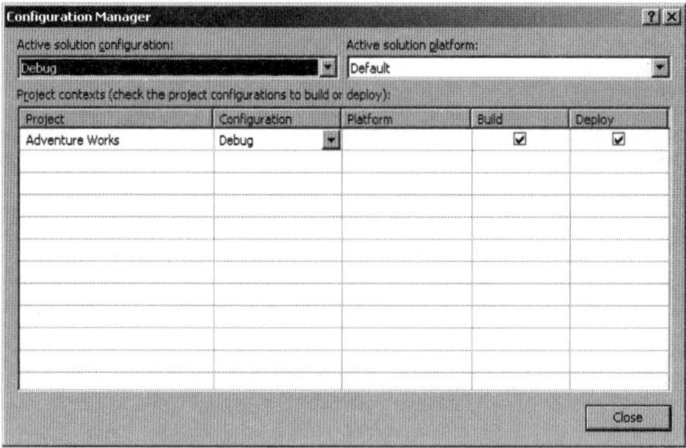

5. Click Close, and then click OK.
6. On the Build menu, click Deploy Adventure Works.

   The Output window displays the progress of deployment. Deployment of the solution is complete when you see messages in the Output window announcing that the build and deploy operations succeeded:

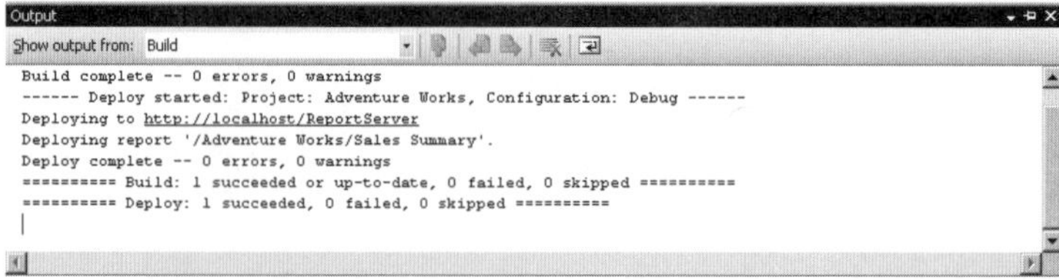

Instead of deploying an entire solution, you also have the option to deploy a single report or multiple reports within a project or solution. A report is published by using one of these deployment options to transfer it from Visual Studio to the Report Server. You can alternatively publish a report programmatically using a script or manually using the Web application called Report Manager, which you'll learn about in Chapter 9.

Managing a Report

You can manage published reports by using Report Manager, which is supplied by Reporting Services. Management of reports includes such activities as setting report properties and execution properties, managing content in folders, and applying security on the Report Server to control how users access and interact with reports. You perform only a few management tasks in this chapter. (You'll learn about all the management tasks in Part III, "Managing the Report Server.")

Reviewing Report Properties

Each report has a set of properties pages that you must manage. You need to know how to use the Report Manager to find these properties and to review the types of properties you can manage.

In this procedure, you'll navigate from the Home page of Report Manager to the Properties page of your report.

Open the report's Properties page

1. Open Internet Explorer.
2. Type the URL ***http://localhost/Reports*** to open the Report Manager.

   The Home page of Report Manager is displayed:

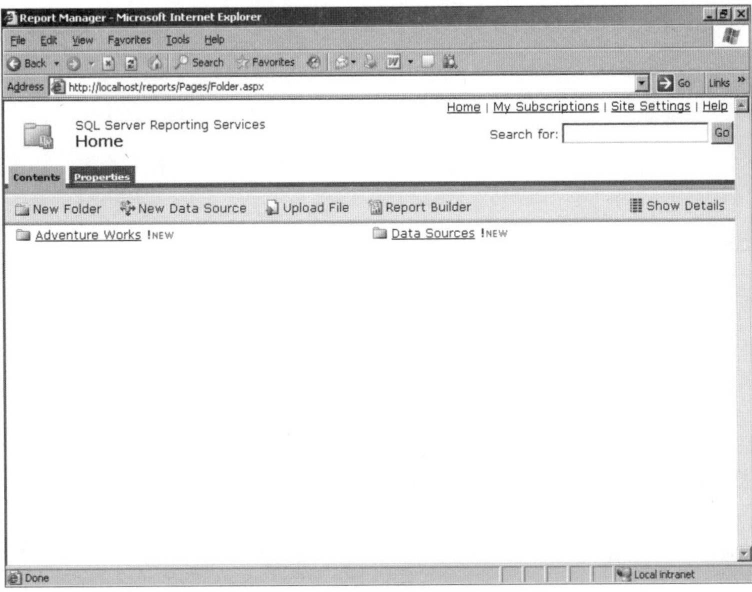

3. Click the Adventure Works folder link.

The folder contents are displayed:

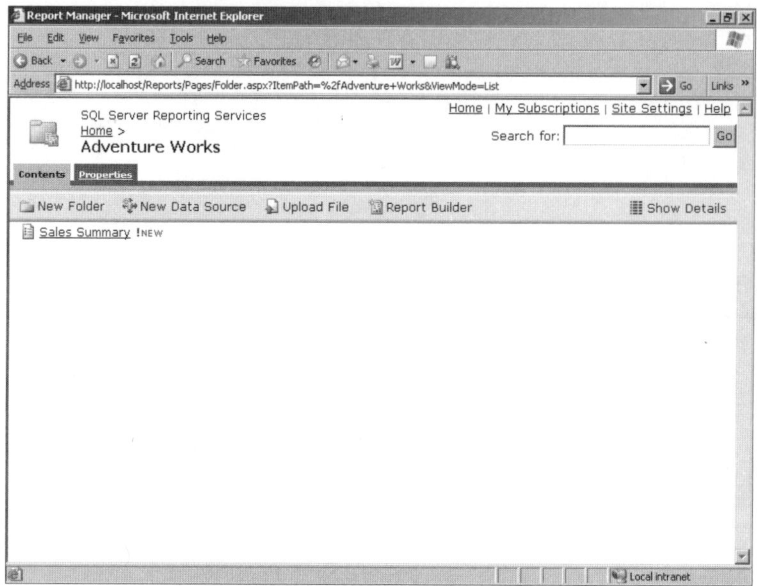

Notice that this page has a Properties tab in addition to the Contents tab. (You'll learn more about managing folder properties in Chapter 9.) Currently, the Adventure Works folder contains only one report, the Sales Summary report that you just published.

4. Click the Sales Summary link.

   Reporting Services generates and displays the Sales Summary report:

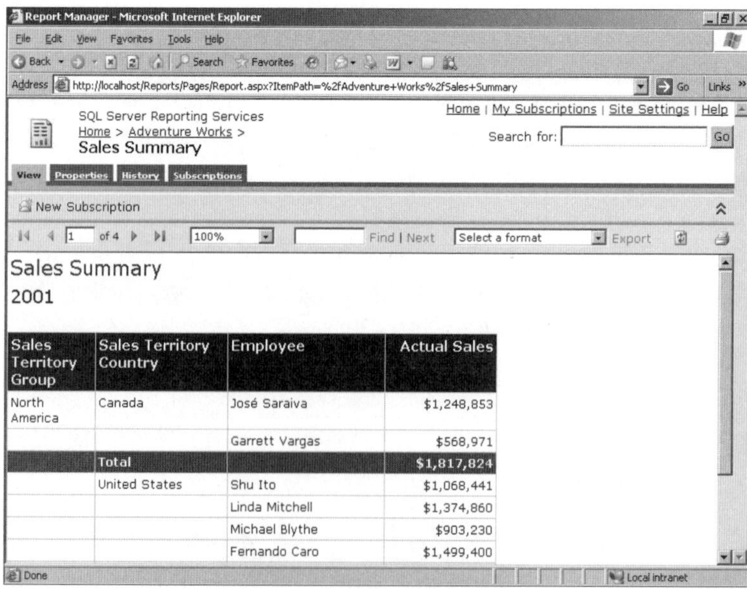

The View tab is displayed by default when you open a report. Three other tabs are available for this report: Properties, History, and Subscriptions. In this section, you review the Properties page. Later, in Chapter 7, you'll learn more about the other tabs.

Tip You don't have to wait for the report to be displayed before clicking another tab.

5. Click the Properties tab.

   The Properties page for the Sales Summary report is displayed:

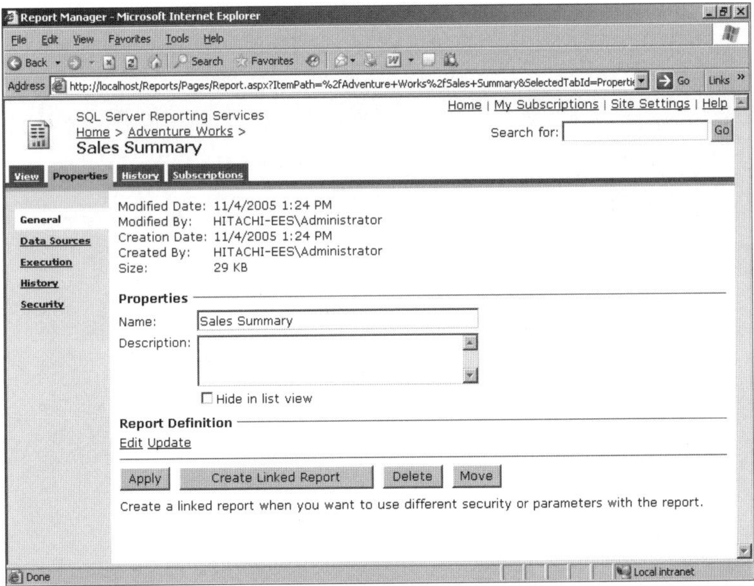

On this page, you can see the author and also the date the report was created. The modification author and date of modification match creation information until the report is subsequently modified. Notice that you can change the name of the report on this page and add a description. The other tasks that you can perform on this page are covered later in Chapter 9.

Notice the links in the left frame of the browser window. The many types of report properties are logically organized into separate pages, where you can apply changes to current settings. Properties determine, for example, how the report appears in Report Manager, how users can interact with the report, and how the Report Server connects to the data sources. You'll review report properties in greater detail in Chapter 9.

Changing Report Properties

Often, you will want to add a description so a user knows what your report contains before opening it. This property is accessible on the main properties page of the report.

In this procedure, you'll add a description and observe how a description is displayed on the Contents page of a folder.

Add a description

1. In the Description box, type **Actual sales by year, territory, and salesperson**.

   Your screen looks like this:

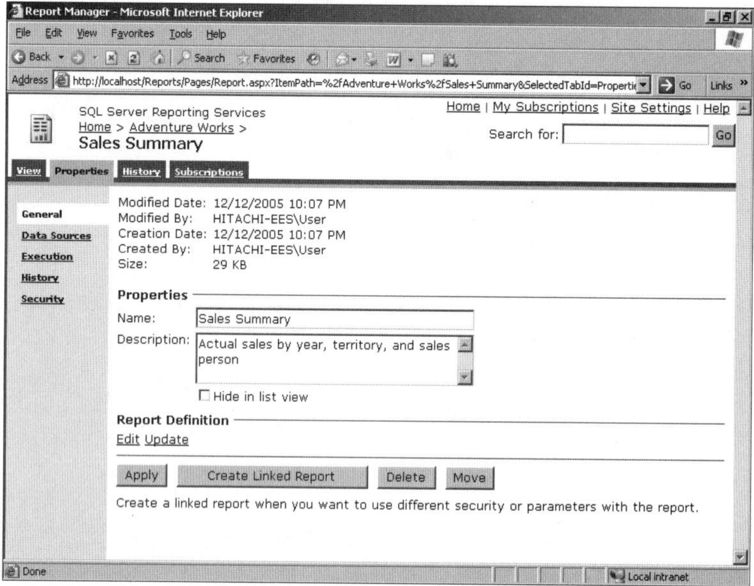

   This report description is displayed on the Contents page and, importantly, is visible only to users who have been granted permission to view the report.

2. Click Apply.

   Clicking Apply doesn't appear to change anything. However, the report description is now visible on the Contents page of the Adventure Works folder.

3. Click the Adventure Works folder link at the top-left corner of the browser window.

Your screen looks like this:

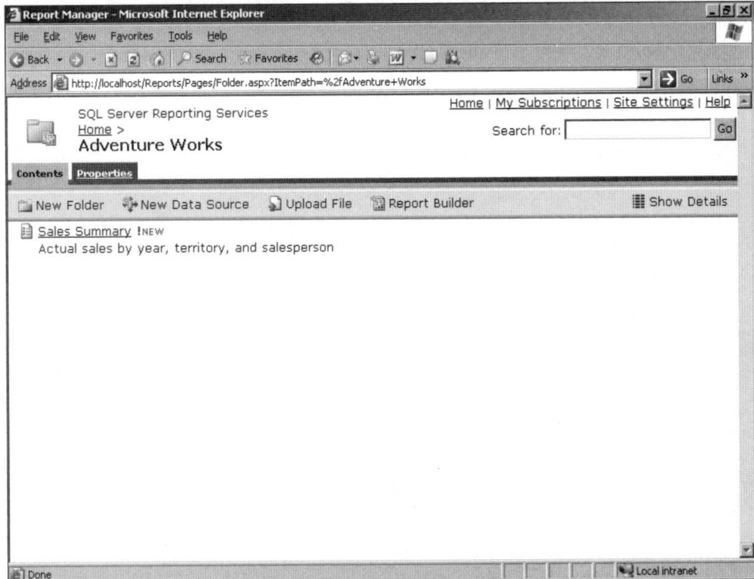

Notice how the report description is displayed below the report name.

Reviewing Execution Properties

Execution properties are a subset of the report properties maintained for each report. When you understand the implications of the execution property settings, you can choose the most appropriate property setting for your reporting environment. Execution properties allow you to manage reports by balancing system resources and performance with the users' information requirements. For example, you set up caching to achieve a reasonable balance when data used in the report is not changing rapidly at the source. To use caching, you first need to change the data sources properties so you can assign logon credentials that will be used to execute the report for the cache. Separate logon credentials are required by Reporting Services to implement report caching in order to make a single report available to many users.

In this procedure, you'll open the Execution Properties page for your report to review the available options.

Open the report's Execution Properties page

1. Click the Sales Summary link.

   Assume for a moment that you've just started a new browser session. Just like the previous time you opened this report, a message is displayed to let you know that several activities are occurring: "Report is being generated". Each time a report executes on demand, as you initiated in this step, a query is executed to retrieve data from the rs2005sbsDW database. The data is processed with the report, which is then rendered into the HTML display in your browser window.

2. Click the Properties tab.
3. Click the Execution link in the left frame of the page.

   The Execution Properties page is displayed:

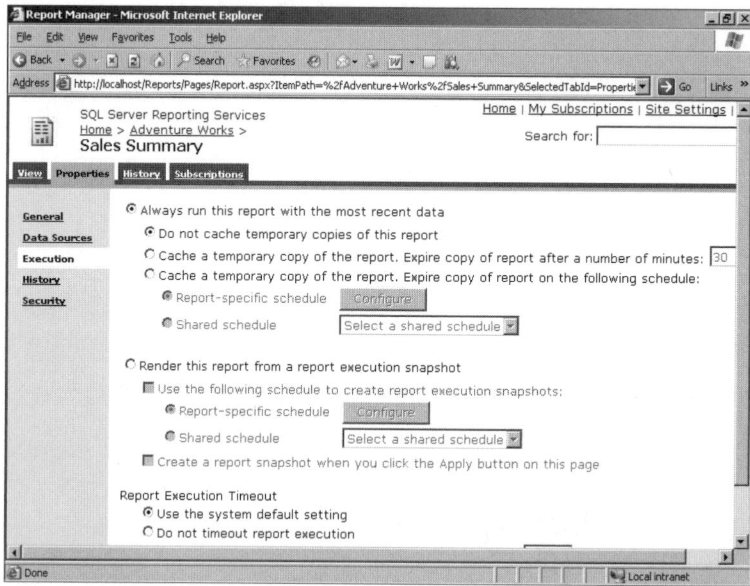

Notice that you can render the report either on demand or on a scheduled basis. When rendered on demand, the report typically displays the most recent data and may or may not use caching. By default, a report renders on demand without caching. When rendered on a scheduled basis, the report is stored as an execution snapshot, which captures data for the report at a point in time.

Execution properties control when report processing occurs. When a report executes on demand, which occurs every time another user opens the report, the defined query runs and the query results are merged with the report definition to produce the HTML output format. You can alternatively set the execution properties to process the report at a scheduled time so the report is ready when accessed. However, if you choose to do this, let users know that the data in the report is not current. Another option is to cache a report temporarily to make the same output available to several users for the duration of a specified timeframe. The key difference between a snapshot and a cached report is that the snapshot is stored permanently until physically deleted, while the cache is stored temporarily with a predetermined expiration. The options for specifying execution properties are covered in Chapter 9.

Changing Data Sources Properties

Data sources properties define the connection to be used for query execution. You can change these properties to override the credentials used for authentication when the report executes. Queries that run unattended, such as when a report is cached or scheduled for execution, require stored credentials. These credentials are encrypted when stored in the ReportServer database. (You'll learn more about using secured credentials in Chapter 9.) To set up a cache for your report, you need to change the credentials information in the data sources properties.

Use secured credentials

1. Click the Data Sources link in the left frame of the page.
2. Click the Credentials Stored Securely In The Report Server option.
3. Type **ReportExecution** as the user name.

   This SQL Server login was added when you installed the sample databases.
4. Type **ReportExecution** as the password.

> **Important** In a production environment in which you are using stored credentials, it's important to test the report by viewing it to ensure that you have entered the user name and password correctly. The credentials will not be validated until the report executes.

Your screen now looks like this:

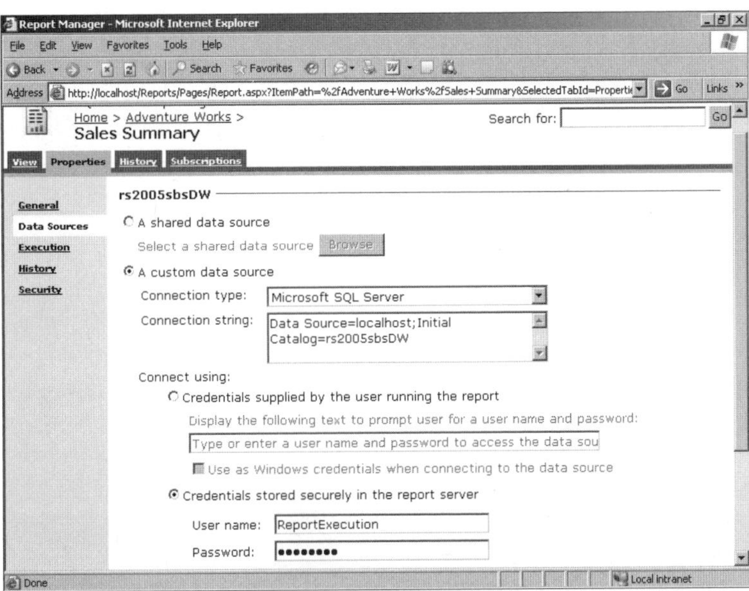

5. Click Apply.

Changing Execution Properties

You might want to temporarily cache a report to improve performance. When a user first opens the report, a copy of the report is placed in temporary storage and made available to other users who open the same report. You can also assign a time limit for the cache so that the report can be periodically refreshed with more current data.

> **Note** The type of caching discussed in this chapter refers to the access of a single report by multiple users. When you open a report, the report is automatically cached for you as part of your browser session. You can then return to this report repeatedly during the same session without having to wait for the query to execute again, regardless of the current setting of the report's execution properties. When you close the browser window, the report is removed from this cache. You'll learn more about session caching in Chapter 9.

In this procedure, you'll change the report execution properties to cache your report, and set the cache to expire after 60 minutes.

Define a report cache

1. Click the Execution link.
2. Click the Cache A Temporary Copy Of The Report. Expire Copy Of Report After A Number Of Minutes option to cache the report and expire after a specified number of minutes. Change the number of minutes to **60**.

   Your screen looks like this:

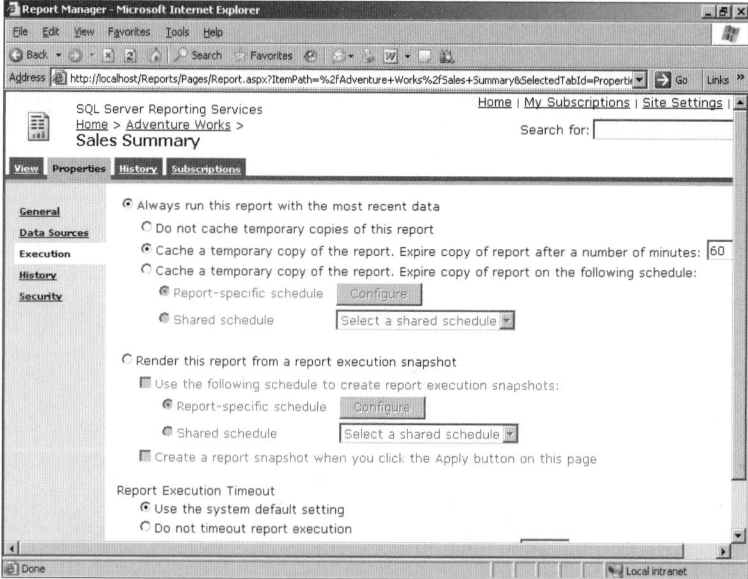

3. Click Apply at the bottom of the page.

   The next time this report is opened, a temporary copy of it will be placed in the cache to speed up its display for any later requests by other users within the same hour. At the end of 60 minutes, the temporary copy is removed from the cache. A new copy is only placed in the cache when a user requests the report again.

   As mentioned earlier, by using the caching option, you can improve performance for the next user who opens the same report. Any subsequent request for a report results in the display of the cached copy of the report rather than in the execution of the query and processing of the report. That is, any subsequent request displays the cached report until the cache expires. The purpose of expiring the cache on a periodic basis is to force the report to be refreshed with the most current data when the next user accesses the report. The result is a new cached instance of the report until the next scheduled expiration.

> **Tip** The caching feature is useful when you have a query that takes a few minutes or more to execute and many people want to see the same report. It minimizes the demand for resources on the database server, reduces the level of network traffic associated with transporting the data from the database server to the Report Server, and speeds up the display of reports when requested. For more details about report caching, refer to Chapter 9.

Accessing a Report

Each published report has its own URL on the Report Server. Instead of using the Report Manager to navigate through folders to find a report, you can enter the report's URL address into your browser. You can also use this URL in a hyperlink that you add to a custom HTML page. (In fact, you could even include additional characters in the URL to control the behavior of the report, such as formatting the report with a different rendering extension, but you'll learn how to do that in Chapter 18, "Building Custom Reporting Tools.") For now, it's easiest to use the Report Manager to find and view a report online and to export the report to another format.

Displaying a Report

Now that you successfully authored and managed your report, you are ready for the access stage of the reporting life cycle. When you access a report online, you can use a toolbar in the viewer to help you explore your report. After opening the report, you can navigate through its pages or search for specific text so you can jump forward in it.

In this procedure, you'll explore each page of your report.

View report pages

1. Click the View tab.

   The first page of the report, for calendar year 2001, is displayed. This presentation of the report is nearly identical to the version you saw in the Report Designer. You now have the HTML viewer that includes a report toolbar to help you explore and interact with the report. For example, you can use controls in the toolbar to page through the report, to search for a string in the report, or to export the report to another format. The HTML Viewer is covered in more detail in Chapter 12, "Accessing Reports."

2. Click the Next Page button on the View toolbar to view the sales data for each year.

Searching a Report

Sometimes the information you're looking for can be difficult to find in a lengthy or multipage report. The HTML Viewer provides a feature to help you find a text string anywhere in the report, from your current position to the end of the report.

In this procedure, you'll use the search feature to locate specific text in the report.

Find text in a report

1. In the Find text box, located in the center of the View toolbar, type **Linda**. Click the Find link.

   Your screen looks like this:

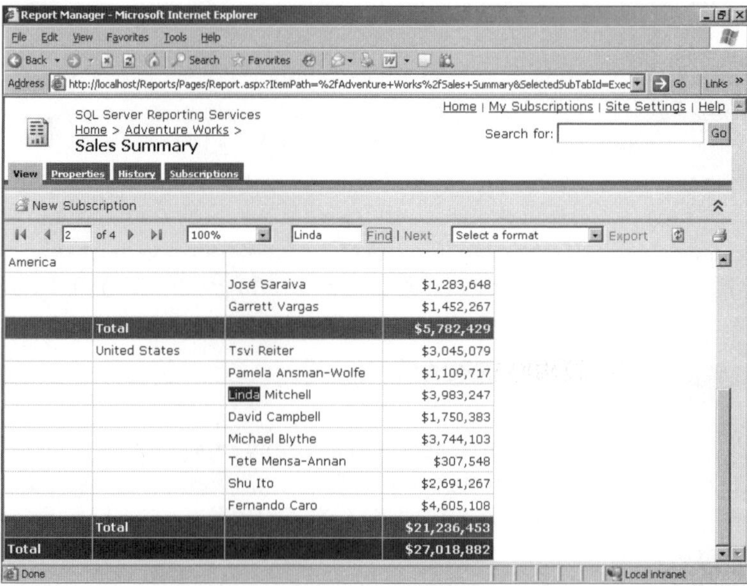

The Find link is not enabled until you type a string into the associated search box. When you click this link, the report scrolls to the first occurrence of this string in the report.

2. Use the Next link to find the next occurrence of the string.

   The search operation begins in the currently selected page or section and continues across each page of the report until the end of the report is reached.

> **Tip** You don't need to worry about using the correct case, because the search operation is not case-sensitive. However, you are limited to a string length of 256 characters.

Exporting a Report

The HTML format is not the only format you can use to view your report. You can also export the report to another format that allows you to create a file that you can open immediately or save to your computer. The View toolbar includes a drop-down list from which you can choose an export format. (Reporting Services includes several export formats, also referred to as rendering formats, which you'll review more closely in Chapter 13, "Rendering Reports.") This feature gives you the flexibility to produce several versions of your report from a single platform.

In this procedure, you'll complete your tour of Reporting Services by exporting your report to an Excel format, opening the generated Excel workbook, and examining each sheet in the workbook, comparing them with the rendering of your report as HTML.

Export to Excel

1. Click Excel in the drop-down list at the far right of the View toolbar.

   Your screen now looks like this:

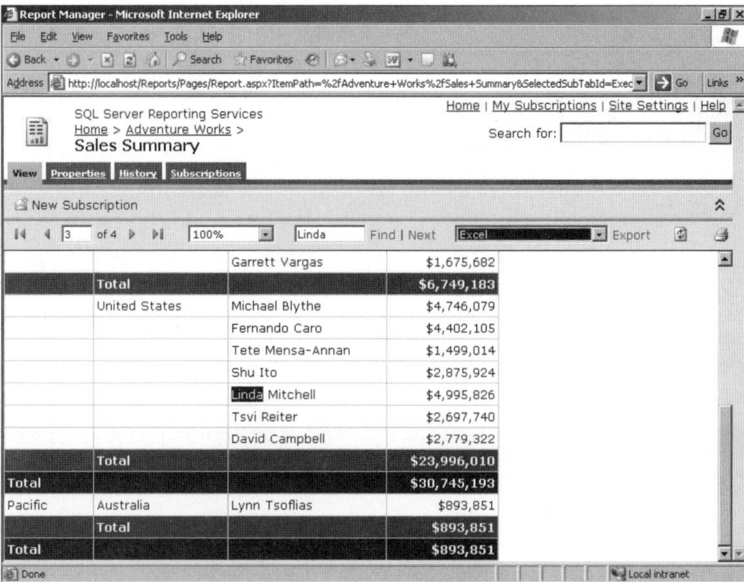

As mentioned earlier, the Export feature of the HTML view gives you the ability to view the report in a different format. When you export the report, if a viewer is available for the selected format, a new browser window opens. For example, to export to the Excel format, you must have Microsoft Excel installed on your computer.

2. Click the Export link.

   A new browser window opens and the File Download dialog box is displayed:

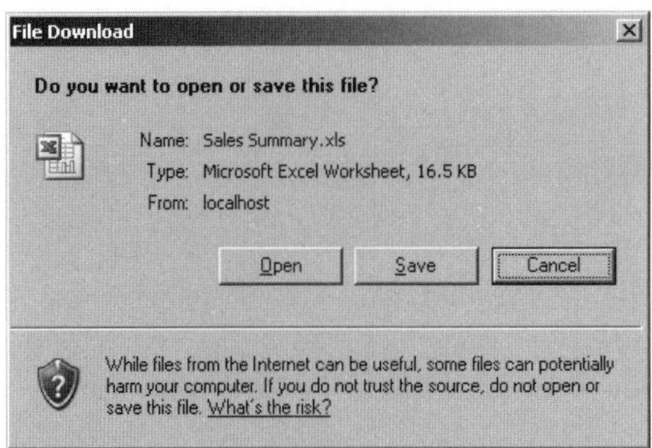

   You can open the file to view it now, or you can save the file to view it later.

3. Click Open.

   The Report Server renders the report as an Excel file that downloads to your computer. Microsoft Excel opens, and the report is displayed:

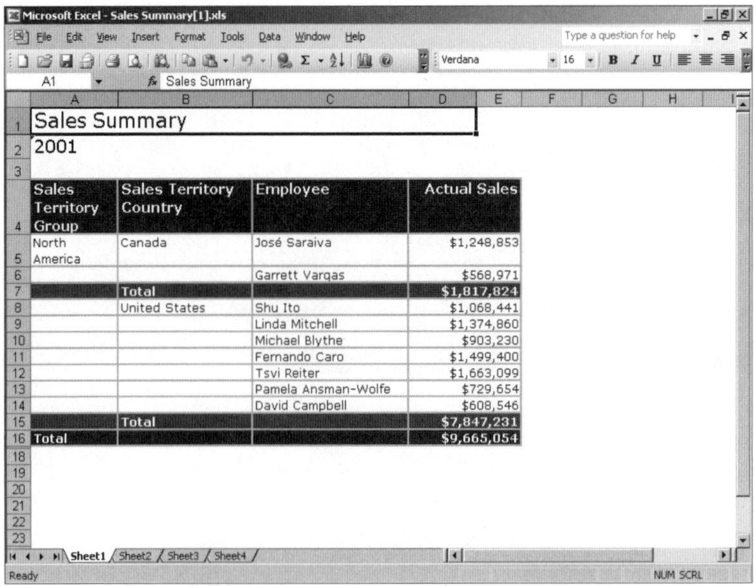

Sales Summary

2001

Sales Territory Group	Sales Territory Country	Employee	Actual Sales
North America	Canada	José Saraiva	$1,248,853
		Garrett Vargas	$568,971
	Total		$1,817,824
	United States	Shu Ito	$1,068,441
		Linda Mitchell	$1,374,860
		Michael Blythe	$903,230
		Fernando Caro	$1,499,400
		Tsvi Reiter	$1,663,099
		Pamela Ansman-Wolfe	$729,654
		David Campbell	$608,546
	Total		$7,847,231
Total			$9,665,054

Notice that the report style in Reporting Services is closely reproduced in the Excel version of the report. Much of the color style, font style, and layout that you see in the HTML version of the report also appears in the Excel version. Each page has been placed on a separate worksheet in the Excel workbook.

4. Click each worksheet tab to review the sales data for each year.

   With the report in this format, you can take advantage of all of Excel's features to interact with the report data and perform additional analysis that was not possible using the static report in the browser.

Chapter 3 Quick Reference

To	Do this
Start the Report Server Project Wizard	Start a new project in Visual Studio (SQL Server Business Intelligence Development Studio) and select Report Server Project Wizard from the Business Intelligence Projects folder. You must provide a name for the project and solution and designate a folder location for the solution.
Add a data source using the Report Wizard	On the Select The Data Source page, enter a name for the data source; select a connection type; and enter a connection string, or use the Edit button to access the Connection Properties dialog box to generate the connection string automatically. For example: `Data Source=localhost;Initial Catalog=rs2005sbsDW`
Add a query string using the Report Wizard	On the Design The Query page, enter or paste in a query string, or click the Query Builder button to open the Query Builder.
Select a report type using the Report Wizard	On the Select The Report Type page, click either the Tabular or Matrix option.
Arrange the data using the Report Wizard	On the Design The Table page, assign fields to the Page, Group, and Details sections. In the Design The Matrix page, assign fields to the Page, Columns, Rows, and Details sections.
Select a table layout using the Report Wizard	On the Choose The Table Layout page, select Block or Stepped, or optionally include subtotals. If you choose the stepped layout, you can enable drilldown.
Apply a style template using the Report Wizard	On the Choose The Table Style page or the Choose The Matrix Style page, click a style name.
Assign a deployment location and a report name using the Report Wizard	On the Choose The Deployment Location page, enter the URL for the Report Server to host the report. For example: *http://localhost/ReportServer* Optionally, enter a folder name. The folder will be created on deployment if it does not already exist. The final page of the Report Wizard requires a report name.
Preview a report	In Visual Studio, click the Preview tab.

To	Do this
Adjust the size of a column in a table	In Visual Studio, click the table to display the column and row handles, and then drag the column handle to the left to make the column smaller or to the right to make it larger. Alternatively, set the *Width* property for the selected column.
Publish a report solution	On the Build menu of Visual Studio, click Deploy *projectname*.
Open Report Manager	Enter the URL in your browser. For example: *http://localhost/Reports*.
View a report	In Report Manager, navigate the folder hierarchy to the report, and then click the report link.
Manage report properties	With the report open in Report Manager, click the Properties tab. Use the applicable link in the left frame to access the set of properties to be managed. Set a property by clicking an option or selecting a check box, and then clicking the Apply button.
Export a report	With the report open in Report Manager, select the export format from the list box and click the Export link.

Part II
Authoring Reports

In this part:

In Part I, "Getting Started with Reporting Services," you learned how the activities of enterprise reporting are fully supported by the Reporting Services platform. You also explored the reporting life cycle by using Reporting Services to author, manage, and access a simple report. In the five chapters of Part II, you focus on the authoring stage of the reporting life cycle by developing a variety of reports that use the range of features provided by the report design environment. In Part III, "Managing the Report Server," you'll learn how to manage the reports you create.

Chapter 4

Developing Basic Reports

After completing this chapter, you will be able to:

- Add a new report to a project.
- Define data for a report.
- Add a table to a report.
- Add sorting to a table.
- Group data in a table.
- Add items to a report.
- Edit properties of report items.

This chapter shows you how to use the Report Designer in Microsoft Visual Studio so you can prepare, structure, and format a tabular report. This chapter begins by explaining the output of the authoring stage–a report definition file.

Understanding a Report Definition File

Reporting Services generates a report by using a *report definition*, which describes the report's data, layout, and properties. Rather than build a report using a programming language to create a series of instructions, you can use Reporting Services to define exactly how you want the report to look. Using a definition, as contrasted with a series of instructions, is known as a *declarative model*. Regardless of the language later used to generate the report from this definition, the result is the same and can be produced in many different formats.

The declarative model used by Reporting Services is constructed as a collection of XML elements that conform to a specific XML schema definition known as *Report Definition Language* (RDL). RDL is an open schema that can be extended by third parties, such as application developers and commercial software companies, to support specialized features. Microsoft developed RDL to promote the exchange of report definitions between report producers and report consumers.

A *report producer* is an application that is used to create a report definition. This application typically has a graphical user interface (GUI), which allows the report developer to create a report definition without writing any code. A developer could also build a custom application to generate a report definition completely from code–ultimately, it's the report definition that matters, not the means by which it is produced.

A report definition is transformed into the desired output format by an application known as a *report consumer*. The report consumer's job is to use the query embedded in the RDL to get data for the report and to merge the results with the set of instructions that define the report's layout and properties. Most commercial reporting applications produce reports in a proprietary format that can be used only within the vendor's report execution environment. By separating production and consumption, reports can be ported easily from one vendor's reporting platform to another, such as Reporting Services.

Preparing a Report Using Report Designer

In Chapter 3, "Building Your First Report," you built a simple report by using some of the features of Report Designer. As you recall, Report Designer is integrated with Visual Studio. Because Report Designer generates a report definition, it is therefore a report producer. The integration of Report Designer into Visual Studio allows you to take advantage of a fully featured programming environment to develop many types of reports, from the most basic reports to quite complex ones. Many people find Report Designer easier to use than Microsoft Access to build reports. As you work in Visual Studio, the Report Designer automatically converts your report layout into RDL.

Even if you don't know any programming languages or XML, the Report Designer is easy enough to use to create attractive and information-rich reports. If, however, you're already an experienced programmer, you'll find that Report Designer has all the tools you need to extend the capabilities of your reports. You'll learn how to add custom development to your reports in Chapter 16, "Report Authoring with Custom Development."

In this section, you use the Report Designer to prepare a report by creating a report project and adding a report to this new project. You then add a data source to the project to define the connection information that Reporting Services will use to get data for the report. To finish preparing the report, you create a dataset to define the data that will be displayed in the report.

Creating a New Report Project

In Chapter 3, you learned how to create a new project using the Report Server Project Wizard. Here, you'll use the Report Server Project template to create a project to contain your report.

In this procedure, you'll add a new project, My Adventure Works, not by using the wizard, but by using the Report Server Project template.

Use the Report Server Project template

1. If necessary, start SQL Server Business Intelligence Development Studio.
2. On the File menu, point to New, and then click Project.

3. In the New Project dialog box, click the Report Server Project template in the Business Intelligence Projects folder.
4. Type in a name for the project: **My Adventure Works**.
5. If necessary, type the following location for the project: **C:\Documents and Settings \<username>\My Documents\Microsoft Press\rs2005sbs\Workspace**, and then click OK.

Creating a New Report

Now you're ready to add a report to your project. You still have the option to use the Report Wizard to help you set up a new report. However, in this section, you'll create a blank report without using the wizard. As you progress through this chapter, you'll add items to this report.

In this procedure, you'll add a new item to your project using the Report template.

Add a new item to a project

1. In Solution Explorer, right-click the Reports folder, point to Add, and then click New Item.

> **Note** Notice that Add New Report is an available option. If you click Add New Report, the Report Wizard that you learned how to use in Chapter 3 is launched.

2. In the Add New Item dialog box, click the Report template.

   Notice that you can launch the Report Wizard from this dialog box as well.
3. Type a report name: **Product Profitability.rdl**.

> **Important** You must include the .rdl extension in the name of the report to ensure that Report Designer interacts properly with the report definition file.

4. Click Add.

Your screen looks like this:

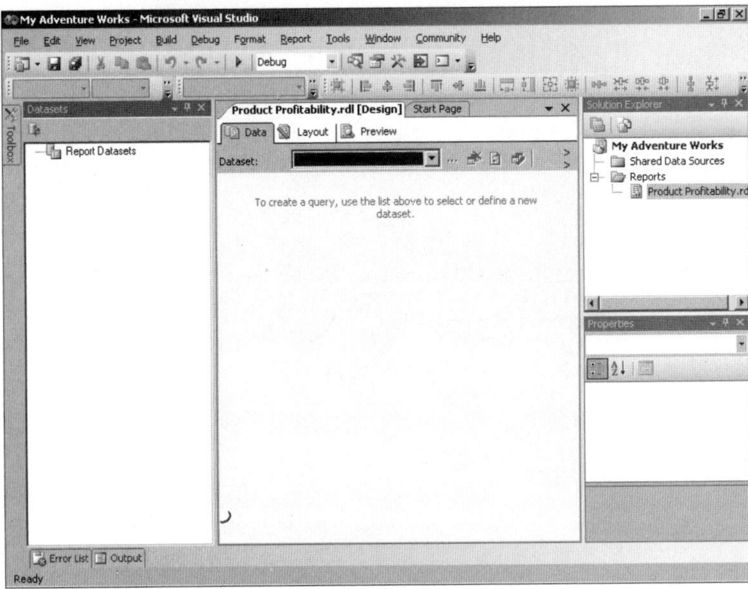

The My Adventure Works project now contains the new report. The Document window displays the report in the Data view.

Connecting to a Data Source

You already learned in Chapter 3 that a data source must include location information for the data that will be used in the report. At minimum, the data source includes the server, database name, and user credentials for authentication. The specific information contained by the data source depends on the type of database in which the data is stored.

A data source can be report-specific or shared. In Chapter 3, you created a report-specific data source that cannot be used in other reports in the project. Now you'll learn how to create a shared data source that can be used by several reports. By using a shared data source, you can more easily manage changes when the location of data or authentication information changes–you need to update only the shared data source instead of update each report that uses a report-specific data source.

In this procedure, you'll create a shared data source to define the connection to the rs2005sbsDW database in your SQL Server using Windows authentication.

Add a shared data source

1. In Solution Explorer, right-click the Shared Data Sources folder, and then click Add New Data Source.

2. Change the name of this data source from DataSource1 to **rs2005sbsDW**.
3. Click Edit.

   The Connection Properties dialog box is displayed. By default, the data provider is Microsoft SQL Server (SqlClient). Reporting Services can work with any OLE DB .NET data provider; you simply click Change and select the appropriate provider.
4. In the Connection Properties dialog box, type the server name: **localhost**.
5. Click Use Windows Authentication.
6. In the Select Or Enter A Database Name drop-down list, select rs2005sbsDW.
7. Click OK to return to the Shared Data Source dialog box.
8. Click OK to complete the creation of the shared data source.

   The Solution Explorer window looks like this:

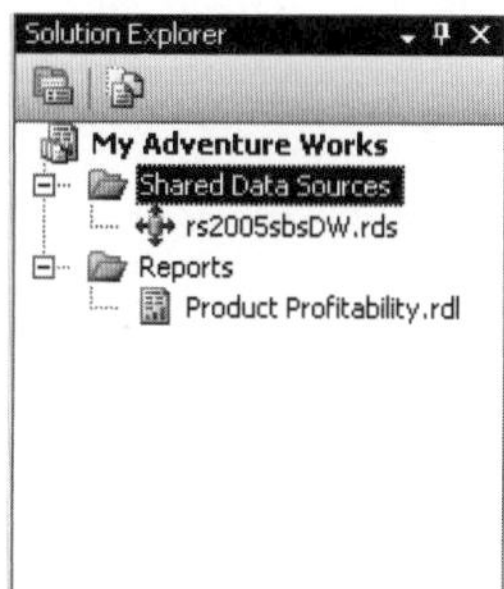

   The Shared Data Sources folder now contains a shared data source item, rs2005sbsDW.rds.

Working with Datasets

A report definition can include one or more datasets. Each dataset is essentially a query used to gather data for the report, but it also contains a pointer to the data source and other information about the data, such as collation and case sensitivity. (If you're unfamiliar with these terms, you should ask your database administrator what settings are appropriate for the data source you're using to build your report.) Each column from the dataset query becomes a field that can be used in the report. In Chapter 3, you used the Report Wizard to add a single dataset to your report. (You'll learn how to use multiple datasets in Chapter 7, "Building Advanced Reports.") In this section, you'll work with just a single dataset in your report, but you'll create it without the help of the wizard.

In this procedure, you'll enter a SQL query that returns data from a view that summarizes costs, sales amounts, and order quantities by product, product subcategory, and product category in January 2003.

Add a dataset

1. On Dataset toolbar, select <New Dataset...> from the drop-down list, as shown here:

The Dataset dialog box is displayed:

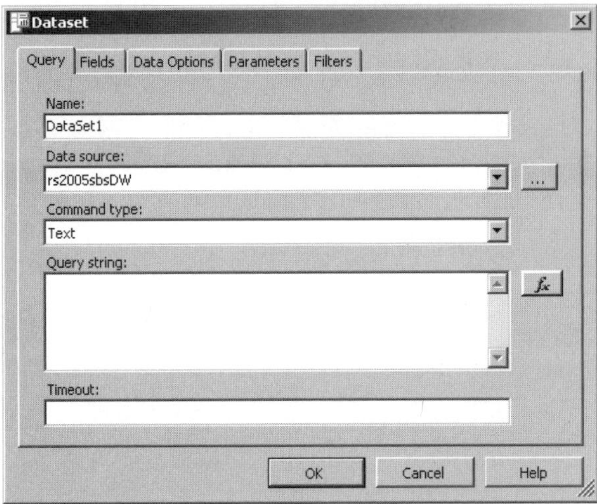

Notice that the data source defaults to the shared data source you created earlier, labeled rs2005sbsDW. You can also create a new private data source for the report by selecting New Data Source in the Data Source drop-down list.

2. Replace the name of the dataset with **DataDetail**.

Important The name of the dataset cannot contain a space.

3. Type the following SQL statement to define a query string for the dataset:

```
select * from vProductProfitability
where Year = 2003 and
MonthNumberOfYear = 1
```

This query uses a view in the rs2005sbsDW database, which was prepared specifically to provide data for reporting.

Tip It's a good idea to use a view rather than a table when extracting data for reporting purposes. If business rules change for the reports, you can make the necessary updates to the view rather than modify each report using the modified table—avoiding a maintenance nightmare. Another way to manage future changes to the report is to use a stored procedure, which you'll learn how to do in Chapter 7.

4. Click OK.
5. Click Run on the Dataset toolbar to test the query and see the result set.

   The Run button is represented as an exclamation point in the Dataset toolbar. You might need to resize the Document window to view the entire toolbar.

   The Document window now looks like this:

   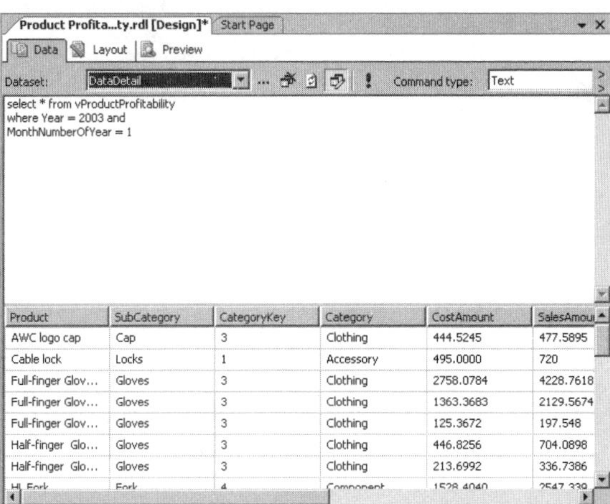

   The Data view page shows the dataset in the Generic Query Designer layout. The query is displayed in the top section of the page, and the query results are shown in a grid in the bottom section. The query results are not stored with the report definition, but they are displayed here to help you validate that you are retrieving the expected data.

   Each column in the grid becomes a field available for use in the report. These fields do not change over time unless you change the query in the dataset. Of course, as the data changes in the source database, the rows that appear in this grid, and eventually in the report, change when the query is executed.

6. Click the Generic Query Designer button (to the left of the Run button) to toggle the Query Builder on.

   You can use the Query Builder to help you create a query using a graphical interface rather than simply typing a completed query, as you did in this procedure. You'll learn how to use the Query Builder in Chapter 7.

7. On the File menu, click Save All.

Structuring a Report Using Report Designer

Once you complete the preparatory steps to define a data source and to create a dataset, you are ready to work on the structure of your report. As you learned in Chapter 3, a data region is a report structure that contains the data. You'll learn how to use the matrix, list, chart, rectangle, and subreport data regions in Chapter 6, "Organizing Data in Reports." In this chapter, you work only with the table data region. You start by placing the table in the report body. Then you add fields to the table, add interactive sorting to allow the user to change the sort direction of data in the table, and define groups to organize the data into logical sections.

Adding Items from the Toolbox

The Toolbox window contains all the *report items* available. Report items can be data regions, graphical elements, and free-standing text. You can choose from six data regions: table, matrix, rectangle, list, subreport, and chart. Graphical elements you can add include a line and an image. You can add one or more of these report items to your report. You can even add multiple data regions, which you'll learn how to do in Chapter 6. You'll learn how to add the other types of report items later in this chapter.

In this procedure, you'll add a table to the design grid.

Add a table

1. Click the Layout tab.
2. In the Visual Studio Window on the left side of your screen, hover the pointer over the Hammer and Wrench icon to open the Toolbox window.

   If the Toolbox window is not visible and the Hammer and Wrench icon is not in the toolbar, click Toolbox on the View menu to show it.

3. In the Toolbox window, click Table.
4. Point to the intersection of the top row and first column of grid lines in the body of the report, and then click to add a table.

If you are using the Visual Studio default layout for Windows, your screen looks like this:

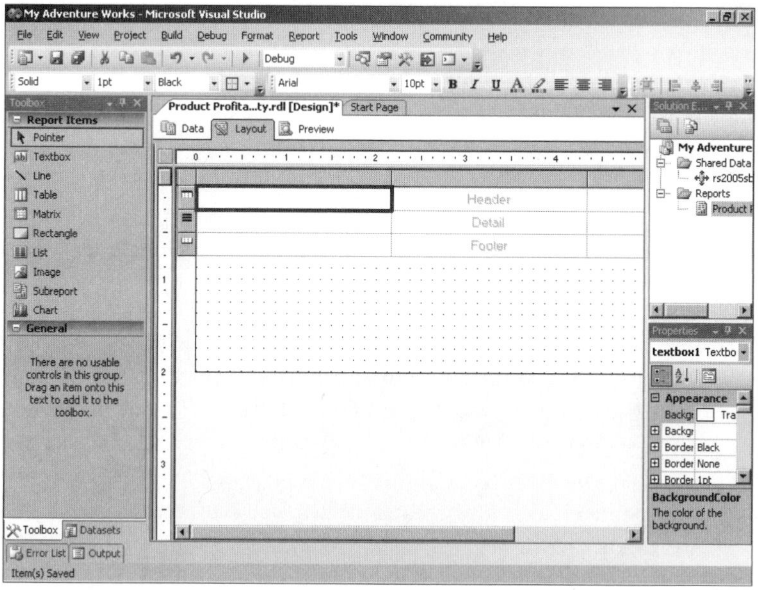

You'll learn how to place the other items in the design grid later in this chapter and in Chapter 6.

> **Tip** You can also drag an item from the Toolbox window and drop it on the design grid in the desired location.

Notice that the initial layout of the table has three columns and three rows. Each row handle–the shaded area on the left border of the table–has a unique icon to represent the row type. The first row is a table header, the second row is a detail row, and the third row is a table footer. The detail row repeats for each row in the dataset. The header and footer rows each appear only once in the table.

Working with Table Rows

A *table* is a collection of cells. Each cell of the table is initially filled with a textbox. A textbox can contain either static text or a formula. The formula can refer simply to a field from a dataset, or it can include more complex calculations.

In this procedure, you'll add fields to each row of the table.

Add fields to a table

1. From the View menu, select Datasets to display the Datasets window if necessary.

2. In the Datasets window, expand DataDetail, click Product, and drag the field to the first cell of the detail row.

   Your table looks like this:

Product	Header	
=Fields!Product.Value	Detail	
	Footer	

   Notice that the field name is automatically placed in the table header of the first column as static text. An expression is added to the first column's detail row:

   ```
   =Fields!Product.Value
   ```

   This expression is evaluated when the report is processed and replaced with values in the Product column of the dataset you created. Expressions that place a field value into a textbox always use this syntax. If you prefer to type a field expression into a textbox directly, just place the field name between the exclamation point and the period. However, dragging and dropping is safer because it ensures proper spelling of the expression.

> **Tip** Because the field name can be used in the table header row, build your query to give columns a report-friendly name. For example, if the table column in the database is labeled vProduct, consider writing your query as follows:
>
> ```
> Select vProduct as Product…
> ```
>
> Reporting Services automatically converts underscores to spaces and adds a space before capital letters in the middle of a word. For example, both Product_Name and ProductName would appear as Product Name. Each row of the dataset becomes a separate detail row in the table when the report is processed. The size of the table adapts dynamically to the number of rows returned by the dataset's query. By default, the table is added with three columns. You'll add an additional column to this report in Chapter 5, "Working with Expressions."

3. Make sure the first column is approximately 2 inches wide. If necessary, position your pointer between the first and second columns and drag to widen the column to 2 inches.

4. In the Datasets window, click *SalesAmount* and drag to the second cell of the detail row.

   Notice that the field name *SalesAmount* is automatically changed to Sales Amount in the table header. Notice also that the string in the table header and the expression in the detail row of the second column are right-justified. The field *SalesAmount* is a numeric column to which Report Designer automatically applies right justification.

5. Resize the second column to approximately 1.5 inches.
6. In the Datasets window, click OrderQuantity and drag to the third cell of the detail row.
7. Resize the third column to approximately 1.5 inches.
8. In the Datasets window, click SalesAmount and drag to the second cell of the table footer.

   Your table now looks like this:

   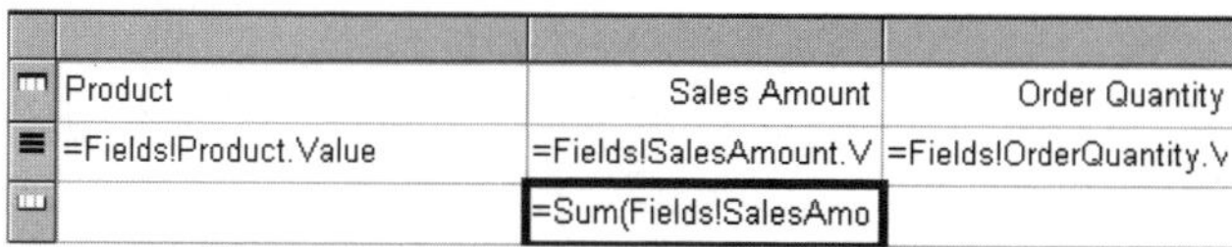

Product
   Sales Amount
   Order Quantity
   =Fields!Product.Value
   =Fields!SalesAmount.V
   =Fields!OrderQuantity.V
   =Sum(Fields!SalesAmo

   When you add a numeric field to a table header or table footer, the Report Designer automatically adds a *Sum* function to the expression to aggregate the values in the column to which the field was assigned. In this case, when the report is processed, the sum of SalesAmount is calculated from the detail rows in the dataset and is displayed in this table footer cell.

9. In the Datasets window, click OrderQuantity and drag to the third cell of the table footer.
10. Click the first cell of the table footer, and then type **Grand Total**.

    You can enter a string into any cell. The string is treated as a constant when the report is processed.

> **Tip** It's good practice in report design, when using aggregate functions like *Sum* in a table header or table footer, to add descriptive text to the same row so the reader understands what the value represents.

11. On the File menu, click Save All.
12. Click the Preview tab.

The top of your report looks like this:

Product	Sales Amount	Order Quantity
AWC logo cap	477.5895	85
Cable lock	720	48
Full-finger Gloves, L	4228.761875	176
Full-finger Gloves, M	2129.56744	87
Full-finger Gloves, S	197.548	8
Half-finger Gloves, M	704.0898	46
Half-finger Gloves, S	336.7386	22
HL Fork	2547.339	15
HL Headset	276.9006	3
HL Mtn Frame - Black, 38	8171.2143	9
HL Mtn Frame - Black, 42	9987.0397	11

There is one row for the table header, which shows the field names in the header row, and one detail row for each row in the dataset.

13. Click the Next Page button in the Preview toolbar.
14. Scroll to the bottom of the page.

    The table footer displays the string Grand Total and the sum of the detail rows for SalesAmount and OrderQuantity.

Sorting Table Rows

A new feature in Reporting Services 2005 is the ability to add interactive sorting to a column so the user can change the sort direction while viewing the report. For example, the report may display data in an ascending sort order, but if you enable interactive sorting, the user can click on an icon and reverse the sort order. You enable interactive sorting by changing textbox properties. Typically, you select the textbox that serves as a label for the column or row to be sorted, access its properties, and enable the interactive sorting.

When a user accesses a report that uses this feature, each textbox for which you have enabled interactive sorting will include an icon with two small arrows positioned to the right of the text. When the user clicks on this icon, the data is sorted in ascending order and the icon changes to an arrow pointing upward. If the user clicks on the icon again, the data is then sorted in descending order and the icon changes to an arrow pointing downward. The direction of the single arrow indicates the sort order, while the presence of the two arrows indicates that the report's default sort order is used.

In this procedure, you'll add interactive sorting to the table.

Add interactive sorting

1. Click the Layout tab.
2. Right-click the textbox in the first column of the table header row that contains the constant value Product, and then click Properties.

3. In the Textbox Properties dialog box, click the Interactive Sort tab.
4. Select the Add An Interactive Sort Action To This Textbox check box.
5. Select =Fields!Product.Value in the Sort Expression drop-down list.

   The Textbox Properties dialog box looks like this:

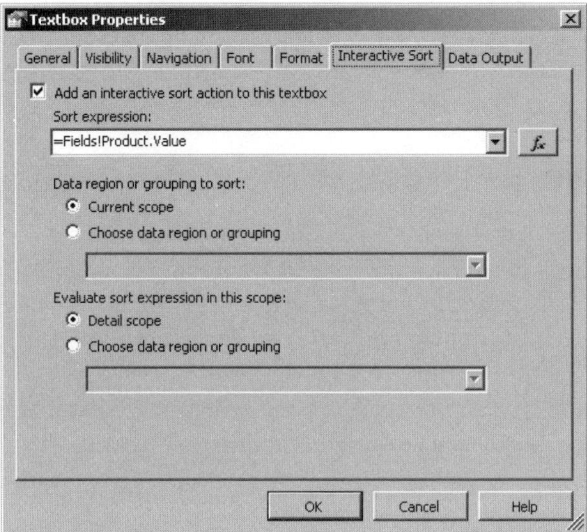

6. Click OK.
7. Click the Preview tab.

   The top of your report looks like this:

Product ⇕	Sales Amount	Order Quantity
AWC logo cap	477.5895	85
Cable lock	720	48
Full-finger Gloves, L	4228.761875	176
Full-finger Gloves, M	2129.56744	87
Full-finger Gloves, S	197.548	8
Half-finger Gloves, M	704.0898	46
Half-finger Gloves, S	336.7386	22
HL Fork	2547.339	15
HL Headset	276.9006	3
HL Mtn Frame - Black, 38	8171.2143	9
HL Mtn Frame - Black, 42	9987.0397	11

Notice the double-arrows icon that appears next to the Product column label. This icon indicates that this column can be sorted interactively. When you first open a report, the default sort order is determined by the order defined by the dataset, unless you override that sort order by changing the sorting within a data region, as you will learn in Chapter 6.

8. Click the double-arrows icon next to the Product column label.

   Now the icon is an arrow pointing upward, which indicates that the data is now sorted in ascending order. However, in this case, there is actually no change in the sort order because the dataset already sorted the products in ascending order.

9. Click the sort icon again to change the sort order to descending.

   You can toggle between ascending and descending by clicking the arrow icon to reverse the current direction. The only way to restore the default sort order, however, is to click the Refresh button on the Preview toolbar.

Grouping Data in a Table

When a report has many detail rows, it is often helpful to organize the detail rows into groups. A *group* is a set of detail rows that have something in common. For example, in your report's dataset, each detail row has a unique product name, but many products share the same product category. If a group is added to the report based on a product's category, all products for one category are arranged together and then followed by another set of detail rows with a different category. You can also nest a group within a group. Because each product category has several product subcategories, you can add another group to further divide the detail rows into smaller sets.

You can insert groups into the table to improve the arrangement of data. After adding the groups, you add fields to the group headers and a function to subtotal the detail rows within each group.

In this procedure, you'll add two groups to the table to organize detail rows by Category and SubCategory.

Add groups to the table

1. Click the Layout tab.
2. Click the table to display the row and column handles.
3. Right-click the row handle for the detail row, and then click Insert Group.

The Grouping And Sorting Properties dialog box is displayed:

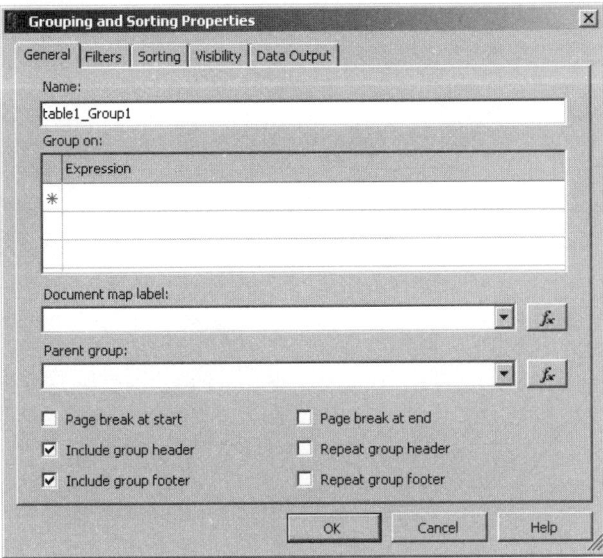

A default name is assigned to the group: table1_Group1. Every item, including a group, that you add to a report is assigned a name. The table you are working with is table1, so the first group added to this table is named table1_Group1. You have the option to keep this name or supply a new name.

> **Tip** Assigning a new name to a group makes it easier to remember how the group is being used. For example, you could use the field name by which the table detail rows will be grouped.

4. Change the name to **table1_Category**.
5. Click =Fields!Category.Value in the first Expression drop-down list.

When you display the Expression drop-down list, the Grouping And Sorting Properties dialog box looks like this:

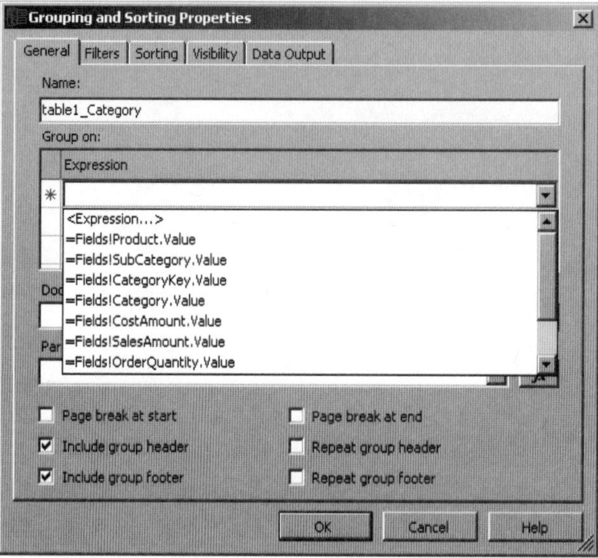

Notice that each item in the list is an expression formed from each field in the dataset. For each unique value of the selected expression, there is a group in the table.

Also notice from the checked options that, by default, the group header and group footer are included. When a group header and group footer are included in a table, the result is the Stepped layout that you reviewed in Chapter 3. Excluding the group header and group footer results in a table with the Block layout you saw in that chapter.

The Grouping And Sorting Properties dialog box contains several tabs you can use to manage properties for a group. You'll learn more about using the other properties in Chapter 5 and Chapter 6.

6. Click OK.
7. Right-click the row handle for the detail row, and then click Insert Group.

> **Note** The placement of the new group relative to existing groups is determined by the row you right-click. When you select the detail row, the new group is nested between the existing groups and the detail row. If you select an existing group, the new group is added between the selected group and either the other existing groups, if any, or the detail row when there are no other existing groups.

8. Change the name to **table1_SubCategory**.
9. Click =Fields!SubCategory.Value in the first Expression drop-down list.

10. Click OK.
11. On the File menu, click Save All.
12. Click the Preview tab.

    The top of your report looks like this:

Product	Sales Amount	Order Quantity
AWC logo cap	477.5895	85
Full-finger Gloves, L	4228.761875	176
Full-finger Gloves, M	2129.56744	87
Full-finger Gloves, S	197.548	8
Half-finger Gloves, M	704.0898	46
Half-finger Gloves, S	336.7386	22

    Now you can see that products are arranged in groups, but you cannot determine from the report how each group is defined. You need to add more information to the report.

Adding Group Headers

A group header gives context to the set of detail rows associated with each group. As with any other textbox in a table, the group header can contain static text, a field value, or a calculation that might reference a field. Usually, group headers include the same expression used to define the group.

In this procedure, you'll add the *Category* and *SubCategory* fields to the respective group headers.

Use field names as a group header

1. Click the Layout tab.
2. In the Datasets window, click Category and drag to the first cell in the table1_Category header, which is the row just below the table header.

   Your table now looks like this:

Product	Sales Amount	Order Quantity
=Fields!Category.Value		
=Fields!Product.Value	=Fields!SalesAmount.V	=Fields!OrderQuantity.V
Grand Total	=Sum(Fields!SalesAmo	=Sum(Fields!OrderQuar

When the report is processed, the group header displays the value of the field that you placed in this row. All detail rows with the same value for the field that are selected in the Grouping And Sorting Properties dialog box will be organized together in the report between the group header and footer rows. This means that you could group detail rows by one field and display a header, or caption, for the group using another field. However, more commonly, you'll use the same field in both places.

3. In the Datasets window, click SubCategory and drag to the first cell in the table1_SubCategory header, which is the row just above the detail row.
4. Click the Save All button on the toolbar.
5. Click the Preview tab.

   The top of your report looks like this:

Product	Sales Amount	Order Quantity
Clothing		
Cap		
AWC logo cap	477.5895	85
Gloves		
Full-finger Gloves, L	4228.761875	176
Full-finger Gloves, M	2129.56744	87
Full-finger Gloves, S	197.548	8
Half-finger Gloves, M	704.0898	46
Half-finger Gloves, S	336.7386	22

   Now you can see the category and subcategory displayed in separate rows above each group of detail rows.

Computing Group Subtotals

Subtotals can be created for each group by placing a function to sum the detail rows into either a group header or group footer. You can also use other aggregate functions in these rows, such as an average, which you'll learn how to do in Chapter 5.

In this procedure, you'll add static text as a caption in each group footer row, and then insert the *Sum* aggregate function in the group footer cells for SalesAmount and OrderQuantity.

Add the *Sum* function to group footers

1. Click the Layout tab.
2. Click the first cell of the table1_Category footer, which is the row just above the table footer, and then type **Category Total**.
3. Click the second cell of the table footer, and then, while pressing Ctrl, click the third cell of the same row to select both cells.
4. Right-click one of the selected cells, and then click Copy.

5. Right-click the second cell of the table1_Category footer, and then click Paste.

   The table now looks like this:

Product	Sales Amount	Order Quantity
=Fields!Category.Value		
=Fields!SubCategory.Value		
=Fields!Product.Value	=Fields!SalesAmount.V	=Fields!OrderQuantity.V
Category Total	=Sum(Fields!SalesAmo	=Sum(Fields!OrderQuar
Grand Total	=Sum(Fields!SalesAmo	=Sum(Fields!OrderQuar

   Even though the same formula now appears in the table1_Category footer and the table footer, the results will be different because of the context of the rows. The table footer sums all detail rows in the table, whereas the table1_Category footer sums detail rows for each category separately.

6. Click the first cell of the table1_SubCategory footer, which is the row below the detail row, and type **SubCategory Total**.
7. Right-click the second cell of the table1_SubCategory footer, and then click Paste.
8. On the File menu, click Save All.
9. Click the Preview tab.

   You can see that on the first page of the report, several SubCategory subtotals are interspersed between groups. You need to scroll about halfway down the page to find the first Category subtotal. However, the group headers and footers aren't noticeably different from detail rows, which make them difficult to pick out.

Formatting a Report Using Report Designer

After defining the data to be gathered for the report and structuring the data within the report, the next step in authoring a report is to apply formatting and set properties for each report item. This step is necessary to control the appearance and behavior of the items in your report. You start with basic formatting to display numeric values properly and to set font styles and colors for different sections of the report. You continue adjusting the formatting of your report by designing your report for the printed page and controlling the visibility of selected report items across pages. Then you finish your report by adding graphical elements to make it more attractive.

Setting the *Format* Property

Sometimes you might want to change the format of the data retrieved for your report. Often, numeric and date or time values require a change from the default format. The *Format* property in the Properties window can be edited to adjust the format of a string in a textbox.

In this procedure, you'll format the SalesAmount column of the table as Currency, and the OrderQuantity column as a number with no decimals.

Format numeric values

1. Click the Layout tab.
2. Click the column handle for the second column, which contains Sales Amount values.

   All cells in the column are selected when you click the column handle.
3. In the Properties window, find the *Format* property, and then type **C0**.

   Properties in the Properties window are arranged alphabetically, first by property category and then by name.

> **Note** The Report Designer uses Visual Basic .NET formatting strings. The first character represents the data format. The most common data formats you're likely to use are C for currency, N for numbers, and P for percents. The digit following any of these characters specifies the number of decimal places, or precision. You can omit the digit if you want to use the system default for the specified data format. You can find out more about the system defaults for numeric data formats at *http://msdn.microsoft.com/library/en-us/cpguide/html/cpconstandardnumericformatstrings.asp*.

   When you select multiple cells, such as all cells in a column, the property setting that you apply affects all selected cells. You can also change several properties at once to update the cells while they remain selected.

4. Click the column handle for the third column, which contains Order Quantity values.
5. In the Properties window, find the *Format* property and type **N0**.
6. On the File menu, click Save All.
7. Click the Preview tab.

   The numeric values are now formatted correctly.

Applying Styles

You can edit style properties for every item in a report, such as background colors, border styles, font styles and colors, and padding values. Like the *Format* property, style properties can be edited in the Properties window. Not all style properties are available to every report item. For example, only items that can contain text have font style properties. The easiest way to apply common styles is to use the Report Formatting toolbar.

In this procedure, you'll use the Report Formatting toolbar to set the background color of the detail row and the font styles of the headers and footers for the table and groups.

Use the Report Formatting toolbar to set color and font style properties

1. Click the Layout tab.
2. Click the row handle of the detail row to select the entire row.
3. On the Report Formatting toolbar, click the Background Color button.

   The Background Color button looks like this:

> **Note** If the Report Formatting toolbar is not visible, right-click any Visual Studio toolbar, and then click Report Formatting. You might need to rearrange the toolbars to view the entire Report Formatting toolbar.

4. On the Web tab, click Silver, and then click OK.

   The new background color is applied to the detail row.
5. Click the row handle for the table header, and then, while pressing Ctrl, click the table footer row handle to select both rows.

> **Tip** When you want to apply the same formatting styles to several rows, select each row handle while pressing Ctrl.

6. On the Report Formatting toolbar, click 12 in the Font Size drop-down list, click the Bold button, and then click the Background Color button.
7. On the Web tab, click Black, and then click OK.
8. On the Report Formatting toolbar, click the Foreground Color button, which is to the left of the Background Color button.
9. Click the Web tab, click White, and then click OK.

> **Note** Alternatively, you can set these properties directly in the Properties window. The Background Color button sets the *BackgroundColor* property, and the Foreground Color button sets the *Color* property.
>
> Expand the Font category to access the font properties. The Font Size list box selection sets the *FontSize* property. The Bold and Italic buttons set the *FontWeight* and *FontStyle*, respectively. Finally, the Underline button sets the *TextDecoration* property, which is not categorized with the other font properties.

10. Click the table1_Category header row handle, and then click the table1_Category footer row handle while pressing Ctrl to select both rows.
11. On the Report Formatting toolbar, click 12 in the Font Size drop-down list, click the Bold button, then click the Background Color button.
12. On the Web tab, click Gainsboro, and then click OK.
13. Click the table1_SubCategory header row handle, and then click the table1_SubCategory footer row handle while pressing Ctrl to select both rows.
14. On the Report Formatting toolbar, click 11 in the Font Size drop-down list, and then click the Bold button.
15. On the File menu, click Save All.
16. Click the Preview tab.

    The top of your report looks like this:

Product	Sales Amount	Order Quantity
Clothing		
Cap		
AWC logo cap	$478	85
SubCategory Total	**$478**	**85**
Gloves		
Full-finger Gloves, L	$4,229	176
Full-finger Gloves, M	$2,130	87
Full-finger Gloves, S	$198	8
Half-finger Gloves, M	$704	46
Half-finger Gloves, S	$337	22
SubCategory Total	**$7,597**	**339**

    By applying different format styles to each section of the report, the distinctions between the table headers and footers, the group headers and footers, and the detail rows are clearer.

Editing Properties

The Report Formatting toolbar contains only some of the properties available for editing. To access all formatting properties, use the Properties window. For example, you might want to adjust the padding within a textbox. *Padding* is the white space between the sides of a textbox and the text inside the textbox, just like a margin is the white space between the sides of a page and the text on the page. You can adjust the amount of padding on any side of the textbox: top, bottom, left, or right. The default padding of each side of the textbox is 2 points.

In this procedure, you'll adjust the padding in the first column of the detail row and the table1_SubCategory group header and footer to indent the column values in these rows.

Indent a column

1. Click the Layout tab.
2. Click the first cell in the detail row, which is the Product cell.
3. In the Properties window, click the plus sign to expand the Padding category.
4. In the *Padding Left* property field, type **22pt**.

   Your Properties window looks like this:

> **Note** In the Properties window, some properties, such as *Padding* properties, are arranged in categories. The category name appears in the Properties list with a plus or minus sign so you can expand or collapse the category. By default, the category is collapsed to make finding a property easier. When the category is expanded, you can modify any individual property that category contains. The field to the right of the category name has the values of all properties in the category. If you know the position of the property you want to change, you can edit the category values.

> **Note** In the example in this procedure, you can replace 2pt, 2pt, 2pt, 2pt, with **22pt, 2pt, 2pt, 2pt**. The sequence of values from left to right in the category field corresponds to the properties grouped in the category from top to bottom. So, for the Padding category field, the sequence of values corresponds to Padding Left, Padding Right, Padding Top, and Padding Bottom.

5. Click the first cell in the table1_SubCategory header, and then, in the Properties window, type **12pt** in the *Padding Left* property field. Repeat for the first cell in the table1_SubCategory footer cell.
6. On the File menu, click Save All.
7. Click the Preview tab.

The top of the report now looks like this:

Product	Sales Amount	Order Quantity
Clothing		
Cap		
AWC logo cap	$478	85
SubCategory Total	**$478**	**85**
Gloves		
Full-finger Gloves, L	$4,229	176
Full-finger Gloves, M	$2,130	87
Full-finger Gloves, S	$198	8
Half-finger Gloves, M	$704	46
Half-finger Gloves, S	$337	22
SubCategory Total	**$7,597**	**339**

Adding Floating Headers

The ability to add floating headers is a feature that is similar to Freeze Panes in Microsoft Excel, which keeps a header row in place while the user scrolls vertically through a document. This feature is particularly useful for documents that contain more data than can be shown on the screen. When working with a matrix data region, you can also use this feature with rows to help users navigate data horizontally.

In this procedure, you'll add floating headers to a table.

Add floating headers

1. Click the Layout tab.
2. Click the table to display the row and column handles.
3. Right-click the table handle, which is located in the top-left corner of the table, and then click Properties.
4. In the Table Properties dialog box, select the Header Should Remain Visible While Scrolling check box.

The Table Properties dialog box looks like this:

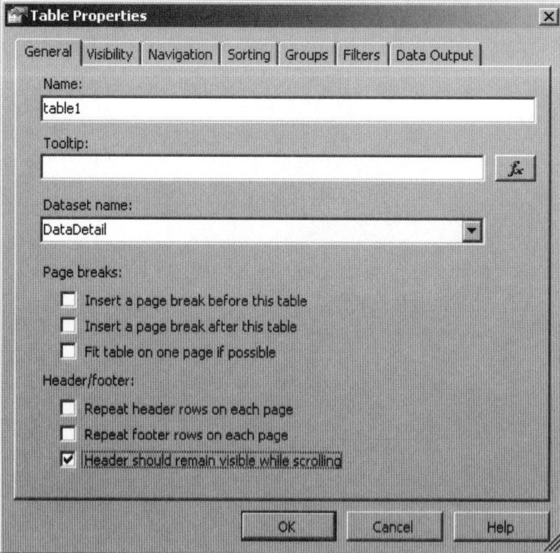

5. Click OK.
6. Click the Preview tab and scroll to the bottom of the page.

   Your screen should look similar to this:

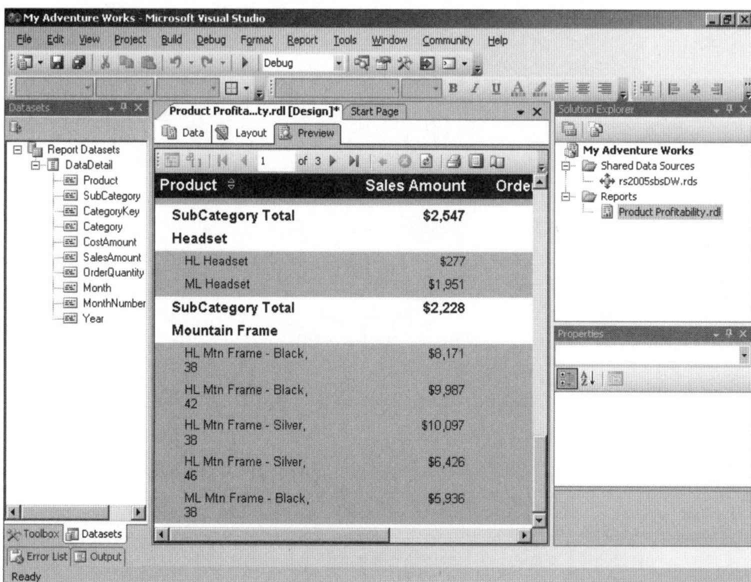

Even though you have scrolled to the bottom of the page, the header columns remain visible.

Triggering Page Breaks

When the report was added to the project, the *PageSize Width* property of the report was set by default to 8.5in and the *PageSize Height* was set to 11in. When you render the report to preview it, the rendering engine determines the number of rows that can fit on a page and creates page breaks automatically. However, you can specify your own trigger for a page break, such as a change in a group value or following a selected report item. You'll learn how to design pages for other rendered formats in Chapter 13, "Rendering Reports."

In this procedure, you'll add a page break to the table1_Category group.

Add pagination

1. Click the Layout tab.
2. Click the blank area in the Document window below the design grid.

   The Report properties display in the Properties window. Note the default settings for the *Margin* and *PageSize* properties.
3. Click the table to display the row and column handles.
4. Right-click the table1_Category footer row handle, and then click Edit Group.
5. Select the Page Break At End check box.
6. Click OK.
7. On the File menu, click Save All.
8. Click the Preview tab.

   Your report now has four pages, one for each category. Notice that the number of detail rows per page is different. The rendering engine still inserts a page break if there are more detail rows within a category than will fit on a single page. However, the group page break forces a new page when the category changes, regardless of the number of detail rows.

Note If Reporting Services followed the page break instruction literally, it would put a page break after the last category, putting the Grand Total on a page by itself. However, Reporting Services doesn't do this.

Adding a Textbox

So far, you've been working with textboxes that are organized as a table. A textbox can also be placed into the report as a separate report item. For example, to add a static title, or report header, to the report, you can add a textbox. You'll learn other uses for an independent textbox in Chapter 5 and Chapter 6.

In this procedure, you'll add a textbox to the design grid and insert static text to create a report header.

Add static text

1. Click the Layout tab.
2. Click the handle in the top-left corner to select the entire table. If you can't see the table handles, click the table first.
3. Drag the table down to place the top of the table approximately 1.5 inches from the top of the report body.
4. In the Toolbox window, click Textbox.
5. Click the top-left corner of the report body, and then drag the corner of the textbox to the right and down to create a textbox approximately 3.5 inches wide and 1.25 inches high.

> **Note** You can also use the *Size Width* and *Height* properties in the Properties window to set the size of the textbox once it is placed in the report body. Another option is to drag the sides of the textbox to resize it as desired.

Your screen now looks like this:

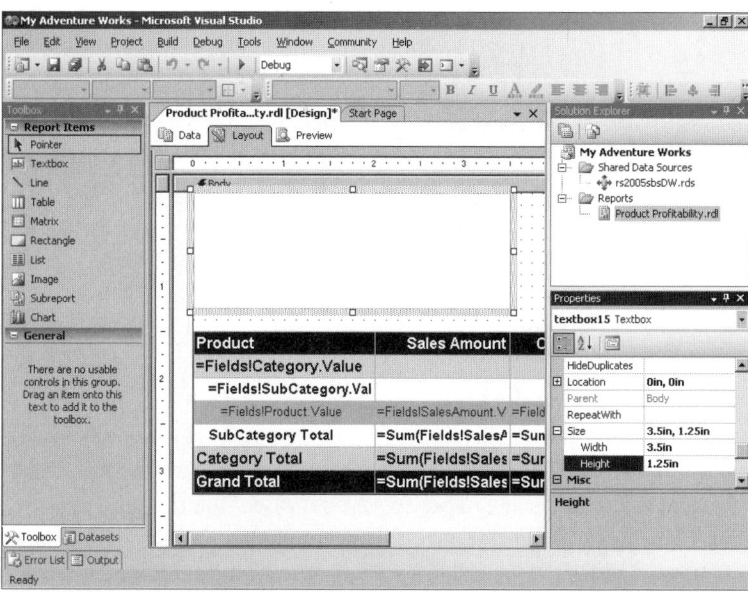

The textbox was added as a report item and automatically assigned a name, similar to textbox15.

6. Click inside the textbox, and then type **Adventure Works Product Profitability Report**.

> **Note** Text will wrap to a new line automatically to fit the width of the textbox, but will never expand the textbox horizontally. In the rendered report, the textbox will expand vertically to display all text contained in the textbox if its *CanGrow* property is set to True, which is the default. You can force a new line in the text by pressing Shift+Enter at the desired position.

7. Make sure the textbox is still selected in the design grid, click 20 in the Font Size drop-down list, and then click the Bold button in the Report Formatting toolbar.

> **Note** Unlike the way you apply formatting in a word processing application, you don't need to select the text in the textbox before applying the formatting styles. You only need to have the textbox selected.

8. On the File menu, click Save All.
9. Click the Preview tab.

   The top of the report looks like this:

   Adventure Works Product
   Profitability Report

Product	Sales Amount	Order Quantity
Clothing		
Cap		
AWC logo cap	$478	85
SubCategory Total	**$478**	**85**

   Notice that the text does not get truncated.

10. Click the Next Page button.

    The textbox you added does not appear on this or any other page because you added it above the table. In this usage, the textbox acts as a report header because it is not contained within a repeating region and consequently only appears once. (You'll learn more about repeating regions in Chapter 6.) Also, notice that the table header is not repeated. Even though the table header is a collection of textboxes that *is* contained in a repeating region, its designation as a table header results in rendering that is different from other rows in the same table. By default, the table header is displayed only on the first page.

Setting Table Properties

As you learned in the previous procedure, a table header is displayed only on the first page that contains the table. If you want to repeat the table header on every page, you can edit the *RepeatOnNewPage* property for the row. The table header will then be repeated, but only on the pages that include the table.

In this procedure, you'll edit the table property to force the table header to repeat on each page of the report.

Repeat the table header

1. Click the Layout tab.
2. Click the table, and then click the table header row handle.

   The properties for this item, TableRow1, are displayed in the Properties window.
3. Scroll to the bottom of the Properties window to locate the *RepeatOnNewPage* property in the Layout section.
4. In the Properties window, click True in the drop-down list for the *RepeatOnNewPage* property.

> **Note** Similarly, group headers and footers appear only at the beginning or end of a group. You can edit the group to set options in the Grouping And Sorting Properties dialog box so you can force the group header or footer to repeat on each page, or you can select the group row in the table and set the *RepeatOnNewPage* property in the Properties window.

5. On the File menu, click Save All.
6. Click the Preview tab.
7. Click the Next Page button.

   The top of the second page of your report looks like this:

Product	Sales Amount	Order Quantity
Accessory		
Locks		
Cable lock	$720	48
SubCategory Total	**$720**	**48**
Pumps		
Mini-pump	$636	53
SubCategory Total	**$636**	**53**
Helmet		
Sport-100 helmet, Black	$1,009	50
Sport-100 helmet, Blue	$1,352	67
Sport-100 helmet, Red	$1,009	50
SubCategory Total	**$3,371**	**167**

Working with Page Headers

When you want to repeat the same content at the top of every page, you can use a page header. A page header can contain textboxes and images, but it cannot contain data regions, subreports, or any item that directly references a field.

In this procedure, you'll add a page header containing a textbox that will be suppressed on the first page, but printed on every other page.

Add a page header

1. Click the Layout tab.
2. Right-click the blank area in the Document window to the left of the report body, and then click Page Header. Alternatively, on the Report menu, you can click Page Header.

   Your screen looks like this:

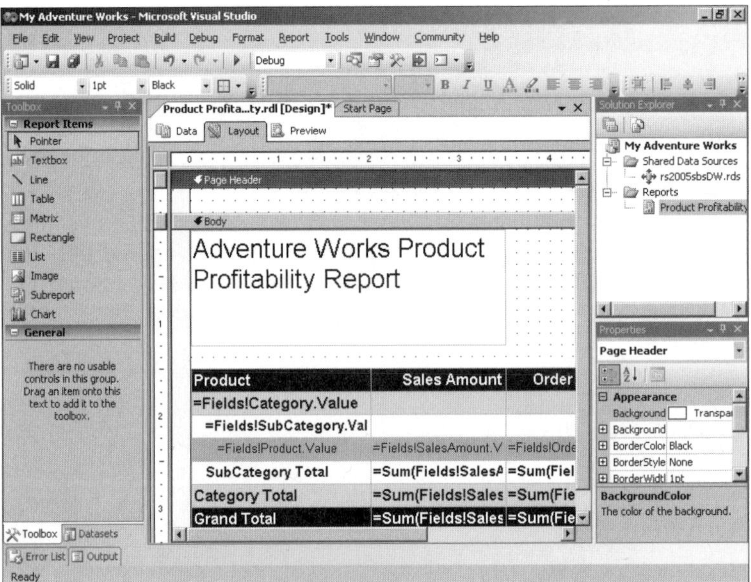

3. In the Toolbox window, click Textbox.
4. Click the top-left corner of the page header section, and then drag the corner of the textbox to the right and down to create a textbox approximately 5 inches wide and 0.25 inches high.
5. In the Properties window, select Right in the Text Align drop-down list.

   The page header will now align with the right edge of the table. If you add more columns or additional items later that increase the width of the report, you'll also need to adjust the location of the textbox in the header.
6. Click the textbox to select it, and then enter **Product Profitability Report**.

> **Tip** If the right edge of the report is hidden by Solution Explorer, you might not be able to see the text as you type. In that case, simply use the horizontal bar to scroll the Document window to the right or resize windows to confirm the text is entered properly. Another option is to Auto Hide the Solution Explorer and Properties windows.

7. In the Properties window, select Page Header in the report item drop-down list at the top of the window (or click anywhere in the page header's design grid), and then scroll to the bottom of the window to find the properties in the Misc group.

> **Tip** Type **P** after opening the Properties report item drop-down list to jump to the report items beginning with that letter instead of scrolling. This list can get long when you're building complex reports.

8. Click False in the *PrintOnFirstPage* property drop-down list.
9. Make sure True is the current setting for the *PrintOnLastPage* property.
10. On the File menu, click Save All.
11. Click the Preview tab.
12. Click the Next Page button.

    The page header appears only on pages 2 through 4.

Working with Page Footers

Like a page header, you can use a page footer to repeat content on every page of the report. The same rules regarding what can be placed in this area of the report apply. You can also choose whether to suppress the page footer from the first or last page of the report.

In this procedure, you'll add a page footer with static text that will print on every page of the report.

Add a page footer

1. Click the Layout tab.
2. Right-click the blank area in the Document window to the left of the report body, and then click Page Footer.

   You might need to close the Output window to view the newly added page footer.
3. In the Toolbox window, click Textbox.

4. Click the top-left corner of the page footer section, then drag the corner of the textbox to the right and down to create a textbox approximately 2.0 inches wide and 0.25 inches high.
5. Click the textbox to select it, and then type **Company Confidential**.
6. In the Report Formatting toolbar, click the Italic button.
7. In the Properties window, click Page Footer in the report items drop-down list.

   The *PrintOnFirstPage* and *PrintOnLastPage* properties are both set to True by default.
8. On the File menu, click Save All.
9. Click the Preview tab.

   The page footer is displayed on the first page.
10. Click the Next Page button to check the existence of the page footer on all other pages.

Adding Graphical Elements

Lines and images are graphical elements you can use to give your report an attractive, professional appearance. These report items are added to the report from the Toolbox window like the other report items you've learned how to use. You can use the graphical interface to resize the graphical elements as desired, or you can use the Properties window to edit properties.

In this procedure, you'll add a line to the top of the report to separate the report body from the page header.

Add a line

1. Click the Layout tab.
2. In the Toolbox window, click Line.
3. Click the top-left corner of the report body, and then drag the line to the right to match the width of the table.

> **Tip** Adding a line to the design grid is easier if, before you start, you make the window large enough to show the beginning and end of the line. If you do not, you'll spend time moving and resizing your line to get it right.

Your screen looks similar to this:

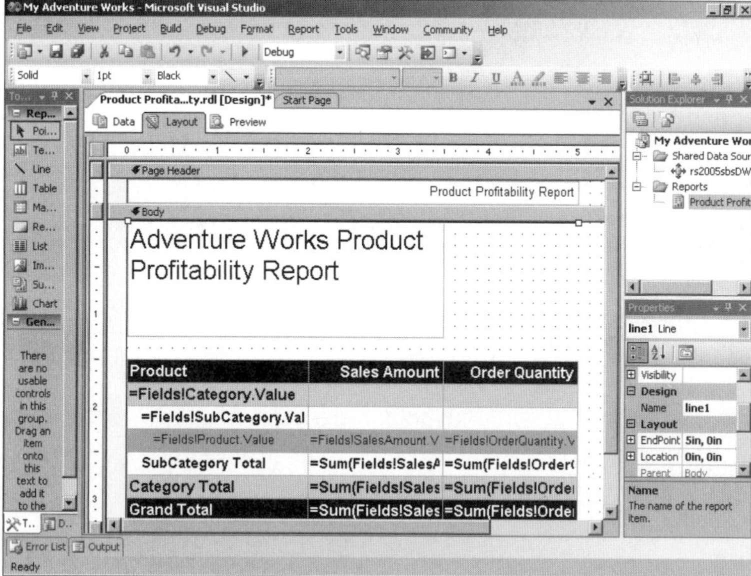

Because the line is small, it might be hard to see in the design grid right now. You should be able to see the line handles at each end. You can use these to lengthen or shorten the line as needed. In the Properties window, you can view the properties for the new report item, line1.

4. In the Properties window, scroll up to find the *LineWidth* property in the Appearance category, and then change the property value to **12pt**.
5. If the line covers some of the text in the textbox containing the report title, drag the textbox a little lower on the design grid.

   As you add report items to the design grid, you will probably need to tweak their arrangement to prevent one item from obscuring another.
6. On the File menu, click Save All.
7. Click the Preview tab.

The top of the report looks like this:

Adventure Works Product
Profitability Report

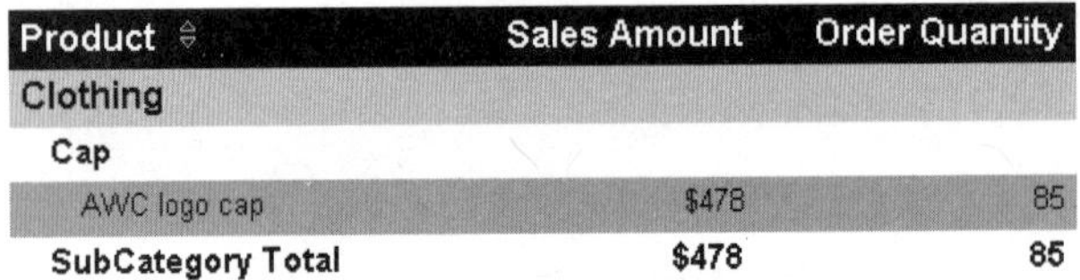

Product	Sales Amount	Order Quantity
Clothing		
Cap		
AWC logo cap	$478	85
SubCategory Total	$478	85

Because the line was added to the report body, it is displayed only on the first page. If you want a line to repeat, you must add it to a repeating section of a data region, such as a group header, a group footer, or a detail row.

Adding Images

In addition to containing data regions and free-standing textboxes, a report can contain logos and other types of graphical images. You can embed an image within the report itself or reference an image that is stored on the Report Server. Often, an image is included in a report as a free-standing item, like the report header you added earlier in this chapter. However, you can also use images in detail rows if you have stored images in a database, such as product images for a catalog.

In this procedure, you'll add the Adventure Works logo as an embedded image at the top of the report.

Use the Image Wizard to add an embedded logo to a report

1. Click the Layout tab.
2. In the Toolbox window, click Image.
3. Click the top-right corner of the report body just below the line and to the right of the textbox you created as a report header.

   The Image Wizard is launched.
4. Click Next.

The Select The Image Source page of the Image Wizard is displayed:

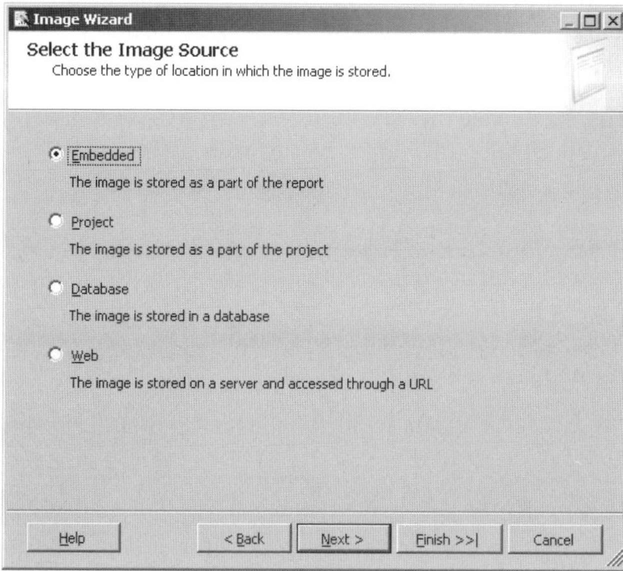

Here you specify where the image to be added to the report is stored: embedded, project, database, or Web.

- An embedded image is converted to a Multipurpose Internet Mail Extension (MIME) object, which allows the image to be stored as text in the report definition file. Using an embedded image ensures that the image is always available to the report, but it also makes the report definition file much larger.

Important ASP.NET imposes a 4-MB limit on items that are posted to the server. Report definition files rarely exceed this limit unless you use embedded images. You can increase this limit by changing the *maxRequestLength* element in the Machine.config file, but by doing so, you also increase the vulnerability of the server to denial of service attacks. Editing this file is beyond the scope of this book. If you need to use multiple images in a report, include them as shared resources in the project or store them in a database field.

- A project image is an image that is stored as an item in the project. You can choose an image that was already added to the project, or you can use the wizard to add an image. When publishing the project, the report definition and the image files are placed on the Report Server separately. As a result, the report definition file is smaller than it is when using an embedded image. Using project images is a good strategy when you want to use the same image within several reports, such as a company logo.

- A database image is retrieved as binary data by the query in the dataset and is included in the detail row. You specify the dataset, the column of query results containing the image, and the MIME type. Because the image is part of the dataset, the images are not stored in the report definition file.
- A Web image is an image that can be accessed from a Web server by using a URL address. You specify the full address to the image, such as *http://<servername>/Images/myImage.jpg*.

5. Click Embedded, and then click Next.
6. Click New Image.
7. Open the image at C:\Documents and Settings\<username>\My Documents\Microsoft Press\rs2005sbs\chap04\logopart.jpg.
8. Click logopart name in the Name column and enter **Logo** to replace the default name.

> **Tip** Choose a name for the image with care so you can find it easily when working with your report.

9. Click Next, and then click Finish.

   The image is now embedded in the report as an independent report item.

> **Tip** You can also use an image with any item in the report that has the *Background-Image* property. For example, you can use an embedded image as a background for a table or textbox.

10. Click the image, and then drag down so that the height of the image matches the height of the report header textbox.

    The top of the design grid looks like this:

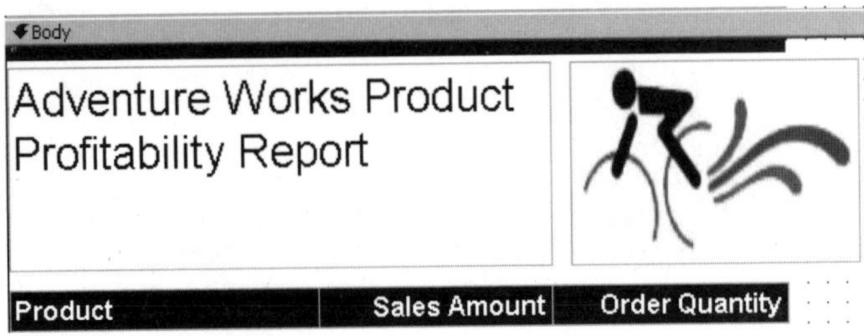

11. On the File menu, click Save All.
12. Click the Preview tab.

The top of the report looks like this:

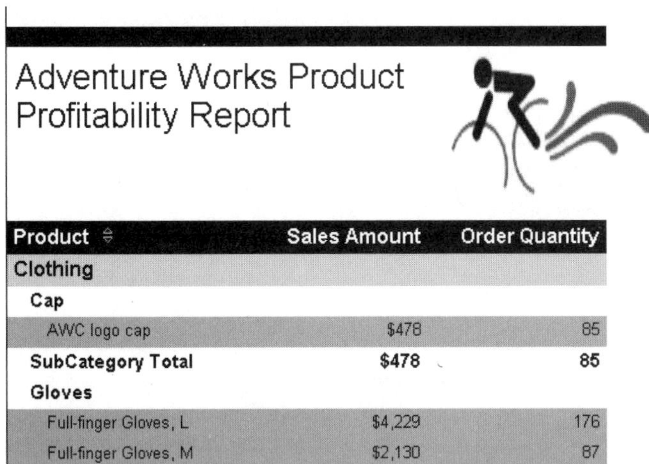

Adventure Works Product Profitability Report

Product	Sales Amount	Order Quantity
Clothing		
Cap		
AWC logo cap	$478	85
SubCategory Total	**$478**	**85**
Gloves		
Full-finger Gloves, L	$4,229	176
Full-finger Gloves, M	$2,130	87

The Adventure Works logo appears only on the first page because it was added to the report body, not to the page header.

Chapter 4 Quick Reference

To	Do this
Create a new report project	On the File menu in Visual Studio, point to New, and then click Project. Choose the Report Server Project template to create an empty report project. Enter a name and a physical folder location for the project.
Add a blank report to a project	In Solution Explorer, right-click the Reports folder of a project, point to Add, and then click New Item. Select the Report template, type a report name with an .rdl extension, and then click Open.
Add a shared data source	In Solution Explorer, right-click the Shared Data Sources folder, and then click Add New Data Source. In the Shared Data Source dialog box, select a provider and enter a server name and credentials for authentication, if needed; and select a database name.
Add a dataset	On the Data tab of the Report Designer, click <New Dataset...> in the Dataset list box, change the name of the dataset if desired, enter a query string, and then click OK.
Add a data region	Open the Toolbox window, click the desired data region, point to the target destination in the report body, and then click to place the data region.
Add fields to a table	In the Datasets window, click the field to be added and drag to a data region cell or textbox. *or* Type a field expression directly in the cell or textbox. For example: **=Fields!Product.Value**.

To	Do this
Sorting Table Rows	Right-click on a textbox (such as a table header), select Properties, click the Interactive Sort tab, and then select the Add An Interactive Sort Action To This Textbox check box.
Add a group to a table	Click the table to display the row handles. Right-click a row, and then click Insert Group. Change the name of the group, if desired, and select one or more expressions from the list box to use for grouping detail rows.
Include subtotals in a table	Copy an expression that returns a numeric value from the table footer and paste into a group header or group footer row. *or* Type an aggregate expression in a group header or group footer cell. For example, to compute a subtotal: **=Sum(Fields!SalesAmount.Value)**.
Create a floating header	Right-click the table handle, select Properties, and then select the Header Should Remain Visible While Scrolling check box.
Format a numeric value	Click the textbox (or multiple textboxes) containing the numeric expression to format and edit the *Format* property in the Properties window. Use Visual Basic .NET formatting strings, such as C2, N0, or P1.
Apply formatting styles to text	Click the textbox (or multiple textboxes), and then click the applicable style button in the Report Formatting toolbar or edit the applicable style property in the Properties window.
Add a page break	To insert a page break between report items, such as between a report and a chart, click a report item, and then edit the *PageBreakAtEnd* or *PageBreakAtStart* property in the Properties window to apply the page break accordingly. To insert a page break in a table, click the table to display the row handles. Click the row you want to use to trigger a page break when the value changes, and then edit the *RepeatOnNewPage* property in the Properties window.
Add a page header or page footer	Right-click the empty space in the Document window surrounding the design grid, and then click either Page Header or Page Footer.
Add a free-standing textbox	Open the Toolbox window; click Textbox; point to the target destination in the report body, page header, or page footer; and then click to place the data region.
Suppress page headers or page footers from the first or last page	Click Page Header or Page Footer in the report item list box of the Properties window, and then set the *PrintOnFirstPage* or *PrintOnLastPage* property to False.
Repeat table rows across pages	Click the table to display row handles, click the table row to repeat on each page, and then, in the Properties window, set the *RepeatOnNewPage* property to True.
Add a graphical element	Open the Toolbox window, click the graphical element (either Line or Image), and then point to the target destination in the report body, page header, or page footer. If adding a line, drag the cursor across the page to the desired length. If adding an image, click to place the image in the report and use the Image Wizard to locate the image and define the storage for the image.

Chapter 5

Working with Expressions

After completing this chapter, you will be able to:

- Use global object collections in expressions.
- Create expressions with aggregate functions.
- Change the report appearance with expressions.

In the previous chapter, you started a report project to which you added a report containing a table data region and other report items. You also edited properties of these report items to manipulate their appearance and behavior in the report. In this chapter, you expand the same report. You build some expressions that perform calculations on values in the dataset and build others that use information that is available only after the report is processed. You also use aggregate functions in various places in the report to learn how the location of a function affects the context of the aggregate. Finally, you change properties by using expressions that are based on conditions or values in the report. Since these expressions are evaluated at run time, the appearance and behavior of the report can change dynamically.

Using Expressions to Calculate Values

You started working with expressions in Chapter 4, "Developing Basic Reports," by adding fields to the table. When you drag a field from the Datasets window and drop it into a cell, the Report Designer inserts a field expression into that cell. For example, the first cell of the detail row in your report contains the following expression: `=Fields!Product.Value`. An expression that points to a field is the simplest expression of all. Like all expressions, it starts with an equal sign (=) and is written in Microsoft Visual Basic. This expression refers to the *Product* field by using standard Visual Basic collection syntax, in which *Fields* is the name of the object collection, *Product* is the name of an object in the collection, and *Value* is the property of the object. In this case, for each row, the expression returns the value of the *Product* field in the *Fields* collection for the current row.

You can create more complex expressions by using functions or by combining field expressions with mathematical operators to perform a calculation. The expression in the second cell in the table footer, `=Sum(Fields!SalesAmount.Value)`, is an example of an expression that uses an aggregate function, which you learn more about later in this chapter. Expressions are commonly used to display field values and calculated values in a report.

Once you have data for your report, you often need to perform additional calculations using this data to derive values that aren't stored in the database. For example, you might need to include the product margin in the report. The *margin* is the difference between the amount for which the product sold and the cost of making or acquiring it. Even though margin isn't stored as a value in the database, it can be derived from other values that are stored in the database by building an expression that subtracts CostAmount from SalesAmount. An expression can be added as a *calculated field* to the dataset, and then used in a table as if it were part of the original dataset.

Not all expressions are based on fields in the dataset. Another type of expression that you might want to use in a report can be created using a *global variable*. Reporting Services makes available certain information about a report, such as page numbering, which you can access through the *Globals* collection. For example, to keep track of the number of pages in a report, you can use the *PageNumber* and *TotalPages* global variables to access the numbering that Reporting Services stores for you. You can create a calculated field to store a global variable expression, or you can type the expression directly into a textbox. In this way, you can avoid writing code to access page numbering.

A third type of expression that is handy to use in reports is a *report item expression*. To create a report item expression, you use the *ReportItems* collection to access the value stored in a textbox. A value in the textbox, if derived from a field expression, such as the margin example discussed earlier in this section, doesn't come directly from the dataset but is stored there to be displayed in the report or for use in another expression. You can think of the textbox as not just a display item, but also as a holding area for a value that can be used as part of another calculation.

Creating Calculated Fields

The Datasets window initially displays the list of database fields contained in the dataset you create. You can add expressions as calculated fields to this list. Once a calculated field is created in the dataset, you can use it in a report just like a database field. It's evaluated the same way, too, for each row in the dataset. If an expression needs to be used in several places, create a calculated field so that, if you need to change the expression, you can edit the expression in one place. However, you can also enter an expression directly into a textbox when it's used in only one or two places in a report.

In this procedure, you'll create a field to compute each product's margin. After you finish creating the calculated field, you will carry out another procedure to add the calculated field to a new column in the report.

Create a field to compute *Margin*

1. Start SQL Server Business Intelligence Development Studio and open the solution My Adventure Works you saved in the C:\Documents and Settings\<username>\My Documents\Microsoft Press\rs2005sbs\Workspace\My Adventure Works folder.

> **Note** If you skipped Chapter 4, open the solution My Adventure Works in the C:\Documents and Settings\<username>\My Documents\Microsoft Press\rs2005sbs \Answers \chap04\My Adventure Works folder.

2. Open the Product Profitability report, if it isn't already open, by double-clicking the report name in Solution Explorer.
3. In the Datasets window, expand DataDetail, right-click anywhere in the same window, and then click Add to display the Add New Field dialog box. Remember that when you add a field to a cell in a heading row, the name of the field, and not the field expression, is inserted.

> **Tip** If you right-click when pointing to an existing field, and then click Edit, you can make changes to that field. For example, if the name of a database field isn't user-friendly, you could change the name directly in the *Fields* collection. As you recall from Chapter 4, the name of the field is automatically added to a table header. While you can override the name in the table header textbox, you may find it more efficient to rename the field in the *Datasets* window if you reuse this field several times in the same report.

4. Type a name for the field: **Margin**.
5. Select the Calculated Field option, and then click the Expression button that appears to the right of the Calculated Field textbox.

   The Edit Expression dialog box is displayed:

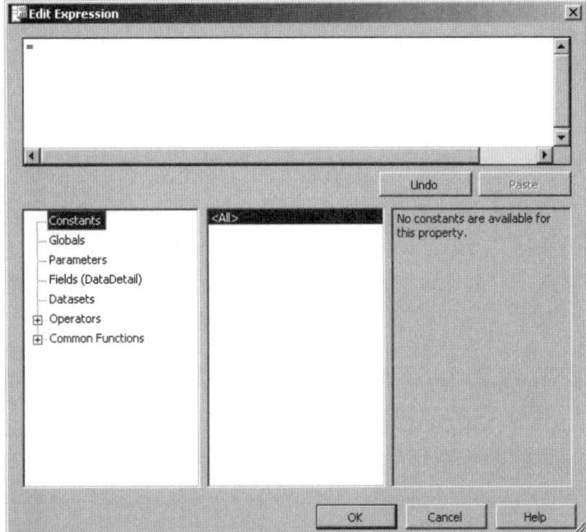

Notice five object collections in the list on the bottom left of the dialog box: *Constants, Globals, Parameters, Fields (DataDetail),* and *Datasets*. You'll be working with the *Fields*

(*DataDetail*) collection in this procedure and with the *Globals* collection later in this section. Each collection contains objects you can use in an expression. In addition to object collections, you can use Operators and Common Functions to build an expression.

6. Click *Fields (DataDetail)* to view its members.
7. Double-click *SalesAmount* to add it to the Expression pane.
8. In the Expression pane, place the cursor after `=Fields!SalesAmount.Value` and then type – (minus sign).
9. Double-click the *CostAmount* field in the Fields pane to finish the expression so the Edit Expression dialog box looks like this:

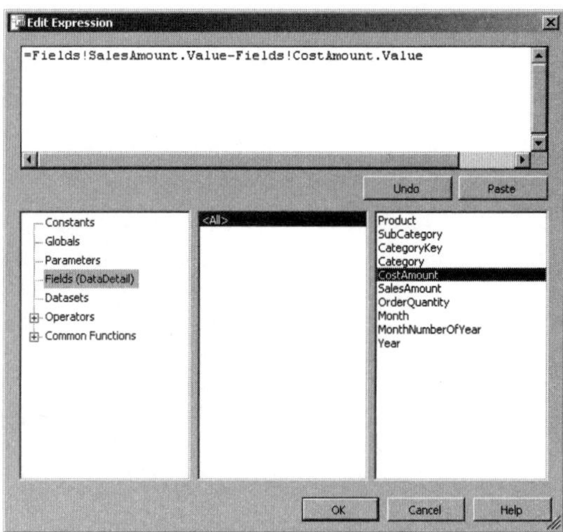

Alternatively, you can type the expression in the field directly. By double-clicking objects from the *Fields* collection to insert the field names, you can be sure that you're not introducing a spelling error.

> **Important** When multiple database fields are used in the same expression, all the fields must come from the same dataset. Also, Microsoft Visual Basic .NET is case-sensitive, so you must use field names correctly. If you don't use the proper case, the field name is not recognized, and you won't be able to view the report because of the resulting compilation error.

10. Click OK to close the Edit Expression dialog box.

The expression is inserted into the Calculated Field textbox, as shown here:

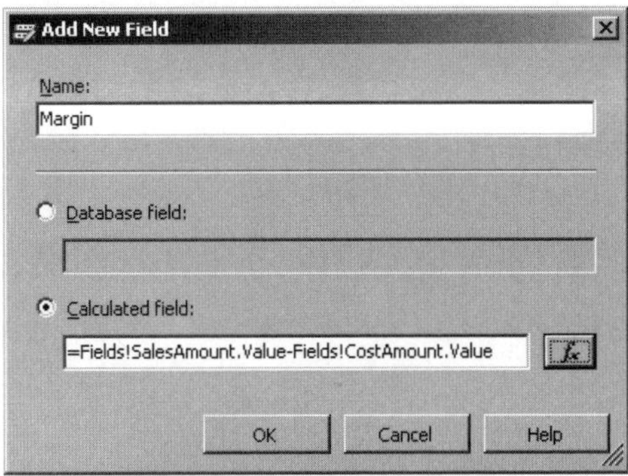

11. Click OK to close the Add New Field dialog box.

    The *Margin* field is now part of the dataset and appears in the Datasets window, as shown here:

    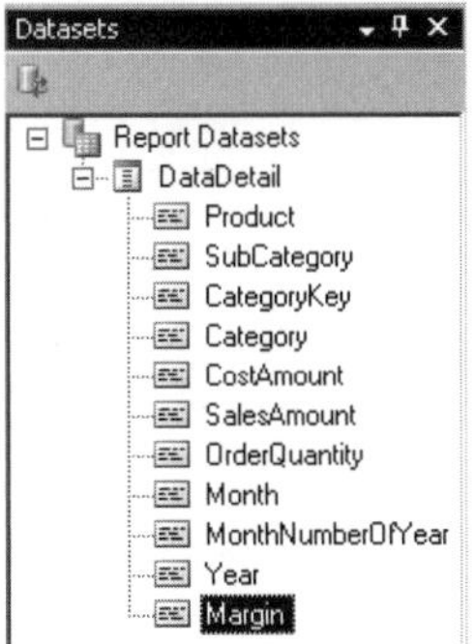

12. Save your report.

In the next procedure, you'll add a new column to the table in your report, into which you add the calculated field–*Margin*–to the detail row and an expression to compute margin subtotals in the footer rows.

Add *Margin* to the table

1. Click the table to display its handles. Right-click the column handle for the third column (Order Quantity), and then click Insert Column To The Right.

Your screen looks like this:

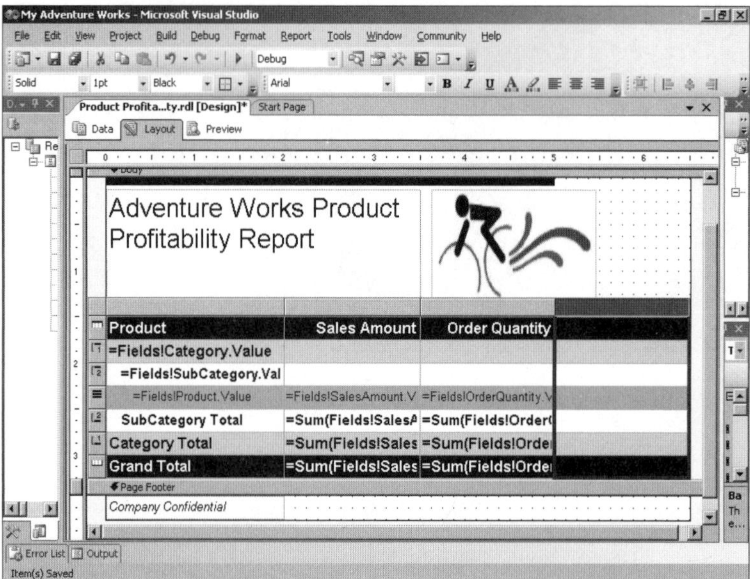

A new column appears in the table. The new column has the same formatting properties as the column you selected. In this case, the *Format* property of the Order Quantity column is set to N0, which is the value automatically assigned to the *Format* property for the new column. Notice that the style formatting of each row of the Order Quantity column is also duplicated in the new column.

> **Note** You can also insert rows into a table by right-clicking a row handle and clicking Insert Row Above or Insert Row Below. The inserted row becomes the same row type as the selected row, such as a detail or footer row.

2. Click Margin in the Datasets window and drag the field to the last cell in the detail row.

   Notice that the field name is added to the table header automatically. Also, the expression placed in the detail row is an expression that references the *Margin* field and is not the underlying expression you assigned to the field.

3. Drag Margin from the Datasets window to the last cell in the table1_SubCategory footer, just below the detail row.

   The *Sum* function is added automatically to the field expression because this row is a footer row.

4. Press Enter to select the expression in this cell. Copy this expression to the clipboard, click the cell beneath it in the table1_Category footer twice so the cursor appears in the textbox, and then paste the contents of the clipboard (the expression itself) into the cell.

> **Note** There is a difference between copying an expression and copying a cell. Copying an expression does not copy the formatting to the destination cell. Copying a cell, by contrast, also copies the formatting to the target cell.

5. Click the last cell in the table footer twice, and then paste the expression that is still in the clipboard into that cell.
6. Click the column handle for the *Margin* column to select all cells in the column, and then type **C0** in the *Format* property in the Properties window to display margin values as currency without decimals.
7. Save the solution files, and then preview the report to confirm that the top of your report looks like this:

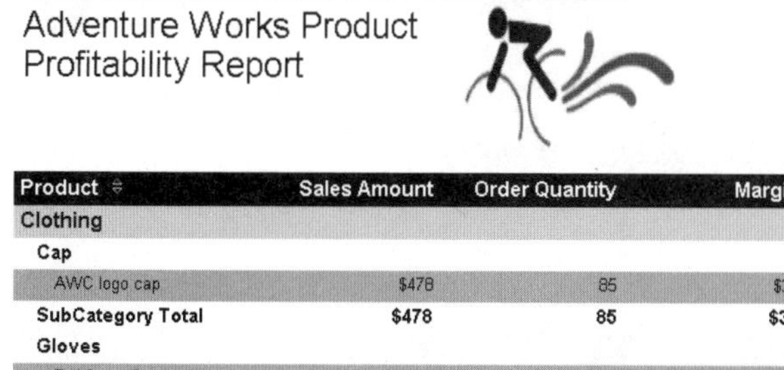

Product	Sales Amount	Order Quantity	Margin
Clothing			
Cap			
AWC logo cap	$478	85	$33
SubCategory Total	$478	85	$33
Gloves			
Full-finger Gloves, L	$4,229	176	$1,471
Full-finger Gloves, M	$2,130	87	$766

Using Global Variables

Global variables are members of the *Globals* collection, in which Reporting Services tracks information unique to a report. You can display this information in the report by including a global variable in an expression placed in a textbox. Six global variables are available for you to use. They are especially useful for embedding report information in printed reports.

The global variables *PageNumber* and *TotalPages* can be used only in the page header or footer. However, the other global variables can be used anywhere that you can place a report item. You can use *ExecutionTime* to include the date and time that the report was executed so users know how current the report is. To help users locate the report online, you can include the report name and location information by using *ReportName*, *ReportServerUrl*, and *ReportFolder* (which includes the full path to the report without the URL).

Global variables are different from fields. Reporting Services does not have values for the global variables until *after* the report is processed, but it can access these values *before* the report is rendered. Fields, on the other hand, are populated with values *during* processing and then are no longer accessible by Reporting Services once processing has completed. As you learned in Chapter 4, the report data is independent of the report layout to enable rendering in any format. Consequently, some information is simply not available until the query is processed and merged into the report layout. Take, for example, page numbering. A report rendered for online viewing in HTML has a different page-numbering system than the same report rendered for print. Until the report has been processed and prepared for rendering, neither the current page number nor the total number of pages are available as global variable values.

In this procedure, you'll edit expressions in textboxes displayed in the page header and report body to incorporate the global variable, *ReportName,* in the report title.

Add global variables to the report

1. Click the Layout tab, right-click the textbox in the page header, and then click Expression.
2. Replace the existing expression, Product Profitability Report, with = (equal sign).
3. Click *Globals* in the leftmost pane, click *ReportName* in the middle pane, and then click the Paste button.

   The Paste button inserts an expression that references the selected item, in this case, Globals!ReportName, into the Expression box, as shown below:

   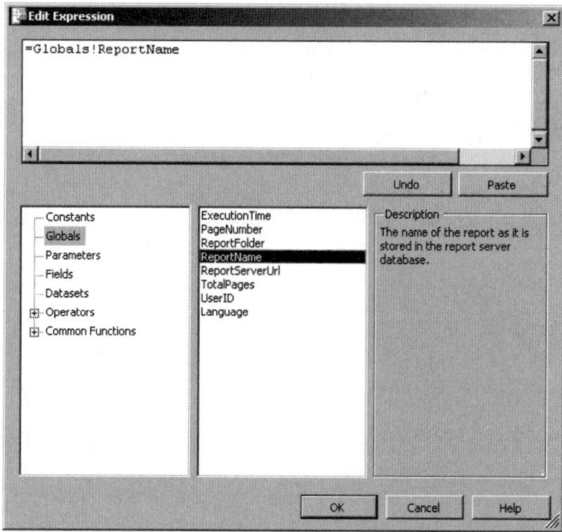

   Notice the other global variables that you can use in an expression.

4. Type **+ "Report"** at the end of the expression so the edited expression looks like this:

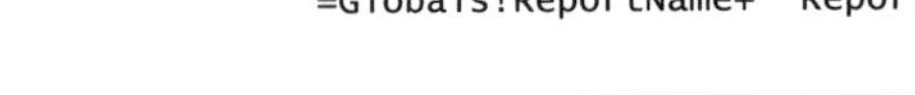

```
=Globals!ReportName+" Report"
```

> **Note** Be sure to include the space between the quotation mark and the word *Report* to properly separate the text when the expression is evaluated and displayed in the report.

5. Click OK.
6. Right-click the textbox that contains the report title in the body of the report, and then click Expression.
7. Replace the existing expression by typing this: **="Adventure Works "+**.
8. Click *Globals* in the leftmost pane, and then double-click *ReportName* in the middle pane.
9. To finish the expression, type **+ " Report"** at the end. The complete expression looks this:

```
="Adventure Works "+ Globals!ReportName+" Report"
```

10. Click OK.
11. Save your report and preview it to check the results.

    Notice that the current title of the report is Adventure Works Product Profitability Report.
12. Click the Next Page button to confirm the report title in the page header.
13. In Solution Explorer, right-click Product Profitability.rdl, click Rename, and then type a new name for the report: **Product Sales and Profitability.rdl**.
14. Click the Refresh button in the Preview toolbar to reset the session cache.

15. Click the Next Page button to check that the title of the report is updated appropriately, as shown in this illustration:

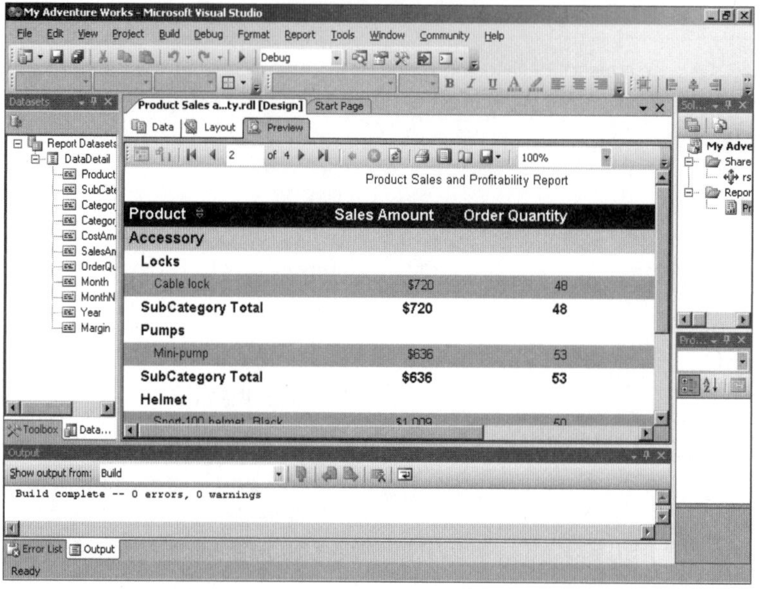

Tip The *ReportName* global variable is useful for reusing report items in many reports to retain a consistent appearance.

Using the *ReportItems* Collection

The *ReportItems* collection contains the report's textboxes as objects. You can use a report item expression to display the value of a textbox in a separate textbox or to use a textbox's value as part of a separate calculation. Report item expressions are similar to global variables because they are evaluated by Reporting Services after processing completes but before rendering. Field expressions in detail and aggregated rows must be evaluated first from the dataset so a textbox has a value that can be used by the report item expression.

Report item expressions, therefore, are useful in situations in which a calculation can be performed only after the dataset is aggregated, and the calculation cannot be derived directly from the dataset. For example, to calculate subtotals in the table, the *Sum* function is used with a field expression. However, if the field expression evaluates as a percentage, the *Sum* function is no longer applicable because percentages are not additive. Specifically, a percentage value in the table footer cannot be calculated by summing percentage values in the detail rows. When working with nonadditive values like ratios or percentages, you must perform the division on aggregated values. To accomplish this, you can use a report item expression to summarize percentage values in rows in which you are using subtotals.

A report item expression used in a textbox that is inside a data region can retrieve the value of a textbox that is either on the same level or a higher level if the data region has grouping defined. This means that you cannot use an expression in a summary row that refers to a textbox in a detail row. Essentially, this is because the report item expression in a data region is acting as a pointer to *one* other textbox at a time, and therefore can retrieve only one result. Because multiple rows can be on a lower level, there is no way to identify which one of those rows contains the value that the report item expression should retrieve.

In this procedure, you'll add report item expressions to calculate the margin percentage in the detail and summary rows of the table.

Add report item expressions to the table

1. Click the Layout tab, click the table, right-click the Margin column handle, and then click Insert Column To The Right.
2. In the last cell of the table header, type **Margin %**.
3. Click the Margin % column handle to select all cells in the column, and then type **P1** in the *Format* property to display the expression as a percentage with one decimal place.
4. Right-click the last cell in the detail row, click Expression, enter the following expression in the Expression pane, and then click OK.

```
=ReportItems!Margin.Value/ReportItems!SalesAmount.Value
```

> **Tip** You can also type the expression directly into the textbox, but the width of the textbox often makes it difficult to see what you're doing when working with longer expressions. Another way to edit the expression is to click <Expression...> in the *Value* property for the textbox in the Properties window.

This expression retrieves the value from the Margin textbox, and then divides the value by the value in the SalesAmount textbox. This calculation is performed for each detail row of the report. You could also use the expression `=Fields!Margin.Value/Fields!SalesAmount.Value` to get the same result, but for now, use the *ReportItems* collection so you can learn something about its behavior in the upcoming steps.

5. Enter the following expression in the last cell of the table footer:

```
=Sum(ReportItems!Margin.Value)/Sum(ReportItems!SalesAmount.Value)
```

> **Note** This expression is *not* valid, but is introduced here to force an error for you to look at shortly.

6. Click the Preview tab. Your screen looks like this (although the sequence of errors may differ):

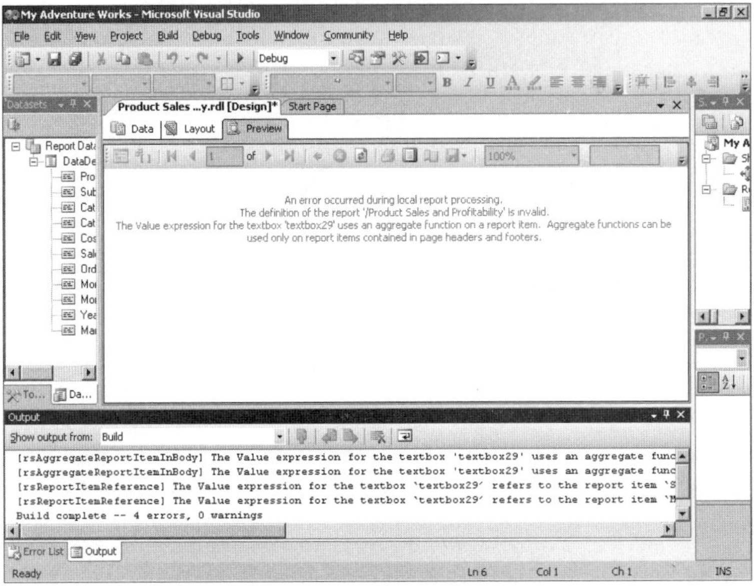

Note There is no error-checking function in Layout mode. To test an expression, you must preview the report.

Two messages refer to the use of an aggregate function in a report item. The same message displays twice because the expression you just added contains two instances of *ReportItems*. Since the textbox is in a table in the report body and not in a page header and footer, you cannot use the *Sum* function in its expression.

The other two messages refer to the use of grouping scope with report items. Here the message displays twice but references the two report items, Margin and Sales Amount, separately. In this case, the error is caused because the expression belongs to an item positioned in a summary row but references an item in a detail row. To avoid this error, the report item expression in this textbox can refer only to another textbox that is in the table footer.

7. Click the Layout tab, click the Sales Amount cell in the table footer, and then change the *Name* property to **SalesAmount_Total** in the Properties window.
8. Click the Margin cell in the same row and change its *Name* property to **Margin_Total**.
9. Enter the following expression for the last cell of the table footer:

```
=ReportItems!Margin_Total.Value/ReportItems!SalesAmount_Total.Value
```

This expression uses the summarized value of Margin divided by the summarized Sales Amount. Importantly, the report item expression refers only to textboxes in the same grouping scope—the table footer—and does not use the aggregate function. The referenced textbox values for *Margin_Total* and *SalesAmount_Total* are already aggregated, so there's no need to apply another aggregate function.

10. Click the Sales Amount cell in the table1_Category footer, and then change the *Name* property to **SalesAmount_Category**.
11. Click the Margin cell in the same row and change its *Name* property to **Margin_Category**.
12. Add the following expression to the Margin % cell in the table1_Category Footer:

```
=ReportItems!Margin_Category.Value/ReportItems!SalesAmount_Category.Value
```

13. Click the Sales Amount cell in the table1_SubCategory Footer, change the *Name* property to **SalesAmount_SubCategory**, and then click the Margin cell in the same row and change its *Name* property to **Margin_SubCategory**.
14. Add the following expressions to the Margin % cell in the table1_SubCategory footer:

```
=ReportItems!Margin_SubCategory.Value/ReportItems!SalesAmount_SubCategory.Value
```

15. Save the solution, and then preview your report.

The top of your report looks like this:

Adventure Works Product
Sales and Profitability
Report

Product	Sales Amount	Order Quantity	Margin	Margin %
Clothing				
Cap				
AWC logo cap	$478	85	$33	6.9 %
SubCategory Total	**$478**	**85**	**$33**	**6.9 %**
Gloves				
Full-finger Gloves, L	$4,229	176	$1,471	34.8 %
Full-finger Gloves, M	$2,130	87	$766	36.0 %
Full-finger Gloves, S	$198	8	$72	36.5 %
Half-finger Gloves, M	$704	46	$257	36.5 %
Half-finger Gloves, S	$337	22	$123	36.5 %

The margin percentages are now correctly displayed in the report.

Using Aggregate Functions

When you add a field to a table, the group footer rows in the table use the default aggregate function, *Sum*, with that field to total the rows in each group. The same function is also used to calculate a grand total for the table in the table footer. In the report body, an aggregate function operates on a set of rows defined by an expression, such as a field, and returns a value, such as a total. Usually, an aggregate function operates on numeric values, but some aggregate functions work with string values. In the page header and page footer, an aggregate function can operate only on report item expressions.

Because the expressions in the report body are evaluated when the report is processed, an aggregate function in the report body has access to the dataset and thus can use a field expression as an argument. However, expressions in the page header and footer are evaluated after the report body is processed and before the report is rendered. If you try to use `=Sum(Fields!SalesAmount.Value)` in the page footer, the report will not compile. Here's where a report item expression comes to the rescue, because it can access information for the processed page and return a value that is displayed in the rendered page. Thus, you can use `=Sum(ReportItems!SalesAmount.Value)` to total the value of all the textboxes labeled SalesAmount on the page.

Reporting Services supports 14 standard aggregate functions, which are shown in the following table:

Use this aggregate function	To do this
Aggregate	Aggregate values as defined by the data provider
Avg	Average nonnull numeric values in the set
Count	Count values in the set
CountDistinct	Count the distinct values in the set
CountRows	Count the number of rows in the set
First	Get the first value in the set
Last	Get the last value in the set
Max	Get the highest value in the set
Min	Get the lowest value in the set
StDev	Find the standard deviation of all nonnull numeric values in the set
StDevP	Find the population standard deviation of all nonnull numeric values in the set
Sum	Total the numeric values in the set
Var	Find the variance of all nonnull numeric values in the set
VarP	Find the population variance of all nonnull numeric values in the set

These functions are typically used in footer rows of a table or a matrix, but can also be used in free-standing textboxes.

Three miscellaneous functions can be used in detail rows to display a previous row value, the current row number, or accumulating values. These functions are shown in the following table:

Use this function	To do this
Previous	Show the value of the expression for the previous row of data
RowNumber	Show the current row count in an accumulating count of rows in the set
RunningValue	Show the current value in an accumulating aggregation of the set

Even though the *Sum* aggregation function is added by the Report Designer as you drop a field into a header or footer row of a table, you can also type an aggregate function directly into the table–for example, when you need to show cumulative values in the detail rows of a report or display averages in the footer row. Aggregates can also be used outside a data region in a free-standing textbox, either in the report body or in the page header or footer. For example, you might want to show a grand total on the first page of a report or display a page total in the footer of each page. In the case of nonnumeric data, such as an employee directory, you might want to show the first and last employee name in a page footer.

Using Aggregate Functions in a Table

When using aggregate functions in a data region, such as a table, you need to consider the scope of the function. *Scope* in the context of a data region determines which rows are included when calculating the aggregated value. Scope can refer not only to a grouping in the data region, but also to an entire data region or even an entire dataset.

Most aggregate functions use the syntax *Function(Expression,Scope)*, but the *RunningValue* function is constructed using the following syntax: *RunningValue(Expression,Function,Scope)*. In this function, *Expression* cannot itself contain an aggregate function; *Function* is the aggregate function to apply (which cannot be *RunningValue* or *RowNumber*); and *Scope* is the name of a data region or a grouping in a data region and is contained within quotation marks.

In this procedure, you'll use the *RunningValue* function to show how many products in a subcategory contribute to 80 percent of product sales in each subcategory.

Add a running total to the table

1. Click the Layout tab, right-click the Sales Amount column handle, and then click Insert Column To The Right.
2. Type **Cumulative** in the new cell in the Category group header (the second row of the table).
3. Click the Align Right button in the Report Formatting toolbar.
4. Add the following expression to the Cumulative cell in the detail row:

```
=RunningValue(Fields!SalesAmount.Value,Sum,"table1_SubCategory")
```

This expression calculates a running total of *SalesAmount* that is reset each time the *Scope* changes. (In this case, the *Scope* is the name of the group based on the *SubCategory* value.)

5. Save the solution, and then click the Preview tab to verify that the top-left section of your report looks like this:

Product	Sales Amount		Order Quantity
Clothing		Cumulative	
Cap			
AWC logo cap	$478	$478	85
SubCategory Total	**$478**		**85**
Gloves			
Half-finger Gloves, S	$337	$337	22
Half-finger Gloves, M	$704	$1,041	46
Full-finger Gloves, S	$198	$1,238	8
Full-finger Gloves, M	$2,130	$3,368	87
Full-finger Gloves, L	$4,229	$7,597	176
SubCategory Total	**$7,597**		**339**

Notice that the Cumulative value increases with each detail row in every subcategory section. The Cumulative value for the last detail row is equal to the subtotal for the subcategory. Then the Cumulative value is reset to zero and increases with each detail row in the next group. Because the Cumulative value is related to the Sales Amount column, you can place a label above the column to better explain what value is accumulating in the Cumulative column.

In this procedure, you'll merge the cells in the table header to center the Sales Amount label above the Actual and Cumulative columns.

Merge cells

1. Click the Layout tab, and then type **Actual** in the Category Header (the second row) of the Sales Amount column.
2. Click the Align Right button in the Report Formatting toolbar.
3. Click the Sales Amount header cell in the table header (the first row), press Ctrl, and click the cell to its immediate right, right-click either of the selected cells, and then click Merge Cells.

   Merging cells is useful for centering text labels over multiple columns in a columnar data region, such as a table or matrix.
4. Click the Center button in the Report Formatting toolbar to center the text across the two cells.

The first three columns of the table in the design grid now look like this:

Product	Sales Amount	
=Fields!Category.Value		Cumulative
=Fields!SubCategory.Value		
=Fields!Product.Value	=Fields!SalesAmount.V	=RunningValue(Fields!S
SubCategory Total	=Sum(Fields!SalesA	
Category Total	=Sum(Fields!Sales	
Grand Total	=Sum(Fields!Sales	

Using Aggregate Functions in a Textbox

Sometimes you might want to display the result of an aggregate function independently of the data region containing the data used by the function. You can place an aggregate function in a free-standing textbox and place it anywhere in your report. If you choose to do this, include a text label, either in a separate textbox or as part of the expression in the same textbox, to indicate the meaning of the value in the report. When using an expression to concatenate a string value with a numeric value, like an aggregate, you need to wrap the *Format* function around the aggregate function to convert the numeric value to a string and apply the proper formatting. The syntax for the *Format* function is *Format(Expression, FormatString)*, where *FormatString* is the same string you would use in the *Format* property.

As stated earlier in this section, the expression used with an aggregate function depends on its location in the report. When using an aggregate function in the report body, you must use a field expression. In the report body, the scope of an aggregate function is always a dataset, which must be specified only when there is more than one dataset in the report. In case you add a dataset later, get into the habit of including the dataset in the *Scope* argument to save edits later. An aggregate function in the page header or footer must instead use a report item expression. *Scope* is never used in this context, because the dataset is no longer accessible.

In this procedure, you'll use the *Sum* function to show total product sales for all categories in the report body rather than in a table.

Add a *Sum* aggregate function to the report body

1. Click the Layout tab, click Textbox in the Toolbox window, and then click the design grid in the spot just right of the image's top-right corner.

2. Use the textbox handles to resize the textbox to approximately 2.5 inches wide and 0.25 inches high so the design grid now looks like this:

3. Add the following expression to the new textbox:

```
=Sum(Fields!SalesAmount.Value,"DataDetail")
```

> **Note** In this example, only one dataset is in the report, so no *Scope* argument is required in the expression. You could enter `=Sum(Fields!SalesAmount.Value)`, but if you add another dataset to the report later, you will need to modify the expression to refer to the appropriate dataset in the *Scope* argument.

4. Click the Preview tab, and then scroll to the right of the report, if necessary.

   You can see that the format of the value needs to be fixed and a label should be added to explain what the value represents. Since the scope of the aggregate function in the report body is the dataset, the sum represents the total of all product sales in the report.

5. Click the Layout tab, and then modify the expression in the textbox as follows:

```
="Total Product Sales: "+Format(Sum(Fields!SalesAmount.Value, "DataDetail"), "C0")
```

   This expression is an example that illustrates how to concatenate an aggregate function with a text label.

6. On the Report Formatting toolbar, click the Italic button.
7. Save the solution and preview your report to confirm that the top looks like this:

Adventure Works Product Sales and Profitability Report

Total Product Sales: $1,582,470

   Now you can have a grand total for all products in the dataset.

In this procedure, you'll use the *First* and *Last* function to show total product sales for all categories in the report body.

Add a *First* and *Last* aggregate function to the page footer

1. Click the Layout tab, click Textbox in the Toolbox window, click the page footer to the right of the existing textbox, and then resize the textbox to about 2 inches in width and 0.25 inches in height and position it so its left edge is aligned with the 2" mark on the horizontal ruler.
2. Click the first cell of the detail row, and then verify that the *Name* property of this textbox in the Properties window is Product.

   The name of the textbox should have been assigned automatically when you dropped the *Product* field into this cell. If for some reason the name is not correct, edit the name now.
3. Click the textbox that you added to the page footer and enter the following expression:

   ```
   =First(ReportItems!Product.Value)
   ```

   This expression will find the name of the product in the first detail row on this page and display the result in the page footer.
4. Click the textbox with the *First* aggregate function, and then click the Align Right button on the Report Formatting toolbar.
5. Click the same textbox, and then, while pressing Ctrl, drag the cell to the right to make a copy of the textbox whose left edge aligns with the right edge of the original textbox and aligned with the 4" mark on the horizontal ruler.
6. Edit the second textbox containing the aggregate function so the expression now looks like this:

   ```
   =" - " +Last(ReportItems!Product.Value)
   ```

   This expression includes a dash as a visual separator between the first and last value displayed in the footer. Reporting Services doesn't let you use two report item expressions in the same textbox, but you can place two textboxes side by side to get the same effect.
7. Click the textbox with the *Last* aggregate function, and then click the Align Left button in the Report Formatting toolbar.
8. Save the solution and preview the report, scrolling to the bottom of the page.

   The bottom of the page looks like this:

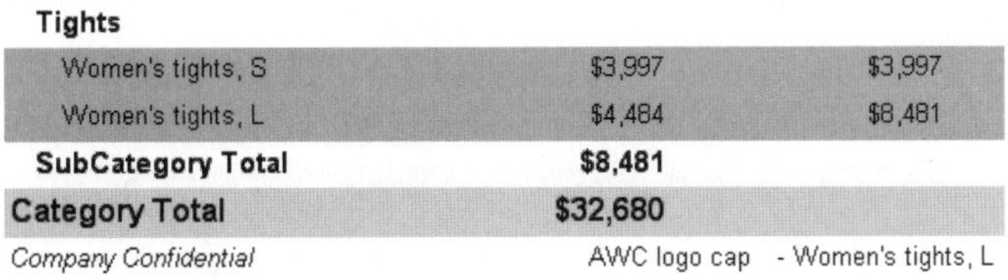

Tights		
Women's tights, S	$3,997	$3,997
Women's tights, L	$4,484	$8,481
SubCategory Total	**$8,481**	
Category Total	**$32,680**	
Company Confidential	AWC logo cap	- Women's tights, L

Using Expressions to Change an Object's Behavior

Even though expressions are often used to display the results of calculations in a report, you can also use them in report item properties to control appearance, such as font color. You can even use expressions to control behavior, such as sort order. You can set many of the properties in the Properties window by using an expression instead of a single value. This feature of Reporting Services provides endless flexibility in designing your reports.

Not every report will need to include expressions to change its appearance or behavior. However, in some situations, you'll find this capability useful. For example, you can find potential problem areas (or highlight areas that are performing well!) by using an expression to change the color of a field when the value falls below a certain threshold instead of using a value in the *Color* property of a report item.

In addition to using expressions to modify the appearance of a report item, you can use expressions to alter the sort order of rows or groups in a table. If you want to sort rows by a derived value rather than by an existing value in the row, you can easily add the expression to the sort definition.

Using Conditional Formatting

Conditional formatting is used to change the font or background color of an item based on the result of evaluating a Boolean expression, which returns either True or False. Often, conditional formatting is used to identify values, known as *exceptions*, that fall outside a specified range to make them easier to locate in a big report. You can also use conditional formatting to create rows with alternating colors.

Conditional formatting is commonly implemented using the *IIf* function, which evaluates an expression to determine whether it's true or false. For example, an expression to change the font color when the margin expression is below 15 percent might look like this: `=IIf(ReportItems!Margin_Percentage.Value<0.15, "Red", "Black")`. The first argument of the *IIf* function, `Margin_Percentage.Value<0.15`, is the condition that is evaluated. If the value is true, the second argument, `"Red"` in this case, is the result of the expression and becomes the value of the *Color* property. If the condition is false, the third argument, `"Black"`, becomes the value of the *Color* property.

In this procedure, you'll use conditional formatting to display detail rows using red text whenever the margin percentage is below 15 percent.

Highlight exceptions

1. Click the Layout tab, click the Margin % cell in the detail row, click Expression in the *Color* property list box, and then replace the default expression with the following expression:

```
=IIf(Me.Value<0.15, "Red", "Black")
```

> **Tip** Use the special word `Me` to refer to the current item so you can reuse the same expression in several textboxes. If you don't, you'll have to create a unique expression for each textbox, even when the expressions are performing the same task. For example, if you wanted to conditionally format the Margin Percentage textbox, you would use `=IIf(ReportItems!Margin_Percentage.Value<0.15, "Red", "Black")`, but you would need to use `=IIf(ReportItems!Margin_Percentage_Total.Value<0.15, "Red", "Black")` to conditionally format the Margin_Percentage_Total textbox. Although both of these expressions are valid, your work is simplified by using `Me`.

2. Copy the expression to the clipboard, and then click OK to close the Edit Expression dialog box.
3. Click the Margin % cell in the table1_SubCategory Footer, press the Ctrl key, click the Margin % cells in the table1_Category footer and the table footer, and then paste the copied expression into the *Color* property in the Properties window to update all three cells in one step.
4. With the Margin % cell in the table footer still selected, click Expression in the *Color* property list box and edit the expression to replace Black with **White**, as shown here:

   ```
   =IIf(Me.Value<0.15, "Red", "White")
   ```

5. Click OK to close the Edit Expressions dialog box.
6. Save your report, and then check the results by clicking the Preview tab.

   Confirm that the Margin % for AWC logo cap and the Cap SubCategory Total are both 6.9% and that they are displayed as red text.

Sorting

The sort order of rows in the table is determined by the order of rows in the dataset. You can use an ORDER BY clause in your query if you want to control the sort order on the database server. Alternatively, you can use a field expression for setting the sort order in Table Properties to change the query's default sort order using the Report Server. If you need to sort rows by a value that is not in the dataset, you can use an expression.

Specifying a sort order in Table Properties affects only the order of the detail rows. If you want to sort the groups, just right-click a group header or footer handle, and then click Edit Groups to access the Grouping And Sorting Properties dialog box. On the Sorting tab, you can select a field expression or enter your own expression to define a sort order for each level of grouping.

In this procedure, you'll sort the detail rows using an expression that calculates the margin percentage.

Sort detail rows using an expression

1. Click the Layout tab; click the table to display the handles; right-click the table handle, which is located in the top-left corner; and then click Properties.
2. In the Table Properties dialog box, click the Sorting tab, select <Expression...> in the Expression drop-down list, and then replace the default expression with the following expression:

```
=Sum(Fields!Margin.Value)/Sum(Fields!SalesAmount.Value)
```

> **Note** You can't use *ReportItems!Margin.Value* in this expression because the Margin textbox is in a detail row, which is not in scope for table properties. Remember that when using the *ReportItems* collection, you can reference only those report items that are on the same level of grouping or higher.

3. Click OK to close the Edit Expression dialog box.
4. Click Descending in the corresponding Direction drop-down list.

   The Table Properties dialog box looks like this:

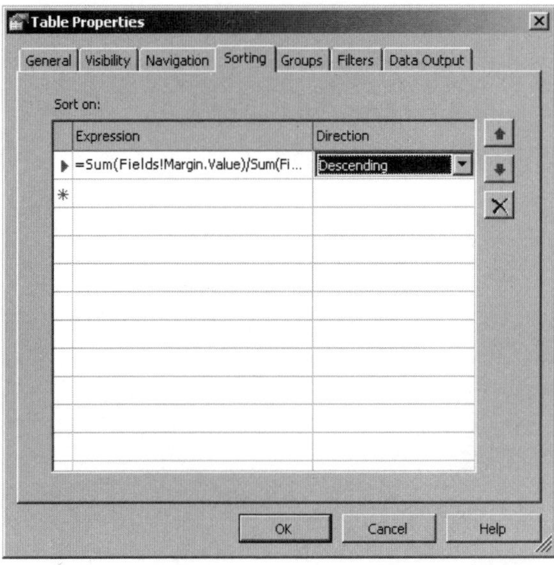

5. Click OK to close the Table Properties dialog box.

6. Click the Preview tab to verify that your report looks like this:

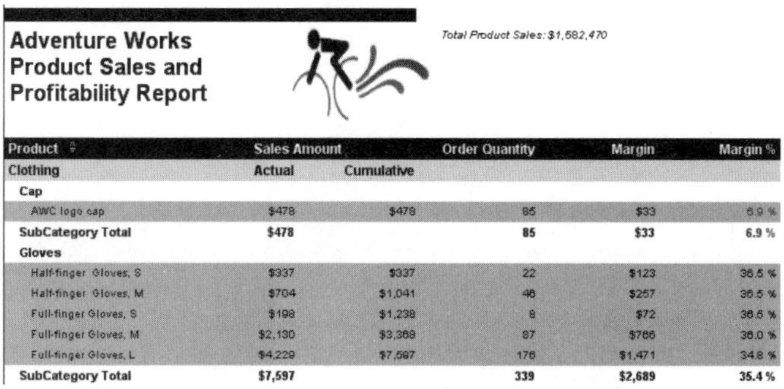

Adventure Works Product Sales and Profitability Report

Total Product Sales: $1,582,470

Product	Sales Amount		Order Quantity	Margin	Margin %
Clothing	Actual	Cumulative			
Cap					
AWC logo cap	$478	$478	85	$33	6.9 %
SubCategory Total	$478		85	$33	6.9 %
Gloves					
Half-finger Gloves, S	$337	$337	22	$123	36.5 %
Half-finger Gloves, M	$704	$1,041	46	$257	36.5 %
Full-finger Gloves, S	$198	$1,238	8	$72	36.5 %
Full-finger Gloves, M	$2,130	$3,368	87	$766	36.0 %
Full-finger Gloves, L	$4,229	$7,597	176	$1,471	34.8 %
SubCategory Total	$7,597		339	$2,689	35.4 %

The detail rows are now sorted in descending order of margin percentage, but only within each subcategory group. Notice that on the first page of the report, the subcategories are still sorting in the order found in the dataset (the default sort order).

7. Save and close the solution.

Chapter 5 Quick Reference

To	Do this
Add a calculated field	Right-click in the Datasets window, and then click Add. Enter a name for the calculated field and click the Calculated Field option. Enter an expression directly into the Calculated Field textbox or click the Expression button to open the expression editor.
Insert a row or column in a table	Right-click the row handle, and then click either Insert Row Above or Insert Row Below. *or* Right-click the column handle and then click either Insert Column To The Left or Insert Column To The Right.
Copy an expression without copying textbox formatting	Click the textbox containing the expression to copy; press Enter to select the expression, and then press Ctrl+C to copy.
Test an expression	Click the Preview tab.
Merge cells	Click the cells to be merged. You can right-click and then click Merge Cells, or click the Merge Cells button in the Layout toolbar.
Use an aggregate function	Use one of the following: *Function(Expression,Scope)* for a standard aggregation. *or* *RunningValue(Expression,Function,Scope)* for a running value aggregation. *or* *RowNumber(Scope)* for a running count of rows.

To	Do this
Apply conditional formatting	Use the *IIf* function to test for a condition and assign a property value for true and false conditions. For example, use the following expression to set the *Color* property of a textbox: `=IIf(Me.Value<0.15, "Red", "Black")`
Sort table rows	Use an ORDER BY clause in the dataset query. *or* Click the table, click the table handle in the top-left corner, and then click Properties. In the Table Properties dialog box, click the Sorting tab, and then click an expression in the Expression list box. If you click <Expression...> in this list box, you can open the expression editor to enter your own expression if you want to sort by a value that is not explicitly contained in the dataset.

Chapter 6

Organizing Data in Reports

After completing this chapter, you will be able to:

- Represent data in a crosstabular form by using a matrix.
- Represent data graphically by using a chart.
- Represent data in a flexible layout by using a list.

In the previous chapter, you finished your report by adding expressions to enhance the information in it and to affect the appearance and behavior of report items. In this chapter, you expand your report design skills using the other data regions supported by Reporting Services. You work with a matrix data region to see how both rows and columns can dynamically adjust to the dataset. You also add a chart data region to a report so you can see how multiple data regions can be combined in a single report and how to manipulate chart properties. To learn how to take advantage of a free-form, repeating data region, you use a list to create grouped sets consisting of a matrix and chart.

Understanding Data Regions

Although a table data region can accommodate most of your reporting needs, you have several other ways to organize data in a report, which you explore in this chapter. Before examining the matrix, chart, and data regions in greater depth, you will compare these data regions with one another and with a table to better understand the general similarities and differences among them. You will also encounter some typical applications of these data regions to help you decide which will be appropriate for your next reporting project.

Comparing Types of Data Regions

As you learned in Chapter 3, "Building Your First Report," a data region is a structure in the report in which data from the dataset is arranged. A data region differs from other report items, such as a textbox or a rectangle, because it repeats data. For example, in the table you built in Chapter 4, "Developing Basic Reports," you defined properties by row, such as the detail row, which were repeated for each record in the dataset.

The following table highlights the differences between the four data regions supported by Reporting Services. You already know that a table data region displays the same number of columns every time the report is executed, but as data changes in the source, the number of rows can vary. In the Product Sales and Profitability report, for example, as new products are sold by Adventure Works, additional rows of data are added to the report. Grouping isn't required in a table, but you did add two grouping levels to the table, Category and SubCategory, to break the product detail rows into smaller sets for which subtotals could be calculated. In this chapter, you work with a matrix, a list, and a chart.

Data region	Description	Grouping levels	Group on
Table	Fixed number of columns with variable number of repeating rows	From zero to many	Rows
Matrix	Fixed crosstab with variable number of repeating rows and columns of aggregate data only	From zero to many	Rows or columns
List	Freeform layout of repeating report items	One	List
Chart	Graphical display of dataset of aggregate data only	Category, Series	Dependent on chart type

Using Data Regions

When designing your report, you need to select a data region that is appropriate for the data you expect to be returned in the dataset. Most of the time, a table will probably satisfy your requirements. However, if you want to use data from the query, such as month names, in the column headers, you need to use a matrix data region. If you need more flexibility in positioning report items, rather than using the fixed row and column structure of a table or matrix, you can use a list.

You also need to consider whether to use multiple data regions. You can nest data regions to repeat the same data region multiple times by placing a list within a list or a table within a list. This is a great way to design one table that is reused many times in the same report. For example, you could use a separate table for each salesperson when reporting sales data. If you wanted to present alternate views of data side by side—which is sometimes the best way to communicate information—you could use a table with detail data and a chart with aggregated data.

Using a Matrix

A matrix data region can be compared to a PivotTable or crosstab-style report, because the number of rows as well as the number of columns adapt dynamically. The number of rows or columns can change as the results of the query change or as selections are made in the report to focus attention on certain data. As in a table, the detail rows of a matrix come from the report's dataset. However, a table has the same number of columns every time the report is executed. The number of columns in a matrix, by contrast, can increase or decrease depending on the query results.

Adding a Matrix Data Region

Adding a matrix data region is as easy as adding any other data region. In the Toolbox window, click Matrix, and then click the report body to position the top-left corner of the matrix. Because the rows and columns of the matrix expand according to the dataset, report items below or to the right of the matrix shift when the matrix adjusts.

> **Tip** If, for some reason, the query returns no data to the dataset, the data region is not rendered. You can choose to display a textbox with a message by entering a value in the *NoRows* property of the data region. This value, when displayed, will use the same style properties, such as *Color* and *Font*, that are defined for the data region. Be sure to supply a value for this property if you want something to appear on the report when no data is returned.

In this procedure, you'll create a new report containing a matrix data region that displays *SalesAmount*.

Add a simple matrix

1. Start SQL Server Business Intelligence Development Studio and open the solution My Adventure Works that you saved in the C:\Documents and Settings\<username>\My Documents\Microsoft Press\rs2005sbs\Workspace\My Adventure Works folder.

> **Note** If you skipped Chapter 5, "Working with Expressions," open the solution My Adventure Works in the C:\Documents and Settings\<username>\My Documents \Microsoft Press\rs2005sbs\Answers\chap05\My Adventure Works folder.

2. In Solution Explorer, right-click the Product Sales and Profitability.rdl report, click Copy, click the Reports folder, and then press Ctrl+V to paste a copy of the report into the folder.
3. Right-click the new report, click Rename, and then type a new name for the report: **Product Sales and Profitability by Month.rdl**.
4. Double-click the Product Sales and Profitability by Month.rdl report in Solution Explorer to display the report in the Document window.
5. Click the table in the new report to display the handles, right-click the table handle in the top left-corner, and then click Delete.

> **Tip** If you plan to use the same dataset in another report, rather than start with a blank report, copy an existing report, and then delete data regions from it. Using this technique, you can also preserve the overall appearance with minimal effort for a consistent look between reports.

6. In the Toolbox window, click Matrix, and then click the left edge of the design grid just below the textbox containing the report title.

   Your screen looks like this:

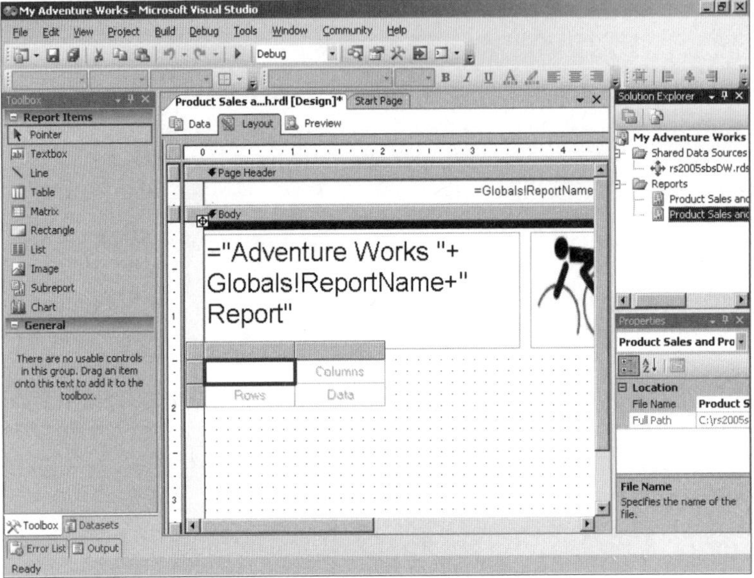

   Notice there are three main areas of the matrix: Rows, Columns, and Data. These are drop zones for fields from the dataset.

7. In the Datasets window, click *SalesAmount* and drag to the Data area of the matrix.

   Notice that the *Sum* function was added to the expression.

> **Note** A matrix data region does not have a detail row and always aggregates numeric data based on the intersection of the rows and columns. The default aggregation function is *Sum*, but you can change this if you need to use a different aggregation.

8. In the Properties window for the SalesAmount textbox, enter **C0** as the *Format* property.

Grouping Rows

You create dynamic row groups using fields in the dataset. Because both the number of rows in each group and the value displayed as the group row header are determined by the dataset, the table grows or shrinks as the dataset increases or decreases. The group row header cell appears, by default, to the left of the numeric value that appears in the Data area of the matrix. You can nest dynamic rows to create multiple grouping levels for rows. The result is similar to the grouping that you added to the table in Chapter 4.

In this procedure, you'll add Category and SubCategory as row groups in the matrix.

Add row groups

1. Drag *Category* from the Datasets window and drop it in the Rows area of the matrix.
2. Drag *SubCategory* and drop it in the same cell, placing the mouse pointer on the right side of the cell as you drop the field so that a new column appears between Category and SalesAmount, as shown here:

   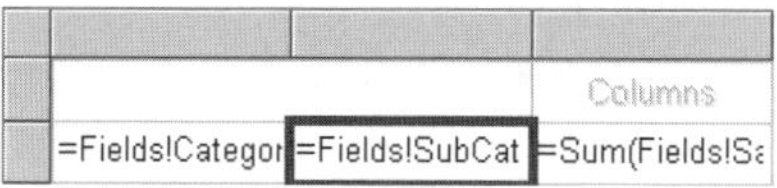

   If the drop zone already contains a field, you can still drop another field into the zone. Instead of inserting a column to the right, you can hold the mouse pointer over the left portion of the Row drop zone, and then drop the field to insert a new column to the left of the existing cell.
3. Click the `=Fields!Category.Value` cell, and then click the Bold button on the Report Formatting toolbar.
4. Save the solution, and then preview the report.

   The top of the report looks like this:

   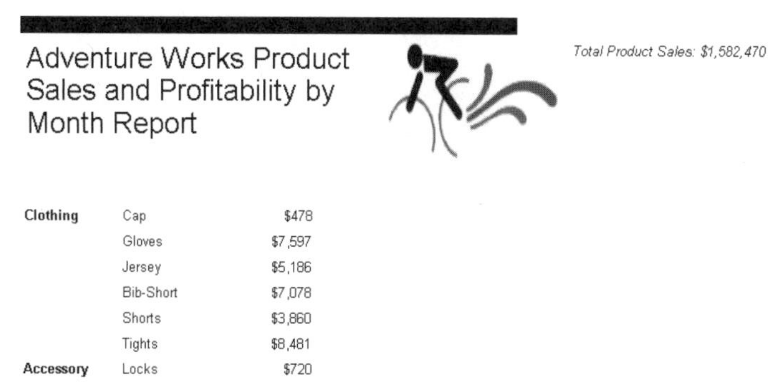

Adventure Works Product Sales and Profitability by Month Report
Total Product Sales: $1,582,470
Clothing Cap $478
Gloves $7,597
Jersey $5,186
Bib-Short $7,078
Shorts $3,860
Tights $8,481
Accessory Locks $720

Sorting Rows

Sorting rows in a matrix is similar to setting sorting properties for a table. You can sort by a field value, or you can add your own expression to control sort order.

In this procedure, you'll edit the matrix properties to apply sorting to each row group.

Define sort order

1. Click the Layout tab, right-click the matrix handle in the top-left corner, and then click Properties.

2. In the Matrix Properties dialog box, click the Groups tab, click matrix1_Category in the Rows pane, and then click Edit.
3. Click the Sorting tab, click `=Fields!Category.Value` in the Expression drop-down list, and then click OK to close the Grouping And Sorting Properties dialog box.
4. Click matrix1_SubCategory, and then click Edit.
5. Click the Sorting tab, click `=Fields!SubCategory.Value` in the Expression drop-down list, and then click OK twice to close all dialog boxes.
6. Save the report, and then preview the report, which now looks like this:

Adventure Works Product Sales and Profitability by Month Report

Total Product Sales: $1,582,470

Accessory	Helmet	$3,371
	Locks	$720
	Pumps	$636
Bike	Mountain Bike	$600,010
	Road Bike	$807,962
Clothing	Bib-Short	$7,078
	Cap	$478

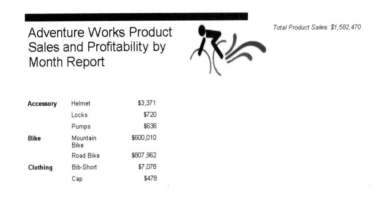

By default, a matrix shows values for only the lowest visible level. In this example, the lowest visible level is the SubCategory group. This report resembles a table. It has yet to show off the power of a matrix because no column groups are defined.

Grouping Columns

A dynamic column group is one of the main differentiators between a matrix and a table. Recall that a table has dynamic rows, but a fixed number of columns. Dynamic column groups work like dynamic row groups, but are laid out from left to right across the page instead of from top to bottom. Also, like dynamic rows, both the number of rows and the value displayed as the column header are determined by the dataset. As with row groups, you can nest dynamic columns to create multiple grouping levels for columns.

> **Tip** If you want some of the data columns to appear to the left of the row headers, use the *GroupsBeforeRowHeaders* property of the matrix. This property uses an integer value to control the number of column groups that are displayed in front of the row header column.

In this procedure, you'll add a column grouping to the matrix to display Sales Amount and Order Quantity by month.

Adding Column Groupings

1. Click the Data tab, and then change the WHERE clause of the query to the following:

```
WHERE Year = 2003 and MonthNumberOfYear IN (1,2,3)
```

   Now the query will return data for January, February, and March of 2003.

2. Click the Layout tab, right-click the matrix handle, and then click Properties.
3. In the Matrix Properties dialog box, click the Groups tab, and then click Add in the Columns pane.

   The Grouping And Sorting Properties dialog box is displayed.

> **Note** You can also drag a field from the Datasets window to the Columns drop zone to add a column. However, by adding a column using the Matrix Properties dialog box, you can also set group properties for the new column right away.

4. Replace the default name of the group by typing **matrix1_Month**.
5. Click `=Fields!Month.Value` in the Expression drop-down list to define the expression to be used to create a column group.
6. Click the Sorting tab, click `=Fields!MonthNumberOfYear.Value` in the Expression drop-down list, and then click OK.

> **Tip** When displaying month names in a report, your query should also include a numeric value of the month that you can use to sort the months in the correct order.

The Matrix Properties dialog box looks like this:

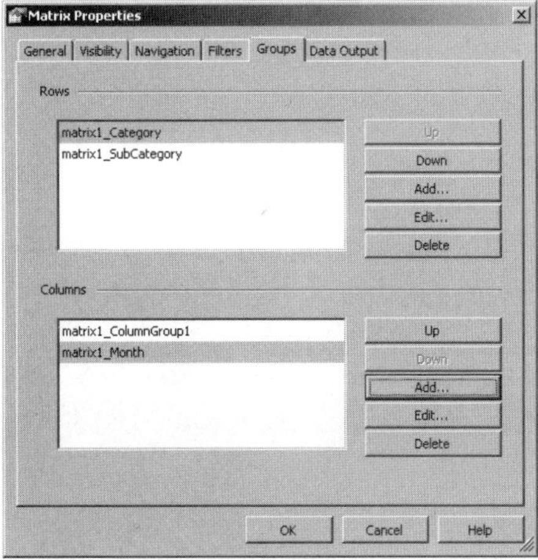

7. In the Matrix Properties dialog box in the Columns pane, click the matrix1_Month group, click the Up button to move matrix1_Month above matrix1_ColumnGroup1, and then click OK. The matrix now looks like this:

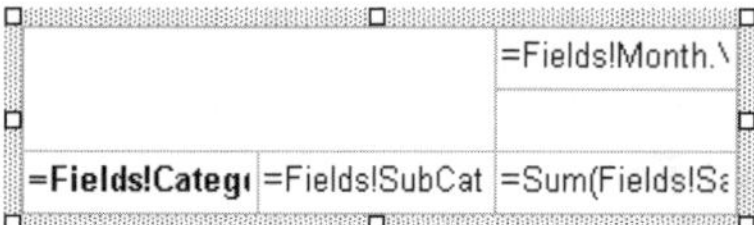

The matrix_ColumnGroup1 group is a static group that consists of a set of columns that will be displayed for each column group. You'll work with the static group later in this chapter. In this case, the static group contains the Sales Amount column. By moving matrix1_Month above the static group, the name of the month is displayed first.

8. Save and then preview your report, which now looks like this:

Adventure Works Product Sales and Profitability by Month Report

		Jan	Feb	Mar
Accessory	Helmet	$3,371	$4,360	$3,932
	Locks	$720	$735	$750
	Pumps	$636	$468	$660
Bike	Mountain Bike	$600,010	$972,136	$698,250
	Road Bike	$807,962	$1,615,294	$934,106
Clothing	Bib-Short	$7,078	$9,183	$7,078

Notice that the month names are not centered above each column. You'll fix the position of the month names in a later procedure.

Your report can now expand vertically as more products are sold by Adventure Works, and horizontally if the query is modified to include more months. You'll learn how to make the query more dynamic in Chapter 7, "Building Advanced Reports," so you don't have to change the query string each time you want to view different data in the report.

Using Subtotals in a Matrix

When working with a single row group, the numeric data in each column is already aggregated, so a subtotal is not necessary. However, when working with multiple groups, you might want to add subtotals to see totals by group. Working with subtotals in a matrix is much different from working with subtotals in a table. In a matrix, the same cell is used to manage the properties of the subtotal label and the numeric values that are displayed in the subtotal row.

You turn on subtotals by selecting the Subtotal command from the shortcut menu for the group heading cell. You format subtotal data values by selecting a small triangle in the corner of the subtotal cell.

In this procedure, you'll add a subtotal to the SubCategory and Category groups.

Add subtotals

1. Click the Layout tab, right-click the SubCategory cell, and then click Subtotal to add a new row to the matrix, which now looks like this:

   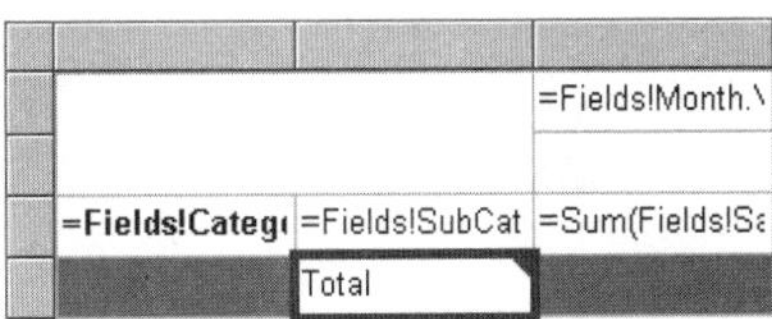

   The result of this subtotal will be the sum of each SubCategory within a Category. In effect, it's really the Category total, which you'll see when you preview the report.

2. Click the Total cell, and then click Bold on the Report Formatting toolbar.

   Now the label for the subtotal is formatted, but you still have to perform additional steps to format the subtotal values.

3. If necessary, open the Properties window, and then click the small green triangle in the top-right corner of the new Total cell.

   The Properties window now displays Subtotal in the report items list box.

4. On the Report Formatting toolbar, click the Bold button.

   The subtotal values are now formatted, even though you can't see the new format in the matrix.

5. Right-click the Category cell, and then click Subtotal.

   Another Total cell appears in the matrix. Because Category is the highest level of the row groups, this subtotal is the equivalent of a grand total.

6. Format the Category Total cell by using the Report Formatting toolbar to set the Font Size to 12, the Background Color to Black, and the Foregound Color to White.

7. Click the green triangle in the Category Total cell to format the values, and then use the Report Formatting toolbar to set the Font Weight to Bold, the Font Size to 12, the Background Color to Black, and the Foreground Color to White.

8. Add a subtotal for months by right-clicking the `=Fields!Month.Value` cell, and then clicking Subtotal.

9. Click the Month Total cell, and then Bold on the Report Formatting toolbar.

10. Save and preview the report, which now looks like this:

Adventure Works Product
Sales and Profitability by
Month Report

		Jan	Feb	Mar	Total
Accessory	Helmet	$3,371	$4,360	$3,932	$11,663
	Locks	$720	$735	$750	$2,205
	Pumps	$636	$468	$660	$1,763
	Total	**$4,727**	**$5,563**	**$5,341**	**$15,631**
Bike	Mountain Bike	$600,010	$972,136	$698,250	$2,270,397
	Road Bike	$807,962	$1,615,294	$934,106	$3,357,362

Notice that the SubCategory totals are bold, the Category totals are bold, and the colors are reversed. You might need to scroll to the bottom of the report to see the Category totals.

Using Static Rows and Columns in a Matrix

You can also add static rows and columns, called Static Groups, to the matrix. By having such rows or columns, you can have multiple aggregations for a single field. For example, your matrix currently displays the aggregated Sales Amount, but you could also add the aggregated Order Quantity. If you have column groups in your report, each column group will display the set of static columns, that is, Sales Amount and Order Quantity. Static columns in a matrix are similar to the columns in a table data region because there is a fixed number of static columns per column group.

In this procedure, you'll add the *OrderQuantity* field to the matrix as a static column.

Add static columns

1. Click the Layout tab, right-click the SalesAmount textbox, and then click Add Column.

   The matrix now looks like this:

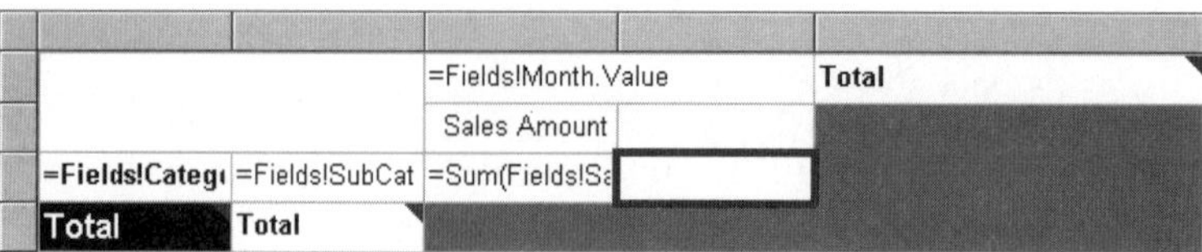

   To the right of SalesAmount, another column is added as a static column to the group. Notice that a column label is also automatically added to the SalesAmount column.

> **Note** To add a static row, right-click a matrix textbox, and then click Add Row. As with a static column, a static row will repeat with each row group.

2. In the Datasets window, click *OrderQuantity* and drag the field to the new data column.
3. Change the *Format* property of the Order Quantity textbox to **N0**.
4. Click the column handle between Sales Amount and Order Quantity columns, and then drag to make the Sales Amount column approximately 1.25 inches wide.
5. Drag the right side of the Order Quantity column handle to extend its width also to approximately 1.25 inches.
6. Click the `=Fields!Month.Value` cell, and then click Center on the Report Formatting toolbar to center the textbox value across the Static Group.
7. Click the Month Total cell, and then click Center on the Report Formatting toolbar to center the subtotal label across the Static Group that isn't visible now but will be rendered.
8. In the first cell of the top row of the matrix, type **Product**.
9. Click all three cells in the top row of the matrix while pressing Ctrl, and then use the Report Formatting toolbar to set the Font Weight to Bold, the Font Size to 12, the Background Color to Black, and the Foreground Color to White.
10. Save the report and preview to verify that the report now looks like this:

Adventure Works Product Sales and Profitability by Month Report

Product		Jan		Feb	
		Sales Amount	Order Quantity	Sales Amount	Order Quantity
Accessory	Helmet	$3,371	167	$4,360	216
	Locks	$720	48	$735	49
	Pumps	$636	53	$468	39
	Total	**$4,727**	**268**	**$5,563**	**304**
Bike	Mountain Bike	$600,010	488	$972,136	781
	Road Bike	$807,962	1,024	$1,615,294	1,863

You can scroll to the right and down to see all the rows and columns on this page. Notice that each month, as well as the month subtotal column, has a column for Sales Amount and Order Quantity.

Using a Chart

You use a chart to display data graphically. Although a chart cannot contain other report items, such as a textbox, it does have many attributes you must manage. Reporting Services supports a wide variety of chart types: column, bar, pie, line, doughnut, area, scatter, bubble, and stock. Standard formatting options allow you to change the chart appearance of the plot and chart areas, the chart axes, and the legend. In addition to choosing colors and styles from a palette, you can use expressions to incorporate conditional formatting into your chart. Many of the chart properties that you might need to change are not accessible in the Properties window, but they are managed in a Chart Properties dialog box associated with the chart.

A chart can be placed into a report all by itself, but many users like to see the data that supports the chart as a separate data region. You can position a chart above, below, or on either side of a data region. At minimum, you need to define a data value to display in the chart, which you can then segment into category and series groups if you like. Reporting Services provides plenty of formatting options and property settings to enhance the appearance of the chart.

Adding a Chart

You can click Chart in the Toolbox window and then click the design grid to add a chart of a fixed size to your report body, or you can drag the mouse pointer across the design grid to set a specific size for the chart. However, whenever you're combining data regions, regardless of type, be sure to allow for the vertical expansion of a table, matrix, or list, and the horizontal expansion of a matrix. You might want to place a chart above a data region rather than below it or to its side to avoid problems with placement.

In this procedure, you'll add a chart to your report to display with the matrix.

Add a chart to a report

1. In Solution Explorer, right-click the Product Sales and Profitability by Month.rdl report, click Copy, click the Reports folder, and then press Ctrl+V to paste a copy of the report into the folder.
2. Right-click the new report, click Rename, and then type a new name for the report: **Product Sales and Profitability Chart.rdl**.
3. Double-click the Product Sales and Profitability Chart.rdl report to open the report in the Document window.

4. Click the matrix to display the handles, and then drag the matrix to a lower position in the report body so the top of the matrix is at about 3.5 inches on the vertical ruler.

   The design grid is not large enough for you to move the top of the matrix to the 3.5-inch mark, but you can move the matrix there in two drag operations by dragging the matrix as far as you can. The design grid will expand vertically to accommodate the matrix, and then you can drag the matrix into position. The additional space will give you more room in the report for working with a chart.

5. In the Toolbox window, click Chart, and then click to the leftmost part of the body just under the report title and above the matrix to place a fixed-size chart in the report body.

6. In the Properties window, change the *Width* property of the new chart1 report item to **6in**, and then change the *Height* property to **2in**.

   The screen looks similar to this:

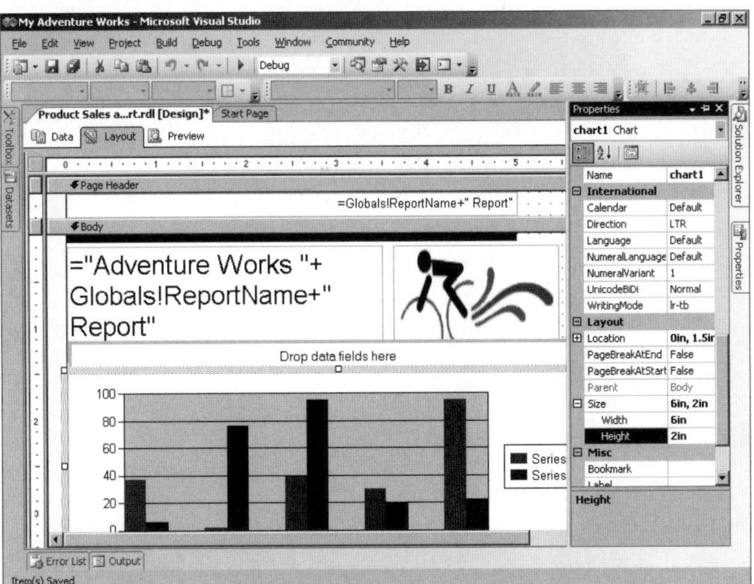

Adding Values and Column Groups to a Chart

A chart must include at least one value. A *value* is the numeric expression represented by a position in a chart, such as a point in a line chart; or by size, such as the length of a bar or the size of a bubble. Values can be grouped by categories, which are basically labels for the values (like a row header). These category groups can be nested, which allows you to break groups down into subgroups, such as years and quarters.

In this procedure, you'll add *SalesAmount* as the chart's value and *Year* and *Month* as its category groups.

Add fields to the chart

1. In the Datasets window, click the *SalesAmount* field and drag it to the area located above the chart labeled Drop Data Fields Here.
2. Drag the *Year* field from the Datasets window to the area located below the chart labeled Drop Category Fields Here.
3. Drag the *Month* field to the same area.
4. Save and then preview the report.

   The chart looks like this:

   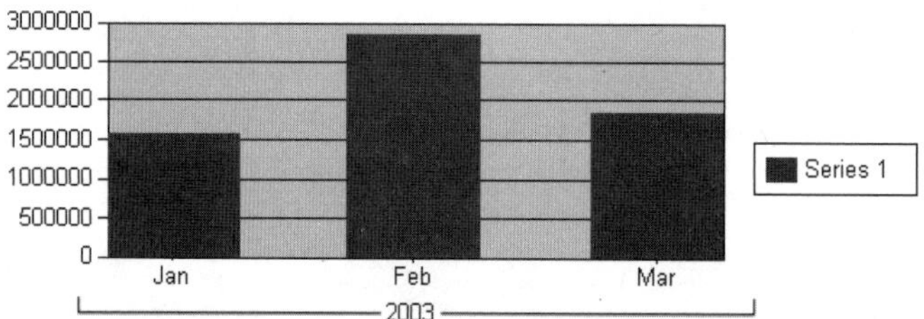

   Take a look at how the category groups are arranged. The first group you added, Year, is displayed as the outermost grouping and includes brackets to indicate how it relates to the next grouping level, Month. If the dataset included an additional year, you would see the second year as another group in the chart.

Grouping Data by Series

A series group adds more information to the report by differentiating the displayed values by yet another group. For example, if your report has category groups for year and quarter, you'll see a separate value in the report for each year and quarter available in the dataset. A series group further subdivides the values by using different colors for the members of the series. So, to continue the example, for a single quarter of a particular year, you can see several values for that quarter, such as a value for each employee's sales. The chart legend is used to map the series color with each series member.

In this procedure, you'll add a series group for SubCategory.

Add a series group

1. Click the Layout tab, right-click the chart, and then click Properties. The Chart Properties dialog box is displayed:

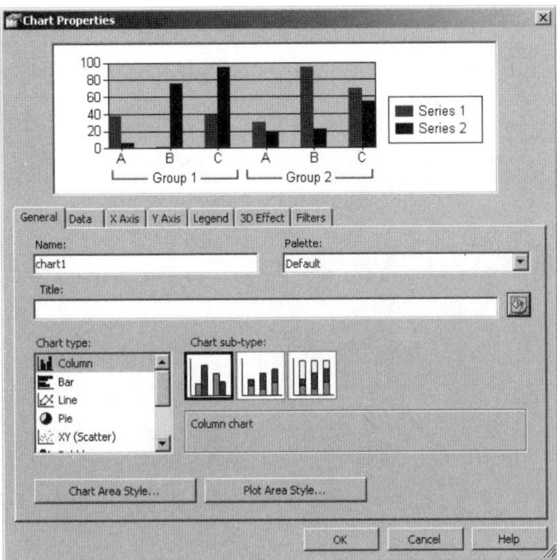

2. Click the Data tab, and then click Add to the right of the Series Groups box.
3. In the Grouping And Sorting Properties dialog box, select `=Fields!SubCategory.Value` in the Expression drop-down list.

   The Series Group is generated dynamically from the *SubCategory* field in the dataset each time the report is rendered.
4. Select `=Fields!SubCategory.Value` in the Label drop-down list.

   The Report Designer uses the label that you specified in the Grouping and Sorting Properties dialog box for the series group. The label doesn't have to be the same value used to create the series group.
5. Click the Sorting tab, select `=Fields!SubCategory.Value` in the Expression drop-down list, and then click OK. Keep the Chart Properties dialog box open for the next procedure.

The Series Group sorts the SubCategory values in alphabetical order. The Chart Properties dialog box now looks like this:

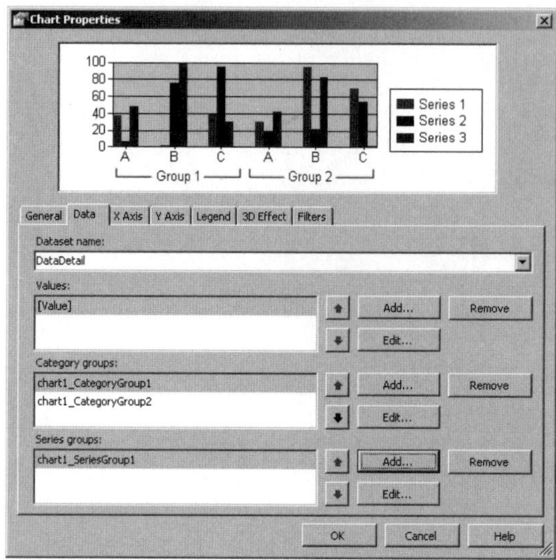

Notice that as you set properties, a generic preview is updated in the Chart Properties dialog box, which helps you see the impact of your changes without previewing the report. Because the preview uses sample data, the chart you see here is just a guideline to illustrate the current property settings.

Adding a Chart Legend

A chart legend describes the values used in your report. If a series group is not added to the chart, you might want to hide the chart legend. You have complete control over its location and appearance.

In this procedure, you'll move the chart legend and format the legend's font text.

Format the chart legend

1. Click the Legend tab.

   The buttons in the Position area are used to position the chart legend relative to the chart.

2. Click the top button in the right column of the Position area of the dialog box to align the legend at the top-right corner of the chart.

The Chart Properties dialog box now looks like this:

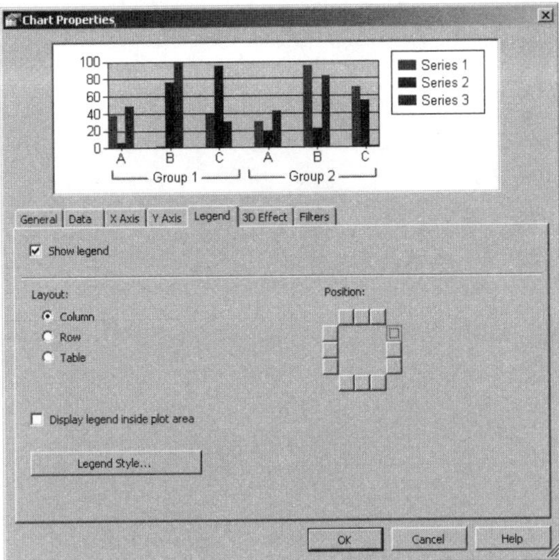

3. Click Legend Style.

   The Style Properties dialog box is displayed:

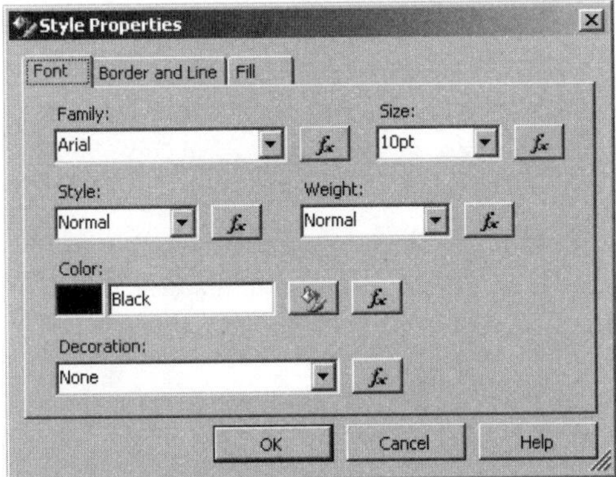

   You can use this dialog box to select a font and to set font size, color, and other style properties. The dialog box also includes tabs for specifying border, line, and fill properties. Notice that every property has an Expression button that allows you to enter a conditional expression to set a property value.

4. Select 8pt in the Size drop-down list, and then click OK to close the Style Properties dialog box.
5. Click OK to close the Chart Properties dialog box and apply the property changes.

6. Save the report, and then preview it to confirm the chart now looks like this:

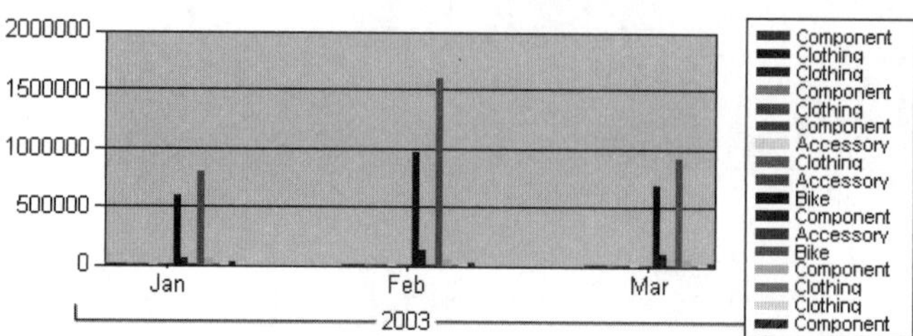

For each month, there is now one column for each member of the series group for which a value exists in that month. The chart legend shows the color assigned to each SubCategory. Now, you can continue to refine the chart's appearance by changing some chart properties.

Setting Chart Properties

The Properties window for the chart data region contains the standard background color, border, and size properties that are associated with the other data regions. However, most of the properties that affect the appearance and behavior of the chart are accessible only in the Chart Properties dialog box. To open the Chart Properties dialog box, you right-click the Chart, and then click Properties.

If you've worked with charting in other applications, most of these properties should be familiar. On the General tab, you can specify a name for the chart for reference in expressions and a title to be displayed in the rendered chart. You can also select from a variety of chart types and subtypes, which are alternate versions of a chart type. You can change style properties for anything you see in the chart: the chart area, the plot area, data values, axis titles, and labels. You can even apply 3-D effects to the chart, if desired.

In this procedure, you'll format the chart.

Format the chart

1. Click the Layout tab, right-click the chart, and then click Properties.

   Take a look at the chart type options, but leave the default chart type. In this dialog box, you can also set the Chart Area and Plot Area styles.

2. Click the Y Axis tab and type **C0** in the Format Code box.
3. In the Title box, type a label for the Y axis: **Sales**.
4. Click the Style Properties icon next to the Title box, click 8pt in the Size drop-down list, and then click OK.

5. Click the 3D Effect tab, select the check box to enable the 3-D settings, select the Cylinder check box, and then move the sliders to change the settings as follows:

Setting	Value
Horizontal rotation	5°
Perspective	0%
Wall thickness	10%
Vertical rotation	0°

6. Click OK.
7. Save and preview the report.

   The chart now looks like this:

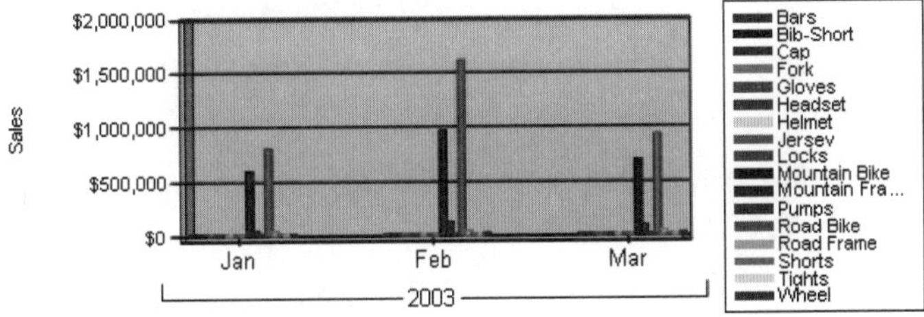

There are, of course, many other properties you can change to make a really nice-looking chart. The best way to learn about them is to experiment by observing the effect of different property settings on your chart. However, remember that the intent of a chart is to convey information. Most users are satisfied with simple chart effects and won't use a report if the chart is too busy or too complicated to decipher.

Using a List

When you use a list, you can combine different types of report items in an unstructured arrangement within the data region. This type of data region repeats each row from a dataset, just like a table or matrix, but has more flexibility. Instead of arranging data in strict rows and columns, you can place textboxes anywhere you want within the data region, regardless of whether your data is dynamic or static. You can even reproduce a columnar look to simulate a table, but you'll spend more time getting report items lined up properly if you do this with a list.

The columnar format of the table and matrix data regions makes aligning data easy. However, other than offering the *Padding* property, which allows you to shift text away from the edges of the column, this format doesn't provide you with much flexibility when arranging data. Using a list, you can arrange report items freely. You can add a grouping level to the list to define how the report items in the list will repeat. You can also nest other data regions in a list, including nesting a list within a list, to take advantage of repeating data regions. Consider these options as just a starting point for using a list, because its free-form nature gives you unlimited possibilities.

Adding a List

You add a list like you add a chart. You can click List in the Toolbox, and then click the design grid to add a list of a fixed size; or, you can drag the mouse pointer across the design grid to create a list of a specific size. The list looks just like a rectangle that is waiting for you to put report items inside it. The difference between a list and a rectangle is that a list repeats for each row of its data set or group when the report is rendered, whereas a rectangle does not repeat. You can also add a list to a report that already contains report items. After adding a list to the design grid, you can drag existing report items into the list.

In this procedure, you'll create a new report to which you add a list data region and associate the data region with a dataset.

Add a list

1. In Solution Explorer, right-click the Product Sales and Profitability Chart.rdl report, click Copy, click the Reports folder, and then press Ctrl+V to paste a copy of the report into the folder.
2. Right-click the new report, click Rename, and then type a new name for the report: **Product Sales and Profitability List.rdl**.
3. Double-click the Product Sales and Profitability List.rdl report in Solution Explorer to display the report in the Document window.
4. Resize the Document window so you can see the full width of the chart. You might need to close some Visual Studio windows, which you can open later using the View menu.
5. Change the *Height* property to **10in** in the Size category of the Body object in the Properties window.

   You won't really need all this space for the finished report, but the design grid is now taller, which gives you more room to work with.
6. Click the matrix, click the matrix handle to select the matrix, and then, while pressing the Ctrl key, click the chart to select both report items.
7. Drag the report items down so that the top of the chart is at the 6-inch mark on the vertical ruler.
8. Click List in the Toolbox window, and then place your mouse pointer just below the bottom-left corner of the report title textbox. Click to create a list of a fixed size.
9. In the Properties window, change the *Width* property to **7.5in** and the *Height* property to **4in**.
10. In the Properties window, scroll to find the *DataSetName* property, and then click *DataDetail* in the property's list box.

> **Note** Each data region is associated with a single dataset. In previous procedures, the *DataSetName* property was updated automatically for you when you added the first field from a dataset to a table or a matrix. However, you need to set this property manually when you add a list to your report. Regardless of the data region, however, if you change the dataset name or remove a dataset from the report, you will need to update the *DataSetName* property; otherwise, the report will not render.

Grouping and Sorting a List

A list can display detail rows or a single grouping level, but not both. Further, a list can have only one level of grouping. (As you learn later in this chapter, you can work around that limitation by nesting a list within a list.)

In this procedure, you'll group data in the list by Category.

Add a grouping level

1. In the Properties window, with list1 selected, click the button with three dots (the Ellipsis button) in the *Grouping* property.
2. Replace the default name of the group with **list1_Category**.
3. Click `=Fields!Category.Value` in the Expression drop-down list.

   As mentioned earlier, a group in a list works the same way as a group in a table. The difference is that a table can have many groups, whereas a list can have only one group.
4. Click the Sorting tab, click `=Fields!Category.Value` in the Expression drop-down list, and then click OK.

   The rows in this list will sort alphabetically by Category. At this point, however, a report preview will not render the list, since fields have not yet been added to the list.

Using Fields in a List

Fields in a free-standing textbox can be used anywhere in a list. Just drag the field from the Datasets window and position the textbox in the desired position. When you add a numeric field to a list that has grouping applied, the *Sum* function is automatically included in the field expression.

In this procedure, you'll add Category to the list to serve as a label.

Add a field to the list

1. In the Datasets window, click *Category*, drag it to the top-left corner of the list, and then drag the right side of the new textbox until it is approximately 2 inches wide.

The list in the design grid looks like this:

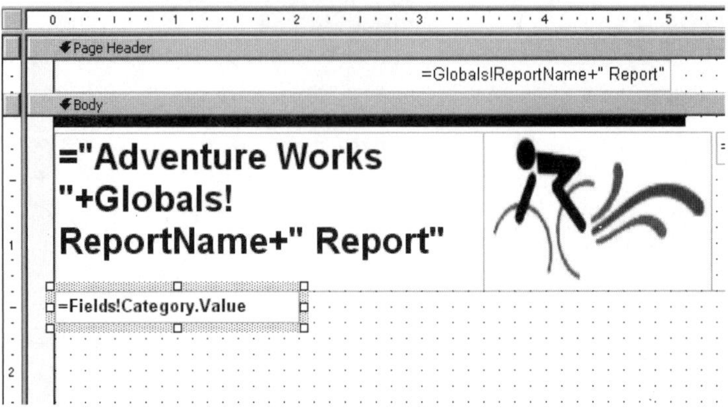

2. Click Bold on the Report Formatting toolbar.

   A basic list data region is created that includes a label to display the current Category when the list repeats the group. Now, you're ready to move the chart and matrix into the list.

Nesting Data Regions

To overcome the limitation that a list can have only one grouping level, you can nest a second list inside the first list. Nested lists increase your flexibility by simulating the effect of grouping. You can also nest other data regions inside a list, thereby enabling a variety of report structures that are limited only by your imagination. When nesting data regions in a list, all data regions must use the same dataset.

In this procedure, you'll nest a chart and a matrix inside the list.

Move a chart and a matrix into the list

1. Click the chart, and then drag the chart into the list just below the Category textbox so the list data region looks like this:

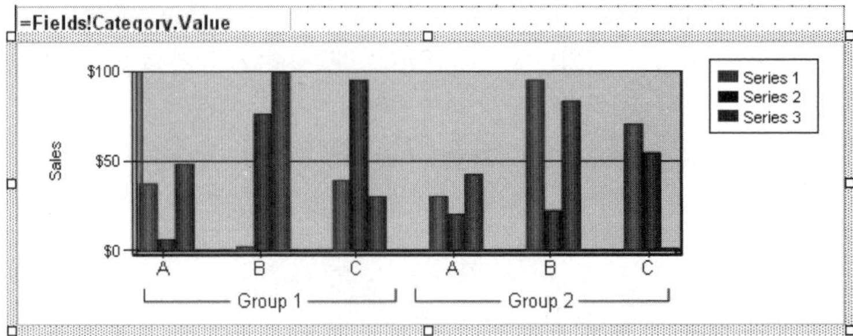

2. Preview the report.

   The top of the report should have four separate charts, one for each category. The list is repeating the textbox and the chart for each member of the Category group. The matrix appears below the list just one time, because it is not yet part of the list.

> **Note** If the chart is not repeating, the chart might not be properly positioned within the list. Try moving the chart so its boundaries are clearly within the boundaries of the list.

3. Click the Layout tab, select the matrix, and then drag the matrix into the list just below the chart.

   At this point, the list should completely surround the chart and matrix.

4. Save and preview the report.

   A portion of the first Category of the list is shown here:

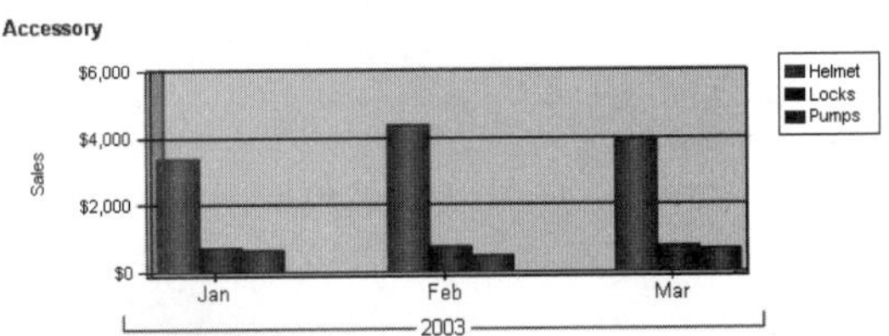

Product		Jan		Feb	
		Sales Amount	Order Quantity	Sales Amount	Order Quantity
Accessory	Helmet	$3,371	167	$4,360	216
	Locks	$720	48	$735	49
	Pumps	$636	53	$468	39
	Total	**$4,727**	**268**	**$5,563**	**304**
Total		$4,727	268	$5,563	304

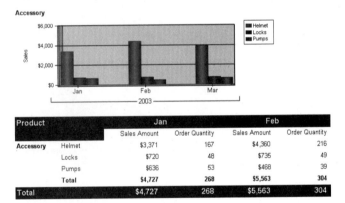

   Now, the scope of each matrix is limited to the Category group, which makes the subtotal for SubCategory redundant. Notice that the bottom two rows of the matrix are identical except for the difference in styles. You can edit the matrix to remove one of the subtotals to fix this duplication.

5. Click the Layout tab, right-click the SubCategory Total cell, and then click Subtotal.

   The Subtotal cell disappears from the matrix.

6. Drag the lower edge of the list up to place it just below the lower edge of the matrix to shrink the space between the repeating regions.

7. Save and preview the report to confirm there is now only one subtotal row.

8. Close the project.

Chapter 6 Quick Reference

To	Do this
Add a data region	Open the Toolbox window, click the desired data region, point to the target destination in the report body, and then click to place the data region.
Add a row group or column group to a matrix	Select a field in the Datasets window and drag to the applicable area, marked Rows or Columns, in the matrix.
Add a static row or column to a matrix	Right-click a textbox in the matrix, and click one of the following: Add Row or Add Column.
Add subtotals to a matrix	Right-click the group cell in a row or column, and then click Subtotal. Format the subtotal value by clicking the green triangle in the new Total cell for the group.
Open the Chart Properties dialog box	Right-click the chart, and then click Properties.
Add values to a chart	In the Datasets window, click the field to be used as a value and drag it to the area of the chart labeled Drop Data Fields Here. *or* Open the Chart Properties dialog box, click the Data tab, and then click the Add button next to the Values box. Click an expression in the Value list box.
Add a category group to a chart	In the Datasets window, click the field to be used as a value and drag it to the area of the chart labeled Drop Category Fields Here. *or* Open the Chart Properties dialog box, click the Data tab, and then click the Add button next to the Category Groups box. Click an expression in the Expression list box.
Add a series group to a chart	In the Datasets window, click the field to be used as a value and drag it to the area of the chart labeled Drop Series Fields Here. *or* Open the Chart Properties dialog box, click the Data tab, and then click the Add button next to the Series Groups box. Click an expression in the Expression list box.
Add a grouping level to a list	Click the list name in the report items list box of the Properties window. Click the Ellipsis button of the *Grouping* property. Click an expression in the Expression list box.
Nest a data region in a list	Open the Toolbox window, click the data region, point to the target destination in an existing list, and then click it. Resize and position as necessary. *or* Drag an existing data region into a list while making sure that the data region is completely surrounded by the list.

Chapter 7
Building Advanced Reports

After completing this chapter, you will be able to:

- Create a report parameter to use as a variable for calculating values in a report.
- Pass a report parameter to a query to filter data at the source.
- Use a report parameter to filter a dataset or a data region in the report.
- Use interactive features to navigate within a report or to jump to information located elsewhere.
- Work with hierarchical data.

In the previous chapter, you created a variety of reports to explore the different ways that data can be organized into data regions. In this chapter, you'll turn your attention to employing advanced techniques to manipulate data in the report. You'll work with report parameters to allow a user to change a report on demand. You'll also add other interactive features to reports to help users navigate within and across reports. Finally, you'll learn how to work with data that is stored using hierarchical data structures. By successfully completing this and the previous three chapters, your report authoring skills will be complete.

Using Parameters to Change Report Data

Using report parameters makes reports more flexible in a number of ways. You can use a report parameter alone to calculate values in the report. Such values may either be displayed as content in the report or used to change properties that affect the behavior and appearance of a report. For example, instead of using a fixed value to control conditional formatting in a report, as you did in Chapter 5, "Working with Expressions," you can add a report parameter that prompts the user to enter a value. The report server then renders the report using the new value to format the report.

You can also create a single report that provides alternate views of data by using a report parameter in combination with a query parameter. This enables a query to be modified on demand, thus changing the query results. A *query parameter* is a placeholder in the WHERE clause of a SQL query that is linked to a report parameter. Reporting Services replaces the placeholder in a query with a report parameter's value and then executes the query. Each time the value of the report parameter changes, the query executes.

Another way to use a report parameter is to filter data in the report after the query executes. This technique is useful when a user wants to quickly switch between different sets of data in the same report. With a filter in the report, a user does not have to wait for the query to execute after changing the value of a report parameter.

Adding a Report Parameter

Every report parameter you add to a report must have a unique name and a data type. The report parameter name cannot contain a space or a special character, because its name will become part of an expression used to access the parameter value. If you use a numeric or time data type, be aware that you'll have to use the *Format* function to control the formatting of the value if you want to display the report parameter's value in a textbox.

A report parameter normally has a prompt, which is a label for the input box or list box that the user sees when the report is displayed. If you don't enter text for a prompt, the user can neither see nor change the report parameter. This is actually a good way to hide a parameter if you're providing the value in some other way, such as administratively, as you'll learn in Chapter 9, "Managing Content," or programmatically, as you'll learn in Chapter 18, "Building Custom Reporting Tools."

When you create a report parameter, you have the option to specify the values that Reporting Services will consider valid. Not only can you prevent a user from using a blank or null value, but you can also provide a list of specific values from which the user must choose. You can create this list manually or by using a query from any dataset in the report to build the list. You can even define a default value so the user can view the report before changing the report parameter value. As with the list of available values, the default value may be entered manually or it may be based on a query.

In this procedure, you'll add a report parameter to prompt the user for a margin percentage value that defaults to 0.15.

Add a report parameter with a default value

1. Start SQL Server Business Intelligence Development Studio and open the solution My Adventure Works that you saved in the C:\Documents and Settings\<username>\My Documents\Microsoft Press\rs2005sbs\Workspace\My Adventure Works folder.

> **Note** If you skipped Chapter 6, "Organizing Data in Reports," open the solution My Adventure Works in the C:\Documents and Settings\<username>\My Documents \Microsoft Press\rs2005sbs\Answers\chap06\My Adventure Works folder.

2. In Solution Explorer, right-click the Product Sales And Profitability.rdl report, click Copy, click the Reports folder, and then press Ctrl+V to paste a copy of the report into the folder.
3. Right-click the new report, click Rename, and then type a new name for the report: **Product Sales and Profitability Parameters.rdl**.

4. Double-click the Product Sales And Profitability Parameters.rdl report in Solution Explorer to display the report in the Document window.
5. Click the Preview tab to view the report.

   In Chapter 5, you added conditional formatting to this report to display margin percentage exceptions with red text when the value was below 15 percent. Now, you'll use a report parameter to allow the user to change the exception definition at execution.
6. Click the Layout tab, and then click Report Parameters on the Report menu to open the Report Parameters dialog box.

   Currently, no report parameters are defined in this report.
7. Click Add to add a parameter and enable the Properties area:

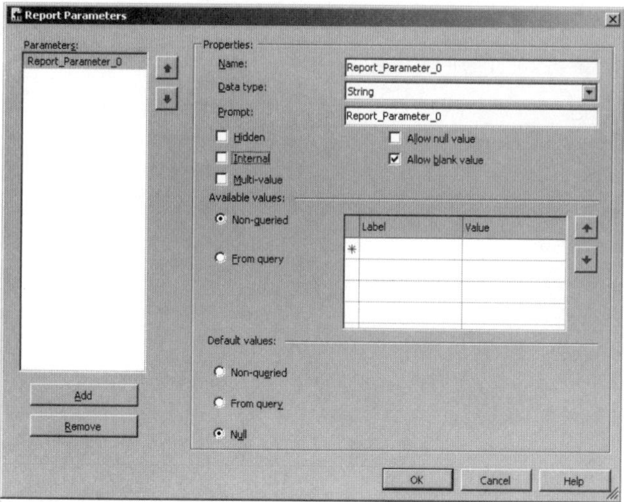

   By default, the name of the parameter is also used as a prompt, which, as you'll see later, is visible to the user when the report is rendered online. Notice the options to control whether the parameter can accept a null or a blank value, or both.
8. Replace the default parameter name with **MarginPercent**.

   Remember that a parameter name cannot include a space or special character.
9. Click Float in the Data Type drop-down list.

   Review the other data type options that are available in the Data Type drop-down list. The default data type is *String*, but you'll need to select a different data type if the expression in which you're using the parameter value requires a different data type. In this case, the value will be used to compare to a percentage value calculated in the report and must, therefore, be typed as **Float**.
10. Replace the default prompt with **Margin %**.

Because the prompt is just a string that is displayed to a user in the HTML viewer, the prompt can contain spaces and special characters.

11. Keep the Available Values option set to Non-Queried.

    If you don't create a list of available values, the user must type in a report parameter value. You'll learn how to provide available values later in this chapter.

12. Click the Non-Queried option in the Default Values pane.

    A default value is required to enable report rendering before the user makes a selection. If you opt to omit a default value, by selecting None, the report will not be rendered until the user enters a value.

13. Enter a default value: **.15**.

    The dialog box looks like this:

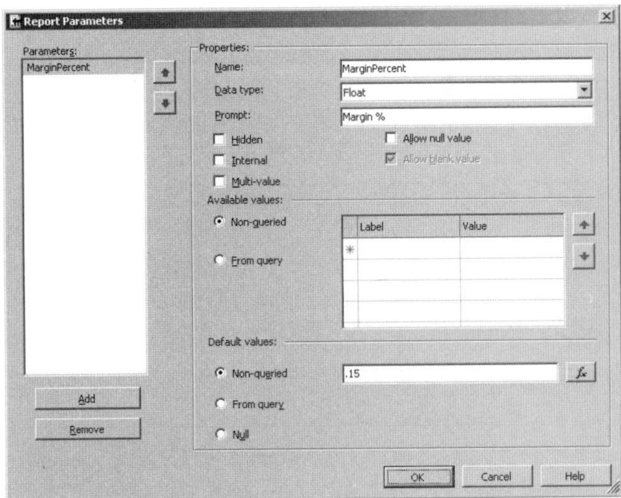

    Notice the Expression button to the right of the Default Value input box. You can click this button to build an expression that calculates the default value rather than use a fixed value.

14. Click OK.

    If you preview the report at this time, you see the report parameter, but because the report definition hasn't been changed yet to use its value, nothing happens if you try to change the value.

Using the *Parameters* Collection

A report parameter is an object in the *Parameters* collection that you can access using either its *Value* or *Label* property. The *Value* property retrieves the current value of the parameter, whereas the *Label* property retrieves the user-friendly name for the parameter that is defined in the list of available values. Using Microsoft Visual Basic collection syntax, you can refer to a report parameter in any expression.

In this procedure, you'll modify the expressions that conditionally format the margin percentage so they use the report parameter value instead of a fixed value.

Change conditional formatting with a report parameter

1. Click the Layout tab, and then Click the Margin % cell, which is the cell in the sixth column of the detail row.
2. In the Properties window, click Expression in the *Color* property for the Margin % cell.
3. Position the cursor after the greater than symbol (<), and then delete 0.15 from the expression.
4. Click the *Parameters* collection to view its members.

   Each time you add a report parameter to the report, a new member is added to the *Parameters* collection for you to use in an expression.
5. Click *MarginPercent*, and then click Paste.

   The Edit Expression dialog box looks like this:

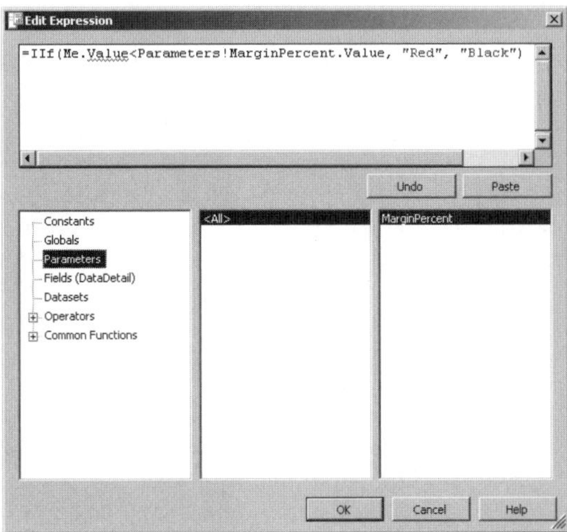

   The *MarginPercent* parameter value, which can be changed at run time by the user, replaces the fixed value of 0.15. Now, the conditional formatting will depend on the value of the parameter supplied by the user to determine whether the margin percentage value in the report is displayed in red or black.
6. Copy the expression to the Clipboard so you can easily update the footer rows, and then click OK.

7. Click the Margin % cell in the table1_SubCategory footer, and then, while pressing the Ctrl key, click the same cell in the table1_Category footer and in the table footer to select all three cells. Paste the expression from the Clipboard into the *Color* property.

8. Select only the Margin % cell in the table footer, click Expression in the *Color* property drop-down list, and then edit the expression to replace Black with **White**, as shown here:

```
=IIf(Me.Value<Parameters!MarginPercent.Value, "Red", "White")
```

   In the table footer, the background is black. If the text color is also black, the margin percentage will not be visible to users when its value is greater than the value supplied for the report parameter. Instead, use white to be consistent with the text color of other cells in this row.

9. Click OK to close the Edit Expression dialog box.

10. Save your report, and then check the results by clicking the Preview tab.

   The report parameter is displayed above the HTML Viewer toolbar:

   You didn't provide a list of available values for this parameter, so a parameter input box is displayed above the report, preceded by its prompt string (Margin %). Because the report parameter has a default value, the report is rendered on demand and the default value is displayed in the parameter's input box.

11. Enter **0.35** for Margin %, and then click View Report.

   Clicking View Report renders the report using the new report parameter value, and now you can see that the Margin % for Full-Finger Gloves, L, and the Clothing category footer are rendered with red text.

> **Tip** Allowing a null value for the report parameter is fine if the expression will evaluate correctly. If you want to allow the user to render this report without any conditional formatting, you can select the report parameter option Allow Null Value. Then, when the report renders, a NULL check box appears next to the *Margin %* parameter. If the user were to select the NULL check box, the expression would return false for all rows, since none of the rows have a margin percentage that is less than null. The false result for the expression would cause all rows to display the margin percentage in black, except the table footer, which would display in white, which effectively removes conditional formatting from the report.

Adding a Query Parameter

You can make a query more flexible by adding a query parameter to the WHERE clause as a placeholder for a value that will be used to filter the data at the source. Always precede the parameter name with the @ symbol. If you have several datasets in the report, you can use the same query parameter in each dataset.

> **Important** Some data sources do not support query parameters. For these data sources, you'll need to use a report filter instead (which you'll learn how to use later in this chapter).

In this procedure, you'll replace the fixed values in the WHERE clause of the dataset query with query parameters.

Add query parameters to the dataset

1. Click the Data tab to view the current query, as shown here:

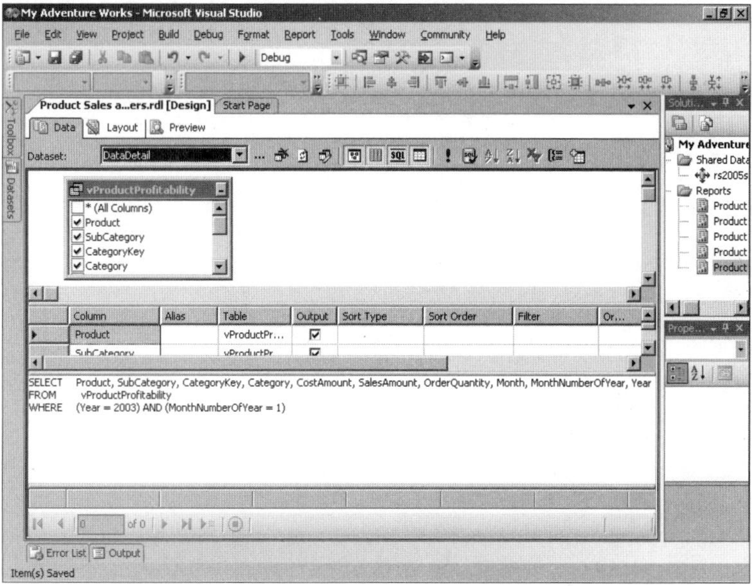

As currently written, this query will create data for a single month only, so a user of the report cannot change the month and year to view results for a different time period.

2. Replace the WHERE clause of the query with the following:

```
WHERE Year = @Year AND MonthNumberOfYear = @Month
```

> **Important** If you're using an Oracle data source with a named query parameter, as in this example, you must select the Oracle data provider instead of the generic Open Database Connectivity (ODBC) data provider in the Data Link Properties of your data source.

3. Click the Edit Selected Dataset button, which is the ellipsis button (...) next to the Dataset drop-down list, to view the Dataset dialog box:

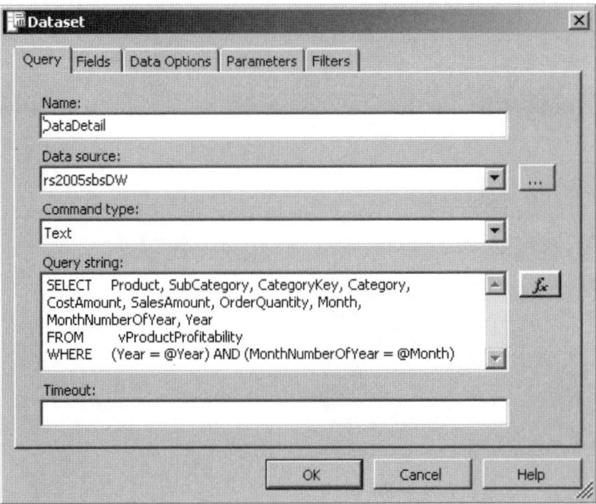

Notice that you can change the dataset name, the data source, and the query, as well as other properties related to the dataset using this dialog box.

4. Click the Parameters tab to view the parameter mappings:

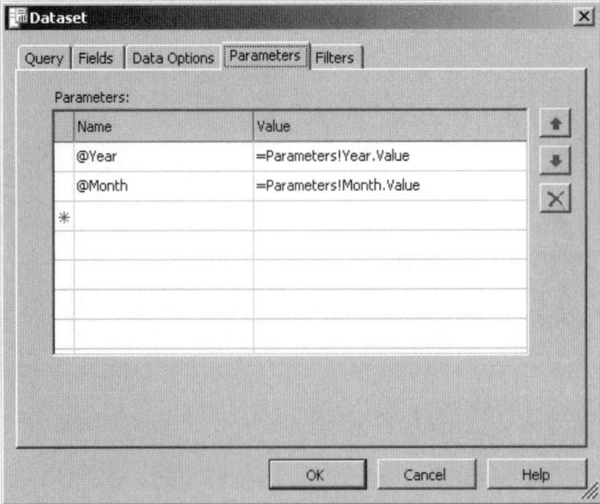

The Report Designer automatically creates parameter expressions to which the query parameters, *@Year* and *@Month*, are mapped.

5. Click Cancel to close the Dataset dialog box.

Supplying Values for a Query Parameter

Before the query executes, Reporting Services replaces the query parameter with the current value of the corresponding report parameter. Even though you could let the user type in a value for a report parameter, a better approach is to create a list of available values for the report parameter to ensure that the user provides a valid value. You can maintain a fixed list of available values for the report parameter, which you'll learn how to do in this procedure, or you can use a query to generate a list of available values, which you'll learn how to do later in this chapter.

A list of available values, regardless of how it is built, always contains labels and values. The label is added to the list of items that the user sees in the report parameter's drop-down list. The value is the corresponding result passed to the report parameter for use in an expression or as a query parameter.

In this procedure, you'll manually enter a list of available values for the *Year* and *Month* report parameters.

Define a list of available values for a report parameter

1. Click the Layout tab, and then click Report Parameters on the Report menu.

   Notice the two new report parameters, *Year* and *Month*.

2. Click *Year* in the Parameters list.

   By default, the name of the parameter is also used as the prompt, the options to allow a null or blank value are cleared, the Available Values option is set to nonqueried, and the Default Values option is set to Null.

3. In the Available Values table, type the following values:

Label	Value
2001	2001
2002	2002
2003	2003
2004	2004

   In this table, the labels and the values are the same because the value in the database is a label that will be understood by the user when choosing a value from the report parameter's drop-down list.

Note Instead of typing in a label or a value for the list, you can use an expression to generate the label or value at run time. Just click the drop-down list in the applicable field to access the Edit Expression dialog box. Alternatively, you can use a query to supply the values for the parameter, which you'll learn how to do later in this chapter.

4. Click the Non-Queried option in the Default Values pane.
5. Enter a default value: **2003**.

   The dialog box looks like this:

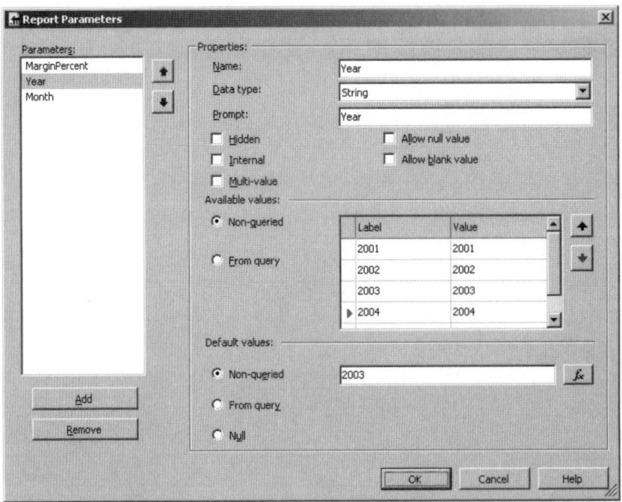

Tip Often, users want to view the most current data in a report. Instead of hard-coding the year, use an expression to calculate the year: `=Year(Now)`. You must make sure that the result is in the parameter's table of Available Values and that the dataset will contain data for the current year; otherwise, the report will be empty.

6. In the Parameters list, click the *Month* parameter.
7. In the Available Values table, type in the following values:

Label	Value
Jan	1
Feb	2
Mar	3

> **Note** In an actual report, you'd supply all months and month values. This example is abbreviated to reduce the amount of typing you need to do for this procedure.

In this example, the labels and values differ because *Month* is stored as a numeric value in the database and needs to be passed to the query as such. Although using a number to represent the month probably wouldn't confuse users, in other situations, a numerical value for the label might be meaningless to the user. For such cases, specify a user-friendly label.

8. Click the Non-Queried option in the Default Values pane.
9. Enter a default value: **1**.

> **Tip** As with the *Year* parameter, you can use an expression to use the current month as the default value for the *Month* parameter. In this case, use the following expression: `=Month(Now)`.

10. Click OK.
11. Save the report, and then preview the results.
12. Click Mar in the Month drop-down list, and then click View Report.
13. Click 75% in the Zoom drop-down list to shrink the report so you can see the full width.

    The Document window looks like this:

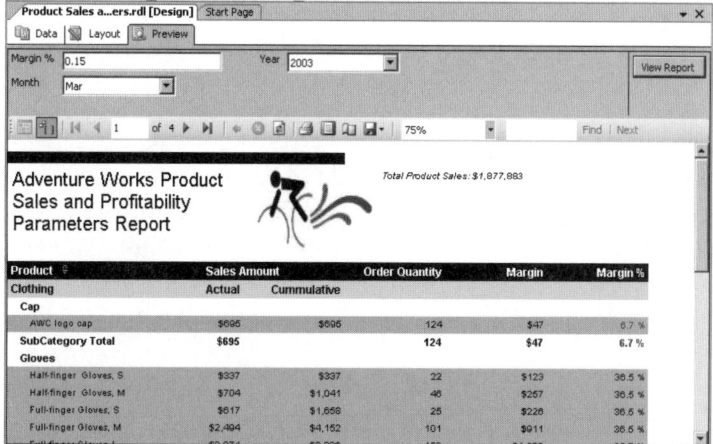

Now you have three report parameters in your report. The first, *Margin %*, is used in an expression in the report to change the report formatting. The other two, *Month* and *Year*, are used to define the query that executes to retrieve data for the report. Since default values were supplied for all the report parameters, the report was executed and rendered using those values. Notice that the report parameters are placed left to right, wrapping to the next row when space is limited, in the same order in which they appear in the Report Parameters dialog box.

Using Input Parameters with a Stored Procedure

Reporting Services supports the use of stored procedures to create a dataset as long as the stored procedure returns a single result set. Creating a dataset that uses a stored procedure is similar to creating a query-based dataset. In the Dataset dialog box, you must name the dataset, set the command type to StoredProcedure, and set the query string to the name of the stored procedure.

You can even use the value of report parameters as input parameters for the stored procedure. The Parameters tab of the Dataset dialog box allows you to map report parameters to the input parameters of the stored procedure. Type the name of the input parameter in the *Name* field, and then select the corresponding report parameter from the Value drop-down list on the same row.

Creating a Report Parameter for a Filter

A filter can be added to a dataset, a data region, or a grouping level. In all cases, the process is very similar. A filter is most commonly based on a report parameter's value, which might be selected from a list that is created from another dataset in the report. It can also be based on any valid expression. Before defining a filter using a report parameter, you must first add the report parameter to the report. Then, you add a filter definition to the applicable object, such as the report's main dataset, using the object's Properties dialog box. It's good practice to display the report parameter's label in the report in case the user decides to save or print the report for future reference.

A filter is similar to a query parameter in that both result in fewer detail rows for the report. However, a query parameter filters data at the data source when the query is executed and returns a filtered row set to the dataset. A filter, by contrast, prevents some rows in the dataset from being displayed in a report, but it does not eliminate them from the dataset. Using a filter can improve report performance when the user changes report parameter values, because data is available for rendering without necessitating another query to the database.

Note A query parameter can also improve report performance by returning fewer rows in the dataset. Whether to use a query parameter or a filter parameter depends on the volume of rows that are being returned from the data source versus the volume of rows that are being filtered out of the dataset for rendering.

As with query parameters, you should make sure that the report parameter value used in a filter is valid. The best way to do this is to use a query to build a list of available values for the report parameter. This query should contain columns only for labels and values. By using a query, you can keep the list of available values up-to-date with actual values contained in the source database.

In this procedure, you'll add a dataset to the report to retrieve valid values for a report parameter.

Add a dataset for report parameter values

1. Click the Data tab, and then click <New Dataset...> in the Dataset drop-down list.
2. Type **Category** as the dataset name, and then click OK.
3. If necessary, click Generic Query Designer on the Dataset toolbar to toggle from the Generic Query Designer to the Query Builder.
4. Right-click in the Diagram pane (the top pane), and then click Add Table.
5. Select DimProductCategory in the list of tables, click Add, and then click Close.

   The DimProductCategory table is displayed in the Diagram pane. You can build a SQL query by using the table diagram to select columns from the table.
6. Select the ProductCategoryKey and ProductCategoryName check boxes in the DimProductCategory table diagram.

   The DimProductCategory table contains only five records that represent the distinct names of all product categories that Adventure Works sells, whereas the vProductProfitability view contains many records for sales transactions that also include category names. You get the same results whether you query the table or the view, but querying DimProductCategory to get values for a report parameter is potentially much faster because fewer records must be scanned.
7. Enter **AS CategoryKey** after ProductCategoryKey in the SQL pane, and then enter **AS Category** after ProductCategoryName so the SQL statement looks like this:

   ```
   SELECT ProductCategoryKey AS CategoryKey, ProductCategoryName AS Category FROM
   DimProductCategory
   ```

   The AS expression creates an alias to replace the actual column name, often to make shorter column names in the result set or to make the original column names more user-friendly in the result set. For example, CategoryName is the alias for ProductCategoryName. You don't have to use an alias for ProductCategoryName, but sometimes, doing so can make expressions in the report easier to read.
8. Click Verify SQL to check the query syntax, and then click OK.

   Now that you've successfully added another dataset to the report, you'll need to update any report item using an aggregate in the report body to associate it with the correct dataset.

9. Click the Layout tab, right-click the textbox in the upper right corner of the report that contains the *Sum* aggregate function, and then click Expression.
10. Add **"DataDetail"** as a *Scope* argument to the expression so that it looks like this:

```
="Total Product Sales: " + Format(Sum(Fields!SalesAmount.Value, "DataDetail"), "c0")
```

> **Tip** The *Scope* argument is now required for aggregate expressions in independent report items, such as a textbox, because your report now contains two datasets. Without the *Scope* argument in aggregate expressions, the report will fail to process. For this reason, it's a good habit to always use a *Scope* argument in a report that contains only one dataset so you can avoid having to fix the expression later if you need to add another dataset.

11. Click OK to close the expression editor.

In this procedure, you'll add a new report parameter that will use the Category dataset to build a list of available values.

Add a report parameter with a query for available values

1. Click the Layout tab, and then click Report Parameters on the Report menu.
2. Click Add.
3. Enter a name: **Category**.
4. Click Integer in the Data Type drop-down list.

   Because you'll be using the value returned from the CategoryKey column as the report parameter, you must change the data type of the report parameter to match the data type of the database value.
5. Enter a prompt: **Category**.
6. Select the From Query option for Available Values.
7. Select Category in the Dataset drop-down list.

   All datasets in the report are available for selection. The two field names created from the query will be assigned to the *Value* and *Label* fields for Available Values. They serve the same purpose as the *Value* and *Label* fields for which you added values earlier in this chapter. The query you use to supply values for a report parameter should include only two columns, one for the value passed to the report, and one for the value displayed to the user.

> **Tip** You can build cascading parameters by using the value of one report parameter as a query parameter in a query used to populate the list of values for another report parameter. This is useful for reducing the size of a list of available values, thereby making it easier for a user to find a desired value.

8. Select CategoryKey in the Value Field drop-down list.
9. Select Category in the Label Field drop-down list.
10. Select the Non-Queried option for Default Values.
11. Enter **4** as a default value so the Report Parameters dialog box now looks like this:

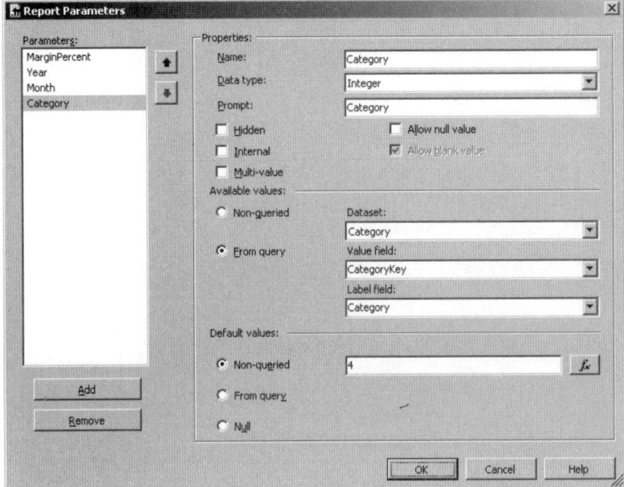

The value 4 corresponds to the Component category. The report parameter list box will display Component by default when the report is rendered. If you decide instead to use a query to set a default value, you must select the dataset and a value field.

Notice that the option to Allow Blank Value is not available. This option is not permitted when the data type is set to Integer. A blank value is possible only when using the string data type.

12. Click OK.

If you preview the report at this point, nothing is changed (other than the addition of the parameter to the Report toolbar) because you have not yet used the report parameter value in an expression.

Adding a Filter

You can apply a dataset filter by editing the properties of a dataset. Reporting Services will filter all data regions that use the filtered dataset in the report. The effect in a rendered report looks the same as it does when using a query parameter in the WHERE clause of a query, but it is different because the full dataset is retrieved from the data source.

You can also filter a single data region in a report and keep the full dataset for other data regions. Say, for example, you have a matrix that shows annual sales for multiple years, but you want to chart sales only for the most recent year. Instead of placing the filter on the dataset, right-click the data region that you want to filter so you can access the data region's

Properties dialog box. The Filters tab in this dialog box is similar to the dataset's Filters tab, but affects only the selected region. Similarly, a grouping level of a data region can be filtered by editing its properties.

In this procedure, you'll apply a filter to the DataDetail dataset based on the value of the *Category* report parameter.

Add a filter to a dataset

1. Click the Data tab.
2. Select DataDetail in the Dataset drop-down list.
3. Click the Edit Selected Dataset button.
4. Click the Filters tab.
5. Select `=Fields!CategoryKey.Value` in the Expression drop-down list.

   You must select this expression because it corresponds to the value returned by the report parameter, *CategoryKey*, and not the label, Category.
6. Select Expression in the Value drop-down list.
7. Click Parameters, click Category, and then click Paste.
8. Click OK.

   The Dataset dialog box should look like this:

   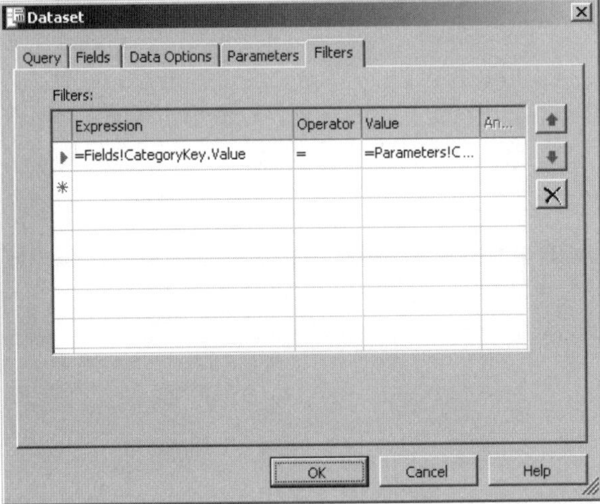

9. Click OK.
10. Save the report, and then preview the results.
11. Select Bike in the Category drop-down list, and then click View Report.

    The report now only shows information for products in the Bike category. Because you used a filter, the dataset query was not executed.

Adding a Parameter Value to a Report

To ensure that users of a report clearly understand that a report has been filtered, include a textbox that displays the current value of the filter. To do so, display the *Label* property of the report parameter that is used as the filter in a textbox.

In this procedure, you'll add a textbox to the top of the report to identify the current filter when the report is rendered.

Display a parameter value in a text box

1. Click the Layout tab, click the Total Product Sales textbox while pressing Ctrl, and then drag below the Total Product Sales textbox to make a copy of it.
2. Right-click the new textbox, and then click Expression.
3. Delete the existing expression, click Parameters, click Category, and then click Paste.
4. Change the expression so it looks like this:

   ```
   ="Filtered by: "+Parameters!Category.Label
   ```

   Even though the value passed to the report parameter is an integer, you have access to the label of the report parameter for display in a textbox.
5. Click OK.
6. Save, and then preview the report.

   The top of your report should now look like this:

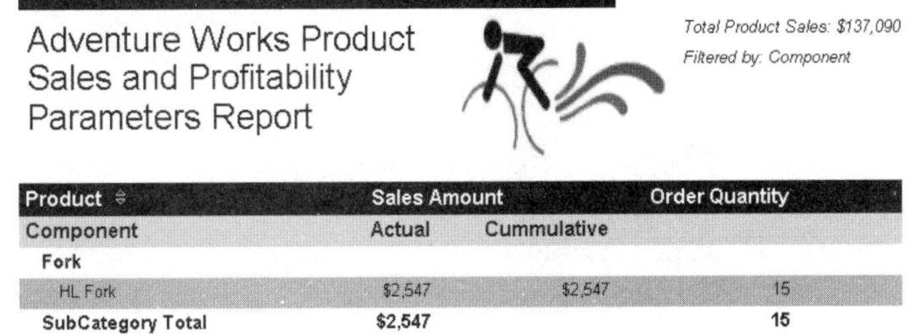

Notice that the *Category* default value, Component, is now displayed at the top of the report.

Linking Information with Interactive Features

Report parameters are a useful interactive feature of Reporting Services that allows a user to manipulate what is shown within a report. Other features are also available–actions, visibility properties, and subreports–to help users interactively navigate reports. Since these features are dependent on interaction with a user, the reports must be rendered on a device that not only supports HTML, but also maintains a connection to the Report Server during the reporting session.

As with many of the features of Reporting Services, the full range of potential applications is impossible to enumerate. One way to think about using these features is to consider how a user generally begins exploring information. A user often starts by examining summary information to determine which detailed data needs to be examined. As with the index at the back of this book, summary information can be used as a pointer to more specific information. Similarly, you can implement actions to allow a user to jump from summary data to detail data, regardless of whether all of the data is included in the same dataset or report. Alternatively, when the summary and detail data can be retrieved from the same dataset, you can build a data region that includes all the data, and then use visibility properties to hide the details until the user chooses to view them. However, there are times when the details come from a different dataset that precludes the use of a single data region, but you can easily solve this problem by nesting a subreport inside a data region.

Choosing the Right Action

An *action* is used to link a report item to information located elsewhere. The type of action you create determines where that information is located and what it looks like. When a user clicks a bookmark action, the report switches to another area of the report, which might be another data region or another page in the same report. Implementing a bookmark action is a two-step process. You have to add the bookmark to a report item (which is not limited to a textbox or an image) that is the destination of the bookmark action, and then add the bookmark action to the report item that serves as the origination point.

A hyperlink, or URL, action launches a Web page when a user clicks a report item. You can define a static URL, or you can use an expression to generate a URL dynamically at run time. You might even consider storing URLs in a relational table that you can query and reference using a field expression. This would allow you to select an appropriate target destination based on current conditions in the source report, or to maintain destinations in a database table to avoid editing the report if a destination changes later.

An action that jumps to another report can simply open another report, or it can pass a value to a report parameter in the target report to control what happens when the report executes or is rendered. For this type of action, you identify the target report, and then, if you're taking advantage of a report parameter, you associate a value in the source report to a specific report parameter in the target report.

Adding Actions

You can add an action either via the Navigation tab of a report item's Properties dialog box or by accessing the *Action* property of the report item in the Properties window. Although you have a lot of freedom to choose the direction an action will take a user, you can add an action only to a textbox or an image in a report.

In this procedure, you'll add an action to the Product textbox in the Orders Detail report to jump to the Products Detail report and display information for the selected product.

Add an action to jump to a report

1. In Solution Explorer, right-click the Reports folder in the project My Adventure Works, point to Add, and then click Existing Item to add the Orders Details.rdl saved in the C:\Documents and Settings\<username>\My Documents\Microsoft Press\rs2005sbs \chap07 folder.
2. Right-click the Shared Data Sources folder, point to Add, and then click Existing Item to add the rs2005sbs.rds data source saved in the C:\Documents and Settings \<username>\My Documents\Microsoft Press\rs2005sbs\chap07 folder.
3. In Solution Explorer, double-click Order Details.rdl to open the report in the Document window, and then click the Preview tab to confirm that the top of the report looks like this:

Wingtip Toys Order Details

Jan 1 2003 through Dec 31 2003

Order	Order Date	Ship Date	Qty	Price	Extended Price
SO8507	9/1/2003	9/8/2003			
LL Mtn Frame - Silver, 44			1	$195.40	$195.40
			1		$195.40
SO8501	12/1/2003	12/8/2003			
Mountain-400-W Silver, 38			2	$554.03	$1,108.07
			2		$1,108.07
All Wingtip Toys Orders			3		$1,303.46

This report uses a table data region to display order detail information used by Customer Service representatives at Adventure Works to verify order status, troubleshoot order complaints, and answer questions from resellers.

4. In the Solution Explorer, right-click the Reports folder in the project My Adventure Works, point to Add, and then click Existing Item to add the Product Detail.rdl saved in the C:\Documents and Settings\<username>\My Documents\Microsoft Press \rs2005sbs\chap07 folder.

5. In Solution Explorer, double-click Product Detail.rdl to open it, and then click the Preview tab, scrolling down to view the product information, which should look like this:

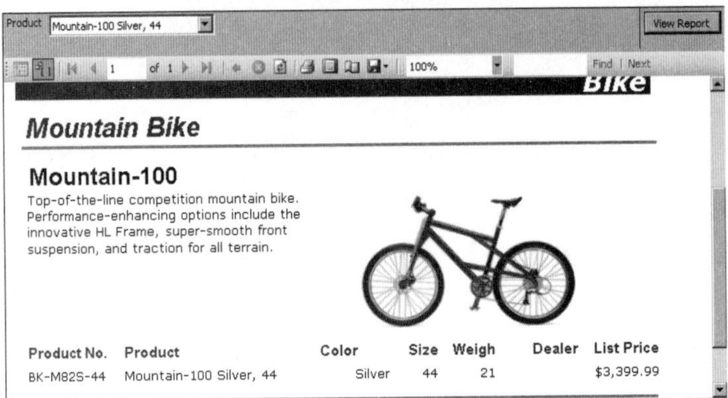

This report is used in conjunction with the Order Details report to aid in responding to resellers' questions. Notice the report parameter to select a product.

6. Close the Product Detail report by clicking Close in the upper-right corner of the Document window.

7. Click the Layout tab of the Order Details report, and then click the Product cell in the first column of the detail row.

8. In the Properties window, click the ellipsis button for the *Action* property, which is near the bottom of the properties list in the Misc section, to display the Action dialog box:

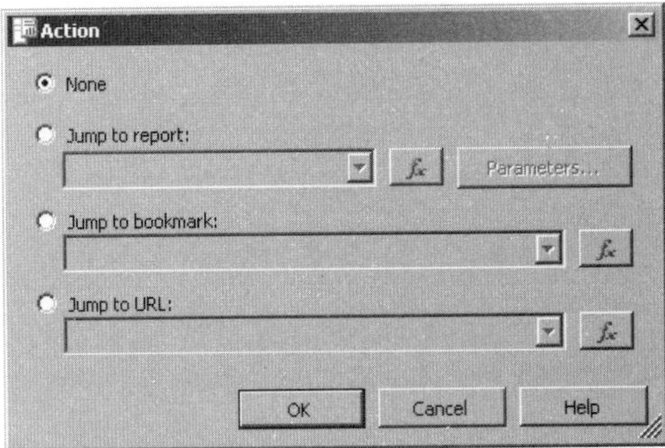

9. In the Action dialog box, click Jump To Report.

10. Select Product Detail in the Jump To Report drop-down list.

    Notice that the only reports available in the list are those located in the same project. Also, notice the Expression button, which you can use to build an expression to assign a report name.

> **Note** You aren't required to use a report from the same project. The list box is just a convenience feature. You can type in the name of a report that is (or will be) on the Report Server. If the target report will not be in the same folder as the source report, you'll need to precede the report name with the absolute or relative folder path on the server.

If you select Jump To Bookmark, you can enter the bookmark identifier, or you can click the Expression button to build your own expression that evaluates to a bookmark identifier. This feature won't work until the bookmark identifier is added to a report item.

11. Click Parameters.

    The Parameters dialog box is displayed. This dialog box allows you to provide a value to pass to the report parameter so the target report can be executed and rendered. The value you supply here overrides the default value, if any, assigned to the report parameter.

12. Select Product in the Parameter Name drop-down list.

    The Parameter Name drop-down list displays all report parameters in the target report. In this case, there is only one report parameter, *Product*.

13. Select `=Fields!Product.Value` in the Parameter Value drop-down list so the Parameters dialog box now looks like this:

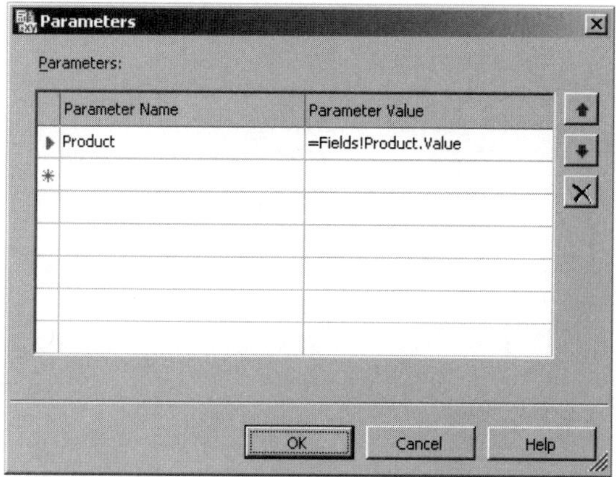

Notice that you can select <Expression...> in the Parameter Value drop-down list to build an expression to return a value to be passed to the target report's report parameter.

14. Click OK twice to return to the Properties window, where the *Action* property contains a value, as shown here:

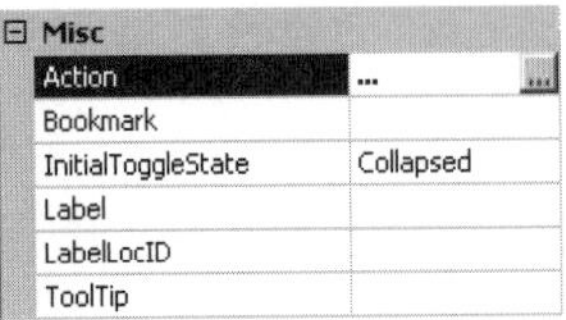

The three dots indicate that an action has been defined for the current report item. You'll have to click the ellipsis button to access the Action dialog box to see what kind of action has been defined.

15. With the Product cell selected in the detail row, click Underline on the Report Formatting toolbar.

Tip If the user points to a report item that has an action defined, the cursor changes to a pointing hand to indicate that clicking the item will launch an action. To provide a visual cue to users that an action exists, it's a good idea to underline the text (if the report item is a textbox) to simulate a hyperlink, which most users recognize as a navigation tool.

16. Save the report, and then preview it to test out the action.
17. Click the LL Mtn Frame – Silver, 44 product in the report to view the Product Detail report, which looks like this:

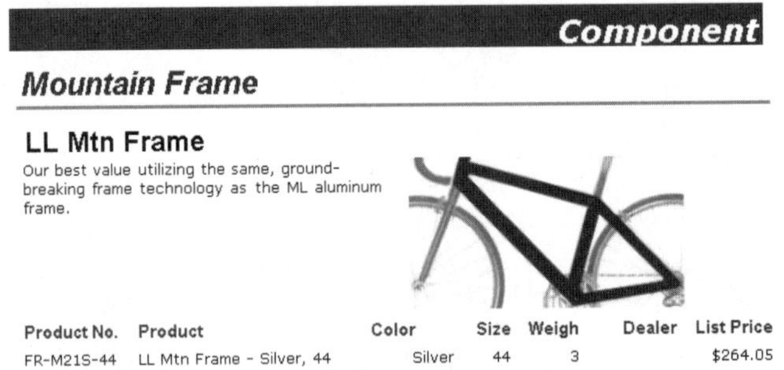

If the report does not refresh, click the action again.

18. On the Preview toolbar, click Back to return to the Order Details preview.

Using the *Hidden* Property

Dynamic visibility in Reporting Services allows you to create a drilldown report. *Drilldown* is a term typically used to describe the ability to click a summary value, which then displays the detail values that contribute to the selected summary value. To implement dynamic visibility, you select the report items to be hidden when the report opens and set the *Hidden* property for these items to True. Then, for these same items, you use the *ToggleItem* property to specify the report item that the user must click to make the hidden report items visible, or to return the visible items to a hidden state.

The *Hidden* property, which appears in the Visibility category in the Properties window, controls the visibility of a report item using the fixed values True or False, or a conditional expression that evaluates as True or False. Although a drilldown report often has all detail rows hidden when the report is initially rendered, you can use an expression to display the detail rows for specific grouping levels while hiding other detail rows for other grouping levels.

In this procedure, you'll hide the detail rows of the table in the Order Details report.

Hide detail rows in a table

1. Click the Layout tab, click the table to display handles, and then click the row handle of the detail row to select the entire row.
2. In the Properties window, expand the Visibility category, and then click True in the *Hidden* property list box.

   The *Hidden* property, when set to True, prevents a report item from appearing in a report. However, the value can still be referenced by an expression associated with another report item.
3. Click the table1_Order footer row handle.
4. In the Properties window, expand the Visibility category, and then select True in the *Hidden* property drop-down list.
5. Save and then preview the report.

   The report should look like this:

   Wingtip Toys Order Details

   Jan 1 2003 through Dec 31 2003

Order	Order Date	Ship Date	Qty	Price	Extended Price
SO8507	9/1/2003	9/8/2003			
SO8501	12/1/2003	12/8/2003			
All Wingtip Toys Orders			3		$1,303.46

   The order detail rows and the order footers (which had the subtotals) are now hidden from view. The table footer still displays and calculates correctly.

Using the *ToggleItem* Property

ToggleItem is another property that is assigned to the Visibility category in the Properties window. The value of this property must be a textbox in the report. When the report is rendered, the specified textbox will be displayed with a plus sign. A user can expand or collapse the visibility of the report item. So, if a detail row is hidden when the report is rendered and its toggle item is a textbox in a header row, when a user clicks that plus sign in that textbox, the detail row is displayed. Conversely, if the detail row is visible, when the user clicks the toggle item, the detail row is hidden.

If group footer totals are in the rows that you are hiding when the report initially opens, you might want to include these totals in a visible group header temporarily. You can then use the *ToggleItem* property for individual cells to hide the totals in the group header when the group footer is visible.

In this procedure, you'll assign the SalesOrderNumber textbox to the *ToggleItem* property of both the detail row and table1_Order footer in the table of the Order Details report.

Toggle the hidden state of an item

1. Click the Layout tab, and then click the row handle of the detail row to select the entire row.
2. In the Properties window, expand the Visibility category, and then select SalesOrderNumber in the *ToggleItem* property drop-down list.

   SalesOrderNumber is the name of the textbox containing the order number in the table1_Order header. By selecting this item as a *ToggleItem*, the SalesOrderNumber textbox will be the item that the user clicks to display the underlying detail rows.
3. Click the table1_Order footer handle to select the entire row.
4. In the Properties window, expand the Visibility category, and then select SalesOrderNumber in the *ToggleItem* property drop-down list.
5. Save and then preview the report to check the results.
6. Expand order SO8501 to confirm that your report looks like this:

   Wingtip Toys Order Details

   Jan 1 2003 through Dec 31 2003

Order	Order Date	Ship Date	Qty	Price	Extended Price
⊞ **SO8507**	**9/1/2003**	**9/8/2003**			
⊟ **SO8501**	**12/1/2003**	**12/8/2003**			
Mountain-400-W Silver, 38			2	$554.03	$1,108.07
			2		**$1,108.07**
All Wingtip Toys Orders			**3**		**$1,303.46**

   Now, when you click a SalesOrderNumber, the detail rows and the order footer are displayed.

In this procedure, you'll use the *ToggleItem* property to display the group footer totals in the group header when detail rows are hidden and hide the group header totals when detail rows are visible.

Show group footer totals in the group header when detail rows are hidden

1. Click the Layout tab to return to the design grid.
2. In the table1_Order footer, click the Qty cell. While pressing Shift, click the Extended Price cell, and then copy the contents to the Clipboard.
3. Click the Qty cell in the table1_Order header, and then paste the contents of the Clipboard to the corresponding cells of the table1_Order header so the table now looks like this:

Order	Order Date	Ship Date	Qty	Price	Extended Price
=Fields!SalesOrderNumt	=Fields!Orde	=Fields!Shipl	=Sum(Fields!		=Sum(Fields!Unit
=Fields!Product.Value			=Fields!OrderQt	=Fields!UnitPric	=Fields!OrderQty.Va
			=Sum(Fields!		=Sum(Fields!Unit
="All " & Parameters!R			=Sum(Field:		=Sum(Fields!Un

   When you copy these textbox formulas, the Visibility settings are not copied because the settings, in this case, are associated with the table rows and not the textboxes.

4. With the three cells still selected, expand the Visibility category in the Properties window, and then select SalesOrderNumber in the *ToggleItem* property drop-down list.

> **Note** Don't change the *Hidden* property. It should still be False.

   When the item is toggled, the values set for the property are hidden. In this case, the totals will be displayed in the group header when the detail rows are hidden. When toggled, the totals will be hidden in the group header.

5. Keep the three cells selected and select Solid in the drop-down list for the *BorderStyle* property.
6. Save the report and then preview it to confirm that your report looks like this:

Wingtip Toys Order Details

Jan 1 2003 through Dec 31 2003

Order	Order Date	Ship Date	Qty	Price	Extended Price
⊞ SO8507	9/1/2003	9/8/2003	1		$195.40
⊞ SO8501	12/1/2003	12/8/2003	2		$1,108.07
All Wingtip Toys Orders			3		$1,303.46

   Notice that the sales order totals are now visible in the order header row.

7. Expand order SO8501 to view the details, which look like this:

Wingtip Toys Order Details

Jan 1 2003 through Dec 31 2003

Order	Order Date	Ship Date	Qty	Price	Extended Price
⊞ SO8507	9/1/2003	9/8/2003	1		$195.40
⊟ SO8501	12/1/2003	12/8/2003			
Mountain-400-W Silver, 38			2	$554.03	$1,108.07
			2		$1,108.07
All Wingtip Toys Orders			3		$1,303.46

Now the totals in the header are hidden, and the detail rows and footer are displayed.

Deciding When to Use a Subreport

A *subreport* is a report item you can use to display another report inside the current report. To filter data in the subreport, you can pass a value from the main report to a report parameter in the subreport.

When you want to represent data from the same dataset in different ways in the same report, use separate data regions for the best performance. Even though the subreport behaves like just another data region, it's really a different report and is treated as such by the Report Server, which must process each subreport separately from the main report. By comparison, the Report Server can process a report containing multiple data regions in one pass. When processing the subreport, the Report Server ignores report items and properties in the subreport that are not a part of the report body, such as page size, or the page header and footer.

Keeping these trade-offs in mind, in a couple of situations, you might find using a subreport useful. For example, even though you cannot nest data regions that use different datasets, you *can* nest a subreport regardless of its dataset. This technique is useful when you need to combine data from disparate data sources. Another reason for using a subreport is to minimize the re-creation of detailed data that is frequently used in many different reports. You can organize this data once, and then reuse it over and over.

Adding a Subreport

Adding a subreport to your report is much like adding a data region. You use the Toolbox window to add a subreport, and then position the subreport in the report body. A subreport can be freestanding in the report, or it can be nested inside a data region. Nesting a subreport allows you to display data from a dataset that is not associated with the data region, and thus is an especially useful feature when you want to provide supporting details that are stored in a separate data source from the summary information. You can even pass a value to the subreport to control the subreport's behavior when it executes or is rendered.

In this procedure, you'll nest the Product Detail report as a subreport in the Product Sales and Profitability report, and then pass the current Product value to a report parameter in Product Detail.

Nest a subreport in a table

1. In Solution Explorer, right-click the Product Sales and Profitability.rdl report and click Copy.
2. Click the Reports folder, and then press Ctrl+V to paste a copy of the report into that folder.

   Because you are working exclusively in the Report Designer, both reports must be in the same folder to preview the reports.
3. Right-click the new report, click Rename, and then type a new name for the report: **Product Sales and Profitability Subreport.rdl**.
4. Double-click the Product Sales and Profitability Subreport.rdl report in Solution Explorer to display the report in the Document window.
5. Click the table, right-click the detail row, and then click Insert Row Below to add a new row.
6. Clear the expression from the *Color* property of the last cell in the new row.

   When you insert a row, the style properties are copied from the row from which you initiated the insert action. Since there is no string text or expression in this cell, the expression in the *Color* property won't do anything. Removing the expression will incrementally improve performance, because there will be one less expression evaluated when the report is processed.
7. In the Toolbox window, click Subreport, and then click the first cell of the empty detail row.
8. Right-click the subreport, and then click Properties.
9. Click Product Detail in the Subreport drop-down list, which should now look like this:

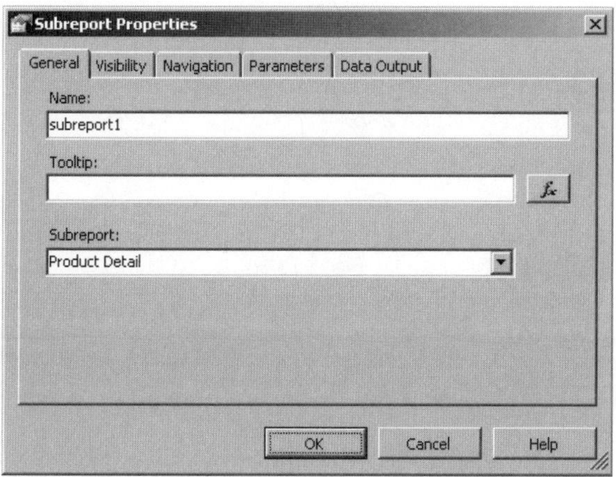

> **Note** As with actions, you aren't required to use a report from the same project. You can type the absolute or relative folder path to the report on the Report Server and the name of the report.

10. Click the Parameters tab.
11. Select Product in the Parameter Name drop-down list.
12. Select `=Fields!Product.Value` in the Parameter Value drop-down list, and then click OK.

> **Note** You must supply a value for each report parameter in the subreport to display the subreport correctly.

13. Click the second detail row, which contains the subreport, to select the entire row.
14. In the Properties window, expand the Visibility category, and then click True in the *Hidden* property.
15. Select Product in the *ToggleItem* property drop-down list.
16. Save, and then preview the report at a zoom factor of 75 percent to check the results.
17. Expand the AWC logo cap item, and then scroll to see the details, which should look like this:

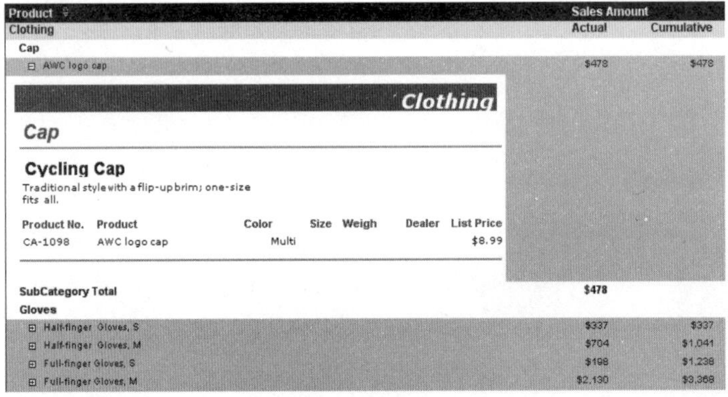

Product
Sales Amount
Clothing
Actual
Cumulative
Cap
AWC logo cap
$478
$478
Clothing
Cap
Cycling Cap
Traditional style with a flip-up brim; one-size fits all.
Product No.
Product
Color
Size
Weigh
Dealer
List Price
CA-1098
AWC logo cap
Multi
$8.99
SubCategory Total
$478
Gloves
Half-finger Gloves, S
$337
$337
Half-finger Gloves, M
$704
$1,041
Full-finger Gloves, S
$198
$1,238
Full-finger Gloves, M
$2,130
$3,368

Now, when you click a product in the detail rows, the subreport for the selected product displays. In this case, the subreport allows access to details from a completely different dataset. This access would not be possible within a table using nested data regions.

Working with Hierarchical Data

In addition to providing interactive features to help you build more sophisticated reports, Reporting Services helps you tackle the challenge of working with hierarchical data in reports.

Specifically, Reporting Services supports the identification of levels in a recursive hierarchy and the aggregation of information across levels within a particular branch of the hierarchy. One type of recursive hierarchy you encounter in data warehousing is a parent-child dimension.

Another hierarchical structure that Reporting Services can access is an Analysis Services online analytical processing (OLAP) database. Analysis Services, like Reporting Services, is bundled with SQL Server. Analysis Services is a server-based OLAP engine that structures data to facilitate fast and powerful queries that would be challenging to reproduce with traditional relational queries. Creating an OLAP database has three main benefits:

- Its hierarchical structure simplifies user navigation.
- An OLAP database can respond to queries faster than a relational database because it uses this hierarchical structure to store precalculated aggregations.
- An OLAP database uses sophisticated analytical formulas on the server, particularly time series analysis, such as year-over-year comparisons.

Many commercial software companies have developed client tools that allow a user to perform interactive analysis directly with the OLAP database. Still, using Reporting Services to access OLAP data using an MDX (multidimensional expressions) query has two main advantages. First, you can provide a simple implementation of a thin-client solution when the majority of users don't need flexible analysis but do want access to the results of server-based calculations. Second, you can reduce the execution time of a report as compared to retrieving the same data from a relational source.

Displaying a Recursive Hierarchy in a Data Region

To add a recursive hierarchy to a data region, you need to modify the data region's grouping properties. The group expression must be the field expression that identifies the unique records in the hierarchy. Then, you specify a parent group expression that identifies the parent records. For example, in a table that describes the organizational relationship between employees and managers, each employee record has a key column to uniquely identify the employee and a parent key column that points to the parent record—the employee's manager—in the same table. You can group employees by manager using these key columns and perform aggregations of values within these groupings, such as counting employees by manager or totaling the employees' salaries.

In this procedure, you'll add a grouping level to a table for a recursive hierarchy that has employees as unique records and supervisors as parent records.

Define a parent group for a recursive hierarchy

1. In Solution Explorer, right-click the Reports folder in the project My Adventure Works, point to Add, and then click Existing Item to add the Employee Salaries.rdl saved in the C:\Documents and Settings\<username>\My Documents\Microsoft Press\rs2005sbs \chap07 folder.

2. Double-click the Employee Salaries.rdl report to open it in the Document window, and then click the Preview tab to confirm the top of the report looks like this:

Employee Salaries

Employee Name	Title	Level	Employee Count	Individual Salary	Total Salary
Terri Lee Duffy	VP Engineering			$129,461	
Wang	Engineering Manager			$88,269	
John Wood	Marketing Specialist			$29,423	
Sheela Word	Purchasing Manager			$61,200	
Annette Hill	Purchasing Assistant			$26,010	
Reinout Hillmann	Purchasing Assistant			$26,010	
Gordon L Hee	Buyer			$37,269	
Erin M Hagens	Buyer			$37,269	
Eric S Kurjan	Buyer			$37,269	
Ben Miller	Buyer			$37,269	
Linda Meisner	Buyer			$37,269	
Fukiko Ogisu	Buyer			$37,269	
Frank Pellow	Buyer			$37,269	
Mikael Sandberg	Buyer			$37,269	
Arvind B Rao	Buyer			$37,269	
Dylan Miller	Research & Development			$102,981	

You'll be changing this report to group employees by supervisor.

3. Click the Layout tab, click the table, and then click the detail row to select the row.
4. In the Properties window, click the ellipsis button for the *Grouping* property.
5. In the Details Grouping dialog box, type **RecursiveGroup** as the name.
6. Select `=Fields!EmployeeKey.Value` from the Expression drop-down list.
7. Select `=Fields!ParentEmployeeKey.Value` from the Parent group drop-down list so the Details Grouping dialog box now looks like this:

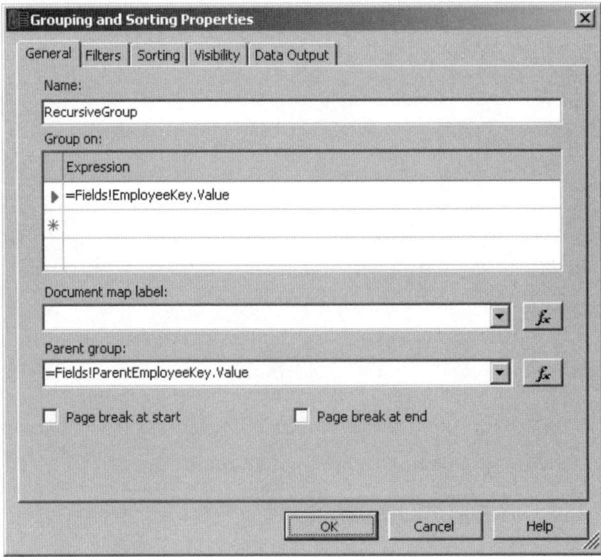

8. Click OK.
9. Click the table, right-click the table handle in the top-left corner, and then click Properties.

10. Click the Sorting tab.
11. Select `=Fields!Salary.Value` in the Expression drop-down list, select Descending in the Direction drop-down list, and then click OK.
12. Save and then preview the report at a zoom factor of 75 percent to check the results.

    Now, employees are sorted in groups by supervisor, and sorted within the group by salary in descending order. However, the layout still doesn't clearly distinguish supervisors from employees.

Using the *Level* Function

The *Level* function is used with recursive hierarchies to identify the relationship of the current row to the top of the hierarchy. The syntax of this function is *Level(Scope)* where *Scope* is the name of a grouping, data region, or dataset. If you omit *Scope*, the current scope of the expression is used. The function returns an integer value that starts at 0 for the top of the hierarchy and increments by 1 for each subsequent level. The most common use of this function is to change style properties for different levels of a hierarchy.

In this procedure, you'll use the *Level* function to display the current level of the hierarchy and to format cells by level.

Use the *Level* function in an expression

1. Click the Layout tab, right-click the Level cell in the detail row, and then click Expression.
2. Type the following expression:

```
=Level("RecursiveGroup")
```

   The scope of the function is *RecursiveGroup*, which is the employee grouping you created in the previous procedure.

3. Click OK.
4. Save and then preview the report, which should now look like this:

Employee Salaries

Employee Name	Title	Level	Employee Count	Individual Salary	Total Salary
James R Hamilton	VP Production	0		$171,635	
Shai Bassli	Facilities Manager	1		$49,039	
Christian Kleinerman	Maintenance Supervisor	2		$41,683	
Pat Coleman	Janitor	3		$18,870	
Jo Berry	Janitor	3		$18,870	
Magnus Hedlund	Facilities Assistant	2		$19,890	
Bob Gage	VP Sales	0		$147,115	
Stephen Yuan Jiang	North American Sales Manager	1		$98,126	
Tete Mensa-Annan	Sales Representative	2		$47,077	
David Campbell	Sales Representative	2		$47,077	
Fernando Caro	Sales Representative	2		$47,077	
Shu Ito	Sales Representative	2		$47,077	
Linda Mitchell	Sales Representative	2		$47,077	
Tsvi Reiter	Sales Representative	2		$47,077	
Garrett R Vargas	Sales Representative	2		$47,077	
Jae B Pak	Sales Representative	2		$47,077	

Now, you can see the employee groupings more easily, but formatting would make the groups stand out even better.

5. Click the Layout tab, and then click the first cell in the detail row.
6. In the Properties window, expand the Padding category, and then select <Expression...> in the *Left* property drop-down list.
7. Replace the default expression with the following:

```
=2 + (Level("RecursiveGroup") * 20) & "pt"
```

This expression increases the padding used to indent the detail row as the level number increases.

8. Click OK.
9. Click the detail row handle in the table.
10. In the Properties window, expand the *Font* property, and then select <Expression...> in the *FontWeight* property drop-down list.
11. Replace the default expression with the following:

```
=IIf(Level ("RecursiveGroup")=0, "Bold", "Normal")
```

This expression uses bold text when rendering the highest-level employees in the report.

12. Click OK.
13. Save and then preview the report, which should now look like this:

Employee Salaries

Employee Name	Title	Level	Employee Count	Individual Salary	Total Salary
James R Hamilton	VP Production	0		$171,635	
Shai Bassli	Facilities Manager	1		$49,039	
Christian Kleinerman	Maintenance Supervisor	2		$41,683	
Pat Coleman	Janitor	3		$18,870	
Jo Berry	Janitor	3		$18,870	
Magnus Hedlund	Facilities Assistant	2		$19,890	
Bob Gage	VP Sales	0		$147,115	
Stephen Yuan Jiang	North American Sales Manager	1		$98,126	
Tete Mensa-Annan	Sales Representative	2		$47,077	
David Campbell	Sales Representative	2		$47,077	
Fernando Caro	Sales Representative	2		$47,077	
Shu Ito	Sales Representative	2		$47,077	
Linda Mitchell	Sales Representative	2		$47,077	
Tsvi Reiter	Sales Representative	2		$47,077	
Garrett R Vargas	Sales Representative	2		$47,077	
Jae B Pak	Sales Representative	2		$47,077	

Using the *Recursive* Keyword

The *Recursive* keyword acts as a modifier to any aggregate function with the purpose of returning a value that includes not only the detail rows, but also the value of the parent row in a group. The keyword must be placed after the *Scope* argument in an aggregate function.

In this procedure, you'll use the *Recursive* keyword with the aggregate functions *Count* and *Sum*.

Use *Recursive* aggregate functions

1. Click the Layout tab, right-click the Employee Count cell in the detail row, and then select Expression.
2. Enter the following expression:

```
=Count(Fields!EmployeeKey.Value,"RecursiveGroup",Recursive)
```

3. Click OK.
4. Right-click the Total Salary cell in the detail row, and then click Expression.
5. Modify the expression so it looks like this:

```
=Sum(Fields!Salary.Value,"RecursiveGroup",Recursive)
```

   This expression calculates the total salaries for the employees in levels below the current row *and* includes the salary for the current row.

6. Click OK.
7. Right-click the Salary of Reports cell in the detail row, and then click Expression.
8. Change the expression so it looks like this:

```
=Sum(Fields!Salary.Value,"RecursiveGroup",Recursive)-Sum(Fields!Salary.Value)
```

   This expression subtracts the salary of the current employee from the recursive aggregation so only the value of the employees below the current employee is returned.

9. Click OK.
10. Save and then preview the report using a zoom factor of 75 percent to confirm that the top of the report now looks like this:

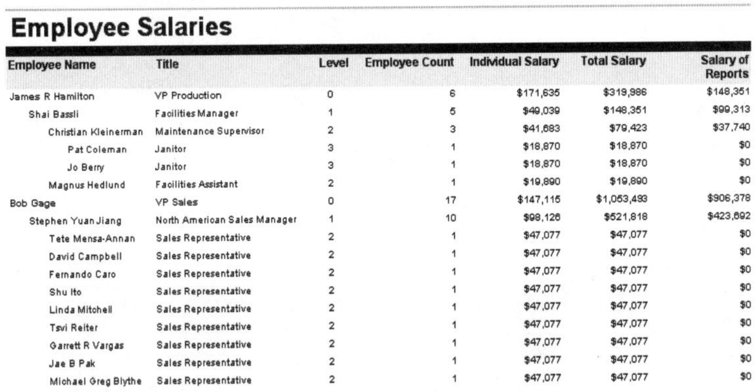

Employee Salaries

Employee Name	Title	Level	Employee Count	Individual Salary	Total Salary	Salary of Reports
James R Hamilton	VP Production	0	6	$171,635	$319,986	$148,351
Shai Bassli	Facilities Manager	1	5	$49,039	$148,351	$99,313
Christian Kleinerman	Maintenance Supervisor	2	3	$41,683	$79,423	$37,740
Pat Coleman	Janitor	3	1	$18,870	$18,870	$0
Jo Berry	Janitor	3	1	$18,870	$18,870	$0
Magnus Hedlund	Facilities Assistant	2	1	$19,890	$19,890	$0
Bob Gage	VP Sales	0	17	$147,115	$1,053,493	$906,378
Stephen Yuan Jiang	North American Sales Manager	1	10	$98,126	$521,818	$423,692
Tete Mensa-Annan	Sales Representative	2	1	$47,077	$47,077	$0
David Campbell	Sales Representative	2	1	$47,077	$47,077	$0
Fernando Caro	Sales Representative	2	1	$47,077	$47,077	$0
Shu Ito	Sales Representative	2	1	$47,077	$47,077	$0
Linda Mitchell	Sales Representative	2	1	$47,077	$47,077	$0
Tsvi Reiter	Sales Representative	2	1	$47,077	$47,077	$0
Garrett R Vargas	Sales Representative	2	1	$47,077	$47,077	$0
Jae B Pak	Sales Representative	2	1	$47,077	$47,077	$0
Michael Greg Blythe	Sales Representative	2	1	$47,077	$47,077	$0

Compare the difference in the results of the Total Salary column and the Salary of Reports column. If you want a parent row's value aggregated with the lower levels, simply use an aggregation with the *Recursive* keyword to get a result like the Total Salary column. If you don't want the parent row's value included, you'll need to deduct the current row to get results shown in the Salary of Reports column.

Creating an Analysis Services Data Source and Dataset

Using Analysis Services data in a report is very similar to using relational data. You still need to define a data source, create a dataset, and add fields to the report. However, when creating a dataset, you write a query using MDX instead of SQL. The procedures in this section will lead you through the creation of an Analysis Services data source and dataset, as well as an examination of an existing report to put these concepts into context.

> **Important** To perform the procedures in this section, you must have Analysis Services installed on your computer, and you must have restored the Analysis Services database by following the instructions in "Installing and Using the Practice Files" in the Introduction to this book.

Analysis Services uses MDX to query its OLAP database. An MDX query is similar to a SQL query in that it has a SELECT, FROM, and WHERE clause. However, where SQL is designed to deal with only a two-dimensional structure of rows and columns, MDX is designed to deal with the multidimensional OLAP structure. Because of its structural differences from SQL, you can add an MDX query to a dataset using either the Generic Query Designer or the MDX Query Builder graphical user interface (GUI).

If you're new to OLAP, MDX queries can seem pretty daunting to construct, but with lots of practice, you'll be rewarded with access to a rich and powerful source of data for reporting. A more complete explanation of MDX is beyond the scope of this book, but you can start learning more about this subject using SQL Server Books Online.

The easiest way to build an OLAP report is to use the MDX Query Builder to create datasets. You can drag and drop OLAP attributes and measures to define what OLAP objects should be included in the MDX SELECT statement and which objects should be included in the MDX WHERE clause. The data source used specifies the information for the From statement.

In this procedure, you'll use the MDX Query Builder to create an Analysis Services data source and datasets for the Year Over Year Sales report.

Build an Analysis Services Data Source and Dataset

1. Right-click the Reports folder in the project My Adventure Works, point to Add, and then click Existing Item to add the Year over Year Sales.rdl saved in the C:\Documents and Settings\<username>\My Documents\Microsoft Press\rs2005sbs\chap07 folder.

This report compares sales amounts for the selected year to those of the prior year. Using an MDX query makes this comparison very easy, because the previous period can be defined as a calculation in the database.

2. Double-click Year over Year Sales.rdl to open the report, and then click the Data tab. Click OK to close the error message that indicates the connection to the database cannot be made.

   You'll correct the connection error by creating a new dataset for this report.

3. Click the Edit Selected Dataset button to the right of the Dataset drop-down list to display the Dataset dialog box..

4. In the Data Source drop-down list, click New Data Source.

5. Change the name of this data source from DataSource1 to **rs2005sbsOLAP**, and then click Microsoft SQL Server Analysis Services in the Type drop-down list.

6. Click Edit, enter **localhost** in the Server Name box, click rs2005sbs in the Select Or Enter A Database Name drop-down list, and then click OK three times to close all dialog boxes.

   The MDX Query Builder is now open, and your screen looks like this:

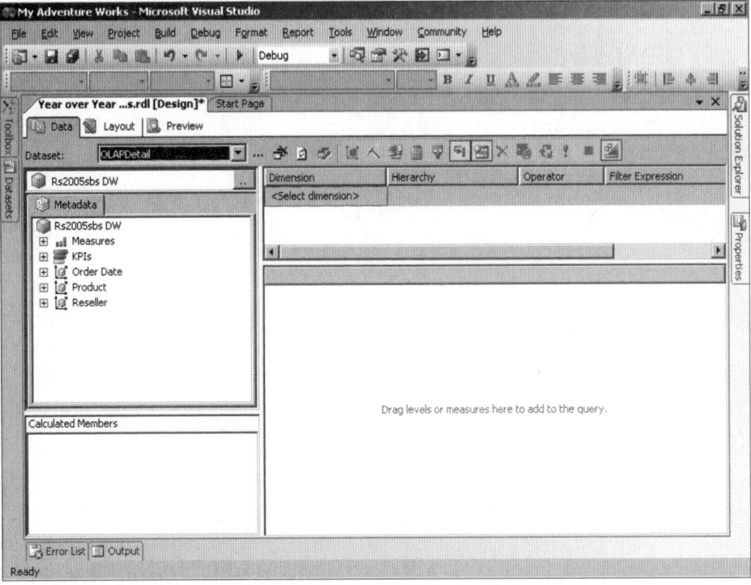

7. Expand Product in the Metadata tree, drag Product Categories to the area of the MDX Query Builder labeled Drag Levels Or Measures Here To Add To The Query.

8. Expand OrderDate in the Metadata tree, and then drag CalendarYear to the right of the Product column in the query builder.

9. Expand Measures, and then drag Prior Year Sales to the position to the right of the CalendarYear column.

10. Expand the two Reseller Sales folders below the Measures folder, and then drag Sales Amount to the position to the right of the Prior Year Sales column.

    All of the columns in the query builder will be included in the MDX SELECT statement, and will be available as dataset fields that are used in the Year Over Year Sales report.

11. In the Dimension drop-down list above the query builder columns, select Order Date. Select CalendarYear in the Hierarchy drop-down list, select 2004 in the Filter Expression drop-down list, and click the Parameters check box.

    Your screen should look like this:

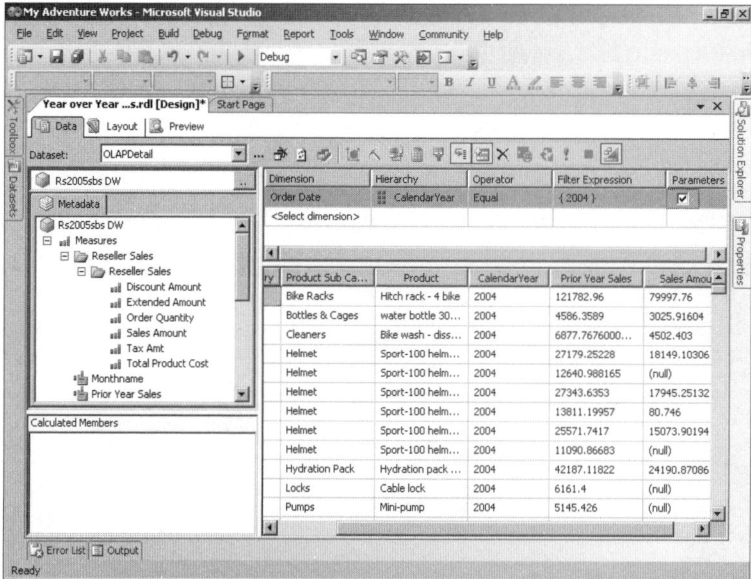

Setting criteria in this area of the query builder creates a subcube for your query to limit the amount of data that must be read to resolve the query. In this case, the query will be limited to the part of the cube that contains data for the year 2004. By specifying this criteria as a parameter, a second dataset is automatically created, OrderDateCalendarYear. This second dataset will execute a query at run time to build a list of years that will be used for the Available Values dataset of a report parameter. The default value is 2004.

Using an Analysis Services Dataset

Once the Analysis Services dataset is created, you can use field expressions in a data region or report item to organize data in your report. When the MDX query executes, the result is a flattened rowset that can be used almost like the results from a SQL query. You can also use the

Hidden and *ToggleItem* properties on group rows to create a drilldown report similar to the one you developed earlier in this chapter.

In this procedure, you'll examine the use of aggregate functions and report parameters with Analysis Services data.

Explore the use of Analysis Services data in a table

1. Click the Layout tab, click the table, and then click the table1_Category header to select the entire row so the table looks like this:

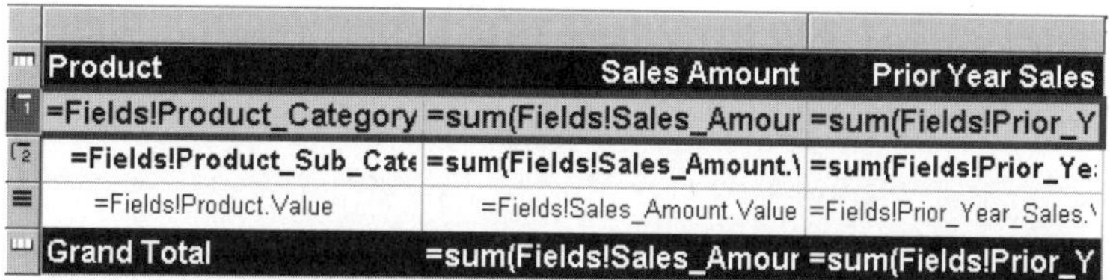

Product
Sales Amount
Prior Year Sales
=Fields!Product_Category
=sum(Fields!Sales_Amour
=sum(Fields!Prior_Y
=Fields!Product_Sub_Cate
=sum(Fields!Sales_Amount.\
=sum(Fields!Prior_Ye:
=Fields!Product.Value
=Fields!Sales_Amount.Value
=Fields!Prior_Year_Sales.\
Grand Total
=sum(Fields!Sales_Amour
=sum(Fields!Prior_Y

   Notice the use of the *Sum* function in the header rows with the Sales Amount and Prior Year Sales measures, just like with a SQL dataset.

2. Click Report Parameters in the Report menu. Change the Prompt from CalendarYear to **Year**.

   This parameter was created when you selected the Parameters check box while creating the OLAPDetail dataset. At that point, the fields *ParameterValue* and *ParameterCaption* were created as part of a new dataset, OrderDateCalendarYear. Additionally, the *OrderDateCalendarYear* report parameter was created.

3. Click OK, save the project, and then click the Preview tab to view the report. Spend some time exploring the report by toggling the category and subcategory rows to review the product details, and then close the project when you've finished.

Chapter 7 Quick Reference

To	Do this
Use a report parameter value as a variable	Click Report Parameters on the Report menu while a report is in Layout mode, click Add, and then provide a name and data type for a report parameter. Optionally, provide a list of available values or a default value. Use the report parameter value in an expression using the following syntax: *Parameters!ObjectName.Value*.
Display the label of a report parameter	Add the following expression to a textbox in a report: **Parameters!ObjectName.Label**.
Use a query parameter	Add a parameter to the WHERE clause of a dataset query, such as: `WHERE Year = @Year`. Update the corresponding report parameter, such as *Year*, to specify the appropriate data type, and optionally the list of available values or a default value.

To	Do this
Use a report parameter as a filter	To filter all data regions in a report, click the Data tab, click the dataset in the Dataset drop-down list, and then click the Edit Selected Dataset button. Click the Filters tab, and then select the expression that corresponds to the report parameter's value. *or* To filter a data region, right-click the data region in the design grid, and then click Properties. Click the Filters tab, and then select the expression that corresponds to the report parameter's value. *or* To filter a grouping level, right-click the group row in the design grid, and then click Properties. In the Properties window, click the ellipsis button for the *Grouping* property, click the Filters tab, and then select the expression that corresponds to the report parameter's value.
Add an action	Right-click a textbox or an image, click the ellipsis button for the *Action* property in the Properties window, and then click the option for the type of action to add. Enter the bookmark identifier, report name, or URL to which the action will direct the user. If a target report has a report parameter, click Parameters, and then select a report parameter in the Parameter Name drop-down list and an expression in the Parameter Value list box.
Create a drilldown report	Click the row handle of the detail row and change its *Hidden* property to True in the Properties window. In the *ToggleItem* property for the same row, click the name of the textbox to use as a toggle for the visibility of the detail row.
Add a subreport	Open the Toolbox window, click Subreport, point to the target destination, and click to place the subreport. Right-click the subreport, and then enter the name of the subreport if it isn't in the same project folder as the host report, or click to select a report from the Subreport list box if it is in the same project folder.
Group relational data in a recursive hierarchy	In the Properties window, click the ellipsis button in the *Grouping* property for the detail row of a data region or click Edit Group to open the *Grouping And Sorting Properties* dialog box for the group row in a data region. Click the field expression in the Group On list box to identify a unique row and select the field expression in the Parent Group drop-down list to identify a parent row.
Identify levels in a recursive hierarchy	Use the *Level* function in an expression, using the group name as scope. For example, for the group RecursiveGroup, use the following expression: `=Level("RecursiveGroup")`.
Aggregate data in a recursive hierarchy	Add the *Recursive* keyword to the aggregate function, `=Function(Expression,Scope,Recursive)`. For example, to count employee rows in a recursive group and the parent row, use the following expression: `=Count(Fields!EmployeeKey.Value, "RecursiveGroup", Recursive)`.
Query an Analysis Services database	Create a dataset using the Microsoft OLE DB Provider for OLAP Services 9.0, and then, using the MDX Query Builder, drag objects from the Metadata tree to build an MDX query.

Chapter 8

Building Report Models

After completing this chapter, you will be able to:

- Create a report model project to support ad hoc reporting.
- Use the Report Model Wizard to autogenerate a model.
- Use Visual Studio to format, reorganize, and extend a report model.
- Deploy and secure a report model.

In the preceding chapters of Part II, "Authoring Reports," you learned how to use the Visual Studio environment to develop reports for broad distribution. Authoring reports for Reporting Services requires you to understand the data structures and relationships of the source data as well as how to create queries that return the data that will be presented in reports. This level of understanding is expected when you are an IT professional responsible for supporting reporting in an organization and is common among many power users in departmental workgroups. Most of the reporting community doesn't typically possess the technical knowledge required to use Visual Studio to author reports, although many would certainly benefit from the ability to create their own reports on demand. To make the process of accessing data and constructing reports easier for this group, you can create a user-friendly abstraction of SQL Server data structures, known as a *report model*. In this chapter, you learn about the composition of a report model, how to create and maintain a report model, and how to put a report model into production.

Understanding Report Models

A report model describes tables and columns found in a data source as well as the relationships between them in order to shield the complexities of the underlying data source from users who want to create their own simpler reports. A report model is stored in a Semantic Model Definition Language (SMDL) file, which is an XML schema analogous to Report Definition Language (RDL) in that it is a definition that can be used by another application to eventually produce a report. In Chapter 15, "Creating Reports with Report Builder," you'll learn how to use the report model file to easily create ad hoc reports.

A report model contains a hierarchy of objects whose purpose is to represent the data structures and relationships in business terms. A folder is an optional object at the highest level of the hierarchy within a model and is used to organize objects logically within the model to help users find related information or to extend access to certain objects to a limited group of users. A model always contains at least one entity, which can also be the highest level in the model hierarchy if it isn't moved into a folder. By default, one entity is created for each table in the data source view (DSV) and contains a collection of attributes corresponding to the collection of columns in the related table. Additionally, an entity might contain special attributes that don't exist in the DSV, such as expressions that perform calculations on data selected for a report or aggregations to sum or average numeric values. An entity can also contain a role, which is a special object that defines a relationship between entities. Fundamentally, these report model objects are used to construct a SQL query based on the placement of these objects in a report layout designer.

Creating a Report Model

To create a report model, you can use the Model Designer that is integrated with Visual Studio as one of the business intelligence project templates. This method offers the most flexible approach for designing a report because you have control over which rules are used to generate the model, and you can change the model after it's generated. You can also generate models using SQL Server Management Studio or Report Manager.

Generating a report model in Visual Studio is quite easy. You start by creating a report model project, and then you add a data source to connect to a SQL Server database. After defining this connection, you create a DSV to identify the specific tables to be used for building a report model as well as the logical relationships between those tables. Once these two items are added to your project, you use the Report Model Wizard to automatically generate a report model based on the definitions contained in the DSV.

Adding a Report Model Data Source

You learned about data sources in Chapter 3, "Building Your First Report." A data source for a report model project is similar to a data source for a report project. It defines the server and database that contains the data to be used in ad hoc reports as well as the credentials used for authentications when queries are executed. However, a data source created for a report project cannot be added to a report model project. You must create a new data source definition to use the Model Designer in Visual Studio. Alternatively, you can add a data source from an Analysis Services project to the report model project. In either case, it's important to understand that a data source for a report model project can use the SQL Server provider only.

In this procedure, you'll create a new report model project and add a data source to connect to the rs2005sbsDW database using Windows authentication.

Add a report model data source

1. Start SQL Server Business Intelligence Development Studio. On the File menu, click New, and then click Project.
2. In the New Project dialog box, click the Report Model Project template in the Business Intelligence Projects folder.

3. Type in a name for the project, **Reseller Sales Report Model**, and, if necessary, type the following location for the project: **C:\Documents and Settings\<username>\My Documents\Microsoft Press\rs2005sbs\Workspace**. Click OK.
4. Right-click the Data Sources folder in Solution Explorer, and then click Add New Data Source to open the Data Source Wizard.
5. Click Next to go past the welcome page, and then click New.
6. In the Connection Manager dialog box, type the server name **localhost**, click rs2005sbsDW in the Select Or Enter A Database Name drop-down list, and then click OK.

> **Note** If you already have a connection created for the rs2005sbsDW database, you can skip this step.

7. On the Select How To Define The Connection page of the Data Source Wizard, make sure localhost.rs2005sbsDW is selected, click Next, and then click Finish.

Adding a Data Source View

A *data source view* (DSV) is an XML file which contains the metadata about the structures and relationships in a data source. It isn't necessary to create a report model that uses all tables or views in the underlying data source. Using the DSV, you can use a subset of tables and views to control access to the data. You can also consolidate information from multiple tables into a logical table known as a *Named Query*, which is like creating a view in a relational database. Similarly, you can use a *Named Calculation* to add a column to a table, much like creating a derived column in a view. Whether using a Named Query or a Named Calculation, no change is made to the underlying relational database. Thus, using a DSV to manipulate table structures is quite advantageous when you don't have permissions to change physical structures, but need to restructure data for reporting purposes.

In this procedure, you'll create a DSV from a subset of tables in the rs2005sbsDW database.

Add a DSV

1. Right-click the Data Source Views folder in Solution Explorer, and then click Add New Data Source View to open the Data Source View Wizard.
2. Click Next to bypass the welcome page, click Rs2005sbs DW in the Relational Data Sources list if it isn't already selected, and then click Next.
3. Move the following tables from the Available Objects list to the Included Objects list: DimGeography, DimProduct, DimReseller, DimSalesTerritory, DimTime, and FactResellerSales.

The Data Source View Wizard dialog box looks like this:

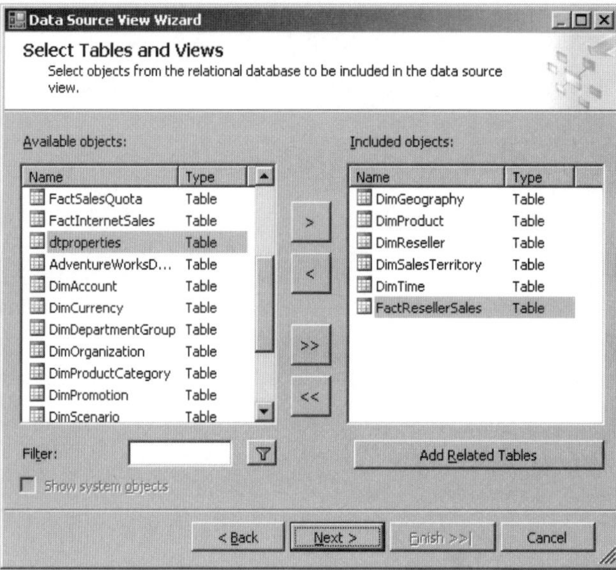

4. Click Next, and then click Finish to close the wizard.
5. Double-click Rs2005sbs DW.dsv in Solution Explorer to open the DSV.

   Your screen looks similar to this:

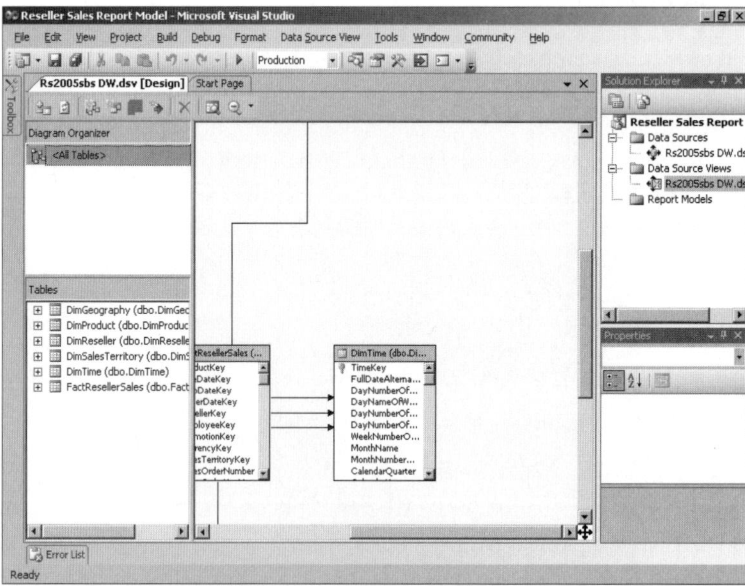

In the rs2005sbsDW database, there are three tables that contain product information: DimProduct, DimProductSubCategory, and DimProductCategory. However, including these three tables in the DSV will create three entities in the report model, which can be confusing to users when they navigate the model while building a report. To avoid this confusion, you can replace the DimProduct table with a Named Query that includes data from all three tables. This consolidation of tables in the DSV will result in a single Product entity in the report model.

6. Locate the DimProduct table, right-click the table caption, point to Replace Table, and then click With New Named Query.

> **Note** With a higher screen resolution, you can see a larger section of the DSV at once. You can use the horizontal or vertical scroll bars to navigate to other sections of the DSV.

7. Click the Add Table button in the Query Definition toolbar, click DimProductCategory, and then, while pressing Shift, click DimProductSubCategory in the Query Definition Window.
8. Click Add, and then click the Close button to close the Add Table dialog box.
9. In the Diagram pane, select the ProductSubCategoryName check box in the DimProductSubCategory table and select the ProductCategoryName check box in the DimProductCategory table.

   Your screen looks similar to this:

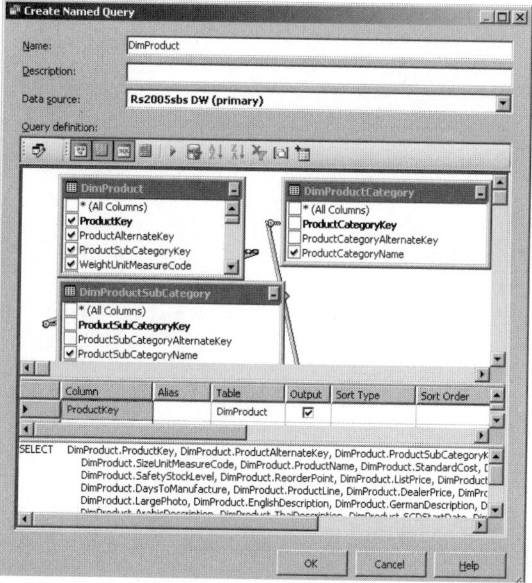

The columns from these two additional tables will now be included in the entity created for DimProduct.

10. Click OK.

    Notice that the existing relationships defined in the relational database are included in the DSV, as indicated by the lines connecting the related tables, which join a foreign key in one table to a primary key in another table. Also notice the key icon that identifies the primary key in each table in the DSV.

    The FactResellerSales table does not have a primary key defined, because typical data warehouse design does not require this definition. However, in order to include this table as an entity in the report model, there must be a primary key. The collection of key columns in this table can be used as a composite key because each combination of keys by row is unique. You can create a logical primary key in the DSV to identify this collection of keys.

11. In the FactResellerSales table, click the *ProductKey* field, and then, while pressing Ctrl, click to select each of the other key fields, the last of which is SalesTerritoryKey.

12. Right-click the currently selected group of fields, and then click Set Logical Primary Key.

    Your screen looks similar to this:

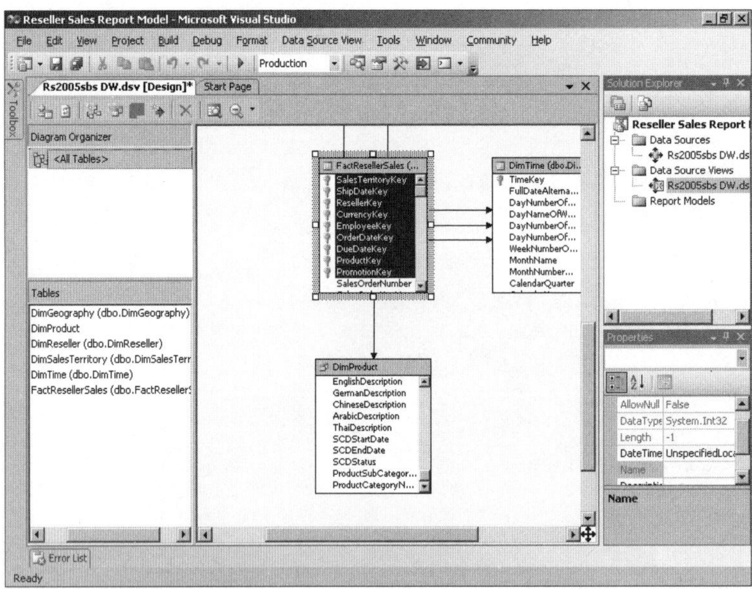

Adding a Report Model

The Report Model Wizard available in the Model Designer produces a report model from a DSV you specify. The selected DSV must be based on one data source only and that data source must be a SQL Server database. Using the wizard, you can change the rules used to generate the model. Until you better understand the purpose of each object in a report model and their interrelationships, you should keep the default selections, but it's nice to have the ability to make changes under certain circumstances. For example, you might have tables that contain columns that are never used. There is a special rule—disabled by default—that you can select in the Report Model Wizard to create attributes only for columns that contain data. By enabling this rule, you won't have to perform an extra step to delete unnecessary attributes later.

In this procedure, you'll use the Report Model Wizard to generate a report model from the rs2005sbs DW DSV you created in the previous procedure.

Use the Report Model Wizard

1. Right-click the Report Models folder in Solution Explorer, and then click Add New Report Model.
2. Click Next on the welcome page of the wizard, ensure that Rs2005sbs DW.dsv is selected on the Available Data Source Views page, and then click Next.

   Your screen looks like this:

   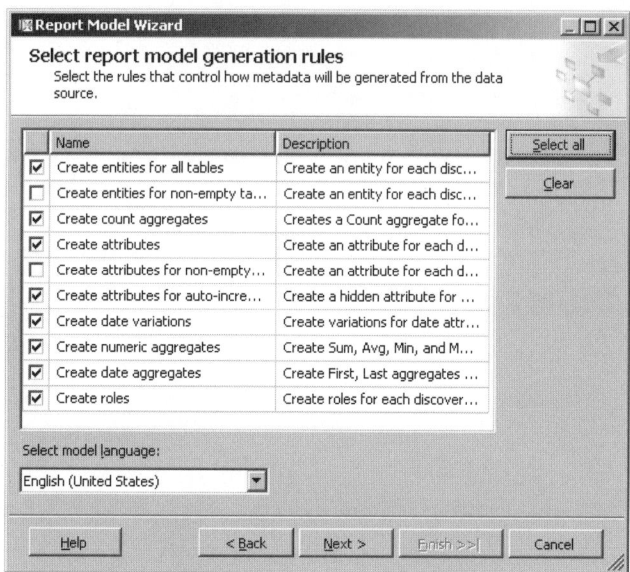

   As you can see here, there are many rules used to generate a report model. You can learn more about the purpose of each rule at *http://msdn2.microsoft.com/en-us/library/ms183622.aspx.*

3. Keep the default selections on the Select Report Model Generation Rules page, and then click Next.

   Since you just created a DSV, the statistics in that file are current.

4. On the Collect Model Statistics page, select Use Current Model Statistics Stored In The Data Source View.

Your screen looks like this:

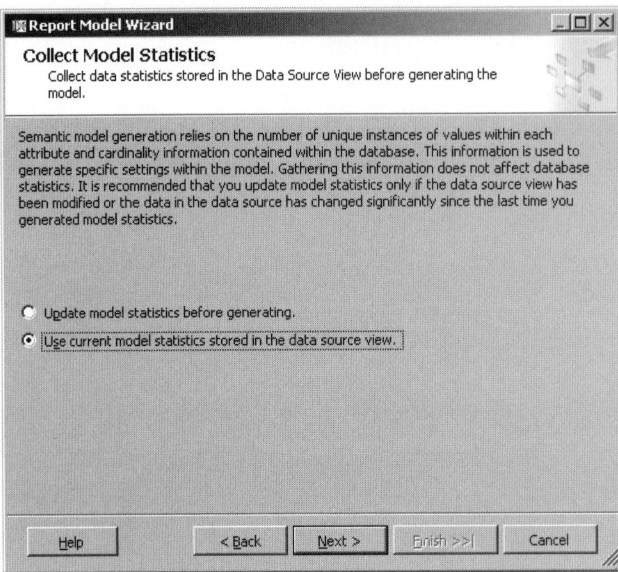

5. Click Next, name the model **Reseller Sales**, and then click Run to generate the report model.

   When the wizard has completed creating the report model, your screen looks like this:

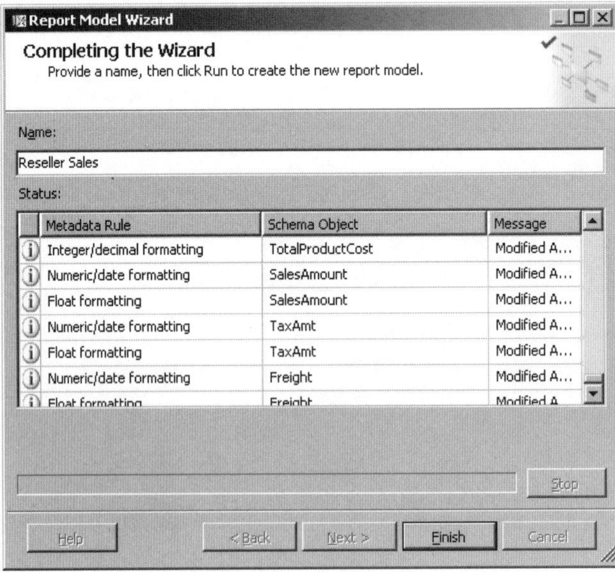

6. Click the Finish button.

You have just successfully created a report model that can be deployed to the Report Server. Once deployed, the report model is available for use in creating ad hoc reports using Report Builder. However, you should review the model first to make sure that the model will be useful to your ad hoc reporting community.

Using Management Tools to Build a Report Model

You can also generate a report model from SQL Server Management Studio or from Report Manager. The report models generated from these management tools are identical to report models generated using the Report Model Wizard. When using the management tools, you can also use an Analysis Services cube as a data source, but you are still limited to one data source per report model. In SQL Server Management Studio, you connect to Reporting Services, right-click a data source, and then click Generate Model. In Report Manager, you open a shared data source, and then click Generate Model.

Regardless of the type of data source, you won't be able to change the rules used to generate a report model. The report model is automatically deployed to the report server after it is generated. If you want to edit a report model that is based on a SQL Server database, you can download it from the report server and use the Model Designer to make any desired changes. However, you don't have the ability to edit a report model based on an Analysis Services cube.

Reviewing a Report Model

The Report Model Designer has two views: Tree View and Detail View. The Tree View displays on the left side of the designer and contains a list of entities. To the right side of the Tree View, the Detail View displays a list of objects, such as attributes and roles, that are associated with the currently selected entity in the Tree View. An attribute is created for each column in the entity's related table (or named query), but there are also additional attributes that don't correspond to a table column. For example, at the top of the list for each entity, there is an aggregate attribute that counts the number of records in the entity. Roles enable Report Builder users to navigate between entities when building a report. You learn about navigating a report model in Report Builder in Chapter 15.

In this procedure, you'll explore the report model generated in the previous procedure.

Examine a report model

1. Review the layout of the Report Model Designer.

   Your screen looks like this:

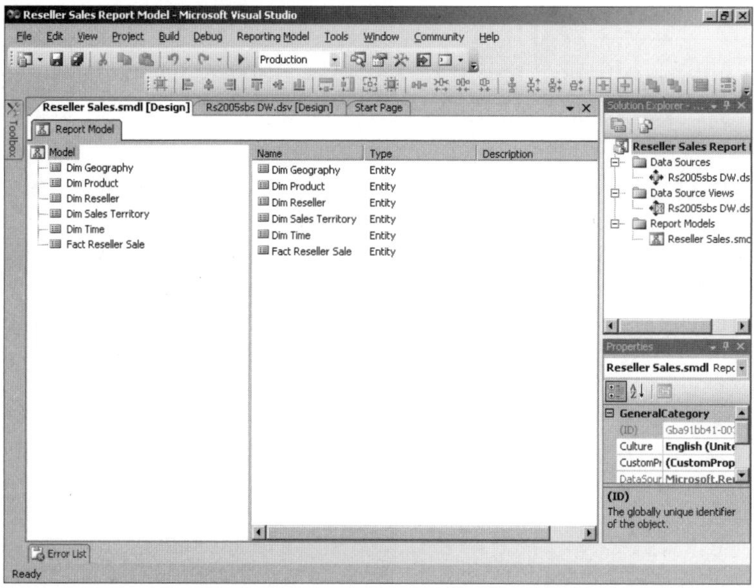

   Notice there is one entity per table included in the DSV. The default name of the entity is the name of the table. If the table name includes a capitalized letter in any position after the first left, a space is inserted before that letter. Additionally, any underscore is converted to a space. Therefore, a table name like Dim_Product or DimProduct would result in an entity named Dim Product. Often, the table names used in a database must conform to certain naming conventions that are not necessarily user-friendly. You can edit the default names assigned by the Report Model Wizard to a more suitable name, which you'll do later in this chapter.

2. Click the Dim Product entity in the Report Model Tree View.

Your screen looks like this:

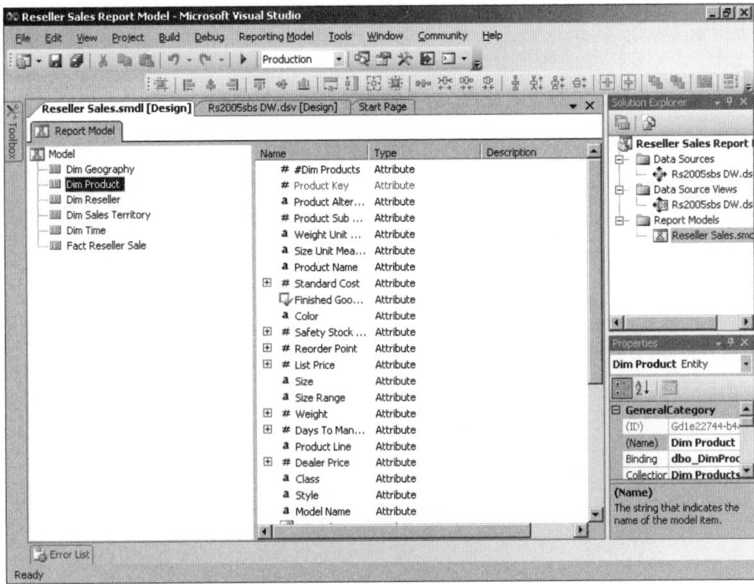

Here you can see that each attribute is preceded by a symbol indicating its data type. Attributes with a string data type, such as *Color* or *Model Name*, are indicated by an icon depicting the letter "a." Decimal, float, and integer data types are indicated by an icon depicting the symbol "#," as you can see for attributes such as *Standard Cost* and *Safety Stock Level*. Attributes with a data type of date, such as *Slowly Changing Dimensions* (SCD) *Start Date*, have a calendar icon, while a check box icon is used to identify the Boolean data type for attributes such as *Finished Goods Flag*.

Toward the bottom of the list in the Detail View of the report model is an item named Fact Reseller Sales. Note that this item is not an attribute, but a role. As a role, this item represents the relationship defined in the DSV between the DimProduct and FactResellerSales tables. The Fact Reseller Sales role is indicated by a multilayer icon, which lets you know there is a one-to-many relationship between the two tables. One-to-one relationships are identified with a single-layer icon.

3. Click the Fact Reseller Sale entity in the Report Model Tree View, and then expand the *Unit Price* attribute.

Your screen looks like this:

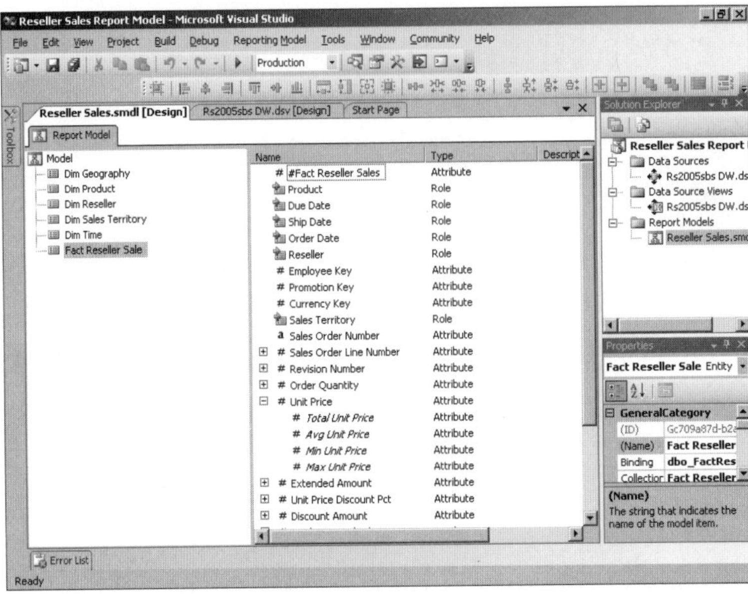

For each numeric attribute, the Report Model Wizard creates *Total*, *Avg*, *Min*, and *Max* numeric aggregations. These aggregate attributes provide an easy way for users to include aggregate functions in their reports.

4. Click the *Unit Price* attribute in the Detail View, and then, in the Properties window, find the *DefaultAggregateAttribute* property.

   The Properties window looks like this:

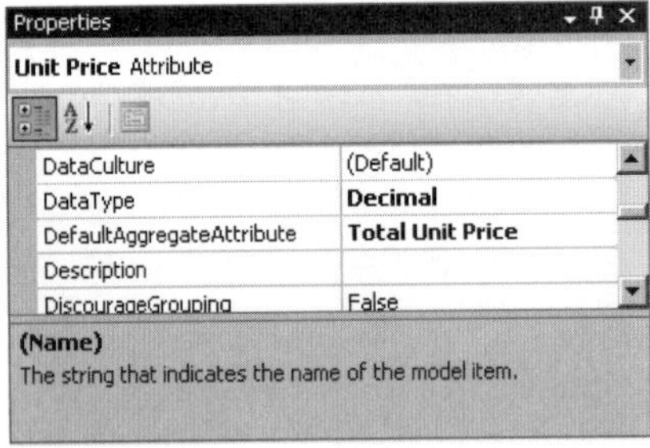

   This property determines which aggregate a Report Builder user will see first when browsing the attributes in the Fact Reseller Sale entity. In this case, Report Builder users can expand Total Unit Sales to see the associated aggregate attributes: *Avg Unit Sales*, *Min Unit Sales*, *Max Unit Sales*, and *Unit Sales*.

5. Click the Dim Time entity in the Tree View, and then expand the *Full Date Alternate Key* attribute.

Your screen looks like this:

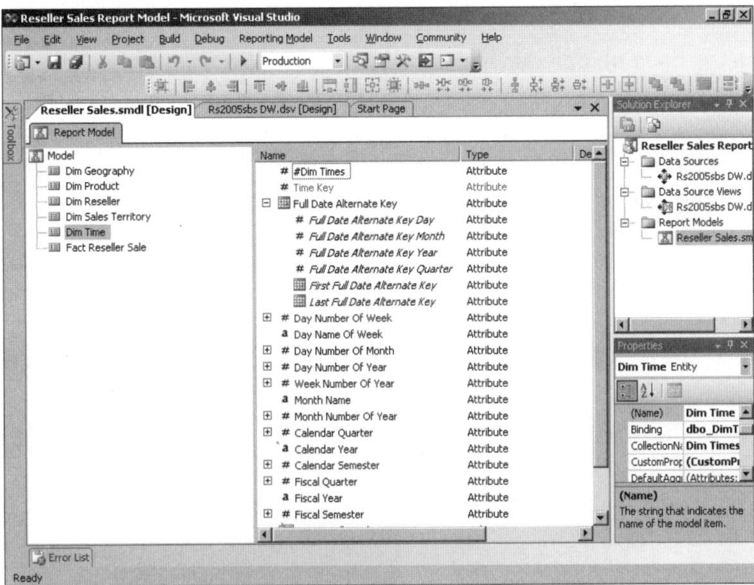

For date attributes such as this, the Report Model Wizard creates year, quarter, month, and day variations, as well as a first and last aggregation. Report Builder users can choose to use any one of these attributes in a report.

The *Full Date Alternate Key* attribute represents a date value, but this would not be obvious to a user who wants to include a date in a report. In this case, you should rename the attribute so it is clearer to users what the attribute represents. You'll perform this task later in this chapter.

Modifying a Report Model

You can use the Model Designer in Visual Studio to edit a report model that is based on a SQL Server data source, whether you use the Model Designer or SQL Server Management Studio to generate the report model. You will likely want to rearrange objects to simplify navigation, modify object properties to change default behavior, and add new objects to extend the range of information that users can include in reports. You should plan to go through several cycles of fine-tuning your report model as users get more experience working with Report Builder and are able to provide more specific feedback about desired report model improvements.

Before releasing a report model to production, you should review the report model and consider whether any structural changes are required. Most often, you'll want to change object names to reflect the way users think about the business. You should also review object properties that affect formatting, sorting, and other aspects of data presentation, and make changes to these properties so that users can focus on creating and sharing information rather than improving the appearance of reports.

In addition to changing objects themselves, you might need to rearrange objects to make it easier for users to find and use the report model objects to create reports using Report Builder. One way to organize objects is to create folders to group similar objects together, while alternatively, you can use perspectives to narrow the scope of available objects for different groups of users. Another way to improve the report model's structure is to change the sequence of objects by placing frequently used objects at the top of a list.

Restructuring a model by adding new objects is yet another option. Over time, your DSV might need to be updated to reflect new columns in the underlying data source. You can then update the report model by adding source fields that correspond to these new columns. You might also discover you need to add expressions to the report model to have a central location for commonly used calculations so users don't need to continually re-create them in each ad hoc report.

Changing Model Objects

While generating a report model automatically from a DSV saves you a lot of time by relieving you from building each object manually, it's unlikely that the generated report model is the best possible model for your users. For example, database naming conventions usually have meaning for database administrators and application developers, but often these naming conventions don't correspond to business terms familiar to users. One of the first tasks to undertake after generating a report model is to assign objects more suitable names wherever necessary.

Additionally, you should change object properties so users can produce nicely formatted reports with minimal effort. Even though users can apply the same changes using Report Builder features, they will appreciate having a model that defines behaviors like appearance, sort direction, and alignment so they won't have to repeatedly make these changes in each report they build. You should also review each attribute for appropriateness and delete those users won't need to reduce clutter in the report model.

In this procedure, you'll change the name of entities, attributes, and roles.

Rename report model objects

1. Right-click Fact Reseller Sale, click Rename, and then type **Reseller Sales**.
2. Click Dim Geography in the Tree View. In the Properties window, change the *(Name)* property to **Geography**.

   You can change the name of the object either by changing its *(Name)* property value in the Properties window or by renaming it directly in the designer. The result is exactly the same.

3. Click #Dim Geographies in the List view, and then change its *(Name)* property to **Count Geographies**.
4. Click Dim Resellers, and then change its *(Name)* property to **Resellers**.
5. Repeat the previous three steps for each of the other entities by removing Dim from the entity name and renaming the count attribute to replace #Dim with **Count** and renaming roles to remove the word Dim or Fact from the autogenerated name.
6. Click Product in the Tree View, and then rename Fact Reseller Sales as **Reseller Sales**.
7. Click Time in the Tree View, click Full Date Alternate Date Key and change its *(Name)* property to **Date**. In addition, rename the three roles to remove the word Fact from the name: **Reseller Sales**, **Reseller Sales (Due Date)**, **Reseller Sales (Ship Date)**.

   Your screen looks like this:

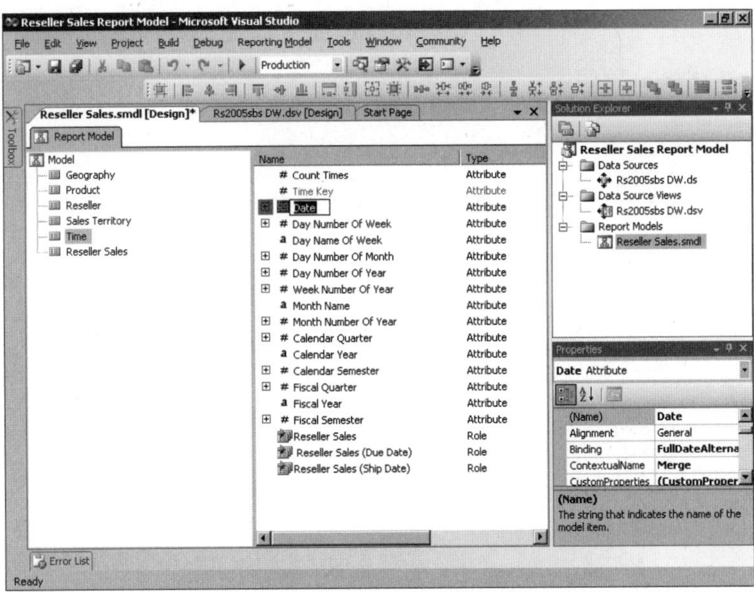

In this procedure, you'll change the *Format* property for selected attributes.

Format numeric values

1. Click the Reseller Sales entity in the Tree View.
2. In the Detail View, click Sales Amount, find the *Format* property in the Properties window, and then type **C2**.

   This property value will format the data as currency with two decimal places. You use the same Visual Basic .NET formatting strings for report models that you use in the Report Designer, as you learned in Chapter 4, "Developing Basic Reports."

> **Tip** Even though you can make formatting changes in Report Builder, such changes must be repeated for each report. To maintain the same formatting for attributes across all reports and to simplify the process of building a report, it is recommended to set the desired formatting for attributes in the report model.

3. Expand Sales Amount, and then repeat the previous step for the aggregate attributes of Sales Amount: *Total Sales Amount*, *Avg Sales Amount*, *Min Sales Amount*, and *Max Sales Amount*.

4. Change the *Format* property for Order Quantity and its four numeric aggregations to **N0**.

   This property value will format the data as numeric with no decimal places.

In this procedure, you'll modify the *SortDirection* property for selected attributes.

Change sort direction

1. In the Tree View, click the Time entity.

   Currently, the *Calendar Year* and *Fiscal Year* attributes are sorted in ascending order, while the *Calendar Quarter* and *Fiscal Quarter* attributes are sorted in descending order. You'll change these attributes' properties so Report Builder users see the most recent year first (descending) and see quarters listed in ascending order.

2. Click the *Calendar Year* attribute, and, in the Properties window, change the *SortDirection* property to Descending.

3. Repeat the previous step for the attribute *Fiscal Year*.

4. Click the *Calendar Quarter* attribute, and in the Properties window, change the *SortDirection* property to Ascending.

5. Repeat the previous step for the attribute *Fiscal Quarter*.

In this procedure, you'll change the *Alignment* property of selected attributes.

Change alignment

1. Click the Reseller Sales entity in the Tree View, and then click the *Order Quantity* attribute.

2. In the Properties window, locate the *Alignment* property, and then select Right in the property value's drop-down list.

3. Repeat the previous step for each of the aggregate attributes of Order Quantity and for the *Sales Amount* attribute, as well as each of its aggregation attributes.

In this procedure, you'll delete selected attributes.

Delete objects

1. Click the Product entity, right-click the *German Description* attribute, click Delete, and then click OK to confirm deletion.

   If a table column won't be used in any report model contained in the same project, it can be removed from the DSV. If it will be used in one or more report models, but not all report models, it can be removed from a specific report model. Later in this chapter, you'll learn how to selectively include attributes in a simplified view of a report model by using a perspective as an alternative to deleting attributes.

2. Repeat the previous step to remove each of the non-English product descriptions: Chinese Description, Arabic Description, and Thai Description.

3. Click the Time entity, right-click the *Count Times* attribute, click Delete, and then click OK.

   When working on a model created by the Report Model Wizard, you'll want to carefully review all attributes that were created and prune the model by deleting any unwanted attributes. There are many more attributes in this particular model that should be considered for deletion, but since this model won't be used for production, you don't need to be as thorough as you should be with your own models.

Organizing Model Objects

In addition to changing model objects, you can improve a report model by changing the arrangement of objects within the report model. You can use folders to group related entities or attributes together so users can find them more easily. Regardless of whether you decide to use folders, you can rearrange objects in the Tree View or the Detail View of the Model Designer as another method for organizing related items. For example, you can change the order of attributes to show the most frequently used attributes first or to arrange attributes in a sequence that is familiar to users so they can navigate the report model efficiently when using Report Builder.

Once you've organized objects by using folders and by changing the sequence of objects, you might want to create limited views of objects by adding perspectives to the data model. A *perspective* is simply a subset of the entities and attributes available in a model. This feature is handy when you want to build one model, but different groups of users require only some of the objects from the model. Each perspective appears as a separate model to users of Report Builder.

In this procedure, you'll add a folder to the report model and move entities into the folder.

Place objects in a folder

1. Right-click Model in the Tree View, point to New, and then click Folder.
2. In the Tree view, rename NewFolder as **Geographies**.

   Your screen looks like this:

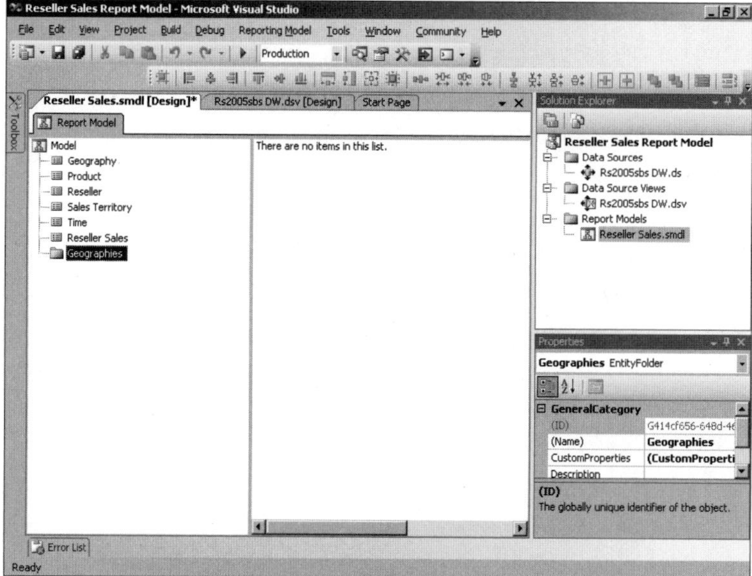

3. Click the Geography entity and drag it into the Geographies folder.
4. Repeat the previous step to move the Sales Territory entity into the Geographies folder.

In this procedure, you'll change the sequence of attributes within the Geography entity.

Rearrange objects

1. Open the Geographies folder, click the Geography entity, right-click the *Country Region Name* attribute, and then click Move Up. Repeat until *Country Region Name* is listed below the *Geography Key* attribute.
2. Repeat the previous step to move *State Province Name* below *Country Region Name*.

Your screen looks like this:

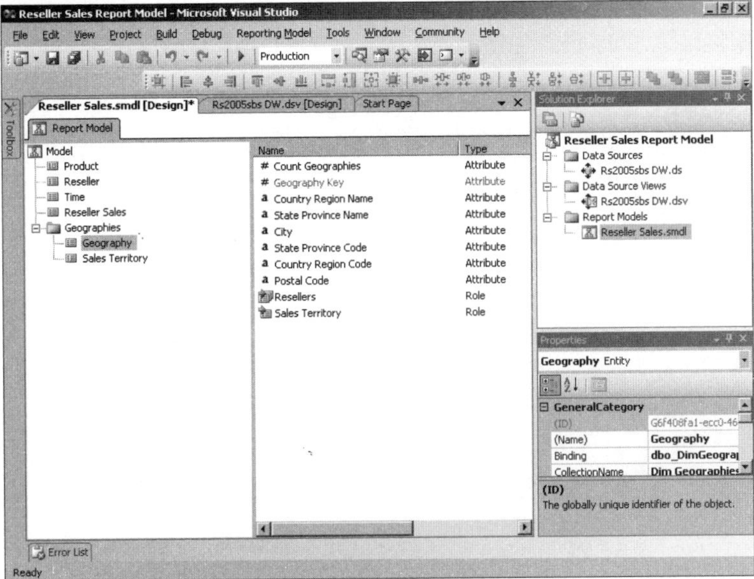

In this procedure, you'll add a perspective to the report model that includes only selected attributes from the Product, Time, and Sales Territory entities.

Create a perspective

1. Right-click Model in the Tree View, click New, and then click Perspective to display the Edit Perspective dialog box.
2. Expand Product to show its attributes, clear the Product check box to deselect all of the attributes, and then select the following attributes: *Color*, *Size*, *Weight*, *Model Name*, *Product Category Name*, and *Product Sub Category Name*. In addition, select the Reseller Sales role.

The Edit Perspective dialog box looks like this:

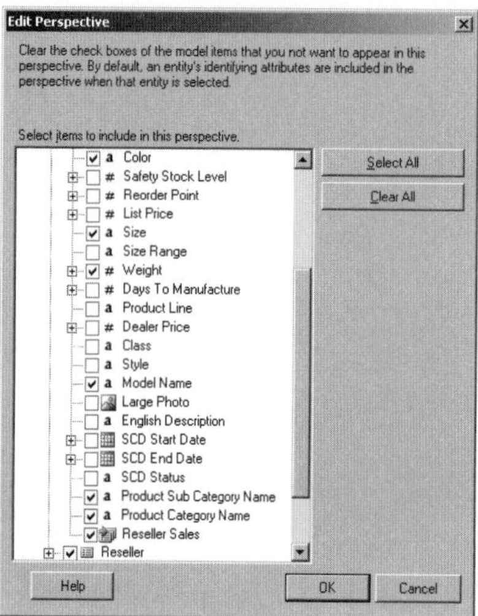

Notice that the *Product Name* and *Product Alternate Key* attributes are not shown in the listing. These were identified by the Report Model Wizard as identifying attributes for the Product entity, and therefore will be included in all perspectives automatically. You can see the identifying attributes for an entity by clicking the ellipsis button in the entity's *IdentifyingAttributes* property.

3. Scroll down to locate the Time entity, expand the Time entity, and deselect all attributes except *Month Name*, *Calendar Quarter*, *Calendar Year*, *Fiscal Quarter*, and *Fiscal Year*. Select the three associated Time roles.

   The Edit Perspective dialog box looks like this:

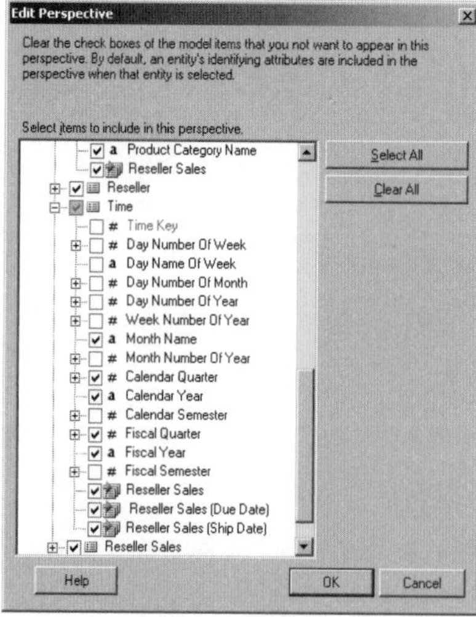

4. Expand the Geographies folder, expand the Sales Territory entity, and then deselect all attributes except *Sales Territory Country* and *Sales Territory Group*. Select the associated roles.

   The Edit Perspective dialog box looks like this:

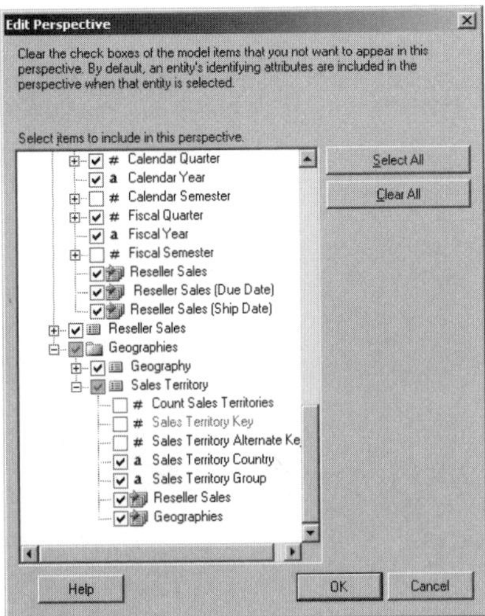

5. Click OK to close the Edit Perspective dialog box.
6. Right-click the perspective, click Rename, and type **Simple Reseller Sales**.

   Your screen looks like this:

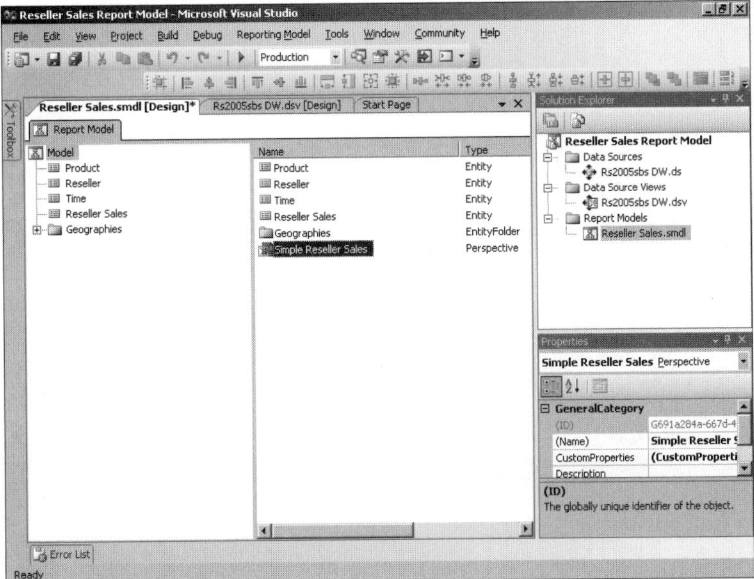

Adding Source Fields

Changing business requirements often drive changes to data structures in source systems used for reporting. Such changes could be made physically to the database tables or logically within the DSV. When these changes occur after you've created a report model, you can incorporate new columns by adding a *source field* to the report model. You can also regenerate the report model, but any objects you deleted will be added to the report model again.

In this procedure, you'll create a derived column in the DSV and add it to the report model as a source field.

Add a source field

1. In Solution Explorer, double-click Rs2005sbs DW.dsv to open the DSV, right-click the DimProduct table caption, and then click Edit Named Query.
2. In the SQL query window, type a comma after the *DimProductCategory.ProductCategory Name* field, and then type the following SQL expression:

```
ListPrice - StandardCost AS StandardMargin
```

3. Click OK to close the Edit Named Query dialog box.

   The Edit Named Query dialog box looks like this:

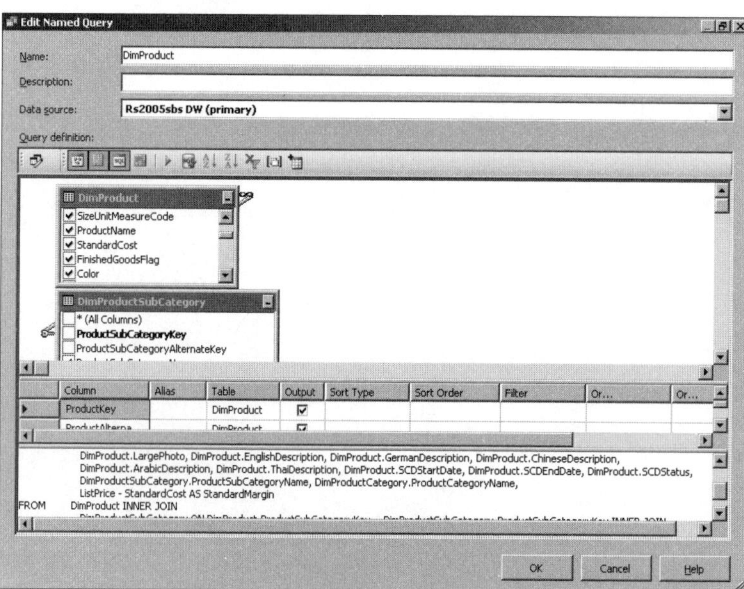

4. Save the DSV.
5. Switch to the Model Designer, right-click Product in the Tree View, click Autogenerate, and then click Yes to confirm.

6. Click Next on all pages of the Report Model Wizard to accept all defaults, click Run on the Completing the Wizard page, and then click Finish.

   Now that you added the StandardMargin column to the Named Query, the Report Model Wizard detects it. The *Standard Margin* attribute and aggregate attributes are added to the model–along with all the attributes that you deleted in an earlier procedure! In situations when you don't want to delete the undesired attributes once again, you can simply manually add the derived column as a source field.

7. Change the *Format* property for the *Standard Margin* attribute and its aggregation attributes to **C2**.

   After creating a new attribute, be sure to set the *Format* property. You should also evaluate whether the new attribute should be included in any of the report model's perspectives and add it where applicable.

8. Click Model in the Tree View, right-click the Simple Reseller Sales perspective, click Edit, expand the Product entity, and then select the check box for Standard Margin to add the attribute to the perspective.

   Your screen looks like this:

   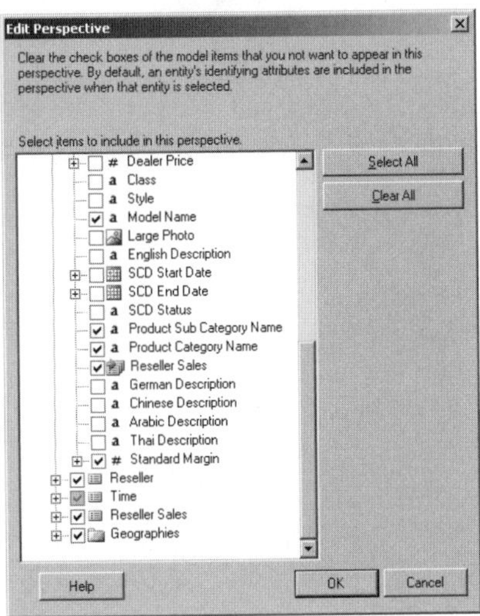

   Notice that selecting the attribute will automatically select its aggregation attributes as well. You can deselect any of the aggregation attributes if you prefer not to include them in the perspective.

9. Click OK to close the Edit Perspective dialog box.

Adding Expressions

You can use expressions to add calculations to a report model. To build an expression, you can use standard mathematical operations with attributes defined in the report model. As an example, you can compute an extended amount for a sales order line item by multiplying the quantity attribute by the amount attribute. The Model Designer also provides a variety of functions that you can use to create more complex expressions. Using these functions, you can create expressions that perform logical operations, manipulate strings or dates, convert data types, or aggregate numerical data.

In this procedure, you'll add an expression to the report model that sums the values of three attributes.

Add an arithmetic expression

1. Click Reseller Sales in the Tree View, right-click a blank area of the Detail View, point to New, and then click Expression.

   The Define Formula dialog box looks like this:

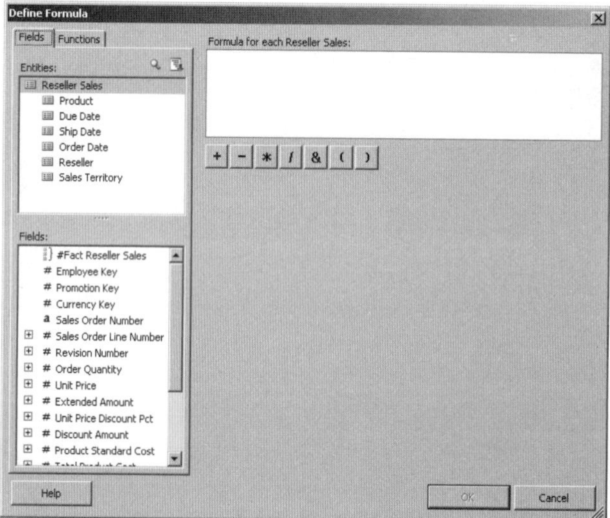

2. Click the Functions tab, and then expand the folders to review the available functions.

   Although you won't be using functions to build this expression, you should be familiar with the functions that are available. Functions are organized by type into separate folders.

3. Click the Fields tab. In the Fields list, double-click Sales Amount to add it to the Formula box, click the Plus Sign button, double-click Tax Amt, click the Plus Sign button again, and then double-click Freight.

The Define Formula dialog box looks like this:

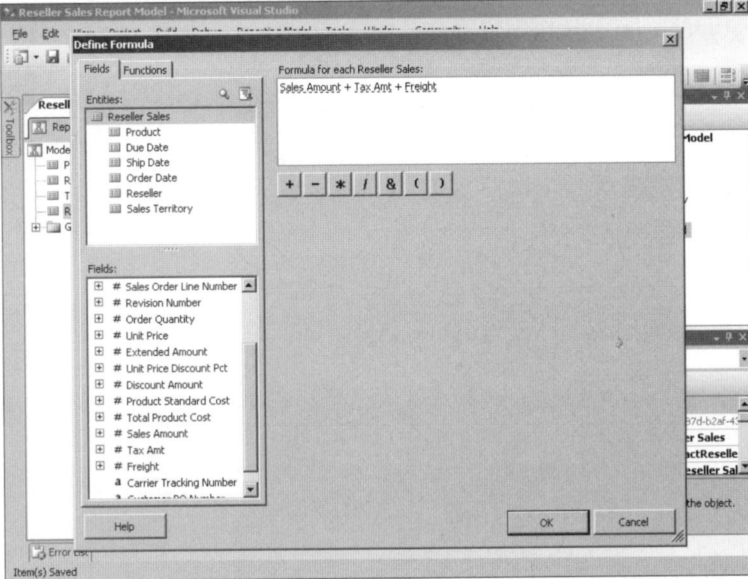

4. Click OK to close the Define Formula dialog box.
5. In the Detail View, click the *NewExpression* attribute, and then, in the Properties window, change its *(Name)* property to **Total Due**.
6. In the Properties window, change the *Nullable* property of the *Total Due* attribute to True.

   The *Nullable* property must be set to True for expressions even if the *Nullable* property of the component attributes is set to False.
7. Click Model in the Tree View, right-click the Simple Reseller Sales perspective, click Edit, expand the Reseller Sales entity, and then select the Total Due check box to add the attribute to the perspective, and then click OK to close the Edit Perspective dialog box.

Managing a Report Model

Because a report model is simply a definition file, it's pretty easy to manage. You make it available to users by publishing it to a report server and then control access by applying security. Once a report model is in production, you might need to update the report model to reflect changes in the underlying data source, in which case you edit the report model and republish the updated SMDL file to the report server. Remember, however, that you can only modify a report model when it's based on a SQL Server database. You need to regenerate a report model file when an Analysis Services cube is the data source.

After you create and refine a report model, you're ready to place the report model on the report server so it can be used by users to build ad hoc reports. You use the Deploy command in Visual Studio if you created the model using the Model Designer. A report model that you create from the management tools, either Report Manager or SQL Server Management Studio, is automatically deployed after it's generated. Once a report model has been deployed, you'll need to apply security using your preferred management tool to restrict access to the report model to authorized users.

Publishing a Report Model

A report model file is added to the report server just like a report file. That is, if you are working with a project in Visual Studio, you can use the Deploy command to add it to the server. When you use the Deploy command, not only is the report model made available on the server, but the data source is also added to the server if it doesn't already exist. You need to be careful when deploying a report model to avoid overwriting an existing model with the same name; otherwise, any reports that were based on the original report model will no longer function.

In this procedure, you'll deploy the Reseller Sales Report Model.

Deploy a report model project

1. Right-click the Reseller Sales Report Model project in Solution Explorer, and then click Deploy.
2. When the deploy process is completed, open Microsoft Internet Explorer, and then type the URL ***http://localhost/Reports*** to open the Report Manager.
3. Click the Models folder link.

Your screen looks like this:

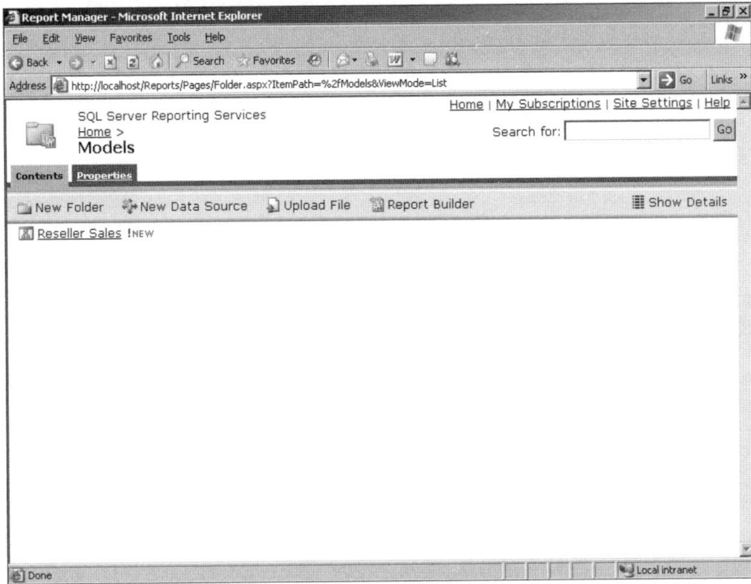

The Models folder was created during the deployment process based on the project properties, in the same way that a project folder for standard reports is created when they are deployed from Report Designer. It contains a link to Reseller Sales, which you can identify as a report model by its icon.

4. Click the Reseller Sales report model link.

   Your screen looks like this:

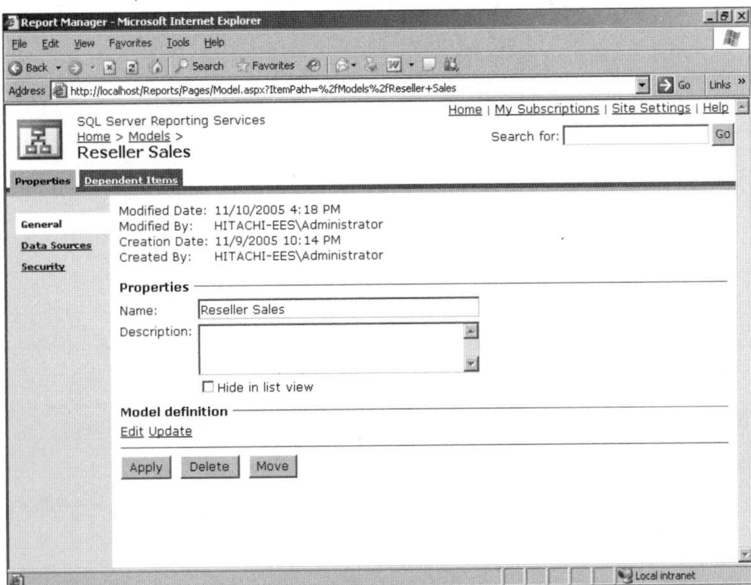

On the Properties tab, you can add a description to the report model, modify data sources, and set security. The Dependent Items tab shows all reports created with Report Builder from this report model, but because this report model was just deployed, there are currently no reports. In Chapter 15, you learn how to use this report model to create ad hoc reports.

5. Click Back in Internet Explorer to return the Contents tab of the Models folder.

   Notice the Report Builder button on the Report Manager toolbar. This button is used to launch the Report Builder application and is available from any folder in Report Manager as long as permissions have been granted. You'll learn how to set security for a Report Model in the next procedure.

Securing a Report Model

You apply security to a report model in exactly the same way that you secure other items deployed to a report server. When a report model is deployed to the server, it inherits the security of its parent folder. Unless you change the project properties, the default folder is Models, to which access is originally granted only to the Content Managers role. Users won't be able to build reports using a report model until you add a Browser role to the item's security definition. Roles, folder security, and item security (which applies to the report model) is covered in much more detail in Chapter 10, "Managing Security." In this section, you learn only the basic steps required to grant access to a report model.

In this procedure, you'll grant Browser permissions to the Everyone group for the Reseller Sales report model.

Add a Browser role to a report model

1. Click the Reseller Sales report model link in the Models folder, and then click the Security link on the Properties page.

Your screen looks like this:

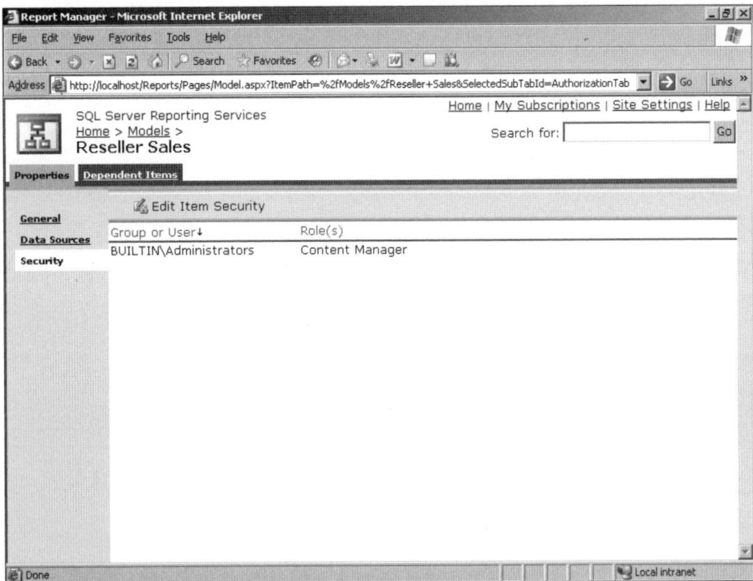

Both the Models folder and the Reseller Sales report model have inherited permissions from the Home folder for the group and user roles listed on the Security page. You can change these settings here.

Notice the only role available now is Content Manager for the Administrators group.

2. Click the Site Settings link (located in the top-right corner), click the Configure Item-Level Role Definitions link, and then click the link for the Content Manager role.

   Your screen looks like this:

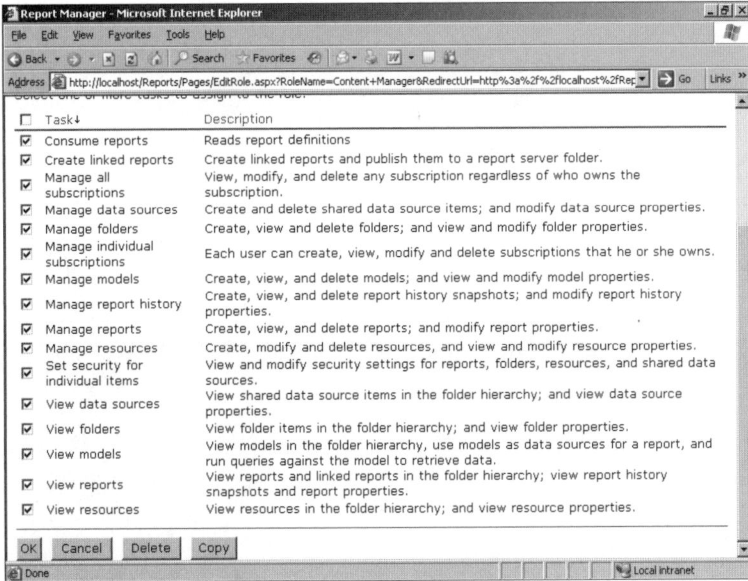

Notice that Manage Models is selected, which allows Content Managers to add, change, or delete models and their properties. Also, since the View Models task check box is selected, Content Managers are, by default, granted permission to use the models to build reports. Using the Item-Level Role Definitions, you can set default permissions by role. You'll learn more about using role-level security in Chapter 10.

3. Click the Home link at the top of the page, click the Models link, click the Reseller Sales report model link, click the Security link, click Edit Item Security, and then click OK in the message dialog box.
4. Click New Role Assignment, and then click the Browser link.

   Your screen looks like this:

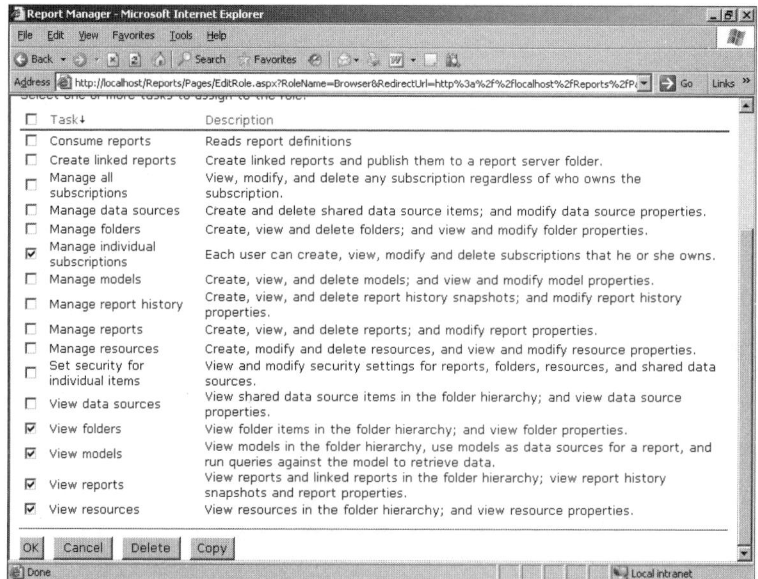

   Here you can see that Browsers have the ability to view and use models, but not to manage models. You can always create a separate role for browsers that should not have access to models. In this case, you're just confirming that the Browser role still defaults to allow use of report models.

5. Click OK.
6. Type a group name **Everyone**, select Browser check box, and then click OK.

   Now each user assigned to the Everyone group on the report server will be able to use the Reseller Sales report model. You learn how to build reports using this report model in Chapter 15.

Chapter 8 Quick Reference

To	Do this
Create a Report Model project	In Visual Studio, click New on the File menu, click Project, click Report Model Project, and then type a name and location for the project.
Add a data source to a report model project	In Solution Explorer, right-click the Data Sources folder, click Add New Data Source, click Next to go past the welcome page of the wizard, click the New button, type the server name, and then click the database name in the Select Or Enter A Database Name list box, click OK, and then click Finish.
Add a data source view to a report model project	In Solution Explorer, right-click the Data Source Views folder, click Add New Data Source View, click Next to pass the welcome page of the wizard, click the data source in the Relational Data Sources list, add tables or views to the Available Objects list, click Next, and then click Finish.
Replace a table with a named query in the DSV	In the Data Source View Designer, right-click the table caption, point to Replace Table, click With New Named Query, and then update the SQL statement with additional columns, joins, or filters in the WHERE clause as needed.
Create a report model using the Report Model Wizard	In Solution Explorer, right-click the Report Models folder, click Add New Report Model, click Next on the welcome page of the wizard, select a DSV, click Next, select rules, click Next, select an option to use current statistics or create new statistics, click Next, assign a name to the report model, and then click Finish.
Rename a report model object	Right-click the object, click Rename, and then type the new name. *or* Edit the *(Name)* property of the object in the Properties window.
Apply a formatting string to an attribute	In the Detail view, select the attribute, and then, in the Properties window, type a Visual Basic.NET formatting string in the *Format* property box.
Change the sort direction of data associated with an attribute	In the Detail view, select the attribute, and then, in the Properties window, click the applicable sort direction in the *SortDirection* property box.
Change the alignment of text data associated with an attribute	In the Detail view, select the attribute, and then, in the Properties window, click the applicable alignment option in the *Alignment* property box.
Delete an object	Right-click the object, and then click Delete.
Add a folder to a report model project and move objects into the new folder	In the Tree view, right-click the item that will become the parent item for the new folder, click New, click Finish, change the *(Name)* property of the new folder as appropriate, and then drag objects into the new folder.
Change the order of an entity's attributes	In the Detail view, right-click an attribute, and then click Move Up or Move Down to reposition the attribute.

To	Do this
Create a perspective	Right-click Model in Tree View, or right-click an entity, click New, and then click Perspective. Select or deselect attributes as needed to limit the perspective to specific attributes, and then assign a name to the perspective.
Add a new attribute to the report model	In the Data Source View Designer, replace the source table with the same table to include the updated version of the table, or right-click the table caption, click Edit Named Query, and then type a valid SQL expression with an alias to name the derived column. In Tree view, right-click the applicable entity for the new attribute, click New, click Source Field, click the *NewAttribute* attribute in the Detail view, click the appropriate value for the *Binding* property in the Properties window, and modify its properties as necessary.
Add an expression to an entity	Right-click the background of the Detail View, click New, and then click Expression. You can type an expression directly into the dialog box, or drag and drop objects and functions from the Fields and Functions tabs, respectively. Change the expression's *(Name)* property as desired and change the *Nullable* property to True.
Deploy a report model project using Visual Studio	Right-click the report model project in Solution Explorer, and then click Deploy.
Grant user permissions to a report model for ad hoc reporting at the item level	In Report Manager, click the link to the report model, click the Security link, click Edit Item Security, click OK in the message dialog box, click the New Role Assignment button, type a group or user name in the Group Or User Name box, select the Browser role check box, and then click OK.

Part III
Managing the Report Server

In this part:

By completing Part II, "Authoring Reports," you learned not only the basics of authoring reports, but also advanced techniques you can use to produce a wide variety of useful reports for your organization. The three chapters of Part III provide you with the skills to properly manage and secure the reports you create as well as to perform administrative tasks on the Report Server. These activities are all part of the managing stage of the reporting life cycle.

Chapter 9

Managing Content

After completing this chapter, you will be able to:

- Publish report definitions and other resources to the Report Server.
- Arrange content on the Report Server.
- Create a linked report.
- Use report properties to manage report content.
- Control report execution with report properties.

In this chapter, you'll learn how to manage the content on the Report Server. You start by publishing several reports. Then, you reorganize content on the Report Server by adding folders, moving content into the new folders, and creating linked reports. You'll also work with report properties to control both how reports interact with data sources to retrieve data and how reports are processed and rendered.

Your ability to publish and manage reports is determined by the permissions assigned to you. This chapter assumes that you are a local system administrator on the Report Server, which allows you to perform all the tasks described here. Specific information regarding how to use security permissions to limit a user's actions on the Report Server is covered in Chapter 10, "Managing Security."

Publishing Reports

When you publish a report, Reporting Services stores the report definition in a SQL Server database named ReportServer (as introduced in Chapter 2, "Installing Reporting Services"). You can also publish other items, such as images referenced by reports or other file types that need to be accessed by the reporting community. If you're a report author, you will generally use Microsoft Visual Studio to publish reports. If you're a report administrator, you can use either Report Manager or a small utility named Rs.exe to move previously created reports to the ReportServer database. You can even use a custom application for publishing reports by using the Reporting Services Web Services application programming interface (API), which is covered in greater detail in Chapter 17, "Programming Report Server Management."

As a report author, you can use standard deployment procedures in Visual Studio to publish content to the Report Server. Before you start, you must define deployment properties for each project that contains objects to be deployed. Then, you choose what you want to deploy and launch the process.

If you're a report administrator and not a report author, you might not have access to Visual Studio to deploy reports to the Report Server. One option you can use is to upload files individually to the Report Server using the Report Manager application. You can upload reports, data sources, and other resources that need to be available to the reporting community.

Another option for publishing reports is the *rs* utility (Rs.exe), which is a command-line utility you can use to run scripts that manage the Report Server. The *rs* utility uses a script file to execute commands on the Report Server. You'll learn more about other ways to use this utility in Chapter 17. A script to publish reports to the server comes as a sample with Reporting Services. To publish reports with this utility, you need to have a script that provides the details regarding the reports to be published. Then, you execute the *rs* utility, passing any arguments used to modify the behavior of the script at run time.

Defining Deployment Properties by Project

You cannot deploy content until you update a project's deployment properties with a target Report Server for each project that has content to be deployed. The *TargetServerURL* property must contain a valid URL, which is not validated until you try to deploy. When you use the Report Wizard to create a report, you must supply a URL for the Report Server before you can complete the wizard, but when you start authoring with a blank report, you must add a value to the *TargetServerURL* property of the report's project.

You should also review the other project deployment properties to ensure you get the results that you want when content deploys. By default, the target folder, which is defined by the *TargetReportFolder* property, will be the same as the project name. This folder will be created, if it does not exist, as a path on the root node of the Report Server, which is the Home page you view using Report Manager. For example, for the My Adventure Works project, a corresponding default folder will be added to the Home page of the Report Manager. You can also create nested folders by adding a relative path folder structure, such as Adventure Works/My Adventure Works, to create a folder called My Adventure Works that is contained within the Adventure Works folder on the Home page.

Another project deployment property is *OverwriteDataSources*. This controls whether shared data sources in the project will be published to the server if the data souce file already exists. The default value of False causes a shared data source to be written to the server only if the data source doesn't already exist. The *OverwriteDataSources* property is discussed in the context of managing data sources later in this chapter. Data sources can be maintained in a separate folder from reports, which by default is specified by the *TargetDataSourceFolder* property with a value of Data Sources.

In this procedure, you'll set the deployment properties for the My Adventure Works project.

Set project deployment properties

1. Start SQL Server Business Intelligence Development Studio and open the solution My Adventure Works that you saved in the C:\Documents and Settings\<username>\My Documents\Microsoft Press\rs2005sbs\Workspace\My Adventure Works folder.

> **Note** If you skipped Chapter 7, "Building Advanced Reports," open the solution My Adventure Works in the C:\Documents and Settings\<username>\My Documents \Microsoft Press\rs2005sbs\Answers\chap07\My Adventure Works folder.

2. In Solution Explorer, right-click the My Adventure Works project, and then click Properties.
3. In the My Adventure Works Property Pages dialog box, type ***http://localhost /ReportServer*** as the *TargetServerURL* so the dialog box looks like this:

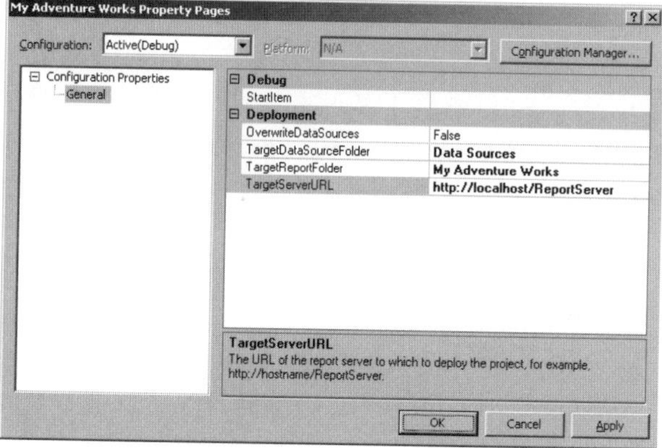

> **Important** You must supply a valid URL for the *TargetServerURL* before a report can deploy because no default URL is supplied automatically for you. If you have multiple projects contained in a single solution, you must enter this URL in each project's properties individually. The URL must be the virtual directory of the Report Server, which is *http://localhost/ReportServer* if you used the default installation of Reporting Services on your computer.

Deploying Reports

You can choose to deploy a single object, such as a report or a shared data source, in a project. You can also decide to deploy an entire project or just some objects in a particular project.

In this procedure, you'll deploy the My Adventure Works project.

Deploy a solution

1. On the Build menu, click Deploy My Adventure Works. Alternatively, you can right-click the project in Solution Explorer, and then click Deploy.

> **Tip** For a situation in which you've already deployed a project to which you later add a report, you can deploy the report individually without deploying the entire solution again. Just right-click the report in Solution Explorer, and then click Deploy. You can also use this procedure to deploy a data source.

2. Review the results of the deployment in the Output window, which should look like this:

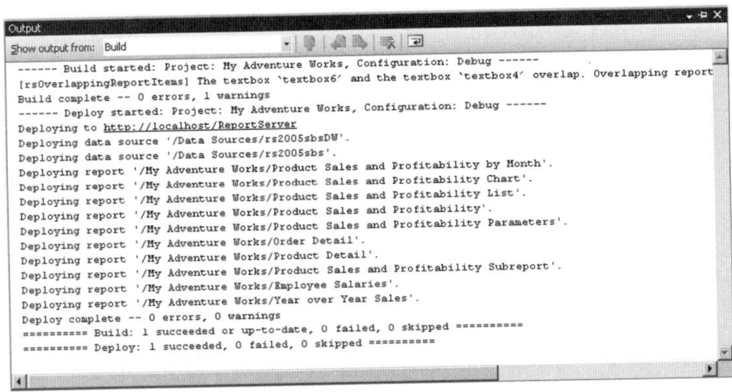
Output
Show output from: Build
------ Build started: Project: My Adventure Works, Configuration: Debug ------
[rsOverlappingReportItems] The textbox 'textbox6' and the textbox 'textbox4' overlap. Overlapping report
Build complete -- 0 errors, 1 warnings
------ Deploy started: Project: My Adventure Works, Configuration: Debug ------
Deploying to http://localhost/ReportServer
Deploying data source '/Data Sources/rs2005sbsDW'.
Deploying data source '/Data Sources/rs2005sbs'.
Deploying report '/My Adventure Works/Product Sales and Profitability by Month'.
Deploying report '/My Adventure Works/Product Sales and Profitability Chart'.
Deploying report '/My Adventure Works/Product Sales and Profitability List'.
Deploying report '/My Adventure Works/Product Sales and Profitability'.
Deploying report '/My Adventure Works/Product Sales and Profitability Parameters'.
Deploying report '/My Adventure Works/Order Detail'.
Deploying report '/My Adventure Works/Product Detail'.
Deploying report '/My Adventure Works/Product Sales and Profitability Subreport'.
Deploying report '/My Adventure Works/Employee Salaries'.
Deploying report '/My Adventure Works/Year over Year Sales'.
Deploy complete -- 0 errors, 0 warnings
========== Build: 1 succeeded or up-to-date, 0 failed, 0 skipped ==========
========== Deploy: 1 succeeded, 0 failed, 0 skipped ==========

If the deployment fails, you need to review all errors given in the Error List window and take the appropriate action to resolve the problems.

3. To confirm the successful deployment of your solution, start Report Manager by navigating to *http://localhost/Reports* in Internet Explorer.

The Home page of the Report Manager looks like this:

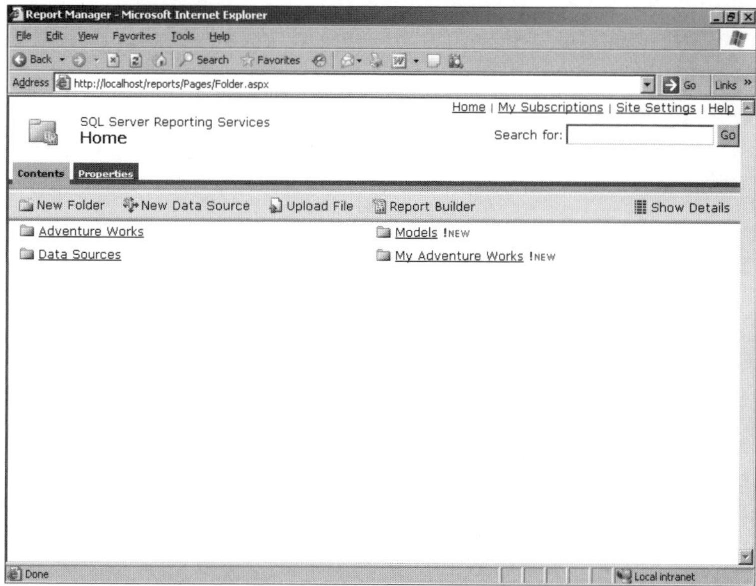

The My Adventure Works folder corresponds to the single project in the solution you just deployed. If you have deployed other projects, you'll see additional folders on this page. For example, if you completed Chapter 3, "Building Your First Report," you will see the Adventure Works folder and the Data Sources folder.

4. Click the My Adventure Works folder link to see its contents in the list view, which looks like this:

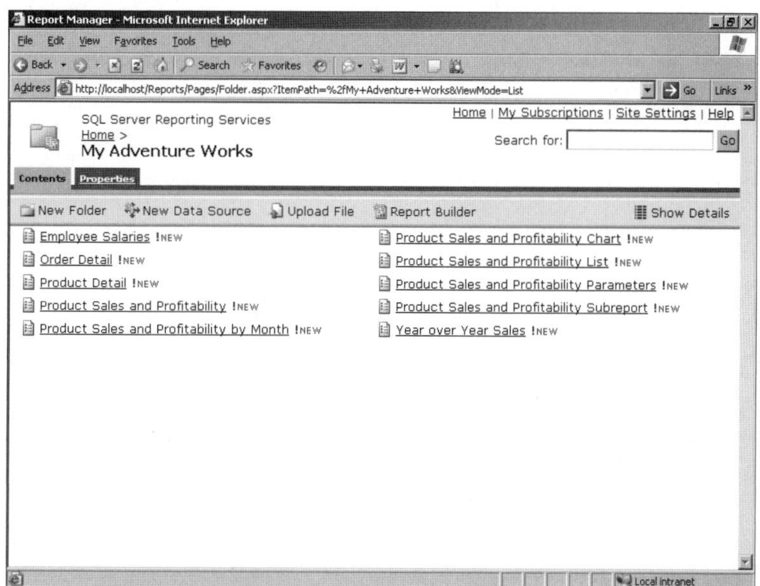

Report Manager queries the ReportServer database to retrieve a list of the resources, such as reports and shared data sources, that are associated with the current folder, My Adventure Works. Notice that the list view displays the folder contents as two columns, with items in alphabetical order.

5. Click the Product Sales and Profitability report link to view the report, which looks like this:

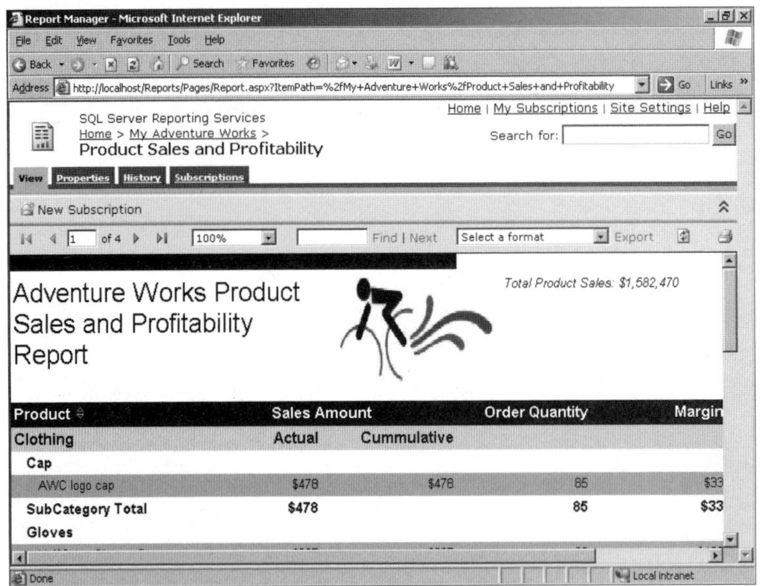

Report Manager passes the request for the report to the Report Server, which, in turn, manages the processes that produce a report you can now view in your browser.

Republishing Reports

Sometimes a report needs to be modified, perhaps as a result of issues discovered during testing or because of the development of new business requirements. After making changes to the report, you can redeploy the modified report to the Report Server. When you redeploy a report, the original report definition stored in the ReportServer database is replaced with the new report definition.

Report properties (such as execution, parameters, history, security, and subscription properties) that you assign by using Report Manager will continue to apply after you redeploy a report. Redeployment updates only the report definition.

Uploading Reports

You can use the Upload File feature in Report Manager to navigate to a file on your computer or on a network file share that you want to upload to the Report Server. Like deploying reports with Visual Studio, the upload process actually stores the file in the ReportServer database. You can upload only one file at a time using this method.

In this procedure, you'll upload the definition of Product Sales YTD using Report Manager.

Upload a report file to the My Adventure Works folder

1. In Report Manager, click the My Adventure Works link in the top-left corner of the browser window.
2. Click Upload File on the Report Manager toolbar, and then click Browse to navigate to the C:\Documents and Settings\<username>\My Documents\Microsoft Press \rs2005sbs\chap09\ folder and open the file Product Sales YTD.rdl.

   Your screen looks like this:

   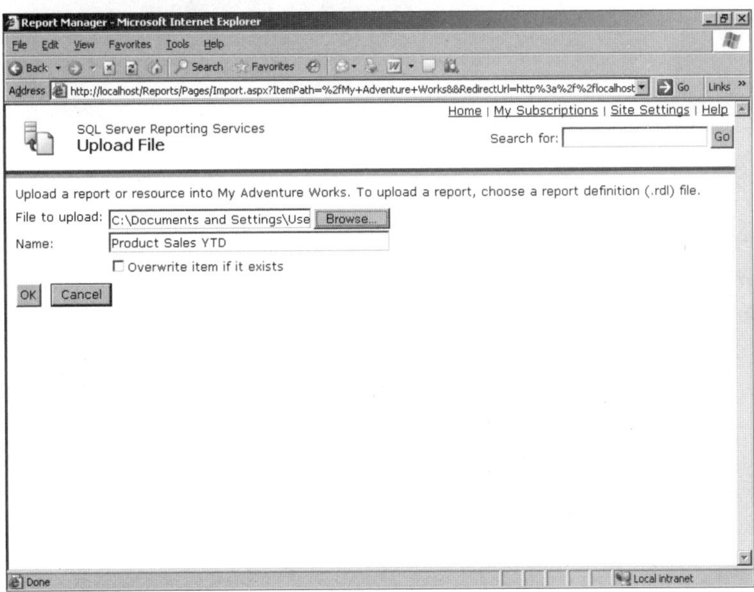

   If you prefer, you can type the path and filename in the File To Upload box and the name in the Name box.

   If the file already exists in the current folder, an error message will be displayed when you click OK, unless you select the Overwrite Item If It Exists check box. If this check box is already selected, the overwrite of the file is performed without any warning.

3. Click OK.

   Report Manager uploads the file and places it in the ReportServer database. The name of the report now displays in the Contents page of the My Adventure Works folder.

4. Click the Product Sales YTD report link to open the report, which looks like this:

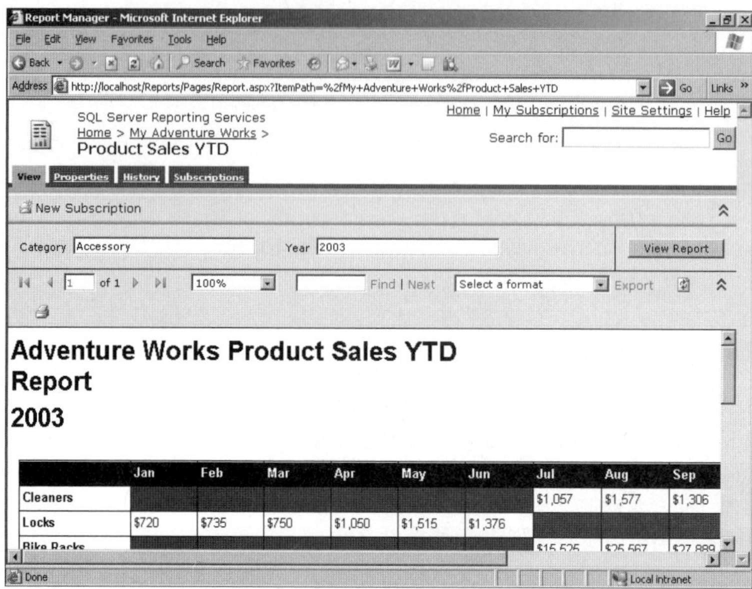

You should always test an uploaded report in Report Manager to confirm that the Report Server can connect properly to the data source, execute the report's query, and render the report.

> **Uploading Resources**
>
> You can also use Report Manager to upload additional items, known as resources, to the Report Server for storage in the ReportServer database. Resources are items such as images–for example, JPEG files–that might be referenced as a link in a report. However, you can also add resources that are not used in a report, such as Microsoft Word or Microsoft Excel files, or even text files. If a user opens a resource, Reporting Services does not process the resource, but instead downloads the resource for saving or for viewing, if the client computer has the requisite application. After a resource is uploaded, it can be moved to another folder just like a report. You'll learn more about moving reports and resources later in this chapter.

Creating a Script File

The *rs* utility requires an input file with an .rss file extension that is written in Microsoft Visual Basic .NET or Microsoft Visual C# .NET. Reporting Services ships with a sample Visual Basic .NET script file, PublishSampleReports.rss (located in the C:\Program Files\Microsoft SQL Server\90\Samples\Reporting Services\Script Samples folder, but you must first install the Microsoft SQL Server 2005 Samples from the Sample program group, which is located in the

Documentation and Tutorials program group of Microsoft SQL Server 2005), which you can adapt to your needs. The script file used in the following procedure is a simplified version of the official sample script.

Using the *rs* Utility

When you want to use the *rs* utility to publish reports, you need to provide at least two arguments, the name of the script file and the URL for the Report Server, using this syntax: `rs -i inputfile -s ReportServerURL`. The current Windows credentials are used for authentication to the Report Server, unless you use arguments to pass a user name and password. To view a description of all available arguments, use the following syntax: `rs -?`. You'll learn more about the *rs* utility in Chapter 17.

In this procedure, you'll execute the *rs* utility using the publishReports.rss script file as an input file.

Execute the *rs* utility

1. On the Start menu, click Run, type **cmd**, and then click OK to open a Command Prompt window.
2. Type **cd C:\Documents and Settings\<username>\My Documents\Microsoft Press\rs2005sbs\chap09** at the command prompt to navigate to the folder that contains the script file.
3. Type **rs -?** and press Enter to view the online help for this utility.
4. Run the *rs* utility by typing the following: **rs –i PublishReports.rss –s http://localhost/ReportServer**. Then press Enter.

   Your screen now looks like this:

```
C:\WINDOWS\system32\cmd.exe
C:\Documents and Settings\User\My Documents\Microsoft Press\rs2005sbs\chap09>rs
-?
Microsoft (R) Reporting Services RS
Version 9.00.1399.00 x86
Executes script file contents against the specified Report Server.
RS -i inputfile -s serverURL [-u username] [-p password]
   [-l timeout] [-b] [-e endpoint] [-v var=value] [-t]

        -i  inputfile   Script file to execute
        -s  serverURL   URL (including server and vroot) to execute
                        script against.
        -u  username    User name used to log in to the server.
        -p  password    Password used to log in to the server.
        -e  endpoint    Web service endpoint to use with the script.
                        Options are:
                        Exec2005 - The ReportExecution2005 endpoint
                        Mgmt2005 - The ReportService2005 endpoint
                        Mgmt2000 - (Deprecated) The ReportService endpoint
        -l  timeout     Number of seconds before the connection to the
                        server times out. Default is 60 seconds and 0 is
                        infinite time out.
        -b              Run as a batch and rollback if commands fail
        -v  var=value   Variables and values to pass to the script
        -t  trace       Include trace information in error message

C:\Documents and Settings\User\My Documents\Microsoft Press\rs2005sbs\chap09>rs
-i PublishReports.rss -s http://localhost/ReportServer
Parent folder created: Adventure Works Samples
Report: Actual Vs Quota published successfully with no warnings
Report: Employee Product Sales published successfully with no warnings
Report: Product Catalog published successfully with no warnings
The command completed successfully

C:\Documents and Settings\User\My Documents\Microsoft Press\rs2005sbs\chap09>
```

5. To confirm that the reports were successfully published, open the Home page of Report Manager in Internet Explorer. If the Home page is already open, click Refresh on the Internet Explorer toolbar to update the page.

6. Click the Adventure Works Samples folder link.

   There should be three reports in this folder: Actual Vs Quota, Employee Product Sales, and Product Catalog.

7. Click each report link to confirm the reports execute successfully.

Organizing Content

You are not limited to using the folders created as part of the publishing process. In addition, you can add more folders to create a hierarchical organization, much like the hierarchy you use in a file system on your computer. You can move reports and resources from their original folder to a new folder quite easily. As part of the content management process, you can also create linked reports to create custom versions of a report without physically reproducing the report definition.

Report Manager offers several features to help you organize and manage content on the Report Server. You can add, move, or delete folders to manage a logical grouping of items on the server. Once you've structured folders to your liking, you can move reports, resources, and shared data sources to folders other than the ones to which they were originally published. You can create linked reports to generate alternate versions of a report so you can use different parameter values or security settings for different groups of users. Finally, you can use folder properties and report general properties to modify names and descriptions to help users locate information more easily.

Working with Folders

Folders are an important tool for organizing reports and resources on the server. In addition, folders are used to apply security to groups of items, which you'll learn about in Chapter 10. The folders you create and access in Report Manager do not physically exist as folders in a file system, but are recognized by the Report Server as containers to logically organize content on the server.

To create a folder, you must navigate to the folder that will become the parent folder or navigate to the Home page if the folder will not be nested. You can move a folder after it has been created to nest it within another folder. If you want to rename a folder, add a description, or hide the folder name from the list view in Report Manager, you can make the necessary changes on the folder's Properties page. If you delete a folder, all of its contents will also be deleted, so be careful to check the contents of a folder beforehand.

Some folders are reserved and cannot be moved, renamed, or deleted. These reserved folders are Home, My Reports, and Users. The latter two folders exist only if you enable My Reports on the Report Server, which is discussed later in this chapter.

In this procedure, you'll add a folder to contain shared data sources.

Add a folder

1. In Report Manager, click the Home link, and then click New Folder on the Report Manager toolbar.
2. Replace the default name with **Adventure Works Data Sources** so your screen looks like this:

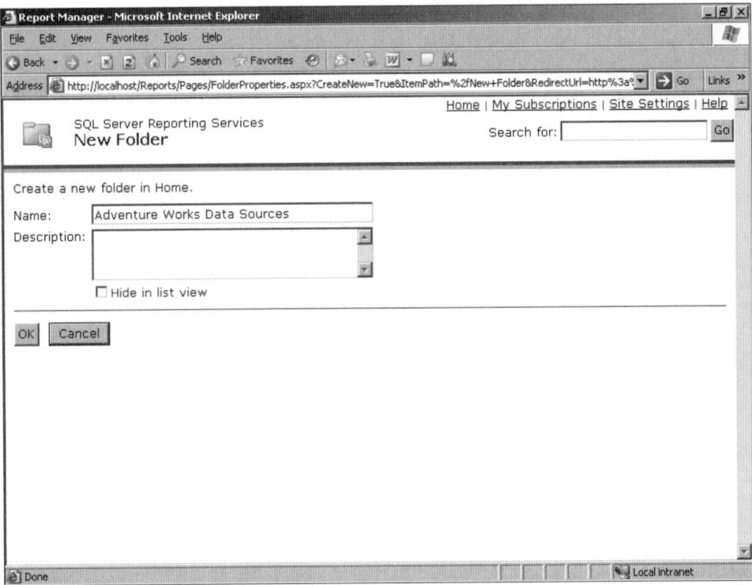

   Notice the option to hide the folder from the list view.

3. Click OK.

   The Home page of Report Manager now includes another folder, Adventure Works Data Sources. You're ready to move content into the new folder.

> ## Using My Reports
>
> My Reports is an optional feature of Report Manager and is disabled by default. It provides a personal workspace for each user to use for such things as private, personalized reports or perhaps reports that are being tested before deployment to the user community. Users cannot share the content of their folders with other users within the Report Manager interface. (However, a user can export a report to another file format and share the exported content through e-mail or placement on a network file share.)
>
> To enable My Reports, click the Site Settings link, and then select the Enable My Reports... check box. You can use roles to modify what a user can do with My Reports. You'll learn all about roles in Chapter 10.

Moving Content

As a report administrator, you can move reports, linked reports, resources, folders, and shared data sources from one folder to another. If you move a report, all its properties will remain the same in its new location and its history will follow the report if it exists. Similarly, when you move a shared data source, its relationship to reports and subscriptions is maintained.

Reorganizing files and folders is particularly useful with data sources. You might refer to the same logical data source from several different projects. On the server, you can put one copy of the data source into a special folder and point to that one data source from all the reports and folders.

In this procedure, you'll move shared data sources from the Data Sources folder to the Adventure Works Data Sources folder.

Move shared data sources

1. On the Report Manager Home page, click the Data Sources folder link.
2. Click Show Details on the Report Manager toolbar to see the details view, which looks like this:

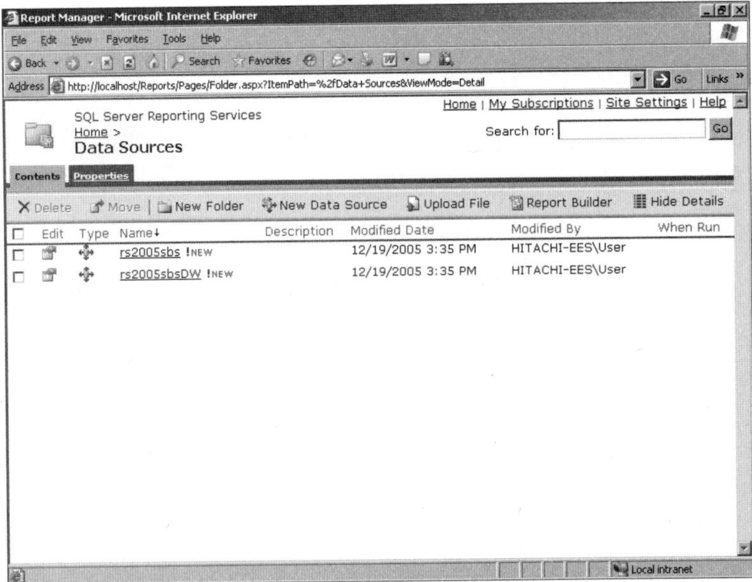

Report Manager now displays the contents of the folder as a single list with check boxes to the left of each item and the item details, such as modification date and author. Notice that the Move button is currently unavailable. You must first select one or more items in the folder to enable this button.

3. To select all data sources in this folder, select the check boxes for rs2005sbs and rs2005sbsDW, and then click Move on the Report Manager toolbar.

The folder hierarchy of the Report Server displays in the Move Multiple Items page. You can navigate this hierarchy to locate a target folder for the items selected from the previous page. Alternatively, you can enter the folder's path in the Location box.

4. Click the Adventure Works Data Sources folder, as shown here, and then click OK:

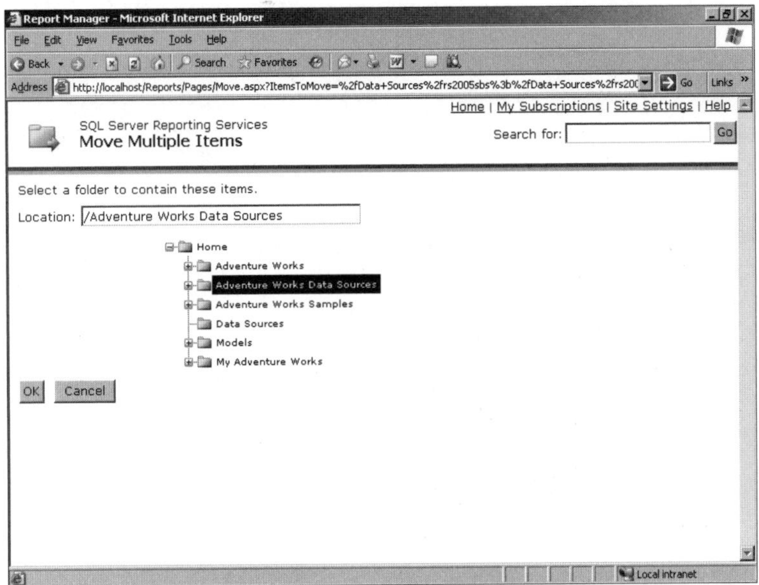

5. Click the Home link, and then click the Adventure Works Data Sources folder link to confirm that the data sources have been moved, as shown here:

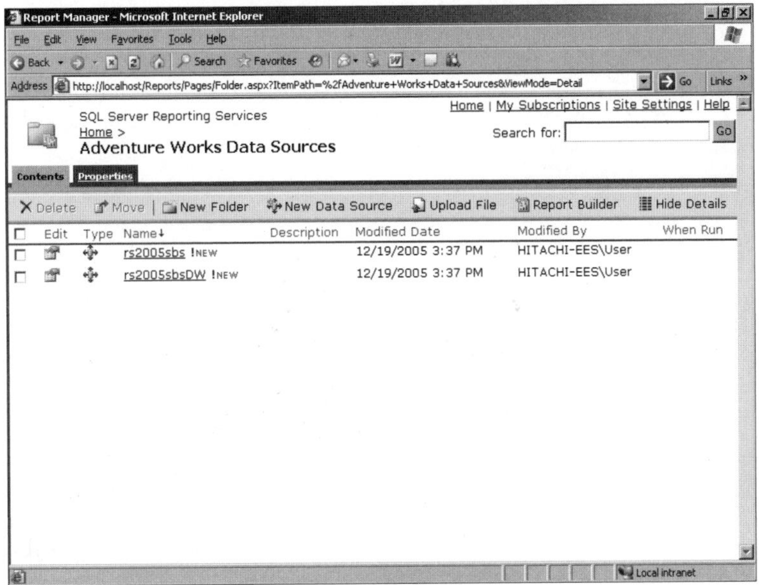

6. Click the rs2005sbsDW data source link, and then click the Dependent Items tab to see the list of associated reports, which looks like this:

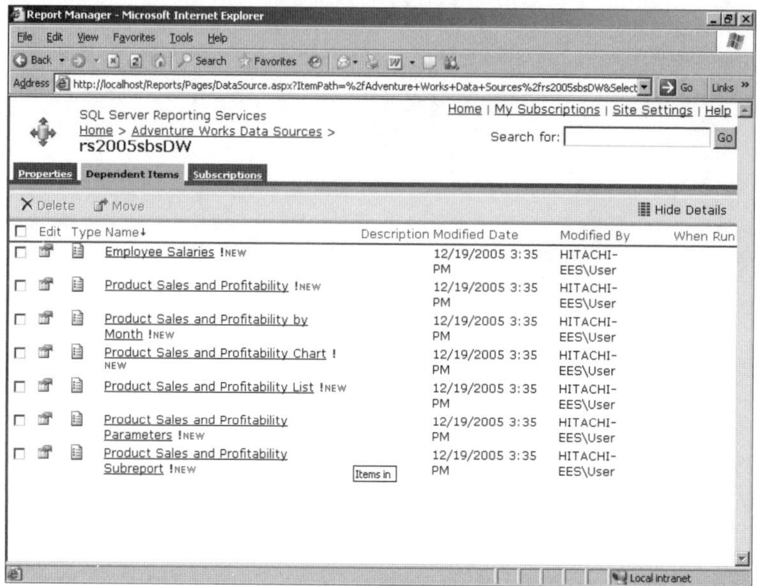

The reports that were associated with this data source during the authoring stage will continue to use the data source, even though it's been relocated to another folder.

Note When you upload a shared data source to the server and then move that data source to a new folder, Visual Studio considers the data source as nonexistent and uploads a new copy to the server during deployment, even if *OverwriteDataSources* is set to False. The data source is not used (because the report now points to the data source in the new folder), but it might be confusing to users. The simplest solution is to hide the new copy of the data source by using item-level security, which you'll learn about in Chapter 10. The other alternative is to delete the unused data source following each deployment using Visual Studio.

Linking Reports

Creating a *linked report* is an easy way to customize report output for users. You can use one report as a base from which to create many representations of report data without physically duplicating reports. A linked report uses the same report definition and data source property as its base report, but can have its own execution, parameter, subscription, and security properties. For example, you can create a linked report that uses the Product Sales and Profitability Parameter report as a base, and then assign a different default value for the *Category* report parameter. If you place the linked report in a separate folder, you can limit access to the report to those users who need to see data related to a particular category. Be careful with linked reports, however. If you delete the base report, any reports linked to it won't work anymore!

In this procedure, you'll create a linked report and store it in a new folder.

Add a linked report

1. Click the Home link in the Report Manager, and then click New Folder on the Report Manager toolbar.
2. Replace the default name with **Adventure Works Bikes**, and then click OK.
3. Click the My Adventure Works folder link, click the Product Sales and Profitability Parameters report link, and then click the Properties tab.

   You don't need to wait for the report to display before you click the tabbed pages of this report.
4. Click Create Linked Report.
5. Enter a name for the linked report: **Bike Sales and Profitability**.

   If you click OK now, the linked report will be added to the current folder, My Adventure Works. However, linked reports are often placed in separate folders to take advantage of the ability to manage permissions by folder.
6. Click Change Location, click Adventure Works Bikes in the folder hierarchy, and then click OK so your screen now looks like this:

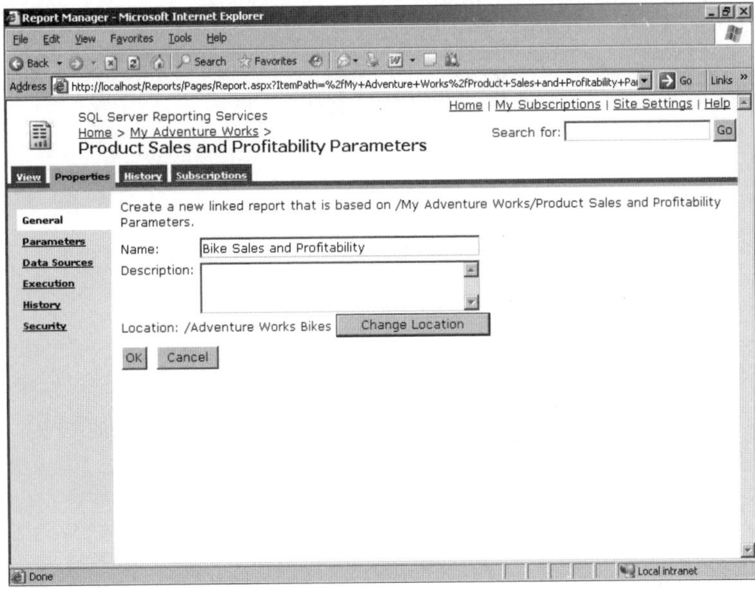

7. Click OK.

   The linked report now displays in the browser window. This linked report is not a physical copy of the base report, but rather a version rendered online that uses the same report definition and data source as the base report. You'll need to change the report's properties to display only the Bike category, which you'll learn how to do later in this chapter.

Working with General Properties

In addition to creating a linked report, you can use the General Properties page of a report to change its name or description. When you create a name, you cannot use special characters, but you have more flexibility in the report's description. Only users who have access to a report can view its description. You can also use the General Properties page of a report to move a report from one folder to another on the Report Server or to delete the report from the server. If you delete a report, any linked reports will be broken and all history, report-specific schedules, and subscriptions associated with the report will also be deleted.

The General Properties page of a report also allows you to access and update the report definition. The Edit link only allows you to extract the report definition for read-only purposes. Any edits you make to the extracted file do not change the report definition used by the Report Server. However, you can save the file to a network share, and then use the Update link to replace the server's report definition.

In this procedure, you'll add a description to the Bike Sales and Profitability report.

Change general properties

1. With the Bike Sales and Profitability report still open in Internet Explorer, click the Properties tab to view the report's general properties, which look like this:

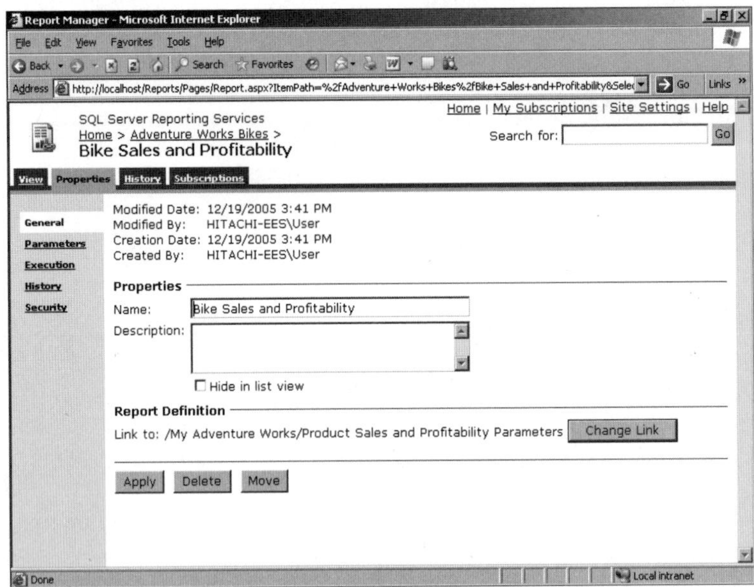

Notice that you can change the name of the report on this screen as well as add a description. This page also includes options that allow you to modify this report. They are as follows:

- **Change Link** allows you to associate the current report with a different report definition. You might need to do this if the original base report changes or is deleted. Only the report definition for the linked report changes; the linked report's properties remain unchanged.
- **Delete** allows you to delete the linked report from the current folder and any subscriptions, schedules, or history associated with the linked report. Deleting the linked report does not have an impact on the base report.
- **Move** allows you to move the linked report from the current folder to another location in the Report Server's folder hierarchy.

2. Type the following description: **Bike sales amount, order quantity, margin amount, and margin percentage by month and year. Margin percentage exceptions at 15% or below, customizable**.

> **Tip** A description should provide users with enough information to let them know what kind of data the report includes as well as apprise them of any unique interactivity features.

3. Click Apply.
4. Click the Adventure Works Bikes link at the top of the browser window to view the report description.
5. Click Hide Details on the Report Manager toolbar so your screen looks like this:

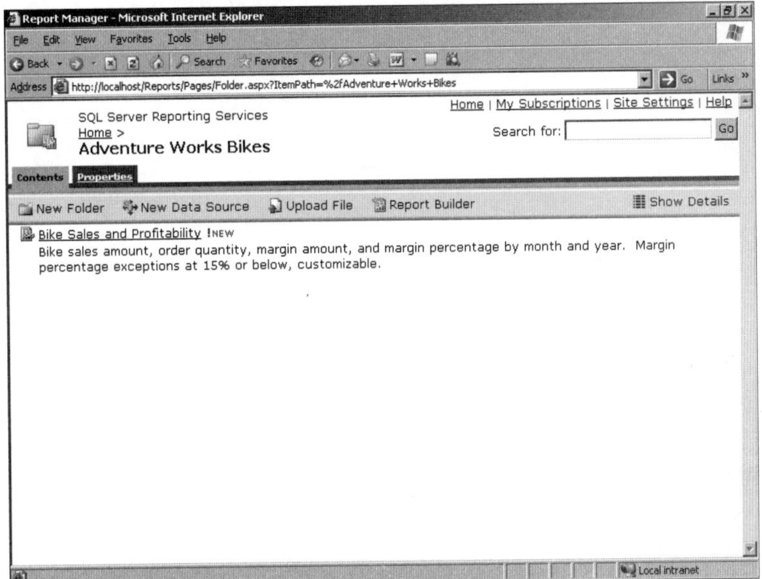

Using Properties to Manage Report Content

In addition to accessing a report's general properties as part of the management of the Report Server's content, you can use Report Manager to manage report properties that affect the content of reports. A data source is needed to connect to the database that is hosting the source data required for the report and to authenticate the connection so the report's query will execute. If the connection or authentication fails, data cannot be displayed in the report. You can override the data source associated with the report when the report was published by changing its data source properties.

Report content can also be affected by changing parameter values. You can override a default parameter value provided in the report definition with a new value using parameter properties. Although you can still permit the user to select a different value, you can also hide the parameter altogether to prevent a change.

Working with Data Sources

Often, you want to manage a report's data source on the Report Server independently of the data source in Visual Studio. For example, while developing a report, you might use a small sample database as the data source, but once the report is on the server, you want it to access the full production database. Likewise, in development, you might want to use integrated security for the data source, but in production, store the user name and password in the report. You can use Report Manager to update the data source and overwrite the report's data source properties that are stored in the ReportServer database. The *OverwriteDataSources* property for the project in Visual Studio controls whether redeploying a report will overwrite changes you make on the Report Server. By leaving *OverwriteDataSources* with the default value of False, you keep the development and production data sources decoupled, which is convenient in most situations.

Selecting a shared data source or creating a custom data source, which requires a data processing extension and a connection string, are pretty straightforward processes. However, you need to give some careful thought to the way that credentials are used to connect to the data source. Most of the time, storing the credentials securely with the report in the database is best. These are not the credentials used to access the report, but the credentials used by the report to access the source data. You most likely don't want to give report users even read access to the source database. In rare cases, you might want to use prompted credentials or Windows credentials, but these can be used only when the user accesses reports in real time. If your database does not require credentials to read the data, you can create a data source using no credentials, but this is an uncommon scenario, since it's good practice to require credentials on all databases.

If reports will be executed as an unattended process, such as for scheduled snapshots and subscriptions, you must use *stored credentials*, because the Report Server executes a scheduled report without a user context. Stored credentials are stored in reversible encryption in the ReportServer database and are not stored in the report definition. The same credentials will be used each time the report is processed for all users of a report that is configured to use stored credentials.

In this procedure, you'll modify the shared data source rs2005sbs to prompt the user for credentials.

Configure credentials supplied by the user

1. In Report Manager, click the Home link, click the Adventure Works Data Sources folder link, and then click the rs2005sbs shared data source link.
2. Below Connect Using, select the Credentials Supplied By The User Running The Report option so your screen looks like this:

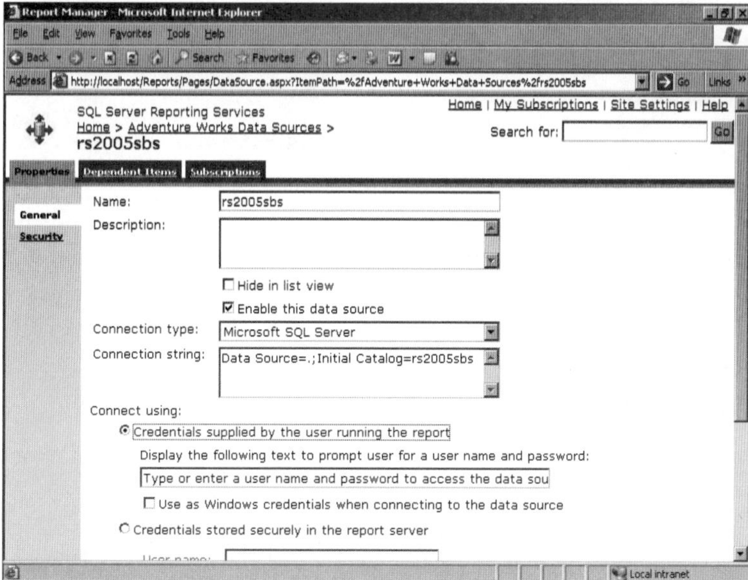

If the database to which the data source connects uses Windows authentication, you can select Use As Windows Credentials When Connecting To The Data Source, but for this example, you should skip this option.

> **Important** You should prompt the user for credentials or use integrated security only when users will be accessing a report in real time. These types of authentication require a user to be physically connected (and possibly to have responded to the authentication prompt) before the report's query can execute.

3. Click Apply at the bottom of the page.

   You'll test this data source later in this chapter when you execute a report on demand.

In this procedure, you'll create a custom data source that uses stored credentials for the Product Sales and Profitability Parameters report.

Configure stored credentials

1. In Report Manager, click the Home link, click the My Adventure Works folder link, and then click the Product Sales and Profitability Parameters report link.
2. Click the Properties tab, and then click the Data Sources link in the left frame of the page.
3. Select A Custom Data Source.
4. Enter a connection string: **data source=localhost;initial catalog = rs2005sbsDW**.

> **Note** Unlike the Report Designer, the Report Manager does not provide a dialog box to help you build a connection string. You will have to enter the connection string manually or copy it from another source.

5. Below Connect Using, select Credentials Stored Securely In The Report Server, and then enter **ReportExecution** as the user name and **ReportExecution** as the password.

> **Note** The ReportExecution user is a special account created as a generic SQL Server account with read access to the rs2005sbs and rs2005sbsDW databases. This user was created with a script that executed during installation of the sample files for this book. When you set up stored credentials for your production environment, you can use either a Windows logon or a database-specific logon for stored credentials.

The data source section of the screen should look like this:

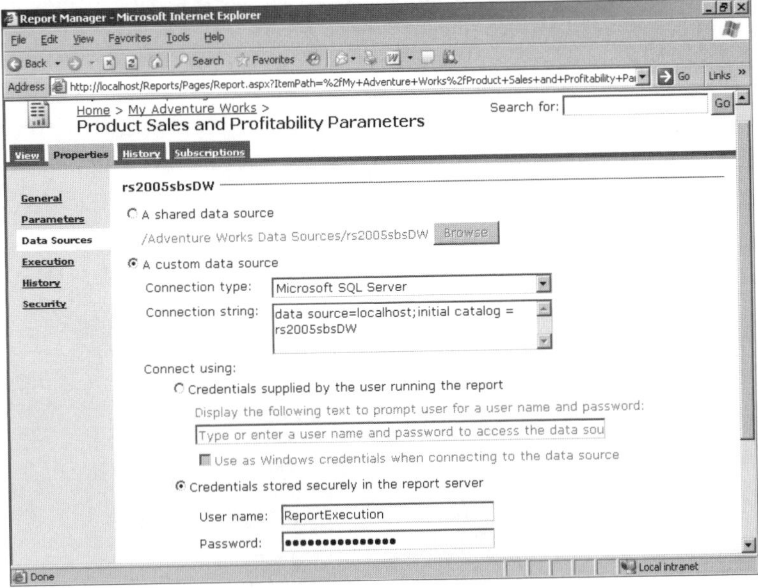

6. Click Apply.

   The Product Sales and Profitability Parameters report now uses a custom data source and is no longer associated with the rs2005sbsDW shared data source. The shared data source continues to use the user's Windows authentication, while the custom data source uses a special SQL Server login account for authentication. This means that a preview of the report in Visual Studio will use a different data source from the production report (which might simply be different credentials, but could also be a different database). You may or may not want that difference.

> **Tip** If you have many reports that need to use a special account, you should instead set up a shared data source rather than a custom data source so you have one place to manage the data source. It's okay to have several different data source definitions that connect to the same database, but use different authentication methods.

The linked report, Bike Sales and Profitability, is also affected by the change to the data source. The data source property is the only property of the base report that cannot be managed separately in the linked report.

Specifying a Default Value

If a report parameter has been defined with a default value in the authoring stage, you can override this value by using Report Manager to update the report's parameter properties. This is a useful technique, in combination with linked reports, to generate separate reports by parameter value. For example, if product categories are managed by different departments, you can create a folder for each department, and then create a linked report that has the default parameter value changed to reflect the applicable category for the folder in which it's placed.

You can also disable a default value that has been provided in the report definition. When you disable the default value, the report will not execute until the user supplies a value for the report parameter.

In this procedure, you'll set the default value for the *Category* report parameter to 2, which is the key value for the Bike category.

Change a parameter's default value

1. In Report Manager, click the Home link, click the Adventure Works Bikes folder link, and then click the Bike Sales and Profitability report link.
2. Click the Properties tab, and then click the Parameters link in the left frame of the page.
3. Change the default value for Category from 4 to **2** so your screen looks like this:

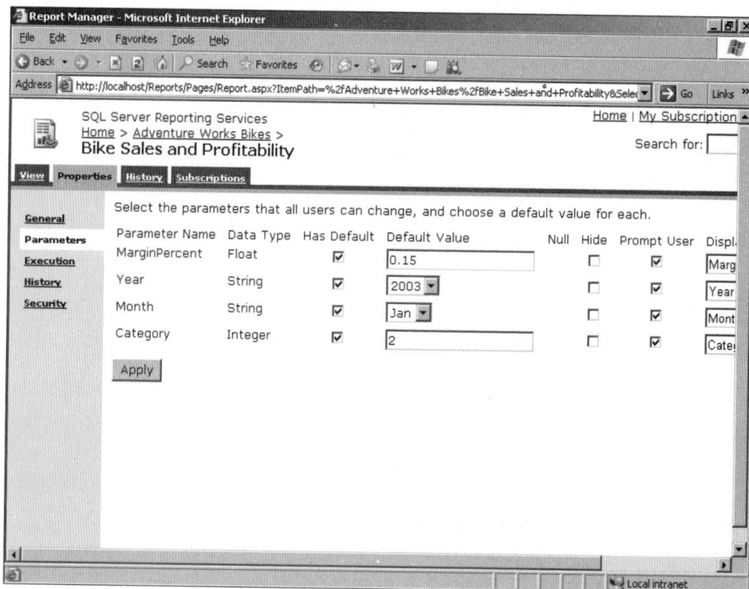

   The value 2 is the CategoryKey value that corresponds to Bike.

4. Click Apply.
5. Click the View tab.

   The report executes using the Bike category as a default. Notice that you can still select a different category. If you don't want the user to view another category, you must remove the prompt.

Disabling a Parameter Prompt

When you don't want a user to be able to change a report parameter value, you can remove the prompt so that a new value cannot be entered or selected from the list of available values. If you decide to use separate folders for linked reports using different parameter values, you can use this technique to prevent users from viewing another category. You can also remove a prompt from reports that run unattended, as long as you make sure the report has a default value for the parameter; otherwise, the report will never execute.

In this procedure, you'll disable the prompt for the *Category* report parameter.

Hide a parameter prompt

1. Click the Properties tab for the Bike Sales and Profitability report, and then, if necessary, click the Parameters link.
2. Clear the Prompt User check box for the *Category* parameter.

> **Important** Don't disable the prompt without providing a default value. Otherwise, the report can't execute and the user has no way to provide a value for the report parameter. The result is an empty report.

3. Click Apply.
4. Click the View tab to confirm the Category prompt was removed, as shown in this report:

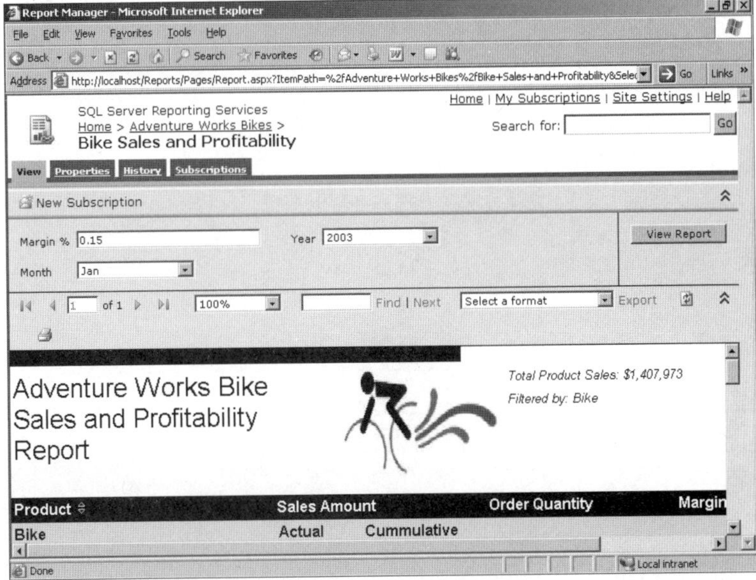

Notice that the Category prompt is no longer displayed. The textbox in the upper-right corner of the report properly indicates that the report is filtered by the Bike category and the table contains only data for the Bike category.

Managing Report Execution

Report execution is the process of turning a published report into a rendered report. More specifically, Reporting Services retrieves the data defined by the query in the dataset, and then combines the report's layout definition with the resulting data to produce an intermediate version of the report. Reporting Services then uses a rendering extension with this intermediate report to produce the report in its final format, which is, in turn, delivered to users. You can optimize report execution by controlling whether the processing steps occur when the user is accessing a report online or before the user opens the report.

When deciding how to manage report execution, you'll need to balance the users' needs for timely data and fast response with the Report Server's ability to process reports. If the user needs access to real-time data or data that is relatively recent *and* the report query can execute and return results in a reasonable amount of time, you can consider the On Demand execution options. When using On Demand execution, you need to decide whether to cache a report. If users need access to historical data *or* a report takes a long time to process, consider using Scheduled execution options to maintain a snapshot or to build a history of reports on a manual or scheduled basis. The On Demand and Scheduled execution options are compared in the following table. The remainder of this chapter reviews each option in detail.

	On Demand		Scheduled	
	Non-Cached	**Cached Instance**	**Snapshot**	**Report History**
Stored Credentials	No	Yes	Yes	Yes
Storage	Each time report is opened	First time report is opened	In advance	In advance
Limits (per report)	None	One per combination of parameter values	One	Multiple
Persistence	Temporary	Expires	Is replaced	Configure as either limited or unlimited number; specific history deletion

You can use the default execution properties for reports that query frequently changing source data or when there is no particular advantage to having a report ready in advance of browsing. If the data in a frequently accessed report needs to be relatively fresh but does not have to be as current as the data source, you can configure the report's execution properties to use a cached instance.

Executing Reports with Current Data

When a report is configured to use the default execution properties, Reporting Services processes a report on demand each time a user requests the same report, which results in a new query for each request. The overhead of all these queries might have negative performance consequences on the source database as well as the Report Server, so you must weigh this against the benefits of providing users with access to the up-to-date data.

To improve the experience of report viewing and navigation with Report Manager, Reporting Services uses session management. A session begins when a user opens a report for viewing in a browser or client application. After the intermediate format of the report is created, a copy is placed in the session cache, which is maintained in the SQL Server database ReportServer-TempDB. The session ends when the user closes the browser or client application. If a report's definition changes while a user is viewing it in an active session, the user will not see the updated version of the report until the user manually refreshes the report, which retrieves the current version from the ReportServer database.

In this procedure, you'll execute a report on demand and respond to prompted credentials.

Execute a report on demand with prompted credentials

1. In Report Manager, click the Home link, click the My Adventure Works folder link, and then click the Order Details report link to see this report:

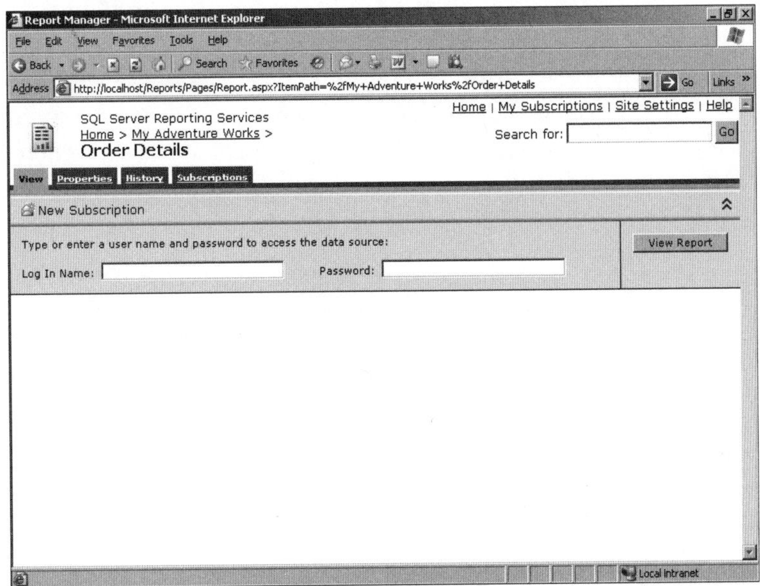

The *Reseller* report parameter in this report is dependent on a query that uses the rs2005sbs data source that you converted to prompted credentials earlier in this chapter. Even though a default value has been defined for this report parameter, the query must execute to build the list of available values for Reseller. Accordingly, the user must enter a login name and a password.

2. Enter **ReportExecution** as the login name and **ReportExecution** as the password.
3. Click View Report to confirm that the top of your screen looks like this:

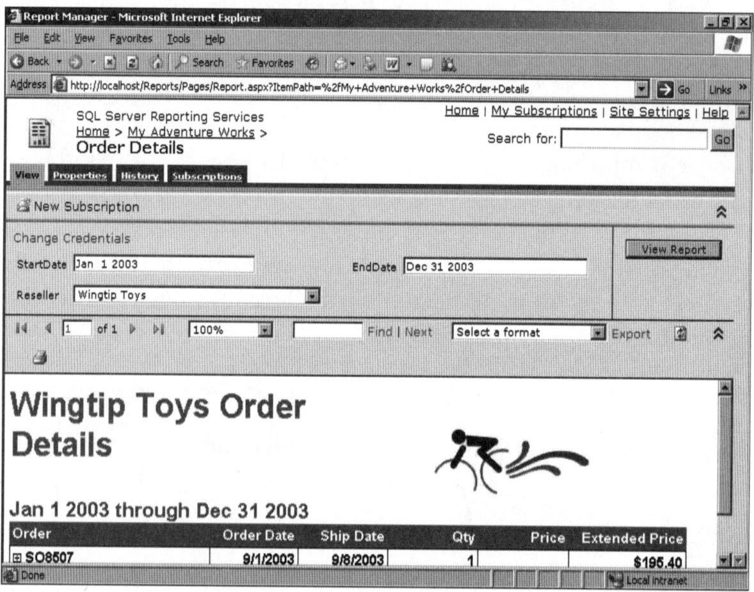

The query for the *Reseller* report parameter executes, and because the report parameter includes a default value, the report query also executes. Now the report is visible and you can change any report parameter value to update the report. The credentials are retained in the report for use in the next query, which is triggered when you click View Report.

> **Note** Technically, the report is not executed on demand each time you view it. The report is stored in the session (in ReportServerTempDB) and subsequent refreshes of the page in the same session retrieve the same report. In effect, the session is a private cache of the report. To force the report to retrieve new data, you must click Refresh on the Report Manager toolbar.

Implementing Cached Instances

A cached instance of a report is like a session report, except that the same intermediate report can be shared between multiple users. Using a cached instance of a report reduces the number of queries to the source database and potentially improves the performance of report execution. In this case, Reporting Services starts the process with the intermediate format of the report, which is stored temporarily in the ReportServerTempDB database. This intermediate report is flagged as a cached instance and is used for rendering in response to subsequent requests for the same report until the cached instance expires.

If a report uses query parameters, the query parameters are applied when the cached instance is created. This means that if the user selects a different parameter value that changes the value of a query parameter, a new cached instance is placed in the ReportServerTempDB database, but only if a cached instance with that parameter value doesn't already exist. Consequently, it's possible to have a cached instance for every combination of parameter values in a report.

Whereas a change in a query parameter triggers a new cached instance, a filter based on a report parameter value is applied each time to the existing cached instance. In this case, each change in a filter value renders the report again without the advantage of storing the results as a cached instance.

When you change a report's execution properties to use a cached instance, you limit the amount of time that it persists in the ReportServerTempDB database by establishing an expiration rule for caching. You can expire a cached instance at regular intervals or according to a report-specific schedule or shared schedule. Regardless of how you choose to expire a cached instance, the report must use a data source that draws on stored credentials.

In this procedure, you'll configure a report as a cached instance that expires on a report-specific schedule.

Configure a cached instance

1. In Report Manager, click the Home link, click the Adventure Works Bikes folder link, and then click the Bike Sales and Profitability report link.
2. Click the Properties tab, and then click the Execution link.

3. Click the third rendering option, Cache A Temporary Copy Of The Report. Expire Copy Of Report On The Following Schedule, so your screen looks like this:

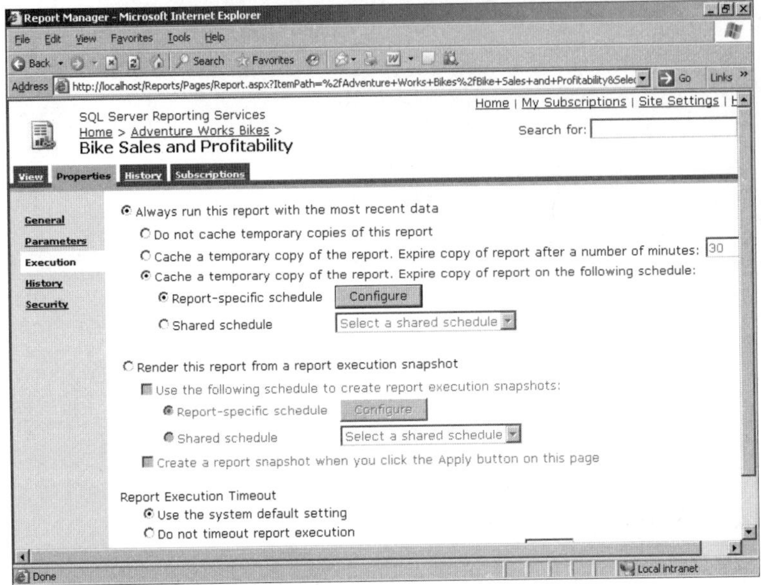

4. With Report-Specific Schedule selected, click Configure.

> **Tip** If you want the cache instance of several reports to expire at the same time, consider using a shared schedule.

5. Keep the default values, which indicate a schedule that executes on every day of the week.

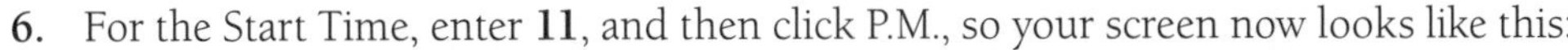

6. For the Start Time, enter **11**, and then click P.M., so your screen now looks like this:

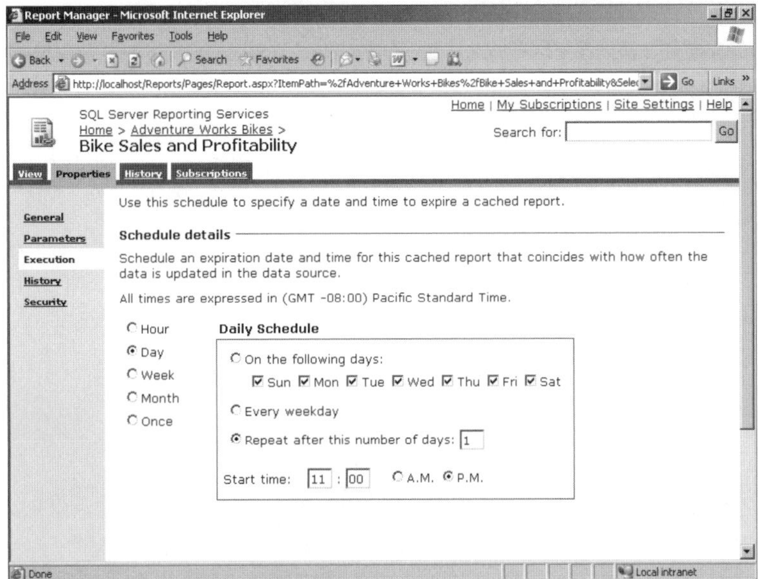

Notice at the bottom of the screen that you can optionally specify a start date or an end date for the schedule, or both.

7. Click OK, and then click Apply to complete the configuration.
8. Click the View tab to browse the report.

A cached instance of the report was just created and will expire at 11 P.M. this evening. If another user opens this report, Reporting Services does not execute the report query, but instead retrieves the cached instance from the ReportServerTempDB and renders the report for viewing.

Working with Shared Schedules

Before you can begin scheduling reports, you must define a schedule. Then, you can use the schedule to create a snapshot of a report that can be accessed later by users, or to build a history of a report to capture information at fixed intervals of time. Although you can define a unique schedule for each report, a more efficient approach is to create a shared schedule that can trigger several activities according to the same time intervals. You can use a shared schedule to manage snapshot creation, cache expiration, and subscription delivery for multiple reports.

In this procedure, you'll create a shared schedule to execute tasks on the first day of every month.

Create a shared schedule

1. In Report Manager, click the Site Settings link.
2. Scroll to the bottom of the page to find the section titled Other, and then click the Managed Shared Schedules link.
3. Click New Schedule on the Report Manager toolbar.

   The Scheduling page is nearly identical to the page you used to create a report-specific schedule earlier in this chapter.
4. In the Schedule Name box, type **Beginning of Month**.
5. Below Schedule Details, select Month.
6. Below Monthly Schedule, select On Calendar Days, and then replace the default value with **1** to execute this schedule on the first day of the month.
7. In the Start Time hours box, type **05** so your screen now looks like this:

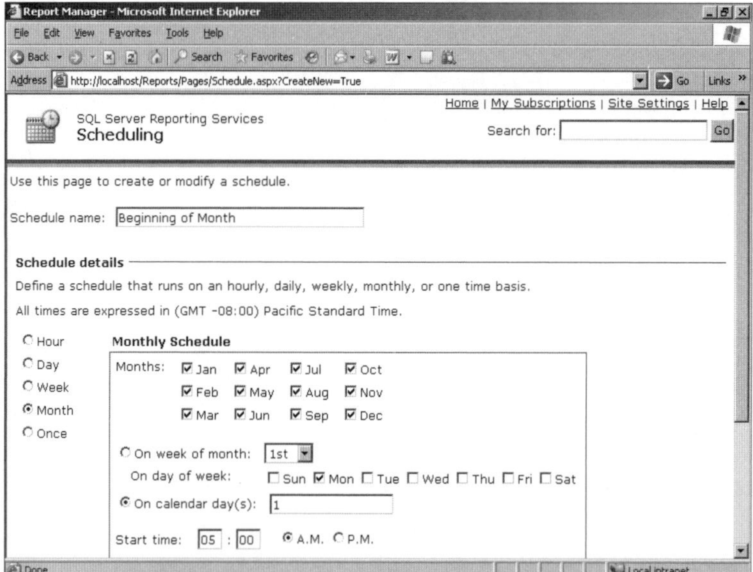

8. Click OK to see the schedule display on the Shared Schedules page, as shown here:

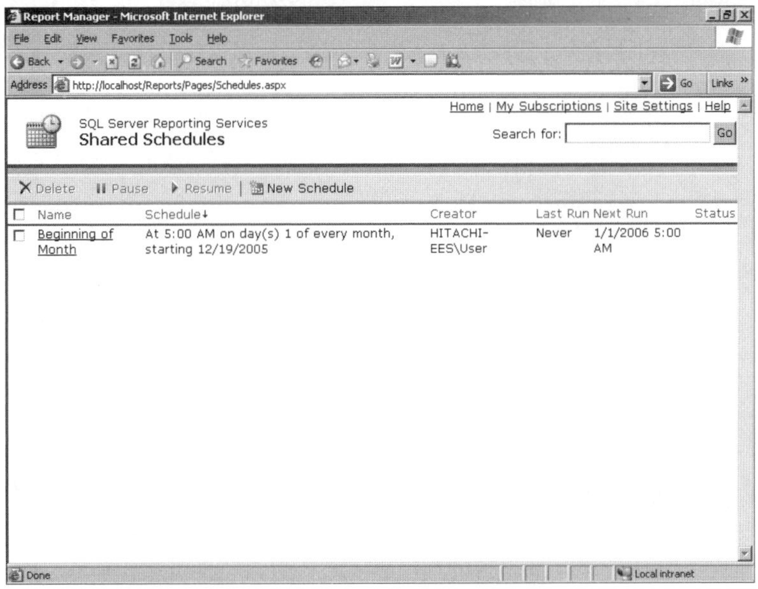

Important In order to add a Shared Schedule, SQL Server Agent must be running. Otherwise, you will receive an error when you click OK to create the shared schedule.

You can select schedules on this page to which you want to apply an action. After you select one or more schedules by selecting the appropriate check boxes, you can click Delete to permanently remove a selected schedule, Pause to temporarily disable a selected schedule, or Resume to enable a selected schedule that had been previously paused.

Managing Snapshots

If a report is configured to render from a snapshot, Reporting Services performs the data retrieval and processing before a user opens the report. This can be useful when you need to capture data in a report as of a particular point in time, such as a financial statement at month-end, or when queries take a long time to execute, such as year-to-date queries in a large transactional database. You can create a snapshot manually, but typically, a snapshot is created on a scheduled basis to update a report with more current data. Either way, Reporting Services uses the query results and the report layout to create an intermediate report that is stored as a snapshot in the ReportServer database. When a user requests the report, Reporting Services retrieves the intermediate report for rendering and delivery to the user.

As with a cached instance, query parameters are applied when the snapshot is created. A snapshot is not an interactive report, so parameter values cannot be changed once the snapshot has been created. However, report parameter values used as filters are applied against the snapshot during browsing, which can be an alternative approach to filtering data with query parameters.

You can create a snapshot manually or on a regular basis by using either a report-specific schedule or a shared schedule. However, only one snapshot at a time can exist. Each subsequent snapshot replaces the previous one. To configure a report to execute as a snapshot, you must select a data source that uses stored credentials for the report.

In this procedure, you'll use a shared schedule to regularly create a snapshot for the Product Sales and Profitability Parameters report.

Schedule a snapshot

1. Click the Home link, click the My Adventure Works folder link, click the Product Sales YTD report, and then click the Properties tab.
2. Click the Data Sources link, and then select the option Credentials Stored Securely In The Report Server. Use **ReportExecution** as the user name and **ReportExecution** as the password. Then, click Apply.

> **Note** When you plan to schedule snapshots for a report, the report's data source must use stored credentials. It doesn't matter whether you use a shared or custom data source. You can skip this step when your report is already using a data source with stored credentials.

3. Click the Execution link.
4. Select Render This Report From A Report Execution Snapshot, select the Use The Following Schedule To Create Report Execution Snapshots check box, and then select Shared Schedule.

   Notice that Beginning Of Month is available in the Shared Schedule drop-down list. Because it is the only shared schedule, it is automatically selected. The schedule details appear below the selected schedule.

5. To prevent a snapshot from being created now, clear the Create A Report Snapshot When You Click The Apply Button On This Page check box so your screen now looks like this:

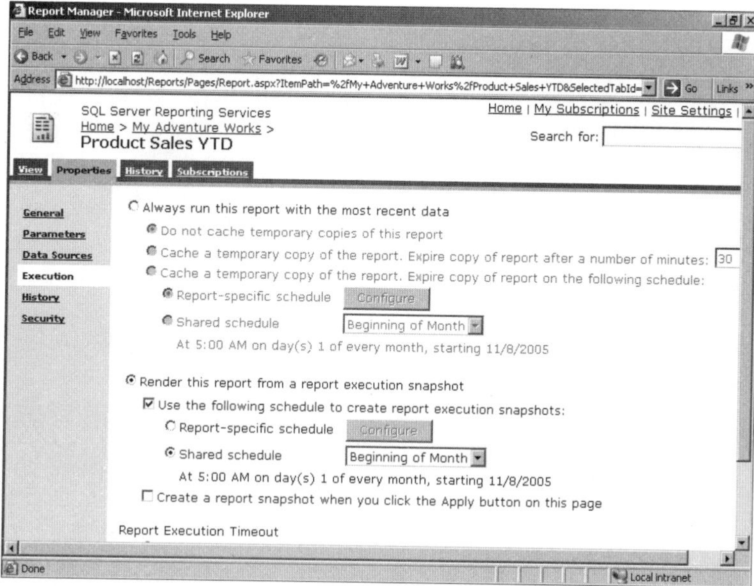

6. Click Apply.

> **Note** If the data source you're using for the current report is not using stored credentials, you will get the following error message when you click Apply: "Credentials used to run this report are not stored." You must change the data source to use stored credentials before you try to assign a snapshot schedule to the report.

7. Click the View tab to view the error message that is displayed when a snapshot is not yet ready:

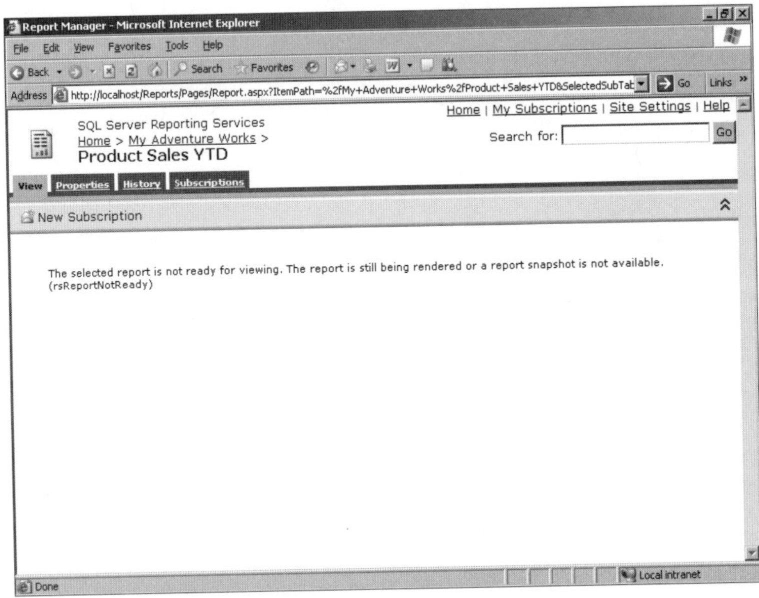

The report will not be available until it executes for the first time, which will be the first day of the next month.

Using Report History

If you want to save snapshots for future reference, you can enable a report's history properties. Then, you can add a snapshot to report history manually or automatically each time a snapshot is created. Alternatively, you can use a schedule to update report history with the current snapshot, which Reporting Services creates if a current snapshot doesn't already exist. Because the report is executed as a snapshot, the report must use a data source that draws on stored credentials.

Although you can keep an unlimited number of snapshots in report history, you might want to establish a maximum limit to keep the number of accumulated snapshots under control. You can set a global limit to apply to all reports that use report history, but you can override this number for any report. You can change the global or report-specific limit any time, but be careful when decreasing the number of snapshots in history. The oldest snapshots will be eliminated immediately, and users might not appreciate losing access to these reports without advanced notice. You can also delete individual snapshots in report history manually, but there isn't a utility for deleting report history in bulk apart from deleting the report itself.

In this procedure, you'll configure report history to store all report snapshots.

Store snapshots in history

1. Click the Properties tab of the Product Sales YTD report, and then click the History link.
2. Select Store All Report Execution Snapshots In History.
3. Below Select The Number Of Snapshots To Keep, select Limit The Copies Of Report History, and then type **12** in the box so your screen looks like this:

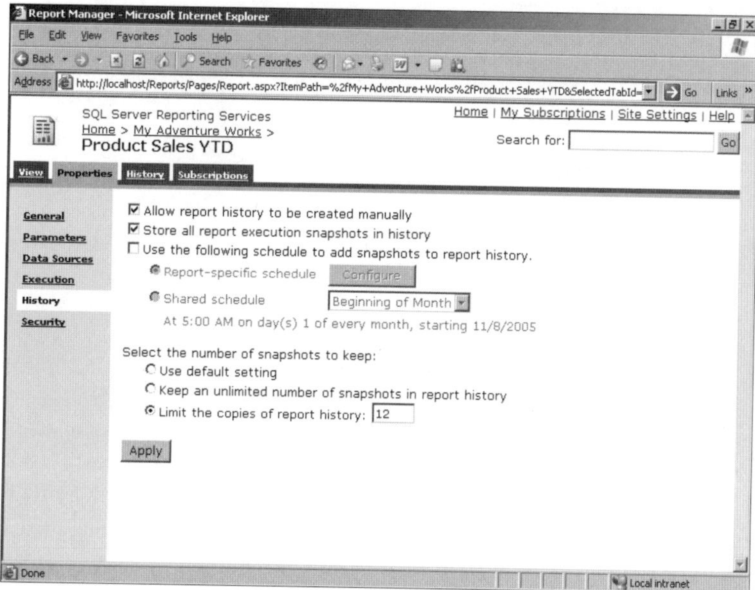

4. Click Apply, and then click OK to confirm the message that warns you about changing the report history.
5. Click the Execution link.
6. Select Create A Report Snapshot When You Click The Apply Button On This Page, and then click Apply.
7. Click the View tab.

   You can view the report now that a snapshot is created ahead of schedule. Notice that you cannot change the report parameter values.

8. Click the History tab to confirm that your screen looks similar to this:

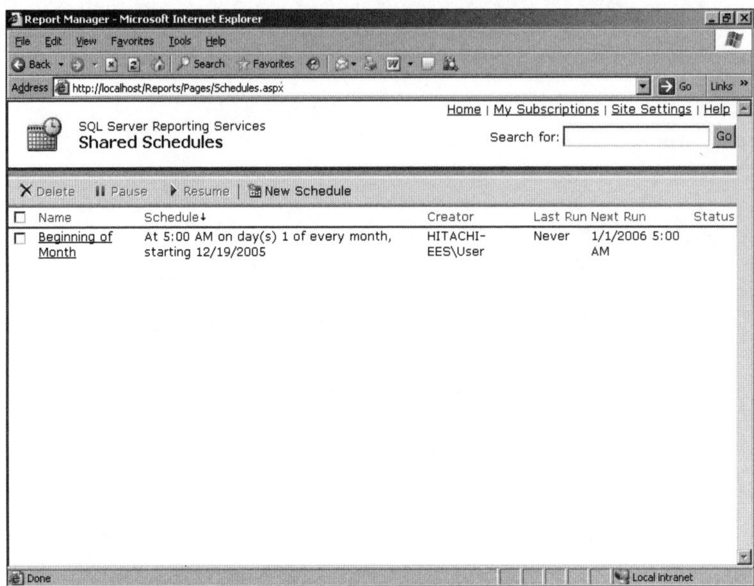

The snapshot you created manually is now available in the History list and is listed by date and time of creation. The list will grow as the Beginning of Month shared schedule executes each month. When the thirteenth snapshot is added to the list, the oldest snapshot will be deleted from the list so that only 12 snapshots are in the list, as defined in the History properties.

Note You can click New Snapshot on the History tab of the current report to add snapshots to the list manually. This button is enabled only when the report uses a data source with stored credentials *and* the option to Allow Report History To Be Created Manually is enabled on the History Properties page.

Chapter 9 Quick Reference

To	Do this
Set project deployment properties	In the Solution Explorer window of Visual Studio, right-click the project name, and then click Properties. At a minimum, enter a TargetServer-URL. For example: ***http://localhost/ReportServer***.
Set the project context properties for deployment	In the Properties dialog box for the project, click Configuration Manager and set Build and Deploy to control deployment behavior.
Publish an object using Visual Studio	In Solution Explorer, right-click the object or objects to deploy. If the object is a solution, click Deploy Solution. For all other objects, click Deploy.

To	Do this
Open Report Manager	In Internet Explorer, enter the Report Manager's URL. For example: ***http://localhost/Reports***.
Upload resources by using Report Manager	In Internet Explorer, open Report Manager, click the folder links to navigate to the parent folder for the resource, and then click Upload File on the Report Manager toolbar. Enter the resource filename, or use the Browse button to navigate to the resource by using the file system.
Publish reports with the *rs* utility	Prepare a script file that uses the Web Service proxy object *rs* and the methods *CreateFolder* and *CreateReport*. Then, use this file as an input argument to the *rs* utility by using the following syntax: `rs -i inputfile -s ReportServerURL`.
Add a folder	In Report Manager, navigate to the parent folder, and then click New Folder on the Report Manager toolbar.
Move a resource	In Report Manager, navigate to the resource's parent folder, and then click Show Details on the Report Manager toolbar. Select the check box for the resource, and then click Move on the toolbar.
Link a report	In Report Manager, open the base report, and then click the Properties tab. On the General Properties page, click Create Linked Report and name the linked report. Click Change Location to select a different folder.
Change a report's name or description	In Report Manager, open the base report, and then click the Properties tab. Enter a revised name or description.
Configure credentials for a data source	In Report Manager, navigate to the shared data source or open a report, click the Properties tab, and then click the Data Sources link. Select the applicable Connect Using option to apply one of the following: prompted credentials, stored credentials (which will require supplying the login name and password), Windows NT credentials, or no credentials.
Change a report parameter's default value or prompt	In Report Manager, open the report, click the Properties tab, and then click the Parameters link.
Change a report's execution properties	In Report Manager, open the report, click the Properties tab, and then click the Execution link.
Enable report history	In Report Manager, open the report, click the Properties tab, and then click the History link to select a method for adding snapshots to report history. You can also specify a limit to the number of snapshots kept in history.

Chapter 10

Managing Security

After completing this chapter, you will be able to:

- Use item-level role assignments to secure items in groups or individually.
- Define administrative permissions with system-level role assignments.
- Combine roles with parameters to secure data in linked reports.
- Use a permissions table to restrict access to data in reports.

After publishing content on the Report Server, which you learned how to do in Chapter 9, "Managing Content," it's important to implement security. At a minimum, you need to grant users access to the Report Server and its contents. In this chapter, you'll learn how to use role-based security to control not only what users can see on the Report Server, but also what they can do. You'll also learn three different techniques to restrict data within a report based on the user currently accessing the report. This chapter assumes that you're a local system administrator on the Report Server so you have appropriate permissions to perform all the tasks described here.

Using Report Server Security

Reporting Services uses role-based security to allow individual users or groups of users to perform specific activities. In a role-based security system, *roles* are used to establish groups of activities based on the functional needs of users. For example, some Reporting Services users only need to view reports, so all activities that relate to viewing items on the Report Server are organized into a predefined role. Similarly, other users need to be able to publish reports, so activities related to viewing, publishing, and managing reports are organized into another predefined role.

Reporting Services has 16 predefined user activities, or *tasks,* and nine predefined system tasks. These tasks include everything that a user or administrator can do in Reporting Services. You cannot create or delete tasks. A specific list of tasks that can be associated with a role is known as a *role definition*. Reporting Services provides five item role definitions and two system role definitions. You can use the role definitions as provided, modify them, or create your own.

An *item role assignment* associates a Microsoft Windows user or group, an item role, and a single *item*, such as a report or a folder. Item role assignments are used to apply security at the item level to manage what users can do with each item. A *system role assignment* associates a Windows user or group with a system role. System role assignments determine who can perform certain administrative tasks on the Report Server, such as managing schedules.

You implement security on the Report Server and its contents by using Report Manager or by using Microsoft SQL Server Management Studio. You might need to edit the existing roles or add your own roles to organize tasks into functional groupings that are appropriate for your environment. To grant access to the Report Server to other users, you must assign each user, either individually or as part of a group, to an existing role for the items on the Report Server with which they can interact. You might also want to create system role assignments for other administrators and for users who need to perform administrative tasks on the Report Server.

Adding Role Assignments

In the standard security model, Reporting Services requires users to be authenticated by the Windows operating system. It is possible to create a custom security extension when you need to use a different method to authenticate users. (Creating custom extensions is discussed in Chapter 18, "Building Custom Reporting Tools.") Using the standard security model, you must use existing local or domain user accounts or groups in order to create a new role assignment.

For any one item, a user or group can have only one role assignment. You can, however, establish a role assignment for a user who is also a member of a group with a role assignment for the same item. Reporting Services grants that user permissions for all the tasks in the role definitions of both the user and group role assignments.

In theory, you could create a unique role assignment for a single user for every report on the server, but a much simpler approach is to place role assignments on folders. The items contained in a secured folder, as well the contents of the folders it contains, inherit the parent folder's security settings. You can break the chain of inheritance at any level, either for a branch of the folder tree, or for an individual report, resource, or data source.

The five default roles provided with Reporting Services will likely meet most of your security requirements. Browser is the most restrictive role and limits users to navigating through the folder hierarchy and opening reports. The Report Builder role has the same permissions as Browser, but includes the ability to load report definitions from the report server into a local instance of Report Builder. My Reports, which assumes that you enabled the My Reports feature on the Report Server, allows users to manage their own reports separately from the main folder hierarchy. Publisher allows users to add content to the Report Server. Content Manager, the broadest role, allows a user to take ownership of the item, including the ability to manage security. Incidentally, as a member of the local system administrators on the Report Server computer, you are automatically granted the permissions of the Content Manager role, which gives you the ability to set security.

The following table shows a checkmark for tasks enabled by default for each role. In general, the term *manage* in a task means the ability to add, change, or delete the item.

Default Task	Browser	Report Builder	My Reports	Publisher	Content Manager
Consume reports		✓			✓
Create linked reports			✓	✓	✓
Manage all subscriptions					✓
Manage data sources			✓	✓	✓
Manage folders			✓	✓	✓
Manage individual subscriptions	✓	✓	✓		✓
Manage models				✓	✓
Manage report history			✓		✓
Manage reports			✓	✓	✓
Manage resources			✓	✓	✓
Set security for individual items					✓
View data sources			✓		✓
View folders	✓	✓	✓		✓
View models	✓	✓			✓
View reports	✓	✓	✓		✓
View resources	✓	✓	✓		✓

In this procedure, you'll add a role assignment to the Home folder for the group AWSalesAnalyst.

Add a Browser role assignment

1. Open Report Manager in Internet Explorer at *http://localhost/Reports*.
2. Click the Properties tab.

The Security Properties page for the Home folder is displayed:

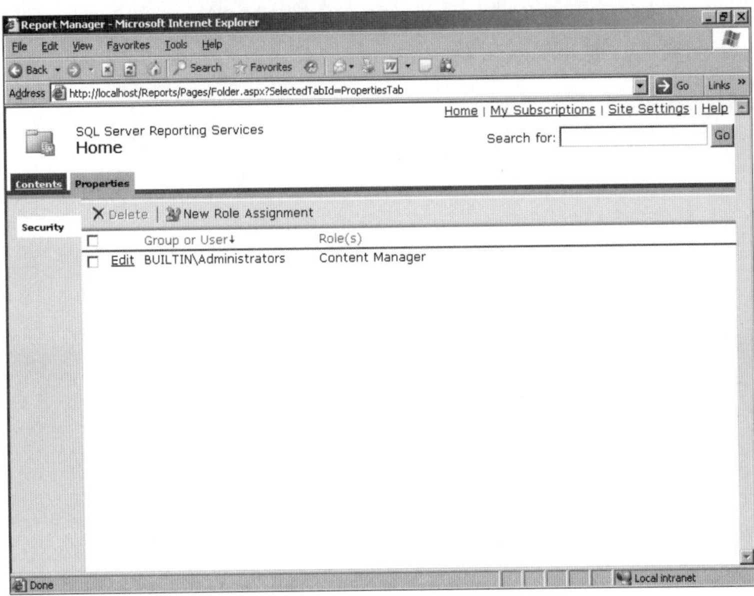

The default role assignment for the Home folder is Content Manager, to which the local system administrators group, BUILTIN\Administrators, is assigned.

3. Click New Role Assignment on the Report Manager toolbar.

   The New Role Assignment page is displayed:

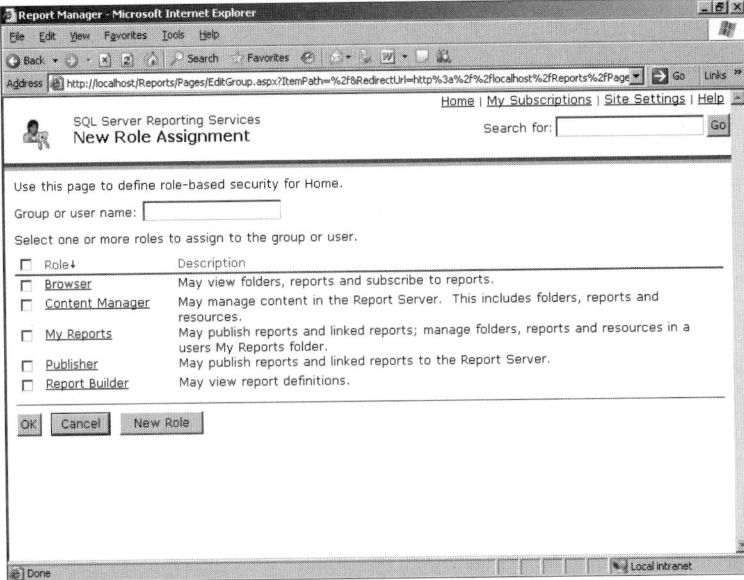

4. Click the Browser link to view the tasks in the role definition, as shown here:

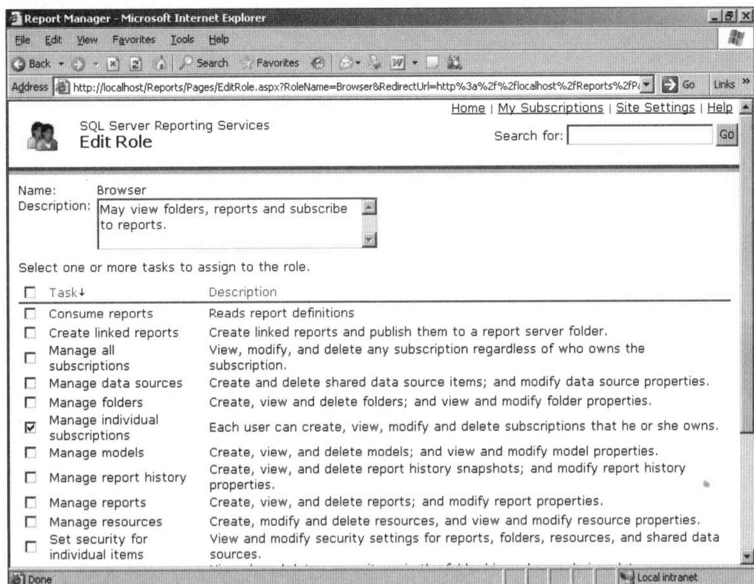

Note You can also reach this page to add a new role or edit an existing role at any time by using the Site Settings link at the top of any Report Manager page. Follow the Configure Item-Level Role Definitions link to access the Item-Level Roles page.

Here you can see a full description of each task to help you decide the task assignments for the current role.

Important Be careful when adding or removing tasks from the role definition. The impact can be far-reaching, because every role assignment with the modified role will be immediately changed across the Report Server. If an item does not currently have an explicit role assignment, remember that its security is inherited from its parent folder (which might, in turn, inherit from a higher-level parent folder).

5. Click Cancel.
6. In the Group Or User Name box, type **AWSalesAnalyst**.

Note The AWSalesAnalyst is a Windows group you should have added to the local groups on your computer as part of the installation of the practice files. If you skipped this step, please refer to this book's Introduction for the specific instructions.

7. Select the Browser check box to select this role.

   You can assign a user or group to multiple roles. If you select the Role check box above the list of roles, you can select all roles with a single click.

   Notice that you can add another role by clicking New Role. You can also edit the existing roles, or even just take a look at the current settings, by clicking the link for the role you want to review.

8. Click OK.

   The Security Properties page of the Home folder is displayed:

   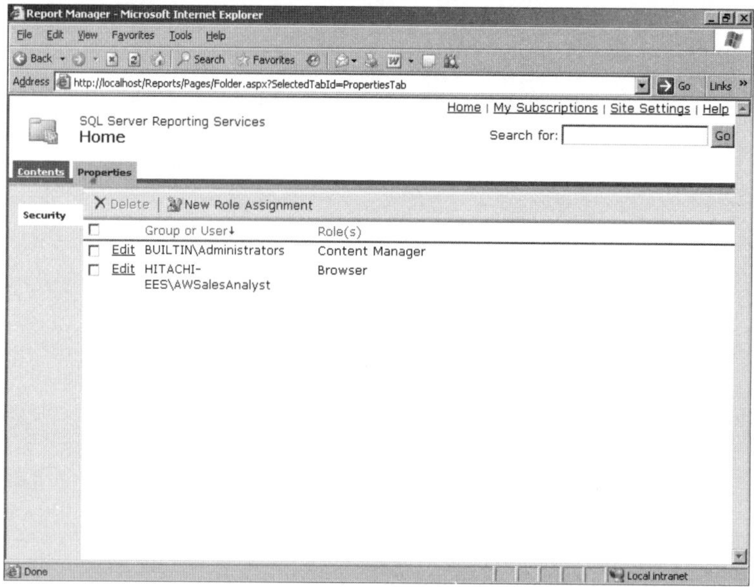

   Now the AWSalesAnalyst group has access to all folders and reports, because each folder nested under the Home folder inherits the security properties of the Home folder.

In this procedure, you'll add a role assignment to the Home folder for the group AWSalesDirector.

Add a Content Manager role assignment

1. On the Properties page of the Home folder, click New Role Assignment on the Report Manager toolbar.
2. In the Group Or User Name box, type **AWSalesDirector**.

> **Note** The AWSalesDirector is a Windows group you should have added to the local groups on your computer as part of the installation of the practice files. If you skipped this step, please refer to this book's Introduction for specific instructions.

3. Select the Content Manager check box to select this role.
4. Click OK.

   The Security Properties page of the Home folder is displayed:

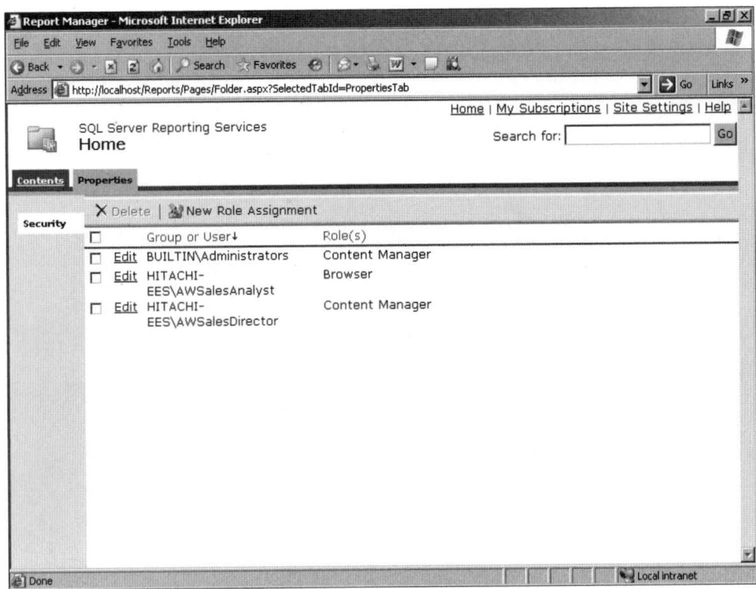

   Now the AWSalesDirector group can perform any task assigned to the Content Manager role for any folder and its contents on the Report Server.

Applying Item Security

When you apply security to a folder, the items within that folder and its nested folders inherit the same security settings. If you take away the ability to view a report or other item, the user will not even see that item on the Contents page. Whenever possible, organize content by folder so you can take advantage of this functionality and also minimize the administrative overhead of managing security for individual items. To handle exceptions to the rule, you can override security on individual items by adding role assignments to reports, resources, or data sources. After choosing to override security on an item, you'll have the option to restore the parent folder's security settings when needed.

In this procedure, you'll restrict access to the Adventure Works Bikes folder by removing a role assignment for the group AWSalesAnalyst to this folder.

Edit report security

1. On the Security Properties page of the Home folder in Report Manager, click the Contents tab.

> **Note** If you skipped Chapter 9, to follow the procedures in this chapter, run publishChap10.cmd in the C:\Documents and Settings\<username>\My Documents \Microsoft Press\rs2005sbs\chap10 folder so you can publish the reports you need. You will need to refresh the Home page after publishing the reports.

2. Click the Adventure Works Bikes folder, click the Properties tab, and then click the Security link.

   The Security Properties page of the Adventure Works Bikes folder is displayed:

   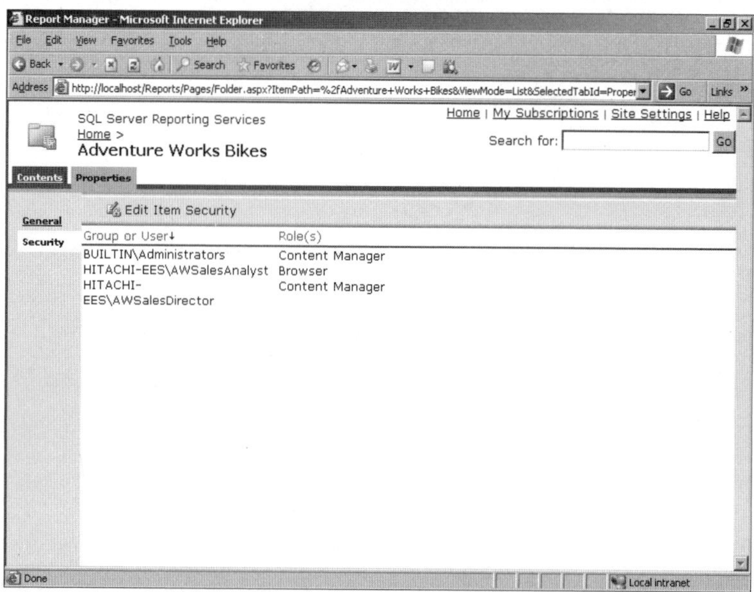

   The same role assignments appear in this folder because they were inherited from the Home folder.

3. Click Edit Item Security.

   A warning message is displayed:

   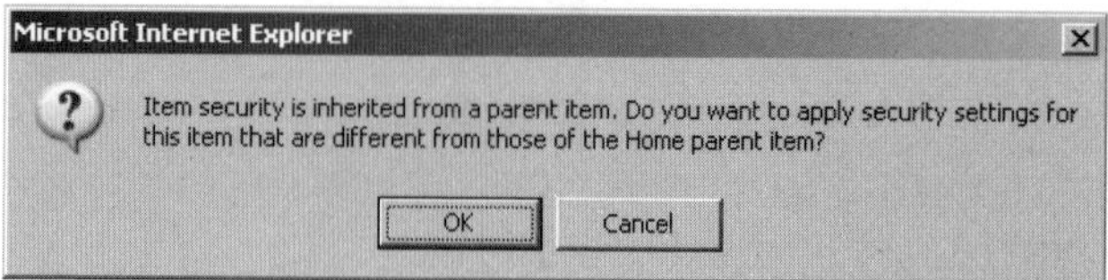

   This message is a reminder that, if you proceed, the Adventure Works Bikes folder will no longer inherit security settings from the Home folder.

4. Click OK.

   The Security Properties page of the Adventure Works Bikes folder is displayed:

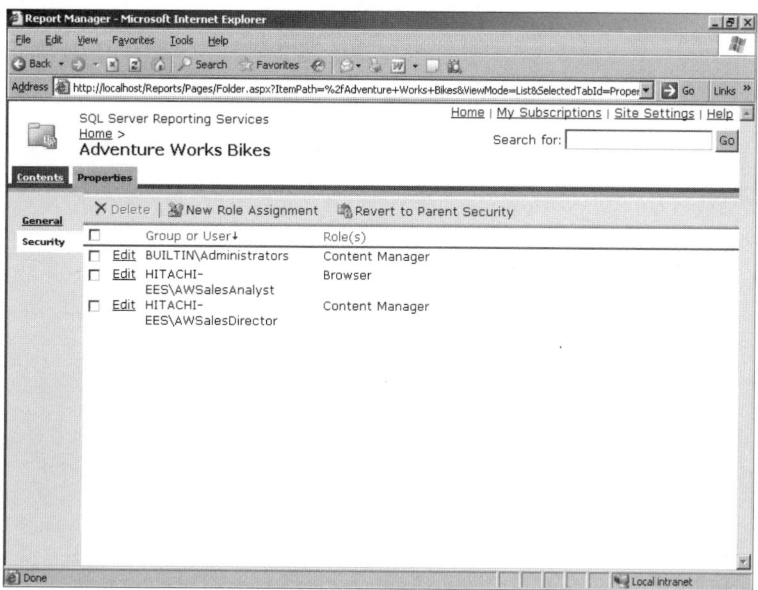

   Notice that a new button, Revert To Parent Security, appears on the Report Manager toolbar. If you change your mind about security settings for the Adventure Works Bikes folder, this button provides an easy way to reset the security settings to match the parent folder, Home.

5. Select the AWSalesAnalyst check box, and then click Delete on the Report Manager toolbar.
6. Click OK to confirm the deletion.

   The AWSalesAnalyst role no longer has access to the Adventure Works Bikes folder, but continues to have access to all other folders.

7. Close Internet Explorer.
8. Click Start, point to All Programs, right-click Internet Explorer, and then click Run As.
9. Select The Following User, and then type **SalesAnalyst** as the user and **SalesAnalyst** as the password.
10. Open Report Manager at *http://localhost/Reports.*

> **Note** The security settings on your computer may require you to enter credentials again. Simply type **SalesAnalyst** again for both the user and password.

The Home page is displayed:

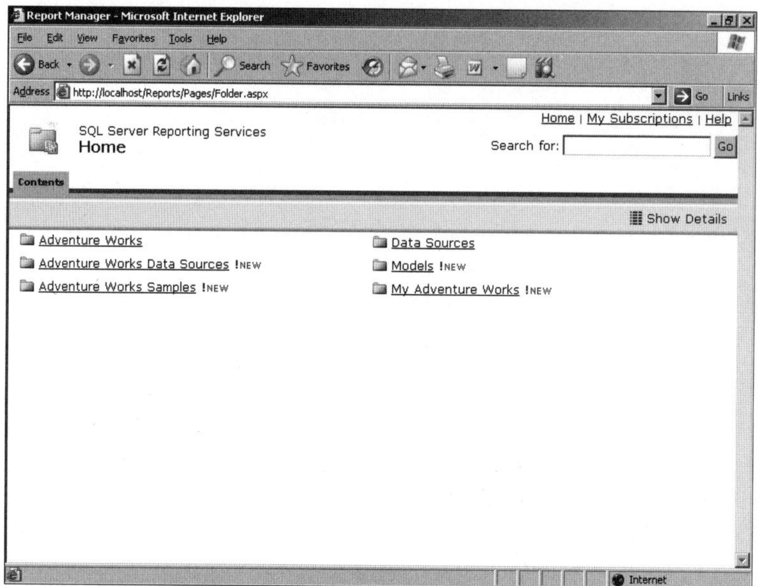

Notice that the Adventure Works Bikes folder is not visible to the SalesAnalyst user. Also, notice that the Properties tab is not available for the Home folder. Members of the AWSalesAnalyst group do not have access to the Site Settings link either because the Browser role is limited to folder and report links.

Important If you still have access to the Adventure Works Bikes folder after completing this step, check the members of the Administrators Windows group on your computer. If NT Authority\Authenticated Users is a member of this group, then the SalesAnalyst will still have access to the folder because the BUILTIN\Administrators permissions are instead used to authenticate and authorize this user. To test this procedure, NT Authority\Authenticated Users cannot be a member of your computer's Administrators group.

11. Close Internet Explorer.

Applying System Security

System role assignments allow selected users or groups to perform system administration tasks that are independent of content managed on the server. System roles provide access only to server activities. If a user is assigned to a system role, but is not assigned to an item-level role and is not a local system administrator, that user cannot view any content on the Report Server.

As a protective measure, local system administrators can always access a Report Server to change site settings. This way, if someone inadvertently creates role assignments that lock out all the users, a local administrator can still reset security. However, in case you need to restrict a local system administrator from opening confidential reports, you will have to implement security at the data level, which is discussed later in this chapter.

Reporting Services has two default system roles that you can use unchanged or extend to better meet your needs. The System User role, by default, allows access to the Site Settings page so that role members can view the server properties and shared schedules. Any user who needs to use a shared schedule for executing scheduled reports or creating subscriptions must be assigned to this role. The default tasks for the System Administrator role include not only managing server properties and shared schedules (which can be viewed *and* edited), but also managing running jobs, system role assignments, and role definitions.

The following table shows a checkmark for tasks enabled by default for each system role.

Default Task	System User	System Administrator
Execute report definitions	✓	✓
Generate events		
Manage jobs		✓
Manager report server properties		✓
Manage report server security		✓
Manage roles		✓
Manage shared schedules		✓
View report server properties	✓	
View shared schedules	✓	

In this procedure, you'll assign the AWSalesAnalyst group to a new role based on the System User role with permission to view shared schedules only.

Add a system role assignment

1. Open Report Manager in Internet Explorer at *http://localhost/Reports*.
2. Click the Site Settings link at the top-right corner of the Home page.

   Anyone with a system role assignment that includes View Report Server Properties or Manage Report Server Properties will have the Site Settings link on any page in Report Manager.

3. Click the Configure Site-Wide Security link.

   The System Role Assignments page is displayed:

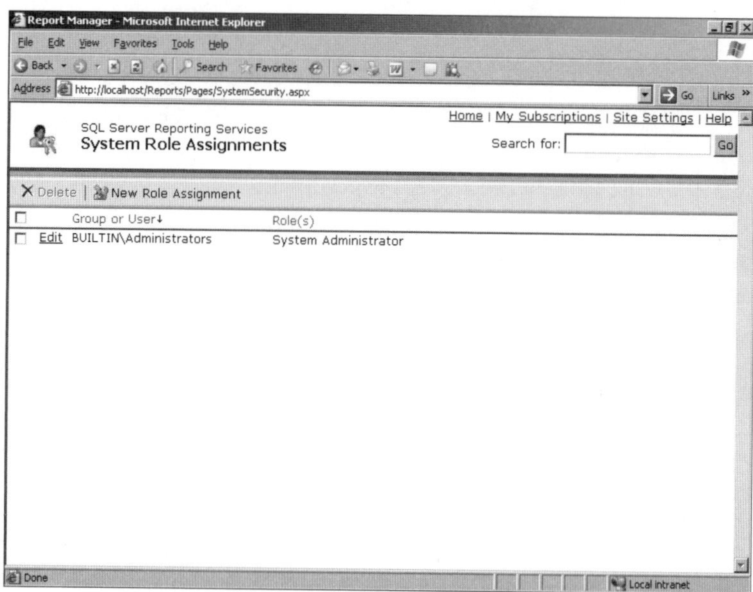

   Notice the default system role assignment of the local system administrators group, BUILTIN\Administrators, as System Administrator. You'll always need at least one System Administrator role assignment.

4. Click New Role Assignment on the Report Manager toolbar.

   The New System Role Assignment page is displayed:

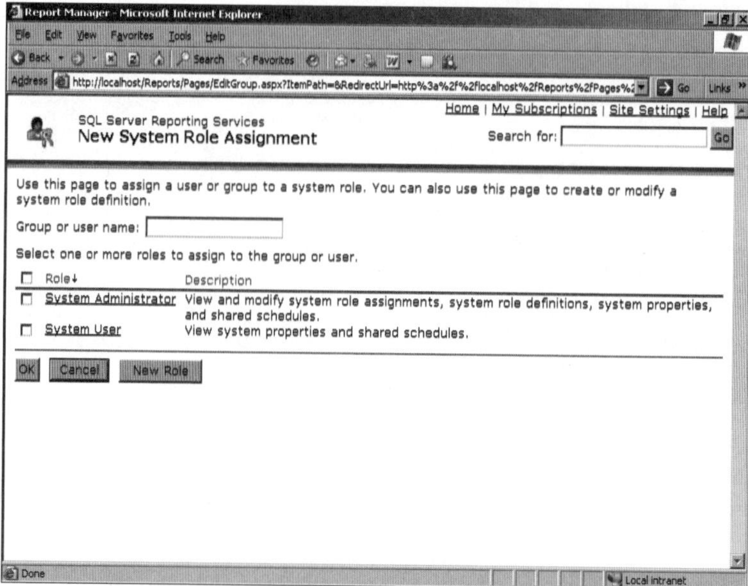

As with item-level role assignments, you can assign a user or group to multiple roles. If you select the Role check box above the list of roles, you can select all roles.

You can also add another role by clicking New Role, or edit the existing roles by clicking the role link.

5. Click the System User link.
6. Click Copy.

   A new role is created with the same tasks that are assigned to the System User role.
7. Enter a name for the new role: **Shared Schedule User**.
8. Add a description that details the assigned tasks: **View shared schedules**.

Tip By listing the tasks in the description, a System Administrator won't have to open the role definition to see the task assignments in the New System Role Assignment page.

9. Clear the Execute Report Definitions check box and the View Report Server Properties check box.

   Your screen should look like this:

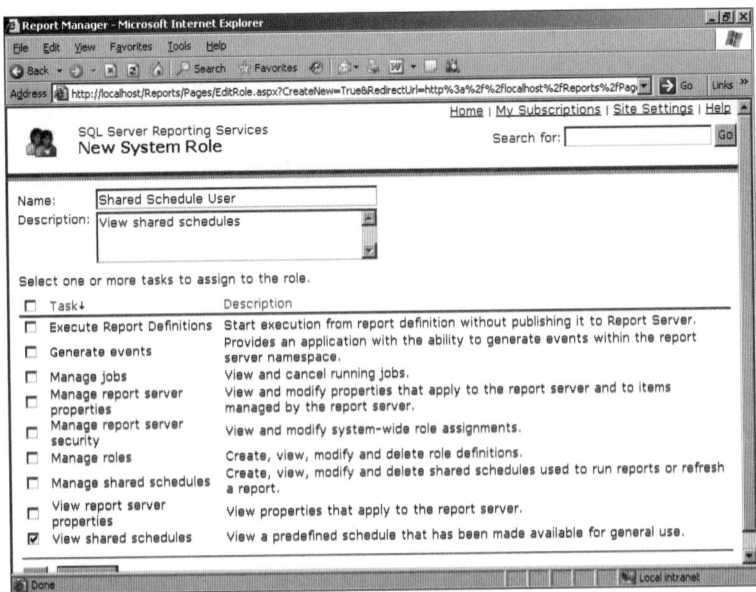

Tip You can also add a new system role or edit an existing system role whenever necessary by using the Site Settings link at the top of any Report Manager page. Click the Configure System-Level Role Definitions link to access the System Roles page.

10. Click OK.

11. In the Group Or User Name box, type **AWSalesAnalyst**.
12. Select the Shared Schedule User link check box.

    Your screen looks like this:

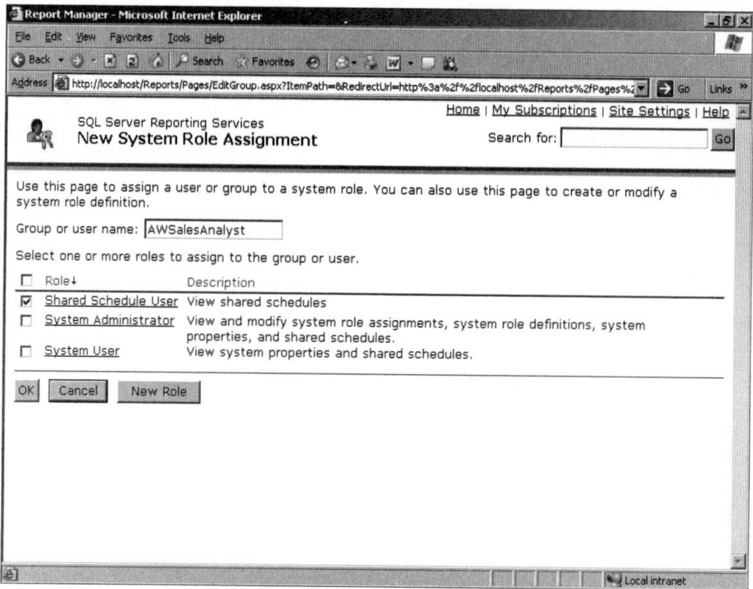

13. Click OK.

    The System Role Assignments page is displayed:

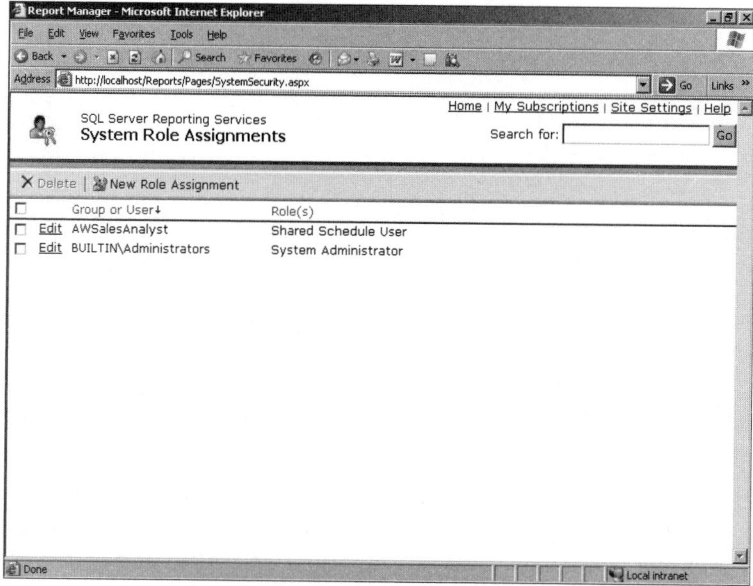

Now the AWSalesAnalyst role can use shared schedules with the reports it can access as defined by item-level role assignments.

Applying Data Security

Sometimes different users need access to the same report, but each user is allowed to see only some of the data. For example, a sales territory manager might be allowed to view only data that pertains to his or her sales territory. In this case, using item-level security works only if you create a separate report using a different query in each report to restrict the data to a single sales territory. If many reports require a similar separation for different groups of users, the administrative overhead of maintaining and securing all the variations can quickly become overwhelming. Instead, you can choose a technique that leverages the use of one report, yet still satisfies the requirement to restrict data by user.

The simplest way to restrict the data a user can see in a report is to use linked reports with parameters. Using this approach, you can easily control which data is displayed in the report, and then use item-level security to control access to each linked report. Alternatively, you can design a report that takes advantage of the *User* function from the global parameters collection to identify the current user. You can pass the user identification either to a query parameter or to a filter to restrict the data in the report.

Using Roles and Parameters to Restrict Data

As you learned in Chapter 7, "Building Advanced Reports," you can use a report parameter to filter data at the source with query parameters or to filter the report data after the full dataset has been retrieved. You can then set a different parameter value in each linked report, which you learned how to do in Chapter 9. By removing the parameter prompt, you prevent users from changing the parameter value and thereby restrict the report to the data defined by the parameter value. You can store each linked report in a separate folder to which you add role assignments to secure access, or you can add role assignments to each linked report to manage security at the report level.

In this procedure, you'll create a linked report from the Actual Vs Quota report, using a parameter and item-level security to restrict access to user EuropeDirector and local system administrators.

Use a query parameter in linked reports to restrict data

1. If the Report Manager isn't already open, launch it in Internet Explorer at *http://localhost/Reports*.
2. Click the Home link at the top of the page, click the Adventure Works Samples folder link, click the Actual Vs Quota report link, and then click the Properties tab.
3. Click the Security link.
4. Click Edit Item Security, and then click OK to confirm the folder setting changed from its parent's setting.
5. Select the AWSalesAnalyst and the AWSalesDirector check boxes, and then click Delete.

6. Click OK to confirm the deletion.
7. Click the General link.
8. Click Create Linked Report.
9. Type a name for the report, **Actual Vs Quota Europe**, and then click OK.

> **Note** Remember that it's easier to maintain security on a report by folder. In a production environment, create a separate folder for the linked report, if one is not already available, and then create the linked report with that folder's location specified. Item-level security can then be set on the folder rather than on its contents separately. These steps are omitted here to focus on using parameters as part of your security solution.

Notice that the *Group* parameter defaults to North America. For this linked report, you need to change this value to Europe, and then hide the parameter prompt.

10. Click the Properties tab, and then click the Parameters link.
11. Type **Europe** in the *Group* parameter's Default Value box.
12. For the *Group* parameter, clear the Prompt User check box.

    The Parameters Properties page looks like this:

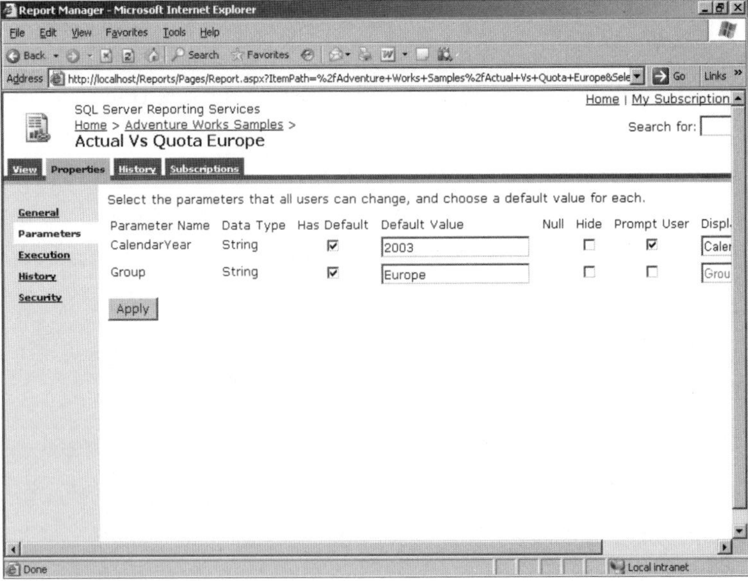

13. Click Apply.
14. Click the Security link.

15. Click Edit Item Security, and then click OK to confirm the folder setting change from its parent's setting.
16. Click New Role Assignment.
17. Type **EuropeDirector** in the Group Or User Name box.

> **Note** The EuropeDirector is a Windows user that you should have added to the local users on your computer as part of the installation of the practice files.

18. Select the Browser check box.
19. Click OK.

    The Security Properties page of the Actual Vs Quota Europe report looks like this:

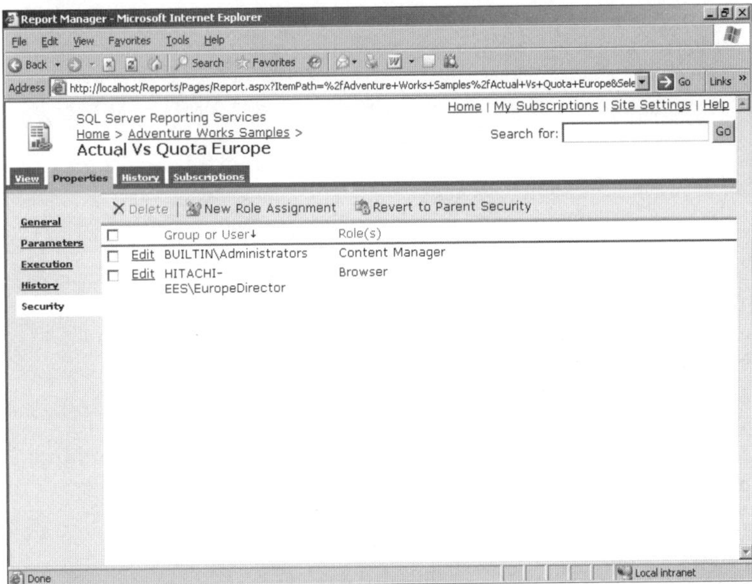

20. Close Internet Explorer.
21. Click Start, point to All Programs, right-click Internet Explorer, and then click Run As.
22. Click The Following User, and then type **EuropeDirector** as the user and **EuropeDirector** as the password.
23. Open Report Manager at *http://localhost/Reports.*
24. Click the Adventure Works Samples folder link, and then click the Actual Vs Quota Europe report.

    Notice that the Actual Vs Quota report is no longer visible.

25. Click the View tab, click Full Screen to expand the view, and then scroll down to view the whole table.

    The report page looks like this:

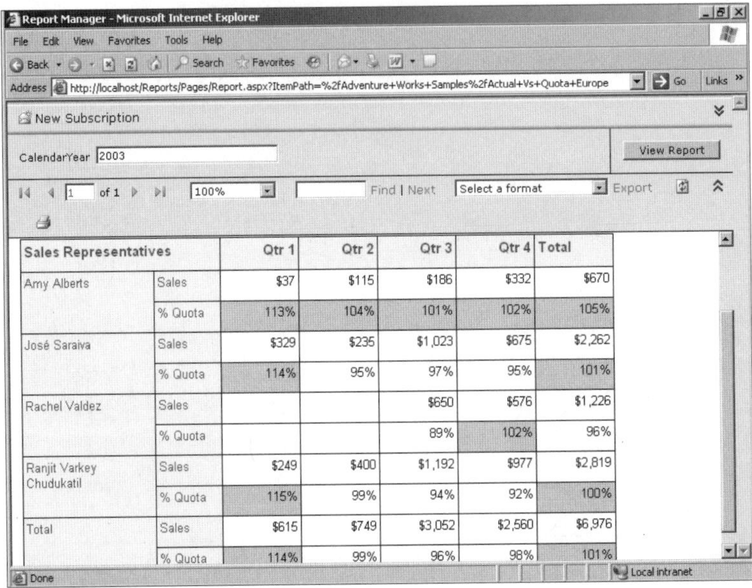

Sales Representatives		Qtr 1	Qtr 2	Qtr 3	Qtr 4	Total
Amy Alberts	Sales	$37	$115	$186	$332	$670
	% Quota	113%	104%	101%	102%	105%
José Saraiva	Sales	$329	$235	$1,023	$675	$2,262
	% Quota	114%	95%	97%	95%	101%
Rachel Valdez	Sales			$650	$576	$1,226
	% Quota			89%	102%	96%
Ranjit Varkey Chudukatil	Sales	$249	$400	$1,192	$977	$2,819
	% Quota	115%	99%	94%	92%	100%
Total	Sales	$615	$749	$3,052	$2,560	$6,976
	% Quota	114%	99%	96%	98%	101%

    You should see only the following Sales Representatives for Europe: Amy Alberts, José Saraiva, Rachel Valdez, and Ranjit Varkey Chudukatil.

26. Close Internet Explorer.
27. Click Start, point to All Programs, right-click Internet Explorer, and then click Run As.
28. Select The Following User, and then type **NADirector** as the user and **NADirector** as the password.
29. Open Report Manager at *http://localhost/Reports.*
30. Click the Adventure Works Samples folder link.

    Neither the Actual Vs Quota nor the Actual Vs Quota Europe is available to the NADirector, since the item-level security doesn't include a role assignment for this user.

31. Close Internet Explorer.

Restricting the Source Query by User

Using parameters and linked reports to restrict access is a good approach when you're not concerned about local system administrators opening these reports. Even if a Content Manager removes the BUILTIN\Administrators role assignment from a report, a local system administrator still has the ability to reset security and the potential to open restricted reports. To protect confidential data, you can design a report that uses a query parameter to filter the dataset at the source based on the current user (which should be a domain user account rather than a local user account to further tighten security).

This technique requires you to create and maintain a permissions table that maps a Windows user account with a value used to restrict the data. For example, you can map the user account EuropeDirector to value Europe. The permissions table includes a column for the user account and a column for the value filter. Then, you add the permissions table to the dataset query in the confidential report and join the value filter column in the permissions table to the corresponding column in an existing table in the query. You also add a query parameter to the WHERE clause of the query that compares the user account column in the permissions table to a query parameter. This query parameter will be used differently from the way you learned to use a query parameter in Chapter 7 because its value comes not from a report parameter, but from the operating system. To get the value from the operating system, you use the expression `=User!UserID`.

When you use the *@UserID* query parameter in a dataset, the report must always run on demand to set the proper user context. Therefore, you'll have many more queries against the source database than would result if you instead filtered the dataset, which you'll learn how to do later in this chapter. Because the query returns fewer rows than it would without the *@UserID* query parameter, the query might run faster, but you will need to weigh performance against the impact of more database queries when designing restricted reports for your organization.

In this procedure, you'll add a query parameter to a report's dataset to pass the current user as a filter in the source query.

Add a query parameter to a report

1. Open SQL Server Management Studio and connect to the Database Engine.
2. Expand the (localhost) server (or the instance to which you installed Reporting Services and the practice files) and navigate to the Tables folder of database rs2005sbsDW.
3. Right-click PermissionsSalesTerritory table, and then click Open Table.

   The data in this table is displayed:

	UserId	SalesTerritoryG...
	HITACHI-EES\Administrator	Europe
	HITACHI-EES\EuropeDirector	Europe
	HITACHI-EES\NADirector	North America
	HITACHI-EES\Administrator	North America
	HITACHI-EES\PacificDirector	Pacific
	HITACHI-EES\Administrator	Pacific

Note This table is populated when you install the practice files. The domain name of the users in the UserId column should match your computer name.

This table maps users to sales territory groups so you can customize the Securing-SourceQuery report for each territory group director. You must create a similar table to use with your data sources when you need to restrict data by user. You can certainly include other columns in your own permissions table, but at minimum, you need a column for the full name of the Windows account and a column to hold the value to filter the data at the source.

4. Close SQL Server Management Studio.
5. Start SQL Server Business Intelligence Development Studio and open the solution DataSecurity in the C:\Documents and Settings\<username>\My Documents \Microsoft Press\rs2005sbs\chap10\DataSecurity folder.
6. In Solution Explorer, double-click SecuringSourceQuery.rdl to open the report.
7. Click the Data tab.
8. Click Show/Hide Grid Pane on the Query Designer toolbar, and then click Show/Hide Result Pane to make some room for the Diagram and SQL Panes.
9. With Detail selected in the Dataset drop-down list, click Add table on the Query Designer toolbar.
10. Double-click the PermissionsSalesTerritory table, and then click Close.
11. Click the *SalesTerritoryGroup* field in the DimSalesTerritory table and drag the mouse to the *SalesTerritoryGroup* field in the PermissionsSalesTerritory table.

    Your Diagram pane, when fully visible, should look similar to this:

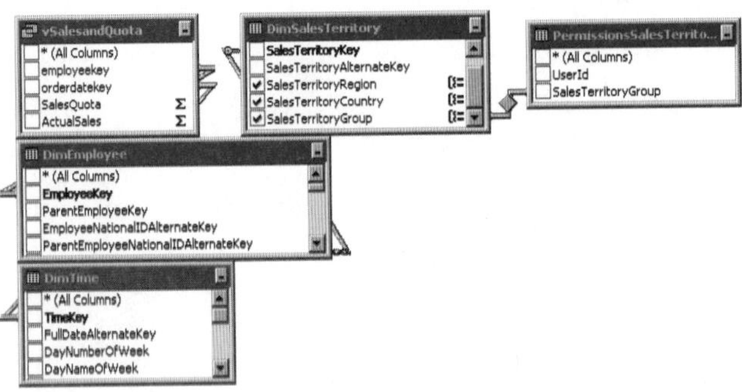

    The PermissionsSalesTerritory table is now joined to the DimSalesTerritory table on the SalesTerritoryGroup column. However, the query still needs to be modified to use this join to filter the dataset by user.

12. Add the following to the end of the WHERE clause:

```
and PermissionsSalesTerritory.UserId = @UserID
```

13. Click Edit Selected Dataset to the right of the Dataset drop-down list.

14. Click the Parameters tab in the Dataset dialog box.

15. In the Parameters list, change the value for the *@UserID* query parameter to `=User!UserID`.

    The Dataset dialog box looks like this:

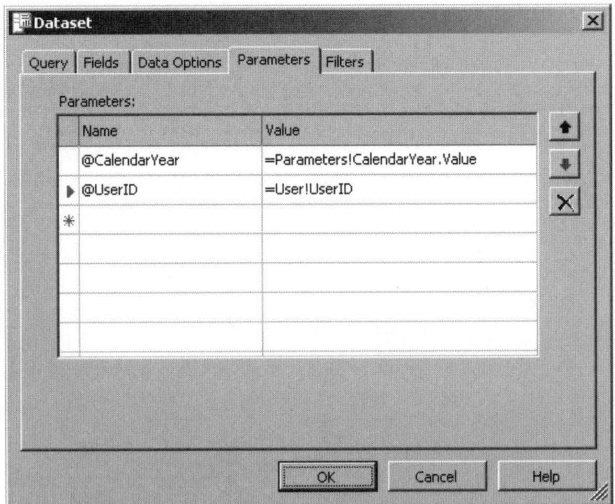

    The expression `=User!UserID` returns the Windows account for the user running the report, a value that is contained in the User global collection.

16. Click OK.

17. Click the Layout tab, and then click Report Parameters on the Report menu.

18. Click UserID in the Parameters list, click Remove, and then click OK.

    When you add a query parameter, a corresponding report parameter is added to the report. However, in this case, the value for the query parameter is provided from an expression, so the report parameter should be removed.

    Save the solution, and then click the Preview tab to test the report.

Your screen should look similar to this:

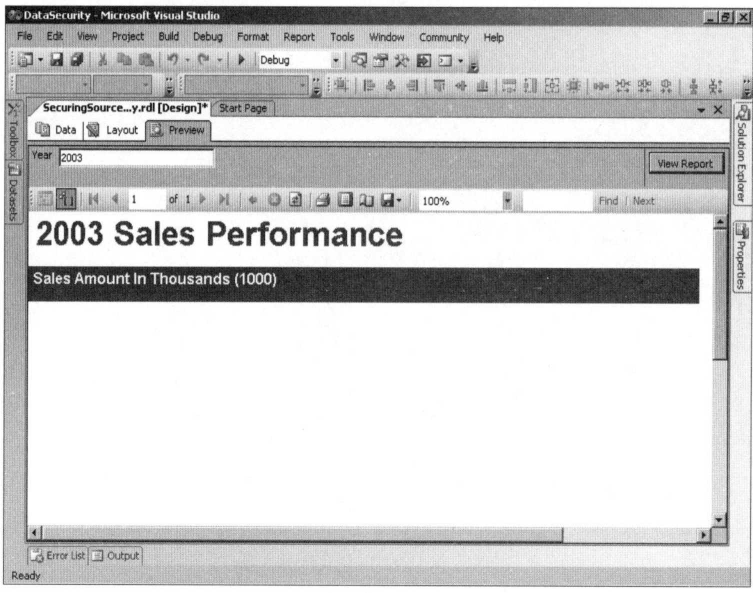

Because your Windows account is not in the permissions table, you cannot see any data in the report.

> **Tip** When developing reports for your organization, add your Windows account to the permissions table to properly test reports before deployment.

19. In Solution Explorer, right-click the SecuringSourceQuery.rdl report, and then click Deploy.
20. Click Start, point to All Programs, right-click Internet Explorer, and then click Run As.
21. Click The Following User, and then type **EuropeDirector** as the user and **EuropeDirector** as the password.
22. Open Report Manager at *http://localhost/Reports.*
23. Click the DataSecurity folder link, and then click the SecuringSourceQuery report link.

The top of the report looks like this:

2003 Sales Performance

Sales Amount In Thousands (1000)							
Sales Reps			Qtr 1	Qtr 2	Qtr 3	Qtr 4	Total
United Kingdom	José Saraiva	Sales	$329	$235	$1,023	$675	$2,262
		% Quota	114%	95%	97%	95%	101%
	Total	Sales	$329	$235	$1,023	$675	$2,262
		% Quota	114%	95%	97%	95%	101%
Germany	Rachel Valdez	Sales			$650	$576	$1,226
		% Quota			89%	102%	96%
	Total	Sales			$650	$576	$1,226
		% Quota			89%	102%	96%
France	Ranjit Varkey Chudukatil	Sales	$249	$400	$1,192	$977	$2,819
		% Quota	115%	99%	94%	92%	100%
	Total	Sales	$249	$400	$1,192	$977	$2,819
		% Quota	115%	99%	94%	92%	100%

If you scroll through the report, you can see that the data in the report includes only United Kingdom, Germany, and France. If a user who is not listed in the permissions table tries to open this report, no data will be displayed, as you experienced when previewing the report in Visual Studio.

24. Close Internet Explorer.

Filtering the Report Data by User

Another way to protect confidential data is to design a report to use the expression `=User!UserID` to filter the dataset after the query executes. As with the query parameter approach, this approach requires a table of users that can be joined to the dataset. Using this scenario, you still join the permissions table to an existing table in the query. However, instead of using the WHERE clause of the query to filter the data by user, you add the UserId column from the permissions table to the SELECT clause so it becomes a field in the dataset. Then, you add a filter to the dataset that compares the field value with the value returned by the expression `=User!UserID`.

When you filter the dataset by user, the full query runs against the source database each time the report executes. However, the filter is applied only when the user is browsing the report. As a result, this method allows you to execute the report on a schedule to minimize the potential impact on the underlying database of running the full query.

In this procedure, you'll add a filter to a report's dataset to limit the display of data in the report during browsing based on the current user.

Add a filter to a report

1. In Solution Explorer in Visual Studio, double-click SecuringReportData.rdl to open the report.
2. Click the Data tab.
3. With Detail selected in the Dataset drop-down list, click Add Table on the Query Designer toolbar.
4. Double-click the PermissionsSalesTerritory table, and then click Close.
5. Click the *SalesTerritoryGroup* field in the DimSalesTerritory table and drag the mouse pointer to the *SalesTerritoryGroup* field in the PermissionsSalesTerrritory table.
6. In the PermissionSalesTerritory table, click UserId to add the column to the query's SELECT clause.
7. Click Edit Selected Dataset to the right of the Dataset drop-down list.
8. Click the Filters tab in the Dataset dialog box.
9. Click `=Fields@UserId.Value` in the Expression drop-down list.
10. Click <Expression...> in the Value drop-down list.
11. Click Globals in the Fields list, click UserID, and then click Paste. Alternatively, you can type **=User!UserID** in the Expression box.

    The Dataset dialog box looks like this:

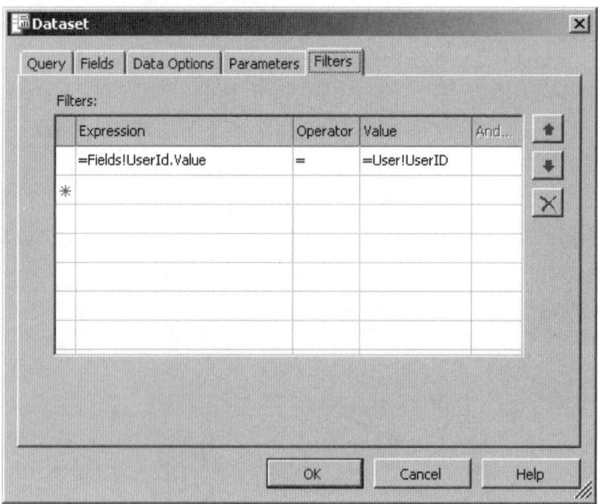

12. Click OK.
13. Save the solution, and then click the Preview tab.

    As with the SecuringSourceQuery report, you cannot see any data in the report because your user account is not in the permissions table.

14. Right-click the SecuringReportData.rdl report in Solution Explorer, and then click Deploy.
15. Click Start, point to All Programs, right-click Internet Explorer, and then click Run As.
16. Select The Following User, and then type **NADirector** as the user and **NADirector** as the password.
17. Open Report Manager at *http://localhost/Reports*.

    Click the DataSecurity folder link, and click the SecuringReportData report.

    The top of the report looks like this:

    2003 Sales Performance

    Sales Amount In Thousands (1000)

Sales Reps			Qtr 1	Qtr 2	Qtr 3	Qtr 4	Total
United States	David Campbell	Sales	$379	$417	$1,124	$860	$2,779
		% Quota	111%	88%	103%	103%	101%
	Fernando Caro	Sales	$918	$1,279	$1,252	$953	$4,402
		% Quota	109%	93%	107%	98%	102%
	Linda Mitchell	Sales	$926	$1,164	$1,623	$1,284	$4,996
		% Quota	108%	114%	106%	101%	107%
	Michael Blythe	Sales	$821	$1,227	$1,498	$1,200	$4,746
		% Quota	113%	103%	95%	99%	102%
	Shu Ito	Sales	$525	$626	$948	$777	$2,876
		% Quota	112%	113%	101%	114%	110%

    If you scroll through the report, you can see that the data in the report includes only North American territories–the United States and Canada.

18. Close Internet Explorer.

Chapter 10 Quick Reference

To	Do this
Add an item-level role assignment to a folder	Navigate to the folder in Report Manager, click the Properties tab, and then click the Security link. Click New Role Assignment, type a Windows user or group account, and then select one or more roles to assign.
Add an item-level role assignment to a report, resource, or data source	Open the item in Report Manager, click the Properties tab if necessary, and then click the Security link. Click Edit Item Security and click OK to confirm the change from the folder's security settings. Click New Role Assignment, type a Windows user or group account, and then select one or more roles to assign.
Add an item-level role	Click the Site Settings link in Report Manager, click the Configure Item-Level Role Definitions link, and then click New Role. Type a name and a description for the new role, and then click the tasks to be assigned to the role.
Add a system role assignment	Click the Site Settings link in Report Manager, and then click the Configure Site-Wide Security link. Click New Role Assignment, type a Windows user or group account, and then select one or more roles to assign.
Add a system role	Click the Site Settings link in Report Manager, click the Configure System-Level Role Definitions link, and then click New Role. Type a name and description for the new role, and then click the tasks to be assigned to the role.
Restrict data using linked reports with a query parameter and item-level security	In Report Manager, open the base report, and then click the Properties tab. On the General Properties page, click Create Linked Report and name the linked report. Click the Properties tab, and then click the Parameters link. Enter a default value for the parameter and clear the Prompt User check box, if necessary. Then, click Apply. Click the Security link, and then click Edit Item Security to make role assignments as needed.

To	Do this
Restrict data using a query parameter and permissions table	Create a permissions table that contains user accounts and filter values. Join the permissions table to a table in the dataset query on columns containing the filter value, and then add a query parameter to the WHERE clause of the query that references the permission table's user account column. For example: `and PermissionsSalesTerritory.UserId = @UserID` Click Edit Selected Dataset, click the Parameters tab, and then change the Value for the query parameter to **=User!UserID**. Click the Layout tab, click Report Parameters on the Report menu, click UserID in the Parameters list, and then click Remove.
Restrict data using a dataset filter and permissions table	Create a permissions table that contains user accounts and filter values. Join the permissions table to a table in the dataset query on columns containing the filter value, and then add the permission table's user account column to the SELECT clause of the query. Click Edit Selected Dataset, and then click the Filters tab. Click `=Fields!UserID` in the Expression list box. Click <Expression...> in the Value list box, and then enter **=User!UserID** as an expression.

Chapter 11

Managing Server Components

After completing this chapter, you will be able to:

- Use configuration files to modify Reporting Services components.
- Monitor Reporting Services performance with execution logging.
- Terminate or suspend jobs.
- Manage the Reporting Services databases.

In the previous two chapters, you learned how to publish and secure content on the Report Server as part of the management stage of the reporting life cycle. Another aspect of management concerns the maintenance of the components that support the reporting life cycle. In this chapter, you'll learn how to configure these Reporting Services components. You'll also learn several ways to monitor activity on the Report Server so you can tune the design of reports or the configuration of server components for optimal performance. In addition, you'll encounter the options for limiting or temporarily suspending the execution of reports so you can proactively manage activity on the server. Management of the server also includes monitoring database growth and protecting the data in the case of disaster, so this chapter closes by showing you which tables require the most attention (and why) and by recommending a backup strategy for your databases.

Configuring Reporting Services

Settings that you can change to control the behavior of Reporting Services components are contained in four configuration files. Some of the settings in these configuration files are supplied by you during installation; the remaining settings have default values you can change as needed. Each configuration file is associated with a separate component, which is shown in the following table:

Component	Configuration File	Default Installation Folder
Report Server engine	rsreportserver.config	Program Files\Microsoft SQL Server\MSSQL.3\Reporting Services\ReportServer
Report Server service	ReportingServices-Service.exe.config	Program Files\Microsoft SQL Server\MSSQL.3\Reporting Services\ReportServer\bin
Report Manager	RSWebApplication.config	Program Files\Microsoft SQL Server\MSSQL.3\Reporting Services\ReportManager
Report Designer	RSReportDesigner.config	Program Files\Microsoft Visual Studio 8\Common7\IDE\PrivateAssemblies

Notice that Report Server has two configuration files. One–ReportingServicesService.exe.config–controls only the trace logs, which will be covered later in the chapter. The other–RSReportServer.config–controls everything else. Of all the configuration files, RSReportServer.config is the most important.

Report Manager and Report Designer are applications that are separate from the core report server engine. If you use a custom or third-party application instead of these applications, you don't need to concern yourself with configuring Report Manager and Report Designer. However, if you do use either of these applications and need to make a configuration change, such as add a rendering extension, you modify the corresponding configuration files.

In addition to the four main configuration files just described, the two Web services–Report Manager and the Report Server–each have a Web.config file, like many ASP.NET Web applications. You might want to modify these configuration files to control trace logs or to add configuration settings for your own custom applications that use the Reporting Services platform.

Reporting Services also includes some configuration files that are internally managed and should not be modified. For example, RSPreviewPolicy.config (for Report Designer), rsmgrpolicy.config (for Report Manager), and rssrvpolicy.config (for the Report Server Service) all manage encrypted keys for critical trusted services. There are also some .ini configuration files that are used for internal purposes and should not be modified.

If you need to change the default behavior of Reporting Services, you can use an XML editor to modify the rsreportserver.config file. Connection information stored in rsreportserver.config is encrypted, so naturally, you cannot simply edit the XML file. You must use a connection utility that is installed with Reporting Services to make changes to the encrypted data.

Editing the rsreportserver.config File

The rsreportserver.config file contains all the settings that apply to the report server engine (except the trace log settings). These settings include the connection string for the ReportServer database, thread and memory management settings, time-out values, Simple Mail Transfer Protocol (SMTP) server settings, and an open connection limit setting for a single user. (For a complete list of settings in this and other configuration files, refer to SQL Server Books Online.) This file also contains configuration information about delivery, rendering, data, and security extensions, so if you create a custom extension (as discussed in Chapter 18, "Building Custom Reporting Tools"), you'll need to modify this file.

> **Note** The RSWebApplication.config file contains settings needed by the Report Manager application. Report Manager needs to know the URL for the Report Server Web service, so if you change the location of the Report Server service, you need to change the URL stored in the RSWebApplication.config file.

In this procedure, you'll edit the rsreportserver.config file in Microsoft Visual Studio to change the number of active sessions permitted per user.

Change unencrypted information in the RSReportServer.config file

1. Using Windows Explorer, make a backup copy of the rsreportserver.config file in the C:\Program Files\Microsoft SQL Server\MSSQL.3\Reporting Services\ReportServer folder (assuming you used the default installation location for Reporting Services).

> **Important** Before making changes to configuration files, you should always make a copy of the file for restoring settings in case a change you make causes a problem.

2. Using Visual Studio, open rsreportserver.config. Alternatively, you can use any XML editor, or even Microsoft Notepad, to open a configuration file and make modifications.

   Your screen should look similar to this:

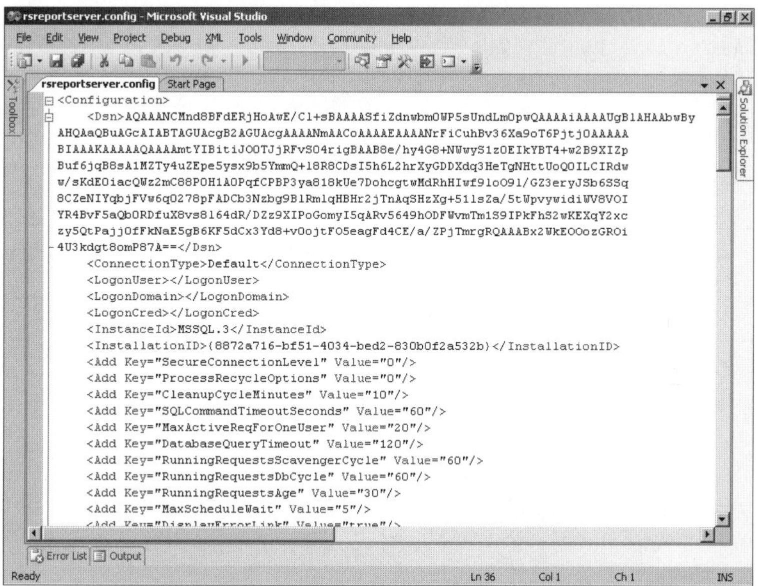

   Notice the encrypted data in the *<Dsn>*, *<LogonUser>*, *<LogonDomain>*, and *<LogonCred>* elements. You need to use a utility to change this data, and you'll learn about how to use this utility later in this chapter.

3. Scroll through the file (or press Ctrl+F to use the Find feature) to find the *<UnattendedExecutionAccount>* element.

   This section of the configuration file looks like this:

```
<UnattendedExecutionAccount>
   <UserName></UserName>
```

```
    <Password></Password>
    <Domain></Domain>
</UnattendedExecutionAccount>
```

The elements nested in the *<UnattendedExecutionAccount>* element currently have no values (assuming you're never used the *rsconfig* utility to add credentials for unattended reports). Because the data stored here must be encrypted, you can't provide credentials using the XML editor at this point, but in the next procedure, you'll learn how to update these values.

4. Scroll up from the *<UnattendedExecutionAccount>* element to find the setting *Max-ActiveReqForOneUser*, and then change its value from 20 to **10**.

   This section of the configuration file looks like this:

```
<Add Key="MaxActiveReqForOneUser" Value="10"/>
```

> **Important** Before making any changes to a configuration file, take the time to review the description of the configuration settings in SQL Server Books Online to be sure you understand the purpose of a setting and the type of values that are appropriate for each setting.

By changing this setting, you are limiting each user to a maximum number of 10 active requests on the Report Server.

5. Save and close the file, but keep Visual Studio open for the next procedure.

   Configuration changes are seamlessly integrated into the running application, so you will not have to stop and restart the service.

Changing Encrypted Configuration Information Using the *rsconfig* Utility

As you have just seen, to keep the connection information Reporting Services uses to connect to the ReportServer database properly secured, the values for the connection information elements in the RSReportServer.config file are encrypted. When you need to change the name of the ReportServer database, the server instance where the database is located, or the credentials used to connect to the database, you must use the *rsconfig* utility supplied with Reporting Services.

You must have administrator privileges on the Report Server to use the *rsconfig* utility. Here is the syntax for using this utility on the Report Server using Windows authentication:

```
rsconfig -c -m computername -s SQLServername -d ReportServerDatabaseName -a windows -u
[domain\]username -p password
```

You can omit the *-m* argument if you are running the utility on the Report Server. The *-s* argument isn't needed if the ReportServer database is located in a local default SQL Server instance. If the database is located in a named instance, use `servername\instancename` for the *-s* argument. For the *-a* argument, you will need to instead use `sql` rather than `windows` if you are using a SQL login to connect to the server. You can add an additional *-t* argument (with no value) to add trace information to error messages.

> **Note** When you use the *-c* argument with the *rsconfig* utility, the values in the *<Dsn>*, *<LogonUser>*, *<LogonDomain>*, and *<LogonCred>* elements are updated with encrypted values. One common scenario that requires using this utility is a change to the credentials used to connect to the ReportServer database. Another common situation is the movement of the ReportServer database to a remote SQL Server instance, which requires a change to the connection information that can only be made using the *rsconfig* utility.

If you have reports that run unattended (scheduled reports and subscriptions) and use a data source that does not require credentials, the Report Server still needs credentials to connect to the computer hosting a remote data source. You use the *rsconfig* utility to store the credentials to connect to the remote computer as encrypted data in the Report Server's configuration file.

> **Note** This situation should be pretty rare, since all of your data sources should be secured. However, there may be a circumstance where you have a database that contains general reference information that doesn't require security. If an unattended report using such a database tries to run when Report Server has no credentials to use to connect to the host computer, the execution will fail.

The syntax to use to add credentials for unattended report processing is

```
rsconfig -e -m computername -s SQLServername -u [domain\]username -p password
```

Again, you can omit the *-m* and *-s* arguments if you're running the on a ReportServer with a local SQL Server instance. The *-t* argument can also be used to add trace information to error messages when configuring the unattended report execution credentials.

In this procedure, you'll add credentials for the Report Server to use when running unattended reports.

Encrypt credentials for unattended reports

1. On the Start menu, click Run, type **cmd**, and then click OK to open a Command Prompt window.
2. Type **rsconfig -?** to view the online help for this utility.

3. Run the *rsconfig* utility by typing the following: **rsconfig -e -u *YourUserName* -p *YourPassword*** (replacing *YourUserName* and *YourPassword* with a valid domain\user name and password).

> **Note** The syntax used in this step assumes that you have all components installed on your local computer. If you later want to use your local installation of Reporting Services in a production environment, use the *rsconfig* utility to assign the appropriate credentials. If you don't want to assign any credentials for unattended reports, you can edit the XML file to clear the values for the elements nested in the *<UnattendedExecutionAccount>* element—but don't remove the element tags.

4. Using Visual Studio, open the rsreportserver.config file in the C:\Program Files \Microsoft SQL Server\MSSQL.3\Reporting Services\ReportServer folder (assuming you used the default installation location for Reporting Services).
5. Scroll through the file to find the *<UnattendedExecutionAccount>* element.

   This section of the configuration file looks similar to this:

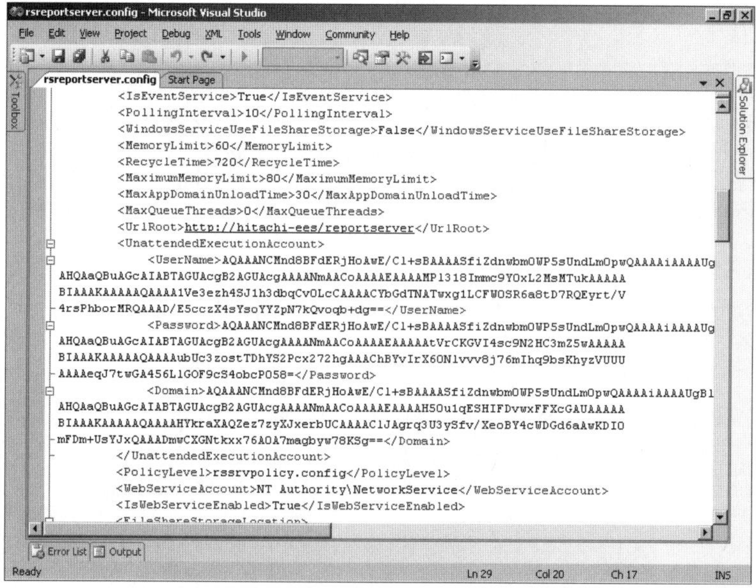

   The elements nested in the *<UnattendedExecutionAccount>* element now have values, each of which is encrypted.

6. Close the file, but keep Visual Studio open for the next procedure.

Configuring Tracing on the Report Server

Reporting Services records information about server operations in trace logs that are located in the C:\Program Files\Microsoft SQL Server\MSSQL.3\Reporting Services\LogFiles folder. Each day, beginning with the first traceable activity that occurs after midnight (local time for the Report Server) or again if Reporting Services is restarted, new trace logs are created. There are four types of trace log files:

- **ReportServerService_main_<*timestamp*>.log** Logs operations of the Report Server Windows and Web services, such as server resource allocation and initialization of settings defined in the configuration files.
- **ReportServerService_<*timestamp*>.log** Records details about operations, such as the initialization of certain service settings as well as the status of polling activities related to schedules, subscriptions, and delivery notifications.
- **ReportServerWebApp_<*timestamp*>.log** Captures information about Report Manager operations, such as HTTP headers and stack trace information, as well as SOAP envelopes and exceptions.
- **ReportServer_<*timestamp*>.log** Logs various information for the Report Server engine, such as exceptions and warnings generated by the Report Server or calls to perform actions like processing reports, creating folders, or deleting items.

These trace logs can be quite helpful when you are debugging a custom application that uses the Report Server, or if you need to troubleshoot a problem that appears in the event log or execution log. (You'll learn more about these other logs later in this chapter.) You can control the amount of detail that is recorded in the trace log files by changing the value of the *DefaultTraceSwitch* setting in the ReportingServicesService.exe.config file and the Web.config file (found in the C:\Program Files\Microsoft SQL Server\MSSQL.3\Reporting Services\ReportServer\bin). You can also disable tracing with this setting, but Microsoft recommends that you always trace at some level in case you ever need to troubleshoot an issue. The possible values for this setting are shown in the following table.

Value	Tracing Level
0	Disables tracing
1	Exceptions and restarts
2	Exceptions, restarts, and warnings
3	Exceptions, restarts, warnings, and status messages (Default setting)
4	Verbose mode

You can also change settings in the ReportingServicesService.exe.config file to route tracing to a debug window instead of to a file. You can use another setting in this file to limit tracing to a single component. By default, trace logs are created for the Report Server, Report Server Web Application, and Report Server service. In addition, you can change the number of days for which trace logs are kept. As a reminder, before making any changes to a configuration file, first read the description of the configuration settings in SQL Server Books Online.

In this procedure, you'll change the ReportingServicesService.exe.config file to keep log files for 10 days only.

Edit the ReportingServicesService.exe.config file

1. Using Visual Studio, open the ReportingServicesService.exe.config file in the C:\Program Files\Microsoft SQL Server\MSSQL.3\Reporting Services\ReportServer\bin folder (assuming you used the default installation location for Reporting Services).

   The top of the configuration file looks like this:

```
<configuration>
  <configSections>
       <section name="RStrace" type="Microsoft.ReportingServices.
           Diagnostics.RSTraceSectionHandler,
           Microsoft.ReportingServices.Diagnostics" />
   </configSections>
   <system.diagnostics>
         <switches>
               <add name="DefaultTraceSwitch" value="3" />
         </switches>
   </system.diagnostics>
   <RStrace>
         <add name="FileName" value="ReportServerService_" />
         <add name="FileSizeLimitMb" value="32" />
         <add name="KeepFilesForDays" value="14" />
         <add name="Prefix" value="tid, time" />
         <add name="TraceListeners" value="debugwindow, file" />
         <add name="TraceFileMode" value="unique" />
         <add name="Components" value="all" />
   </RStrace>
```

   Notice the default value of 3 for the *DefaultTraceSwitch* setting that controls the level of tracing.

2. Change the setting *KeepFilesForDays* value to **10**.

   You can increase or decrease this number as desired to control the length of time that trace logs are kept. When the number of days is exceeded, the trace logs are deleted from the file system.

3. Save and then close the file.

Managing the Report Server

In addition to using trace logs to capture details about Reporting Services operations, you can use an *execution log* to help you manage report execution. An execution log provides even more detail about the reports that are processed than you'll find in the trace log. With an execution log, you can monitor the duration and success rate of report executions; identify bottlenecks by examining execution times; and optimize report executions by using request frequency, execution times, and user information to help you choose an appropriate execution method for each report.

Besides monitoring activity on the server, Reporting Services provides several methods you can implement to proactively manage the resources on your server. You can use time-out settings to stop queries or report executions that take too long. In addition to this automatic approach to shutting down jobs, you can manually cancel a job whenever necessary. You can also temporarily suspend jobs by disabling either a shared data source or a shared schedule.

Using Performance Counters

Reporting Services also includes ASP.NET performance counters for you to monitor the performance of the services. Reviewing these performance counters can help you make decisions about how to best manage your server. Performance counters belong to two performance objects. One object, *MSRS 2005 Windows Service*, includes counters for all activity that happens on the server, whether scheduled or interactive. The second object, *MSRS 2005 Web Service*, includes counters for activity initiated through a scheduled operation. Many counters appear in both objects, some are specific to the *MSRS 2005 Windows Service* object, and others are specific to the *MSRS 2005 Web Service* object.

Some counters show current state (for example, Active Sessions), some show current rates (for example, Requests/Sec), and some show a cumulative total since the service was last started (for example, Total Requests). To find instructions for using the Windows Performance tool, search the help file for your operating system. Details about the performance counters themselves are in SQL Server Books Online.

Here are some performance counters you might monitor regularly:

- Active Sessions, to obtain the count of all active browser sessions
- Reports Executed/Sec, to determine the volume of successful report execution
- Requests/Sec, to compare with Reports Executed/Sec to evaluate the proportion of reports executed to reports returned from the cache
- Total Requests, to track the number of requests since the service started
- Total Processing Failures, to monitor failure rates since the service started as compared with Total Requests

How to Monitor Performance

You can monitor report execution performance using execution logs. Execution logs differ from trace logs because the latter are stored in a set of files, whereas execution logs are stored in the ReportServer database. Because execution logs are intended for continual analysis, the data is stored relationally. The information that is stored in the ExecutionLog table of the ReportServer database isn't the best format for general reporting and analysis, but you can create your own logging database to which you can export logging records on a periodic basis. Reporting Services supplies you with the following tools to facilitate reporting on the logs:

- A script to create tables in your own database
- A SQL Server 2005 Integration Services (SSIS) package to load logging records into this database
- Reports that allow you to review the execution information loaded into the new database

You will work with these tools later in this chapter. You can schedule the SSIS package to perform periodic extracts from the ExecutionLog table to keep your logging database current and to allow you to delete rows from the log tables.

Managing Execution Logging

You can use the Site Settings page in Report Manager to start or stop execution logging at any time. You must be assigned to the System Administrator role in SQL Server to be able to change this setting. By default, execution logging is enabled, and log records will be kept for only 60 days. You can increase or decrease the number of days as desired to limit the amount of logging history that accumulates in the ExecutionLog table in the ReportServer database. Logging records that exceed the specified number are removed each day at 2:00 A.M. (local time for the Report Server). Alternatively, you can remove this limitation if you want to allow logging records to accumulate indefinitely. If you use the SSIS package mentioned earlier to copy the logs to a reporting database, you can delete logs as soon as they are copied to the logging database by adding an additional package step.

In this procedure, you'll open the Site Settings page in Report Manager to review the current execution logging settings.

Review current execution logging settings

1. Open Report Manager in Internet Explorer at *http://localhost/Reports*.

2. Click the Site Settings link to review the settings shown here:

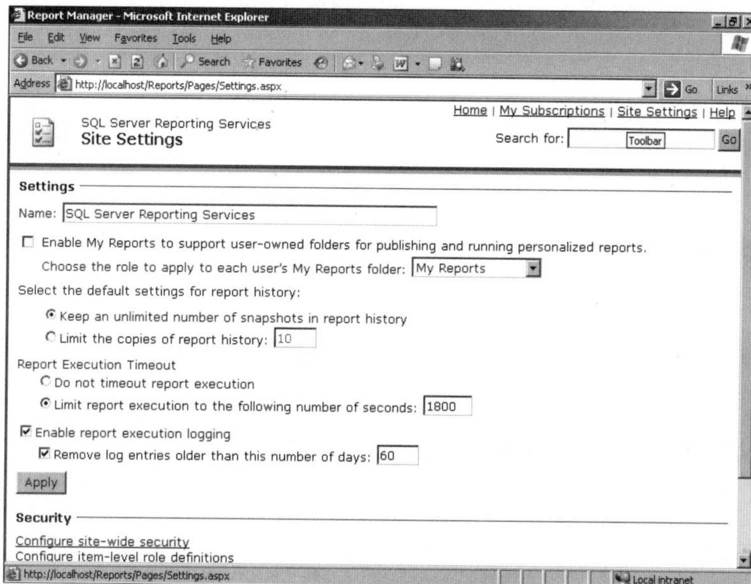

If you want to disable execution logging, you can clear the Enable Report Execution Logging check box. Notice that you can type a different number of days to change the frequency with which logging records are removed from the ExecutionLog table. To make the changes take effect, click Apply.

Initializing an Execution Log Database

Reporting Services provides the tools you need to effectively report and analyze information related to report processing. To get started, you will need to create a SQL Server database, and then you can use a supplied script to build the necessary tables in your new database. After creating the tables, you can use the SSIS package supplied by Reporting Services to load the new tables with data from the ExecutionLog table.

In this procedure, you'll create the RSExecutionLog database in which you'll create tables using a script and then use a SSIS package to load data into the tables.

Create and load the execution log database

1. Open Microsoft SQL Server Management Studio and connect to the Database Engine.
2. Right-click the Databases folder, and then click New Database.
3. Type a name for the database in the New Database properties dialog box: **RSExecutionLog**.
4. Click Options, set the Recovery Model to Simple, and then click OK.
5. Click Open File on the toolbar, navigate to the C:\Documents and Settings\<username>\My Documents\Microsoft Press\rs2005sbs\chap11 folder, open the createtables.sql file, and connect to the Database Engine.

> **Note** The createtables.sql file is included for your convenience in the practice files. Reporting Services supplies this file in the SQL Server 2005 samples. After you install the samples, you'll find this file in the C:\Program Files\Microsoft SQL Server\90\Samples\Reporting Services\Report Samples\Server Management Sample Reports\Execution Log Sample Reports folder.

6. Click RSExecutionLog in the Availalbe Database drop-down list.
7. Click Execute (or press F5) to run the createtables.sql script.

   The results of the query execution are displayed in the Messages tab on the Results pane:

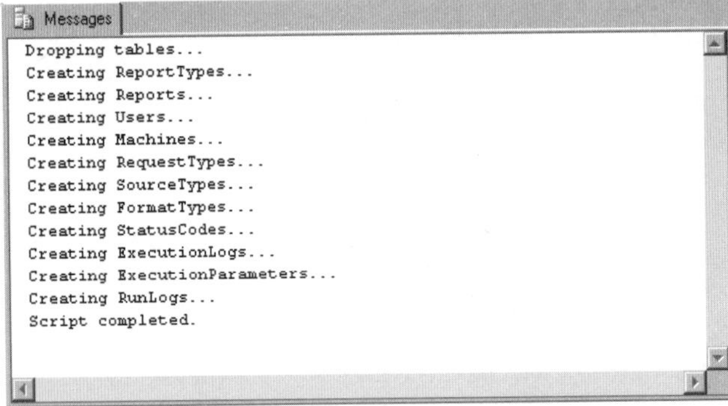

Messages
Dropping tables...
Creating ReportTypes...
Creating Reports...
Creating Users...
Creating Machines...
Creating RequestTypes...
Creating SourceTypes...
Creating FormatTypes...
Creating StatusCodes...
Creating ExecutionLogs...
Creating ExecutionParameters...
Creating RunLogs...
Script completed.

8. In Windows Explorer, double-click the RSExecutionLog_Update.dtsx file in the C:\Documents and Settings\<username>\My Documents\Microsoft Press\rs2005sbs\chap11 folder.

   The Execute Package Utility dialog box is displayed:

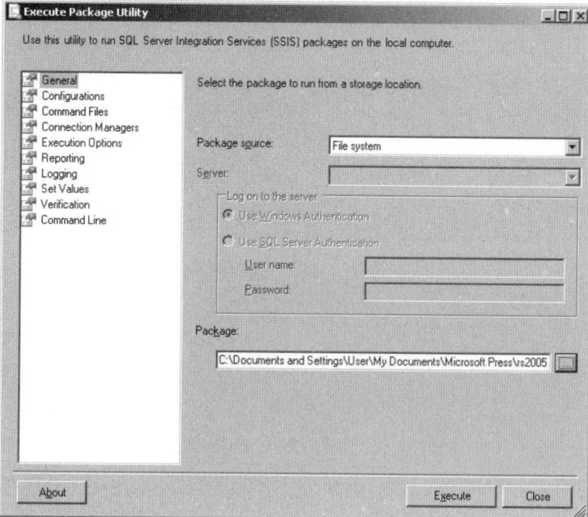

9. Click Execute to start running the package.

> **Note** As with the script file you just used, the RSExecutionLog_Update.dtsx file is also included for your convenience in the practice files. You can find this file if you installed the SQL Server 2005 samples section in the C:\Program Files\Microsoft SQL Server\90\Samples\Reporting Services\Report Samples\Server Management Sample Reports\Execution Log Sample Reports folder.

When package execution is complete, your screen looks like this:

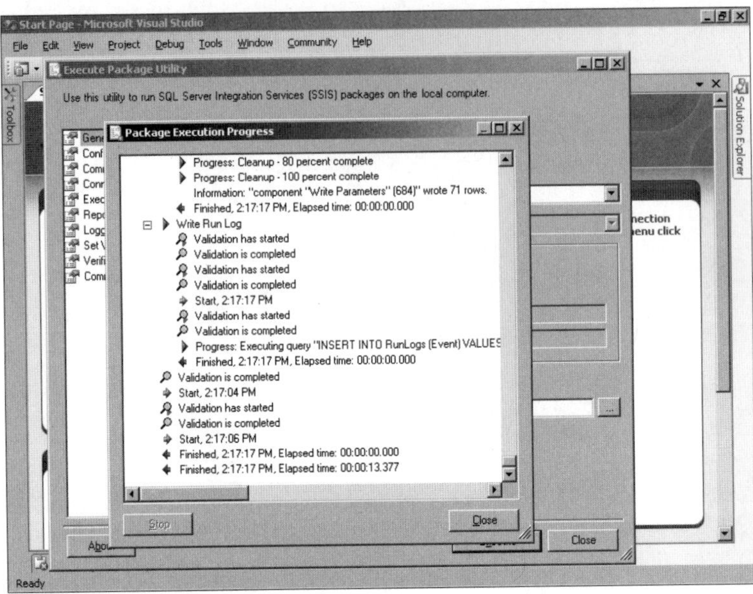

10. Click Close. Leave the Execute Package Utility open because you'll use it again in a later procedure.

Using an Execution Log Report

To help you review the information extracted to the RSExecutionLog database, Reporting Services supplies several sample execution logging reports. The practice files supplied with this book include several more reports to review execution log information. You can use the reports with or without modification, or add your own reports to use the execution logging information in different ways.

In this procedure, you'll deploy the execution logging reports, review the Average Report Execution Times report, and then deploy reports for comparing execution times.

Deploy execution logging reports

1. Using Visual Studio, open the ExecutionLog solution in the C:\Documents and Settings\<username>\My Documents\Microsoft Press\rs2005sbs\chap11\Execution Log folder.

The Solution Explorer window looks like this:

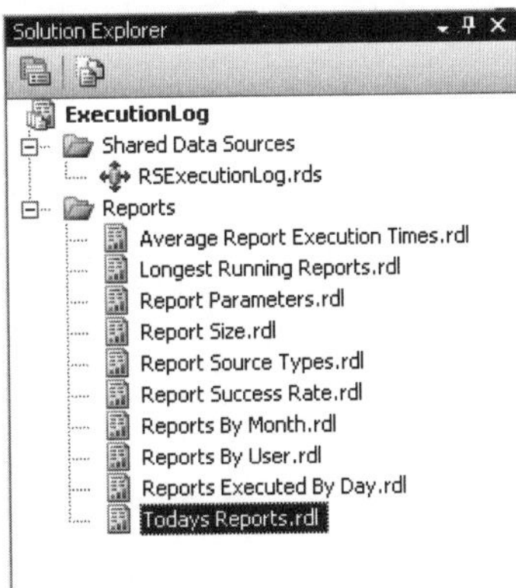

Note The shared data source in this solution assumes you've named the new database RSExecutionLog, as described in the previous procedure, and that the database is on the local server.

2. Right-click the ExecutionLog project, and then click Deploy.
3. When the project successfully deploys, open the Home page in Report Manager.
4. Click the Example Reports folder link, click the Execution Log Reports folder link, and then click the Average Report Execution Times report link.

   The top of the report looks similar to this:

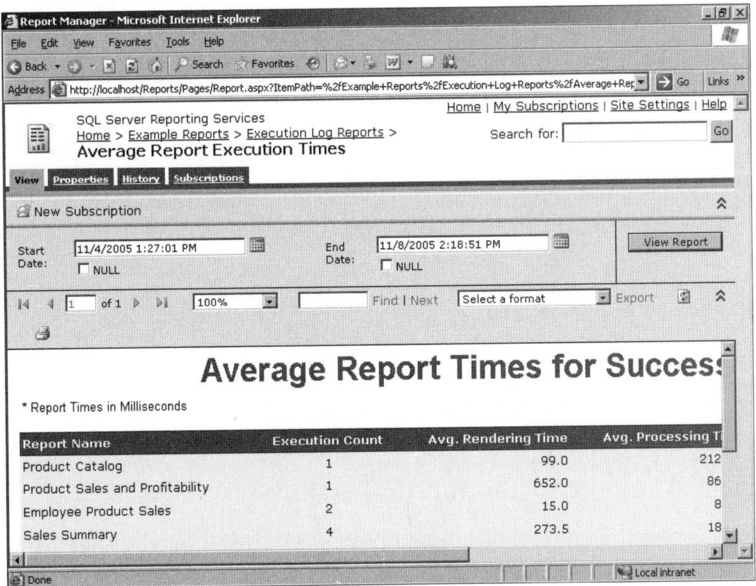

You'll see report names and metrics in this report that correspond to your usage of Reporting Services, but the speed of your computer might result in times different from those shown in this report. You'll need to scroll horizontally to see all averages calculated for a report. Notice the report parameters to select a start and end date for the report. The default values for these report parameters are calculated from the earliest and latest dates in the RSExecutionLog database tables.

In the sample report shown here, the Product Sales and Profitability report has the longest rendering time. Your computer might render faster or slower. As you review the details of this report, you can see that the reports are listed in descending order of average total execution time. This execution time includes data retrieval, processing, and rendering time, which are displayed in separate columns for comparison.

5. Using Visual Studio, open the Filter vs Parameter solution in the C:\Documents and Settings\<username>\My Documents\Microsoft Press\rs2005sbs\chap11\Execution Log folder.
6. On the Build menu, click Deploy Filter vs Parameter.

   The two reports in this solution use identical queries. You will execute these reports to compare the difference between the time to execute a report that uses a dataset filter, Product Profitability Filter, and the time to execute a report that uses a query parameter, Product Profitability Query Parameter.
7. When the project successfully deploys, switch from Visual Studio to Report Manager, and then click the Execution Log Reports link.
8. Click the Product Profitability Filter report link to execute the report.

   The execution time required for this report includes data retrieval, report processing, and rendering time, because this is the first time the report has been executed since deployment to the Report Server.
9. In the Category drop-down list, select Accessory, and then click View Report.

   Since this report uses a dataset filter, there is no execution time for data retrieval or report processing when you change the category value. Only rendering time will be required to display Accessory data in this report.
10. In the Category drop-down list, select Bike, click View Report, and then repeat this step for the Clothing category.
11. Click the Execution Log Reports folder link.
12. Click the Product Profitability Query Parameter Report link to execute the report.
13. In the Category drop-down list, select Accessory, click View Report, and then repeat this step for the Bike category, and then again for the Clothing category.

    This report is created with query parameters, so each time you click View Report, execution time includes data retrieval, report processing, and rendering time.

14. Click the Execution Log Reports folder link.
15. Click the Average Report Execution Times report link.

    Notice that neither the Product Profitability Filter report nor the Product Profitability Query Parameter report is displayed in this report. The execution log reports are dependent on the data that currently exists in the RSExecutionLog database, which was extracted *before* you executed the product reports. You need to update the RSExecutionLog database to append records for the execution logging for the product reports.

Adding Current Data to the Execution Log

The RSExecutionLog is not designed to stay synchronized with the execution logging data in the ReportServer database. You need to determine a reasonable frequency for updating the RSExecutionLog database with new execution logging records, and then schedule the SSIS package to execute with this frequency. (Refer to SQL Server Books Online for more information about scheduling an SSIS package.)

In this procedure, you'll update the RSExecutionLog database by executing the RSExecutionLog_Update package.

Update the execution log database

1. Switch to the Execute Package Utility, and then click Execute.
2. Click Close twice.

   The SSIS package appended new records to the RSExecutionLog database.

> **Note** Rather than append records to the logging database, you might want to remove records for older data. You can use the cleanup.sql script in the C:\Documents and Settings\<username>\My Documents\Microsoft Press\rs2005sbs\chap11 folder. This file is also located in the C:\Program Files\Microsoft SQL Server\90\Samples\Reporting Services\Report Samples\Server Management Sample Reports\Execution Log Sample Reports folder if you installed the SQL Server 2005 samples.

3. Close the Execute Package Utility.

In this procedure, you'll use execution logging reports to compare the performance of the Product Profitability Filter and Product Profitability Query Parameter reports.

Compare execution performance

1. In Report Manager, return to the Execution Log Reports page, and then click the Average Report Execution Times report link.
2. If necessary, replace the values in the Start Date and End Date boxes with the current date and time in the End Date box, and then click View Report. You might need to scroll through the report to find the product reports.

The averages for the product reports should look similar to this:

Average Report Times for Successf

* Report Times in Milliseconds

Report Name	Execution Count	Avg. Rendering Time	Avg. Processing Time	Avg. Data Retrieval Time	Avg. Total Time
Product Profitability Filter	1	95.0	348.0	1404.0	1847.0
Product Profitability Query Parameter	4	35.8	88.5	142.3	266.5

Note The report shown in this example was exported to Microsoft Excel and reformatted to better display all data for these two reports. You might need to scroll horizontally to view the values in each column in Report Manager.

The averages shown in your report will differ because of variations in server configurations. Using the report illustrated here, you can see that the relative performance of the two reports is similar. The average rendering time of the two product reports in the previous illustration is nearly the same, because rendering was required when each report was opened and each time View Report was clicked. The processing time and data retrieval time is greater for the Product Profitability Filter report, even though the query executed only once. However, the query retrieved data for all categories, which increased the data retrieval time as well as the processing time of the report. In the case of the Product Profitability Query Parameter report, the use of query parameters to retrieve a smaller dataset actually resulted in faster performance overall compared to the other report.

As indicated in the Average Report Execution Times report, the times displayed in the report are milliseconds, so any delay experienced by the user in executing these reports is not particularly noticeable. However, when you are working with reports including production data, you can use the information in the Average Report Execution Times report to help you discover bottlenecks so you can take appropriate action to resolve report problems. For example, if you see that data retrieval is consuming a considerable amount of the overall processing time, you might try to improve the performance of the SQL query. If, on the other hand, you see processing is taking a long time, you might look for ways to reduce the complexity of the report.

3. Click the Execution Log Reports folder link, and then click the Report Parameters report link.
4. Expand Product Profitability Filter, and then expand Product Profitability Query Parameter.

The top of the report looks similar to this:

Report Parameter Summary

* Report Times in Milliseconds

Report/Parameter Name	Execution Count	Avg Total Time
⊟ Product Profitability Query Parameter	12	266.5
Month	4	266.5
1	4	266.5
Category	4	266.5
Component	1	371

This report lets you compare and contrast the average total execution time by report parameter. This average is computed by dividing the total execution time for the report by the number of report executions.

5. Click the Execution Log Reports folder link, and then click the Report Source Types report link.
6. Expand Product Profitability Filter, and then expand Product Profitability Query Parameter.

   The top of the report looks similar to this:

Report Source Type Summary

* Report Times in Milliseconds

Report Name / Start Time	Source Type	Report Execution Time
⊞ Average Report Execution Times		1535
⊟ Product Profitability Query Parameter		1066
11/9/2005 2:26:00 PM	Live	240
11/9/2005 2:25:55 PM	Live	297
11/9/2005 2:25:50 PM	Live	158
11/9/2005 2:25:40 PM	Live	371

Here, you can see execution times by source type. Possible source types are Snapshot, Live, Cache, and History. Because the source type can affect execution times, you should review this report when evaluating the performance of a report.

Applying Time-outs to Source Queries

You can only add a source query time-out to a report during the authoring stage. When the report executes, if the query doesn't finish before the query time-out is exceeded, the report execution will fail. You can use a query time-out to protect the source database from the effect of unexpectedly long-running queries. Each dataset in a report has its own query time-out setting.

In this procedure, you'll change the query time-out to the Product Profitability Query Parameter report.

Add a time-out to a source query

1. In Visual Studio, open the Product Profitability Query Parameter report. If you closed the solution after completing the previous procedure, open the Filter vs Parameter solution in the folder C:\Documents and Settings\<username>\My Documents\Microsoft Press\rs2005sbs\chap11\Execution Log, and then open this report.
2. Click the Data tab, select Category in the Dataset drop-down list, and then click Edit Selected Dataset.
3. Type **60** in the Timeout box.

   The Dataset dialog box looks like this:

   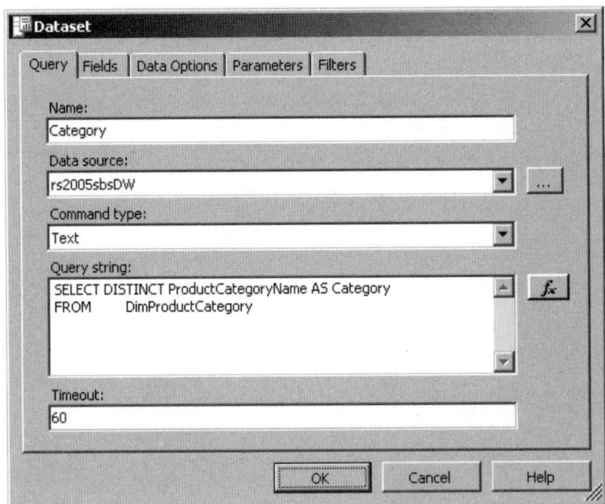

4. Click OK, and then save the project.

   If you were to deploy the report, the query time-out would be applied each time the Category query executes.

Applying Time-outs to Report Execution

Another option for managing server resources is to use Report Manager to establish time-outs for report execution. You can set a global time-out value that applies to all reports on the Report Server, or you can override the global value on individual reports. You also have the option of not using time-outs for report execution.

In this procedure, you'll review the global time-out value and apply a time-out value to the Average Report Execution Times report.

Add a time-out to report execution

1. In Report Manager, click the Site Settings link.

The Site Settings page looks like this:

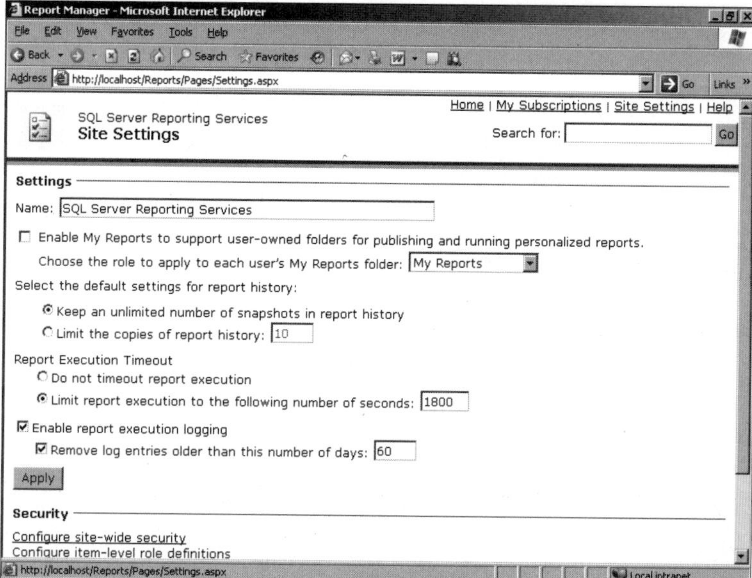

Notice that the current default setting for Report Execution Timeout is set to 1800 seconds. This setting will apply to all reports that execute on the Report Server unless you override the setting for an individual report.

2. Click the Home link.
3. Click the Example Reports folder link, click the Execution Log Reports folder link, and then click the Average Report Execution Times report link.
4. Click the Properties tab, and then click the Execution link.
5. If necessary, scroll to the bottom of the page to find the Report Execution Timeout section.
6. Click Limit Report Execution To The Following Number Of Seconds and type **60** in the box.

The bottom of the screen looks like this:

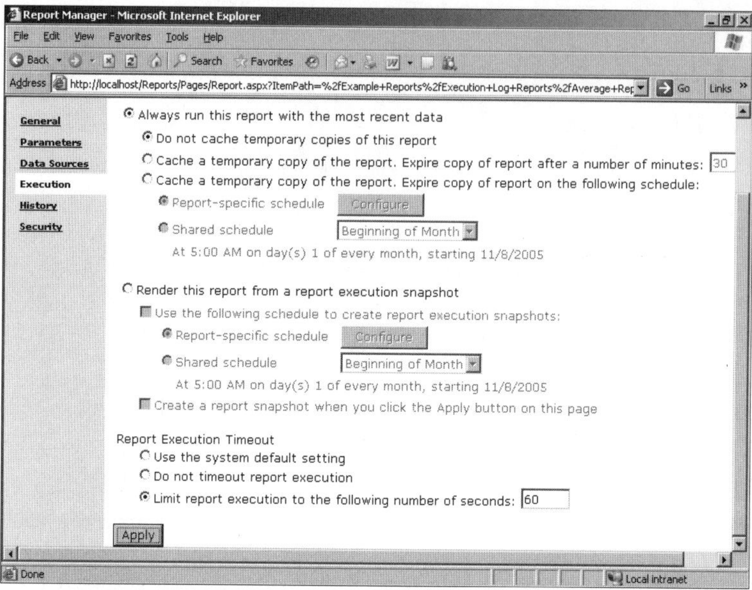

7. Click Apply.

   Now this report will fail when execution takes longer than 60 seconds. Of course, you'll need to monitor reports in your own production environment to determine an appropriate time-out value globally or for individual reports.

Canceling Jobs

In addition to using time-outs to stop a report, you can manually cancel a report by using the Report Manager. From the Site Settings page, you can access the Manage Jobs page to display jobs that are currently executing. You can select one or more jobs to cancel on this page. However, bear in mind that killing the job with Report Manager doesn't necessarily kill the corresponding process in the source database.

In this procedure, you'll execute a report to see how jobs appear in the Manage Jobs page. To perform this procedure, you'll need to have two instances of Internet Explorer running Report Manager.

Review the Manage Jobs page

1. In the first instance of Internet Explorer, use Report Manager to navigate to Site Settings.
2. At the bottom of the Site Settings page, click the Manage Jobs link.

   This page currently has no jobs to display.

3. In a second instance of Internet Explorer, use Report Manager to open the Reports Executed By Day report, which is found in the Execution Log Reports subfolder of the Example Reports folder.
4. Switch to the first instance of Internet Explorer, and then click Refresh on the Internet Explorer toolbar to update the page. You might need to click Refresh a few times in quick succession to see the job appear on this page.

Note If, after a few seconds, you still don't see the job appear, you might not have switched between applications quickly enough. In that case, click the Execution Log Reports link and open another report. Quickly switch to the Manage Jobs page, refreshing the page repeatedly until the job appears. If you still can't see the job, it might be that your computer is too fast for the job to display on this page. In a production environment, you'll likely have an opportunity to monitor jobs on this page.

The Manage Jobs page looks like this:

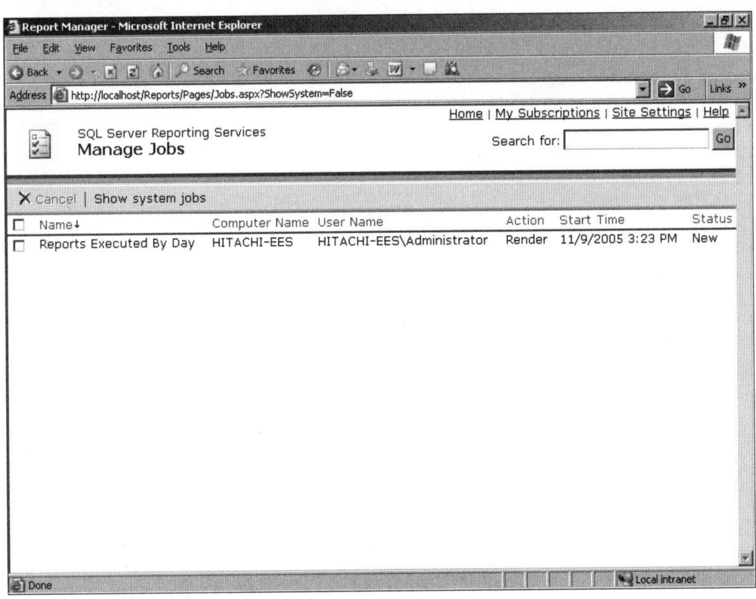

If you need to cancel one or more jobs, you can select the job's check box, and then click Cancel on the Report Manager toolbar.

Disabling a Shared Data Source

Sometimes, you might want to temporarily prevent reports from executing altogether. You might need to suspend jobs while performing maintenance on a source database or when troubleshooting data issues. Any reports that had been assigned to the disabled shared data source can't execute until the shared data source is enabled or a new data source is assigned.

Subscriptions using a disabled shared data source are also prevented from executing. Disabling a shared data source is an easy way to temporarily suspend many reports with one step. You should consider using shared data sources whenever possible so you can take advantage of this feature, because you can't disable custom data sources.

In this procedure, you'll suspend the rs2005sbsDW shared data source in the Execution Log Reports subfolder.

Suspend jobs by disabling a shared data source

1. In Report Manager, open the rs2005sbsDW shared data source in the Execution Log Reports subfolder of the Example Reports folder.
2. Click the Dependent Items tab.

   Your screen looks like this:

   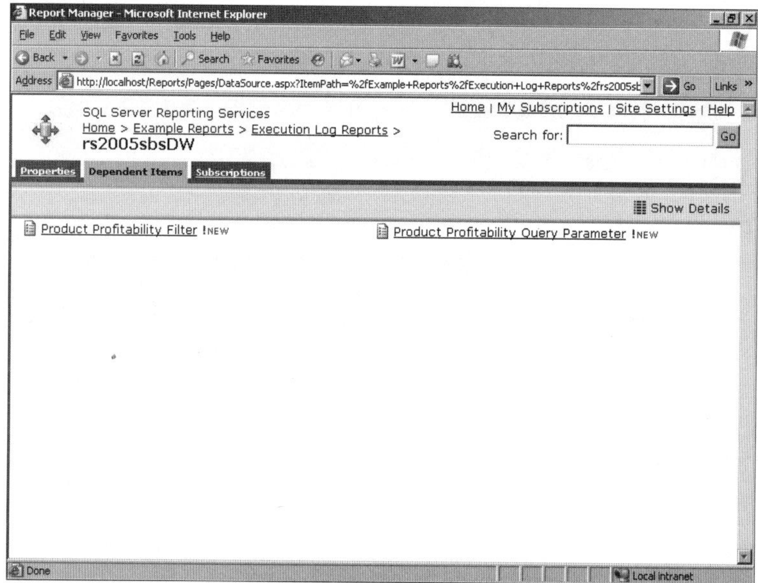

   A list of reports that are associated with the current shared data source is always available. This feature gives you the opportunity to assess the impact of disabling the shared data source. Notice also the Subscriptions tab, which serves the same purpose for subscriptions dependent on the current shared data source.

3. Click the Properties tab.
4. Clear the Enable This Data Source check box.

Your screen looks like this:

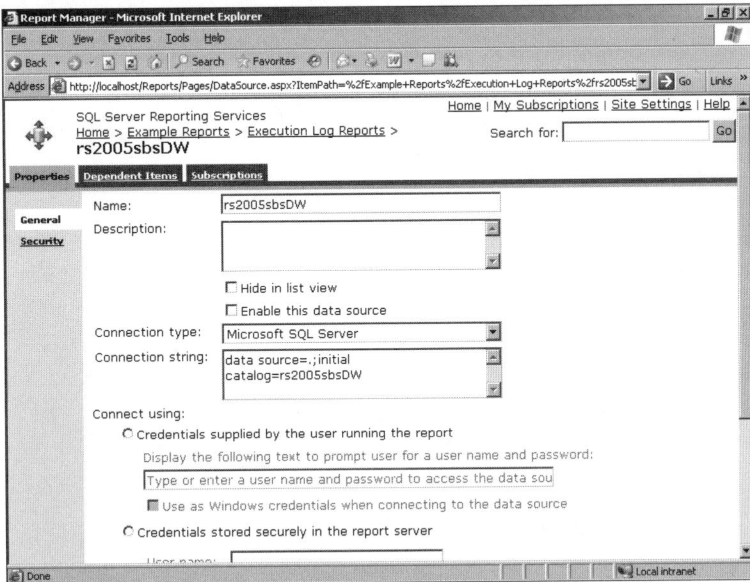

5. Click Apply.

   Now any reports or subscriptions that use this shared data source will be suspended.

6. Click the Execution Log Reports link, and then click the Product Profitability Filter report link.

   Your screen looks like this:

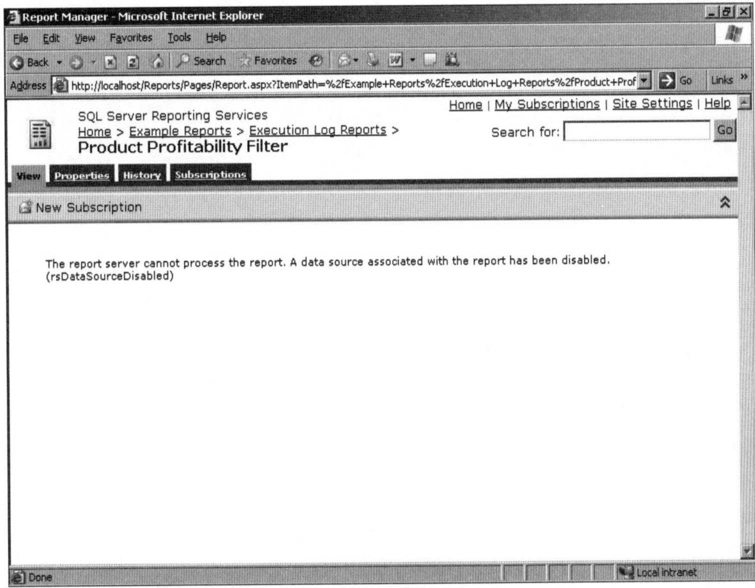

If a user attempts to execute an on-demand report that uses a disabled shared data source, an error message is displayed. However, a snapshot of the report can still be viewed.

Pausing a Shared Schedule

You can also pause a shared schedule to temporarily suspend jobs. In Chapter 9, "Managing Content," you learned how to create a shared schedule by accessing the Shared Schedules page from the Site Settings page. You were also introduced to the Report Manager toolbar buttons that allow you to pause or resume a schedule. By pausing a schedule, you suspend related jobs, such as report executions and subscriptions. However, there is no list of reports or subscriptions provided for you to examine before pausing the schedule. Also, as with disabling a shared data source, pausing a shared schedule is an easy way to temporarily suspend many reports with one step, which isn't possible when using a custom schedule.

Administering Reporting Services Databases

You learned about the .ReportServer and the ReportServerTempDB databases while learning how to deploy reports and manage report execution. Now it's time to take a closer look at these databases from an administrative perspective. To manage these databases, you need to understand the factors that affect their size so you can manage your disk space resources appropriately. You also need to implement an appropriate disaster recovery strategy for these databases.

You use standard SQL Server tools to monitor the size of the tables in the ReportServer and ReportServerTempDB databases. You will need to understand how Reporting Services implementation decisions can increase or decrease their space requirements. To protect the data from disaster, you can use SQL Server backup utilities. However, because some information in the ReportServer database is encrypted, you'll also need to use the Reporting Services *rskeymgmt* utility to back up the encryption key.

Monitoring Database Storage Consumption

Reporting Services uses the ReportServer database as its primary storage component not only for reports, but also for configuration information, security assignments, and schedules. As such, Reporting Services cannot operate without the ReportServer database. The ReportServerTempDB database is also a storage component, but only for temporary data, such as session and caching information. The following table compares the contents of each database:

ReportServer	ReportServerTempDB
Folders, reports, resources	User session information
Shared data sources	Session caching
Snapshots and report history	Cached instances

ReportServer	ReportServerTempDB
Security	
Schedules	
Subscriptions and notifications	
Configuration	
Execution Log	

Most tables in either database don't consume much space, with the exception of the ChunkData table. In the ReportServer database, the ChunkData table contains snapshots and report history. Because snapshots and report history are stored in the intermediate format of a report, they also include all the report data, and consequently, consume a higher percentage of disk space than other tables in the database. The ChunkData table in the ReportServer-TempDB database contains the session cache and the cached instances, which also store reports in an intermediate format with data, so it, too, requires a large amount of disk space relative to other tables.

Check the ChunkData table size

1. Open Microsoft SQL Server Management Studio and connect to the Database Engine.
2. Expand the Databases folder, and then click ReportServer.
3. On the Summary tab, click the drop-down list arrow next to Report.
4. Choose Disk Usage Report.
5. Expand the Disk Space Used By Tables section.

   Your screen looks similar to this:

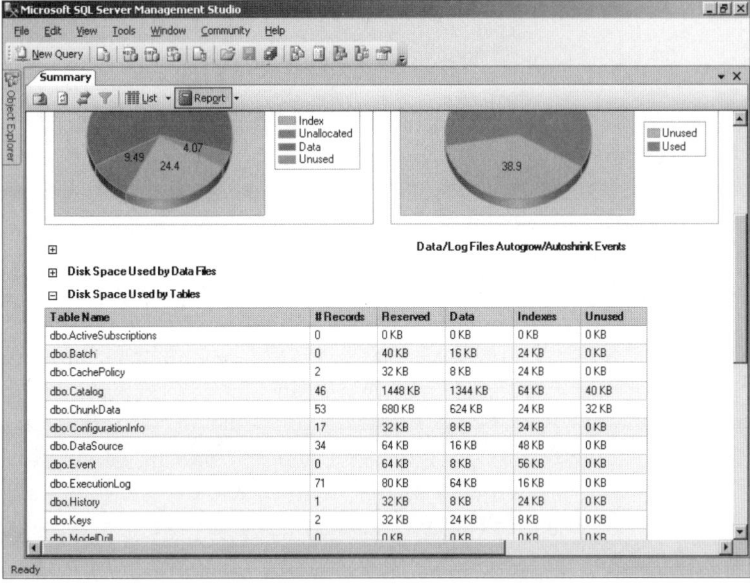

6. Scroll through the list to find the ChunkData table.

   As you add snapshots and report history, this table will continue to grow much faster than the other tables in this database. You can use this report to monitor its size. If it starts getting too large (which really depends on your specific environment), you might want to work with users to determine which snapshots are appropriate to take or how much report history is really needed.

Evaluating Disk Space Requirements

Because so many variables contribute to disk space consumption, there's no specific formula you can use to estimate disk space. However, the following list provides some general areas you can review when evaluating the impact of implementation decisions on server disk space:

- Total number of reports
- Total number of snapshots
- Total number of snapshots saved in report history
- Total size of intermediate reports (which include report data) in snapshots and report history
- Total number of cached instances resulting from different combinations of report parameters
- Total number of users affecting session cache
- Session cache time-out length

Implementing a Backup and Restore Strategy

You can take advantage of the backup and restore utilities provided with SQL Server 2005 as part of your disaster recovery plan. Backing up your ReportServer database, as well as the master and mdb databases, on a regular basis is critical because together they contain everything that Reporting Services needs to function. (The master database contains user accounts and msdb contains the scheduled jobs.) However, you really only need to back up the ReportServerTempDB database one time so you have something to restore in the event of disaster. As users browse reports, data will cache as needed–either as a session cache or as a cached instance.

If you need to restore the ReportServer database, you'll also need to restore the key that is used to store the encrypted data in that database. For example, if you migrate the ReportServer database to a new SQL Server instance, you will also need to migrate the encryption key. As you learned earlier in this chapter, Reporting Services uses encryption for several purposes–storing the connection string and credentials used to connect to the Reporting Services databases, storing the credentials to use for running unattended reports, and storing credentials for selected data sources. To encrypt and decrypt this data, Reporting Services uses a public key and a symmetric key that are created at installation. Migrating the ReportServer database "breaks" the symmetric key such that Reporting Services is no longer able to decrypt the connection strings or credentials. As a result, an unauthorized migration of the database is foiled and the security of your Reporting Services implementation is protected.

Important Moving the ReportServer database is not the only event that modifies the symmetric key. The symmetric key is also affected by renaming the server or changing the service account that runs the ReportServer Windows service.

To help you manage changes to the server infrastructure that affect the symmetric key, Reporting Services includes the *rskeymgmt* utility. This utility allows you to back up this key. After an event occurs which invalidates the symmetric key, you can use the *rskeymgmt* utility to restore the original version of the symmetric key.

Use the following syntax on the Report Server to back up the encryption key:

```
rskeymgmt -e -f [drive:][folder\]filename -p password
```

The *-e* argument instructs the utility to extract the encryption key to the file identified with the *-f* argument. If you want to save the symmetric key to a different drive or foler, be sure to provide the driver letter and folder name with the file name, such as D:\MyFolder\RSKey, for example.The *-p* is a password that is used to scramble the symmetric key and is required if you later need to restore it. After you store the symmetric key in an external file, you can move it to a secure location. To restore the symmetric key, use the following syntax:

```
rskeymgmt -a -f [drive:][folder\]filename -p password
```

After restoring the key, you must restart Internet Information Services (IIS) for the change to take effect.

Important When using the *rskeymgmt* utility, you need to have local system administrator privileges on the server. This utility must be run locally on the server.

If, for some reason, you don't have access to the backup of the encryption key (or forget the password), and the ReportServer database becomes disabled due to a problem with the symmetric key, you can also use the *rskeymgmt* utility to delete the encrypted data in the ReportServer database. In this case, just use `rskeymgmt -d` and then restart IIS. Then, you can use the *rsconfig* utility to specify the connection information to be encrypted. You may then use the *rskeymgmt* utility to create a new backup of the encryption key. (You can learn more about the *rskeymgmt* utility in SQL Server Books Online.)

If you delete the encrypted data in the ReportServer database and had previously configured credentials for unattended report processing, you will need to run the *rsconfig* utility again to add these credentials back to the Report Server configuration file (as explained earlier in this chapter). For each report and shared data source that uses stored credentials, you'll need to update the credentials individually, since this data is wiped out when you use the *–d* argument with the *rskeymgmt* utility. You will also need to open and save each subscription, since they are also affected by the deletion of encrypted credentials. This is a lot of work to do if you have a lot of items using stored credentials or subscriptions, so take care to back up the symmetric key!

In this procedure, you'll use the *rskeymgmt* utility to back up the symmetric key.

Back up the symmetric key

1. On the Start menu, click Run, type **cmd**, and then click OK to open a Command Prompt window.
2. Run the *rskeymgmt* utility by typing the following: **rskeymgmt –e –f RSkey –p <*YourPassword*>** (replacing <*YourPassword*> with a password of your choosing).

> **Important** This password is used to encrypt the key in the extracted file. You will need this password if you need to reapply the key to a Reporting Services instance.

3. Type **Y** to confirm that you want to extract the key, and then press Enter.

   When the file is created, the screen looks like this:

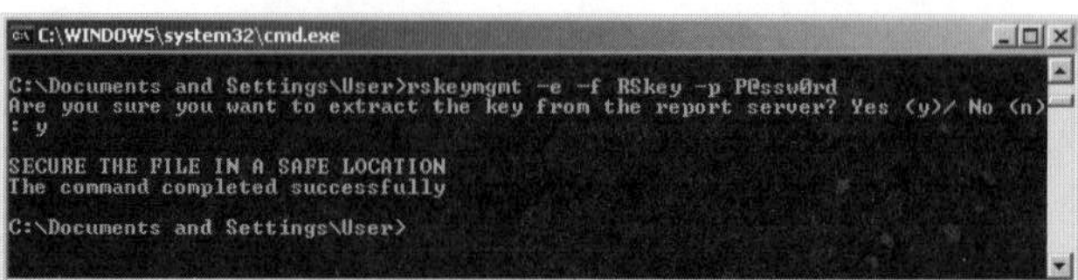

   Now, you can move the RSKey file to a secure location in your environment.

Chapter 11 Quick Reference

To	Do this
Edit a configuration file	After reviewing valid values for modifiable configuration settings in SQL Server Books Online, open the applicable configuration file with any XML editor and edit the file. You can edit the following files: RSReportServer.config RSWebApplication.config ReportingServicesService.exe.config RSReportDesigner.config

To	Do this
Change connection information for the Report Server database	Use the *rsconfig* utility at the command line using the following syntax: `rsconfig -c -m computername -s SQLServername -d ReportServerDatabaseName -a windows|sql -u [domain\]username -p password`
Encrypt credentials for unattended reports	Use the rsconfig utility at the command line using the following syntax: `rsconfig -e -u [domain\]username -p password`
Change tracing levels on the Report Server	Edit the ReportingServicesService.exe.config file using any XML editor and change the value for the configuration setting *DefaultTraceSwitch*. Valid integer values are 0 to disable tracing or 1 through 4 to enable tracing with successively greater detail.
Create an execution logging database	Create an execution logging database in Microsoft SQL Server Management Studio, and then run the createtables.sql script.
Load the execution logging database with current data	Execute the SQL Server 2005 Integration Services (SSIS) package RSExecutionLog_Update.dtsx and schedule for periodic execution to keep the execution logging database relatively current.
Analyze data in the execution logging database	Use the Report Designer in Visual Studio to create your own reports or deploy the sample reports in the ExecutionLog solution in the C:\Documents and Settings\<username>\My Doucments\Microsoft Press\rs2005sbs \chap11\ExecutionLog folder.
Apply a time-out to a source query	In Visual Studio, click the Data tab of a report, click the dataset containing the source query in the Dataset drop-down list, and then click Edit Selected Dataset. Enter the time-out value in seconds in the Timeout box.
Apply a time-out to report execution	For a global time-out, click the Site Settings link in Report Manager. Select Limit Report Execution To The Following Number Of Seconds and enter a time-out value in seconds. *or* For a report time-out, open the report, click the Properties tab, and then click the Execution link. Select Limit Report Execution To The Following Number Of Seconds and enter a time-out value in seconds.
Cancel a job	In Report Manager, click the Site Settings link, and then click the Manage Jobs link. Select the job's check box, and then click Cancel.
Disable a shared data source	In Report Manager, open the shared data source, and then clear the Enable This Data Source check box.
Monitor the ChunkData table size	In Microsoft SQL Server Management Studio, expand the Databases folder, click ReportServer, run the Disk Usage Report on the Summary tab, and expand the Disk Space Used By Tables section.
Back up the encryption key	Use the *rskeymgmt* utility at the command line using the following syntax: `rskeymgmt -e -f [drive:][folder\]filename -p password`

Part IV
Delivering Reports

In this part:

You learned a great deal about the first two stages of the reporting life cycle in Part II, "Authoring Reports," and Part III, "Managing the Report Server." The third and final stage of the reporting life cycle includes accessing and delivering reports, which is covered in the four chapters of Part IV. You'll learn how features of Report Manager help you view and save reports, how report design affects report rendering, and how subscriptions to deliver reports are created and managed. In Part V, "Programming Reporting Services," you'll explore ways to build custom scripts and applications to automate each stage of the reporting life cycle.

Chapter 12

Accessing Reports

After completing this chapter, you will be able to:

- Use Report Manager's navigation features to locate and view reports.
- Add content to the My Reports folder.
- Save a report.
- Print a report.

This chapter begins by teaching you how to retrieve reports from the Report Server. You learn the available options for locating reports on the server, exploring the contents of a report online, and changing the size of the report in your browser. The latter half of this chapter shows you how to preserve the report and its data on the Report Server, on your computer as a local file, or as a printed report.

Finding and Viewing Reports

Using Report Manager to open and view a report has already been introduced in earlier chapters of this book, but there are a few more activities to learn that are related to finding and viewing reports. As you already know, you can use folder links to reach a report when you know the location. When you aren't sure where a report is found, you can search all or part of the Report Server to find it.

After you open a report, the report remains available "as is" in your browser so you can return later to the same view of the report for as long as your browser session is active, even if the report definition or the underlying data changes. However, the HTML Viewer in which Report Manager displays your report provides you with the option of reloading the report to get the most current report definition and to update the data. This option to refresh a report is one of several features of the HTML Viewer you can use while working with your report online.

To view a report using Report Manager, you simply click the report link on a folder's Contents page. The trick is knowing which folder contains the report that you're looking for. You can use Report Manager's folder links to move deeper into a folder hierarchy or use navigation links to move in the opposite direction until you find the desired report. When you have a lot of folders to traverse using this method, finding a report can become a tedious process. You can eliminate this hassle by using Report Manager's search feature. You don't even need to know the report's complete name to search for it–just enter a string of characters to find reports that contain that same string in either the report name or its description.

If you return to a report you viewed earlier in the same browser session, you'll be viewing the version of the report retrieved from the session cache. The report is retained in the session cache for the duration of the browser session. If you suspect that a report definition or the source data has changed during your current session, you can force Report Manager to reload the report definition from the Report Server and to execute the report query. To do so, you use the Refresh button on the report toolbar in the HTML Viewer. The report toolbar contains several other features that allow you to interact more effectively with a report. For example, you can resize the report to better fit your browser window, or you can search the contents of a report for a specific string (which is different from the search feature in Report Manager described earlier). Finally, if you want easy access to a report that uses default parameter values that are different from those defined by the Content Manager, you can–if you have the right permissions and the feature is enabled–create a personal linked report to store in your private workspace, the My Reports folder.

Navigating the Folder Hierarchy

You can review the contents of the Report Server by browsing the folder hierarchy. Folders can be created by the report author if the report is deployed using the Report Designer (as you learned in Chapter 9, "Managing Content"); by a Content Manager if reports and resources need to be relocated after deployment (as you also learned in Chapter 9); or by a script or application (as you'll learn in Chapter 17, "Programming Report Server Management") for automated content management. The folder hierarchy works much like the arrangement of folders you use to navigate the Microsoft Windows file system, in which folders can contain items or other folders that also contain items or additional folders. However, in Report Manager, the hierarchy is not represented as a tree view, but rather as separate pages. You can see only those folders and items for which you have the appropriate permissions (as explained in Chapter 10, "Managing Security").

To open a folder, you click the folder link in the Contents page. The path to the current folder is displayed at the end of a series of navigation links in the top-left corner of the browser window, beginning with the Home folder and continuing with each nested folder. You can quickly jump to a higher-level folder using these links.

In this procedure, you'll explore the Adventure Works Chapter 12 folder hierarchy in Report Manager.

Use navigation links

1. Run publishChap12.cmd in the C:\Documents and Settings\<username>\My Documents\Microsoft Press\rs2005sbs\chap12 folder to create the folders and publish the reports that you need to follow the procedures in this chapter.
2. Open Report Manager in Internet Explorer at *http://localhost/Reports*.

3. Click the Adventure Works Chapter 12 folder link to display its contents, as shown here:

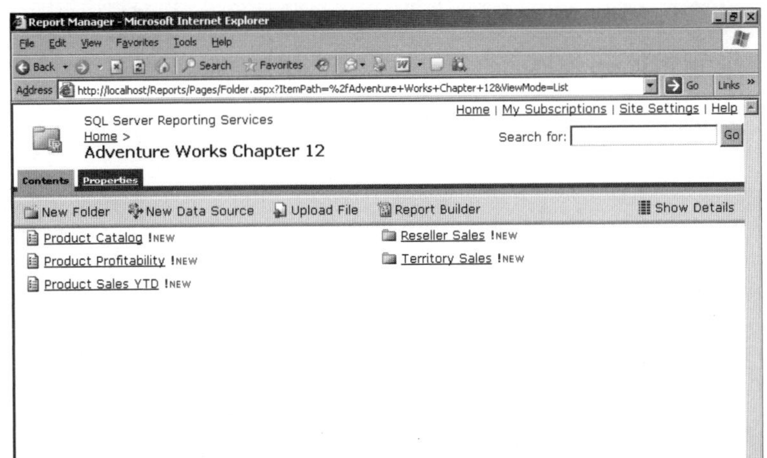

This folder contains three reports and two folder links. Notice the link for the Home folder in the top-left corner of the window. Whenever you browse folders and open items, the folder links always appear in this location to identify your current location in the folder hierarchy and to help you quickly return to a folder at a higher level.

The Home link in the top-right corner of the browser window also takes you to the Home folder, and is always available whether you are browsing the folder hierarchy or managing server settings, which are accessed independently of the folder hierarchy.

4. Click the Reseller Sales folder link, and then click the Reseller Sales report link.

   The navigation links at the top of the screen look like this:

   Home > Adventure Works Chapter 12 > Reseller Sales >

   The complete series of links shows the path to the current report, beginning from the Home page. Rather than use the Back button in your browser, you can quickly jump to another folder in this path by using the navigation link.

5. Click the Adventure Works Chapter 12 navigation link.

   With one click, you have moved to a folder two levels above the report you were viewing.

6. Leave the Report Manager open for the next procedure.

Refreshing Reports

You can also use the Back button to return to folders or reports that you have previously opened. Whereas the Contents page of a folder will display new contents that were added since you previously viewed the page, an on-demand report will not reflect any changes made to the report after you initially opened it–as long as you're still using the same browser session.

As you learned in Chapter 11, "Managing Server Components," the ReportServerTempDB stores the session cache version of the report to speed up delivery of the same report during a single browser session. If you suspect that the report definition or source data has changed during your session, you can use the Refresh button to force a cached report to be reloaded from the ReportServer database and a new query to be executed against the source database.

In this procedure, you'll use the Refresh button to load a revised report definition into the session cache.

Replace the session cache

1. Run updateResellerSales.cmd in the C:\Documents and Settings\<username>\My Documents\Microsoft Press\rs2005sbs\chap12 folder to publish a revised version of the Reseller Sales report.

   This batch command file will publish a revised report definition of the Reseller Sales report and overwrite the existing report definition.

2. In Report Manager, use the Back button to return to the Reseller Sales Report.

   A portion of the report is shown here:

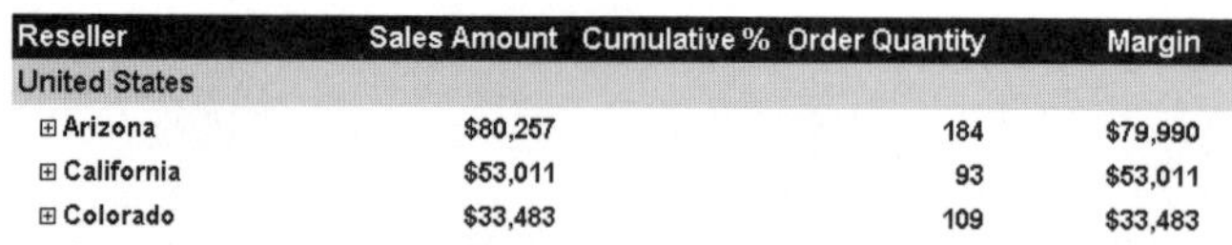

Reseller	Sales Amount	Cumulative %	Order Quantity	Margin
United States				
⊞ Arizona	$80,257		184	$79,990
⊞ California	$53,011		93	$53,011
⊞ Colorado	$33,483		109	$33,483
⊞ Connecticut	$61,097		93	$61,044

   Even though a new version of the Reseller Sales report has been stored on the Report Server, the version of the report in the session cache is displayed. Notice in this version of the report that the group header row, which currently displays United States, includes no other data.

3. Click Refresh on the Report Manager toolbar.

Note If you use the browser's Refresh button, or if you press Ctrl+F5, the report is reloaded from the cache without the report definition.

The top of the report looks like this:

AdventureWorks Reseller Sales Report

Jan 2003

United States

Reseller	Sales Amount	Cumulative %	Order Quantity	Margin
United States	$1,183,477		2,204	$1,175,303
⊞ Arizona	$80,257		184	$79,990
⊞ California	$53,011		93	$53,011
⊞ Colorado	$33,483		109	$33,483
⊞ Connecticut	$61,097		93	$61,044

The report is reloaded from the Report Server and the query is executed again. In this case, the source data hasn't changed, but the report definition has been updated to include subtotals in the group header row to the right of United States.

Searching for Reports

If you aren't sure where to begin looking for a report, you can use the Search feature in Report Manager to find a report by name or by description. In fact, you can also use this feature to search for folders, shared data sources, and resources. However, you can't search for a specific snapshot in report history or a subscription, nor can you search for schedules or role assignments.

To search, you type in a search string using all or part of the folder or item name (or its description) in the Search For box in the top-right corner of Report Manager. Reporting Services will begin the search in the current folder and will continue through all the nested folders below the current location. Report Manager won't search a folder or return an item for which you don't have permissions.

In this procedure, you'll search for reports that include "product sales" in the report name or description.

Search for reports using a partial name

1. Click the Home link to return to the Home page.
2. By searching from the Home page, all folders to which you have permission will be searched.
3. Type **product sales** in the Search For box, as shown here:

4. Click Go.

The Search page looks similar to this:

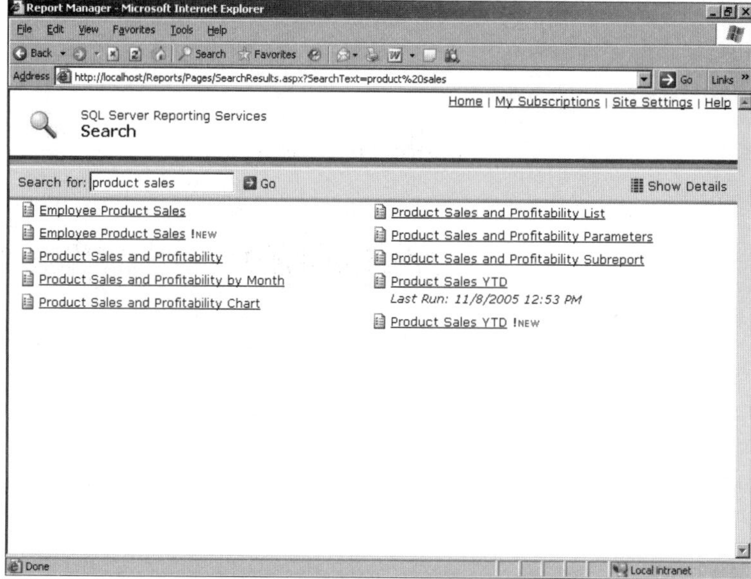

Depending on the reports you have on your server, the list of reports might be different from those shown in the illustration.

5. Click Show Details.

Your screen looks like this:

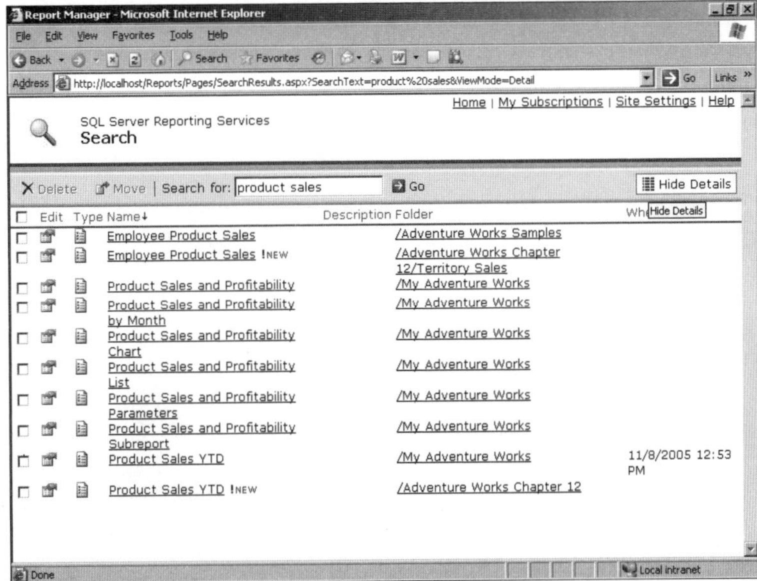

Now you can see not only the reports that met the search criteria, but also in which folder each report is stored. If the report is a snapshot, you will also see the last execution date in the When Run column. You can click on a folder link to navigate to the Contents page of that folder, or you can click on a report link to view the report.

6. Click the Employee Product Sales report link (in the Adventure Works Chapter 12/ Territory Sales folder) to view the report, and then leave this report open for the next procedure.

Using the HTML Viewer

The HTML Viewer is supplied by Reporting Services to view reports online in HTML format. Above the report is a parameters section (if report parameters are used and the prompt is enabled) and a report toolbar. The report toolbar has useful features that allow you to explore your report more easily as well as change your viewing options.

In the parameters section of the HTML Viewer, you change the value either by selecting a value from the parameter drop-down list or by entering a new value. The report will render with the new value only after you click View Report. (Whether the report requeries the data source before rendering depends on how each parameter is configured, as discussed in Chapter 7, "Building Advanced Reports.")

Beneath the parameters section in the HTML Viewer is the report toolbar, which looks like this:

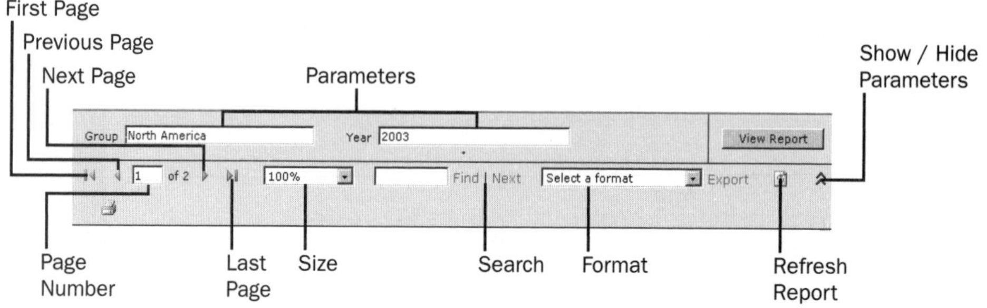

The following table describes how to use the features of the report toolbar.

To	Do this
Jump to the beginning or end of a report	Click the First Page or Last Page button.
Scroll the previous or next page	Click the Previous Page or Next Page button.
Jump to a specific page	Type a page number in the Current Page box, and then press Enter.
Change the size of the report page	Select a percentage in the size drop-down list. You can also select Page Width if you want the report resized to fit the horizontal width of your browser, or select Whole Page if you want the report resized to fit vertically within your browser.
Search for the first occurrence of text on any page of a report	Type the search string in the Find Text box, and then click Find. This is available only when you enter a search string.
Search for the next occurrence of text within a report	Click Next. As with Find, this is not available until you enter a search string and click Find once.
View the report in a different format	Click the desired format in the format drop-down list, and then click Export.
Reload the report from the ReportServer database	Click Refresh.
Toggle the display of the report parameters	Click Show / Hide Parameters.
Toggle the display mode of the report	Click Full Screen to view the report in the full screen mode and click Restore Down to return to the default display mode.

In this procedure, you'll explore some of the features of the report toolbar.

Use the report toolbar

1. If you skipped the previous procedure, open Report Manager and open the Employee Product Sales report open, located the folder path Adventure Works Chapter 12/Territory Sales. Click Full Screen on the report toolbar.

   The screen looks like this:

   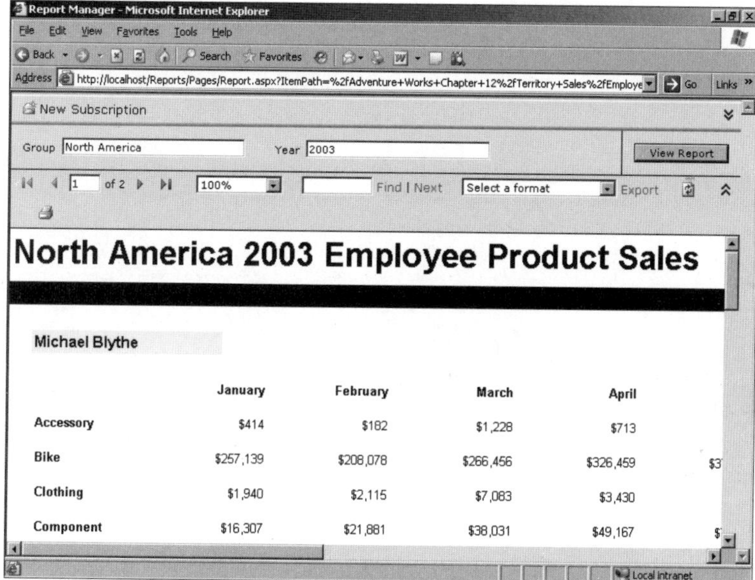

   More space in the browser is dedicated to the report, but it still doesn't quite fit the screen.

2. Click Show / Hide Parameters.

   Even more space is allocated to the report. You can also adjust the size of the report to view more data in the browser at a time.

3. Select 75% in the size drop-down list.

   Now, you can see more months of the year in the browser. The exact number that you see will depend on your screen resolution.

4. Click Next Page to view the second page of the report.

5. Click Restore Down to restore the Report Manager interface, as shown here:

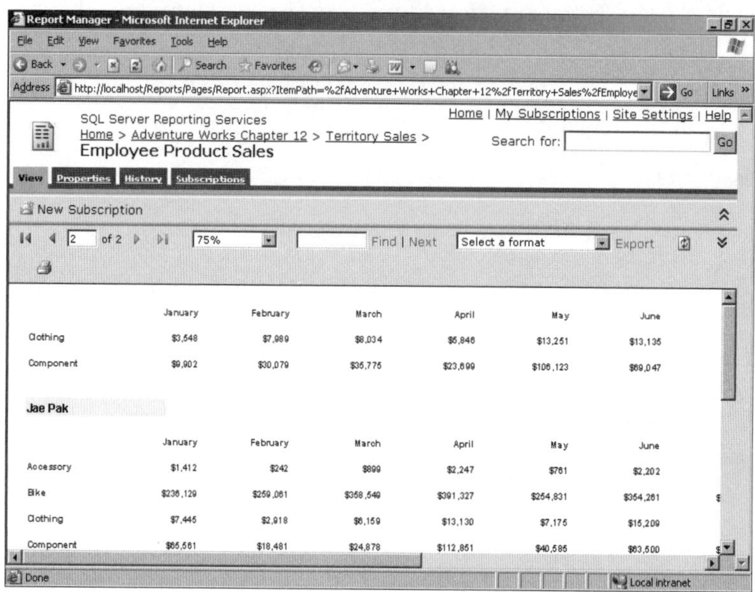

6. Keep the report open for the next procedure.

Using My Reports

If the My Reports feature is enabled on the Report Server, the My Reports folder appears on the Home page. With this feature enabled, each user has his or her own My Reports folder as a personal workspace to which no one else has access, except for report administrators. As you learned in Chapter 10, there is a default role definition for My Reports, which a report administrator can use to limit the tasks that users can perform in this workspace. If you have permissions to create a linked report from an existing report, you can create a personal linked report to access in your My Reports folder, and then you can set your own default parameter values.

You can also upload a report definition or resource file for storage in My Reports or, if you're a report author, you can create and publish a report to My Reports using Report Designer–assuming, of course, that you have the appropriate permissions. If you publish a report from Report Designer, set the project deployment folder to Users Folders/*computername username* /My Reports.

In this procedure, you'll create a personal linked report from the Employee Product Sales report.

Create a personal linked report

1. If My Reports isn't already enabled, click the Site Settings link in Report Manager, click Enable My Reports To Support User-Owned Folders For Publishing And Running Personalized Reports, and then click Apply.
2. If you accessed the Site Settings using the same browser session you used in the previous procedure, click Back twice to return to the Employee Product Sales report.
3. Click the Properties tab, and then, if the General Properties page isn't currently displayed, click the General link.
4. Click Create Linked Report.
5. Type a name for the report: **My Employee Product Sales**.

   Your screen looks like this:

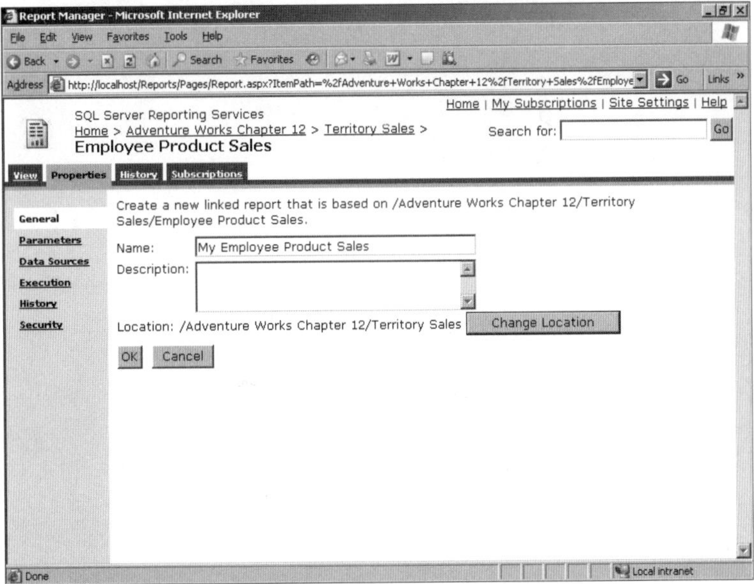

6. Click Change Location.

The screen looks similar to this:

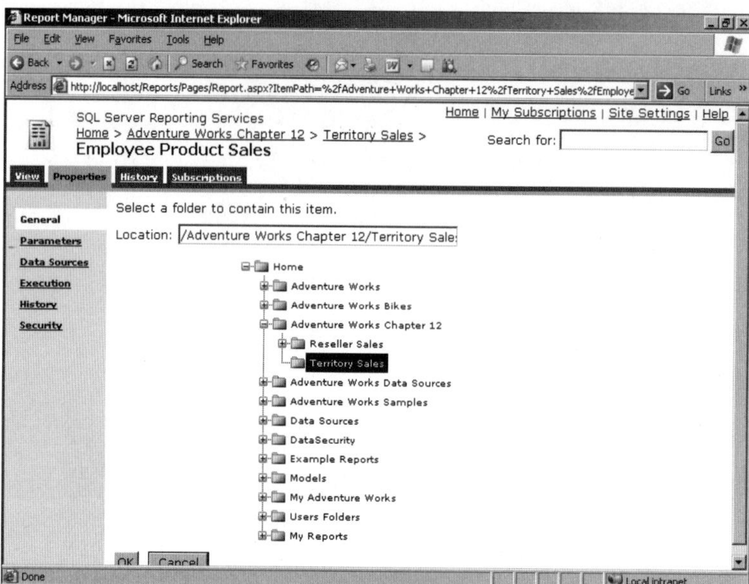

If you did not complete all the procedures in the preceding chapters, you will see fewer folders in the location tree.

7. Click My Reports.

   Notice the folder path that appears in the Location box: /My Reports.

8. Click OK to confirm the My Reports location, and then click OK again to create the personal linked report.

The screen looks similar to this:

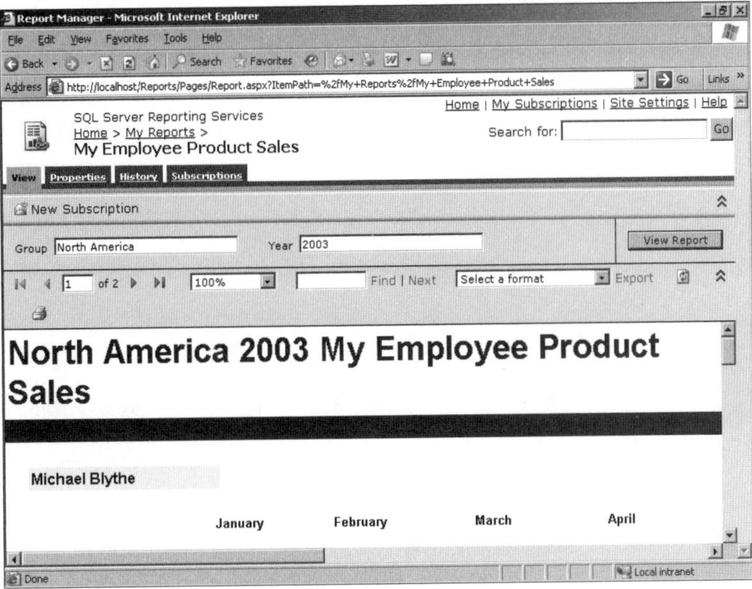

Notice the navigation links in the top-left corner of the browser window that now indicate your current location in the My Reports folder.

9. Click the Properties tab, and then click the Parameters link.
10. Change the Default Value for the *Group* parameter to **Europe**.

The Parameters Properties page looks like this:

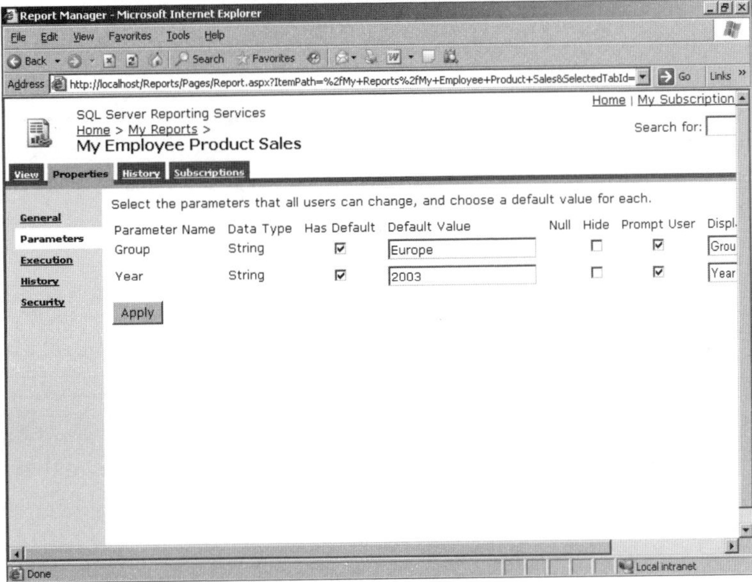

11. Click Apply.
12. Click the Home link.

    Notice the folder on the Home page: My Reports. This is a new folder if you enabled My Reports in this procedure, but it might not be labeled as new. If you're a report administrator, you'll also see a folder titled Users Folders, in which you will be able to open each user's My Reports folder to review content placed there.
13. Click the My Reports folder link, and then click the My Employee Product Sales report link.

    The top of the report looks like this:

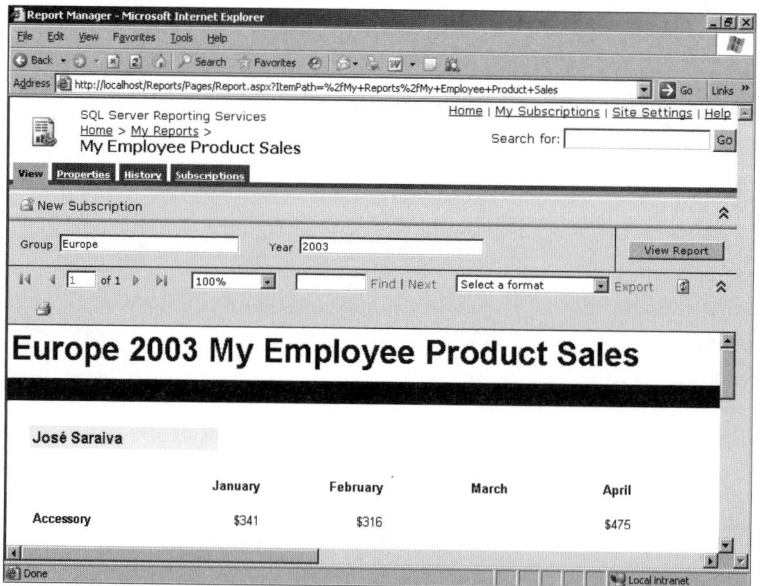

The advantage of creating a personal linked report is the ability to set the default values of each parameter that presents the data the way you want to see it when you open the report. If the base report gets deleted, however, your personal linked report will no longer operate. You will then need to manually delete the report from the My Reports folder.

Saving Reports for Future Reference

Whether a report runs on demand or on a scheduled basis, the information in the report is generally dynamic. That is, when the source data is refreshed periodically, the report eventually reflects changes in the data. If you want to have a permanent record of the data at a certain point in time, you'll need to save the report. To store the report and its data on the Report Server, you can create a report snapshot. You also have the option to store the report as a file on your computer or on a network share. Alternatively, you can create a printed copy of the report for your personal use or for distribution across the organization.

Basically, there are two ways to make a permanent copy of a report. One way is to keep the report copy as a snapshot in report history, which requires you to have access to the Report Server whenever you want to view this copy of the report. Another way is to export the report to another format, which can then be printed or saved to a local file. If you export the report to a file, you can view the file even when you can't connect to the Report Server. Of course, if you save the file to a network share, you need to be able to navigate the network's file system to open the report. Further, your computer must have the appropriate software installed before you can view the file. For example, if you export a report as an Microsoft Excel file, you must have Microsoft Office XP or a later version installed on your computer to view the file contents.

Creating a Report History Snapshot

In Chapter 9, you learned how a report administrator can enable a report's history properties so snapshots can be saved for reference at some point in the future. Commonly, a schedule is used to put a snapshot into report history on a regular basis. For example, you might have a schedule to place a snapshot of financial statements into report history at the end of each month. However, there may be occasions when users want to manually add a snapshot to report history as well. Just as with scheduled snapshots, the report must be configured to use a data source with stored credentials before anyone can add a snapshot to report history manually.

In this procedure, you'll use the New Snapshot button to add a snapshot to the report history of the Employee Product Sales report.

Create a manual snapshot for report history

1. In Report Manager, click the Home link, click the Adventure Works Chapter 12 folder link, click the Territory Sales folder link, and then click the Employee Product Sales report.
2. Click the Properties tab, and then click the Data Sources link.
3. Click Credentials Stored Securely In The Report Server, and then type user name **ReportExecution** and password **ReportExecution**.

   You can create a snapshot only when the data source uses stored credentials.
4. Click Apply.
5. Click the History tab, and then click New Snapshot.

The screen looks similar to this:

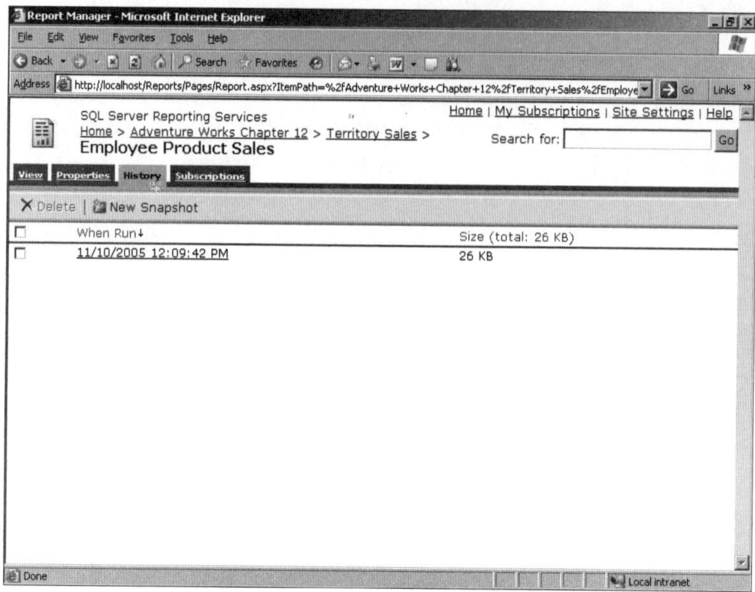

The snapshot will remain in report history until the limit of snapshots defined globally or specifically for this report is exceeded. If no limit is defined, the snapshot will remain in report history until it's manually deleted using Delete on this page.

6. Click the snapshot link.

   A new browser window is opened with a snapshot that looks similar to this:

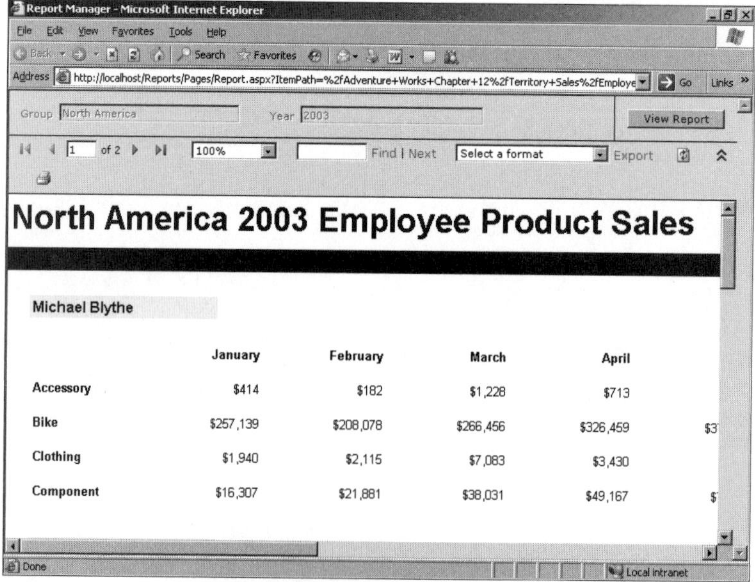

As with a snapshot that replaces an on-demand report, you can't change the report parameter values in a snapshot placed in report history. The snapshot is created using the default parameter values.

7. Close the snapshot's browser window.

Saving Reports to Local Files

You can save a report to a local file and thereby create the equivalent of a snapshot. By saving to a local file, you can access the report anytime without connecting to the Report Server. To create a local file, you use the Export feature in the HTML Viewer. The best formats to use for saving a report as a local file are Excel, Web archive, Acrobat Portable Document Format (PDF), and TIFF. You'll explore these and other rendering formats in greater detail in Chapter 13, "Rendering Reports."

The export format you choose determines which features of the online report can be reproduced. For example, a document map is a feature that enhances navigation in a very large report that you view using the HTML Viewer. The document map can also be rendered in a PDF file to facilitate navigation when viewing the report with Acrobat Reader. You'll learn more about the effect of rendering on specific report features in Chapter 13.

In this procedure, you'll save the Product Catalog report as a PDF file.

Save a report as a PDF file

1. In Report Manager, click the Adventure Works Chapter 12 navigation link, and then click the Product Catalog report.

   Your screen looks like this:

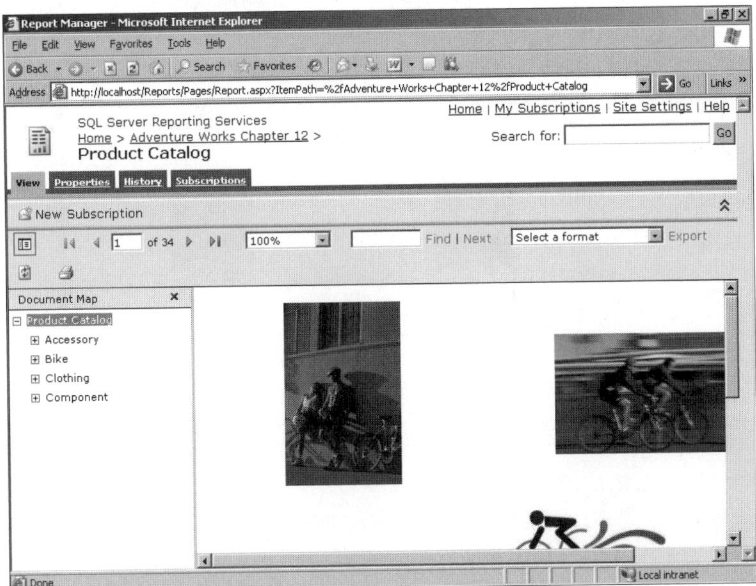

Notice the Document Map pane that appears on the left portion of the page. The Document Map is a feature added during the report-authoring stage and is used to jump to a corresponding location in the report. You'll learn more about creating a Document Map in Chapter 13.

2. Expand the Bike item, expand Road Bike, and then click Road-150.

   The information in the Product Catalog related to the Road-150 bike is displayed. As you can see, a document map is very useful for navigating a large report like the Product Catalog.

3. Select Acrobat (PDF) File in the Export drop-down list, and then click Export.

   You have the option to view the exported file now or to save the report to the file system for viewing later. To view a file that is exported to another format, you must have the appropriate application installed on your computer. In this case, you must have Acrobat Reader.

4. Click Open to download the file and launch Acrobat Reader as the file viewer.

5. Click the Bookmarks tab.

   The screen looks similar to this:

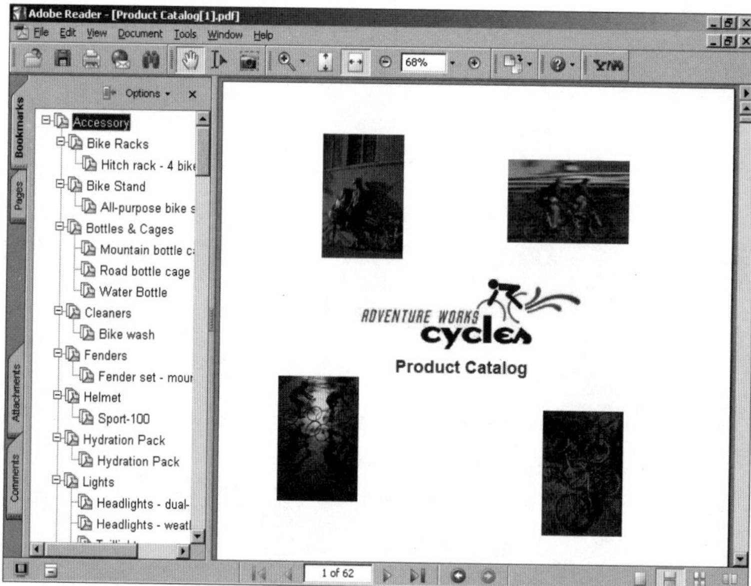

   The document map is converted to bookmarks in the PDF file.

6. Collapse the Accessory category, and then click Road-150.

The screen looks similar to this:

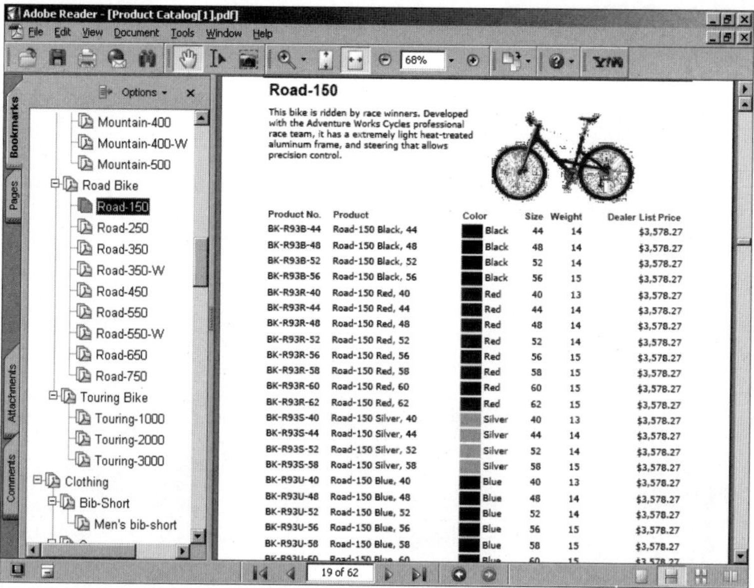

> **Note** The bicycle image in the PDF file is unclear at the current resolution. When viewed at 100 percent, however, the image is quite clear.

Now you have a file that you can share with others who don't have access to the Report Server. As an added bonus, the PDF file contains the navigation functionality that was built into the original report to facilitate finding items of interest in a large report.

7. Close the PDF file.

Printing Reports

Report Manager includes a Print button on the report toolbar in the HTML Viewer. After a report has completed rendering in the viewer, you can click this button, select a printer, and specify printing options, such as margins or specific pages to print. The first time that you try to use the print feature, you'll be prompted to download an ActiveX control.

In this procedure, you'll use the Print button to preview the print version of the Sales Summary report.

Preview the print version of a report

1. In Report Manager, click the Adventure Works Chapter 12 navigation link, click the Territory Sales folder link, and then click the Sales Summary report.
2. Click Print on the HTML Viewer toolbar.
3. Click Preview.

   The screen looks similar to this:

   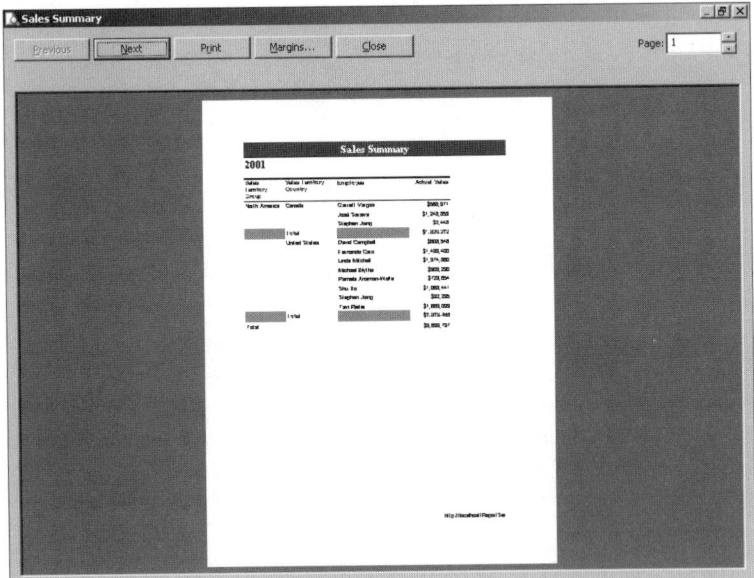

   Scroll through the report to verify that all four pages of the report display as separate pages for printing. If you tried to use the browser's print feature, you could only print one page at a time and the printed version of the report would include the Web elements of the Report Manager application.
4. Click Close, click Cancel, and then close all browser windows.

Chapter 12 Quick Reference

To	Do this
Navigate a folder hierarchy	In Report Manager, use the folder links in the Contents page to move to successively lower levels of the hierarchy; use the navigation links at the top of the page to move to higher levels of the hierarchy.
Replace the session cache with the current report definition and/or current data	In Report Manager, open a report that was opened earlier in the same browser session, and then click Refresh on the report toolbar (not the browser toolbar).
Search for folders or items	In the Search For box in the top-right corner of Report Manager, type the full or partial report name or description, and then click Go.
Create a personal linked report	With My Reports enabled in Site Settings, open the General Properties page of a report, and then click Create Linked Report. Assign the report to the My Reports location. Use the Parameters Properties page of the linked report to change the default values as desired.
Add a manual snapshot to report history	Ensure the report uses a data source with stored credentials, and then click the History tab of the report and click New Snapshot.
Save a report as a local file	With the report open in Report Manager, click a format in the Export drop-down list, and then click Export. Click Save, select a download location for the file, and type a name.
Print a report	With the report open in Report Manager, click Print on the HTML Viewer toolbar, select a printer, and change print options.

Chapter 13

Rendering Reports

After completing this chapter, you will be able to:

- Render a report as a Web document for sharing.
- Convert a report to a page-oriented format for document storage or printing.
- Save a report as a Microsoft Excel workbook for offline analysis.
- Create a structured file for data exchange from a report.

In the previous chapter, you learned how to use the features of Report Manager to locate and view reports. You were also introduced to the Export feature to render reports so that you could save or print a report. In this chapter, you take a closer look at the rendering options. You compare and contrast the rendering formats by exporting reports that contain specific design features. This evaluation of the differences between rendering formats will help you improve the design of your reports by enabling you to make informed choices about available options.

Comparing Rendering Formats

Rendering is the process of converting the report definition and the report data into a specific output format. Report Manager renders reports as HTML documents by default and provides seven alternative rendering formats from which you can choose. Each of these formats will be reviewed in this chapter. You can also add a custom rendering extension to expand the list of available formats in Report Manager, or you can build a custom application to programmatically render reports as desired, which you will learn about in Chapter 18, "Building Custom Reporting Tools." Because rendering is implemented as an extension, it's possible that other rendering extensions might be added in the future (either by Microsoft or by third-party vendors) or that the behavior of existing extensions will change (with service packs).

The HTML rendering format is best for viewing reports online and might include interactive features. Other rendering formats, such as Adobe Acrobat Portable Document Format (PDF) files or TIFF files, are ideal for distributing large, page-oriented reports that can be sent to a printer or viewed using an appropriate client application. Reporting Services also supplies formats that are useful for sharing the data in a report. One way to share data is to export a report to an Excel format so that users can perform more sophisticated interactive analysis of the data. You can also share data using comma separated values (CSV) or XML formats. For example, you might need to supply invoicing data to customers in a structured format that their internal applications can use as input.

Although all the rendering formats support any of the data regions that you can use in a report definition, you will find that some data regions are more compatible with certain formats than with others. The compatibility between data regions and rendering formats will be discussed in more detail later in this chapter. You will also find that some design features are not supported by all formats. Be sure to test a new report in each rendering format to avoid surprises.

Rendering for Online Viewing

In a typical implementation of Reporting Services, users view reports online using Report Manager. A report is rendered as HTML 4.0 if the browser that is used to open Report Manager is Internet Explorer version 5.5 or 6. Otherwise, the report is rendered as HTML 3.2. Reporting Services can also render reports online as Multipurpose Internet Mail Extensions (MIME) Encapsulated Aggregate HTML (MHTML). If you have a multipage report that you want to embed in an e-mail message, you can export your report as MHTML.

Rendering as MHTML

If you want to save or share a report as a Web page, you can use the MHTML format to combine all report items into a single file, even if the report uses a subreport or other external resources, such as images stored separately on the Report Server. The MHTML format can also be used with any data region. This format is best used to combine multiple pages in a report. You can then easily e-mail the MHTML document to share with others.

The MHTML document does not have any interactive features. When you export a report to this format, the current view of the report is rendered. This means that if your report uses dynamic visibility, the items that are visible when you export the report will also be visible in the MHTML version of the report.

In this procedure, you'll export the Product Sales and Profitability Subreport, which includes a subreport with dynamic visibility, as a single-page MHTML document.

Export a multiple page report as a Web Archive

1. In Visual Studio, open the Rendering solution in the C:\Documents and Settings \<username>\My Documents\Microsoft Press\rs2005sbs\chap13 folder.
2. Right-click the solution in Solution Explorer, and then click Deploy. Leave Visual Studio open for use in another procedure later in this chapter.
3. In Report Manager, click the Rendering link, and then click the Product Sales and Profitability Subreport report link.

   This report is designed with dynamic visibility. You can expand a product to view detail information (in the form of a subreport, in this case) about that product.

4. Click the Next Page button on the Report toolbar, and then expand Cable Lock to view the subreport. Click 75% in the Size drop-down list to view the report, as shown here:

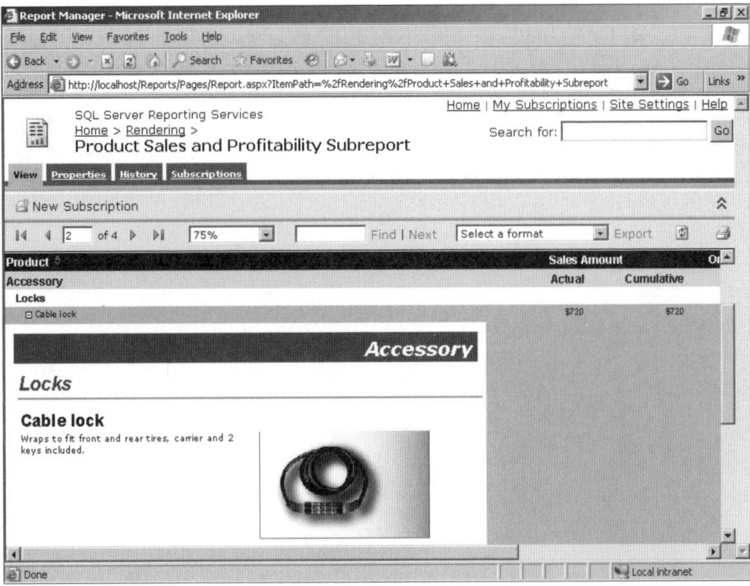

5. Select Web Archive in the Export drop-down list, click the Export link on the Report toolbar, and then click Open in the File Download dialog box.

6. Scroll down the page to find the break between the first page and the second page of the report, as shown here:

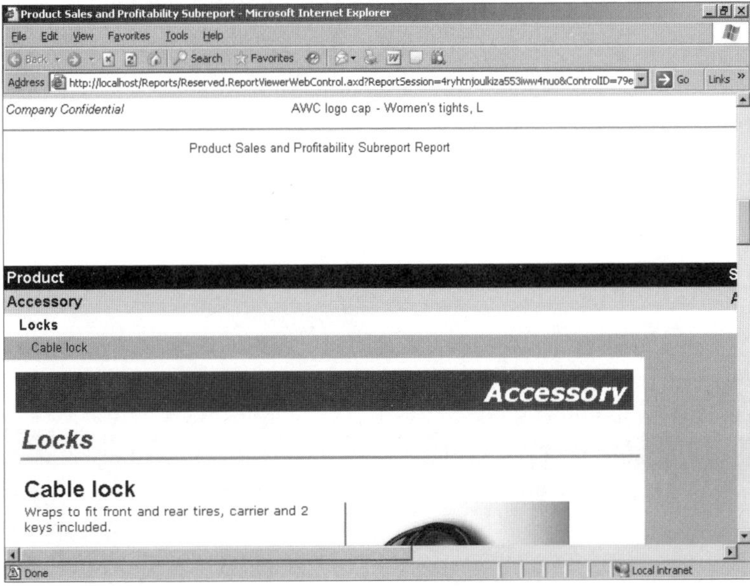

Notice that all four pages of the original report are displayed in a single page in this browser window. The page footer of the first page is immediately followed by the page header of the second page. The subreport is displayed only on the second page below the Cable Lock product.

> **Tip** The MHTML format is great for creating a single Web page from a report, especially a report with multiple pages. However, as you can see from this example, it might not be the best format for a report designed with dynamic visibility, unless you're interested only in highlighting specific details in the report. Expanding each item in the report before you export is not very practical.

7. Close the browser window.

Rendering for Document Management

One benefit of Reporting Services is its role as a central location for the online storage and retrieval of information–which can be incorporated into a comprehensive corporate document management strategy. Two common formats used for document management are PDF files and TIFF files. Reporting Services can render any report into these page-oriented formats.

When you need to provide information to people who don't have access to the reporting platform, you can retrieve a report from Reporting Services and export it as a page-oriented file. The page-oriented formats supported by Reporting Services are TIFF and PDF files. You can export a report as a TIFF file for document archival or for integration with other applications. The TIFF file is intended to be used independently of the reporting platform, so you don't need to be connected to the Report Server to view the file.

Similarly, you might want to use PDF documents offline. For example, you can create a PDF document for a product catalog that sales representatives can keep on their laptops or send to their clients as an e-mail attachment. When authoring a report that is likely to be exported as a PDF document, you can include a document map to serve as an interactive table of contents that allows the user to easily jump to another section of the document.

Rendering as a TIFF File

Reporting Services includes a rendering extension that allows you to generate a TIFF file from a report if needed. All data regions are properly rendered using this format, but only visible items will be displayed if dynamic visibility has been added to the report. Since a TIFF file is a page-oriented format, you will want to carefully check the design of reports during the authoring stage for correct print layout. For example, you'll want to make sure that you have properly set the page size properties *Width* and *Height*, as well as the margin properties *Left*, *Right*, *Top*, and *Bottom*. These properties belong to Report, which you can access in the report item list box in the Properties window or by clicking outside the design grid in the Document window.

Also, during the design process, preview the report frequently and use the Print Preview button to see how the report lays out on a printed page. The TIFF format does not support the use of a document map because TIFF files are primarily used for document storage, printing, or faxing.

In this procedure, you'll correct the layout of the Product Sales and Profitability Chart for printing and export the report as a TIFF file.

Export a report as a TIFF file

1. In Report Manager, click the Rendering link, and then click the Product Sales and Profitability Chart report link. You might need to scroll down the page to see the top of the matrix.

   Your screen looks similar to this:

   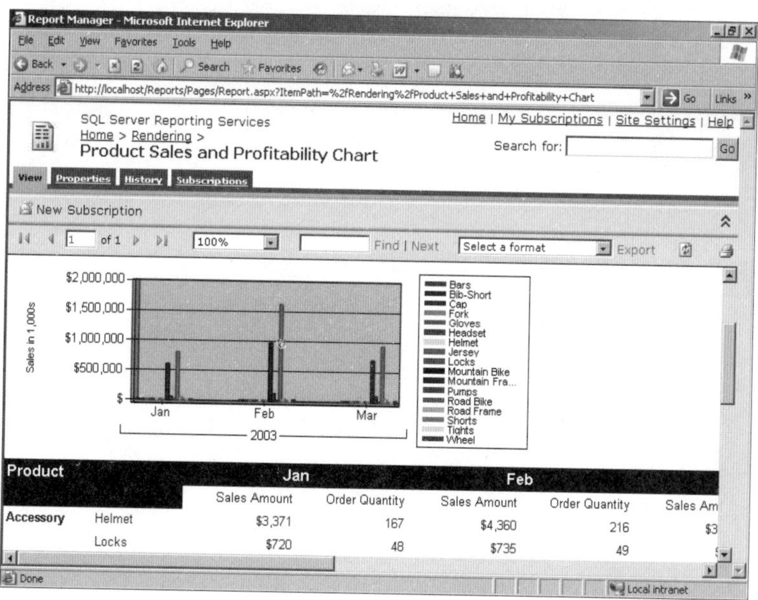

   This report includes both a chart and a matrix. When rendered as HTML, the size of the Web page expands horizontally and vertically to accommodate the contents. However, the chart and the matrix won't fit on a printed page if the report is designed incorrectly.

2. Select TIFF File in the Export drop-down list, click the Export link, and then click Open in the File Download dialog box.

Your default viewer for TIFF files might be different, but the resulting image looks like this:

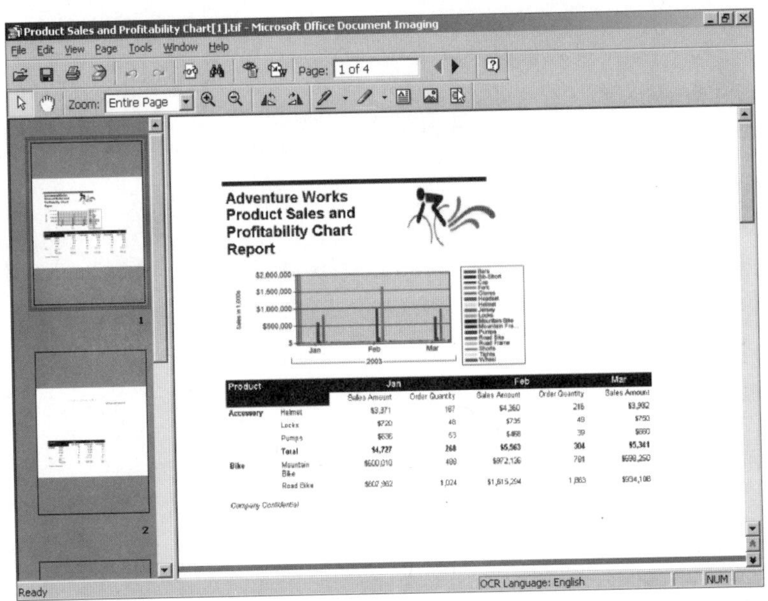

Notice that the report layout has portrait orientation. Although the chart fits well on the page, the matrix is cut off and spreads out across the next three pages. The orientation of this report should be changed to fit on a printed page properly.

3. Close the TIFF viewer.
4. Using Visual Studio, open the Product Sales and Profitability Chart report in the Rendering solution.
5. In the Properties window, the current item should be Report. If it isn't, click Report in the Properties item drop-down list to access the Report's properties.
6. Expand *PageSize*, and then change the *Width* property to **14in** and the *Height* property to **11in**.

Your screen should look similar to this:

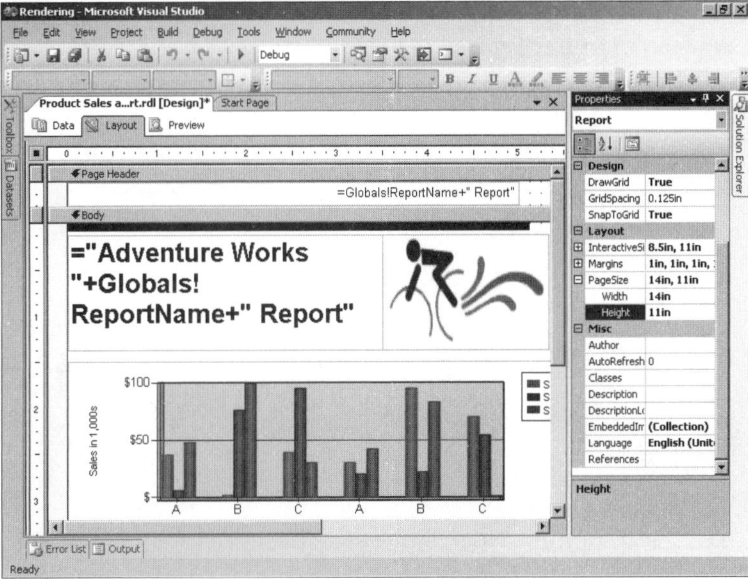

7. Click the Preview tab, and then click the Print Layout button.

   Your screen should look similar to this:

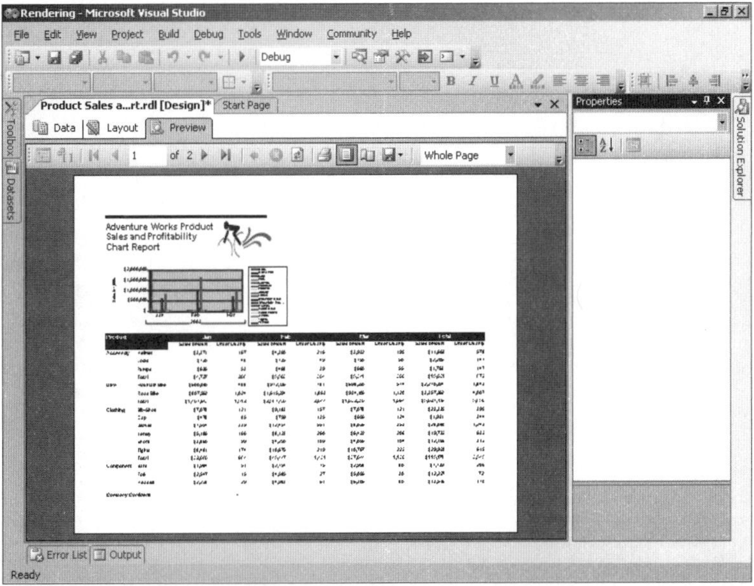

The matrix fits horizontally on the page when you change the dimensions of the page to force a landscape orientation.

8. Click the Next Page button.

   Because the full matrix doesn't fit on the page vertically, a second page is created. Notice that the column headers appear at the top of the matrix on this page.

9. Save and then deploy the report.

10. In Report Manager, with the Product Sales and Profitability Chart open, click Refresh on the Report toolbar to load the updated report definition.

11. Click TIFF File in the Export list box, click the Export link, and then click Open in the File Download dialog box.

    The image looks like this:

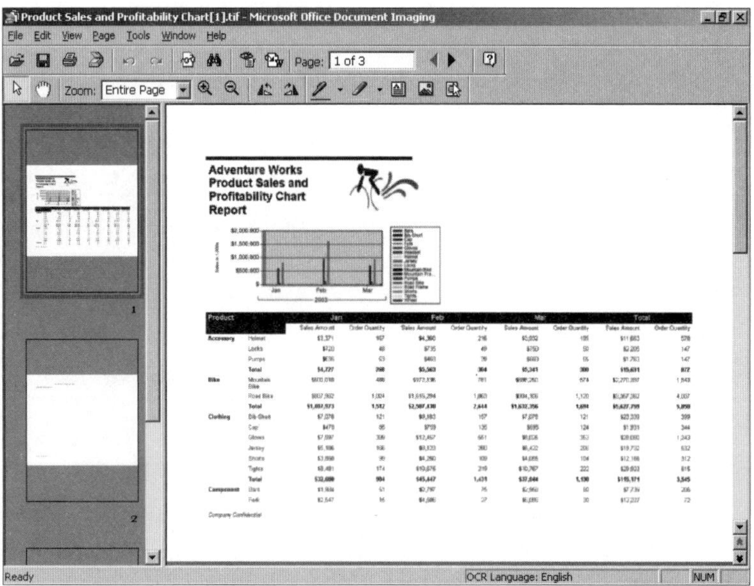

    The TIFF format now displays the complete width of the matrix, just like the print preview you saw in Visual Studio. The second page with the remaining rows of the matrix is part of the same file, which you can view by clicking the Next Page button (Page Down) at the bottom of the viewer.

12. Close the TIFF viewer.

Rendering as a PDF File

A PDF file created by exporting a report from Reporting Services is much like an MHTML document in that what you see in the HTML version is what you get in the exported file. Consequently, the PDF file is not the best format for reports with interactive features like dynamic visibility. However, it's a very good format for large reports that might take some time to render online, for printing reports, and for sharing documents outside of the Reporting Services environment. Because this format renders what you see in the original report, any data region in a report renders properly in the PDF file. Because PDF is a page-oriented format, you must take care in the design of the report to ensure that the report items, when rendered, fit within the defined physical size of the page.

A particularly useful feature in a PDF file is the document map. It renders with the PDF file to help users find specific information within a large report. (You have to wait until all pages of an HTML report finish rendering in the background before the document map is available online, but once a PDF file is created, there's no waiting!) A document map is added in the authoring stage by assigning a label to a group (in a table, matrix, or list).

In this procedure, you'll add another group to the document map for the Product Catalog. In a later procedure, you'll export the Product Catalog as a PDF file.

Add groups to a document map

1. In Report Manager, click the Rendering link, and then click the Product Catalog report link.

   Your screen looks like this:

   When a report is designed with a document map, the document map automatically appears as a frame in the page to the left of the report.

> **Note** Even though the document map appears automatically, it doesn't necessarily appear immediately in all reports. You will see the first page of an HTML document before all pages in the report have been rendered. Reporting Services can't generate the document map until all rendering is complete.

2. Select Clothing in the Document Map pane.

   The report now displays the first product subcategory in this section of the report, Bib-Short. You can continue browsing through the Clothing category by scrolling through this page or by clicking the Next Page button a few times. However, having a more detailed document map would be preferable.

3. Leave the report open in Report Manager, because you will return to this report later in this procedure.

4. Using Visual Studio, open the Product Catalog report in the Rendering solution.

5. Scroll through the report until you see the textboxes that contain field expressions, as shown here:

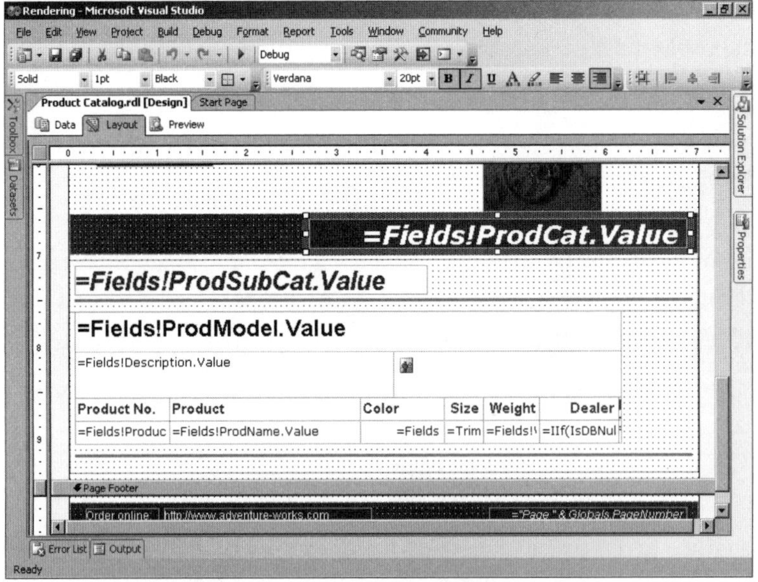

   This report is constructed as a collection of nested lists. The outermost list repeats Category information, which includes the expression `=Fields!ProdCat.Value`. You can't click the design grid to access this list's properties because the grid is fully covered by other report items. Instead, you need to use the Properties window to change the list properties.

6. In the Properties window, select CategoryList in the drop-down list, and then click the *Grouping* property's ellipsis button.

The Grouping and Sorting Properties dialog box is displayed:

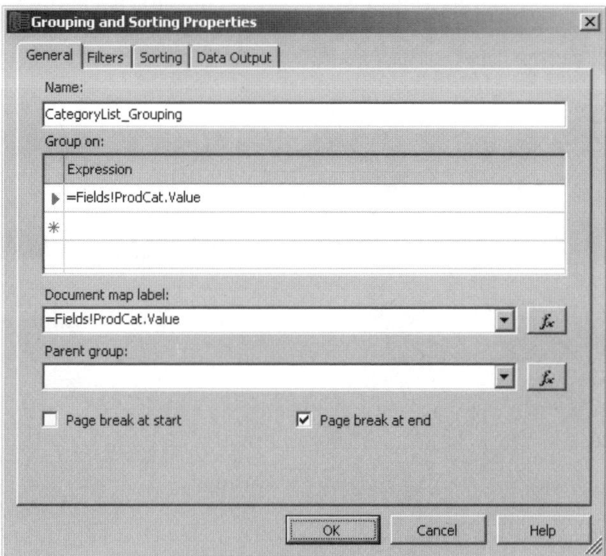

Notice that `=Fields!ProdCat.Value` appears in the Document Map Label drop-down list. This value is used to configure the current document map. In this case, a new group is created in the list for each product category (ProdCat) value. The label that corresponds to the position of a particular group will be the same value. So, for example, the Bike group in the report will be labeled as Bike in the document map.

7. Click Cancel.
8. In the Properties window, select SubCategoryList in the drop-down list, and then click the *Grouping* property's ellipsis button.
9. Select `=Fields!ProdSubCat.Value` in the Document Map Label drop-down list.

   Since SubCategoryList is nested within CategoryList, the label for this group will appear as a node of the category group to which it belongs. In other words, you will expand a category in the document map to view the available subcategories for that category.
10. Click OK.
11. In the Properties window, select ModelList in the drop-down list, and then click the *Grouping* property's ellipsis button.
12. Select `=Fields!ProdModel.Value` in the Document Map Label drop-down list.

    By adding a document map label to this list group, you are adding yet another level to the document map. Specifically, a subcategory will expand to reveal its associated models.
13. Click OK, and then save the report.

14. In Solution Explorer, right-click ProductCatalog.rdl and click Deploy. Keep the solution open in Visual Studio for use in another procedure later in this chapter.

In this procedure, you'll export the Product Catalog as a PDF file.

Export a report as a PDF file

1. In Report Manager, with the Product Catalog open, click Refresh on the Report toolbar to load the updated report definition.

   Notice that the Document Map now has plus signs to indicate each category can be expanded.

2. Select Acrobat (PDF) File in the Export drop-down list, click the Export link, and then click Open in the File Download dialog box.

   Since this is a bigger report than you have previously viewed, the export process might take a little longer.

3. Click the Bookmarks tab to display the document map.

4. In the Document Map, collapse Accessory and Bike to view the Clothing category. In the Jersey subcategory, click Long-Sleeve Logo Jersey to navigate to that product model in the Product Catalog.

   Your screen looks similar to this:

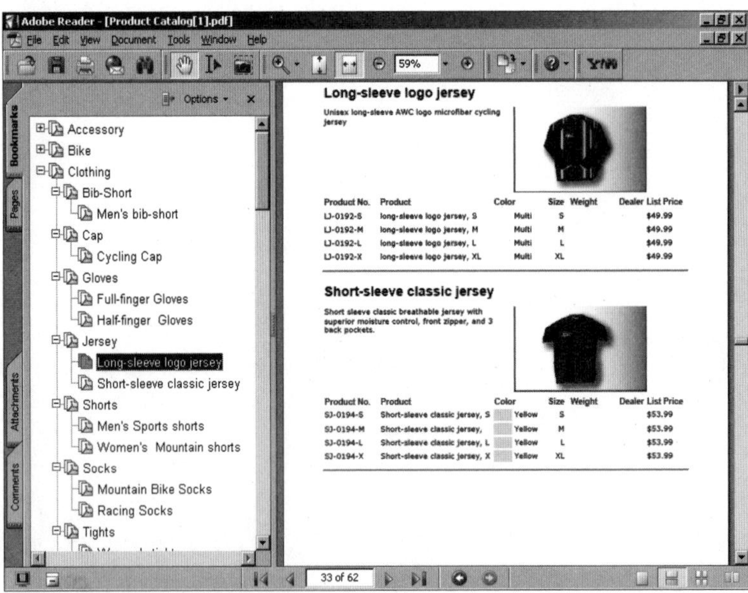

   You can click any level of the document map—category, subcategory, or model—to jump to the section of the report that marks the beginning of the selected group.

5. Close Acrobat Reader.

Rendering for Data Exchange

Besides viewing reports online or creating printable documents from reports, you will likely need to use information contained in reports in other ways. It's a very common requirement of reporting systems to export data to Excel so that users can perform more complex analysis or even integrate data from other sources. For example, if you keep forecast data in an Excel spreadsheet, you could export sales data from Reporting Services to Excel and then add a formula to compute the ratio of actual performance to forecasted performance.

It's also becoming more common for businesses to exchange information electronically. A retailer can submit an order electronically, and a supplier can return an electronic invoice. This information is typically exchanged in a structured format, such as in a delimited file or an XML file. You can use Reporting Services to convert a report to a CSV or an XML file for data exchange.

As you learned earlier in this chapter, you can use a report's interactive features in the default HTML format, and you can also take advantage of PivotTable interactivity by exporting a report to HTML with Microsoft Office Web Components. However, these formats still have a limited scope of interactive features, and you must connect to the Report Server to use the report data. You can export a report to Excel to use the full range of its features to explore and manipulate a local copy of the data. Some interactive features that are integrated into the report, such as actions, are also rendered in the Excel version of the report.

To share data with other applications or external information consumers, you can export a report to a CSV file. This file is intended for use as input into a process or application, and is not intended for a user to read. Rows and columns (which are delimited with a comma by default) are created for the lowest level of detail in the report, regardless of data region. Essentially, the CSV file is a flattened rowset of the report data.

Another way to share data is to export a report to an XML file. As with the CSV file, the XML file is not intended to be read by a user, but instead is meant to be used by another application. The file contains XML elements and attributes that define the structure of the data and also supply the data. However, none of the formatting from the source report is preserved in the XML file. In this case, the XML file contains raw data that retains its original structure rather than getting flattened as data exported to a CSV file does.

Rendering as an Excel File

Excel is a popular application for analyzing data. By exporting data to an Excel file, you have access to the report data even when you're disconnected from the Report Server. You can also add your own formulas or incorporate data from other sources into your Excel workbook.

Though all the data regions that can be in a report are also supported in Excel, the Excel format is best used with a table or a matrix. A chart can be rendered in Excel, but it is rendered as a picture and not as an Excel chart that you can modify. A list will be rendered with repeating groups, as it is in an HTML report, but the items contained in the list will be rendered in positions that correspond to their relative positions in the original report, which might conflict with the position of items that aren't contained in the list. A subreport is not recommended for export to Excel.

The Excel version keeps most of the features and formatting of the original report, including pagination, actions, and a document map. However, if a report has been designed using dynamic visibility, all items hidden in the original report will be visible in the Excel version of the report.

Microsoft Visual Basic .NET formulas are converted to an Excel formula if Excel has an equivalent. The formulas that get translated are those that use report item expressions, not field expressions. Otherwise, the result of the expression is stored in a cell as a constant value. For example, if a textbox contains an expression like `=Sum(Fields!UnitPrice.Value * Fields!OrderQty.Value)`, there is no equivalent in Excel. When a report containing this expression is rendered to Excel, the calculation is performed and the resulting value, rather than the formula, is stored in the Excel cell.

In this procedure, you'll export the Order Details report, which has interactive features such as dynamic visibility and drillthrough, as an Excel file.

Export an interactive table to Excel

1. In Report Manager, click the Rendering link, and then click the Order Details report link.

   Your screen looks similar to this:

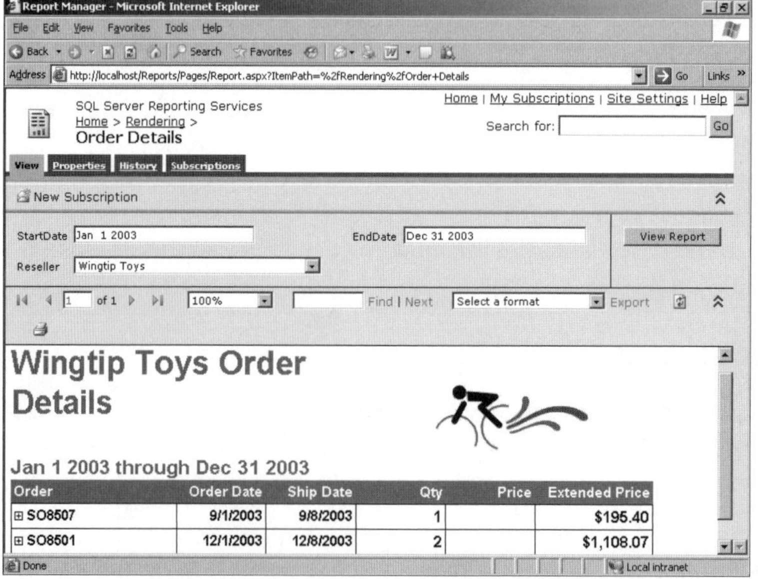

This report includes a table in which dynamic visibility is used to hide the detail rows and a subtotal row when the report is opened. Notice that on the row that contains the order header information (order number and dates), the quantity and extended price are also displayed.

2. Expand order number SO8501 to display the detail rows, as shown here:

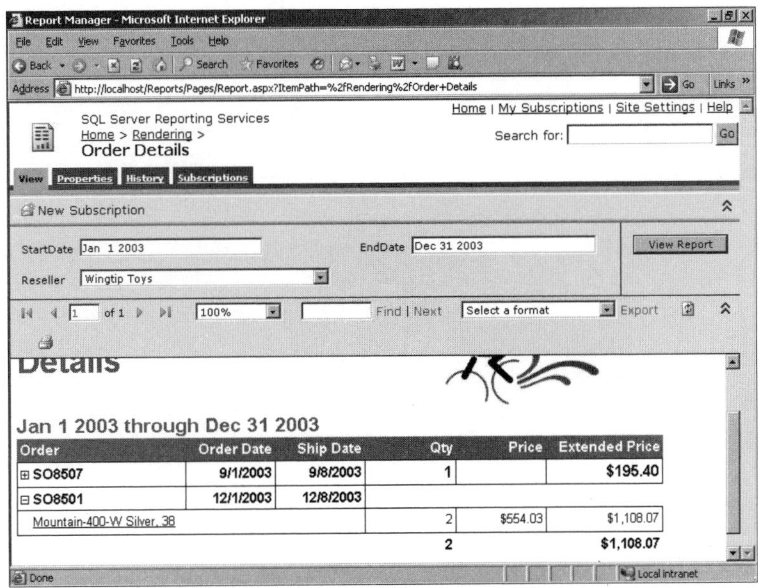

Now the quantity and extended price in the order header row are hidden. The product row and the order subtotal row are displayed below the order header row.

3. Collapse order SO8501.

Now the order header information is again displayed with the quantity and extended price, and the rows below the order header information are hidden.

4. Select Excel in the Export drop-down list, click the Export link, and then click Open in the File Download dialog box to view the Excel report, as shown here:

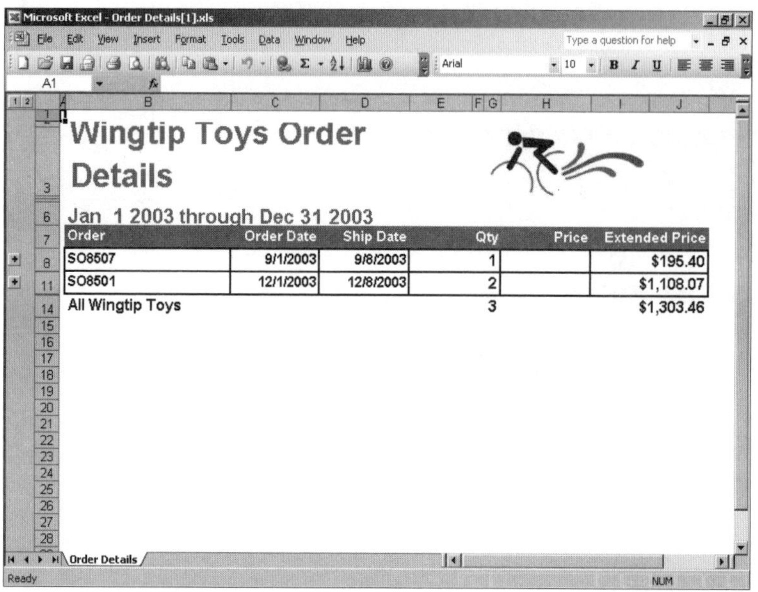

> **Tip** If you save the Excel report directly to disk at this point, you must use Office XP Excel or later to open the file. By clicking Open, you can use the Save As Workbook feature to share the file with users who have an earlier version of Excel.

Here, all detail rows that were hidden in the HTML version of the report remain hidden, but are grouped. You can expand each group to view the details. The quantity and extended price in the order header are also displayed, regardless of whether you choose to display the details. You can see that dynamic visibility is not rendered in the Excel report, but all the data is included in the report.

> **Note** This result of handling dynamic visibility when rendering to Excel is unlike rendering to MHTML or the page-oriented formats, PDF or TIFF. In those formats, only the currently visible rows are rendered. By contrast, all rows—regardless of whether they're visible—are rendered in the Excel format.

5. Expand row 8, and then click the LL Mtn Frame – Silver, 44 link in cell B9.

Your screen looks like this:

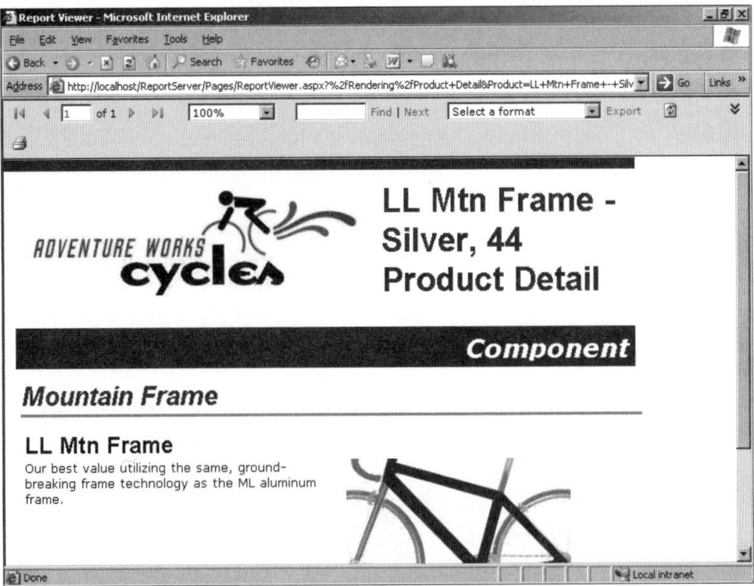

The link in the report is defined as a drillthrough action that opens the HTML version of the drillthrough report in a browser window. Notice that the URL in Internet Explorer's Address bar references the Report Server virtual directory rather than the Reports directory that you have seen with other reports that you access using Report Manager. You'll learn more about accessing reports directly with URLs in Chapter 18.

> **Note** The bookmark and hyperlink actions are also supported in Excel. You can work with the Excel file while disconnected from the network, but you must have connectivity when using the hyperlink action (to access the URL defined for the hyperlink) and when using the drillthrough action (to access the Report Server hosting the drillthrough report).

6. Close the browser window with the drillthrough report and close Excel.

Rendering a Report as a CSV File

If you need to provide information in document form for a person to read and you also need to provide a structured file for input into an application, you can satisfy both requirements with one report in Reporting Services. When you export a report to a CSV file, the data is flattened (or denormalized) so that each row in the file represents the lowest level of detail in the report, with higher-level information incorporated into the row. For example, a textbox that contains the report title will be rendered as a column in the CSV file, so each row will contain the report title even though it appears in the HTML report only once.

The format of the CSV file is predefined as comma-delimited fields with records delimited by a carriage return and line feed. If a delimiter appears in a text string, the string is contained within quotation marks as a text qualifier. The header row of the file contains the names of the report items that correspond to each column. The CSV format just described is used by Report Manager by default. Through programmatic rendering (which is discussed in Chapter 18), you can define different delimiters, specify a different text qualifier, omit the header row, supply a different file extension, or change the default encoding from Unicode.

In this procedure, you'll export the Order Details report as a CSV file.

Export a table as a CSV file

1. In Report Manager, with the Order Details report open, select CSV (Comma Delimited) in the Export drop-down list, click the Export link, and then click Save in the File Download dialog box.

   If you click Open, the file will be opened using Excel, which can be difficult to read.

2. Save the file as Order Details.csv in the C:\Documents and Settings\<username>\My Documents\Microsoft Press\rs2005sbs\Workspace folder.
3. Close the browser window that opened as part of the file download process.
4. Using Microsoft Notepad, open the Order Details.csv file.

   The file looks like this if word wrap is turned off:

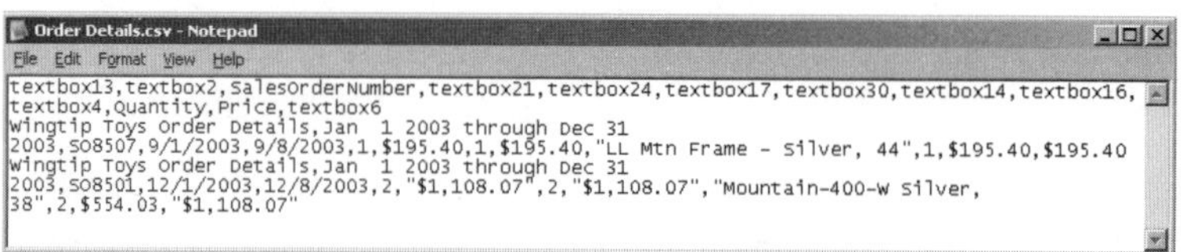

   Notice that the header row contains names of the report items. In this report, the report item names were assigned by default. Normally, this doesn't matter, because the user doesn't see the report item name elsewhere. In a CSV file, however, it's difficult to know exactly what you're looking at without referring back to the report definition.

> **Tip** If you know that a report will be used for export as a CSV file, you should rename the report items in the authoring stage so the output is more meaningful when exported.

In this example, there are only two rows because the table in this report includes only two detail rows, which represent the lowest level of detail in this report. The first two columns of each row are the report title and the date range, which appear above the table in the HTML rendering.

The next five columns in each row represent, respectively, order number, order date, ship date, quantity, and extended price. These latter two columns are the textboxes that are hidden when the detail rows are visible. Just as with Excel rendering, the CSV rendering ignores dynamic visibility and puts all data into the target file. These columns are followed by the data in the subtotal row—again, quantity and extended price. Then, the final four columns represent the data elements found in the detail row. Notice the quotation marks used as a text qualifier when a comma is embedded in a string.

5. Close Notepad.

Rendering a Report as an XML File

You can also create a structured file using an XML format. The hierarchical structure of the data is tagged in the file, unlike the CSV file, which flattened the data to its lowest level. Obviously, the application that will eventually translate this file will need to understand the meaning of this structure. Because report item names are used to distinguish XML elements in the document, you'll need to carefully consider your naming conventions in the report design.

In this procedure, you'll export the Order Details report as an XML file.

Export a table as an XML file

1. In Report Manager, with the Order Details report open, select XML File With Report Data in the Export drop-down list, click the Export link, and then click Open in the File Download dialog box.

   The XML document is displayed in a browser window like this:

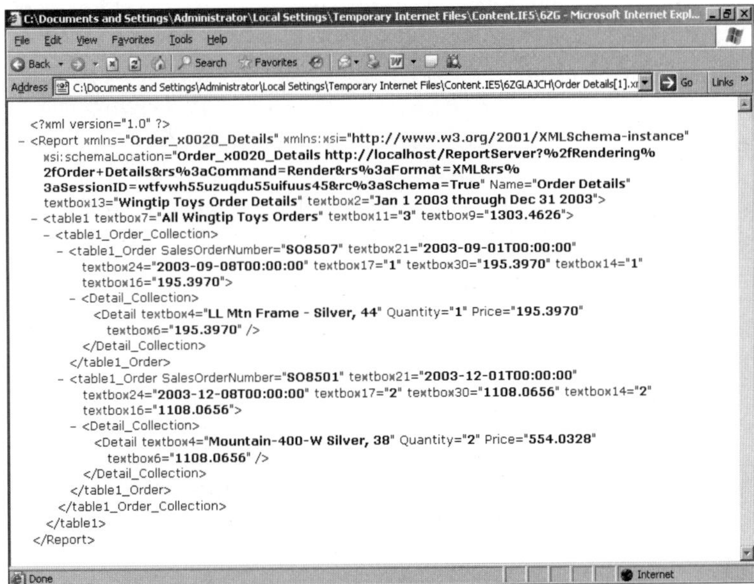

Notice that the outermost element that contains data is the *table1* element. Nested within this element are the elements that define the grouping in the table, *table1_Order*, which are themselves organized into an element called *table1_Order_Collection*, which was created by the XML rendering process. Each *table1_Order* element has a set of attributes that correspond to the report items that make up the order header in the table. Detail rows are also organized into a collection, with attributes to contain the values in each detail row.

Also notice that the subtotal information that has dynamic visibility in the HTML rendering is included twice as attributes of the *table1_Order* element. The first instance corresponds to the values that are displayed in the order header row, and the second instance corresponds to the values that are displayed with the detail rows. Because the rows in which these values appear belong to the *table1_Order* group in the table, they both become attributes of the *table1_Order* element in the XML file.

2. Close all browser windows.

Chapter 13 Quick Reference

To	Do this
Render a multiple page report as a single page	On the Report toolbar in Report Manager, select Web Archive in the Export drop-down list, and then click the Export link.
Add a document map to a report	Open the report using Visual Studio. In the Properties window, click the report item that contains the grouping to be added to the document map, and then click the *Grouping* property's ellipsis button. Click the applicable expression in the Document Map Label list box, such as `=Fields!ProdCat.Value`.
Render a report to a page-oriented format	On the Report toolbar in Report Manager, click either Acrobat (PDF) File or TIFF File in the Export list box, and then click the Export link.
Render a report for offline analysis	On the Report toolbar in Report Manager, select Excel in the Export drop-down list, and then click the Export link.
Render a report as a structured data file for data exchange	On the Report toolbar in Report Manager, select either CSV (Comma Delimited) File or XML File With Report Data in the Export drop-down list, and then click the Export link.

Chapter 14

Managing Subscriptions

After completing this chapter, you will be able to:

- Create a standard subscription to e-mail a report.
- Add a standard subscription to place a report on a file share.
- Define a data-driven subscription to retrieve recipients and subscription options from a relational table.
- Monitor the status of a subscription.
- Delete an inactive subscription.

In the previous two chapters, you learned about accessing reports online and about how reports can be rendered into different formats. You can also use Reporting Services to deliver reports directly to users in any rendering format. In this chapter, you learn how to use subscriptions as an alternative method to execute and deliver reports to users. You also learn how to monitor and manage subscriptions.

Creating a Standard Subscription

Subscriptions allow users to take full advantage of the "push" paradigm that is supported by Reporting Services. In other words, users can decide what information they want sent to them automatically and are not limited to "pulling" information from the reporting platform. A subscription can be defined to deliver a specific report to an e-mail account or to a network file share on a scheduled basis. You can also install a custom or third-pary delivery extension if you have other delivery requirements. For example, you might want to try out the sample delivery extension to send a report to a printer that is described in Reporting Services Books Online.

By default, the Browser role includes the task assignment, "Manage individual subscriptions," that allows a user to add, change, or delete his or her own subscriptions, whereas the Content Manager role is assigned the task, "Manage all subscriptions," that controls all subscriptions defined on the Report Server. Users can create a subscription for any report to which they have access, but only if the report uses stored credentials (because a subscription executes a report in unattended mode).

Delivery of a subscription can be triggered either by a defined schedule or by the update of a snapshot (which can be updated manually or according to a schedule). When the triggering event occurs, the Report Server reads the delivery information from the subscription, which it passes to the delivery extension. The delivery extension is responsible for rendering and delivering the report as defined in the subscription. If an error occurs during delivery, the problem is logged in the ReportServerService_<*timestamp*>.log file.

> **Disabling Subscriptions**
>
> You can prevent users from using subscriptions by removing the "Manage individual subscriptions" task assignment. Users will no longer be able to access the Subscription page of a report when using Report Manager, but any active subscriptions will continue to execute.
>
> Rather than completely disable subscriptions, you might prefer to prevent the use of a specific delivery extension. If you remove a delivery extension from the RSWeb-Application.config configuration file, this extension is no longer available as a report delivery option in Report Manager. You can also remove the delivery extension from the RSReportServer.config file, but any subscriptions that were using that delivery extension will become inactive. Inactive subscriptions, because they don't do anything, don't cause any problems on the Report Server, but it's considered good practice to delete the inactive subscriptions that result from the removal of a delivery extension. (Handling inactive subscriptions is discussed later in this chapter.)

Delivering a Report by E-Mail

Use e-mail delivery when you want to mail a rendered report. If you use the Web Archive rendering option, the report is embedded in the e-mail message. If you do not use this option, the report is sent as an attachment. Alternatively, you can define the subscription to send a link to a report on the Report Server, or even to send just a notification message that a report is ready for viewing on the server.

To use e-mail delivery, you must have a local or remote Simple Mail Transport Protocol (SMTP) server available on the same network as your Report Server. During installation of Reporting Services, you can specify an SMTP server address and an e-mail address that appears as the sender of the message. You can change these values, as well as configure other e-mail delivery settings, by editing the RSReportServer.config file. For example, you can restrict the delivery of reports to specific domains by adding the Data Source Name (DSN) or the IP address to *PermittedHosts*. You can find a complete list of available settings and valid values in SQL Server Books Online.

In this procedure, you'll create a subscription for the Employee Product Sales report that embeds the report in an e-mail message and sends the report.

Create a standard e-mail subscription

1. Run PublishChap14.cmd in the folder C:\Documents and Settings\<username>\My Documents\Microsoft Press\rs2005sbs\chap14 folder to publish the reports you need so that you can follow the procedures in this chapter.

> **Important** To complete the procedures related to e-mail delivery in this chapter, you must have your Microsoft Internet Information Services (IIS) server configured to use SMTP with a local domain alias of adventure-works.com, or substitute your own e-mail address in place of the supplied e-mail address. For specific instructions, refer to the Introduction to this book.

2. Open Report Manager in Internet Explorer at *http://localhost/Reports.*

   If Report Manager is already open, you will need to use Internet Explorer's Refresh button to view the published reports.

3. Click the Delivery folder link.
4. Click Show Details, and then click the Properties icon in the Edit column to the left of the Employee Product Sales report, as shown here:

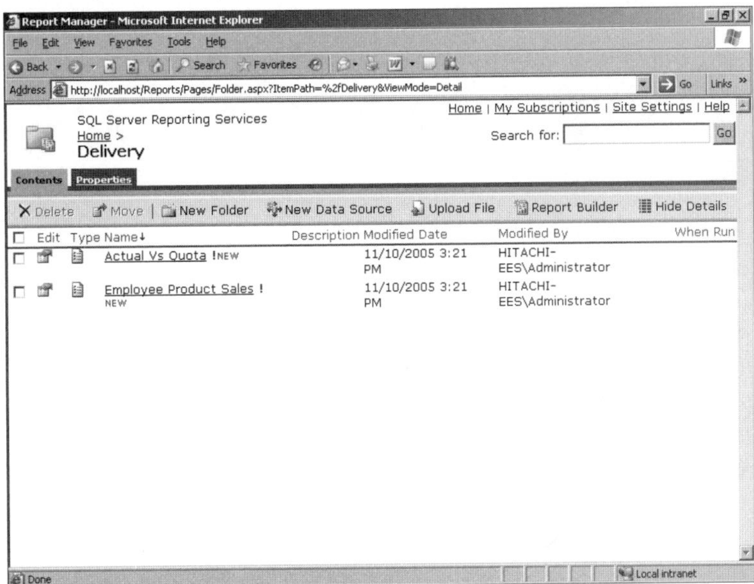

5. Click the Data Sources link, select Credentials Stored Securely In The Report Server, type **ReportExecution** as the user name and **ReportExecution** as the password, and then click Apply.

   You will not be able to add a subscription to a report unless it uses stored credentials.

6. Click the Subscriptions tab.

Your screen looks like this:

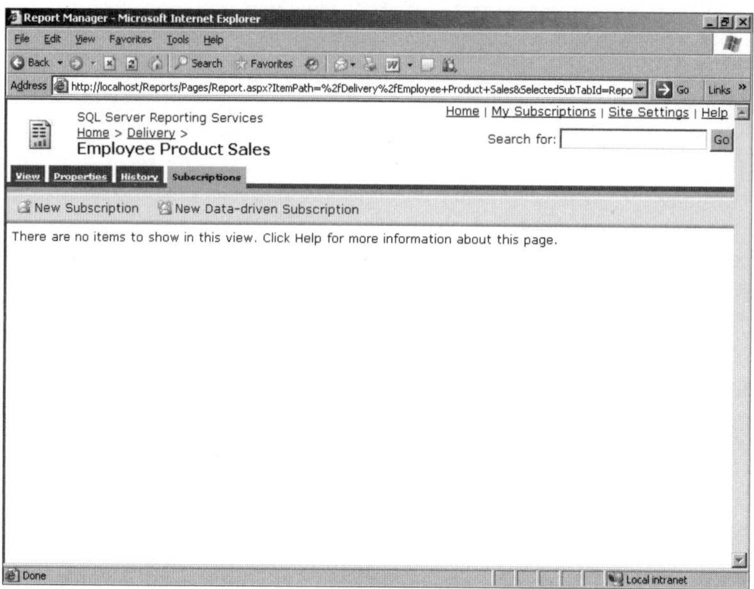

7. Click New Subscription.

   The Subscription definition page is displayed:

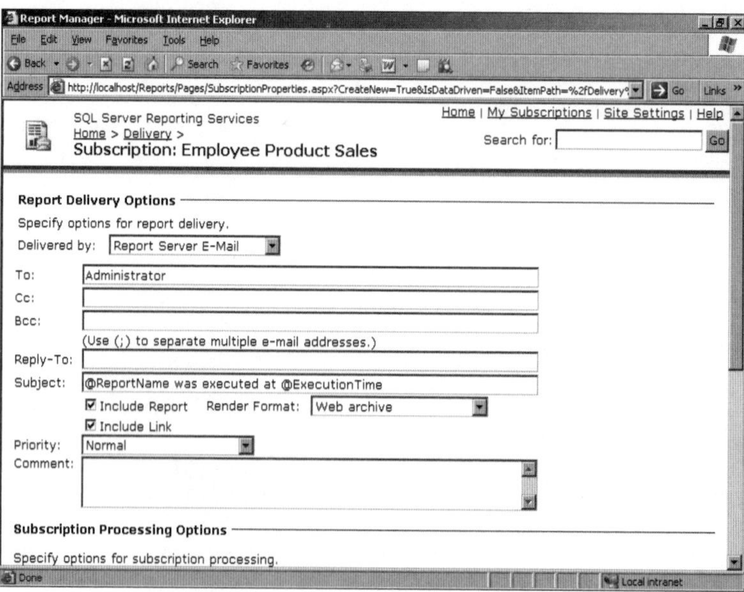

The default delivery method is Report Server E-Mail. In the To text box, the current user name is automatically added as the default recipient. (You can override this behavior by editing the RSReportServer.config configuration file so the To field is not populated automatically.) Also notice the default Subject text box: @ReportName Was Executed At @ExecutionTime. The current report name and the execution name are inserted when the e-mail message is prepared for delivery. These two names match variables in the *Globals* collection in Report Designer, but you cannot use any of the other *Global* variables in the Subject line.

8. Replace the value in the To text box with **PacificDirector@adventure-works.com**.

   As with a regular e-mail message, you can send a subscription to multiple users by separating the e-mail addresses with a semicolon (;), or you can send the report to copied recipients and blind copied recipients. Optionally, you can include a Reply-To e-mail address.

9. Click the Render Format drop-down list to review the available options, but keep the default value of Web Archive.

10. Clear the Include Link check box.

    The Report Delivery Options portion of the page looks like this:

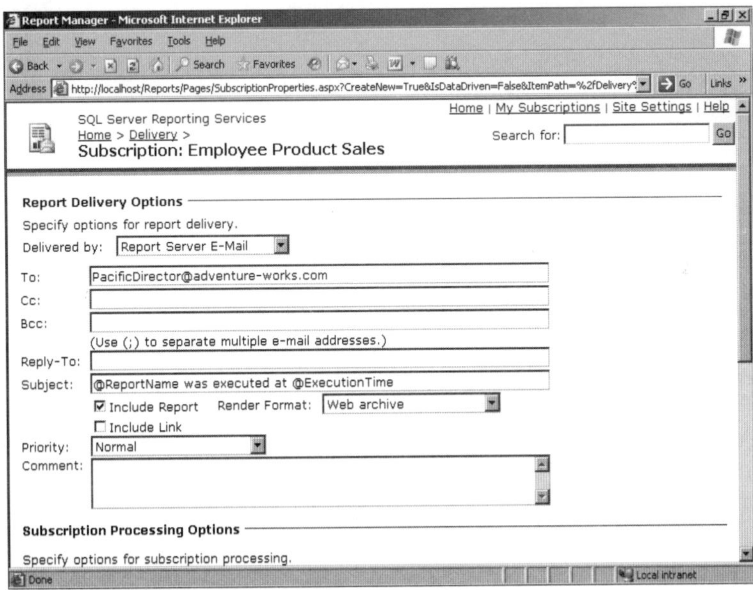

    In this case, only an embedded report will be sent in the e-mail message. If you also clear the Include Report check box, only a notification message will be sent.

11. Click Select Schedule.

12. Click Once to specify the frequency of the report.

    In this procedure, you'll run the subscription one time to generate output. Normally, you would specify a periodic frequency for a subscription schedule. This schedule that you create will apply to the current subscription only.

13. Enter a start time that is 3 minutes ahead of the current time and select the correct A.M. or P.M. option.

    Your screen looks similar to this (with a different time specified):

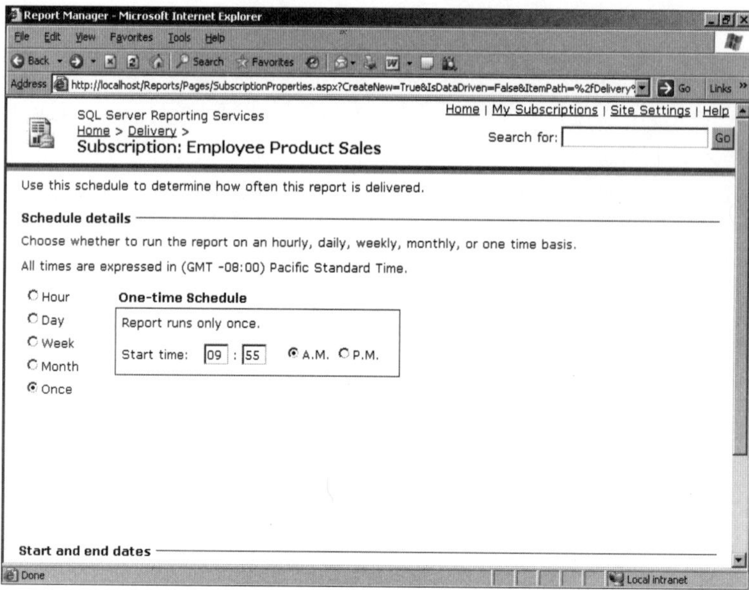

14. Click OK.
15. Replace the *Group* parameter value with **Pacific**.
16. Select the Use Default check box for the *Year* parameter.

Note If you were to select a report snapshot for the subscription, you wouldn't be able to edit parameter values used as query parameters. The values in the rendered report for the subscription will match those of the snapshot. However, if the report parameter is used as a filter, you can modify it in a subscription.

The bottom of the Subscriptions page looks like this:

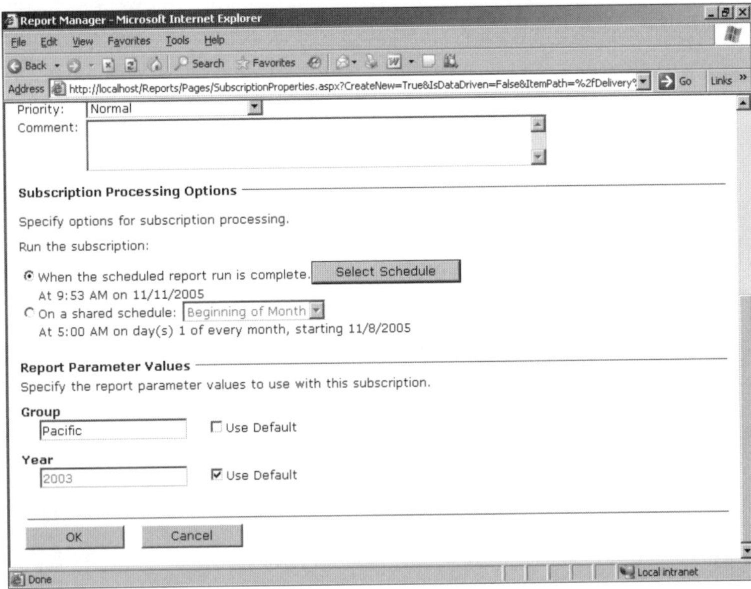

17. Click OK.

The Subscriptions page for the Employee Product Sales report looks like this:

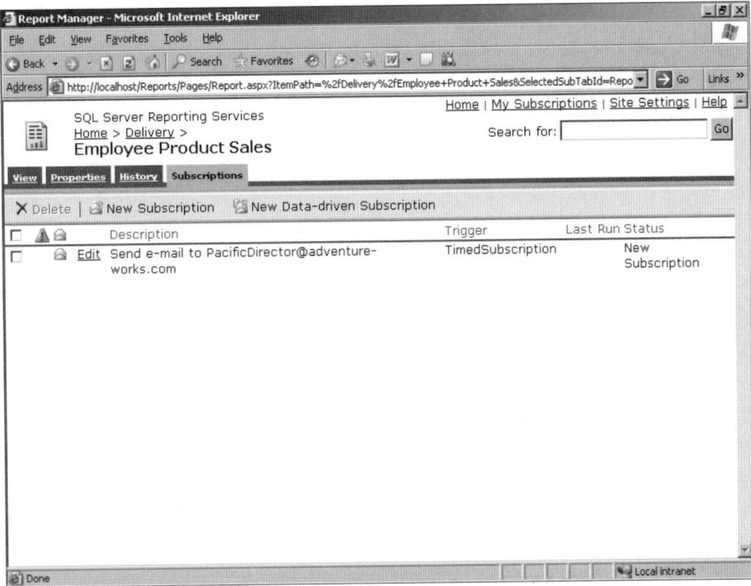

> **Important** The SQL Server Agent must be running to create a subscription. If it isn't running, you'll receive an error when you click OK to create the subscription.

18. After waiting 3 minutes, click Refresh on the Internet Explorer toolbar.

    The Subscriptions page for the Employee Product Sales report looks similar to this:

    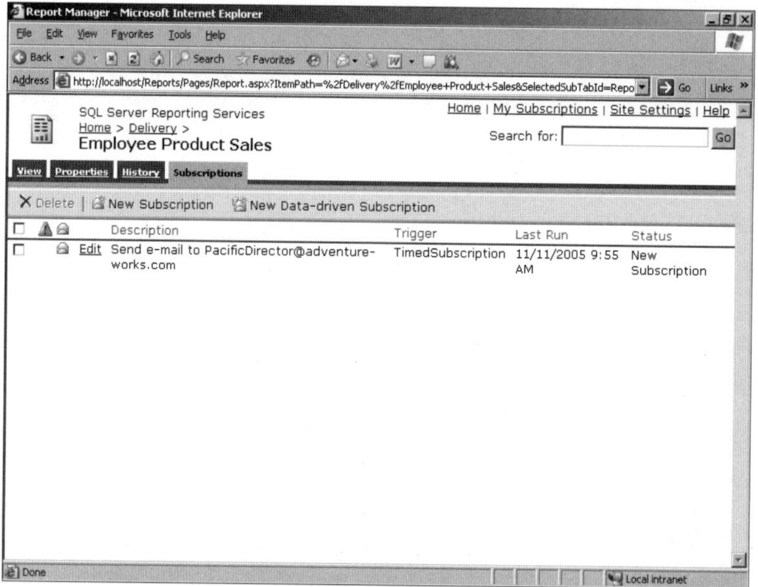

    When the subscription is delivered, the Last Run and Status columns are updated.

19. If you're using a local SMTP Server, open Microsoft Windows Explorer, navigate to the C:\Inetpub\mailroot\Drop folder, and double-click the e-mail file (with extension .eml) located there. Otherwise, if you're using a local Post Office Protocol v3 (POP3) Server, navigate to C:\Inetpub\mailroot\Mailbox\adventure-works.com \P3_PacificDirector.mbx and open the message file in that folder.

Your screen looks similar to this:

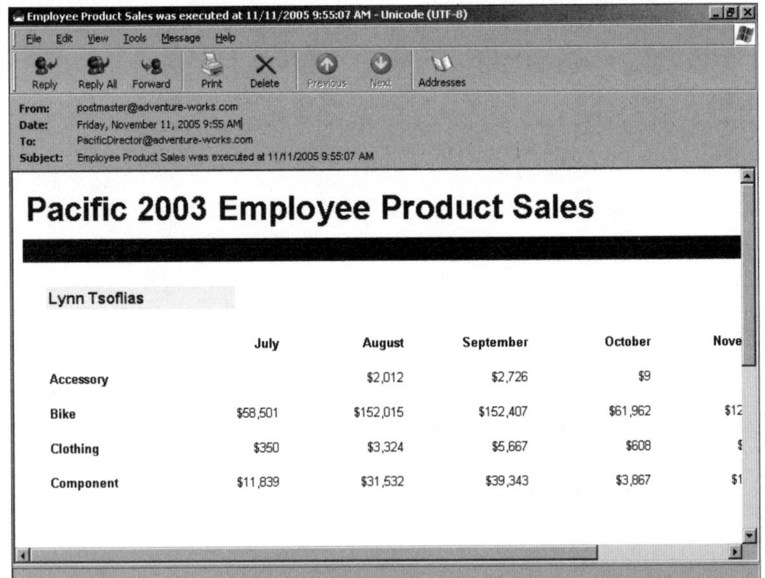

At the scheduled time, Reporting Services executed the report, which it embedded as Multipurpose Internet Mail Extensions (MIME) Encapsulated Aggregate HTML (MHTML) into the body of an e-mail message. Notice that the subject line is updated with the report name and execution time. The From e-mail address is defined in the Report Server configuration file.

Delivering a Report to a File Share

Instead of e-mailing a report to recipients, you can use file share delivery to put a copy of a report on a file share in a designated location. You can use any rendering format. With file share delivery, you can choose to overwrite an existing file or have Reporting Services generate incremental file names to track versions of the same report. You must supply credentials with write permission on the file share.

In this procedure, you'll create a subscription for the Actual Vs Quota report, which renders the report as a Microsoft Excel file and places it on a file share.

Create a standard file share subscription

1. Open Windows Explorer, right-click on the C:\Documents and Settings\<username>\My Documents\Microsoft Press\rs2005sbs\Workspace folder, and then click Sharing And Security.
2. On the Sharing tab of the Workspace Properties dialog box, select Share This Folder, and then click Permissions.

> **Note** The specifics for establishing a file share might vary if you're using a different operating system. The instructions in this procedure are written with the assumption that you are using an edition of Microsoft Windows Server 2003 or Windows XP with simple file sharing disabled.

3. On the Share Permission tab of the Permissions For Workspace dialog box, click Add and type **ReportServer2005** in the Enter The Object Names To Select box. Select Check Names to validate the account, and then click OK.

> **Note** ReportServer2005 is the Windows account added in Chapter 2, "Installing Reporting Services," to run the ReportServer service. You can use another user account in its place if you prefer.

4. Select Change in the Allow column of the Permissions, and then click OK twice to close all dialog boxes.
5. In Report Manager, click the Delivery link.
6. In the Edit column of Actual Vs Quota, click the Properties icon.
7. Click the Data Sources link, click Credentials Stored Securely In The Report Server, type **ReportExecution** as the user name and **ReportExecution** as the password, and then click Apply.
8. Click the Subscriptions tab, and then click New Subscription.
9. In the Delivered By list, select Report Server File Share.

A new Subscription definition page is displayed:

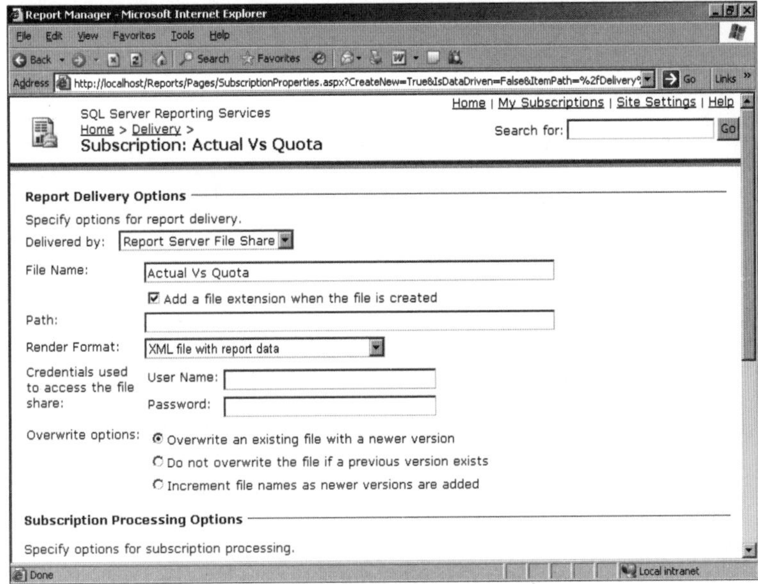

In the Path text box, type ***computername*****Workspace**.

> **Important** Replace *computername* with the name or IP address of your local computer. Do not use localhost. If you do, Reporting Services will not be able to access the correct file share. Whenever you specify a file share path on a remote computer, you must use the Universal Naming Convention (UNC) instead of a mapped network drive.

10. Select Excel in the Render Format list.

    Notice that the only rendering option missing from this list is HTML with Office Web Components. This format doesn't work properly when stored on a file share.

11. Type **ReportServer2005** as the User Name, but leave the password blank for now.
12. Select Increment File Names As Newer Versions Are Added.

Your screen looks like this:

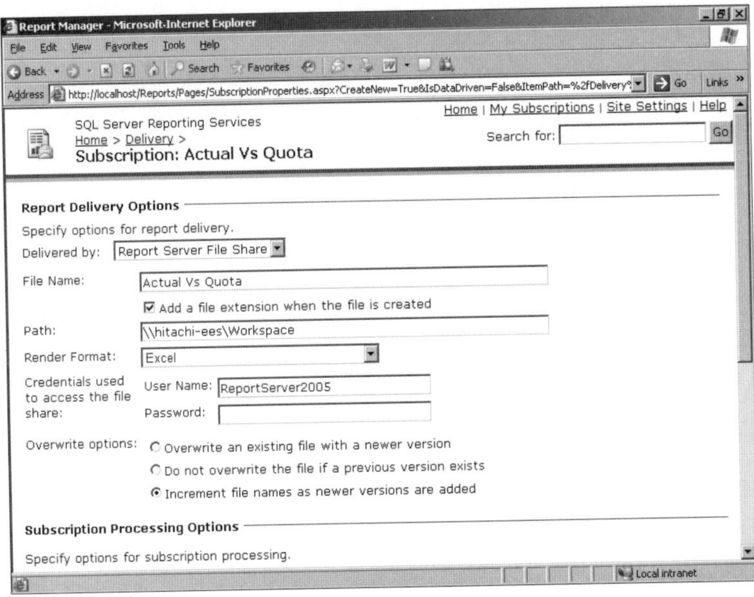

This overwrite option configures Reporting Services to append a number to the file name that increments by one each time this subscripton is executed if there is an existing file of the same name already on the file share. With this option, the existing file is not overwritten, and a separate file–distinguished by a number added to the file name–is placed on the file share.

13. Click Select Schedule.
14. Select Once to specify the frequency of the report.

    In this procedure, you'll run the subscription just once to generate output.
15. Enter a start time that is 3 minutes ahead of the current time and select the correct A.M. or P.M. option.
16. Click OK.
17. Enter the password for the ReportServer2005 account.

> **Note** As with stored credentials used with a data source, the password entered for subscriptions is also encrypted and stored in the ReportServer database.

If you had entered the password directly after you entered the user name, the password would have been cleared because you left the page to make changes to the subscription schedule page. Anytime you return to a page that has credentials, even if you've entered the full credentials earlier, you are always required to enter the password.

18. Select the Use Default check boxes for both the *Group* and *CalendarYear* parameters.

    The bottom of the page looks like this:

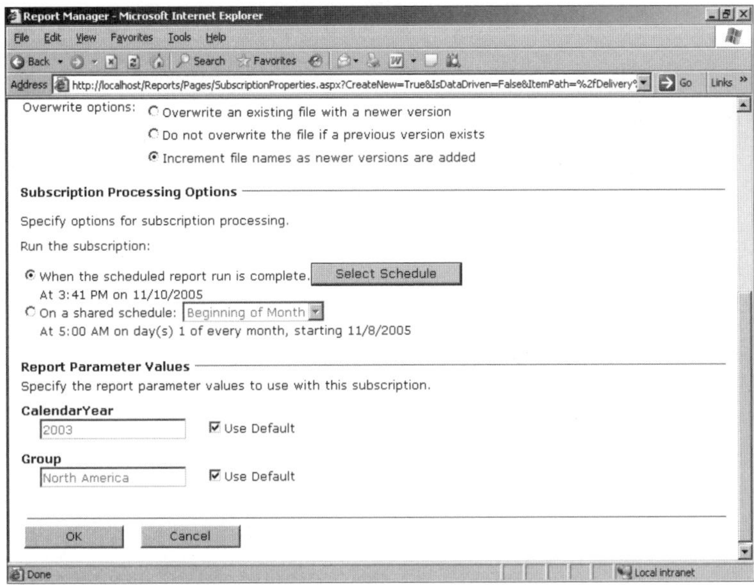

19. Click OK.

    The Subscriptions page for the Actual Vs Quota report looks like this:

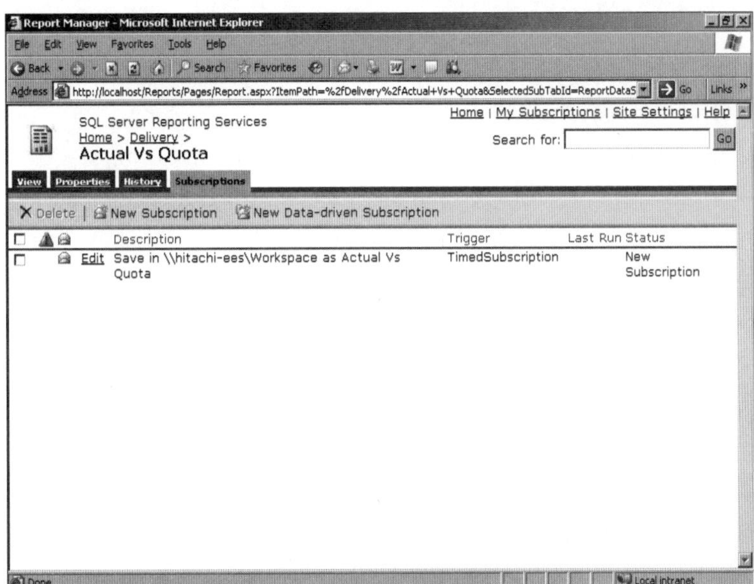

20. After waiting 3 minutes, click Refresh on the Internet Explorer toolbar.

The Subscriptions page for the Actual Vs Quota report looks similar to this:

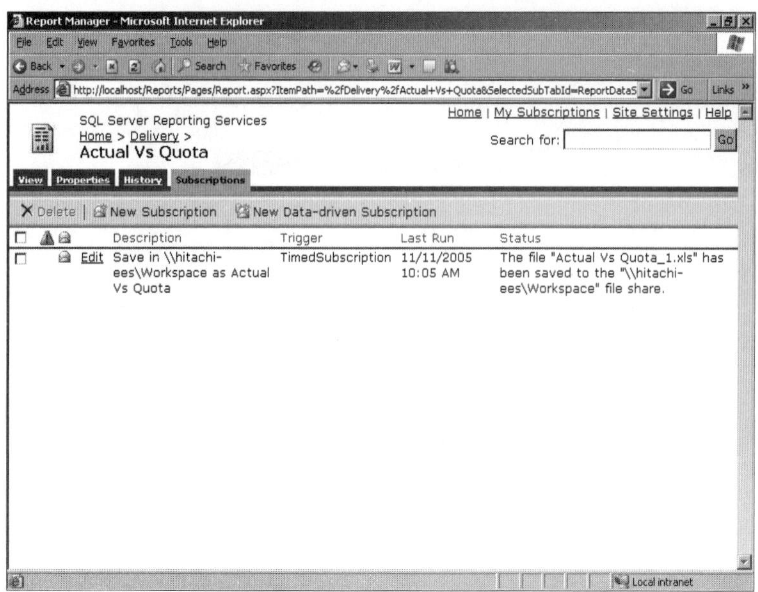

When the subscription is delivered, the Last Run and Status columns are updated.

21. In Windows Explorer, open the C:\Documents and Settings\<username>\My Documents\Microsoft Press\rs2005sbs\Workspace folder.

    The Actual Vs Quota.xls file is in the Workspace folder. Even though you set the Overwrite Option to increment the number added to the file name, the first instance of the file is assigned the same name as the report. The file name is incremented only when a file of the same name already exists.

22. Double-click the Actual Vs Quota.xls file to open the file in Excel.

Your screen looks like this:

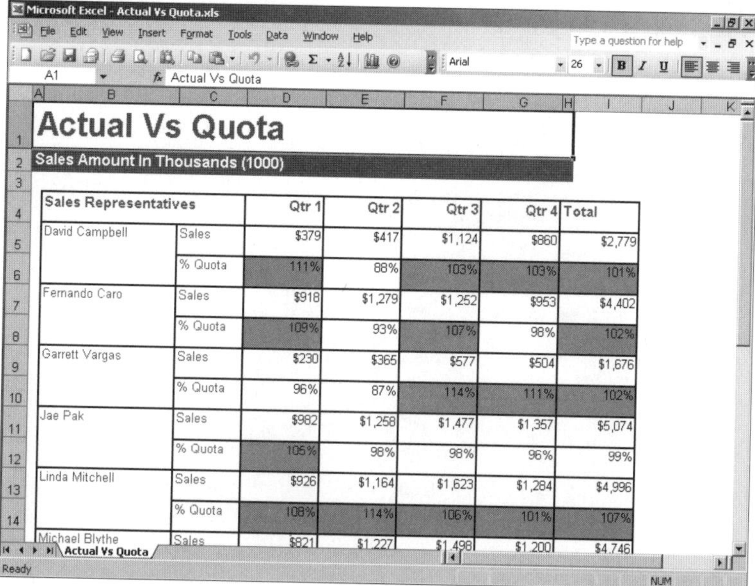

23. Close both Excel and Windows Explorer, but keep the Actual Vs Quota subscription properties page open in Report Manager.

Creating a Data-Driven Subscription

Using a data-driven subscription, Reporting Services can execute a report one time, render it in several different formats, and then send the results to many destinations. Destinations can be e-mail recipients or file shares. With a data-driven subscription, you can e-mail a report to a list of users that can change dynamically over time, and you can customize the rendered format of the report for each recipient. You can even customize parameter values by recipient as well as configure delivery options, such as including a report in an e-mail message or sending a link to the report. You need to create a relational table to manage these settings, and then create a data-driven subscription that queries this table when the report is rendered.

Creating a Subscription Delivery Table

A subscription delivery table allows you to manage a list of destinations with delivery options, rendering preferences, and parameter values. Reporting Services does not provide an interface for you to build and maintain this table, but you can use your favorite SQL Server tool to set up the table and load it with data. At a minimum, you need to define a column for the subscription destination if all you want to do is manage a list of recipients. The main advantage of this table, however, is the ability to configure many options to customize the subscription for each recipient.

In this procedure, you'll review the contents of the SubscriptionGroupDirector table in the rs2005sbsDW database.

Browse the contents of a subscription delivery table

1. Open Microsoft SQL Server Management Studio, expand the local instance (or the instance to which you installed Reporting Services and the practice files), expand the Databases folder, expand the rs2005sbsDW database, and then click Tables.
2. Right-click SubscriptionGroupDirector, and then click Open Table.

   The table looks like this:

	To	IncludeReport	RenderFormat	IncludeLink	GroupParameter
	NADirector@adventure-works.com	True	MHTML	False	North America
	PacificDirector@adventure-works.com	False	Excel	True	Pacific
	EuropeDirector@adventure-works.com	True	PDF	False	Europe
▸*	NULL	NULL	NULL	NULL	NULL

   Notice that the records in this table define subscription options for each Sales Director. You will use this table to apply these options to a data-driven subscription that customizes the delivery of reports to each territory group director. Two of the directors will have the report included in the e-mail message, while one will have a link to the report. Each director will receive a different rendered format, and each will see different data in the report because a different parameter is used to filter the data for each director.

> **Note** The structure of this table is provided as an example. You can create a more complex table if you need to manage additional subscription options.

3. Close Microsoft SQL Server Management Studio.

Creating a Data-Driven Subscription

After you create a subscription delivery table and populate it with data, you are ready to create a data-driven subscription. Rather than set the delivery options directly, as you did with the e-mail delivery, you will define a query that returns rows from the subscription delivery table. You then assign columns of the table to corresponding delivery settings and, optionally, to parameter values. A report is created for each row that is in the table and delivered according to the settings specific to each row.

In this procedure, you'll create a new data-driven subscription to send the Actual Vs Quota report by using the information in the subscription delivery table.

Create a data-driven subscription

1. In Report Manager, on the Actual Vs Quota subscription Subscriptions tab, click New Data-Driven Subscription on the toolbar.
2. Type a description: **Actual Vs Quota Subscription**.
3. Select Report Server E-Mail in the Specify How Recipients Are Notified drop-down list.
4. Keep the default data source option, Specify For This Subscription Only.

   Your screen looks like this:

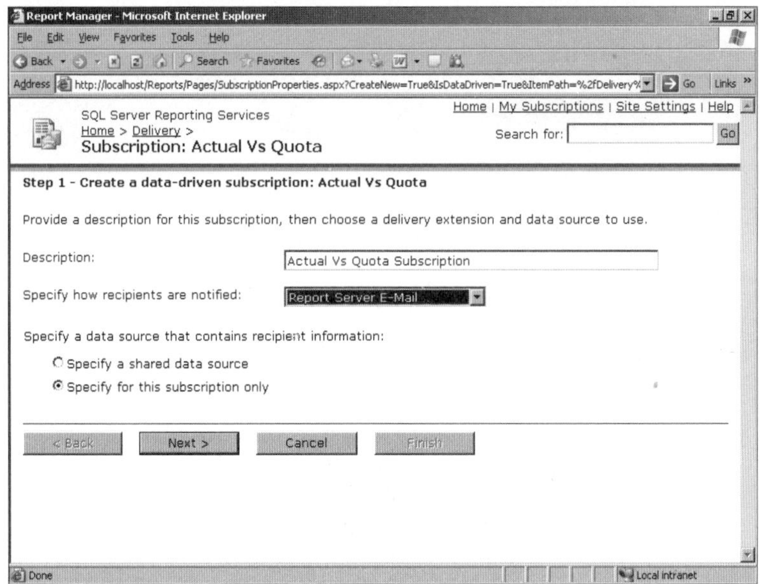

5. Click Next.
6. Type this connection string: **data source=localhost; initial catalog=rs2005sbsDW**.
7. Type **ReportExecution** as the user name and **ReportExecution** as the password.

Your screen looks like this:

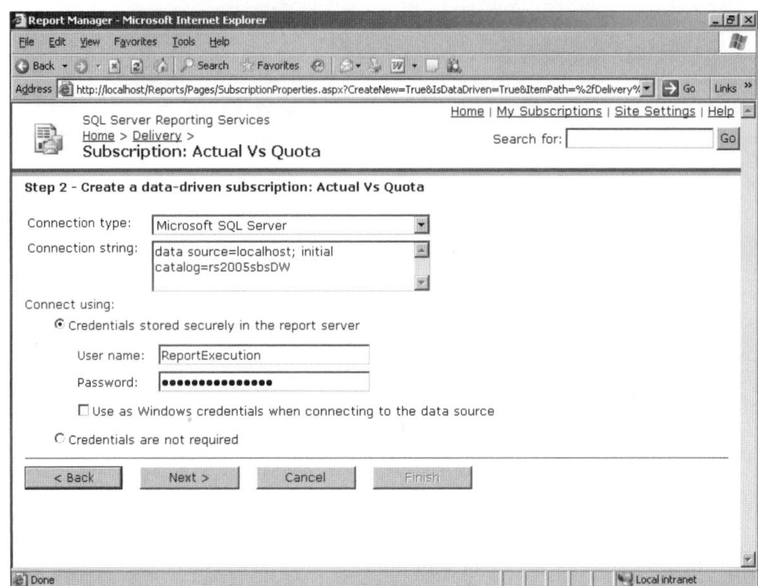

Note The connection string and credentials used here are used to connect to the subscription information table and are not used by Reporting Services to execute the report. For report execution, the data source defined for the report is still used.

8. Click Next.
9. In the text box, type **select * from SubscriptionGroupDirector**.

Note This example retrieves all rows from the SubscriptionGroupDirector table. You can, of course, write a query to filter the table to return only certain rows according to specific criteria.

10. Click Validate.

The lower part of your screen looks like this:

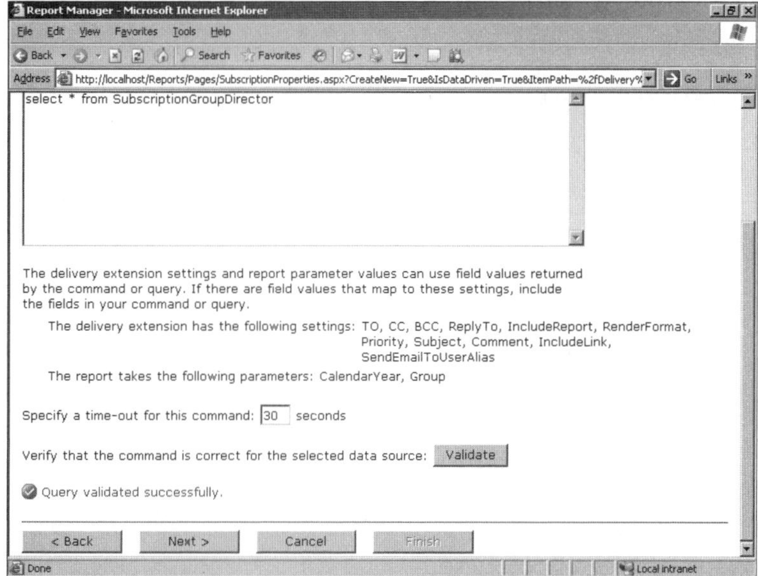

The result of the validation appears as a message at the bottom of the same page. If the validation is unsuccessful, you will not be able to proceed until the query validates, even if you don't click the Validate button. For the query to validate successfully, the data source must be correctly defined and the credentials must be successfully authenticated.

Notice also that you can change the query time-out for this query to retrieve the recipient and subscription options from the subscription delivery table.

11. Click Next.
12. Configure the delivery extension settings according to the following table:

Delivery setting	Option	Value
To	Get the value from the database	*To*
Reply-To	Specify a static value	**Sales@adventure-works.com**
Include Report	Get the value from the database	*IncludeReport*
Render Format	Get the value from the database	*RenderFormat*
Include Link	Get the value from the database	*IncludeLink*

As you can see, each delivery setting can be configured using a column from a subscription delivery table, or by supplying a static value or no value for some settings.

13. Click Next.
14. Select the Use Default check box for the *CalendarYear* parameter.

15. For the *Group* parameter, select Get The Value From The Database, and then select *GroupParameter* in the corresponding drop-down list.

    Your screen looks like this:

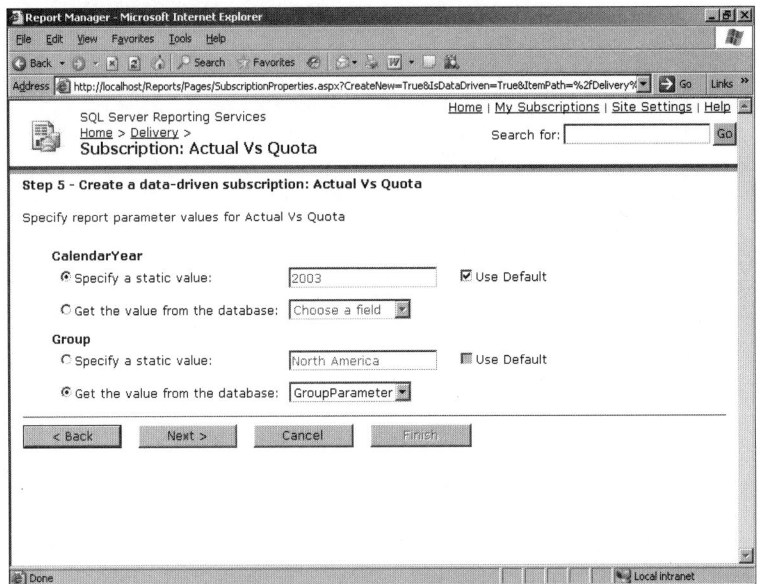

16. Click Next.
17. Select On A Schedule Created For This Subscription, and then click Next.
18. Select Once to specify the frequency of the report.

    You will run the subscription just one time to generate output.
19. Enter a start time that is 3 minutes ahead of the current time and select the correct A.M. or P.M. option.
20. Click Finish.

The *Subscriptions* properties page looks like this:

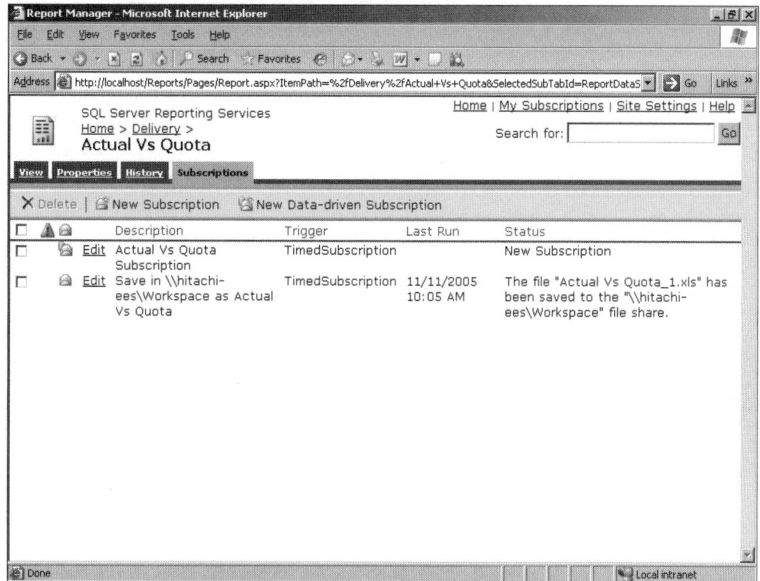

21. After waiting 3 minutes, refresh the Subscriptions page for the Actual Vs Quota report, which looks similar to this:

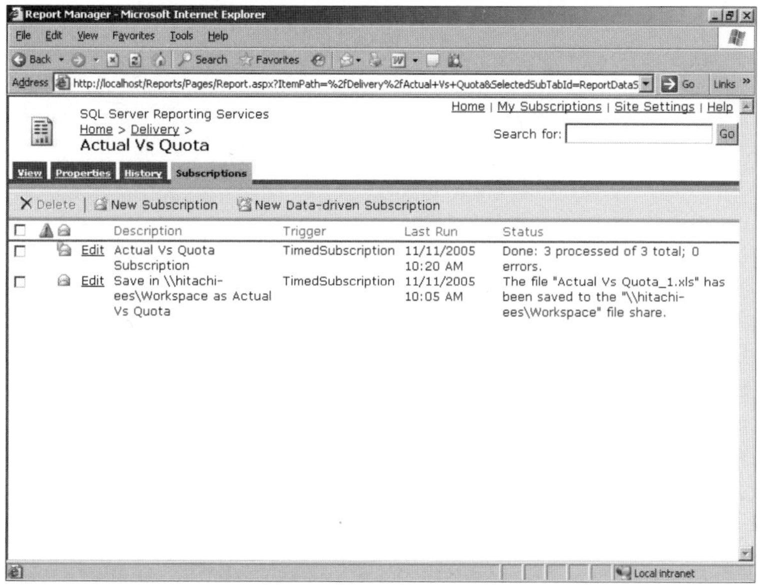

When the subscription is delivered, the Last Run and Status columns are updated. The number of deliveries and the number of errors (if any) are displayed in the Status column.

22. If you're using a local SMTP Server, open Windows Explorer, navigate to the C:\Inetpub\mailroot\Drop folder, and double-click the e-mail file (with extension .eml) located there. Otherwise, if you're using a local POP3 Server, navigate to the C:\Inetpub\mailroot\Mailbox\adventure-works.com folder.

23. If you're using SMTP, check the timestamp of the new e-mail files, and then double-click the first e-mail file that was generated at the time that the data-driven subscription executed. If using POP3, open the P3_PacificDirector.mbx.

    Your screen looks similar this:

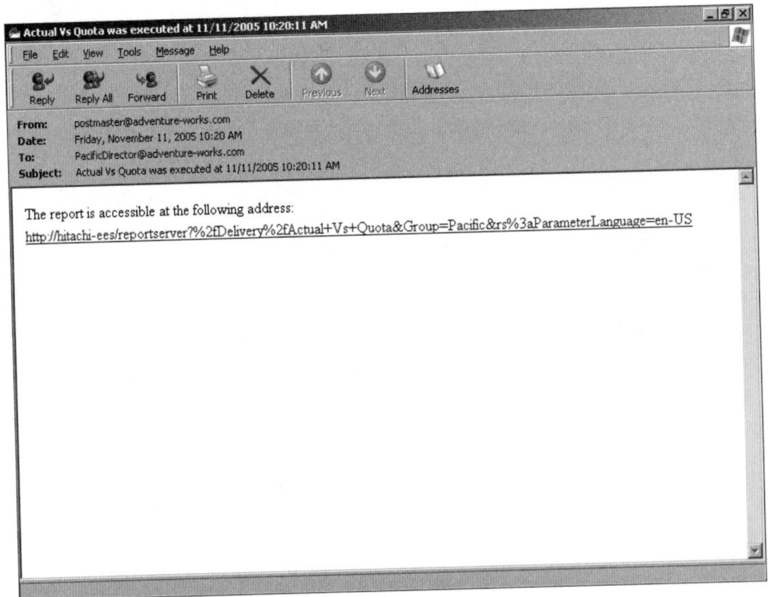

This message to the PacificDirector includes a link to the report. In this case, the report executes on demand. If more sales had been added to the database after the subscription processing completed, the report could contain data different from that of a report that was rendered with the same parameter values and delivered in an e-mail message. You should factor in this possibility when deciding when to schedule subscriptions and which delivery options to use.

24. In Windows Explorer, double-click the second e-mail file that was generated for the data-driven subscription if using the local SMTP server or open the P3_NADirector.mbx mailbox to retrieve the message there.

    Your screen looks similar this:

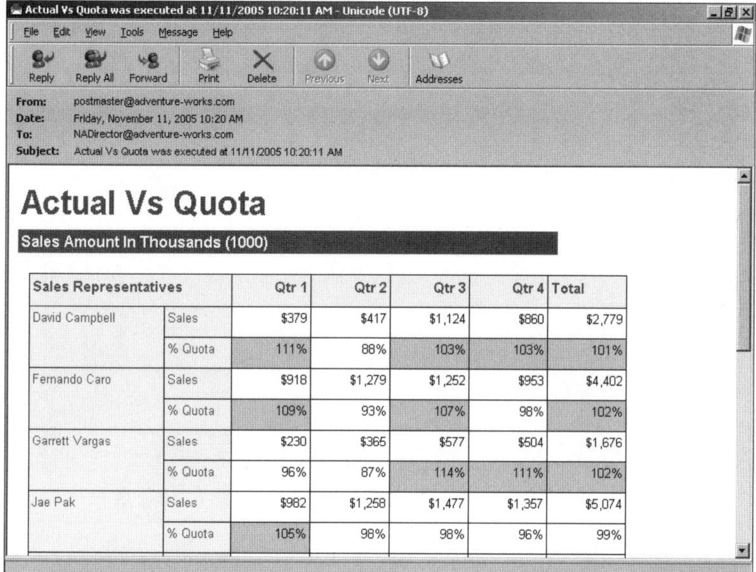

Sales Representatives		Qtr 1	Qtr 2	Qtr 3	Qtr 4	Total
David Campbell	Sales	$379	$417	$1,124	$860	$2,779
	% Quota	111%	88%	103%	103%	101%
Fernando Caro	Sales	$918	$1,279	$1,252	$953	$4,402
	% Quota	109%	93%	107%	98%	102%
Garrett Vargas	Sales	$230	$365	$577	$504	$1,676
	% Quota	96%	87%	114%	111%	102%
Jae Pak	Sales	$982	$1,258	$1,477	$1,357	$5,074
	% Quota	105%	98%	98%	96%	99%

This message to the NADirector has an embedded report. The data in this report is current as of the subscription execution time. The parameter value supplied in the subscription filters the data in this report so that sales data for only North America is sent to the NADirector.

25. In Windows Explorer, double-click the third e-mail file that was generated for the data-driven subscription if using the local SMTP server or open the e-mail message in the P3_EuropeDirector.mbx folder.

Your screen looks similar this:

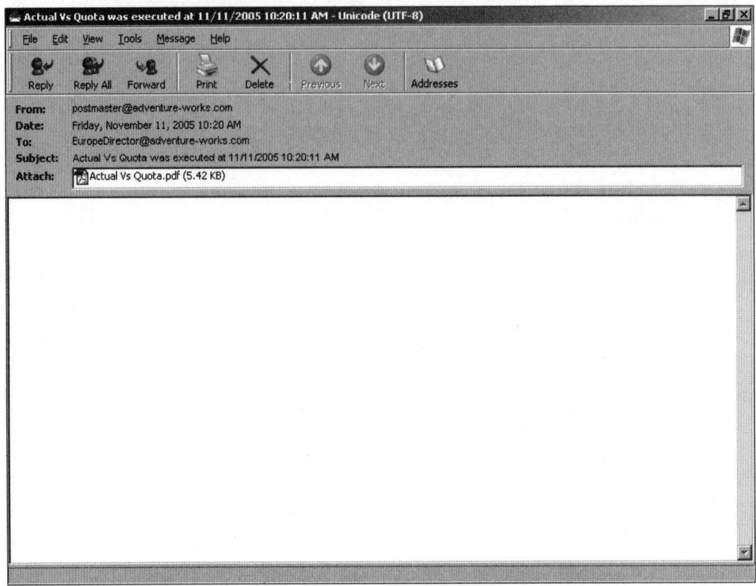

This message to the EuropeDirector has a PDF file attachment.

26. Double-click the Actual Vs Quota.pdf file to view the file.

    As with the embedded report, the data in this report is current as of the subscription execution time. Only Europe sales are shown in this report.

27. Close the e-mail messages and close Windows Explorer.

Managing Subscriptions

The Subscriptions page of a report shows you information about the existing subscriptions and the status of each subscription when it last executed. If a subscription has been created, but not yet executed, the status will be "New Subscription." If you are assigned the "Manage individual subscriptions" task, you can see only your own subscriptions on this page, but if you are assigned the "Manage all subscriptions" task, you can see all subscriptions associated with a report.

Another way to monitor the status of all of your own subscriptions is to use the My Subscriptions page. This page consolidates your subscriptions for all reports on the Report Server. You can also check the log files in the file system to troubleshoot problems with subscriptions. You'll find that certain types of problems can render a subscription inactive. If you're unable to correct the condition that caused a problem, you can delete an inactive subscription.

Using the My Subscriptions Page

The My Subscriptions page is the best way to check the status of your subscriptions because they're all organized into a single page. The link to My Subscriptions is available at all times at the top of any Report Manager page. The subscriptions on this page are only those subscriptions that you create. If your role on the Report Server grants you permission to manage all subscriptions, you must open a specific report and navigate to its Subscriptions page to see the subscriptions created by other users.

The status information for a successful subscription execution depends on the type of subscription. The status of a successful e-mail delivery will show that mail was sent to the recipients. If the Report Server could not connect to the mail server, the status will reflect this failure. Similarly, the status information of a successful file share delivery will note that the file was written to the named location. However, if the file could not be written to the target location, then the status will record the failure.

In the case of a data-driven subscription, the status will include the number of records for which notifications were delivered and the number of errors that were generated. The number of notifications should match the total number of records returned by the query to the subscription delivery table. If the number of errors is greater than zero, you will need to review the trace log to discover what caused the subscription to fail.

In this procedure, you'll review the My Subscriptions page and edit an existing subscription.

Review the My Subscriptions page

1. In Report Manager, click the My Subscriptions link in the top-right corner of the browser window.

Your screen looks similar to this:

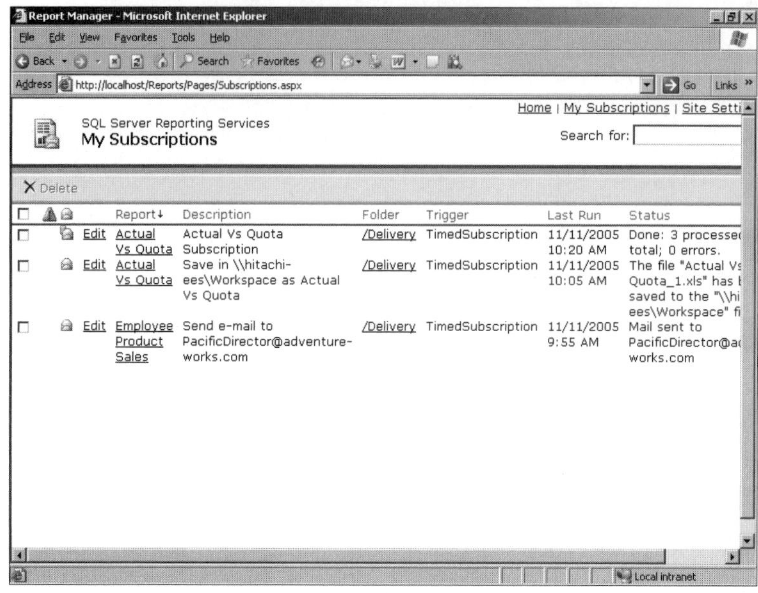

2. Click the Last Run column to change the sort order of the subscriptions.

   The first time you click a column to change the sort order, the subscriptions sort in ascending order. Click the column again to reverse the sort order. Right now, only a few subscriptions appear on this page, so the sorting feature is not particularly helpful. However, as you add more subscriptions, you'll find the ability to sort a long list of subscriptions useful. You can sort the subscriptions using any column on this page. You can also use this page to open a report to which a subscription is attached or even the folder in which the report is stored.

3. Click the Edit link to the left of the file share delivery subscription for the Actual Vs Quota report.

   Now, you'll edit the subscription to execute it one more time. Before it actually executes, you'll change the credentials assigned to the data source to force an error.

4. Click Select Schedule.

5. Change the Start Time of the report to 5 minutes from now, and then click OK.
6. Enter **NADirector** as both the user name and password, and then click OK.
7. Click the Actual Vs Quota report link for the same subscription, click the Properties tab, and then click the Data Sources link.
8. Change the Connect Using option to The Credentials Supplied By The User Running The Report, and then click Apply.

   Because a subscription must use stored credentials to execute, choosing this connection option will cause the subscription to fail.
9. After waiting 5 minutes, click the My Subscriptions link.

   Your screen looks similar to this:

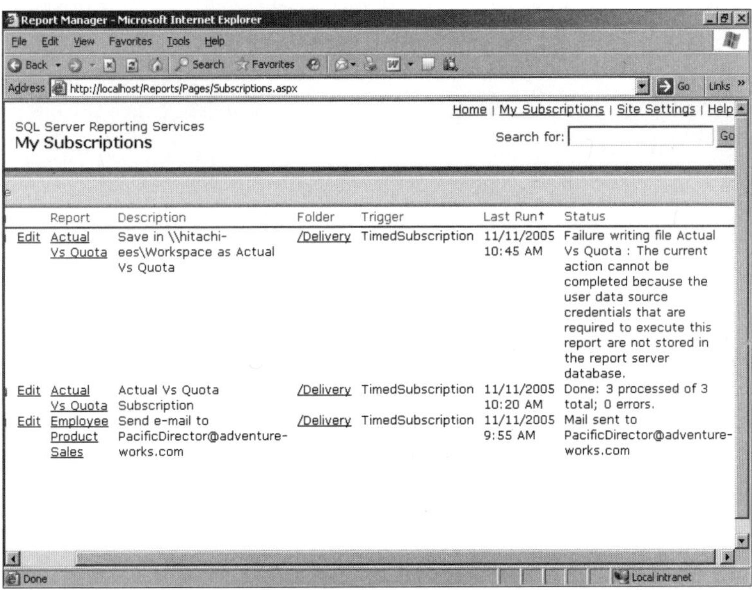

The status for the subscription notes a failure because of the change in the report's use of credentials.

Troubleshooting Subscriptions

If you have permissions to access the trace log files, you can review the ReportServer-Service_<*timestamp*>.log file to get more information related to subscription processing and deliveries. For example, if a data-driven subscription is done processing but includes errors, you can use the log file to investigate the underlying errors. The subscription may have processed just fine, but the delivery extension may not have been able to connect to the mail server to forward the messages. If, for some reason, the mail server might not be available when the Report Server tries to connect, you can configure a certain number of retry attempts. By default, this value is set to three. You can edit the RSReportServer .config file to increase or decrease this setting as appropriate for your environment.

Many other situations can cause a subscription to fail. Usually, the status message or the trace log will indicate what is causing the problem, but in some cases you'll need to peform basic troubleshooting. Here are some options to consider:

- On the Report Server, make sure the delivery extension has not been removed or disabled. (Always back up the configuration file before making changes!)
- Check that the SQL Server Reporting Services (MSSQLSERVER) and the SQL Server Agent (MSSQLSERVER) services are both running.
- Make sure the destination server is running—either the e-mail server or the target computer with a file share, depending on the delivery extension used.
- If using file share delivery, confirm that the file share is configured for write access, that the subscription is using the proper credentials, and that the disk is not full.

Sometimes the problem can be caused by the report itself. If a subscription uses a snapshot, which itself is based on a schedule, confirm that the snapshot schedule is still active. Changing credentials for the data source to anything other than stored credentials will also cause a subscription to fail. Any modifications to the report definition, such as a parameter name or data type, can also invalidate a subscription. Finally, if the report is too big for the recipient's mailbox, the report will be undeliverable.

Deleting Subscriptions

When a subscription can't be processed, it becomes inactive. You will need to resolve the problem that caused subscription processing to fail. You can also delete a subscription when it becomes inactive or when you no longer need it.

You can delete one or more subscriptions on a report's Subscriptions page or on the My Subscriptions page. To delete a subscription, select the subscription's check box and then click Delete. The Delete button is not activated until you select at least one subscription.

In this procedure, you'll delete a subscription.

Delete an inactive subscription

1. On the My Subscriptions page, select the file share delivery subscription for the Actual Vs Quota report.

   Your screen looks like this:

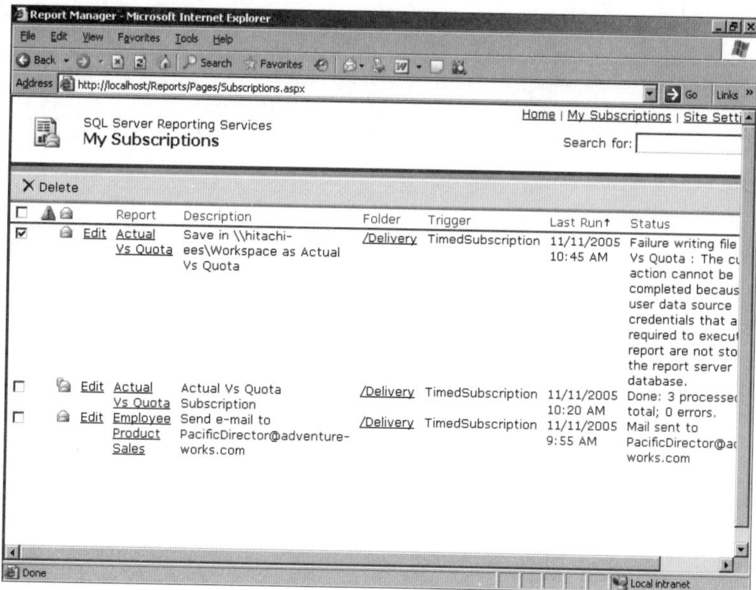

2. Click Delete.
3. Click OK to confirm the deletion.

Chapter 14 Quick Reference

To	Do this
Reconfigure or disable delivery extensions	Edit the delivery extension configuration settings in the RSWeb-Application.config file to modify interaction between Report Manager and delivery extensions. *or* Configure new values for the delivery extension, such as the number of retry attempts, in the RSReportServer.config file, or remove all delivery extension values to disable.
Create an e-mail subscription	In Report Manager, open the Subscriptions page of a report, and then click New Subscription. Use the default delivery method, Report Server E-Mail, and enter one or more recipient e-mail addresses. Specify a rendering format for the report to be sent and choose whether to include the report in the message or a link to the report on the Report Server. Assign a schedule to the report or base the subscription on the update of a report snapshot. If the report has parameters, select the default parameter value or provide a value for this subscription.
Create a file share subscription	In Report Manager, open the Subscriptions page of a report, and then click New Subscription. Change the delivery method to Report Server File Share and enter a file share on the network using a UNC format. Enter credentials for an account with permissions to write to the file share. Specify a rendering format for the report to be placed on the file share and select overwrite options. Assign a schedule to the report or base the subscription on the update of a report snapshot. If the report has parameters, select the default parameter value or provide a value for this subscription.
Create a data-driven subscription	Create and populate a subscription delivery table to contain destination information and subscription options by destination. In Report Manager, open the Subscriptions page of a report, and then click New Data-Driven Subscription. Choose a delivery method and a data source that will be used to connect to the subscription delivery table. Enter a query to retrieve values from the subscription delivery table and map these values to delivery settings and parameter values for the subscription. Assign a schedule to the report or base the subscription on the update of a report snapshot.
Monitor subscriptions	In Report Manager, view the status of a subscription as of its last execution using the report-specific Subscriptions page or the global My Subscriptions page.
View trace logs for subscription processing and delivery information	Review the log entries in the ReportServerService_<*timestamp*>.log file.
Delete a subscription	In Report Manager, open the report-specific Subscriptions page or the global My Subscriptions page, select one or more subscriptions, and then click Delete.

Chapter 15

Creating Reports with Report Builder

After completing this chapter, you will be able to:

- Navigate a report model to select attributes for a report.
- Build a table, matrix, and chart report.
- Apply formatting to a report.
- Add a filter to a report.
- Sort data in a report.
- Publish a report to the report server.

In the previous chapters of Part IV, "Delivering Reports," you learned how to use Report Manager to access and deliver reports that were created using the Visual Studio development environment. Because using this development environment requires a technical understanding of the data to include in a report, the task of building enterprise reports is usually assigned to power users and IT staff. However, the need for information by the rest of the user community often outpaces the ability of these report developers to produce requested reports. The purpose of Report Builder is to fill this gap, providing users who don't have the technical knowledge required for writing T-SQL or MDX queries with easy access to information from SQL Server and Analysis Services databases. In this chapter, you'll learn how to use Report Builder for creating ad hoc reports–one more option you have for delivering information to decision makers in your organization.

Building Basic Reports

When you use Report Builder to create an ad hoc report, you don't need to know anything about how data is structured in the source database. You simply select items from a model of the data and arrange these items in a table, matrix, or chart. You can then view the report in Report Builder. If you want to access the report later or to share it with others, you can even save your report to the report server.

Getting Started with Report Builder

Report Builder insulates users from the technical details of querying a database by using a report model to describe the data elements and the relationship between these data elements in a user-friendly way. As explained in Chapter 8, "Building Report Models," a report model contains a collection of entities, attributes, and roles. In Report Builder, you navigate through the report model by selecting an entity to review its attributes, which you can add to the report layout, or by selecting a role to view attributes for a related entity.

In this procedure, you'll start Report Builder and explore the interface in preparation for developing a report.

Launch Report Builder

1. In Internet Explorer, open Report Manager at *http://localhost/Reports.*

> **Note** If you skipped Chapter 8, open SQL Server Business Intelligence Development Studio, open the Reseller Sales Report Model solution in the C:\Documents and Settings\<username>\My Documents\Microsoft Press\rs2005sbs\Answers\chap08\Reseller Sales Report Model folder. Right-click the Reseller Sales Report Model project in Solution Explorer, and then click Deploy. The report model and its associated data source will be deployed to the report server.

2. Click Report Builder on the Report Manager toolbar.
3. Click Run if the Application Run – Security Warning dialog box displays.

   This dialog box appears only the first time that the Report Builder application is launched on a client workstation.
4. In the Source of Data list in the right pane, expand the Reseller Sales model.

   Your screen looks like this:

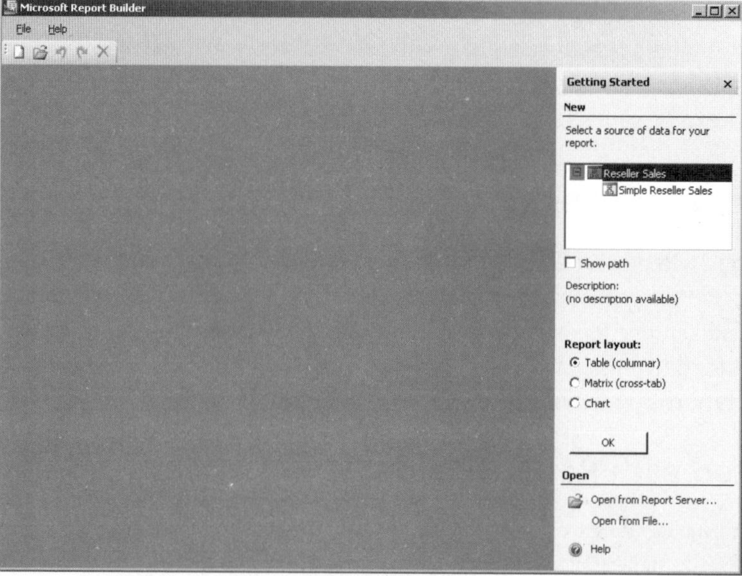

You can select either the entire Reseller Sales report model or the Simple Reseller Sales perspective. The Simple Reseller Sales perspective, which was created in Chapter 8, contains only a subset of objects from the Reseller Sales report model.

Notice the default report layout is Table. You'll create a report using the matrix and chart layouts later in this chapter. While the report designer in Visual Studio allows you to combine multiple data regions in a single report, Report Builder limits you to one at a time.

5. Click Simple Reseller Sales, and then click OK.

   Your screen looks like this:

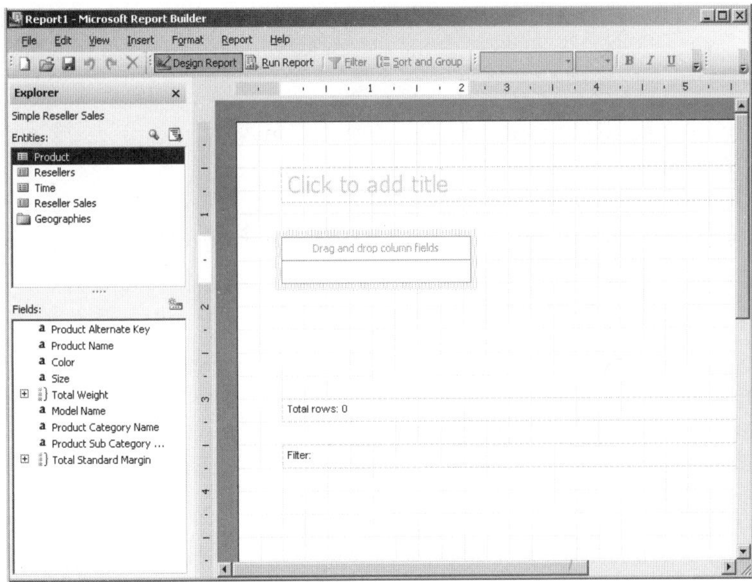

   The Explorer pane on the left displays a list of entities and folders created when you built the report model. Below the Entities list is the Fields list, which displays the attributes for the currently selected item in the Entities list. The main portion of the Report Builder window is the design area in which you work with the report layout.

6. In the Entities list, click Time.

   The attributes in the Fields list are associated with the currently selected entity. Here you see only those attributes that you included in the Simple Reseller Sales perspective as well as any identifying attributes created by the Report Model Wizard. As discussed in Chapter 8, the Report Model Wizard determines which attributes uniquely identify each entity. These identifying attributes are included in all perspectives.

The design area currently contains four report items. There is a textbox at the top that you can use to include a title for the report. Below the textbox is an empty table data region. At the bottom of the report is a textbox that will display the number of rows in the report and another textbox to display the current filter criteria. These report items will be explained in more detail later in this chapter.

7. On the Help menu, click Report Builder Help.

   These help files provide detailed information on how to use Report Builder. There are also tutorials to give you more practice with various features of Report Builder. This information is not included in SQL Server Books Online.

8. Close the Help window.

Building a Report

Once you've selected the type of report you want to build, you explore the report model to find the attributes you want to add to your report. You can double-click an attribute to add it to the report or drag and drop it to the desired location. When you have finished adding attributes to the data region, you run the report. Report Builder uses information about those attributes from the report model to construct a query that retrieves data from the source database and displays the data in the specified structure.

Sometimes, you create an ad hoc report to answer a particular question and don't need to save it for future reference. Other times, you may want to view the report again at a later date with more current information, or you may decide that other people might benefit from the information contained in the report. For those situations, you can publish the report to the report server.

In this procedure, you'll add attributes to a table, provide a report title, and then view and publish the report.

Build a table report

1. In the Entities list, click the Geographies folder, and then click the Geography entity.
2. Drag the Country Region Name from the Fields list onto the Drag And Drop Column Fields area of the table data region.

Your screen looks like this:

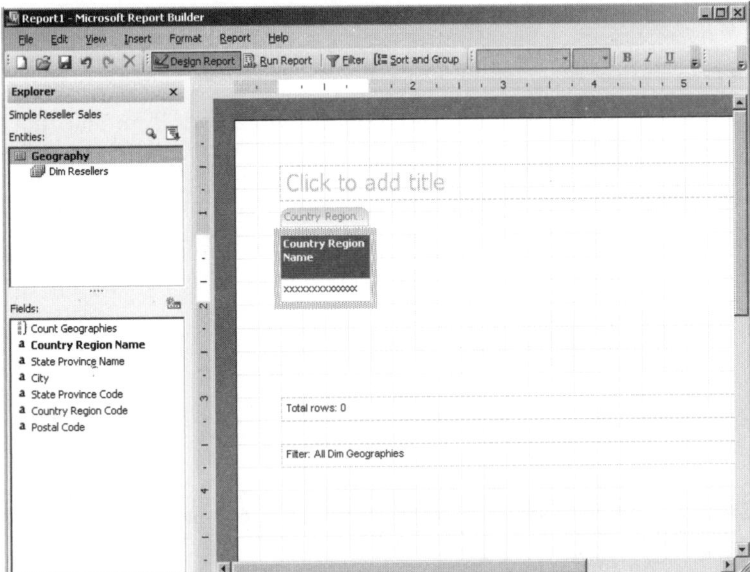

Unlike the table data region in Visual Studio's Report Designer, this table does not have multiple blank cells into which fields can be added. Instead, you drag new attributes, called fields in Report Builder, to the data region and position them relative to fields already in the table to create a new column. Notice that, by adding a field to a detail table, two rows are created in the new column–a header row to display the field name and a detail row to display the field value.

3. Drag State Province Name from the Fields list to the table, and, when you see an I-bar to the right of Country Region Name, drop State Province Name at the insertion point.

4. In the Entities list, click the Dim Resellers role.

   You can navigate from entity to entity within a model by using roles. Remember that roles relate a foreign key in one table with a primary key in another table, as described in Chapter 8. Consequently, when you build a report that includes attributes from one entity and attributes from an entity that is related through a role, the result is a query that creates joins between these tables. However, users don't need to know how these relationships affect a query, but instead should understand that roles help to group information.

   In this case, Geography data can be used to group Reseller data from the Dim Reseller entity. Thus, users should understand that adding fields from the Resellers role will be grouped by the fields added from the Geography entity.

5. Click the Fact Reseller Sales role.

   Fields added from this role will be grouped by fields added from the Dim Reseller entity. However, if there are no Reseller fields in the report, then the fields will be grouped by the Geography entity as a result of the Dim Resellers role. Without roles defined in the report model, users would be limited to using attributes from one entity only.

6. Drag the field *Total Order Quantity* onto the report and drop it at the right edge of the table (when you see an I-bar).

   Subtotals are automatically added to the table for each numeric field. You can disable subtotals by right-clicking the column header or the column's detail row and clearing the Show Subtotal selection.

7. Repeat the previous step to add Total Sales Amount to the report.

8. Double-click the textbox above the table, and then type **Reseller Sales**.

   Your screen looks like this:

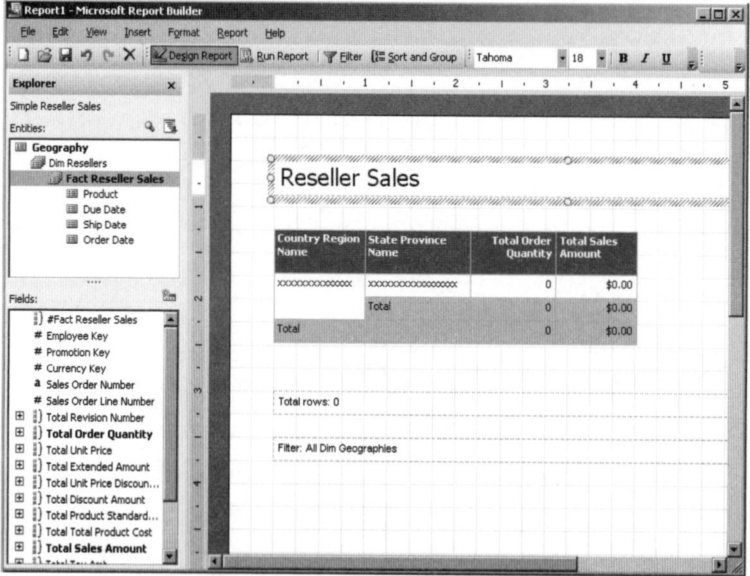

9. Click Run Report on the toolbar to generate the Reseller Sales report.

Your screen looks like this:

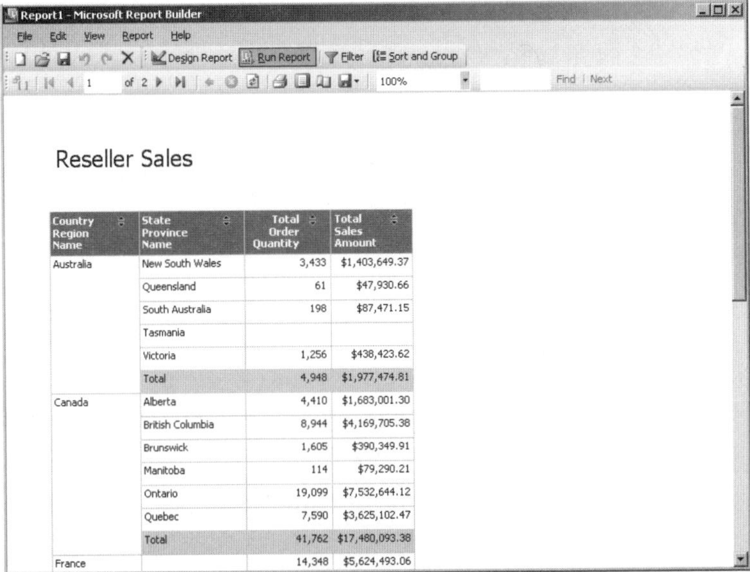

The arrow icons to the right of each column header indicate that interactive sorting is automatically enabled for each column in the table. You can click an arrow to change the column's sort order. If you plan to publish the report and prefer to disable interactive sorting for all fields, you can select Report Properties in the Report menu, and then clear the Allow Users To Sort The Report Data When They View It check box.

10. Scroll down through the first page to review the subtotals for each country.

    Even though subtotals are enabled for the State Province Name group, none are shown here because there are no detail records, which, in this case, would be Resellers. In this report, because the detail row is the same value as the subtotal, the corresponding subtotal row is not generated.

    Also notice that the column headers remain at the top of the page as you scroll. This feature is enabled by default in Report Builder. If you plan to publish the report and want to disable this feature, select Report Properties in the Report menu and then clear the Fixed Headers check box.

11. Click the Next Page button to view the grand total for all countries.

12. Click Save on the toolbar, name the report **Reseller Sales**, and then click Save in the Save Report dialog box.

    When you save a report from Report Builder, you store the report definition on the Report Server along with reports created using Visual Studio's Report Designer. Also notice that you can place the report in any folder to which you have access. You cannot create a new folder here because folders can only be created using Report Manger.

13. Close the Report Builder window, switch to Report Manager, refresh the page, and then open the Reseller Sales report.

    The report accessed in Report Manager is identical to the report you viewed in Report Builder. Now that the report is stored on the report server, you can use Report Manager to perform any of the management tasks you learned about in previous chapters. For example, you can modify the security settings or change the execution properties.

Building a Matrix Report

When you want to view data in a crosstab format, you create a matrix report in Report Builder. Just like a matrix report created in Visual Studio, both the number of rows and the number of columns in the matrix change dynamically according to the results returned by the report query. A matrix report developed with Report Builder, however, automatically collapses multiple groupings in rows or columns to produce a drilldown report. In Visual Studio, by contrast, you must design the report to collapse groups.

In this procedure, you'll create and view a matrix report using Report Builder.

Build a matrix report

1. In Report Manager, click the Home link, and then click Report Builder on the toolbar.
2. On the right side of the screen, select Matrix (Cross-tab) to change the Report Layout option, and then click OK.
3. Double-click the textbox at the top of the design area and enter **Reseller Sales - Matrix**.

   This report will be similar to the table report you created in the previous procedure. In this procedure, however, you'll learn how to work with column groupings.
4. In the Entities list, click the Geographies folder, and then click the Geography entity.
5. Drag the *Country Region Name* field from the Fields window onto the Drag And Drop Row Groups area of the matrix data region.
6. Drag the *State Province Name* field to the matrix and drop it to the right of Country Region Name.
7. In the Entities list, click the Dim Resellers role, and then click the Fact Reseller Sales role.
8. Drag the field *Total Order Quantity* to the Drag And Drop Totals area, and then drag and drop Total Sales Amount to the right of Total Order Quantity.

Your screen looks like this:

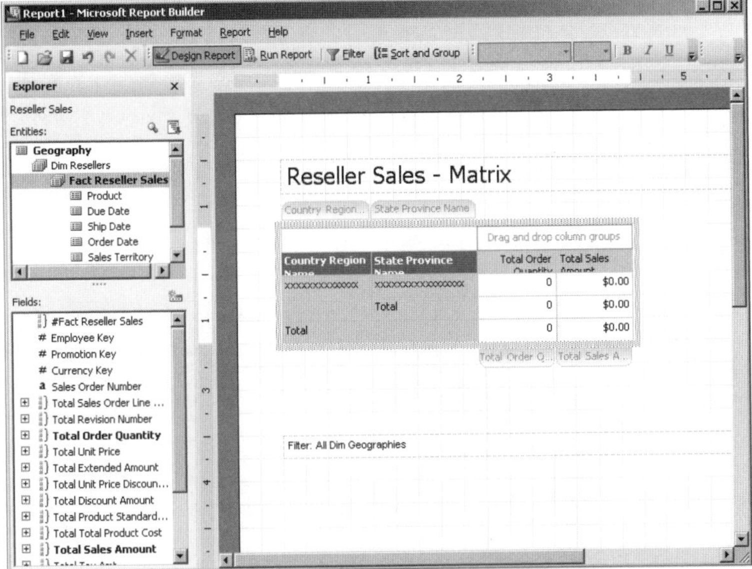

9. Click Run.Report.

   A message box displays:

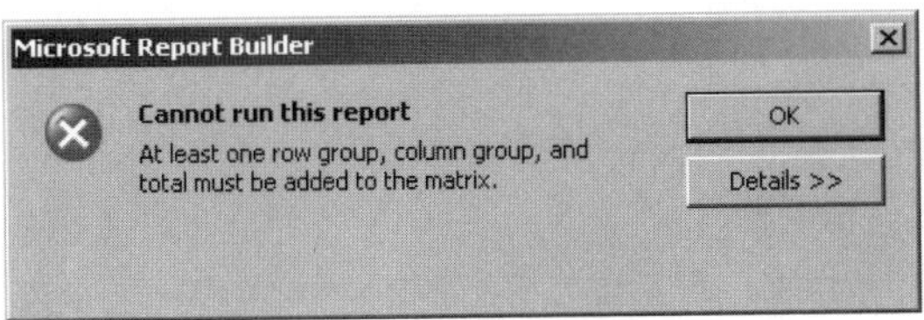

   In Report Builder, you are required to add a row group, a column group, and data element to the matrix. Without including these three elements, you cannot save this report.

10. Click OK, and then click the Order Date role in the Entities list.
11. Drag the *Calendar Year* field to the Drag And Drop Column Groups area.

    Subtotals are automatically added on the right for the Calendar Year column group for both Total Order Quantity and Total Sales Amount.

12. Position the cursor between the header row and detail row so the cursor changes shape, and then drag the cursor down to expand the height of the header row to approximately $^3/_4$" like this:

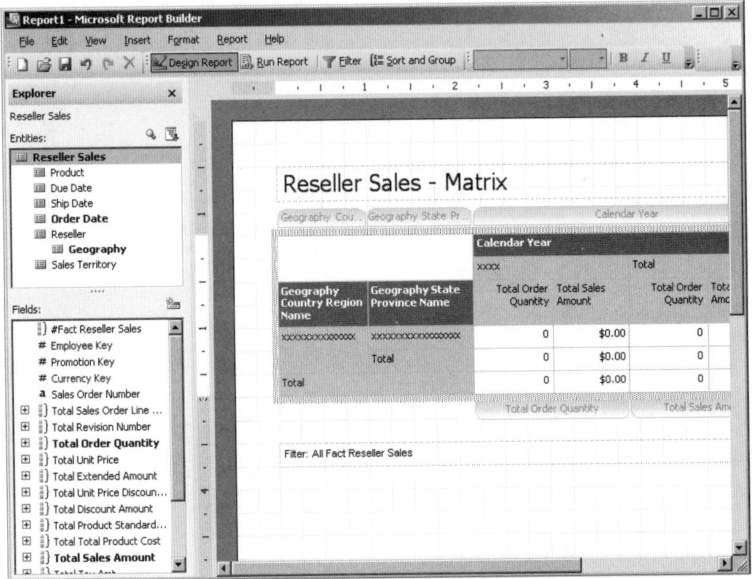

13. Click Run Report.

Your screen looks like this:

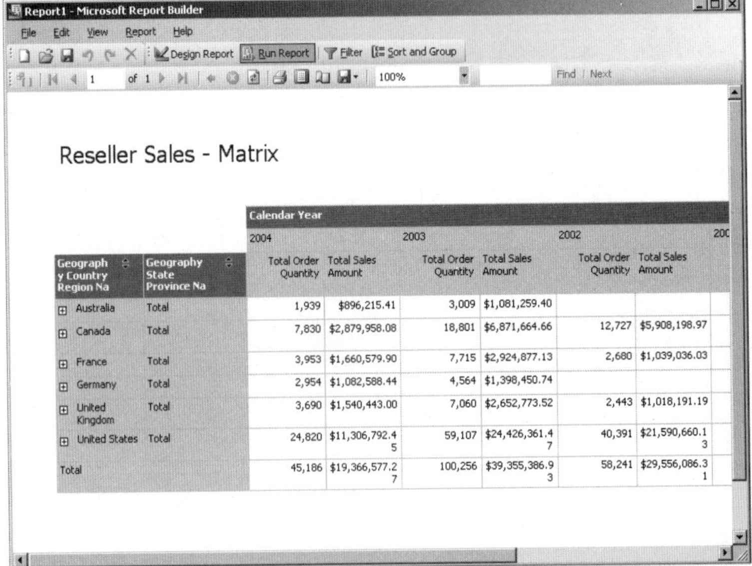

Notice that you can expand each Country Region Name. State Province names are currently hidden. When you add multiple column groups to rows (or columns), you automatically create a drilldown report.

14. Expand Canada to view its details by province. Keep the report open for the next procedure.

    Your screen looks like this:

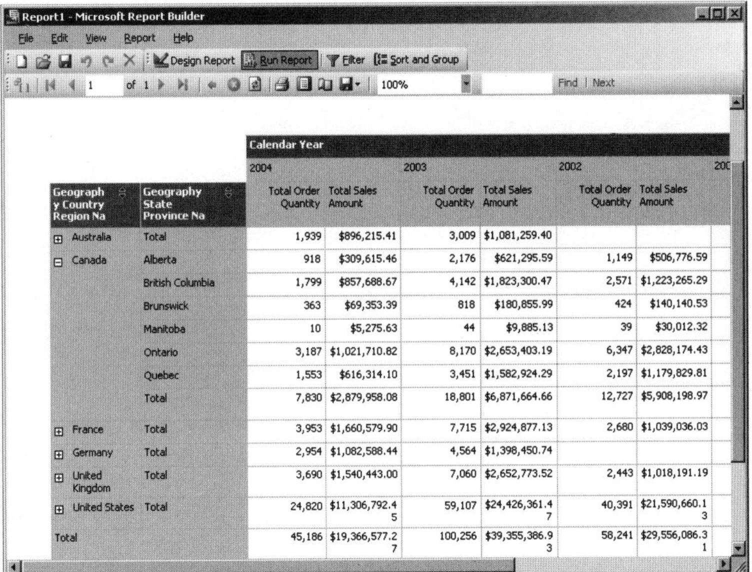

Geography Country Region Na	Geography State Province Na	Calendar Year 2004 Total Order Quantity	2004 Total Sales Amount	2003 Total Order Quantity	2003 Total Sales Amount	2002 Total Order Quantity	2002 Total Sales Amount
⊞ Australia	Total	1,939	$896,215.41	3,009	$1,081,259.40		
⊟ Canada	Alberta	918	$309,615.46	2,176	$621,295.59	1,149	$506,776.59
	British Columbia	1,799	$857,688.67	4,142	$1,823,300.47	2,571	$1,223,265.29
	Brunswick	363	$69,353.39	818	$180,855.99	424	$140,140.53
	Manitoba	10	$5,275.63	44	$9,885.13	39	$30,012.32
	Ontario	3,187	$1,021,710.82	8,170	$2,653,403.19	6,347	$2,828,174.43
	Quebec	1,553	$616,314.10	3,451	$1,582,924.29	2,197	$1,179,829.81
	Total	7,830	$2,879,958.08	18,801	$6,871,664.66	12,727	$5,908,198.97
⊞ France	Total	3,953	$1,660,579.90	7,715	$2,924,877.13	2,680	$1,039,036.03
⊞ Germany	Total	2,954	$1,082,588.44	4,564	$1,398,450.74		
⊞ United Kingdom	Total	3,690	$1,540,443.00	7,060	$2,652,773.52	2,443	$1,018,191.19
⊞ United States	Total	24,820	$11,306,792.45	59,107	$24,426,361.47	40,391	$21,590,660.13
Total		45,186	$19,366,577.27	100,256	$39,355,386.93	58,241	$29,556,086.31

Using Clickthrough

Clickthrough is a special feature of Report Builder that dynamically generates a new report from the data presented in the report you created. The report model design controls whether clickthrough is available and which information appears in the clickthrough report. If the related information, as defined by the relationships specified in the report model, is limited to data for a single record, then Report Builder displays a list in the clickthrough report. Otherwise, when the related information corresponds to multiple records in the source database, Report Builder displays the information in a table.

> **Important** Clickthrough is only available with SQL Server Enterprise edition.

In this procedure, you'll create a clickthrough report.

Use Clickthrough to view details

1. Click the Order Quantity Value for Manitoba for 2002.

   Your screen looks like this:

   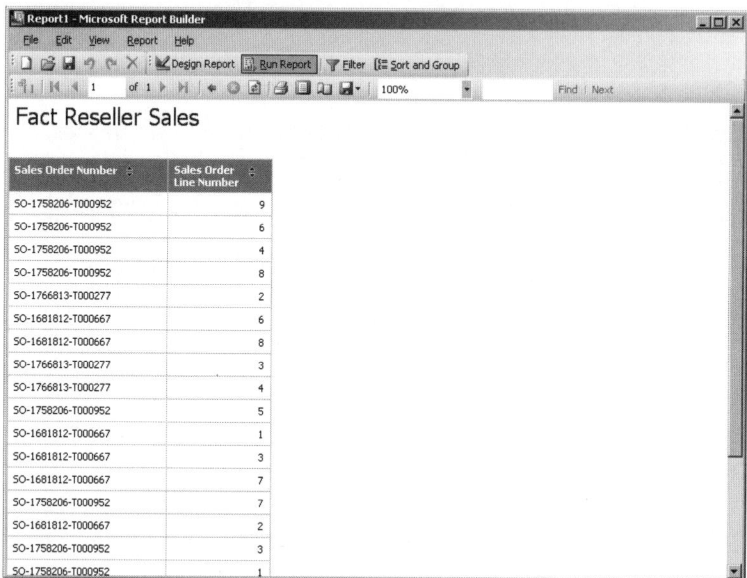

   You can identify a field that supports clickthrough when the cursor changes to a hand. This new report shows the individual sales orders that make up the total order quantity for Manitoba in 2002. By using the clickthrough feature of Report Builder, you can generate report after report without additional development work in anticipation of the need for more detailed reports that support a summary report. The number of relationships between entities and the fields contributing to the cell that you click together determine how many times you can click to generate new reports.

2. Click the first Sales Order Number, SO-1758206-T000952.

Your screen looks like this:

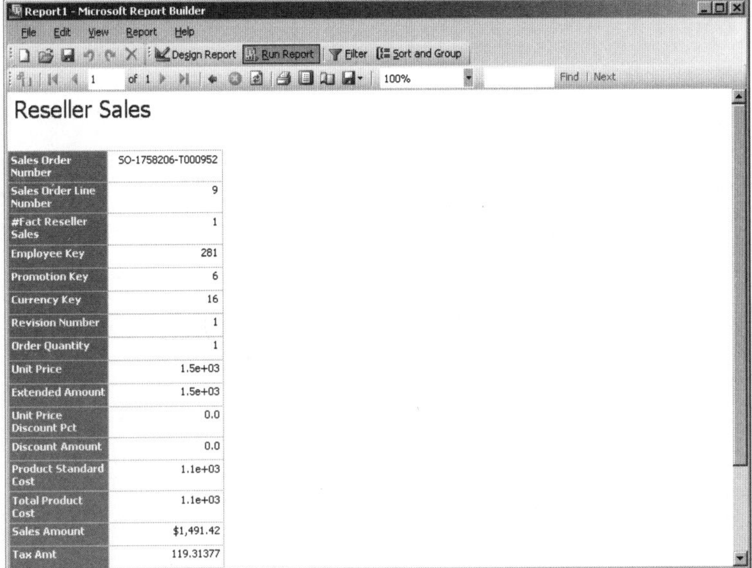

This new report shows the details of the sales order, including the sales amount, total product cost, and the freight amount. From here, you can click through to other reports, but these additional reports are really just variations on the same data you are viewing because the model doesn't support additional relationships with the fields represented here.

Notice several fields require formatting of the values. However, you don't have access to the clickthrough report layout to fix formatting. For this reason, it's important that you review the formatting of each attribute in the report model during its design and then test each attribute by using Report Builder to ensure it displays correctly when click-through reports are generated.

3. Click the Back To Parent Report button on the toolbar twice to return to the original report containing the matrix.

Building a Chart Report

If you prefer to view data graphically, you can create a chart report. Report Builder supports many of the chart types that you can create using Visual Studio: column, bar, area, line, pie, and doughnut. You can use the Chart Options dialog box to change the chart's color palette, format the chart axes and legend, or add 3-D visual effects. If you've created charts using Visual Studio, you'll find your options for creating charts using Report Builder are very similar.

In this procedure, you'll create and format a chart report.

Build a chart

1. Click New on the toolbar, click No when asked if you want to save your current report, select Chart to change the Report Layout option, and then click OK.
2. Double-click the report title textbox, and then type **Reseller Sales – Chart**.
3. Click the chart data region.

   Your screen looks like this:

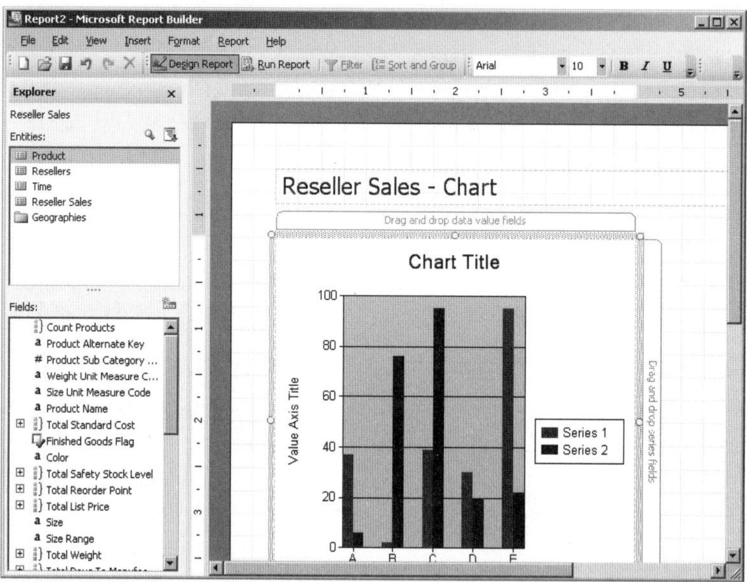

   Similar to a chart data region in Visual Studio's report designer, there are drop areas for category fields, series fields, and data value fields.

4. In the Entities list, click the Geographies folder, click the Geography entity, and then drag the *Country Region Name* field to the area labeled Drag And Drop Category Fields.
5. Click the Dim Resellers role, click the Fact Reseller Sales role, and then drag Total Sales Amount to the area labeled Drag And Drop Data Value Fields.
6. Click Run Report to view the report.

Your screen looks like this:

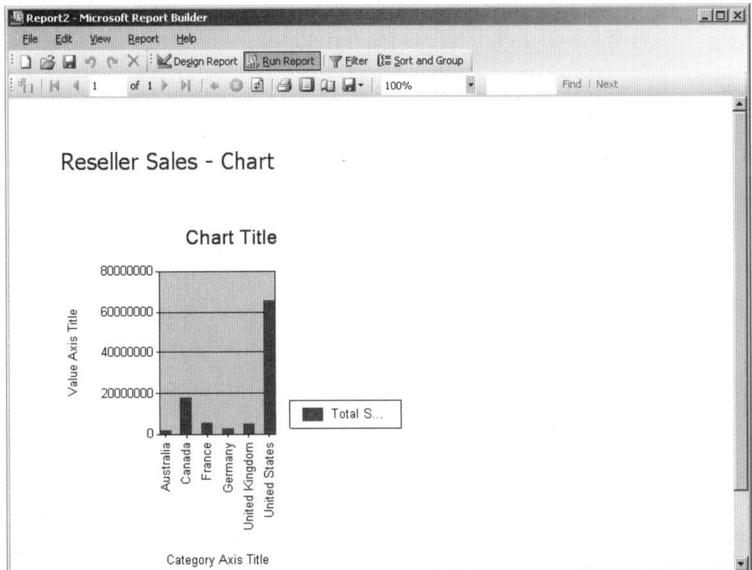

Without formatting, the chart isn't very legible. You'll need to apply some changes.

7. Click Design Report, right-click the Total Sales Amount tag above the chart, and click Format Data Series – Total Sales Amount.
8. Change the text in the Legend Label box to **Sales Amount**, and then click OK.
9. Right-click the chart background, and then click Chart Options.
10. Click the Titles tab, clear the text from the Chart Title box, change the Category Title of Category (X) Axis to **Countries**, and change the Value Title of Category (Y) Axis to **Dollars**.

    The Chart Options dialog box looks like this:

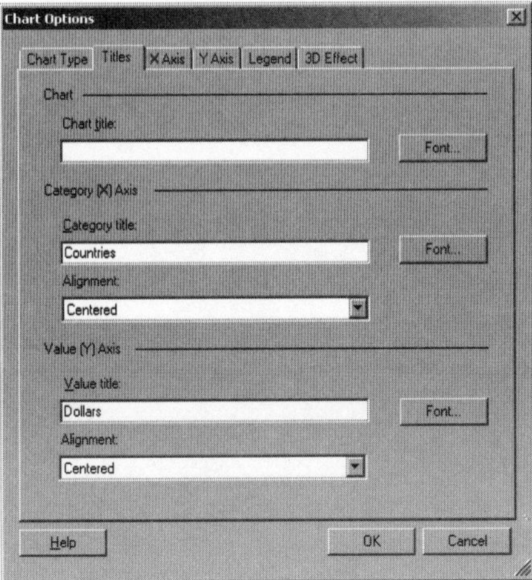

11. Click the Legend tab, and then clear the Show Legend check box.
12. Click the 3D Effect tab, select the Display Chart With 3-D Visual Effect check box, and then adjust the values as shown in the following table:

Property	Value
Horizontal Rotation (Degrees)	5
Vertical Rotation (Degrees)	0
Perspective (%)	0
Wall Thickness (%)	10

13. Click OK to close the Chart Options dialog box.
14. Drag the right edge of the chart region to the 5.5-inch mark on the horizontal ruler and the bottom edge to the 6-inch mark on the vertical ruler.
15. Click Run Report.

    Your screen looks like this:

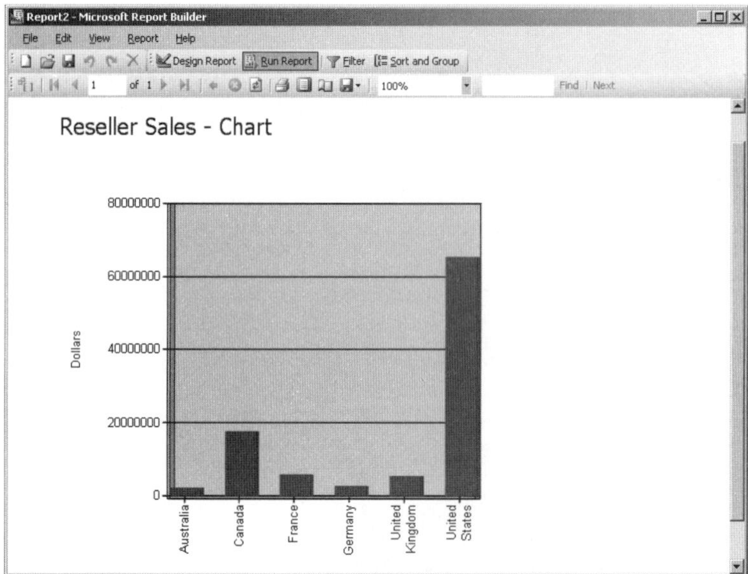

Enhancing Reports

An ad hoc report you create to quickly access to information doesn't typically need to be formatted when you view it once and then discard it. However, if you plan to share your report with others, you might decide to apply formatting to make the report easier to read and more attractive. Report Builder provides formatting tools similar to Microsoft Office, which you can use to quickly and easily to change the appearance of your report.

In addition to modifying the appearance of your report, you can enhance the behavior of your report by using other Report Builder features. For example, you can apply a filter to restrict the information to display in the report. You can also add new information to your report by creating an expression that performs a calculation based on the information retrieved for your report. These features allow you to create a wide variety of reports right from your browser without the need to use the Visual Studio development environment.

Formatting a Report

Even though Report Builder is a simple reporting tool, you have many formatting options to improve the appearance of your report. The Formatting toolbar is available for you to apply standard word processing options, such as font, font size, and font color, among others. You can also change the default text in the column headings or total rows.

In this procedure, you'll rename column headings, change the text alignment and font size of the column headings, specify a different color for a total row, and resize column widths.

Format a table report

1. In Report Builder, click the Open button on the toolbar, click No to decline saving the chart report, select Reseller Sales in the Open Report dialog box, and then click Open.
2. Double-click the column header Country Region Name and change the text to **Country**.
3. Repeat the previous step to change State Province Name to **State / Province**, Total Order Quantity to **Order Quantity**, and Total Sales Amount to **Sales Amount**.

   You can override the column headings by typing a new heading directly in the cell.
4. Click the Country column header, and, while pressing Shift, click Sales Amount to select all four column headers.
5. Click the Centered button on the Formatting toolbar, and then change Font Size to 10.

   Using the Formatting toolbar, you can make changes to the text alignment, the font, and also background and foreground colors. Alternatively, you can right-click a table cell and click Format to open the Format dialog box.
6. Click the Total cell in the State / Province column, and, while pressing Shift, click the last cell on the same row (in the Sales Amount column) to select a total of three cells. Right-click one of these cells, click Format, click the Fill tab, and then select Light Yellow (the third color from the left on the bottom row), and then click OK.
7. Position the cursor between Order Quantity and Sales Amount so that the cursor changes shape, and then drag the cursor until the complete column header text for Order Quantity can be seen without wrapping when you run the report (about 1.75 inches).
8. Resize the column header text for Sales Amount to approximately 1.25 inches wide.

Your screen looks like this:

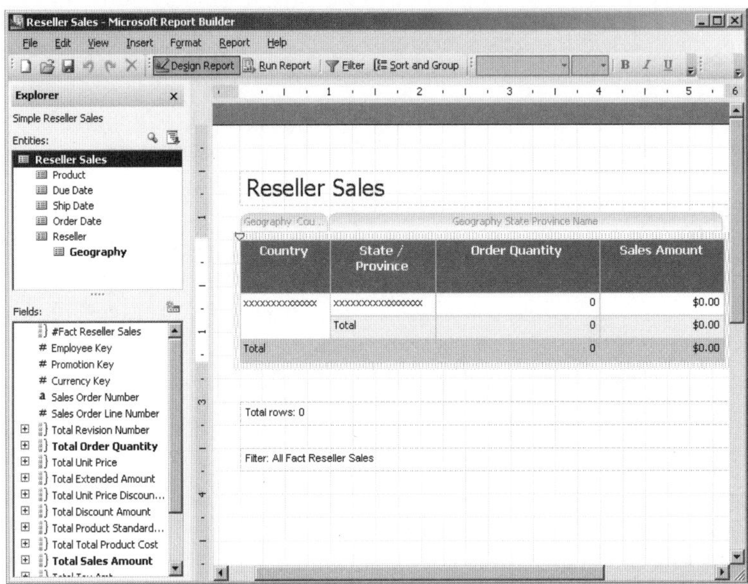

9. Click Run Report to view your report, and then click the Print Layout button on the toolbar.

   Your screen looks like this:

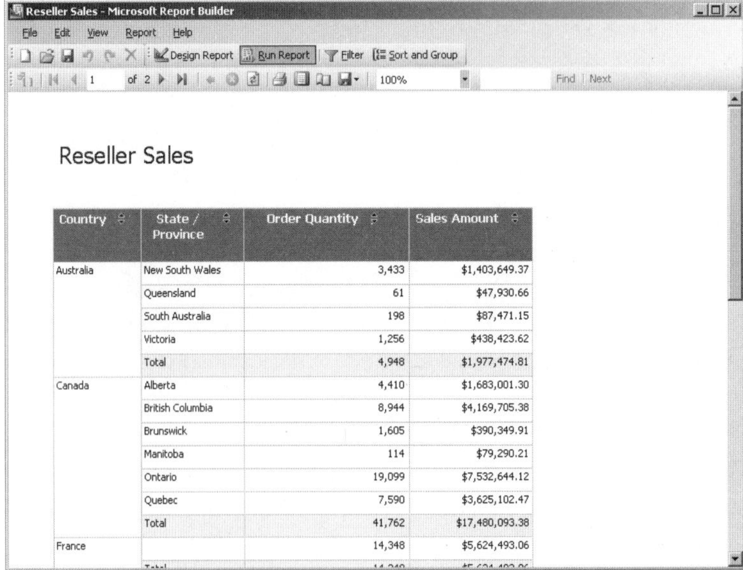

Country	State / Province	Order Quantity	Sales Amount
Australia	New South Wales	3,433	$1,403,649.37
	Queensland	61	$47,930.66
	South Australia	198	$87,471.15
	Victoria	1,256	$438,423.62
	Total	4,948	$1,977,474.81
Canada	Alberta	4,410	$1,683,001.30
	British Columbia	8,944	$4,169,705.38
	Brunswick	1,605	$390,349.91
	Manitoba	114	$79,290.21
	Ontario	19,099	$7,532,644.12
	Quebec	7,590	$3,625,102.47
	Total	41,762	$17,480,093.38
France		14,348	$5,624,493.06

If you plan to print your report, you should check the layout first to make sure the margins and orientation of your report are set correctly. You can make changes to these settings, if necessary, by selecting Page Setup from the File menu.

10. Click the Print Layout button again to return to the online view of your report.

Filtering a Report

Adding a filter to a report modifies the query that Report Builder generates by adding a WHERE clause to restrict the data returned from the source database. You can optionally include a prompt with the filter condition to make it easy for a user to create alternate views of the report. Each time the filter values are changed, a new query executes.

In this procedure, you'll apply one filter condition to prompt the user for one or more countries to include in the report and another filter condition without a prompt to limit the report data to a specific year.

Filter a report

1. Click Filter.

   You can navigate through the report model to select different entities using the Entities list just as you did when building your report. In the Fields list, you select fields to include as the filter criteria.

2. In the Fields list, double-click Country Region Name to add it as a filter condition.
3. Click the word Equals that appears next to Country Region Name, and then select In A List to change the operator in the conditional expression that you are building.
4. Click (No Values Selected), and then select Canada and United States in the drop-down list.
5. Click Geography Country Region Name and select Prompt in the pop-up menu.

The Filter Data dialog box looks like this:

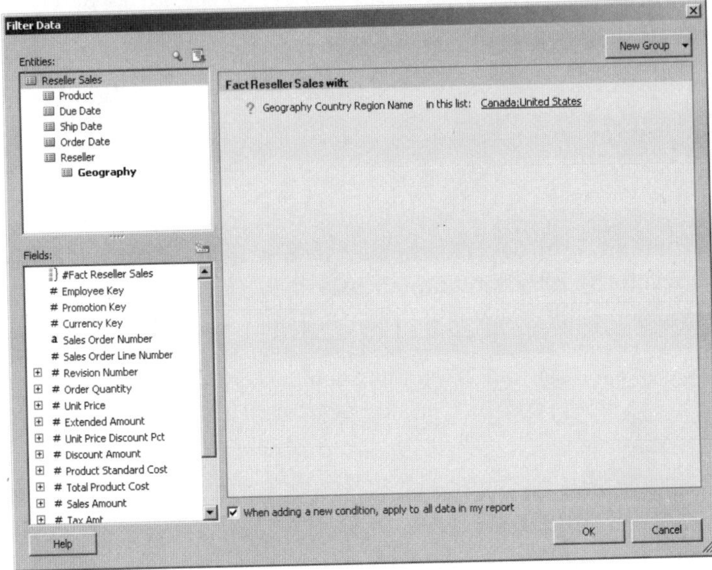

6. In the Entities list, click Dim Resellers, click Fact Reseller Sales, click Order Date, and then double-click Calendar Year in the Fields list.
7. Select 2003 in the drop-down list to the right of Calendar Year.

   The Filter Data dialog box now looks like this:

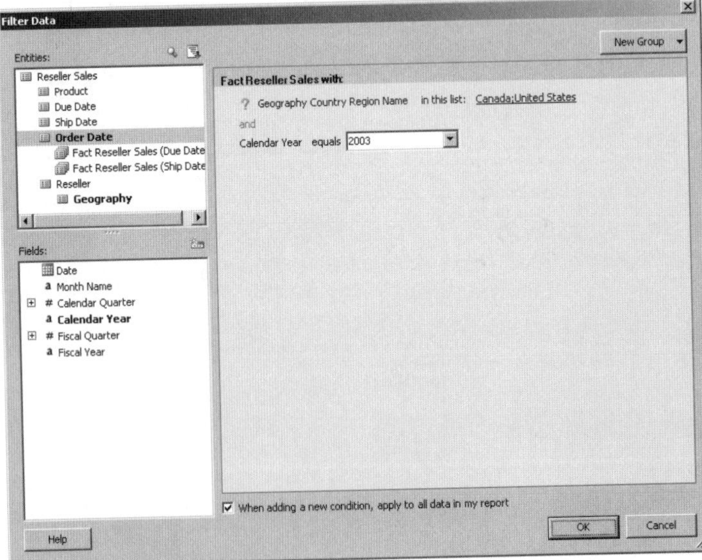

Notice the word *and* that appears between the two conditions. You can click this word to change it to *or*.

8. Click OK to close the Filter Data dialog box.

   Your screen looks like this:

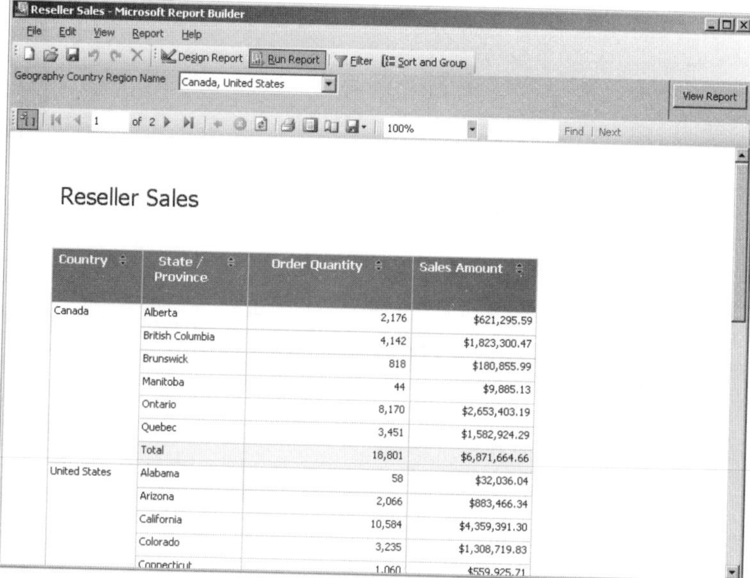

   Now only data for Canada and the United States for the orders placed in 2003 displays in the report.

9. Click Next Page and scroll to the bottom of the page.

   Your screen looks like this:

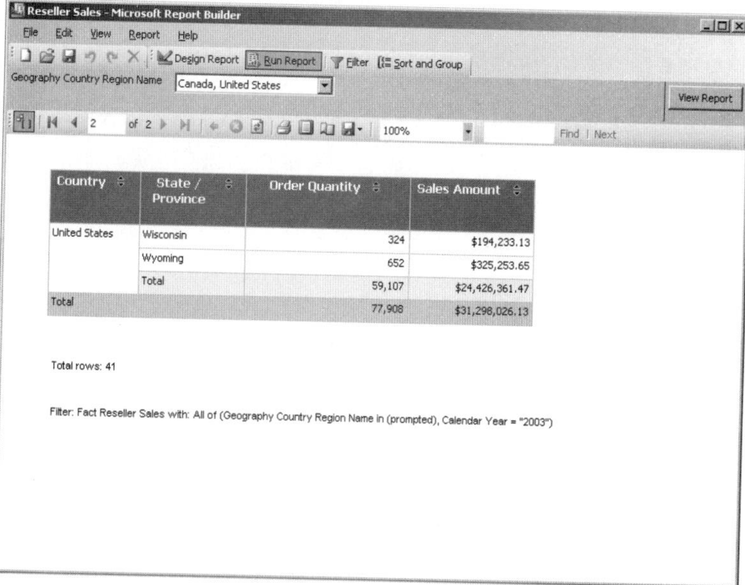

The filter criteria definition is included in the report at the bottom of the second page.

10. In the Geography Country Region Name drop-down list, clear the Canada and United States check boxes, select Australia and France, and then click View Report.

> **Tip** If you add a filter to a report that you view only by using Report Builder, then you can easily change the filter criteria by clicking Filter on the toolbar. However, if you publish the report to the report server, other users of this report will not be able to change the filter values unless you include a prompt for the filter condition.

Adding Expressions

Ideally, any commonly used calculations should be added to the report model to ensure the formulas are designed consistently. Adding calculations as expressions to the report model also saves time for the user who won't have to re-create the calculation each time it's needed in a new report. Nonetheless, you can easily create an expression when you need to enhance the report data.

In this procedure, you'll create an expression that calculates the number of distinct cities.

Add an expression to the table report

1. Click Design Report.
2. In the Explorer pane, select the Geography entity, and then click the New Field button above the Fields list
3. In the Field Name textbox, type **Count of Cities**.
4. Click the Functions tab, and, in the Functions list, expand the Aggregate folder.
5. Double-click COUNTDISTINCT to add it to the Formula box.
6. Click the Fields tab, and then, in the Fields list, double-click City to add it to the Formula box.

The Define Formula dialog box looks like this:

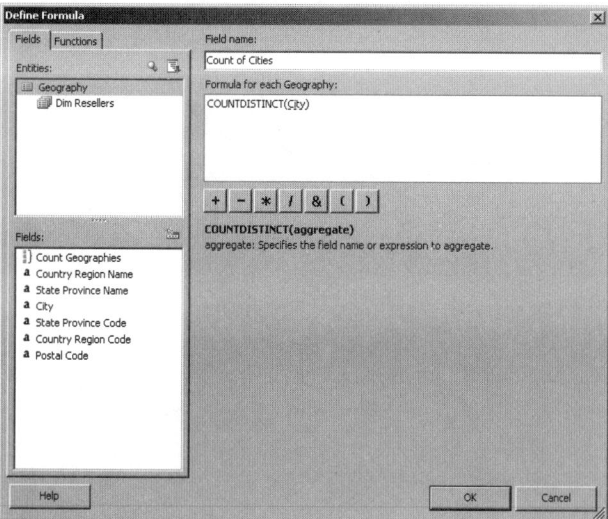

7. Click OK to close the Define Formula dialog box.

   Notice Count of Cities now appears in the Fields list and is indistinguishable from other fields that are defined in the report model. However, it is important to understand that the *Count of Cities* field is associated only with this report. It cannot be reused when creating new reports. If you want to use an expression in multiple reports, it is best to create it in the report model.

8. Drag the *Count of Cities* field to the right edge of the table data region.

   Notice the data values for the new field are left-justified. You can apply formatting to a field that you add to a report.

9. Click the Count of Cities detail cell (the cell that contains 0), press the Shift key, and then click the bottom cell in the same column to select all three data cells in the column. Right-click the selected cells, and then click Format. On the Alignment tab, select Right in the Horizontal drop-down list, and then click OK.

10. Click Run Report.

Your screen looks like this:

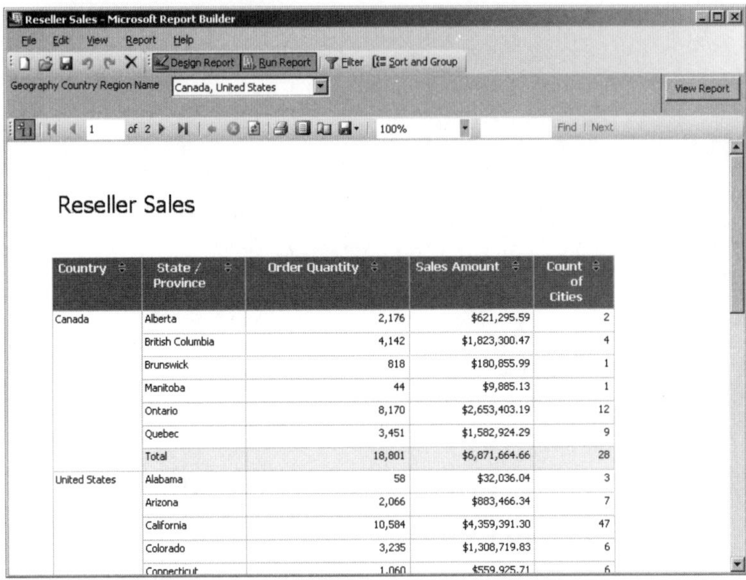

Country	State / Province	Order Quantity	Sales Amount	Count of Cities
Canada	Alberta	2,176	$621,295.59	2
	British Columbia	4,142	$1,823,300.47	4
	Brunswick	818	$180,855.99	1
	Manitoba	44	$9,885.13	1
	Ontario	8,170	$2,653,403.19	12
	Quebec	3,451	$1,582,924.29	9
	Total	18,801	$6,871,664.66	28
United States	Alabama	58	$32,036.04	3
	Arizona	2,066	$883,466.34	7
	California	10,584	$4,359,391.30	47
	Colorado	3,235	$1,308,719.83	6
	Connecticut	1,060	$559,925.71	6

11. Save the report, and then close Report Builder.

Report Builder is a great tool for providing ad hoc reporting capabilities to your user community. The key to successful ad hoc reporting is a well-built report model that uses familiar business terms to describe data and relationships in data. Now that you know how to interact with a report model in Report Builder, you should better understand how your design decisions when building the model will affect the user experience.

Chapter 15 Quick Reference

To	Do this
Create a table report	In Report Builder, start a new report, select the Table report layout, and then drag attributes from the Fields list and drop in the Drag And Drop Column Fields area of the table data region.
Create a matrix report	In Report Builder, start a new report, select the Matrix (Cross-tab) report layout, drag attributes from the Fields list and drop in both the Drag And Drop Row Groups and the Drag And Drop Column Groups areas of the matrix data region, and then drag numeric aggregate attributes to the Drag And Drop Totals area.
Create a chart report	In Report Builder, start a new report, select the Chart report layout, right-click the chart data region, select a chart type or set chart options as desired, drag attributes to the Drag And Drop Category Fields area and optionally to the Drag And Drop Series Fields area, and then drag numeric aggregate attributes to the Drag And Drop Data Value Fields area.

To	Do this
Create a clickthrough report	In Report Builder, create a new report or open an existing report, click Run Report on the toolbar, and then click any field in the report for which the cursor changes to a hand.
Rename a column heading	Click in the table cell and type a new heading in the cell.
Change the appearance of text in a report	Select a cell or press Shift while selecting the first and last cell in a group, and then click applicable buttons on the Formatting toolbar: Font Name, Font Size, Bold, Italic, Underline, Left Justify, Centered, Right Justify, Text Color, and Fill Color. *or* Right-click a cell, select Format, and then change settings in the Format dialog box.
Filter report data	Click Filter, double-click an attribute to create a new filter expression, click the comparison operator to change the default value from equals (if necessary), and then select filter criteria. Click the attribute name and select Prompt to create an interactive filter for the report.
Add an expression to a report	In Report Builder's design mode, select the entity in the Explorer list to contain the expression, click New Field, type a name for the expression, click the Functions tab, double-click a function, click the Fields tab, and then double-click an attribute to complete the expression.
Publish a report to the report server	Click Save on the Report Builder toolbar, name the report, and then click Save in the Save Report dialog box.

Part V
Programming Reporting Services

In this part:

In Part IV, "Delivering Reports," you completed the final stage of the reporting life cycle using Reporting Services. Now, in Part V, you begin the reporting life cycle again, but in these chapters, you'll look at how to author, manage, and deliver reports programmatically. Because Reporting Services has an extensible architecture that uses an open schema for reports and a published application programming interface (API), you can add as little or as much customization as you need to fully support the information requirements of your organization.

Chapter 16

Report Authoring with Custom Development

After completing this chapter, you will be able to:

- Use custom code in expressions.
- Create a custom data processing extension.
- Generate a report definition programmatically.

This chapter explores the types of authoring activities that you can customize. You'll learn how to reuse custom code in your report to handle complex functions–either as embedded code or as a custom assembly. You'll also learn how to build a custom data processing extension to read XML data and how to incorporate that data processing extension into a program that builds a report.

Using Custom Code

When you need to use a complex expression many times in a report, it's usually easier to write the code once as a custom function, and then refer to it as needed. By following this practice, you can minimize the number of places in the report requiring updates if you later want to modify the expression. In particular, you can write procedural code in your custom functions to take advantage of loops using FOR or WHILE, or conditional logic using IF...THEN or CASE statements. You can reference custom functions anywhere that you can use an expression to control report item values, styles, and formatting.

One way that you can implement custom functions is to embed code in your report. However, with this approach, only the report in which you embed the code has access to the custom functions. Also, the embedded code must be written using Microsoft Visual Basic .NET. Another approach with custom functions is to create a custom assembly that can then be referenced by any report. A custom assembly can be written using any language supported by the Microsoft .NET Framework.

Adding Custom Code to a Report

By adding custom code to your report, you can build in additional functionality to expand upon the features provided by Reporting Services. For example, a common issue that must be dealt with in reports that use ratios is the prevention of divide-by-zero errors. In Chapter 5, "Working with Expressions," you created an expression to add a margin percentage to the Product Sales and Profitability report. This expression used the following code in the detail row: `=ReportItems!Margin.Value/ReportItems!SalesAmount.Value`, which, in this case, is equivalent to `=Fields!Margin.Value/Fields!SalesAmount.Value`. Whether you use the *ReportItems* or the *Fields* collection to build this expression, the risk is that a record in the dataset will have a zero value for *SalesAmount*.

It's a common programming practice to test a value for zero before you use it as a denominator in a division operation. Your inclination to fix the expression would probably be to write some code that looks like this: `=IIf(Fields!SalesAmount.Value=0,0,Fields!Margin.Value /Fields!SalesAmount.Value)`. However, Visual Basic .NET evaluates each argument individually–if one argument fails, the whole expression fails. (You can test this with `=IIf(true,1,0 /0)` to confirm that, even though the argument is not returned, the division by zero makes the entire expression fail.)

One approach to solving this problem is to write a custom function to test the denominator before performing the division. Using this method, you still use IF logic to test the denominator before performing the division, but you do it with procedural statements rather than in a single function. This prevents the division if the denominator test fails. The code for this function is then embedded in the report definition and can be referenced by any expression in the report.

In this procedure, you'll embed code to prevent errors caused by dividing by zero.

Embed code in a report

1. Start Microsoft Business Intelligence Development Studio and open the Custom solution in the C:\Documents and Settings\<username>\My Documents\Microsoft Press \rs2005sbs\chap16 folder.
2. In Solution Explorer, double-click the Order Profitability Embedded report.

3. Click the Preview tab to review the report, as shown here:

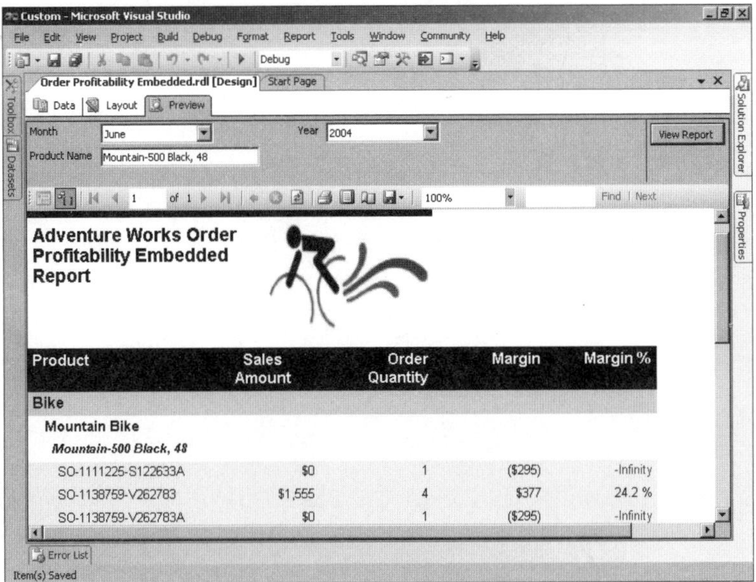

There are two rows in this report where the margin percentage is expressed as –Infinity. This problem is caused because the margin percentage is calculated by dividing the margin amount by the sales amount, which in this case is zero.

4. Click the Layout tab, and then click Report Properties on the Report menu.
5. Click the Code tab and enter the following code in the Custom Code box:

```
Function Divide(Numerator as Double, Denominator as Double)
    If Denominator = 0 Then
        Return 0
    Else
        Return Numerator/Denominator
    End If
End Function
```

> **Tip** Sometimes, you might want want an empty textbox instead of a textbox that displays 0 when the expression cannot perform the division. In this case, just change `If Denominator = 0 Then Return 0` to `If Denominator = 0 Then Return Nothing`.

The Report Properties dialog box looks like this:

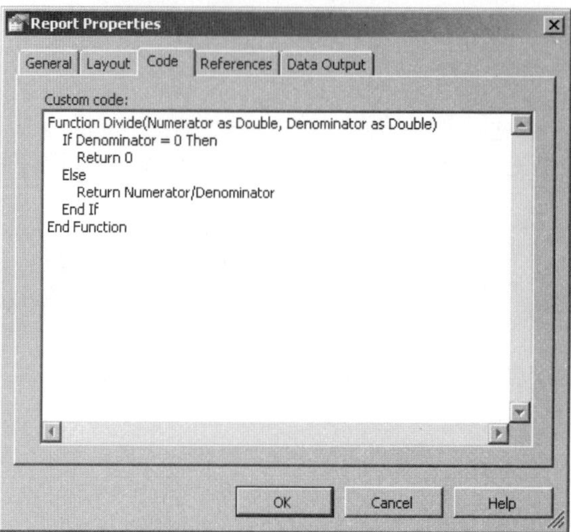

6. Click OK, and then save the report.

Accessing Functions Using the *Code* Global Member

After embedding code in a report, you can access its functions by using the global member *Code*. In any expression that you use to set a report item's value or other properties, you can reference the *Code* member and a specific function using the following syntax: `Code.method(arguments)`. The *Divide* function that you embedded in the report in the previous procedure takes two arguments: a numerator and a denominator.

In this procedure, you'll use the *Divide* function in ratio expressions.

Refer to embedded code in an expression

1. Right-click the margin percentage cell in the detail row of the table, and then click Expression.

2. Replace the existing expression with the following code:

```
=Code.Divide(ReportItems!Margin.Value,ReportItems!SalesAmount.Value)
```

   In this example, the *Divide* method will return zero if the `ReportItems!SalesAmount.Value` evaluates to zero. Otherwise, it will return the result of dividing the numerator, `ReportItems!Margin.Value`, by the denominator, `ReportItems!SalesAmount.Value`.

3. Click OK.

4. Replace the ratio expressions in the remaining cells of the Margin % column, as shown here:

Replace:

```
=ReportItems!Margin_Product.Value/
ReportItems!SalesAmount_Product.
Value
```

With:

```
=Code.Divide(ReportItems!
Margin_Product.Value,ReportItems!SalesAmount_Product.Value)
```

Replace:

```
=ReportItems!Margin_SubCategory.Value/
ReportItems!SalesAmount_SubCategory.
Value
```

With:

```
=Code.Divide(ReportItems!
Margin_SubCategory.Value,
ReportItems!
SalesAmount_SubCategory.Value)
```

Replace:

```
=ReportItems!Margin_Category.Value/
ReportItems!SalesAmount_Category.Value
```

With:

```
=Code.Divide(ReportItems!
Margin_Category.Value,
ReportItems!SalesAmount_Category.Value)
```

Replace:

```
=ReportItems!Margin_Total.Value/
ReportItems!SalesAmount_Total.Value
```

With:

```
=Code.Divide(ReportItems!
Margin_Total.Value,
ReportItems!SalesAmount_Total.Value)
```

5. Save and then preview the report.

The top of the report looks like this:

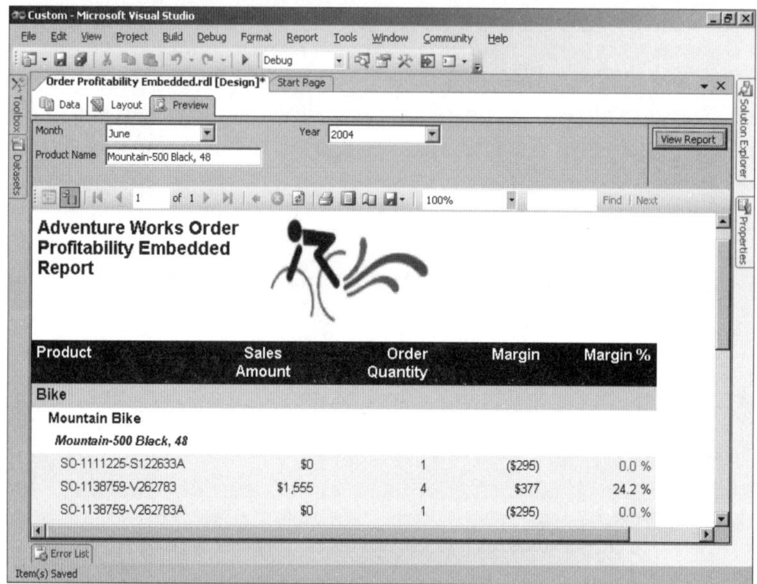

The problem with dividing by zero is now resolved.

6. Close the project.

Creating a Custom Class Library

Instead of limiting the scope of your custom functions to a single report, you can create your own .NET assembly to which you can add the custom functions for reuse in any report. After the assembly has been installed, you add a reference to the custom assembly in your report definition, and then use your custom functions in expressions when building a report.

The first step in building a custom assembly is to create a class library. One benefit of creating a class library for your custom functions is centralizing the code used in report expressions so you can easily use the same function in multiple reports. Another benefit is the ability to use the .NET language of your choice so you can leverage existing skills in your organization or leverage code that you have written for other applications.

In this procedure, you'll add custom functions to a class library to add custom conditional formatting.

> **Note** Steps and illustrations are provided for creating projects using Visual Basic .NET. However, you can find C# code samples in the C:\Documents and Settings\<username>\My Documents\Microsoft Press\rs2005sbs\chap16 folder and completed projects in the C:\Documents and Settings\<username>\My Documents\Microsoft Press\rs2005sbs\Answers\chap16 folder. To use code samples when following the procedures in this chapter, replace VB with **CS** wherever you need to type a name or open a file.
>
> To complete the procedures in this chapter, you must install either Visual Basic or Visual C# for Microsoft Visual Studio 2005.

Create a class library

1. On the File menu, point to New, and then click Project.

   Click the Visual Basic Projects folder, and then click Class Library.

   Change the project name to **AdventureWorks.VB.Extensions** and specify its location as **C:\Documents and Settings\<username>\My Documents\Microsoft Press\rs2005sbs\Workspace**.

   The New Project dialog box looks like this:

   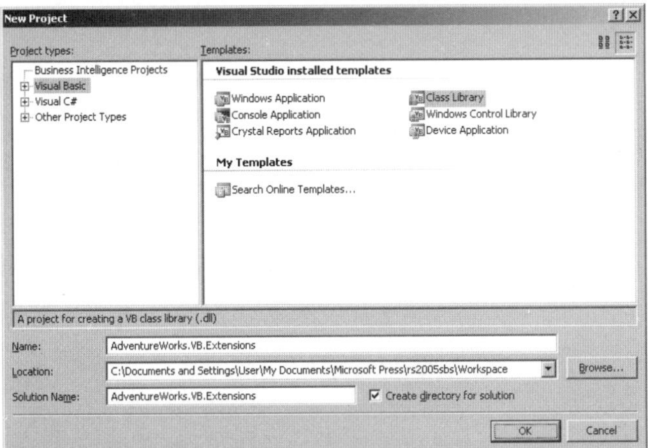

2. Click OK.
3. In Solution Explorer, right-click Class1.vb, click Rename, and then type **Common-Functions.vb**.
4. Add the following code to the class definition (before the *End Class* statement):

```
Public Shared Function GetConditionColor(ByVal Value As Decimal, ByVal CautionValue As
Decimal, ByVal AlertValue As Decimal) As String
Select Case Value
Case Is > CautionValue
Return "Green"
Case Is > AlertValue
```

```
Return "Yellow"
Case Else
Return "Red"
End Select
End Function
```

This function takes three arguments–*Value*, *CautionValue*, and *AlertValue*. The first argument, *Value*, represents the current value of the cell and is compared to the other two arguments to determine the color to be returned by the function. *AlertValue* and *CautionValue* are set by corresponding report parameters for which values are provided by the user at run time. These values define the thresholds for alert conditions and for caution conditions respectively.

5. Save the file.

The document window looks like this:

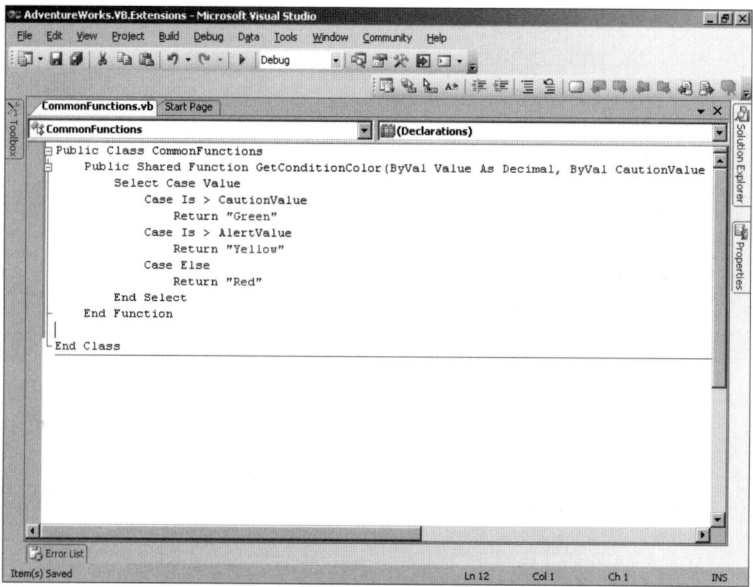

6. Right-click the AdventureWorks.VB.Extensions solution in Solution Explorer, and then click Build Solution.

By building the solution, the AdventureWorks.VB.Extensions.dll file is created in the C:\Documents and Settings\<username>\My Documents\Microsoft Press\rs2005sbs\Workspace\AdventureWorks.VB.Extensions\bin\Debug folder. You will reference this .dll file in reports in which you want to use this custom function, but first, you need to deploy the file so that Report Server and Report Designer can access the custom function.

7. Copy the AdventureWorks.VB.Extensions.dll assembly from the C:\Documents and Settings\<username>\My Documents\Microsoft Press\rs2005sbs\Workspace \AdventureWorks.VB.Extensions\Debug\bin folder to the following locations:

For this component	Copy to this location
Report Server	C:\Program Files\Microsoft SQL Server\MSSQL.3\Reporting Services\ReportServer\bin
Report Designer	C:\Program Files\Microsoft Visual Studio 8\Common7\IDE \PrivateAssemblies

Reporting Services requires custom assemblies to be placed in a common directory with their own assemblies. This means you need to place your assembly's .dll file in the bin folder of Report Server and in the Common7\IDE\PrivateAssemblies folder of Visual Studio, as shown in the table above.

Using Functions from a Custom Assembly

You need to add a reference to your custom assembly in the report definition before you can use its custom functions in expressions in the report. You could add a *<CodeModules>* element to the report definition manually (or programmatically) to add this reference. An easier way, however, is to update the *References* property of the report.

To use a custom function in an expression, you need to reference both the namespace and the class name, and pass any arguments required by the function. You can do so by calling the function from any area that accepts an expression. Rather than use Report Designer, you can replace expressions with function calls directly in the XML representation of the report definition. Because arguments passed to a function can be the result of any expression, you have a lot of flexibility in creating arguments. For example, you can create a dynamic argument whose value can be changed at run time if you use a report parameter as an argument for your custom function.

In this procedure, you'll call a custom function from your custom assembly that is referenced in a report.

Call a function from a custom assembly

1. In Visual Studio, open the Custom solution in the C:\Documents and Settings \<username>\My Documents\Microsoft Press\rs2005sbs\chap16 folder.
2. In Solution Explorer, double-click the Order Profitability Custom Assembly report.
3. Click the Preview tab.

The top of the report looks like this:

Adventure Works Order Profitability Custom Assembly Report

Product	Sales Amount	Order Quantity	Margin	Margin %
Bike				
Road Bike				
Road-250 Red, 44				
SO-1197318-T531889	$7,973	5	$379	4.8 %
SO-1917855-T320885	$10,555	6	$1,443	13.7 %
SO-1881704-U365790	$3,518	2	$481	13.7 %
SO-1397557-S353808	$14,074	8	$1,923	13.7 %
SO-1418482-N516818	$3,518	2	$481	13.7 %

Right now, the margin percentage value is displayed in red when the value is below 15% and black when the value is equal to or greater than 15%. The *Color* property for each cell in the Margin % column uses an expression to determine which color to use. Now, you will replace this expression to allow the report user to customize thresholds for exceptions for two levels–Alert and Caution. Margin percentages below the threshold defined for the Alert level will be displayed in red, and margin percentages between the Alert level and the Caution level will be displayed in yellow. All other margin percentages will be displayed in green.

The *GetConditionColor* function that you added to the custom assembly in the previous procedure can be used to compare the value of the current cell to the values that the user assigns to the *AlertValue* and *CautionValue* parameters. These parameters and their default values are already defined in the report. To use the function, you first need to reference the custom assembly that contains it.

4. Click the Layout tab, and then click Report in the Properties items drop-down list at the top of the Properties window.
5. Click the *References* property, and then click the ellipsis button in the property box.
6. Click the ellipsis button in the Edit References dialog box, and then click the Browse tab in the Add Reference dialog box.
7. Navigate to the C:\Program Files\Microsoft Visual Studio 8\Common7\IDE\PrivateAssemblies folder, select the AdventureWorks.VB.Extensions.dll file, and then click Add (or double-click the file name).

The Add Reference dialog box looks like this:

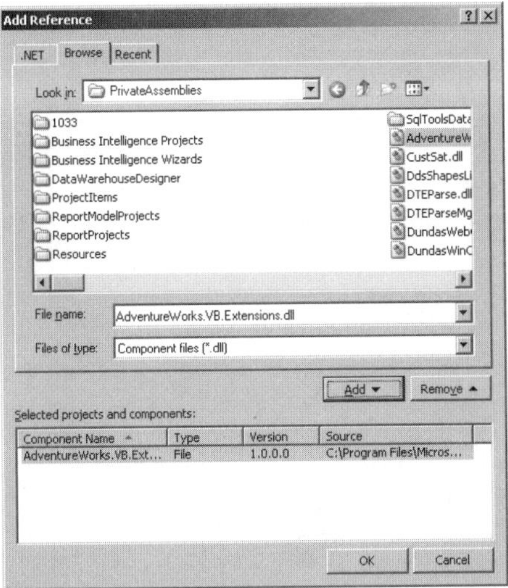

8. Close all dialog boxes by clicking OK in each.

   Now that the reference to the assembly is associated with the report, you are ready to call a function in the assembly using an expression in your report.

9. Save the report.

10. In Solution Explorer, right-click the Order Profitability Custom Assembly report, and then click View Code.

    The XML version of the report is displayed:

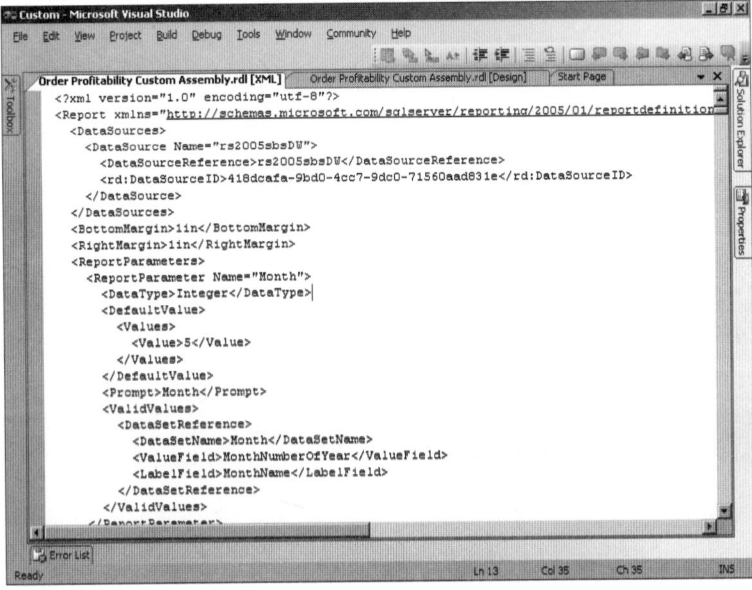

11. Search through the XML to find the <*CodeModules*> element.

    This element references the assembly name, its version number, culture definition, and public key information. This element is required to identify the assembly.

> **Important** If you create a report definition programmatically and use functions from a custom assembly in the report, be sure to include the <*CodeModules*> element and the appropriate attributes. Reports that reference the original version of the assembly won't work if a change to a custom assembly results in an incremented version number. To resolve the problem, you need to update the version number in the <*CodeModules*> element and then republish the reports. See the topic, "Deploying a Custom Assembly," in Reporting Services Books Online for alternative solutions to managing version changes to custom assemblies.

12. Press Ctrl+F, type **"Red"** in the Find and Replace dialog box, and then click Find Next.

    The first occurrence of "Red" is found in the <*Color*> element that belongs to the final textbox of the detail row.

13. Replace the expression in the <*Color*> element with the following code:

```
=AdventureWorks.VB.Extensions.CommonFunctions.GetConditionColor(Me.Value,Parameters!Ca
utionValue.Value,Parameters!AlertValue.Value)
```

Your screen looks like this:

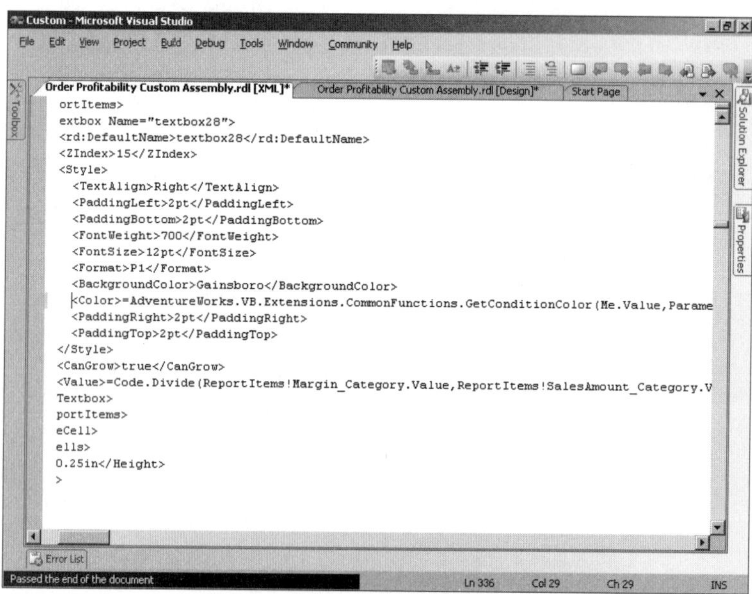

When you pass arguments to the function in the custom assembly, you can use a reference to a member of a global collection in your report, such as *Parameters!CautionValue.Value*.

The *CautionValue* and *AlertValue* parameters have already been added to the report with default values of .20 and .10, respectively.

14. In the Find and Replace dialog box, click Find Next to find the next occurrence of the string, and then replace the expression in the <*Color*> element with the same code used in the previous step. Repeat this step three more times so that a total of five <*Color*> elements contain the custom function.

15. Close the Find and Replace box and then save and close the XML version of the report.

    Preview the report.

16. The top of the report looks like this:

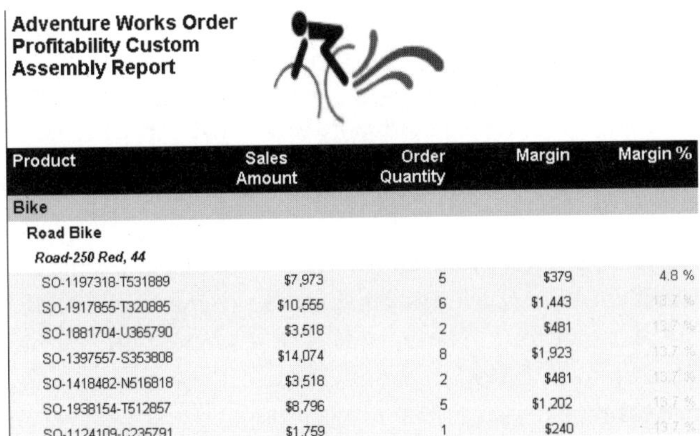

Adventure Works Order Profitability Custom Assembly Report

Product	Sales Amount	Order Quantity	Margin	Margin %
Bike				
Road Bike				
Road-250 Red, 44				
SO-1197318-T531889	$7,973	5	$379	4.8 %
SO-1917855-T320885	$10,555	6	$1,443	13.7 %
SO-1881704-U365790	$3,518	2	$481	13.7 %
SO-1397557-S353808	$14,074	8	$1,923	13.7 %
SO-1418482-N516818	$3,518	2	$481	13.7 %
SO-1938154-T512857	$8,796	5	$1,202	13.7 %
SO-1124109-C235791	$1,759	1	$240	13.7 %

Notice that in the first detail row, the margin percentage is displayed in red because the value is below the default Alert threshold of .1, or 10%. In the second detail row, the margin percentage is displayed in yellow because the value is between the Alert and the Caution thresholds.

17. Type **.15** as the *Caution* < parameter value.

18. Click View Report to preview the report and scroll to the bottom of the page.

    All values between the Alert and Caution thresholds–that is, between 10% and 15%–are displayed in yellow. There is one value displayed in green because the value is not within the range defined for Alert or Caution. If you scroll to the top of the report, you can see one value below the Alert threshold displayed in red.

    By combining a custom function with parameters, you can allow the user to provide the values used to set properties in the report. If you don't want to use parameter values, simply replace the applicable arguments in the expression that is used to call the custom function with constant values or expressions based on conditions elsewhere in the report. Because the function is in a custom assembly, you can reuse this logic in any report that includes a reference to the assembly.

19. Close the project.

Creating Custom Data Processing Extensions

As you explored the stages of the reporting life cycle throughout the earlier chapters of this book, you learned about four different types of extensions used by Reporting Services—data processing extensions, security extensions, rendering extensions, and delivery extensions. Of these four extensions, the easiest one to develop is a data processing extension. If you've created a .NET data provider, you have a good foundation to get started, because you can easily extend a .NET data provider with Reporting Services interfaces for use in your reporting environment.

> **Note** A thorough discussion of writing custom extensions could be a whole book in itself. This chapter focuses on the key issues you need to be aware of when developing and using a data processing extension. Over time, you can expect to see many vendors produce custom extensions that you can integrate into your Reporting Services environment. If your requirements are sufficiently unique to require a custom extension, you can start learning more by reviewing the examples provided in this chapter and in Reporting Services Books Online.

One reason that you might need to write your own data processing extension is to use a file (such as an XML file) that you receive from a third party as a data source. XML files are rapidly becoming the structure of choice for exchanging data, so you might find it practical to develop a data processing extension to read XML data into reports. Reporting Services already provides an XML data processing extension, but in this section, you learn how to construct and implement a very simple XML data processing extension to better understand the process of building one. You can, of course, extend the code in this data-processing extension to add more sophisticated functionality.

To create a custom data processing extension, you build an assembly that defines how Reporting Services connects to a data source, sends a command to the data source, and retrieves data from the data source. You start by defining a namespace, to which you add the classes that contain the constructors, properties, and methods that are used by Reporting Services to interact with the data source. Then, you build classes that include specific namespaces and implement the required interfaces, as shown in the following table:

Object	Namespaces	Interfaces
Connection	*System* *Microsoft.ReportingServices.DataProcessing* *Microsoft.ReportingServices.Interfaces*	*IDbConnectionExtension*
Command	*System* *System.Component.Model* *Microsoft.ReportingServices.DataProcessing*	*IDbCommand*

Object	Namespaces	Interfaces
Data reader	*System* *System.Collections* *System.Globalization* *System.IO* *System.Security* *System.Security.Principal* *Microsoft.ReportingServices.DataProcessing*	*IDataReader*
Parameter	*System* *Microsoft.ReportingServices.DataProcessing*	*IDataParameter*
ParameterCollection	*System* *System.Collections* *System.Globalization* *Microsoft.ReportingServices.DataProcessing*	*ArrayList* *IDataParameterCollection*
Transaction	*System* *Microsoft.ReportingServices.DataProcessing*	*IDbTransaction*

To deploy your custom data processing extension, you move the assembly to the Reporting Services interface directories and configure Reporting Services to use the extension and to grant *FullTrust* permission to your extension.

Assigning a Namespace

You need to assign a namespace to your custom data processing extension so you can uniquely identify your extension in your Reporting Services implementation. When you configure Reporting Services to use your extension, you include this namespace. You also reference this namespace when using the extension in custom applications, such as the report producer application that you build later in this chapter.

In this procedure, you'll assign a namespace to the custom data processing extension.

Assign a namespace to the assembly

1. Using Visual Studio, open the XMLDataExtensionVB solution located in the C:\Documents and Settings\<username>\My Documents\Microsoft Press \rs2005sbs\chap16\XMLDataExtensionVB folder.
2. On the Project menu, click XMLDataExtensionVB Properties.
3. Change both the Assembly Name and the Root Namespace to **AdventureWorks .VB.ReportingServices.XMLDataExtension**.

The dialog box looks like this:

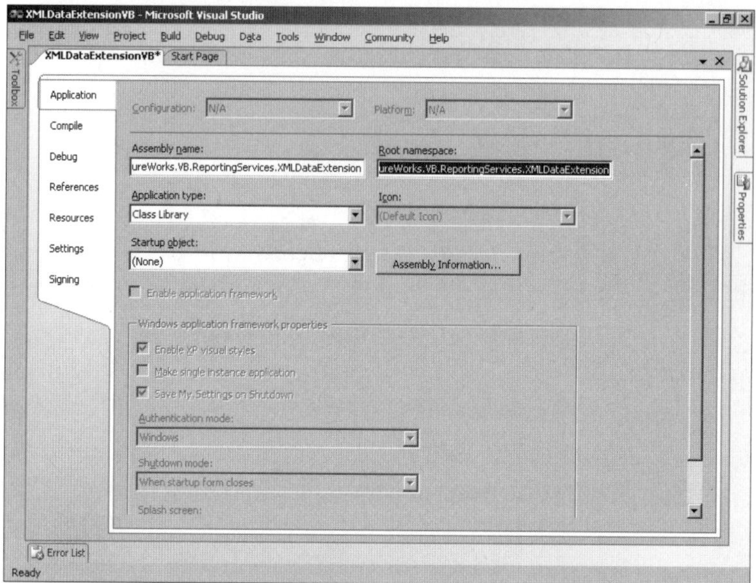

The assembly name is the name assigned to the .dll file that you place in the Reporting Services application directories like you did when you deployed a custom assembly earlier in this chapter. The namespace uniquely identifies the data processing extension to Reporting Services.

4. Choose Save All from the File Menu and close the tab.

Creating a Connection Object

Your custom data processing extension needs a class that allows Report Designer to create a connection object. At the very least, you implement the *IDbConnection* interface to get or set the properties of a connection, such as the connection string. This interface also opens or closes the connection and defines a time-out value for the connection attempt. If you need to support the use of credentials, implement the *IDbConnectionExtension* interface. You can then pass credentials to the connection using integrated security or a specific user name and password that is passed from the user interface. When you inherit either of these interfaces, you must implement all the inherited members whether you need them or not, and then you can add functionality to specific members as required by your data processing extension.

Because *IDbConnection* inherits from *IExtension*, you must also implement the inherited *IExtension* members. This interface is used to display a localized name for the extension in the user interface, such as Report Designer or Report Manager. It can also be used to access configuration information, which you can add as a child element to the <*Extension*> element in the configuration file.

For the simplest possible data processing extension, all you need to add to your connection class is a string for the *m_locname* variable. You also must add a reference to Microsoft .ReportingServices.Interfaces.dll so the compiler can access the interfaces that you will be using in your data processing extension. Then, you need to update the *CreateCommand()* method to return a command object from your command class. If your data source does not support transactions, as is the case with an XML file, the *BeginTransaction()* method should throw an exception. Otherwise, you will need to insert code in this method to initiate a transaction. Finally, if you want to implement a configurable extension–that is, an extension with settings maintained in a Reporting Services configuration file–you can add code to the *SetConfiguration()* method to retrieve the settings from the configuration file.

In this procedure, you'll add a reference to Microsoft.ReportingServices.Interfaces.dll, update the namespace for the *XMLConnection* class, and initialize the localized name for the data extension.

Update the *XMLConnection* class

1. In Solution Explorer, right-click the name of the project, and then click Add Reference.
2. Click the Browse tab, and then navigate to Microsoft.ReportingServices.Interfaces.dll, which by default is located in C:\Program Files\Microsoft SQL Server\MSSQL.3 \Reporting Services\ReportServer\bin. Select the file, click Open (or double-click the file name), and then click OK.
3. In Solution Explorer, double-click the XMLConnection file.
4. Modify line 11 of the file to add the localized name for the data processing extension between the sets of quotation marks: **Adventure Works XML Provider (VB .NET)**.

   The XMLConnection.vb file looks like this:

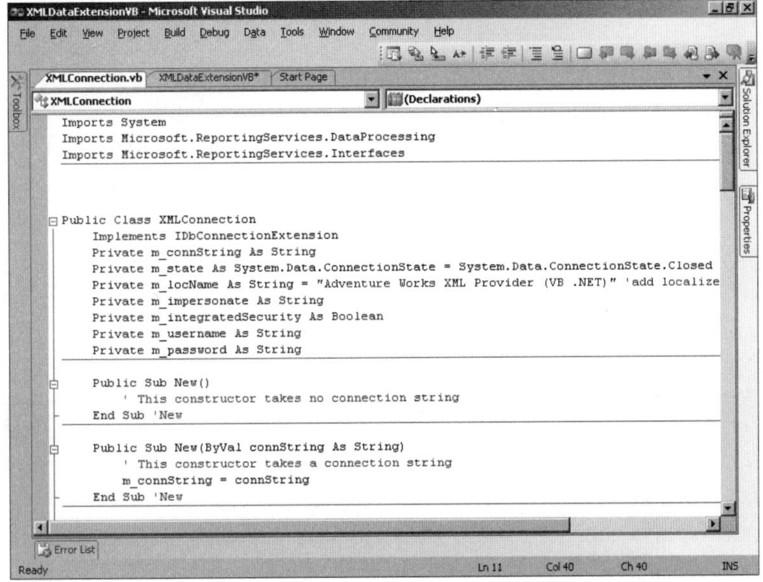

> **Note** The name that you supply here will appear in the list of available data providers when you create a data source in Report Designer or Report Manager.

5. Take a moment to review the code in this class, and then save the file.

   Scroll down in this file and notice the *CreateCommand()* method in this class. This method is used to create and return a command object that is specific to the connection. The command object to be created in this data processing extension is an instantiation of the *XMLCommand* class, which you will review in the next procedure.

Creating a Command Object

Your custom data processing extension also needs a class to create a command object that sends a request to the data source. This command object can include parameters passed from Reporting Services. The command is executed against the data source and the results are returned as a data reader object.

In this class, you must implement the *IDbCommand* interface. This interface is responsible for managing the properties of a command, such as the command text and time-out value for the command execution. It is also used to create a parameter object or to cancel command execution. The code in the *ExecuteReader()* method is specific to your implementation and is the only method that you have to update for your extension. This method is used to execute the command and put the results into a new data reader object.

There are several references to other classes that you might need to update in this class. The *m_parameters* variable and the *Parameters* property both reference the parameters collection class. The *Transaction* property references the transaction class and the *CreateParameter()* method references the parameter class.

You can optionally implement the *IDbCommandAnalysis* interface if you want to include a prompt for parameters when previewing a report with your custom data processing extension in Report Designer. However, it isn't necessary if your extension doesn't support parameters.

In this procedure, you'll review the code for the *ExecuteReader()* method.

Review the *XMLCommand* class

1. In Solution Explorer, open the XMLCommand file to review the program code.
2. Find the *ExecuteReader()* method toward the bottom of the file.

   The code for *ExecuteReader()* method looks like this:

```
Public Overloads Function ExecuteReader() As IDataReader
'
'* ExecuteReader should retrieve results from the data source
'* using a valid and open connection,
```

```
'* and return a DataReader that allows the user to process
'* the results.

If m_connection Is Nothing OrElse m_connection.State <> System.Data.ConnectionState.Open
Then
Throw New InvalidOperationException("Connection must be valid and open.")
End If
' Execute the command.
Dim reader As New XMLDataReader(Me, m_connection)

' This method instantiates a data reader object by passing the current connection
' and command objects

Return reader
End Function 'ExecuteReader
```

Note If you create your own data processing extension, you will need to factor in which arguments, if any, to pass when creating the data reader object. For example, the File Share data processing extension included in the Reporting Services Samples passes only the command text to the data reader. You can find this sample in the C:\Program Files\Microsoft SQL Server\90\Samples\Reporting Services\Extension Samples\FsiData Extension Sample folder. There is a C# version and a Visual Basic .NET version of the sample data processing extension.

3. Save the file.

Creating a Data Reader Object

The next class in your custom data processing extension creates a data reader object to store the results returned when a command is executed against a data source. The *IDataReader* interface that you must implement in this class allows you to read a result set and gives you access to the column types, column names, and values for each row in the result set. Report Designer uses the methods of the data reader class to build the list of fields that you use to place in a report. You might need to add other namespaces if you plan to implement additional interfaces in your data reader class. For example, in the *XMLDataReader* class that you review in the next procedure, the *System.XML* and *System.XML.XPath* namespaces are added to support an *XPath* query. In addition to placing code specific to your data processing extension in the constructor, you need to update the *Read()* method to retrieve the values from the data source for the fields.

In this procedure, you'll update the namespace for the data reader class and add code to construct a data reader object.

Update and review the *XMLDataReader* class

1. In Solution Explorer, open the XMLDataReader file.
2. Using Notepad, open the XMLDataReaderConstructorVB.txt file in the C:\Documents and Settings\<username>\My Documents\Microsoft Press\rs2005sbs\chap16 folder.
3. Copy the contents of the .txt file in Notepad and paste it into the *XMLDataReader* class in Visual Studio at line 31, replacing the placeholder comment on that line.

   The code for *XMLDataReader* constructor looks like this:

```
Friend Sub New(ByVal cmdText As XMLCommand, ByVal connection As XMLConnection)
' This data reader constructor receives the connection and command objects
' as arguments

Dim dataSource As String = Nothing

' Parse the connection string to separate the key/value pair.
' The expected syntax of the connection string is
' data source=path/filename.
' Validate the connection string to ensure that it contains the
' expected elements in the proper sequence and that the file
' exists in the specified location.

Dim connectionPieces As String() = Split(connection.ConnectionString, "=")

If (connectionPieces(0).Trim().ToUpper().Equals("DATA SOURCE")) Then
   dataSource = connectionPieces(1)
Else
   Throw New Exception ("Connection string is invalid")
End If

If dataSource Is Nothing Then
    Throw New Exception("File path missing in connection string")
End If

If File.Exists(dataSource) = False Then
    Throw New Exception("File " + dataSource + " doesn't exist")
End If

' Isolate the starting node from the command text.
' The expected syntax of the command text is
' StartNode; field1, field2, ... field N.
' The StartNode is the path from the root element to the element
' containing the innermost detail row to be returned in the result set.
' The fields are the attributes of the element specified by the StartNode.
' A field can also be a path combined with an element or attribute name.

Dim args As String() = Split(cmdText.CommandText, ";")
Dim startNode As String = args(0)
```

```
' Build the field list and initialize the field metadata arrays
' Metadata is used to generate a list of fields for building the report.
Dim fields As String() = Split(args(1), ",")
m_fieldCount = fields.Length
ReDim m_names(m_fieldCount - 1)
ReDim m_nodes(m_fieldCount - 1)
ReDim m_types(m_fieldCount - 1)
ReDim m_columns(m_fieldCount - 1)

' Prepare objects for an XPath query.
' An XPathDocument is created as a read-only cache for the specified XML file.
' XPathNavigator and XPathNodeIterator objects support the traversal of the nodes
' in the XML document.

Dim doc As XPathDocument = New XPathDocument(dataSource)

Dim nav As XPathNavigator = doc.CreateNavigator()
m_iterator = nav.Select(startNode)
Dim clone As XPathNodeIterator = m_iterator.Clone()
clone.MoveNext()

' Populate the field metadata arrays
Dim i As Integer = 0
Dim field As String

For Each field In fields
    Dim fieldClone As XPathNodeIterator = clone.Current.Select(field)
    fieldClone.MoveNext()
    m_names(i) = fieldClone.Current.Name
    m_types(i) = fieldClone.Current.Value.GetType()
    m_nodes(i) = field
    i += 1
Next
End Sub 'New
```

Note In this example, the syntax used for the connection string and for the command text is implementation-specific. Users of this data processing extension will need to understand how to construct the connection string and command text properly. When building your own custom data processing extension, you should use the standard syntax, if available, for your data provider, and code the data reader constructor to parse these strings accordingly.

4. Take a moment to review the code in this class, and then save the file.

   Notice the *Read()* method that is called by Reporting Services to retrieve the values from the data source. Like the data reader constructor code, the code in this method is implementation-specific.

Understanding Required Classes for a Data Processing Extension

So far, you've reviewed and updated three classes for the XML custom data processing extension. Because this extension needs only to connect to a data source, send a command to a data source, and retrieve data from a data source, these three classes are the only ones where implementation-specific code needs to be placed. However, to satisfy the data processing interface requirements for Reporting Services, you also need to add a parameter, parameter collection, and transaction class to your assembly. These classes are already added to the solution used in this chapter and include the boilerplate code in the methods that will support a basic data processing extension that doesn't use parameters or transactions.

If, however, your data source supports parameters in a query, you can add code to the parameter and parameter collection classes to incorporate parameters into the command execution. You can find more information about the *IDataParameter* and *IDataParameterCollection* interfaces in Reporting Services Books Online. Similarly, if your data source supports transactions, you might need to add code to the transaction class that needs to implement the *IDbTransaction* or *IDbTransactionExtension* interfaces, which are also explained in Reporting Services Books Online.

Deploying a Custom Data Processing Extension

After all the required classes are created, you are ready to deploy your custom data processing extension. You start by building the solution to create the assembly's .dll file, which you then move to the Report Server and also to the client workstation using Report Designer. Report Server requires the .dll file to be placed in the C:\Program Files\Microsoft SQL Server \MSSQL.3\Reporting Services\ReportServer\bin folder, whereas Report Designer requires the .dll file to be placed in the C:\Program Files\Microsoft Visual Studio 8\Common7\IDE \PrivateAssemblies folder.

For Reporting Services to use your custom data processing extension, you need to reference the extension in the Report Server and Report Designer configuration files. Both configuration files require an *<Extension>* element in which you provide a reference to the extension's namespace and *Connection* class as well as the full name of the extension's assembly. In addition, you need to associate the generic query designer with the extension as a *<Designer>* element in the Report Designer configuration file. Then, you need to grant *FullTrust* permission to the extension by adding a corresponding code group to the Reporting Services policy configuration files, Rssrvpolicy.config and Rspreviewpolicy.config.

In this procedure, you'll deploy the XML data processing extension to the Reporting Services environment.

Deploy a custom data processing extension

1. In Solution Explorer, right-click the name of the solution, and then click Build Solution.

   If you performed the previous procedures correctly, the solution successfully builds.

> **Note** If you encounter a problem that you cannot resolve, you can open a completed Visual Basic .NET solution in the C:\Documents and Settings\<username>\My Documents\Microsoft Press\rs2005sbs\Answers\chap16\XMLDataExtensionVB folder. If you prefer, you can open a completed C# solution in the C:\ Documents and Settings\<username>\My Documents\Microsoft Press\rs2005sbs\Answers\chap16 \XMLDataExtensionCS folder. Build the selected solution so that you can perform the following steps successfully.

2. Copy the AdventureWorks.VB.ReportingServices.XMLDataExtension.dll from the C:\Documents and Settings\<username>\My Documents\Microsoft Press\rs2005sbs \chap16\XMLDataExtensionVB\bin folder to the following locations:

For this component	Copy to this location
Report Server	C:\Program Files\Microsoft SQL Server\MSSQL.3\Reporting Services\ReportServer\bin
Report Designer	C:\Program Files\Microsoft Visual Studio 8\Common7\IDE \PrivateAssemblies

3. Close Visual Studio.

> **Important** In order to use the data processing extension, you need to use a new instance of Visual Studio. Otherwise, Report Designer will not recognize the new data processing extension.

4. Make a backup copy of the RSReportDesigner.config file in the C:\Program Files \Microsoft Visual Studio 8\Common7\IDE\PrivateAssemblies folder, and then edit the RSReportDesigner.config file, adding the following code as a child to the *<Data>* element:

```
<Extension Name = "XML_VB"
Type="AdventureWorks.VB.ReportingServices.XMLDataExtension.XMLConnection,AdventureWork
s.VB.ReportingServices.XMLDataExtension"/>
```

5. Continue editing the RSReportDesigner.config file, adding the following code as a child to the *<Designer>* element:

```
<Extension Name="XML_VB"
Type="Microsoft.ReportingServices.QueryDesigners.GenericQueryDesigner,Microsoft.Report
ingServices.QueryDesigners"/>
```

The <*Data*> and <*Designer*> elements of the RSReportDesigner.config file look like this:

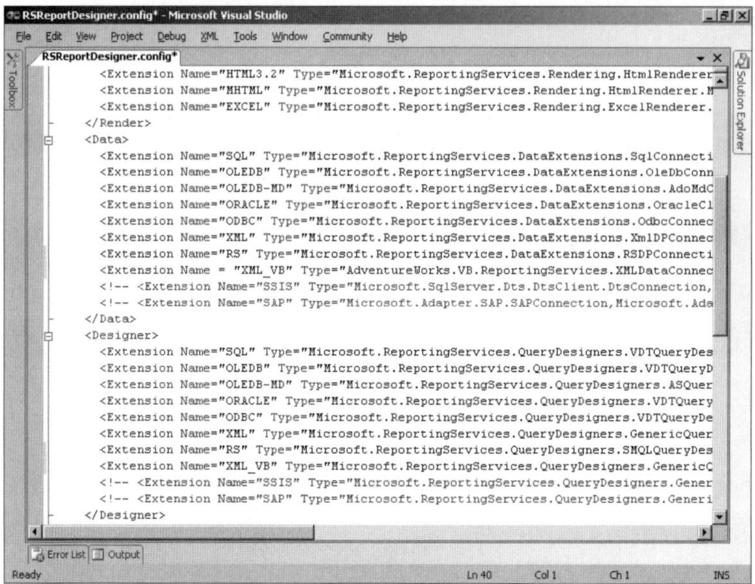

6. Save and close the file.
7. Make a backup copy of the RSReportServer.config file in the C:\Program Files \Microsoft SQL Server\MSSQL.3\Reporting Services\ReportServer folder, and then edit the RSReportServer.config file, adding the following code as a child to the <*Data*> element:

```
<Extension Name = "XML_VB"
Type="AdventureWorks.VB.ReportingServices.XMLDataExtension.XMLConnection,AdventureWork
s.VB.ReportingServices.XMLDataExtension"/>
```

The <*Data*> element of the RSReportServer.config file looks like this:

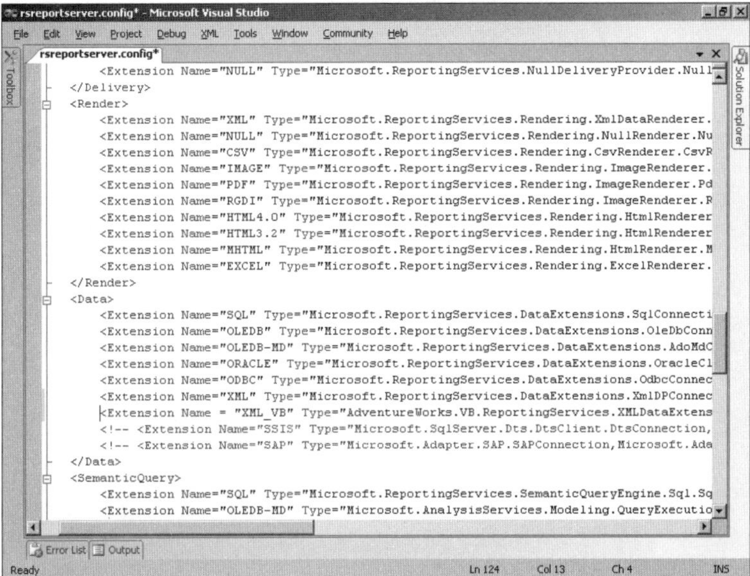

8. Save and close the file.

9. Make a backup of the Rssrvpolicy.config file, which is found in the C:\Program Files \Microsoft SQL Server\MSSQL.3\Reporting Services\ReportServer folder, and then edit the Rssrvpolicy.config file by adding the following code just below the code group with a <*Url*> attribute of "$CodeGen$/*":

```
<CodeGroup class="UnionCodeGroup"
   version="1"
   PermissionSetName="FullTrust"
   Name="XML_VB_CodeGroup"
   Description="Code group for my VB XML data processing extension">
      <IMembershipCondition class="UrlMembershipCondition"
         version="1"
         Url="C:\Program Files\Microsoft SQL Server\MSSQL.3\Reporting
Services\ReportServer\bin\AdventureWorks.VB.ReportingServices.XMLDataExtension.dll"
       />
</CodeGroup>
```

The <*Code Group*> element of the Rssrvpolicy.config file looks like this:

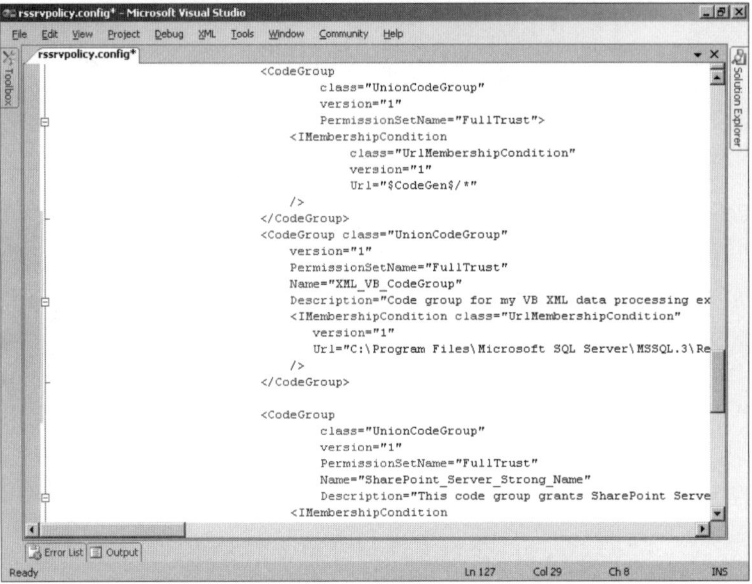

10. Save and close the file.

11. Make a backup of the Rspreviewpolicy.config file, located at C:\Program Files\Microsoft Visual Studio 8\Common7\IDE\PrivateAssemblies, and then add the following code group just below the last code group that you encounter in this file:

```
<CodeGroup class="UnionCodeGroup"
   version="1"
   PermissionSetName="FullTrust"
   Name="XML_VB_CodeGroup"
   Description="Code group for my VB XML data processing extension">
      <IMembershipCondition class="UrlMembershipCondition"
         version="1"
         Url="C:\Program Files\Microsoft Visual Studio
8\Common7\IDE\PrivateAssemblies\AdventureWorks.VB.ReportingServices.XMLDataExtension.d
ll"
       />
</CodeGroup>
```

> **Note** There should be two </CodeGroup> tags below the code group that you added for this data extension. Be sure to place the new code group correctly in this file.

12. Save and close the file.

In this procedure, you'll test the deployment of the custom data processing extension in Report Designer.

Test the data processing extension

1. In Business Intelligence Development Studio, point to New on the File menu, and then click Project.

2. Click Report Server Project in the Business Intelligence Projects folder to create a project named **XMLDataVB** located in the C:\Documents and Settings\<username>\My Documents\Microsoft Press\rs2005sbs\Workspace folder, and then click OK.

3. Right-click the Reports folder in Solution Explorer, point to Add, and then click New Item.

4. Click Report, type a name for the report, **XMLdata.rdl**, and then click Add.

5. Click <New Dataset...> in the Dataset drop-down list, select the data processing extension that you added, and then enter the following connection string: **data source=C:\Documents and Settings\<username>\My Documents\Microsoft Press\rs2005sbs\chap16\Purchase Order Details.xml**.

   The Shared Data Source dialog box looks like this:

   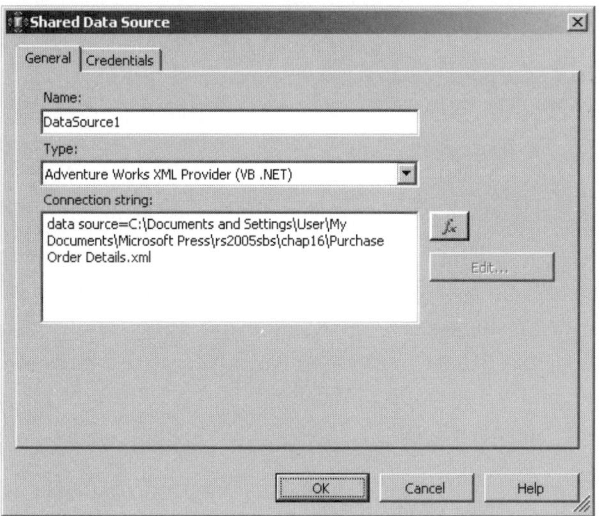

6. On the Credentials tab of the Data Source dialog box, click Use Windows Authentication (Integrated Security), and then click OK.

7. In the Generic Query Designer text box, type the following query string:

```
/PurchaseOrders/PurchaseOrder/items/item;description,qty,price,../../@PO_id,../../
@PO_date,/PurchaseOrders/Customers/Customer
```

   As explained earlier in this chapter, the expected syntax of the command text for this implementation is ***StartNode; field1, field2, ..fieldN***. For example, the Purchase Order Details.xml file, located at C:\Documents and Settings\<username>\My Documents\Microsoft Press\rs2005sbs\chap16, that will be used to test this extension contains purchase order information where the most detailed data is the line item information that includes product, quantity, and price information. This information is contained on the <*item*> node, so the *StartNode* for this query includes the full node path from the root node to the <*item*> node.

The structure of the XML file looks like this:

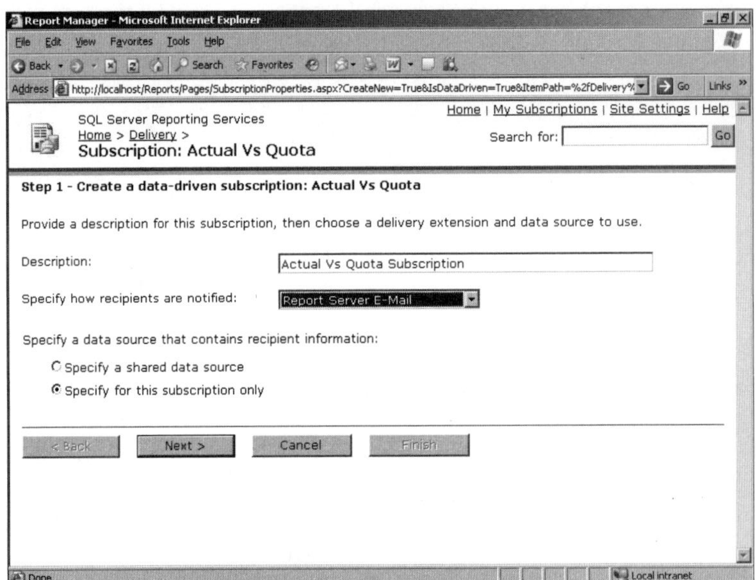

A semicolon (;) is used as a delimiter between the *StartNode* and the fields to be retrieved by the query. Then the field names are listed. The fields must correspond to an element or an attribute in the XML file and are separated by a comma. Notice that the @ symbol is used as a prefix for an attribute name, whereas an element name has no prefix. Also, if a field comes from a different node, you can prefix the field with the absolute path or the relative path from the *StartNode*.

8. Click Run on the Dataset toolbar.

Your screen looks like this:

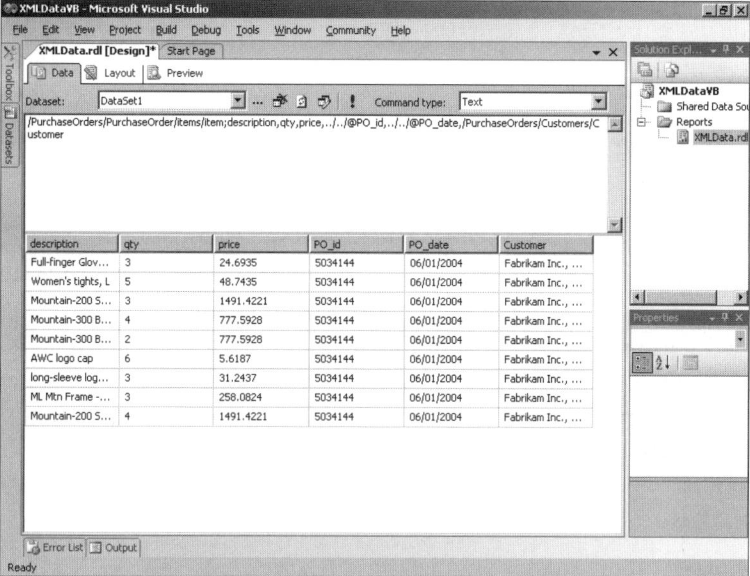

When data from the XML file is displayed in the results pane of the Generic Query designer, you have successfully installed the data processing extension.

9. Click the Layout tab, then display the Datasets window. (Click Datasets in the View menu if you've closed this window.)

   Your screen looks like this:

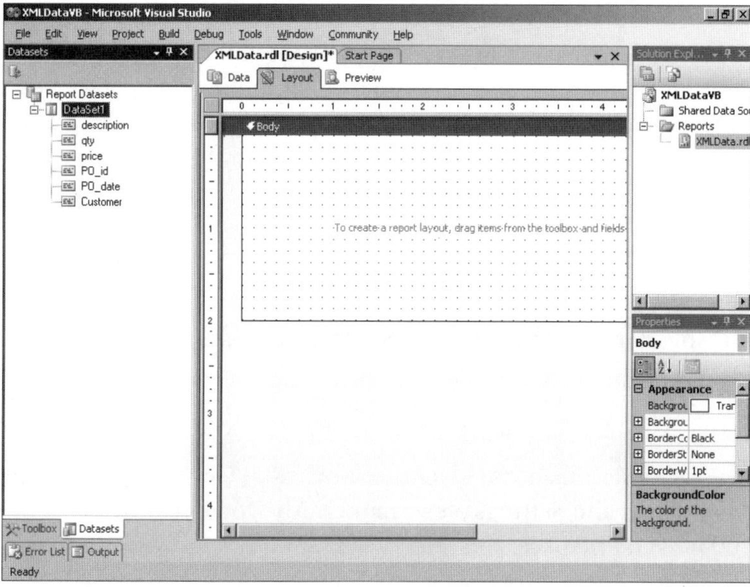

The Datasets window is populated with a list of the fields from the dataset that you use to build a report by placing these fields in freestanding textboxes or data regions. You can also use the XML data processing extension to build reports by using other tools that can access the Reporting Services API, as you'll learn in the next section.

Generating Report Definition Language

You learned in Part II, "Authoring Reports," how to use Report Designer to create report definitions that are published to the Report Server for user consumption. Because Reporting Services is an extensible platform, you aren't restricted to using Report Designer to create reports. As a report producer application, the goal of Report Designer is to create a file that describes a report using Report Definition Language (RDL). Although building a custom application that matches Report Designer feature for feature doesn't make sense, you might have a need to automate the process of creating RDL files. You can do so by creating a simple report producer application to reproduce a specific layout and formatting that you know in advance. Before you begin to develop such an application, you should have a good understanding of the RDL schema.

Regardless of the specific implementation of your application, your RDL generator needs to be able to perform some common tasks. If you will incorporate metadata (such as column names) from your data source in your report, you will need to add a data source connection and command text so the application can query the data to get a current list of fields. You can then use this list of fields when generating the RDL (or you can hard-code field names) for a report.

Creating a Console Application

You can build an RDL generator into any type of application, but, for simplicity, you will create a console application in this chapter. All code in this application is contained in a single *RDLGenerator* class. You can also find a sample RDL generator described in a Reporting Services tutorial that you can find in SQL Server Books Online. In this version of the RDL generator, you'll use the XML custom data processing extension that you created earlier in this chapter.

In this procedure, you'll create a console application based on a template for an *RDLGenerator* class.

Create a console application with an *RDLGenerator* class

1. On the File menu, point to New, and then click Project.
2. Click the Visual Basic Projects folder, and then click Console Application.
3. Change the project name to **AdventureWorksRDLGenerator**, specify its location as **C:\Documents and Settings\<username>\My Documents\Microsoft Press\rs2005sbs\Workspace**, and then click OK.

4. In Solution Explorer, right-click the AdventureWorksRDLGenerator project icon, point to Add, and then click Add Class.
5. Type a name for the class, **RDLGenerator.vb**, and then click Add.
6. Replace the contents of the file with the contents of the RDLGeneratorClassVB.txt file in the C:\Documents and Settings\<username>\My Documents\Microsoft Press \rs2005sbs\chap16 folder, shown here:

```
Imports System
Imports System.Collections
Imports System.Data
Imports System.Data.SqlClient
Imports System.IO
Imports System.Text
Imports System.Xml
Imports AdventureWorks.VB.ReportingServices.XMLDataExtension

Namespace AdventureWorksRDLGenerator
    Class RDLGenerator
        Private m_connection As XMLConnection
        Private m_connectString As String
        Private m_commandText As String
        Private m_fields As ArrayList


        Public Shared Sub Main()
            Dim myRDLGenerator As New RDLGenerator
            myRDLGenerator.Run()
        End Sub 'Main


        Public Sub Run()
            Try
                ' Call methods to create the RDL
                Me.OpenConnection()
                Me.GenerateFieldsList()
                Me.GenerateRDL()

                Console.WriteLine("RDL file generated successfully.")

            Catch exception As Exception
                Console.WriteLine(("An error occurred: " + exception.Message))

            Finally
                ' Close the connection string
                m_connection.Close()
            End Try
        End Sub 'Run


        Public Sub OpenConnection()
        End Sub 'OpenConnection
```

```
        ' TODO: Open a connection to the sample database

        Public Sub GenerateFieldsList()
        End Sub 'GenerateFieldsList

        ' TODO: Generate a list of fields for a report query

        Public Sub GenerateRDL()
        End Sub 'GenerateRdl
    End Class 'RdlGenerator ' TODO: Generate RDL using XmlTextWriter
End Namespace 'AdventureWorksRDLGenerator
```

This code currently has placeholders for functions that you will add in subsequent procedures.

7. In Solution Explorer, double-click the Module1.vb file
8. In main method, enter the code shown here:

```
Dim myRDLGenerator As New AdventureWorks.RDLGenerator myRDLGenerator.Run().
```

9. In Solution Explorer, right-click the name of the project, click Add Reference, click the Browse tab, navigate to C:\Program Files\Microsoft SQL Server\90\SDK\Assemblies, and then double-click Microsoft.ReportingServices.Interfaces.dll.
10. In Solution Explorer, right-click the name of the project, click Add Reference, click the Browse tab, navigate to C:\Program Files\Microsoft SQL Server\MSSQL.3\Reporting Services\ReportServer\bin, and then double-click AdventureWorks.VB.ReportingServices.XMLDataExtension.dll to add a reference to your custom data processing extension.
11. Save the file.

Adding a Data Source Connection

A data source connection is required only if you want to query the data source to get a list of fields to use while building your report. By getting a list of fields before the application generates the RDL, you can create a flexible report that adapts to the current data set. For example, you could reuse the application code to generate a table with three columns in one case and four columns in another case if the query changes between each execution of the application. If your application will produce a report that has a fixed structure, you don't need to implement a method to open the data source connection.

In this procedure, you'll add the *OpenConnection()* method to the application.

Add a method to open an XML connection

1. Switch to the RDLGenerator.vb file, and then replace the code for the *OpenConnection()* method in the project with the contents of the OpenConnectionVB.txt file in the C:\Documents and Settings\<username>\My Documents\Microsoft Press\rs2005sbs \chap16 folder:

```
Public Sub OpenConnection()
            ' Create a connection object
            m_connection = New XMLConnection

            ' Create the connection string
            m_connectString = "data source=C:\Documents and Settings\<username>\My
Documents\Microsoft Press\rs2005sbs\chap16\Purchase Order Details.xml"
            m_connection.ConnectionString = m_connectString

            ' Open the connection
            m_connection.Open()
End Sub 'OpenConnection
```

> **Note** In this example, the connection string is hard-coded into the method. (In order to complete this procedure, the XML data provider extension described earlier in this chapter must be deployed.) Of course, you can create a method that accepts a connection string as an argument. You can also omit this method if you don't need to query the data source to create a list of fields.

2. Save the file.

Generating a Fields List

As described in the previous section, you can create a fields list to use for generating the report definition. You can use a loop in your RDL generator to iterate through the list of fields when you want to assign the same elements and attributes to the report items associated with each field. If you hard-code elements and attributes by field, you can skip the implementation of a method to create a list of fields.

In this procedure, you'll add the *GenerateFieldsList()* method to the application.

Add a method to generate a list of fields

1. Replace the code for the *GenerateFieldsList()* method in the project with the contents of the GenerateFieldsListVB.txt file in the C:\Documents and Settings\<username>\My Documents\Microsoft Press\rs2005sbs\chap16 folder:

```
Public Sub GenerateFieldsList()
        Dim command As XMLCommand
        Dim reader As XMLDataReader

        ' Executing a query to retrieve a fields list for the report
        command = m_connection.CreateCommand()
        m_commandText = "/PurchaseOrders/PurchaseOrder/items/item;" & _
            "description,qty,price," & _
            "../../@PO_id,../../@PO_date," & _
            "/PurchaseOrders/Customers/Customer"

        command.CommandText = m_commandText

        ' Execute and create a reader for the current command
        reader = command.ExecuteReader()

        ' For each field in the result set, add the name to an array list
        m_fields = New ArrayList
        Dim i As Integer
        For i = 0 To reader.FieldCount - 1
            m_fields.Add(reader.GetName(i))
        Next i
End Sub 'GenerateFieldsList
```

Note Here, the command text (which is dependent on the installation of the XML data provider extension) is hard-coded into the method. Another way you might create this method is using an argument to accept command text as input. The *m_fields* array is used to store the list of field names. You can iterate through this list in another method to embed field names into the report definition at run time rather than hard-code field names. The method shown here is for illustrative purposes only—to show how to use the custom data processing extension in a custom application and to show how to get a list of fields from the data source. The *GenerateRDL()* method that you review in the next procedure does not use the resulting list of fields.

2. Save the file.

Generating the RDL

The easiest way to generate the RDL is to use the *XmlTextWriter* class included in the Microsoft .NET Framework. This class lets you write a forward-only stream of text without the overhead of the XML Document Object Model (DOM), which helps the code runs faster. After opening a file stream and instantiating an *XmlTextWriter* object, you create sets of elements and attributes using the *WriteStartElement*, *WriteElementString*, *WriteAttributeString*, and *Write-EndElement* methods. RDL is a declarative model (as explained in Chapter 4, "Developing Basic Reports"), so the sequence of root elements is not important, nor is the sequence of sub-elements. However, the relationship between an element and its descendant elements (which can be nested to a considerable number of levels) is important because it controls the layout of report items and their relative positions. For this reason, you need to ensure that the output of your RDL generator conforms to the RDL specification published by Microsoft.

> **Note** You can download the most current version of this specification at *http://www.microsoft.com/sql/technologies/reporting/rdlspec.mspx.*

In this procedure, you'll add the *GenerateRDL()* method to the application.

Add a method to generate RDL

1. Replace the code for the *GenerateRDL()* method in the project with the contents of the GenerateRDLVB.txt file (or the GenerateRDLCS.txt file) in the C:\Documents and Settings\<username>\My Documents\Microsoft Press\rs2005sbs\chap16 folder.
2. Review the code in this method, and then save the file.

   You can see that this code is fairly extensive to produce a simple report. The resulting report definition contains several required elements that appear at the start of the method: *<Report>*, *<DataSource>*, *<DataSet>*, *<Query>*, *<Fields>*, and *<Body>*. The end tag of the *<Report>* element is the very last string written to the output file in this method. Consequently, the subsequent elements are subelements of the *<Report>* element. The *<DataSource>* and *<Query>* elements contain the connection string and command text used when Reporting Services executes the report. The *<Body>* element contains a *<ReportItems>* subelement in which various data regions and independent report items are placed. In this report, there is a free-standing textbox to hold the report title and a table that contains not only a table header and footer, but also a group header and footer. In addition, dynamic visibility has been used to hide selected elements, such as textboxes in the group header or the detail rows when a report item is toggled.

> **Tip** You can do many things to make this code more flexible. For example, you can create a method to apply the same properties to all cells in a row. When building the elements for the row, you can use a FOR loop to iterate through the list of fields obtained from the data source and then, within the loop, call a method to write out the set of properties for the current field.

In this procedure, you'll run the RDL application and test the results by uploading the report definition to the Report Server.

Run the AdventureWorksRDLGenerator

1. If you are working on a Visual Basic project, click AdventureWorksRDLGenerator Properties on the Project menu, click AdventureWorksRDLGenerator.RDLGenerator in the Startup Object list, and then save the file.
2. On the Debug menu, click Start Without Debugging.

> **Tip** Use Start Without Debugging when you want to view the contents of the console window while the application executes.

A console window opens and displays a message after the generation of the RDL is attempted. If the application completed without throwing exceptions, the message displayed is "RDL file generated successfully." You can, of course, modify this message by changing the line `Console.WriteLine("RDL file generated successfully.")` to write a different string of text.

3. Open the Report Manager, and then click Upload File on the Report Manager toolbar.
4. Click Browse to navigate to C:\Documents and Settings\<username>\My Documents \Microsoft Press\rs2005sbs\Workspace\AdventureWorksRDLGenerator \4AdventureWorksRDLGenerator\Debug folder, select the Purchase Order Details.rdl file, click Open, and then click OK.
5. Click the new Purchase Order Details link in Report Manager.

   Your screen looks like this:

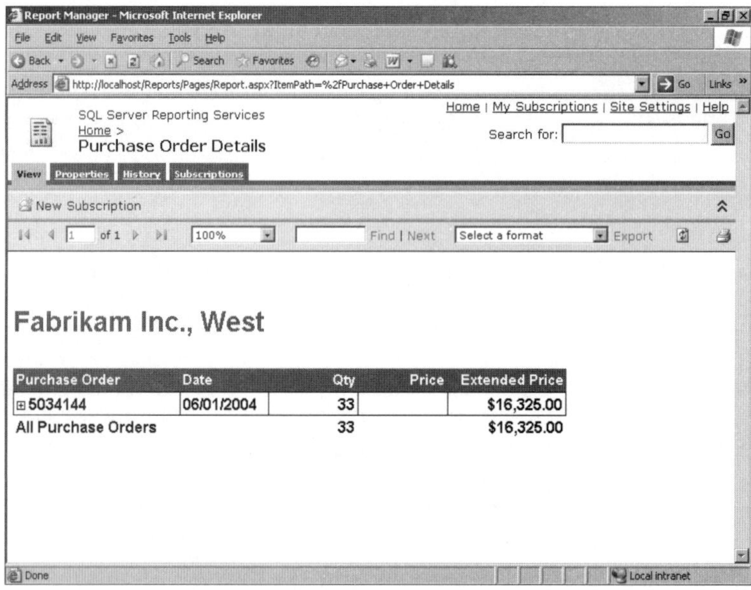

6. Expand the order to view the hidden rows.
7. Click Properties, and then click the Data Sources link.

Your screen looks like this:

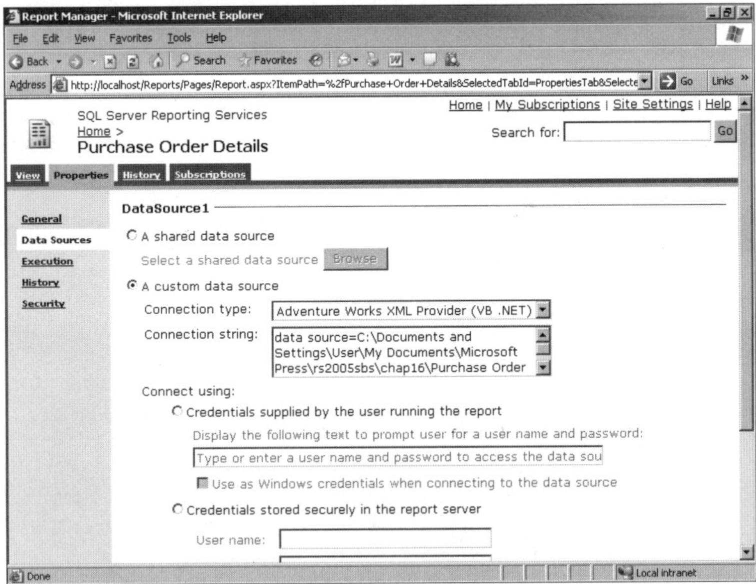

Notice that the custom data processing extension appears as an available connection type for data sources. If you want to use a different XML file for this report, you can change the file name in the connection string. As long as the new file conforms to the same structure as the original file, the data can be read by Reporting Services and displayed in this report.

Chapter 16 Quick Reference

To	Do this
Add embedded custom code to a report	In Business Intelligence Development Studio, click Report Properties on the Report menu, click the Code tab, and then enter a Visual Basic .NET code block in the Custom Code box. Call the function in an expression using the following syntax: `Code.method(arguments)`. For example: `=Code .Divide(ReportItems!Margin.Value,ReportItems!SalesAmount.Value)`
Use a custom assembly in a report	Create a class library using a .NET language. In the Properties window for Report, click the ellipsis button for the *References* property, click Browse in the Add Reference dialog box, and select the .dll file for the assembly. Call a function from the custom assembly using the following syntax: `Namespace.Class.Method(arguments)`. For example: `=AdventureWorks.VB.Extensions.CommonFunctions.GetConditionColor(Me.Value,Parameters!CautionValue.Value,Parameters!AlertValue.Value)`

To	Do this
Create a custom data processing extension	Build a class library to create six required data processing objects that inherit the *Microsoft.ReportingServices.DataProcessing* namespace. Each object is associated with a specific interface and must implement all members of that interface as follows: Connection object: *IExtension*, *IDbConnection*, or *IDbConnectionExtension*. The connection object must also include the *Microsoft.ReportingServices.Interfaces* namespace. Command object: *IDbCommand*. Data reader object: *IDataReader*. Parameter object: *IDataParameter*. Parameter collection object: *IDataParameterCollection*. Transaction object: *IDbTransaction*.
Deploy a custom data processing extension	Place the assembly in the C:\Program Files\Microsoft SQL Server \MSSQL.3 \ReportingServices\ReportServer\bin folder and Program Files\Microsoft Visual Studio 8\Common7\IDE\PrivateAssemblies folder. Then, after backing up the configuration files, add a child element to the <*Data*> element in both the RSReportServer.config file and the RSReportDesigner.config file. Add a child element to the <*Designer*> element in the RSReportDesigner .config file. Add a code group to the Rssrvpolicy.config file and the Rspre-viewpolicy.config file to grant *FullTrust* permission.
Create RDL programmatically	Create an application that includes methods to connect to and read a data source and generate XML tags that conform to the RDL schema. The easiest way to generate RDL is to use the *XmlTextWriter* class.

Chapter 17

Programming Report Server Management

After completing this chapter, you will be able to:

- Use the *rs* utility (Rs.exe) to manage Report Server contents.
- Create a Microsoft Windows application to search and update Report Server Contents.
- Use Windows Management Instrumentation (WMI) classes to review and update configuration settings.

As you learned in Chapter 16, "Report Authoring with Custom Development," the Reporting Services application programming interface (API) allows you to customize all stages of the reporting life cycle. In this chapter, you'll learn how to build a few alternatives to Report Manager for managing Report Server. In fact, anything you can do with Report Manager can be done programmatically by taking advantage of any of the more than 100 functions in the Reporting Services Web Service Library. In this chapter, you'll learn how to use this library to build a Microsoft Visual Basic .NET script and a custom application, which will help you understand the different ways that you can manage the contents of Report Server. Whether you simply want to review the existing contents of Report Server or change its contents by adding or deleting items such as folders or reports, you can build a tool to provide just the range of functionality that you require.

Understanding Web Services

The Reporting Services Web Service is the programmatic interface that all client components use to interact with Report Server. Unlike traditional server applications that run as a service on a Windows server, a Web service doesn't run at all. It simply exists to expose classes and methods when it is called by a client. These classes and methods are encapsulated in a file with an .asmx file extension. The code can also be compiled in a separate assembly file that is placed in the same directory as the .asmx file. If you create a separate assembly, the declaration of the Web Service in the .asmx file includes a reference to that assembly. A client application can access a Web service in several different ways, but as implemented in Reporting Services, the client finds the Web service via a URL that locates the .asmx file. Associated with the .asmx file is an XML-based document known as a Web Services Description Language (WSDL) document that describes all the public members of the Web service available to the client. That is, WSDL is the metadata for the Web Service that exposes its methods, the arguments required by those methods, and their return values.

Once you know how to locate a Web service, all you have to do is code the application to use the Web service's class library. Because the Microsoft .NET Framework includes support for Web services, you're insulated from the details behind how the client application actually communicates with the Web service. You need to understand, however, that the client application and the Web service rely on a Web server to handle the transport of information between the two locations by using HTTP. The structure of the information is packaged as SOAP messages, which are formatted as XML documents. By using open standards such as HTTP, SOAP, and XML, neither the client application nor the Web service is tied to a single platform or language. Each is capable of receiving, translating, and sending SOAP messages that integrate applications and share data.

Typically, you use the components included with Reporting Services, such as Report Designer and Report Manager, to avoid developing and maintaining additional code to perform management tasks. These components communicate with Report Server exclusively through a Web service, which provides the complete range of management functionality required to publish reports and other resources, set item properties, define security roles and assignments, create schedules or subscriptions, and configure server properties. Using the .NET Framework, you have several options for accessing the Reporting Services Web Service. To handle specific functional needs, such as tasks that are frequently repeated, consider developing .NET scripts. You can also add Reporting Services management functionality to a console application or, when a graphical user interface (GUI) is preferred, to a Windows form or a Web application. In all cases, you use a proxy class in your code to gain access to the Web service library.

Using the *rs* Utility

If you need to perform only a simple management task, you don't have to undertake the development of a full-blown application. Instead, you can create a script file that you can execute using the *rs* (Rs.exe) utility. The *rs* utility is the simplest way to use the Reporting Services Web Service, because this utility creates a proxy class for you and automatically connects to the Web service.

You first learned how to use the *rs* utility to publish in Chapter 9, "Managing Content," but this utility can be used to do much more. Because it has full access to the Reporting Services Web Service Library, you can write a script using the *rs* utility to do anything that you can do with Report Manager. Further, when you need to perform several tasks in series, you can create multiple script files and then execute them as a batch process using command-line arguments. (You executed scripts as a batch if you used PublishChap10.cmd or PublishChap 12.cmd when preparing for the procedures in these chapters.)

Anything that you have to do multiple times is a task you should consider automating by using scripts. For example, you might want to script the following repetitive tasks:

- Deploying a set of reports to each Report Server in a Web farm.
- Assigning the same server settings to multiple servers to maintain consistency across environments.
- Applying the same security or subscription settings to multiple reports.

The *rs* utility uses the following syntax:

```
rs -i input_file -s ReportServerURL -i input_file -s ReportServerURL -u username -p password
-l timeout -b -v variable_key=variable_value -t
```

The *input_file* is the name of the script file, which must be fully qualified when it isn't in the same directory as the *rs* utility. The *ReportServerURL* identifies the virtual directory for Report Server on either a local or a remote server. Both of these arguments are required.

The following arguments are optional:

- **-u username and -p password** Use this pair of arguments when you need to override your current Windows logon credentials when connecting to Report Server. The credentials that you use must have local administrator rights on the server that you are targeting with the script.
- **-l timeout** Specify the maximum number of seconds to elapse before ending the attempt to connect to Report Server. The default time-out value is 8 seconds. If you specify 0 seconds, the connection attempt will continue indefinitely.
- **-b** To run the script commands as a batch, use the *-b* argument. If any single command fails that is not handled as an exception in the script, the entire transaction is rolled back. On the other hand, if the exception-handling in your script results in a normal return from the *Main* method, the transaction is committed.
- **-v variable_key=variable_value** Pass a value to a global variable in your script using this argument. No spaces are allowed between the equal operator and the operands variable_key and variable_value. If you have multiple variables, precede each key/value pair with the *-v* flag. Even though you use the global variable in expressions in your script, the global variable is not declared in the script.
- **-t** Enable tracing for the execution of the script to update the trace logs should any error messages result. This optional argument is useful when you are running unattended scripts.

When you execute the *rs* utility, the utility automatically locates the WSDL document for the Reporting Services Web Service on the specified server and creates a proxy class called *rs*. This proxy class serves as the interface that you use in your script to access Web service methods and properties. The *rs* utility also gives you access to four namespaces in the .NET

Framework–*System*, *Sytem.IO*, *System.Xml*, and *System.Web.Services*–that are not declared in the script.

Querying Report Server

The *rs* utility is particularly useful when you need to iterate through a collection of items to perform a particular task, such as to compile a list of items in a particular folder. Two methods are available to retrieve information about Report Server contents–*ListChildren()* and *FindChildren()*. This section shows you how to use *ListChildren()*. You use *FindChildren()* in the next section.

A script requires a *Main* procedure, but you can also create your own subprocedures to modularize functionality within the script. When using *ListChildren()*–or any other Reporting Services Web Service method–in a script, you must use the *rs* reference variable for the Web service proxy class.

> **Note** The Reporting Services Web Service library is documented in SQL Server Books Online. In many cases, the documentation includes code samples to illustrate the usage of Reporting Services methods and properties.

Use the following syntax with *ListChildren()*: `rs.ListChildren(Item, Recursive)`. The *Item* argument is the full path of the parent folder whose contents you want to list. For example, use "/" to list the contents of the root folder (known as the Home folder in Report Manager) or, for nested folders, use a string like "/Example Reports/Execution Log Reports." The *Recursive* argument is a Boolean expression used to specify how much content is retrieved by the method. If True, all items in the specified folder and its nested folders are returned. If False, only the items in the specified folder are returned.

The *ListChildren()* method returns an empty *CatalogItem* object if the specified folder is empty, but returns an array of *CatalogItem* objects if items exist there. You can then use a FOR loop to iterate through the *CatalogItem* objects and read the properties for each object. Because security settings for items as defined in Reporting Services are enforced even when accessing contents programmatically, the array of *CatalogItem* objects might not contain all items that exist in the specified folder. The credentials that you use to run the script are compared with role definitions and assignments to determine what items you can access with Web service methods.

In this procedure, you'll run a script that uses the *ListChildren()* method to display a list of items and selected properties in the command window.

List items in a specified folder

1. Using Microsoft Notepad, open the Contents.rss file in the C:\Documents and Settings\<username>\My Documents\Microsoft Press\rs2005sbs\chap17 folder.

The script looks like this:

```
'The folder for which contents will be listed is passed as an argument in the
'command-line
Dim parentPath As String = "/" + parentFolder

Public Sub Main()
   Dim myCatalogItems() as CatalogItem = Nothing
   'Only the items visible to the current user will display
   rs.Credentials = System.Net.CredentialCache.DefaultCredentials
   Try
       'List only children in current folder - ignore descendants in nested folders
       myCatalogItems = rs.ListChildren(parentPath, False)
   Catch e As Exception
       Console.WriteLine(e.Message)
   End Try

   Dim item As CatalogItem
   Try
       Console.WriteLine("Name".PadRight(40) +
   "Type".PadRight(10) + "Modified Date")
       For each item in myCatalogItems
          Console.WriteLine(Microsoft.VisualBasic.Left(item.Name,39)
     .PadRight(40) + item.Type.ToString().PadRight(10) +
     item.ModifiedDate.ToString())
       Next item
       Console.WriteLine()
       Console.WriteLine(myCatalogItems.Length.ToString() + "
   total item(s)")
   Catch e As Exception
           Console.WriteLine(e.Message)
   End Try
End Sub
```

Notice the reference to the *Microsoft.VisualBasic* namespace in this code. Because the *rs* utility does not provide access to this namespace automatically, you must include this prefix in your Visual Basic .NET script when you need to manipulate a string value. In this case, the *Left* function is used to truncate *Item.Name* so it will fit within a fixed column width structure.

Note You can use any text editor or scripting tool to create the script file, including the Microsoft Visual Studio environment. However, even though the script must be written in Visual Basic .NET, the resulting .rss file will not compile in Visual Studio.

2. Open a command window, navigate to the C:\Documents and Settings\<username>\My Documents\Microsoft Press\rs2005sbs\chap17 folder, and then type the following:

```
rs -i contents.rss -s http://localhost/ReportServer -v parentFolder="My Adventure Works"
```

   When passing a variable as an argument using the *-v* flag, you must be careful to type the variable name and its value on each side of the equal sign (=) with no spaces. Otherwise, an error message will be displayed when you try to run the utility.

> **Important** This procedure assumes that you have completed previous chapters satisfactorily. If you do not have the My Adventure Works folder on your Report Server, substitute a valid folder name to complete this procedure.

3. Press Enter.

   Your screen looks like this:

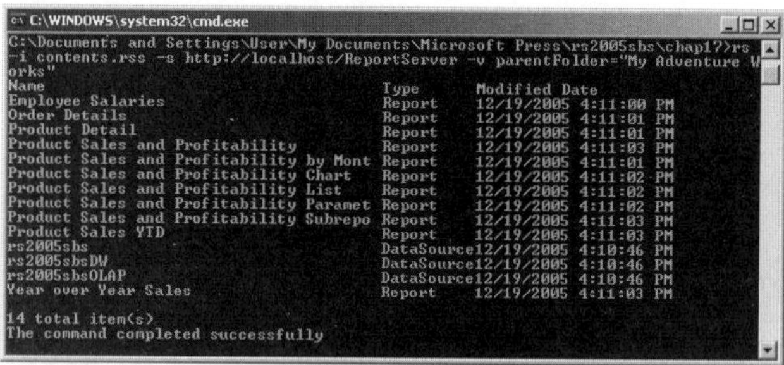

   Notice that some of the report names are truncated to fit the fixed column width defined by the script. You can adjust the script to accommodate longer report names if you prefer.

   Even though the *rs* utility is a handy tool, typing a full set of arguments each time that you want to use the utility can rapidly become tedious. You can use a batch file to simplify running the utility.

4. Create a new file using Notepad and add the following text:

```
rs -i ..\chap17\contents.rss -s http://localhost/ReportServer -v parentFolder=%1
```

5. Save the file to C:\Documents and Settings\<username>\My Documents\Microsoft Press\rs2005sbs\Workspace as **listfolder.cmd**.

6. In the command window, change to the C:\Documents and Settings\<username>\My Documents\Microsoft Press\rs2005sbs\Workspace directory, type **listfolder "My Adventure Works"**, and then press Enter.

Your screen looks like this:

```
C:\WINDOWS\system32\cmd.exe

C:\Documents and Settings\User\My Documents\Microsoft Press\rs2005sbs\Workspace>
listfolder "My Adventure Works"

C:\Documents and Settings\User\My Documents\Microsoft Press\rs2005sbs\Workspace>
rs -i ..\chap17\contents.rss -s http://localhost/ReportServer -v parentFolder="M
y Adventure Works"
                                            Type      Modified Date
Name
Employee Salaries                           Report    12/19/2005 4:11:00 PM
Order Details                               Report    12/19/2005 4:11:01 PM
Product Detail                              Report    12/19/2005 4:11:01 PM
Product Sales and Profitability             Report    12/19/2005 4:11:03 PM
Product Sales and Profitability by Mont     Report    12/19/2005 4:11:01 PM
Product Sales and Profitability Chart       Report    12/19/2005 4:11:02 PM
Product Sales and Profitability List        Report    12/19/2005 4:11:02 PM
Product Sales and Profitability Paramet     Report    12/19/2005 4:11:02 PM
Product Sales and Profitability Subrepo     Report    12/19/2005 4:11:03 PM
Product Sales YTD                           Report    12/19/2005 4:11:03 PM
rs2005sbs                                   DataSource12/19/2005 4:10:46 PM
rs2005sbsDW                                 DataSource12/19/2005 4:10:46 PM
rs2005sbsOLAP                               DataSource12/19/2005 4:10:46 PM
Year over Year Sales                        Report    12/19/2005 4:11:03 PM

14 total item(s)
The command completed successfully

C:\Documents and Settings\User\My Documents\Microsoft Press\rs2005sbs\Workspace>
```

Use the *rs* utility in a batch file for tasks that you repeat often. Adding a batch file argument to pass in a value for a script variable gives you greater flexibility for repeating similar tasks with the same batch command file.

Tip Of course, you can create a batch command to perform many tasks as a single series. Take a look at PublishChap10.cmd in the C:\Documents and Settings\<username>\My Documents\Microsoft Press\rs2005sbs\chap10 folder for an example of how to run scripts to publish data sources, reports, and a linked report by using a batch command. The *rs* utility is also useful not only for querying Report Server, but also for iterative tasks that include publishing reports and other resources, setting properties, establishing a data source for reports, or assigning users to a role definition.

Using a Custom Application to Manage Reporting Services

Even though you can use any method or property included in the Reporting Services Web Service in a script by using the *rs* utility, the utility does not provide for user interaction while it executes. If you require user interaction, you can develop a .NET application to provide a user interface for management tasks. You can either build an application that exclusively performs Reporting Services management tasks, or you can incorporate this management functionality into existing applications. In either case, you need to add code to your application to create a proxy class as an interface to the Reporting Services Web Service.

For each application that you create, you are required to perform specific tasks. You must first create a proxy class for the Reporting Services Web Service. One way to do so is to use Visual Studio to add a Web reference that specifies the location of the WSDL document describing the available methods and properties of the Web service. The location for the WDSL document is specified as a URL, *http://<servername>/reportserver/reportservice2005.asmx?wsdl*. In addition to creating the proxy class, you need to create a reference variable for a ReportingServices object, which will be used as the mechanism for connecting to the Web service and for accessing items on the server. In your application, you must also assign credentials from the local .NET Credentials Cache so that Reporting Services can determine who is trying to access the Web service and enforce the appropriate security role definition.

You can use the Reporting Services Web Service Library in a custom application to review information about Report Server contents or settings. If you're using a Windows form in your application, for example, you can display this information using a *ComboBox*, *ListView*, or *TreeView* control. You can add buttons and other controls that enable the user to perform operations on the server, such as filter a list of items based on specified search criteria. You can also use commands or controls to add or remove content on the server, to change item properties, or to perform other management tasks.

Querying Report Server

You can build a custom browser application or custom management tool to look up information about Report Server items that isn't readily available using Report Manager. For example, you can build a custom application to do any of the following:

- Find reports available to a particular user.
- Find out whether those reports require parameters.
- Find out other pertinent information about those reports, such as subscriptions and security settings.
- Review properties for a set of items before updating those properties.

As you learned earlier in this chapter, one way to retrieve information from Report Server is to use the *ListChildren()* method to navigate through the hierarchy of folders. Another way to get information from Report Server is to use the *FindItems()* method to filter all or part of the folder hierarchy based on search conditions. To use *FindItems()*, use the following syntax: `FindItems(folder, operator, conditions)`. The *folder* argument indicates the highest level folder in a hierarchy to search. The *conditions* argument is an array that stores a minimum of one property name/value pair that is used to search items that have a matching value for the specified property. When you have only one name/value search condition, set the *operator* argument to Nothing. When you have multiple search conditions in the array, set the *operator* argument to AND or OR to indicate how the search conditions are evaluated in combination.

Like the *ListChildren()* method, the *FindItems()* method returns an empty *CatalogItem* object or an array of *CatalogItem* objects matching the specified search criteria, but it returns only those items that can be viewed based on the authenticated user's permissions. Your search can be based on any of the following *CatalogItem* properties: *Name*, *Description*, *CreatedBy*, *CreationDate*, *ModifiedBy*, or *ModifiedDate*.

> **Note** In this chapter, steps and illustrations are provided for creating applications using Visual Basic .NET. Corresponding C# .NET code samples are available in the C:\Documents and Settings\<username>\My Documents\Microsoft Press\rs2005sbs\chap17 folder, and completed C# .NET projects are in the C:\Documents and Settings\<username>\My Documents\Microsoft Press\rs2005sbs\Answers\chap17 folder. To use these alternate code samples when following the procedures in this chapter, replace VB with **CS** wherever you need to type a name or open a file.

In this procedure, you'll add code to a Windows form that uses the *FindItems()* method to display items and selected properties in a *ListView* control.

Search for items by name

1. Start Visual Studio, and then open the myRSManagerVB solution in the C:\Documents and Settings\<username>\My Documents\Microsoft Press\rs2005sbs\chap17\myRSManagerVB folder.
2. In Solution Explorer, right-click the Project folder, and then click Add Web Reference.
3. In the URL textbox, type ***http://localhost/ReportServer/ReportService2005.asmx?wsdl***, and then click Go.

   One Web service–ReportService–is found at this URL.
4. In the Web Reference Name text box, replace the default value with **ReportService**.

   The Add Web Reference dialog box looks like this:

   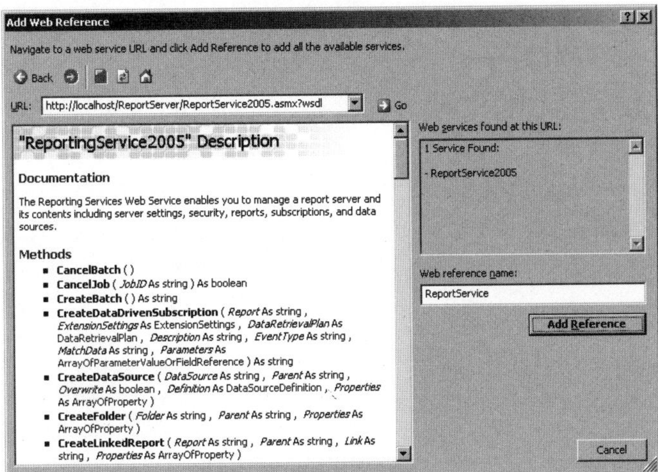

   Though it isn't required, replacing the default Web Reference Name with the Web service name to make it more easily identifiable in the Solution Explorer is a good idea.
5. Click Add Reference.

The Web reference is now added to the solution.

6. Double-click the myRSManager.vb file in Solution Explorer.

   Your screen looks like this:

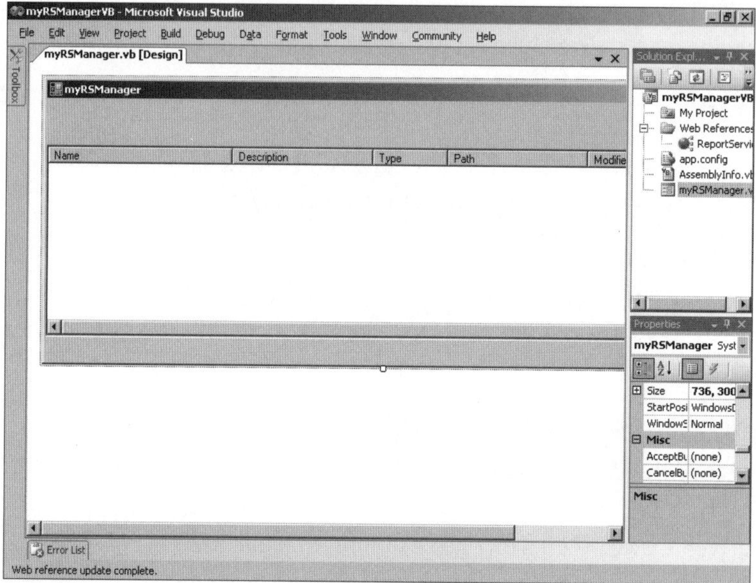

   The myRSManager form currently contains a *ListView* control that will be populated with a list of catalog items based on a search condition specified by the user. You need to add a *TextBox* control for the search condition and a *Button* control to execute the search and load the *ListView* control.

7. In the Toolbox window, double-click *TextBox*, and then double-click *Button* to add these controls to the form.

8. Position the *Button1* control to the right of the *TextBox1* control.

9. Select the *Button1* control, replace the *Text* property value with **Find Items by Name** in the Properties window, and then widen the control so that the button's full text is displayed.

Your screen looks like this:

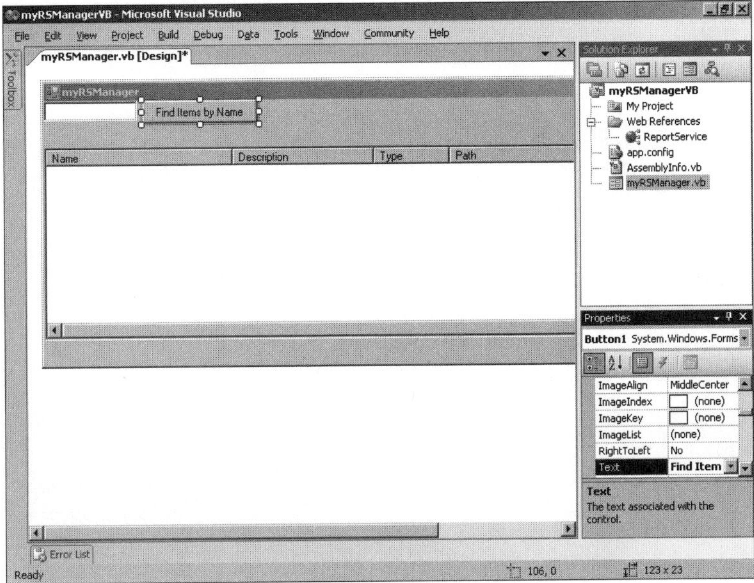

10. Double-click Find Items By Name to open the Visual Basic page for the current form to which a new subroutine, *Button1Click*, is added.
11. Add the following code after the *Inherits* statement at the top of the page:

```
Dim myReportService As New ReportService.ReportingService2005

Dim myCatalogItems As ReportService.CatalogItem()
```

The variable *myReportService* opens the connection to the Web service and is used to pass information to Report Server, such as the user's credentials. The variable *myCatalogItems* is an array of *CatalogItem* objects that will be used to store the results returned by the *FindChildren()* method.

12. Expand Windows Form Designer Generated Code.
13. Type the following code after the *InitializeComponent()* statement:

```
myReportService.Credentials = System.Net.CredentialCache.DefaultCredentials
```

Your screen looks like this:

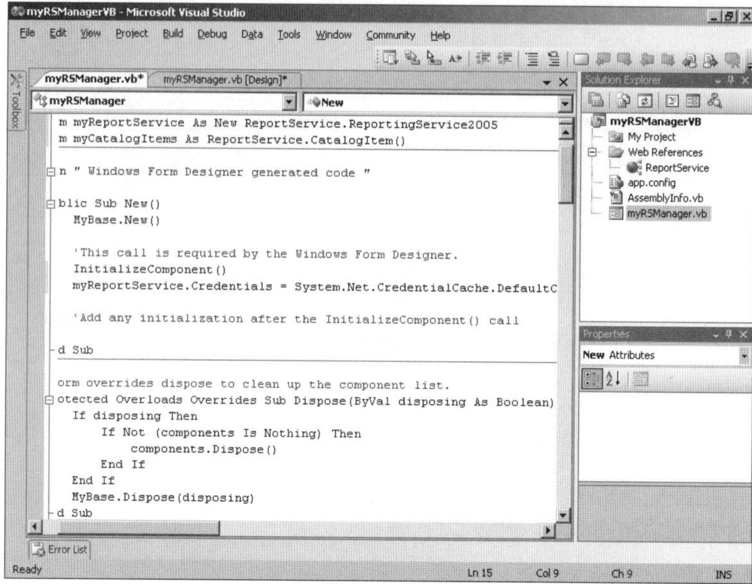

14. Collapse the #Region <;$QD> Windows Form Designer Generated Code <;$QS> section of the page.

15. Copy the contents of the FindItemsButtonVB.txt file in the C:\Documents and Settings\<username>\My Documents\Microsoft Press\rs2005sbs\chap17 folder and paste into the code page within the *Button1Click* subroutine.

    The code looks like this:

```
'Initialize a SearchCondition object to search by item name
'using the value obtained from TextBox1
Dim mySearchConditions(0) As ReportService.SearchCondition
mySearchConditions(0) = New ReportService.SearchCondition
mySearchConditions(0).Name = "Name"
mySearchConditions(0).Value = TextBox1.Text

'Assign the SearchCondition object as an argument for the FindItems method
'and begin the search at the root folder of Report Server to search all content
'on the server. Store the results as an array of CatalogItem objects.
myCatalogItems = myReportService.FindItems("/", Nothing, mySearchConditions)

'Clear the ListView to prepare for loading with new values.
ListView1.Items.Clear()
Try
   If Not (myCatalogItems Is Nothing) Then
    Dim ci As ReportService.CatalogItem
    For Each ci In myCatalogItems
     'Instantiate each object in the array of CatalogItem objects
     'to assign item properties as details for the ListView control
```

```
            Dim newItem As New CatalogListViewItem(ci)
            'Add the current catalog item to the ListView
            ListView1.Items.Add(newItem)
          Next ci
        End If
        'Display the complete list of catalog items
        ListView1.View = View.Details
        'Uncomment the lines below after adding the applicable button
        'Button2.Enabled = True
        'Button3.Enabled = True
    Catch ex As Exception
        'For a production environment, you should create
        'specific error-handling routines
        Throw New Exception("Unable to build tree view.")
    End Try
```

This code assumes that you want to search the entire contents of Report Server. You can extend the code to allow run-time changes to the specified search folder.

Notice that each item in the *ReportingService.CatalogItem* class is instantiated as an object of the *CatalogListViewItem* class. You will add this class later in this procedure.

16. Save the file.
17. In Solution Explorer, right-click the myRSManager project, point to Add, and then click Add New Item.
18. Click Class, change its name to **CatalogListViewItem.vb**, and then click Add.
19. Copy the contents of the CatalogListViewVB.txt file in the C:\Documents and Settings \<username>\My Documents\Microsoft Press\rs2005sbs\chap17 folder and paste into the code page to replace the skeleton class definition.

    The code looks like this:

```
Public Class CatalogListViewItem
    Inherits ListViewItem
    Private m_catalogItem As ReportService.CatalogItem

    Public Sub New(ByVal catalogItem As ReportService.CatalogItem)
        m_catalogItem = catalogItem

        'Retrieve the catalog item properties as subitems for the details
        'setting of the ListView control
        [Text] = m_catalogItem.Name
        Me.SubItems.Add(m_catalogItem.Description)
        Me.SubItems.Add(m_catalogItem.Type.ToString())
        Me.SubItems.Add(m_catalogItem.Path)
        Me.SubItems.Add(m_catalogItem.ModifiedDate.ToString())
        'You can additional properties here to include as details
```

```
        'but you will also need to adjust the Columns property for
        'the ListView control to define a name and column size for
        'the added properties
    End Sub 'New

End Class 'CatalogListViewItem
```

This file also includes code for the *Item*, *Type*, and *Path* properties for the *CatalogListViewItem* class, which is not shown here.

20. Save the file.
21. Right-click the myRSManagerVB project in Solution Explorer, and then click Properties.
22. Click myRSManager in the Startup Object list box, and then save the project.

    Because your Visual Basic application doesn't include a *Sub Main* routine, you need to specify the startup object so that the application will compile and execute.
23. On the Debug menu, click Start to run the form (or press F5).
24. In myRSManager, click Find Items By Name.

    The myRSManager form looks like this:

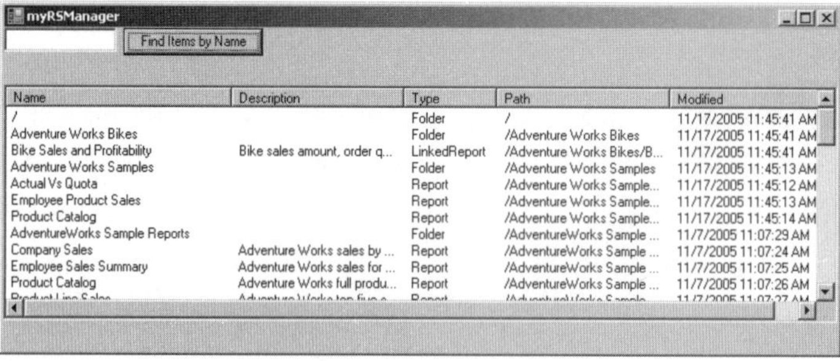

    The names of all items on the server–reports, linked reports, and data sources–appear. You can see the item description, if one has been specified; the item type; the path to the item from the root folder; and the modification date (which is equivalent to the creation date when no subsequent modifications have been made to the item).
25. Type **sales** in the textbox, and then click Find Items By Name.

The myRSManager form looks like this:

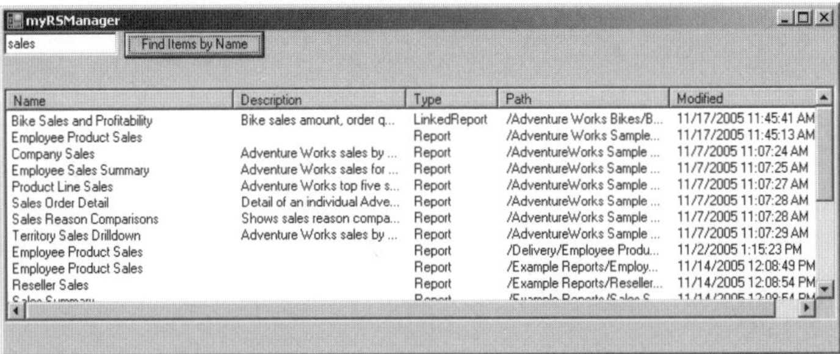

Any item on the server that includes the string "sales" in its name is displayed in the *List-View* control. Notice that the search string is not case-sensitive.

> **Tip** You can extend the code used in this procedure to sort the list by column or to add search functionality for other catalog item properties, such as *CreatedBy*, *Description*, or *ExecutionDate*. You can find a complete list of properties in the topic, "Catalog-Item Class," in SQL Server Books Online.

26. Click Close to close the myRSManager window, but keep the project open.

Managing Reports

In addition to using a custom application to query a Report Server, you can use a custom application to handle routine management tasks on the server. For example, your custom application can include functionality to execute the following operations:

- Add or delete reports, folders, data sources, or other resources.
- Administer security settings.
- Define schedules for report execution or subscriptions.

A complete review of all the possible functionality that you might consider for a custom management tool is beyond the scope of this book. However, this introduction to using the Reporting Services Web Library will give you enough information to understand how to use the Reporting Services API in your own applications.

Perhaps the most common management task that you can include in a custom application is uploading reports to Report Server. The easiest way to do so is to establish a common staging area in which you place report definition files in preparation for upload. Then, you can iterate through these files and use the *CreateReport()* method to add the report to a specified folder. The *CreateReport()* method uses the following syntax:

```
CreateReport(report_name, parent_folder_path, overwrite_flag, report_definition,
report_properties)
```

These arguments have the following requirements:

- **report_name** The report_name must be a string value. This value is associated with the *Name* property of the resulting catalog item in the ReportServer database.
- **parent_folder_path** The parent_folder_path is the full path name of the folder that will contain the report. The path name must begin with the root folder, "/", and include all folder names in the hierarchy to which the report will be added. For example, with a path name like "/Example Reports/Execution Log Reports", the *CreateReport()* method will add a report to the Execution Log Reports folder. If the folder name is invalid, the method will fail.

> **Tip** Your custom application can allow the user to select a target folder for the batch of reports to be uploaded. You will see how to do this in the next procedure.

- **overwrite_flag** This argument is a Boolean expression to indicate whether a report of the same name in the same location should be overwritten.
- **report_definition** The *report_definition* is a byte array that contains the contents of the report definition file. You can load this byte array from a file using the *FileStream* class.
- **report_properties** You can optionally supply an array that contains name and value pairs for system-defined and user-defined properties of a report. If you don't want to set the report properties when you add the report, you need to use *Nothing* (or *null* when coding with C# .NET) as a placeholder for this argument.

Another common management task is deleting content that is no longer needed. The *DeleteItem()* method takes only one argument–the full path name of the item to be deleted. The full path name includes the entire folder path from the root folder as well as the name of the item. For example, to delete the Sales Summary report in the Adventure Works folder, you use the following code: `DeleteItem("/Adventure Works/Sales Summary")`. When using the *DeleteItem()* method, you're not limited to reports. You can also delete folders and other resources contained in folders, as well as subscriptions, schedules, or report snapshots. To use this method, you must have delete permission for the item that you are attempting to delete.

In this procedure, you'll add one button to a Windows form to add reports to a selected folder, and another button to delete selected items.

Create buttons to add and remove content

1. In Visual Studio, switch to the design page of myRSManager to work with the Windows form.
2. In the Toolbox window, double-click the *Button* control twice.

3. Move the two buttons to the right of the Find Items By Name button so that your screen looks like this:

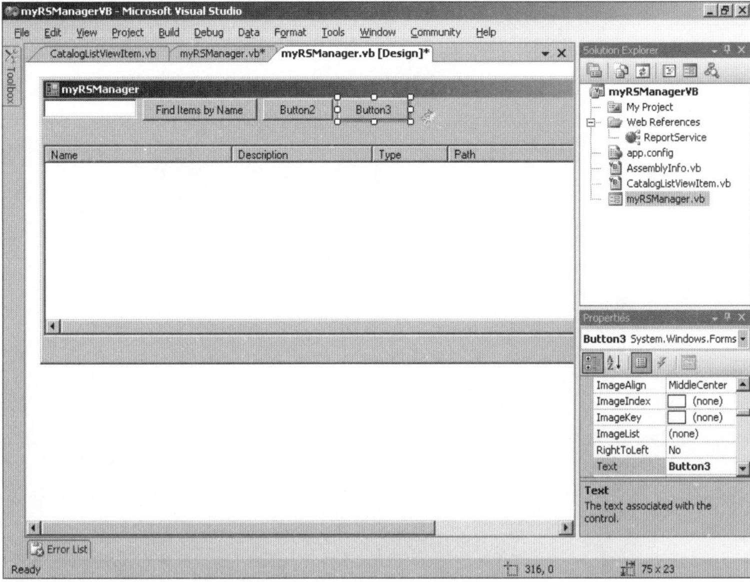

4. Select the *Button2* control, and then type **Add Reports** in the control's *Text* property in the Properties window.
5. Change the *Enabled* property for the *Button2* control to False.

   As you saw in the previous procedure, items do not display in the *ListView* control until you use the Find Items By Name button. By disabling the *Button2* control when the form is first executed, you can require a user to retrieve items first, and then a folder can be selected from the resulting list. You will change the code for the Find Items By Name button (the *Button1* control) to enable the *Button2* control once a list has been created.
6. Select the *Button3* control, and then type **Delete Items** in the control's *Text* property in the Properties window. Resize the button, if necessary, to view the entire text.
7. Change the *Enabled* property for the *Button3* control to False.

   This control works like the *Button2* control and requires a user to select an item before an operation can be performed. Consequently, you will enable this button only when the user has requested a list by using the Find Items By Name button.
8. Switch to the code page (the myRSManager.vb form), and then remove the single quotation mark from the *Button1_Click* subroutine to uncomment the lines `Button2.Enabled = True and Button3.Enabled = True`.
9. Switch back to the design page, and then double-click Add Reports to view the code for the *Button2* control.

10. Copy the contents of the AddReportsButtonVB.txt file in the C:\Documents and Settings\<username>\My Documents\Microsoft Press\rs2005sbs\chap17 folder and paste into the code page within the *Button2_Click* subroutine.

    The code looks like this:

```
     Dim parentfolder As System.IO.Directory
    'For a production environment, you should create a staging area
    'for reports ready for publishing, then change the folder path value below.
    Dim folderPath As String = "C:\Documents and Settings\<username>\My
Documents\Microsoft Press\rs2005sbs\chap17\"
    Dim parentPath As String
    If ListView1.SelectedItems.Count > 1 Then
        'For a production environment, you should create
        'specific error-handling routines
        Throw New Exception("Cannot select more than one parent folder")
    End If

    Dim selectedCatalogItems As ListView.SelectedListViewItemCollection =
Me.ListView1.SelectedItems

    If Not (selectedCatalogItems Is Nothing) Then
        Dim sci As CatalogListViewItem
        For Each sci In selectedCatalogItems
       If sci.Type = ReportService.ItemTypeEnum.Folder Then
           parentPath = GetFolderPath(sci.Path)
       Else
           'For a production environment, you should create
           'specific error-handling routines
           Throw New Exception("Select a folder")
       End If
        Next sci
    End If

    Dim reports As String() = parentfolder.GetFiles(folderPath, "*.rdl")
    Dim report As String

    'Each report in the array will be published to the same folder.
    For Each report In reports
        PublishReport(report, parentPath)
    Next
    'After all reports are published, Button1 (Find Items by Name) is activated.

    Button1_Click(Nothing, Nothing)
```

    At this point, the *GetFolderPath* and *PublishReports* subroutines have not been declared. You will add the code for these subroutines later in this procedure.

11. Copy the contents of the PublishReportVB.txt file in the C:\Documents and Settings \<username>\My Documents\Microsoft Press\rs2005sbs\chap17 folder and paste

into the code page below the *Button2_Click* subroutine to create the *PublishReport* and *GetFolderPath* subroutines.

The code for these two subroutines looks like this:

```
Public Sub PublishReport(ByVal reportPath As String, ByVal parentPath As String)
   Dim definition As [Byte]() = Nothing
   Dim warnings As ReportService.Warning() = Nothing
   Dim warning As ReportService.Warning

   Try
       Dim stream As FileStream = File.OpenRead(parentPath + reportPath)
       definition = New [Byte](stream.Length) {}
       stream.Read(definition, 0, CInt(stream.Length))
       stream.Close()

   Catch e As Exception
       Throw New Exception(e.Message)
   End Try

   Try
       'Parse the report path to separate the report name from its folder path
       Dim reportPieces As String() = Split(reportPath, "\")
       Dim reportName As String = reportPieces.GetValue(reportPieces.Length - 1)
       reportName = reportName.Substring(0, reportName.Length - 4)


       'Publish the report to Report Server using the specified parentPath
       'but do not overwrite an existing report.
       'For production purposes, you need to test whether report exists first.
       warnings = myReportService.CreateReport(reportName, parentPath, False,
definition, Nothing)
       If Not (warnings Is Nothing) Then
         For Each warning In warnings
           Throw New Exception(warning.Message)
         Next warning
       Else
     'You should change this message and move to a new location
     'in the code if you publish a lot of reports using
     'this application.
         MessageBox.Show("Report "+reportName+" added.","Add
Report",MessageBoxButtons.OK)
       End If

   Catch e As Exception
       Throw New Exception(e.Message)
   End Try
    End Sub 'PublishReport

    Public Function GetFolderPath(ByVal currentPath As String) As String
   'Parse the item path to get the folder hierarchy
   Dim pathPieces As String() = Split(currentPath, "/")
   Dim parentLength As Integer = pathPieces.Length - 1
   Dim parentPath(parentLength) As String
```

```
    Dim i As Integer
    For i = 0 To parentLength
        parentPath(i) = pathPieces(i)
    Next i
    If parentPath.Length = 1 Then
        Return "/"
    Else
        Return String.Join("/", parentPath)
    End If
     End Function 'GetFolderPath
```

12. Above the class declaration at the very top of the page, add the following code:

```
Imports System.IO
```

The *PublishReport* subroutine that you added in the previous step uses the *FileStream* class to read a report definition file from the file system. You need to add the *System.IO* namespace to your application in order to use this class.

13. On the design page of myRSReportManager, double-click Delete Items, and then copy the contents of the DeleteItemsButtonVB.txt file in the C:\Documents and Settings \<username>\My Documents\Microsoft Press\rs2005sbs\chap17 folder and paste into the code page within the *Button3_Click* subroutine.

   The code looks like this:

```
Dim selectedCatalogItems As ListView.SelectedListViewItemCollection =
Me.ListView1.SelectedItems

If Not (selectedCatalogItems Is Nothing) Then
    Dim sci As CatalogListViewItem
    For Each sci In selectedCatalogItems
      Try
          myReportService.DeleteItem(sci.Path)
      Catch ex As Exception
          'For a production environment, you should create
          'specific error-handling routines
          Throw New Exception("Attempt to delete item failed.")
      End Try
    Next sci
End If
MessageBox.Show("Item(s) deleted.", "Delete Item", MessageBoxButtons.OK)
Button1_Click(Nothing, Nothing)
```

14. Save the file, and then press F5 to run the project and test the results.
15. In myRSManager, click Find Items By Name, scroll and select My Adventure Works.

The myRSManager form looks similar to this:

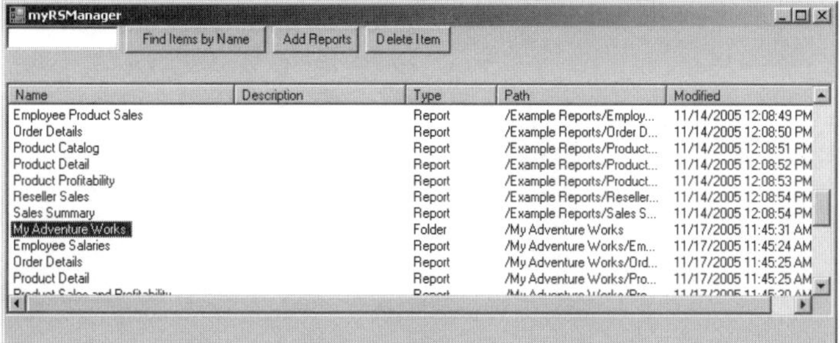

Because you clicked the Find Items By Name button, the Add Reports and Delete Reports buttons are now enabled.

> **Note** The My Adventure Works folder is created as a result of completing the procedures in Chapter 9. If you skipped this chapter, you need to close the myRSManager form. Open Report Manager and add a new folder to the Home page named My Adventure Works. Then, run myRSManager and repeat this step to continue.

16. Click Add Reports.

    This message box is displayed:

    When this message is displayed, the report named Actual Vs Quota Chapter 17, which is stored in the staging area C:\Documents and Settings\<username>\My Documents \Microsoft Press\rs2005sbs\chap17, was successfully published to Report Server.

17. Click OK to close the message box.
18. In the textbox, type **actual**, and then click Find Items By Name. Drag the column handles to make the Description column narrower and the Path column wider.

The myRSManager window looks like this:

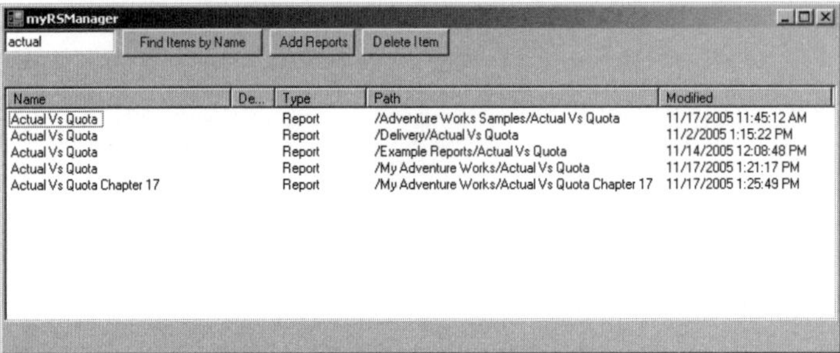

Because the myRSManager is a simple application, it doesn't sort the items in the ListView. The easiest way to find the added report is to use the search feature.

19. Select the Actual Vs Quota Chapter 17 report that you just added to the My Adventure Works folder, and then click Delete Item.
20. Click OK to close the message box.

    The myRSManager window looks like this:

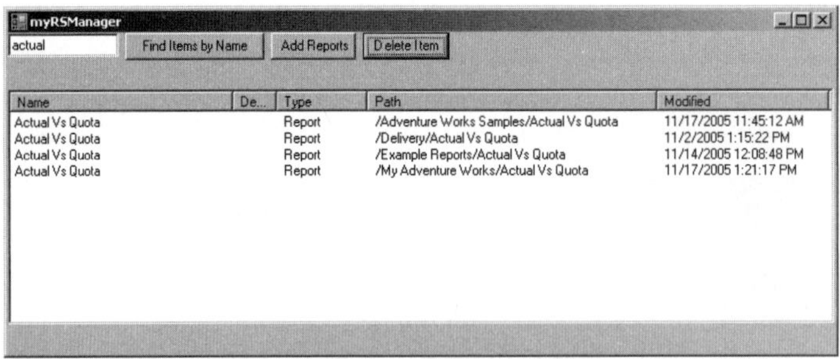

The Actual Vs Quota Chapter 17 report in the My Adventure Works folder was deleted.

21. Close the myRSManager window, and then close the myRSManager project in Visual Studio.

Tip The myRSManager application is intended solely as a simple introduction to using the Reporting Services Web Service Library. Consequently, it has limited functionality and error-handling capabilities. For another approach to building a Windows application to manage Report Server's contents, take a look at the RSExplorer sample application. You can find the files for RSExplorer in C:\Program Files\Microsoft SQL Server\90\Samples\Reporting Services\Application Samples\RSExplorer Sample (if you install samples by running Microsoft SQL Server 2005 Samples from the Microsoft SQL Server 2005/Documentation and Tutorials/Samples program group).

Using the Reporting Services WMI Provider

In addition to the Web service interface that can be used in custom scripts and applications to manage Report Server, Reporting Services includes WMI classes that allow you to programmatically review and manage the configuration settings for Report Server and Report Manager. The following two classes are defined in the namespace located at \root\Microsoft\SqlServer\ReportServer\v9\Admin:

- ***MSReportServer_ConfigurationSetting*** You can use this class to access some of the settings defined at installation and the parameters defined in the RSReportServer.config file. You can also use this class to read the value properties that correspond to settings in the configuration file. Many of these properties are also write-enabled. This class also includes a method to activate a Report Server instance. Not all configuration settings, however, are accessible using this interface.
- ***MSReportServerReportManager_ConfigurationSetting*** You can use this class to get some of the installation settings and some of the parameters stored in the RSWebApplication.config file. You can write to only one of these properties, *URLToReportServer*, which is the URL used to access the virtual directory for Report Server. No methods are included in this class.

Note The Reporting Services WMI classes are documented in SQL Server Books Online.

Querying a Report Server

To quickly check the current settings of a Report Server instance, you can incorporate the Reporting Services WMI classes in a custom application. For example, you might create a console application to iterate through a list of properties and then write a property name and its value to the console window. You can also update some properties using a custom application. Instead of opening the configuration file to change the value of a property, such as *DatabaseQueryTimeout*—which puts a limit on the time that Report Server can attempt to query the ReportServer database—you can programmatically update this value using a custom application.

A custom application to query Report Server settings provides you with a convenient tool to look up the current values instead of opening configuration files individually. To access this information, you must have system administrator privileges on the computer hosting Report Server. If you need to change database-related information, such as database credentials for the ReportServer database or change the name of that database, you must have database administrator privileges. You can use a custom application to find out information in the following areas:

ReportServer database

- Find out whether integrated security is in force and, if it is not, find out the user name used to connect to the ReportServer database. The password is write-only and cannot be accessed.
- If integrated security is not in force, find out whether Report Server is configured to impersonate a Windows user when connecting to the ReportServer database. When impersonation is configured, you can get the impersonated user's domain and user name, but not the corresponding password, because it's write-only.
- View the connection and query time-out values imposed on Report Server when accessing the Report Server database.
- Retrieve the name of the server on which the ReportServer database is installed as well as the name of the SQL Server instance.

Report Server instance

- Show the instance ID and the instance name for the Report Server instance.
- Find the installation path for the Report Server instance.
- Retrieve the virtual root for the Report Server instance.

Unattended execution

- Find out the user's domain and user name used when Report Server connects to a remote server to run unattended reports. (Unattended execution is explained in Chapter 11, "Managing Server Components.") As with the other password properties in this class, the corresponding password is write-only and isn't accessible with this interface.

If you want to use the WMI classes in a custom application, you need to include the following namespaces to the application: *System*, *System.Management*, and *System.IO*. Then, you need to create a *ManagementScope* object to bring the Reporting Services WMI namespace of a specified server into scope. You also need to create a *ManagementClass* object to connect to the management object of a Report Server instance. This *ManagementClass* object is based on the Report Server–specific WMI class definition at \root\Microsoft\SqlServer\ReportServer\v9 \admin:MSReportServer_ConfigurationSetting. Finally, you create a Report Server instance as a *ManagementObject* object, which gives you access to a collection of *PropertyData* objects that describe Report Server.

In this procedure, you'll create a console application to display Report Server settings by using WMI classes.

List current Report Server settings

1. In Visual Studio, create a new project based on the console application template named WMIQueryVB located in the C:\Documents and Settings\<username>\My Documents \Microsoft Press\rs2005sbs\Workspace folder.
2. Add the following code to the top of the page above the *Module* statement:

```
Imports System
Imports System.Management
Imports System.IO
```

3. In Solution Explorer, right-click the WMIQuery project, and then select Add Reference.
4. Select System.Management in the list of components, click Select, and then click OK.
5. Copy the contents of the WMIQueryVB.txt file in the C:\Documents and Settings \<username>\My Documents\Microsoft Press\rs2005sbs\chap17 folder and paste into the code page within the *Main* subroutine.

   The code looks like this:

```
Const WmiNamespace As String = _
"\\localhost\root\Microsoft\SqlServer\ReportServer\v9\Admin"
Const WmiRSClass As String = _
 "\\localhost\root\Microsoft\SqlServer\ReportServer\v9\admin:MSReportServer_Config
urationSetting"

Dim serverClass As ManagementClass
Dim scope As ManagementScope
scope = New ManagementScope(WmiNamespace)

'Connect to the Reporting Services namespace.
scope.Connect()

'Create the server class.
serverClass = New ManagementClass(WmiRSClass)

'Connect to the management object.
serverClass.Get()
If serverClass Is Nothing Then Throw New Exception("No class found")
```

```
'Loop through the instances of the server class.
Dim instances As ManagementObjectCollection = _
serverClass.GetInstances()
Dim instance As ManagementObject
For Each instance In instances
   Console.Out.WriteLine("Instance Detected")
   Dim instProps As PropertyDataCollection = _
   instance.Properties
   Dim prop As PropertyData
Console.WriteLine("Property Name".PadRight(35) + "Value")
   For Each prop In instProps

         Dim name As String = prop.Name
         Dim val As Object = prop.Value
Console.Out.Write(prop.Name.PadRight(35))
         If val Is Nothing Then
               Console.Out.WriteLine("<null>")
Else
               Console.Out.WriteLine(val.ToString())
         End If
   Next
Next
Console.WriteLine("Press ENTER to continue")
Console.ReadLine()
```

6. Save the file.
7. On the Debug menu, click Start Without Debugging.

   The console window looks like this:

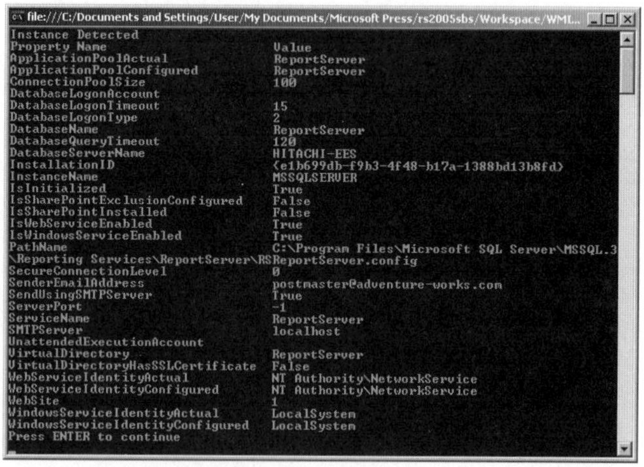

```
file:///C:/Documents and Settings/User/My Documents/Microsoft Press/rs2005sbs/Workspace/WMI...
Instance Detected
Property Name                      Value
ApplicationPoolActual              ReportServer
ApplicationPoolConfigured          ReportServer
ConnectionPoolSize                 100
DatabaseLogonAccount
DatabaseLogonTimeout               15
DatabaseLogonType                  2
DatabaseName                       ReportServer
DatabaseQueryTimeout               120
DatabaseServerName                 HITACHI-EES
InstallationID                     {e1b699db-f9b3-4f48-b17a-1388bd13b8fd}
InstanceName                       MSSQLSERVER
IsInitialized                      True
IsSharePointExclusionConfigured    False
IsSharePointInstalled              False
IsWebServiceEnabled                True
IsWindowsServiceEnabled            True
PathName                           C:\Program Files\Microsoft SQL Server\MSSQL.3
\Reporting Services\ReportServer\RSReportServer.config
SecureConnectionLevel              0
SenderEmailAddress                 postmaster@adventure-works.com
SendUsingSMTPServer                True
ServerPort                         -1
ServiceName                        ReportServer
SMTPServer                         localhost
UnattendedExecutionAccount
VirtualDirectory                   ReportServer
VirtualDirectoryHasSSLCertificate  False
WebServiceIdentityActual           NT Authority\NetworkService
WebServiceIdentityConfigured       NT Authority\NetworkService
WebSite                            1
WindowsServiceIdentityActual       LocalSystem
WindowsServiceIdentityConfigured   LocalSystem
Press ENTER to continue
```

   Now, you have a quick way to check the settings of your Report Server without opening the configuration file.

Chapter 17 Quick Reference

To	Do this

List items on Report Server	Use the *ListChildren*() method. For example, to list all contents of Report Server:
	`rs.ListChildren("/", True)`
	To list only the contents of the specified folder:
	`rs.ListChildren("/", False)`

Search items on Report Server	Use the *FindItems*() method. For example, to search all folders on Report Server, use:
	`FindItems("/", Nothing, myConditions)`
	where *myConditions* is an array containing a name/value pair like:
	`myConditions(0).Name = "Name"`
	and
	`myConditions(0).Value = "sales"`

Add a Web reference to the Reporting Services Web Service	In Solution Explorer, right-click the References folder, and then click Add Web Reference. Type: ***http://localhost/ReportServer/ReportService2005.asmx?wsdl*** in the URL text box, and then click Go. Replace the default Web Reference Name, if desired, and then click Add Reference.

Add a report to Report Server	Use the *CreateReport*() method. For example:
	`CreateReport("Actual Vs Quota", "/Adventure Works",`
	`False, report_definition,`
	`Nothing)`
	where *report_definition* is a byte array created from reading in a report definition file using the *FileStream* class.

Delete an item from Report Server	Use the DeleteItem() method. For example: `DeleteItem("/Adventure Works/Sales Summary")`

Review Report Server and Report Manager management properties	Include the following namespaces: *System*, *System.Management*, and *System.IO*. Create a *ManagementScope* object using the WMI class definition at \root \Microsoft\SqlServer\ReportServer\v9\Admin. Create a *ManagementClass* object using the WMI class definition at \ root\Microsoft\SqlServer\ReportServer\v9 \admin:MSReportServer_ConfigurationSetting. Create a Report Server instance as a *ManagementObject* object. Iterate through this object's *PropertyData* collection. For example:
	`For Each prop In instProps`
	`Dim name As String = prop.Name`
	`Dim val As Object = prop.Value Console.Out.WriteLine("Name:`
	`"+prop.Name)`
	`If val Is Nothing Then`
	`      Console.Out.WriteLine("Value: <null>")`
	`Else`
	`   Console.Out.WriteLine("Value: "+val.ToString())`
	`End If`
	`Next`

Chapter 18

Building Custom Reporting Tools

After completing this chapter, you will be able to:

- Use a URL to access reports and other items from Report Server.
- Add parameters to a URL to control the appearance and behavior of reports.
- Render reports programmatically in an application.

If you completed the previous two chapters, you have already learned a great deal about using Reporting Services as a platform for developing applications that will author and manage reports. Of course, because Reporting Services supports the full reporting life cycle, you can also use it to customize the access and delivery of reports. From including links to current reports in a Web page to creating a customized report viewer, you can choose from a wide range of access and delivery options. You can implement these separately or in combination to make reports available to the user community.

In this chapter, you'll explore some alternatives for accessing reports independently of Report Manager. These alternatives are not full-blown applications, but rather starting points that illustrate the key concepts you need to understand before undertaking development of your own custom application. You'll start with simple URL access and add parameters that allow you to control how a report is accessed from Report Server. Then, you'll learn different ways to render a report in both a Microsoft Windows–based application and a Web application. Finally, you'll learn how to use the Reporting Services Web service to provide an interface for selecting parameter values that are used to render a report. After you complete this chapter, you'll know how to use Reporting Services as a foundation for building your own reporting tools.

Using URLs

Although Report Manager is a great application for accessing reports, some situations require more direct access to reports. For example, you might want to add a link in a corporate portal directly to specific reports and thus bypass Report Manager altogether. Similarly, you might need to add a link to an executive dashboard that downloads a report to a specified format, such as a Microsoft Excel file. Wherever you need to provide access to reports, you can easily embed URLs to link to these reports. This method of accessing reports without Report Manager allows you to keep the features of the HTML Viewer and also provides faster access to reports than using the Web service.

Not only can you use URLs to access reports, but you can also use them to access other items stored in Report Server and to perform several functions supported by Report Manager. You can view the contents of folders, data sources, or resources uploaded to Report Server by using an item's URL. You can also add parameters to a URL to control behavior, such as setting the starting page of a long report. Because parameters control how the report looks, you can specify a rendering format for online viewing or download a file to another format such as Excel.

How to Use URLs to Access Reports

You can navigate Report Server's virtual directory to find a report and to get its URL. You can type this URL into your browser later to retrieve the report again, or you can use the URL as a link by pasting it into an HTML page, Web application, or portal. In addition to using a URL to access a specific report, you can include values in the URL for report parameters to override the default values established by the report author or an administrator. For more control, you can use special parameters known as *URL access parameters* to manage the HTML Viewer or to give Report Server special instructions for handling the report request.

Viewing Reports

The easiest way to access a desired report by using URLs is to use your browser to navigate from the virtual directory of Report Server, *http://localhost/ReportServer*, through the folder hierarchy. When you use this approach, folders, data sources, reports, and resources are all displayed in a list of links that is like a table of contents for the current folder. To the left of each link is either an item identifier–such as <dir> for a folder or <ds> for a data source–or a number that indicates the file size of the report or uploaded resource. You can use these links to view the selected item or to view the list of contents for a nested folder.

Another way to access a report is to enter its URL directly into your browser or to use a link in a Web page that includes the report's URL. Either way, the URL syntax is *http://servername/ReportServer?/item_path*. For *servername*, use localhost or the computer name of the server hosting Report Server. Replace *ReportServer* with the virtual directory name for Report Server only if you specified a different name when installing Reporting Services. Specify the final component of the URL, *item_path*, using the full path of the item to access, which includes all of the item's parent folders and the item name itself. For example, to view the Product Profitability report in the Custom Reporting folder on a local Report Server, use this URL: *http://localhost/ReportServer?/Custom Reporting/Product Profitability*.

Even though you are bypassing Report Manager by using URLs to access items on Report Server, the security permissions still apply. You can open an item or view the contents of a folder only when your role assignment has the correct permissions. If you plan to use the URL in a link that you add to a Web page, make sure you have the correct role assignments defined for the item.

In this procedure, you'll access reports by navigating Report Server's virtual directory and by entering a specific URL.

Display a report

1. Start Microsoft Visual Studio, and then open the Custom Reporting solution at C:\Documents and Settings\<username>\My Documents\Microsoft Press\rs2005sbs\chap18\Custom Reporting.
2. Right-click the solution name in Solution Explorer, and then click Deploy. Keep the solution open in Visual Studio for a later procedure in this chapter.
3. Using Microsoft Internet Explorer, navigate to *http://localhost/ReportServer* to view the contents of the virtual directory root, as shown here:

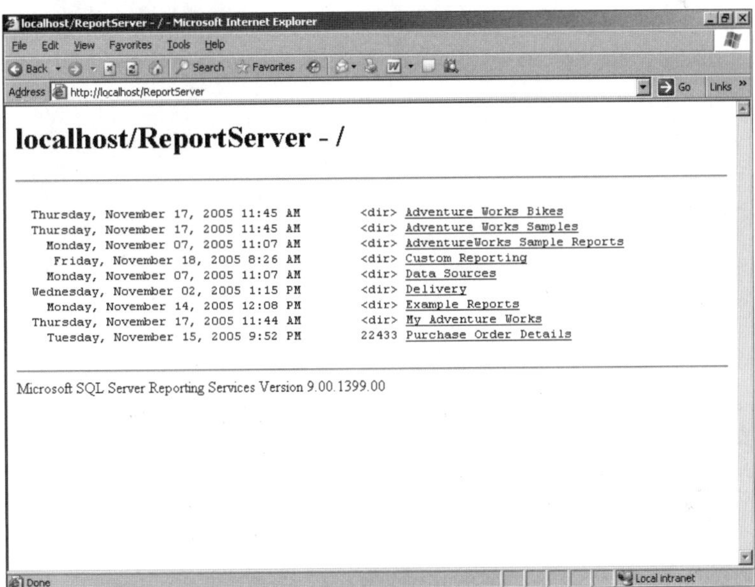

   You can navigate through the folder hierarchy of Report Server directly without the Report Manager interface. The content that you see is identical to the content viewable through the Report Manager interface because the same security permissions apply. Whether you use the Report Server virtual directory, the Report Manager interface, or a custom interface (as you will later in this chapter), you always view the same content because the same security infrastructure is always in force.

4. Click the Custom Reporting link, and then click the Product Catalog report.

Your screen looks like this:

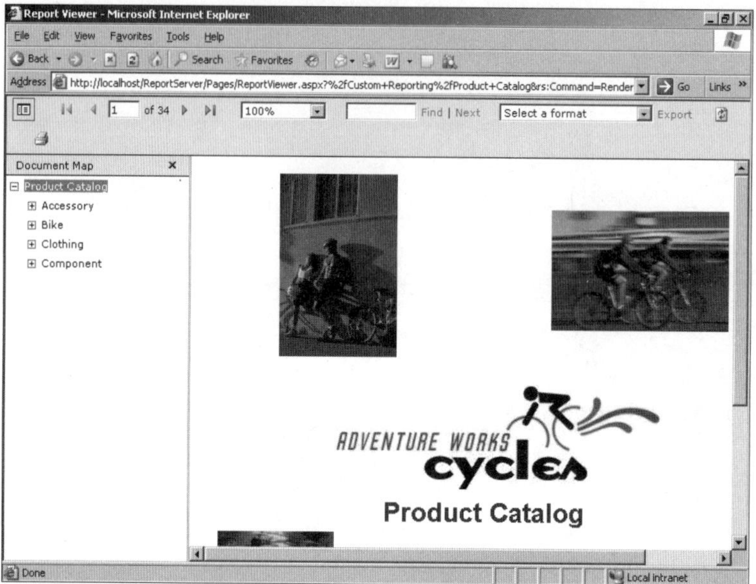

Because the report is rendered as HTML, the browser includes the HTML Viewer toolbar with the report by default. Later in this chapter, you'll learn how to override the default behavior.

Notice the URL for this report in the Address box– *http://localhost/ReportServer/Pages/ReportViewer.aspx?%2fCustom+Reporting%2fProduct+Catalog&rs:Command=Render*. You can copy this URL and paste it into an HTML page or another application to create an external link to this report. As another option, you can programmatically reproduce this URL if you want to integrate reporting functionality into a custom application.

Your browser automatically encodes the URL by replacing each forward slash with *%2f* and each space with + (plus sign). You are not required to create this fully encoded version of the URL when using the URL in your browser or when placing it in a link. When navigating Report Server, you'll notice each link includes *Pages/ReportViewer.aspx*, which is an ASP.NET page used to display reports in Web applications independently of Report Manager. You can create a URL without explicitly including this page because the URL will automatically update to include it. Each link also includes a URL access parameter, such as *rs:Command=Render*, that instructs Report Server how to handle the request for the item. Including this parameter in the URL that you use to access a report is not required, although it is recommended. You'll learn more about this and other URL access parameters later in this chapter.

5. In the Address box of Internet Explorer, type ***http://localhost/ReportServer?/Custom+Reporting/Product+Profitability*** to access the report shown here:

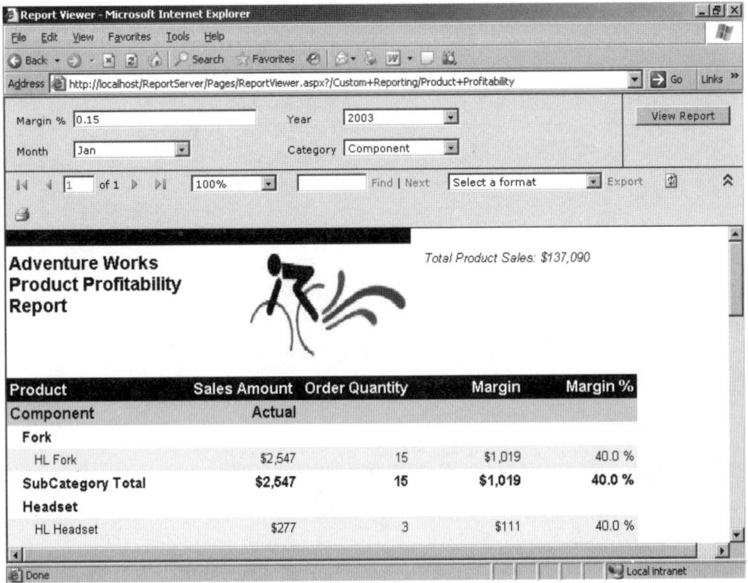

Instead of navigating the folder hierarchy of Report Server, you can go directly to a specific report when you know the URL.

Working with Report Parameters

When using URLs to access reports, you can decide how report parameters should be handled. To override the default values established for the report, you can specify which values should be set when the report is rendered by including a name/value pair for each parameter that you want to change. To do this, add a string to the URL that uses the following syntax: `&rc:ParameterName=ParameterValue`. All URLs are sent as plain text, so use Secure Sockets Layer (SSL) when parameters include confidential data.

By default, the report is displayed in the browser window with the HTML Viewer toolbar, which includes a Parameters area for selecting alternate values. The values that you specify in the URL will be displayed in the Parameters area, but a user can also select new values. If allowing changes to parameters is not required, you can hide the Parameters area by including the following URL access parameter: `&rc:Parameters=false`. Hiding the Parameters area makes more room available for viewing the report in the browser window; it isn't intended as a security feature when accessing reports using URLs. A user can still see the parameter values in the URL string and even change the values by changing the URL string.

In this procedure, you'll change the value of the *Category* report parameter to *Bike*, and then you'll hide the Parameters area of the HTML Viewer toolbar.

Control report parameters

1. In the Address box of Internet Explorer, type ***http://localhost/ReportServer?/Custom+Reporting/Product+Profitability&Category=2***.

   Your screen looks like this:

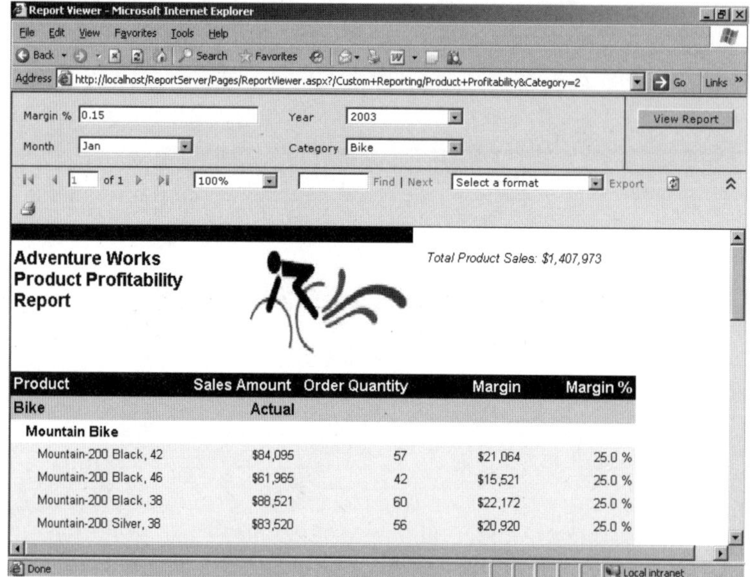

   The *Category* report parameter requires a value in the URL rather than the label that is displayed in the corresponding list box in the report itself. You can still use the list box to change the value for this or any other report parameter associated with this report.

> **Important** When supplying parameter values in a URL, you need to know the valid values. In this example, 2 is the value that the Bike label represents. If you try to use `&Category=Bike` to set the report parameter value in this URL, an error will result.

2. Type the following URL in Internet Explorer: ***http://localhost/ReportServer?/Custom+Reporting/Product+Profitability&Category=2&rc:Parameters=false***.

Your screen looks like this:

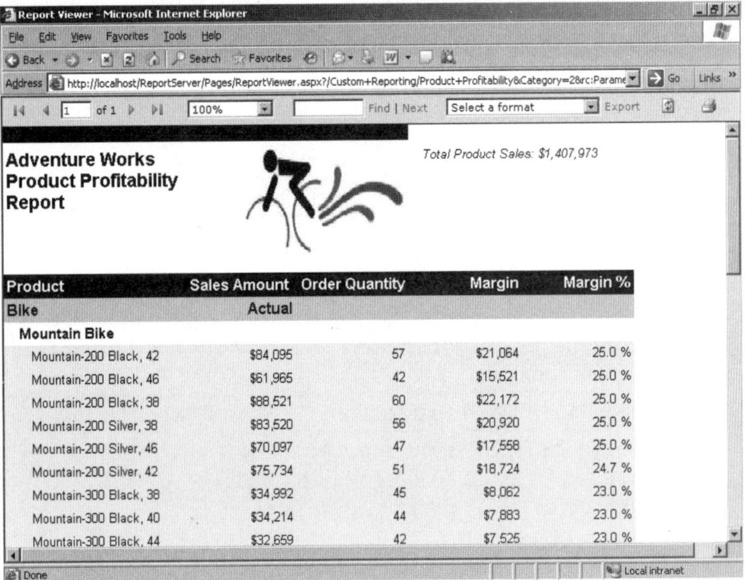

By hiding the Parameters area of the HTML Viewer toolbar, you can see more of the report in the browser window. The only way to change report parameter values now is to change the URL.

Note When you use URL access parameters to access and display a report, the report parameters and their values are visible in the browser. A user can change the URL by replacing parameter values or by removing the parameters from the URL. The only way to keep these details hidden from view is to programmatically render the report, which you'll learn how to do later in this chapter.

Using URL Access Parameters

URL access parameters provide you with additional options for controlling both what you see and what you get. In the previous section, you learned how to hide the Parameters area of the HTML Viewer toolbar. You can also control other features of this toolbar, and thereby affect how the report is displayed, by including the corresponding URL access parameters in the URL request. Some URL access parameters are specific to Report Server and give you control over what is delivered in response to your request, such as a particular rendered format or a report snapshot from a certain point in time. Finally, you can use a pair of URL access parameters to pass credentials to a data source.

All URL access parameters that affect the HTML Viewer use the following syntax: **`&rc:URLAccessParameterName=URLAccessParameterValue`**. The name/value pairs for this group of URL access parameters are shown in the following table:

Use	To	Like this
DocMap	Hide a document map.	`&rc:DocMap=false`
FallbackPage	Display a specific page if a search fails.	`&rc:FallbackPage=1`
FindString	Locate a string in a report. Use with *StartFind* and *EndFind* to define the range of pages to search.	`&rc:FindString=helmet&rc:StartFind=1&rcEndFind=5`
Section	Display the specified page.	`&rc:Section=10`
Parameters	Hide the parameters section of the HTML Viewer toolbar.	`&rc:Parameters=false`
Toolbar	Hide the HTML Viewer toolbar.	`&rc:Toolbar=false`

Zoom	Resize the report to the specified percentage (expressed as an integer) or to the fit defined by *Page Width* or *Whole Page*.	`&rc:Zoom=75`
		 or
		 `&rc:Zoom=Whole Page`

Note You can omit *DocMap*, *Parameters*, or *Toolbar* if you want to display these items. The default value for these parameters is true, and you do not need to explicitly include them in the URL request.

You can also include device-specific information in a URL access parameter using the **`&rc:`** prefix. In this case, the name/value pair is the name of the device information settings element and its corresponding value. For example, if you are rendering to a comma separated file (CSV) format, you can replace the default file extension of .csv with another extension, such as .txt. To do this, use this parameter: *&rc:Extension=.TXT*.

Note There are too many device information settings to be included in this book. However, you can learn more about the settings available for each rendering extension by reviewing the topic, "Reporting Services Device Information Settings," in SQL Server Books Online.

The URL access parameters that control Report Server use the same syntax that you use for parameters affecting the HTML Viewer, except that **`&rc:`** is replaced by **`&rs:`**. You can potentially improve the performance of a request if you use the *Command* parameter. Because the value that you supply for *Command* describes what you're asking for, Report Server does not have to look up the item type and determine the response. When you want to view a report, use *&rs:Command=Render*. If you're interested in seeing a list of items contained in a specified folder, use *&rs:Command=ListChildren*. To view the XML representation of a data source, use *GetDataSourceContents*. Report Server's response to *&rs:Command=GetResourceContents* depends on whether the item can be viewed in the browser and whether Report Server needs to prompt you to open or save the file.

The complete set of URL access parameters that controls Report Server is shown in the following table:

Use	To	Like this
Command	Identify the request to Report Server to improve performance. Valid values: *Render, ListChildren, GetDataSourceContents,* and *GetResourceContents.*	`&rs:Command=ListChildren`
Format	Specify a rendering format. Valid values: XML, NULL, CSV, IMAGE, PDF, RGDI, HTML4.0, HTML3.2, MHTML, and EXCEL.	`&rs:Format=EXCEL`
Snapshot	Render the snapshot created at the specified date and time.	`&rs:Snapshot=2004-06-23T15:45:21`

If the report uses a data source that prompts for credentials, you can pass those credentials as URL access parameters. You pass credentials using the following syntax: *&dsu:DataSourceName=username&dsp:DataSourceName=password*. For example, if your data source is SqlOrder01 and the ReportExecution user has read access to this data source, you can add *&dsu:SqlOrder01=ReportExecution&dsp:SqlOrder01=ReportExecution* to the URL request for a report.

Important Any parameters passed as part of the URL, including credentials, are sent as clear text. Using SSL will encrypt the data during transfer. However, if you embedded a URL that includes credentials in a Web page link, the user will see the unencrypted credentials in the URL that is displayed in the browser.

In this procedure, you'll use URL access parameters to hide the HTML Viewer toolbar as you display a report, to render a report to a Portable Document Format (PDF) file, and to list the contents of a folder.

Add URL access parameters to a URL

1. In Internet Explorer, type the URL: ***http://localhost/ReportServer?/Custom+Reporting/Product+Profitability&rc:Toolbar=false*** to view the report without the toolbar, as shown here:

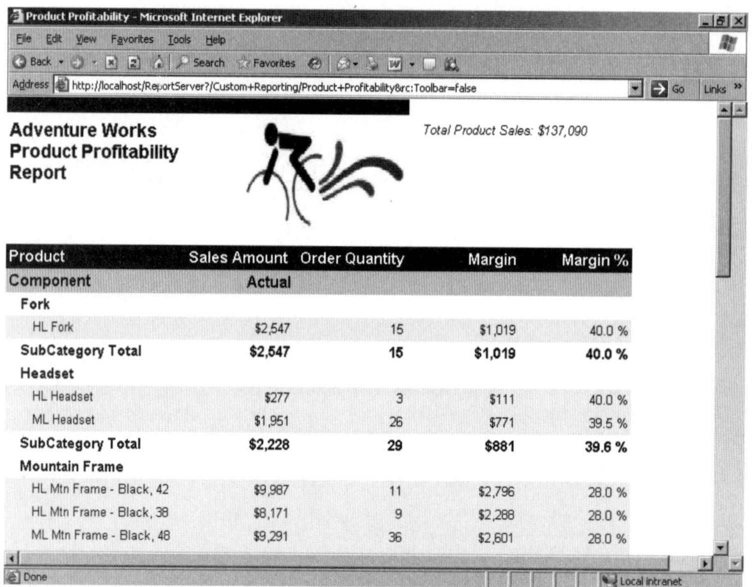

   When you hide the toolbar using the *Toolbar* parameter, you also automatically hide the Parameters area, so you can omit the *Parameters* parameter in the URL.

2. Export the report by typing the URL: ***http://localhost/ReportServer?/Custom+Reporting/Product+Profitability&rs:Format=PDF.***

3. Click Open to view the rendered report, which looks like this:

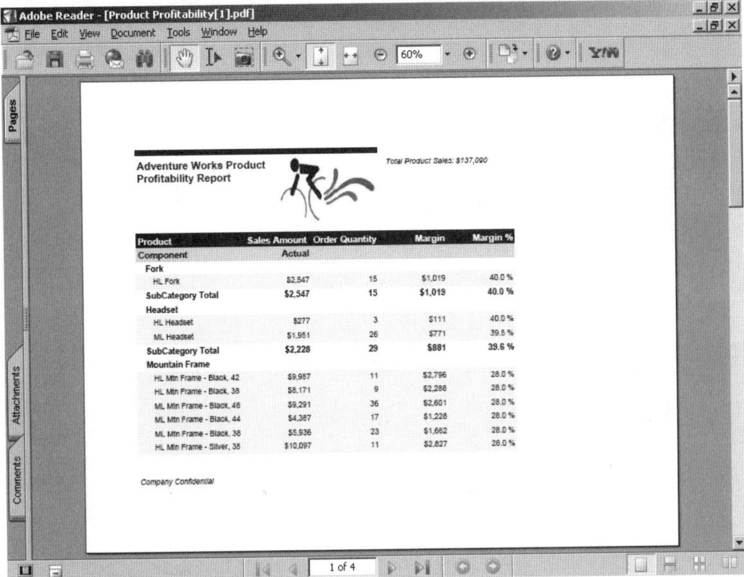

Adventure Works Product Profitability Report

Total Product Sales: $137,090

Product	Sales Amount	Order Quantity	Margin	Margin %
Component	Actual			
Fork				
HL Fork	$2,547	15	$1,019	40.0 %
SubCategory Total	**$2,547**	**15**	**$1,019**	**40.0 %**
Headset				
HL Headset	$277	3	$111	40.0 %
ML Headset	$1,951	26	$771	39.5 %
SubCategory Total	**$2,228**	**29**	**$881**	**39.6 %**
Mountain Frame				
HL Mtn Frame - Black, 42	$9,987	11	$2,796	28.0 %
HL Mtn Frame - Black, 38	$8,171	9	$2,288	28.0 %
ML Mtn Frame - Black, 48	$9,291	36	$2,601	28.0 %
ML Mtn Frame - Black, 44	$4,387	17	$1,228	28.0 %
ML Mtn Frame - Black, 38	$5,936	23	$1,662	28.0 %
HL Mtn Frame - Silver, 38	$10,097	11	$2,827	28.0 %

Company Confidential

You can choose to render a report using a format other than HTML by specifying the desired format in the URL. As long as you have a viewer application for the requested format, such as Adobe Acrobat for the PDF format, you can open the requested report or save the report to your computer.

4. Close the PDF file.

5. To list the contents of the Custom Reporting folder, type the following URL: ***http://localhost/ReportServer?/Custom+Reporting/&rs:Command=ListChildren***.

Your screen looks like this:

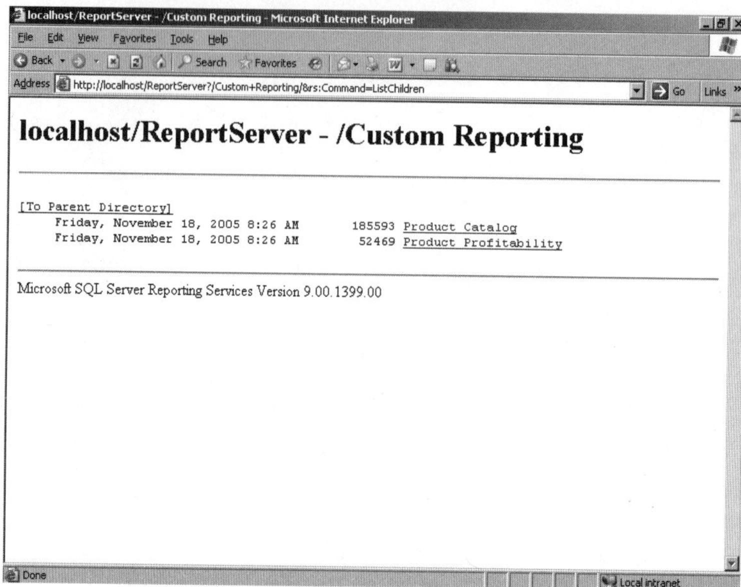

You're not limited to viewing reports when using URLs. You can also view resources or data sources, as well as the contents of a specified folder, as shown in the previous illustration. Alternatively, you could use *http://localhost/ReportServer?/Custom+Reporting* to view the contents of this folder. However, the addition of the *&rs:Command=ListChildren* parameter eliminates the need for Report Server to determine the type of item being requested, thus speeding up the return of the requested information–in this case, the list of items contained in the Custom Reporting folder.

Using the Web Service

When you need a higher degree of integration with existing applications or more control over what users can see or do, you can create a custom reporting tool. If you built a custom management tool, for example, you might want to include the capability to preview a selected report. Whether you need to provide a reporting tool to Windows users or to Web users, you can easily develop an application that provides as little or as much functionality as requirements dictate. You can even build applications to use data from selected reports as a data source for another application, such as an order entry system that can take your Reporting Services purchase orders as input.

In Chapter 17, "Programming Report Server Management," you learned how to use the Reporting Services Web service to manage Report Server. Using the Web service to provide access to reports in a custom application is very similar. For both types of tools, you create an application that includes a Web reference to the Reporting Services Web service and you authenticate the current user. In your reporting tool, you can use the *Render()* method to display a report, incorporate URL access into an application, or use the *ReportViewer* control.

You can build a reporting tool in so many ways that outlining all your possible approaches is a daunting task. Because Reporting Services already provides a feature-rich reporting environment, you should need to develop a custom application to satisfy only specific requirements. Taking a simple approach, you can build a reporting tool that allows the user to render a report by double-clicking a report name that is displayed in a list. You can display the rendered output in the application, display the results in a browser window opened by the application, or write the output to a file in a specified location.

Another approach is to modify the functionality of a report. For example, you can incorporate your own security measures rather than rely strictly on the Reporting Services security model. Additionally, if you want greater control over how users can use parameters, you can wrap an application around a report to provide your own interface for selecting parameter values. In your custom application, you can use a *ListBox* control to allow the user to select multiple values, and then pass the selection to Report Server for rendering the report. With these examples in mind, you can begin to understand how you can leverage the Reporting Services platform to augment the reporting capabilities that it provides.

Rendering a Report

To view a report, you need to send a request to Report Server to either render it or retrieve a rendered report snapshot. The Reporting Services Report Execution Web Service includes the *Render()* method as the interface for packaging this request. At a minimum, you use the *Render()* method to specify the full path to the report and the format to use for rendering. You can also pass arguments to identify a snapshot, provide values for report parameters, specify device-specific information required for rendering, or include credentials for a data source.

You aren't required to display the report returned by the *Render()* method. The result is actually stored as a byte array that you can use any way that you like. For example, you can bind the byte array to a control in a form, or you can generate the results as a file.

The *Render()* method uses the following syntax: `Render(Format, DeviceInfo, Extension, MimeType, Encoding, Warnings(), StreamIDs())`. Only the *Format* argument is required. The *Format* argument is the name of the rendering extension that is defined in the Report Server configuration file. The available rendering extensions included with Reporting Services (if you haven't added extensions or removed any of the default rendering extensions) are XML, NULL, CSV, IMAGE, PDF, HTML4.0, HTML3.2, MHTML, and EXCEL.

The remaining arguments are optional and are described in the following list. Many of them perform functions that are similar to those of the URL access parameters described earlier in this chapter. When using the *Render()* method, however, you still must include a value for each argument by assigning the Microsoft Visual Basic .NET keyword *Nothing* (or *null* if you're using Microsoft Visual C# .NET).

- ***DeviceInfo*** Build an XML string to pass the device information settings, which are specific to the selected rendering extension. For example, you might want to embed a report in an existing HTML page rather than display it as a separate page. In this case, use the string *<DeviceInfo><HTMLFragment>True</HTMLFragment></DeviceInfo>* as the DeviceInfo argument.
- ***Extension*** The Report Server returns the file extension that was used to produce the output stream.
- ***MimeType*** You can test the Multipurpose Internet Mail Extensions (MIME) type returned by Report Server if you want to add code to make sure the browser can handle the MIME type of the report format.
- ***Encoding*** The Report Server also returns the encoding used to render the output.
- ***Warnings()*** You should always test this array of *Warning* objects to uncover any problems encountered during report processing.
- ***StreamIDs()*** You use the Stream IDs when using the *RenderStream()* method to get external resources associated with the report, such as images.

In this procedure, you'll add a control to a Windows application as a container for rendering a report to a CSV format.

Render output to a RichTextBox

1. Copy the myRSManagerVB folder from the C:\Documents and Settings\<username>\My Documents\Microsoft Press\rs2005sbs\chap17 folder to the C:\Documents and Settings\<username>\My Documents\Microsoft Press\rs2005sbs\Workspace folder.

> **Note** If you skipped Chapter 17, copy the myRSManagerVB folder from the C:\Documents and Settings\<username>\My Documents\Microsoft Press\rs2005sbs\Answers \chap17 folder to the Workspace folder. The steps in this procedure build on the application completed in Chapter 17.

2. Start a new instance of Visual Studio and open the myRSManagerVB solution in the myRSManagerVB folder.
3. In Solution Explorer, double-click myRSManager.vb to open the form.
4. In the Properties window, change the *Height* property of the form (in the Size category) to 545.
5. In the Toolbox window, double-click *RichTextBox* to add the control to the form.

6. In the Properties window, change the following properties of *RichTextBox1* to the values indicated in this table:

Property	Value
Size: Width	728
Size: Height	250
Location: X	0
Location: Y	256

Your screen looks similar to this:

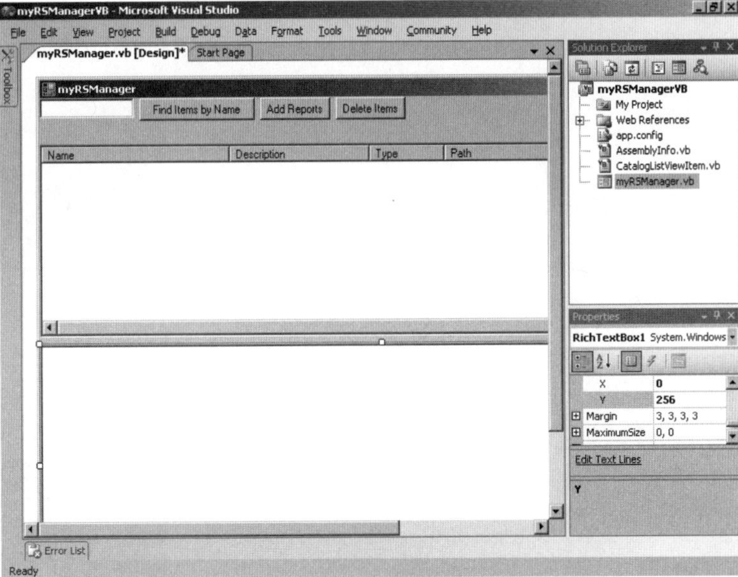

7. Right-click the form, and then click View Code.
8. In the Class Name list at the top of the page, click *ListView1*.
9. In the Method Name list, click *DoubleClick* to add the method to the code page.
10. Copy the contents of C:\Documents and Settings\<username>\My Documents \Microsoft Press\rs2005sbs\chap18\ListView_DoubleClickVB.txt into the *ListView1_DoubleClick* method to add the following code:

```
'Create an instance of the proxy class for the execution service
Dim myReportExecutionService As New ReportExecutionService.ReportExecutionService()
myReportExecutionService.Url = "http://localhost/ReportServer/
ReportExecution2005.asmx?wsdl"
myReportExecutionService.Credentials =
System.Net.CredentialCache.DefaultCredentials
```

```
'Load the report in preparation for execution
Dim execInfo As New ReportExecutionService.ExecutionInfo
execInfo =
myReportExecutionService.LoadReport(myCatalogItems(ListView1.SelectedIndices.Item(
0)).Path, Nothing)

'Declare a byte array to store the results of the Render() method and
'a variable to specify Unicode encoding
Dim myDefinitionBytes As Byte()
Dim myEncoding As System.Text.Encoding = System.Text.Encoding.Unicode

Try
    'Pass the path of the selected item in the ListView to the Render() method
    'and render to a CSV format. Include the Nothing keyword as a placeholder
    'for the optional arguments. Store the results in a byte array.

    myDefinitionBytes = myReportExecutionService.Render("CSV", _
    Nothing, Nothing, Nothing, Nothing, Nothing, Nothing)

    'Place the contents of the byte array into the RichTextBox control
    'after translating the byte array into a Unicode string
    RichTextBox1.Text = myEncoding.GetString(myDefinitionBytes)
Catch ex As Exception
    'For a production environment, you should create
    'specific error-handling routines.
    Throw New Exception("Attempt to render failed.")
End Try
```

Note This example is just one way of handling the output of the *Render()* method. Other options include writing the output to an *HttpResponse* object or to the file system.

11. In Solution Explorer, right-click the Project folder, and then click Add Web Reference.
12. In the URL text box, type ***http://localhost/ReportServer/ReportExecution2005.asmx?wsdl***, and then click Go.
13. In the Web Reference Name text box, replace the default value with **ReportExecutionService**.
14. Click Add Reference.
15. Save the file, and then press F5 to run the application.
16. Type **product profit** in the textbox at the top of the form, and then click Find Items By Name.
17. Double-click the Product Profitability report (with path /Custom Reporting/Product Profitability) to view the report in the form, similar to this:

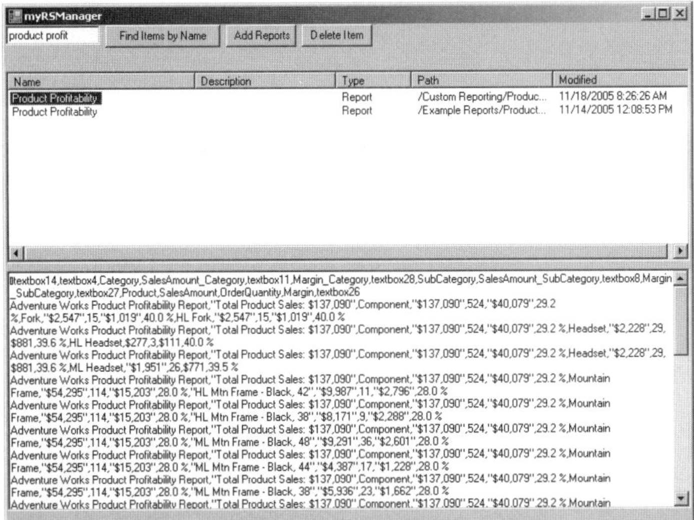

The CSV format of the report is displayed in the *RichTextBox* control. If you need to use information from a report as source data for another application, you can use this form to preview the contents of a report before saving the contents to a file. You can also extend the functionality of this application by adding a button to save the render output to a file or change the functionality of the double-click to open a browser window if you want to view the report in HTML format. In fact, now that you know how to render a report programmatically, there's no limit to the possibilities for incorporating reporting functionality into your own applications.

> **Tip** The FindRenderSave sample application included with Reporting Services shows how to save a rendered report to a file. You can find this application's solution files in the C:\Program Files\Microsoft SQL Server 2005 Samples\ReportingServices\Application Samples\FindRenderSave Sample folder if you have installed the samples that ship with SQL Server 2005.

18. Close the myRSManager application.

Authenticating Users

When you build a custom application, you can integrate with an existing security infrastructure and then pass credentials that are recognized by Reporting Services. The procedures that you have completed in this and the preceding two chapters pass the current user's credentials to Reporting Services. An ASP.NET application will run using its own account, but you can either override this and impersonate the current user or integrate your own authentication process. To impersonate the current user, add the following code to the Web.config file of your application: `<identity impersonate="true" />`.

In this procedure, you'll create a Web application that uses integrated Windows security and impersonates the current user.

Add identity impersonation to a Web application

1. In Visual Studio, create a new website project by using the ASP.NET Web Site template in the Visual Studio installed templates folder. In the Location box, type ***http://localhost/myReportVB***, and then click OK.
2. Open Internet Information Services (IIS) Manager, expand nodes to reach the Default Web Site node, right-click the myReportVB virtual directory, and then click Properties.
3. Click the Directory Security tab of the myReportVB Properties dialog box, and then click Edit for Authentication and Access Control.
4. Clear the Enable Anonymous Access check box, and then, if necessary, select the Integrated Windows Authentication check box.

   The Authentication Methods dialog box looks like this:

   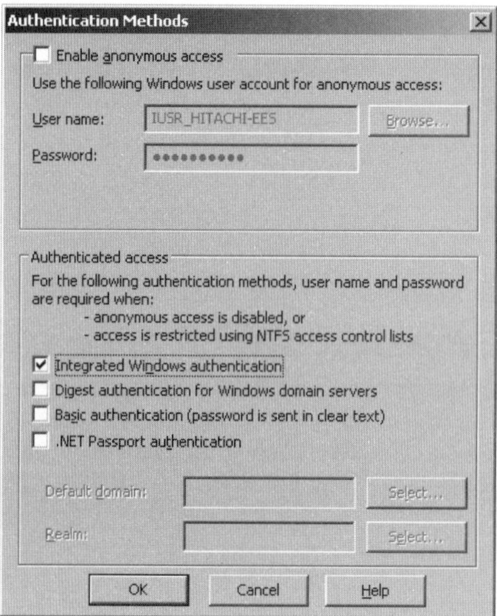

5. Click OK twice to close all dialog boxes, and then close Internet Information Services Manager.
6. In Solution Explorer, double-click the Web.config file, and then add the following code to the Authentication section of the file:

```
<identity impersonate="true" />
```

Your screen looks like this:

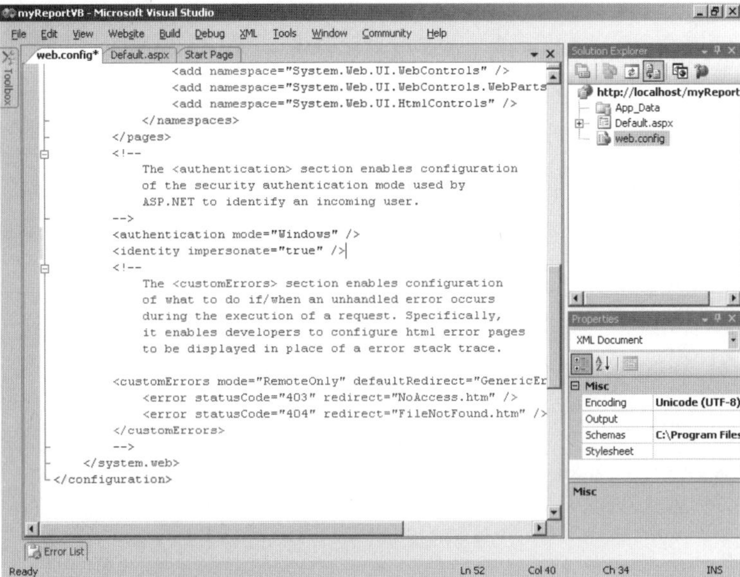

Now the application will authenticate using the current user's credentials rather than use the ASP.NET account.

> **Important** Be sure to use "true" instead of "True" because this value is case-sensitive. Otherwise, you'll get an error when you try to run the application.

7. Save and then close the Web.config file.

   Now you're ready to add functionality to your Web application. In the next two sections, you'll learn how to retrieve report parameters for display in a Web Control and how to render a report as part of a Web application.

Using Report Parameters in a Control

As you learned earlier in this chapter, using a URL to access a report and specify its parameter values isn't secure. A user can easily manipulate the URL to alter parameter values. If you want to prevent a user from viewing or changing the parameter values that are passed to Report Server, you can develop an application to display a report and manage the parameter interface.

As you learned in a previous section of this chapter, you can use the *Render()* method of the report execution Web service to get output from the report server and display that output in a form. Another way to display a report is to use the *ReportViewer* control, which is not a Reporting Services control. It is instead distributed with Visual Studio 2005 because this control has many uses beyond the scope of Reporting Services. In this chapter, you'll learn only how to use the *ReportViewer* control in "remote mode" to render a report stored on a Report Server.

The *ReportViewer* control includes the standard parameter interface, but you aren't required to use it if you prefer greater control. For example, you can filter the available parameter values to display a subset of values, or you can set alternate default values. To create a parameter interface, you first retrieve the parameters by using the *GetParameters()* method of the *ServerReport* class, which is bound to the *ReportViewer* control. Then, you bind report parameters to a control, such as a *ListBox, DropDownList*, or *TextBox*.

In this procedure, you'll add an interface to the Web application that allows selection of report parameter values before rendering a report.

Display available parameter values in a *ListBox* control

1. In Solution Explorer, double-click Default.aspx to open the Web page. Copy the contents of the Table.txt file in the C:\Documents and Settings\<username>\My Documents\Microsoft Press\rs2005sbs\chap18 folder and paste between the *<div></div>* tags so that your screen looks like this:

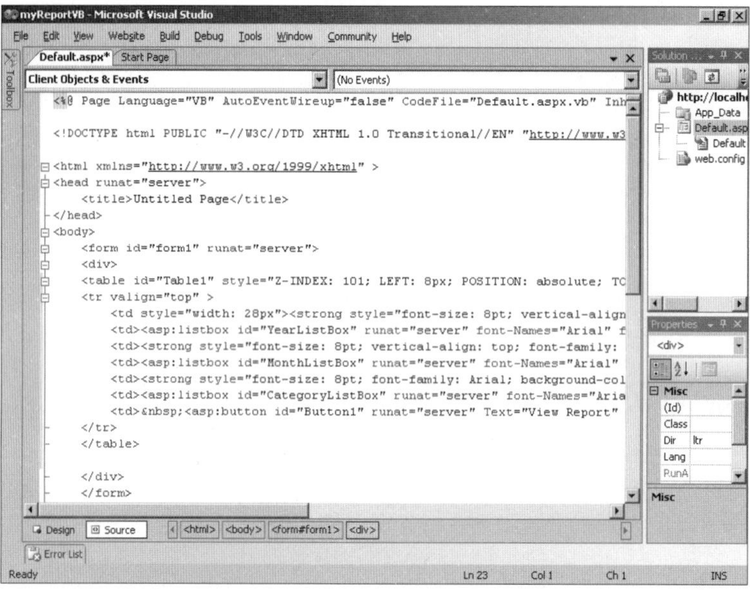

   This HTML code defines a table that contains list boxes to which you will bind parameter values defined for the report.

2. Click the Design tab of the Default.aspx file, drag the *ReportViewer* control from the Toolbox onto the page, right-click the *ReportViewer* control, click Style, click Position, click Absolutely Position in the Position Mode list, and then set properties to values indicated in the following table:

Property	Value
Top	100 px
Left	8 px

Property	Value
Height	400 px
Width	800 px

The Style Builder dialog box looks like this:

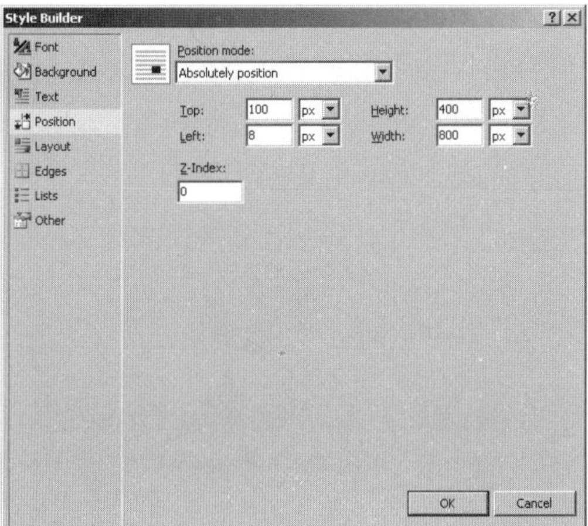

3. Click OK.

   Your screen looks like this:

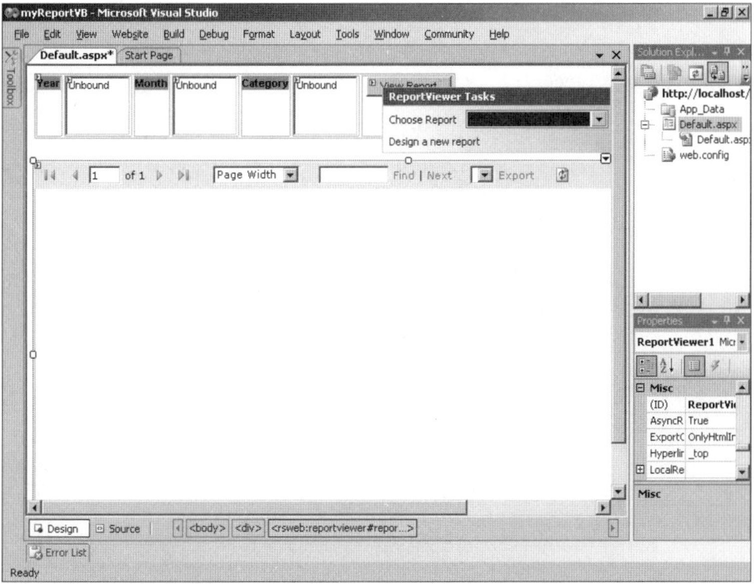

Notice the three list boxes that will contain the available values for the *Year*, *Month*, and *Category* report parameters. List boxes are used in this procedure for simplicity as well as to demonstrate the multiple selection of values later in this chapter. For your own applications, you can also use a drop-down list or a textbox to display parameter values.

4. In the ReportViewer Tasks dialog box, click <Server Report> in the Choose Report list, type ***http://localhost/ReportServer*** in the Report Server Url box, and type **/Custom Reporting/Product Profitability** in the Report Path box.

   These property settings define "remote mode" processing for the Product Profitability report, which will be retrieved from and processed on the specified report server. Using "local mode," you can process and render reports without using Reporting Services. For more information, refer to Microsoft Visual Studio 2005 Documentation.

   The report to render in this application is hard-coded as a property to keep things simple. You learned in Chapter 17 how to retrieve a list of reports and find their paths. After completing this chapter, you could incorporate that logic if you want to practice your skills by adding more flexibility to this application through the programmatic changes to the *ReportServerUrl* and *ReportPath* properties of the report viewer's *ServerReport* object.

5. In the Properties window, locate the *ShowParameterPrompts* property (in the Appearance section) for *ReportViewer1* and change its value to False.

6. Double-click the form background to open the code page.

7. At the top of the page, type the following statement to make the report viewer library available to all members of the web form's class:

```
Imports Microsoft.Reporting.WebForms
```

8. Paste the contents of the PageLoadVB.txt in the C:\Documents and Settings \<username>\My Documents\Microsoft Press\rs2005sbs\chap18 folder into the *Page_Load()* method to add the following code:

```
If Not IsPostBack Then
    'Use the GetParameters() method to retrieve the parameters
    'for the specified report.
    Dim parameters As ReportParameterInfoCollection =
 ReportViewer1.ServerReport.GetParameters()
    Dim i As Integer
    For i = 0 To parameters.Count - 1
        'Check each parameter to see if Available Values have been defined
        'Available Values are stored in the ValidValues property of the parameter
object
        If Not (parameters(i).ValidValues Is Nothing) Then
            'Assign the parameters to a ListBox control
            Select Case parameters(i).Name
        Case "Year"
            SetParameterValuesList(YearListBox, parameters(i))
```

```
Case "Month"
                SetParameterValuesList(MonthListBox, parameters(i))
            Case "Category"
                SetParameterValuesList(CategoryListBox, parameters(i))
                End Select
            End If
        Next
            End If
            'Process and render the report
            ReportViewer1.ServerReport.Refresh()
```

Again, to keep things simple, the assignment of parameters to *ListBox* controls is hard-coded using the *SetParameterValuesList* method that you will add in the next step. You can change this code to dynamically generate one control per parameter to make it more flexible.

9. Copy the contents of the SetParameterValuesListVB.txt file in the C:\Documents and Settings\<username>\My Documents\Microsoft Press\rs2005sbs\chap18 folder below the *Page_Load()* method to add the following code:

```
Private Sub SetParameterValuesList(ByVal CurrentListBox As ListBox, ByVal
CurrentParameter As ReportParameterInfo)
        Dim i As Integer
        'Iterate through each available value and add its label and value as new
ListBox item

        For i = 0 To CurrentParameter.ValidValues.Count - 1
            CurrentListBox.Items.Add(New
ListItem(CurrentParameter.ValidValues(i).Label, _
            CurrentParameter.ValidValues(i).Value))
        Next
        'Set the default value as the selected value in the ListBox
        Dim DefaultValue As String
        Dim item As ListItem
        For Each DefaultValue In CurrentParameter.Values
            For Each item In CurrentListBox.Items
                If item.Value = DefaultValue Then
                    item.Selected = True
                End If
            Next
        Next
    End Sub
```

If you want to limit the range of available values in the list, you can modify this code to evaluate each *Value* against business rules before adding it to the list box. Similarly, you can override the default values found in the *Values* collection of each parameter to set the *Selected* property according to your application's business rules.

10. Save the file, and then press F5 to test. Click OK to modify the Web.config file to enable debugging if prompted.

> **Important** Before deploying an application into production, you should update the Web.config file to disable debugging.

Your screen looks like this:

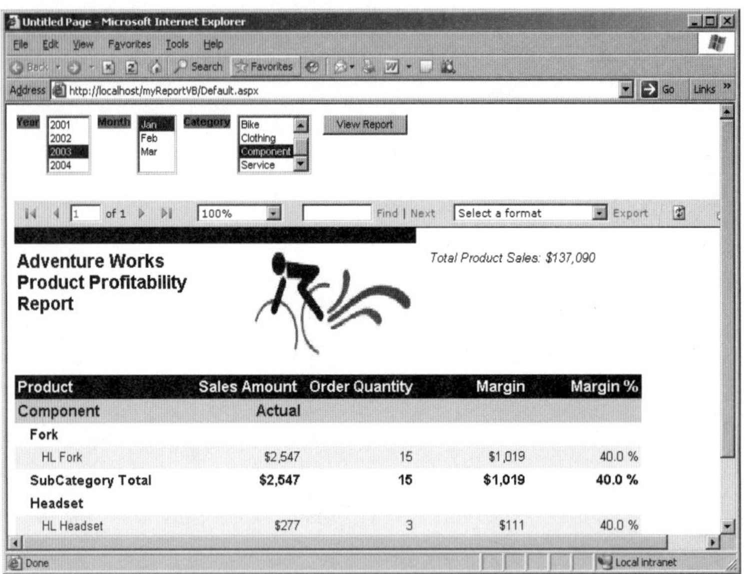

The available values for each parameter are displayed in each *ListBox* control. The selected value in each *ListBox* corresponds to the default value defined for the parameter. Now that you have an interface for displaying parameter values, you need to add code to the View Report button to change the parameters for the instantiated *ServerReport* object.

11. Close the browser window.

12. On the Default.aspx page, double-click View Report to automatically add a *Click* method for this button, and then copy the following code from the Button1_ClickVB.txt in the C:\Documents and Settings\<username>\My Documents\Microsoft Press\rs2005sbs \chap18 folder into the *Button1_Click* method:

```
Try
    'Add the current selected value from each listbox to an array of parameter
objects
    Dim myParameters(2) As ReportParameter
    myParameters(0) = GetParameterSelectedValue(YearListBox, "Year")
    myParameters(1) = GetParameterSelectedValue(MonthListBox, "Month")
    myParameters(2) = GetParameterSelectedValue(CategoryListBox, "Category")
```

```
        'Update the ServerReport object with the selected parameters and refresh
        ReportViewer1.ServerReport.SetParameters(myParameters)
        ReportViewer1.ServerReport.Refresh()

    Catch ex As Exception
        'Insert error-handling code here
    End Try
```

13. Copy the contents of the GetParameterSelectedValueVB.txt in the C:\Documents and Settings\<username>\My Documents\Microsoft Press\rs2005sbs\chap18 folder below the *Button1_Click()* method to add the following code:

```
Private Function GetParameterSelectedValue(ByVal CurrentListBox As ListBox, ByVal
ParameterName As String) As ReportParameter
   Dim parameter As New ReportParameter(ParameterName, CurrentListBox.SelectedValue)
        Return parameter
End Function
```

14. Save the file, and then press F5 to test.
15. Select the parameter values as shown in the table below, and then click View Report.

Parameter	Value
Year	2002
Month	Feb
Category	Bike

Your screen looks like this:

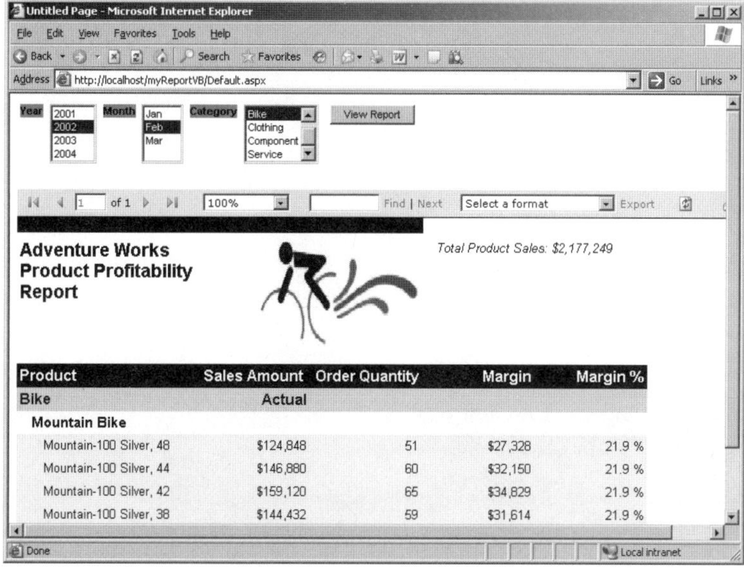

> **Tip** You can use security creatively if you want to control access to reports within Report Manager. You can block users from viewing the folder that contains the report in your application so that users can neither see nor open that folder in Report Manager. However, you can grant permission to the report within that folder so it can be accessed directly by an application. (It can also be accessed directly by URL). This technique is useful when you have reports that you display in a controlled interface, such as the parameter interface implemented here.

16. Close the browser window.

Enabling Multiselect for Parameters

If you want to use multiple values for a parameter, you can design a Web application that uses the multiple selection mode of a *ListBox* control and then transform the selected values into a string collection of report parameters that can be used with the IN operator in the dataset query. This approach requires you to modify the report by adding a new parameter to contain the values selected by the user and by altering the dataset query to use the new parameter.

In this procedure, you'll modify both the report and the Web application to accept multiple values for the *Category* parameter.

Pass multiple values for a parameter as a unit

1. Switch to the Custom Reporting solution, open the Product Profitability report, and then click the Data tab.
2. On the Report menu, click Report Parameter, select Category in the Parameters list, and then select the Multi-value check box.

   The Report Parameters dialog box looks like this:

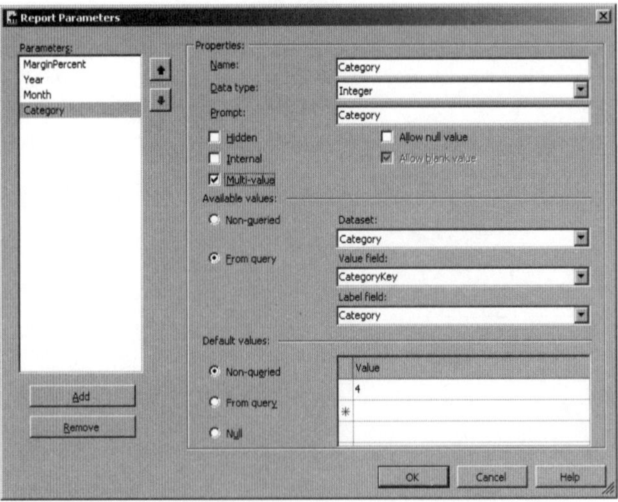

Previously, the *Category* parameter was configured to accept only one value. Now, you have changed it to allow the user to select one or more values.

3. Click OK, and then replace `(CategoryKey = @Category)` with **(CategoryKey IN (@Category))**.
4. Save the file, and then deploy the report.
5. In the myReportVB solution, open the Default.aspx page, click the *CategoryListBox* control (which is third from the left), and then change its *SelectionMode* property to Multiple.

   Your screen looks like this:

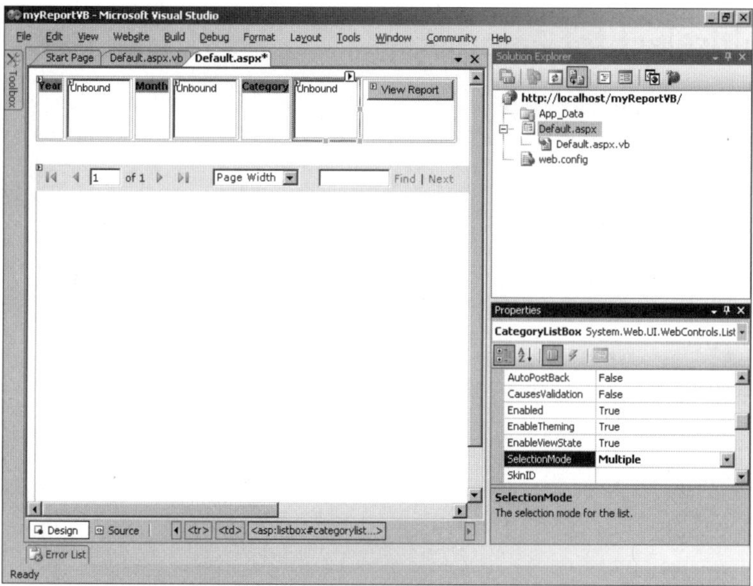

Now, you will need to modify the code that finds the selected value for this *ListBox* control so that you can combine the multiple values for a single report parameter.

6. Copy the contents of the GetParameterMultiSelectVB.txt in the C:\Documents and Settings\<username>\My Documents\Microsoft Press\rs2005sbs\chap18 folder below the *GetParameterSelectedValue()* method to add the following code:

```
Private Function GetParameterMultiSelect(ByVal CurrentListBox As ListBox, ByVal
ParameterName As String) As ReportParameter
        Dim parameter As New ReportParameter
        Dim item As ListItem

        parameter.Name = ParameterName
        For Each item In CurrentListBox.Items
            If item.Selected Then
                parameter.Values.Add(item.Value)
            End If
        Next
        Return parameter
    End Function
```

7. Change the assignment for *myParameters(2)* in the *Button1_Click()* method so that the code looks like this:

```
myParameters(2) = GetParameterMultiSelect(CategoryListBox, "CategoryString")
```

8. Press F5 to start, select Accessory and Bike in the Category list (pressing the Ctrl key to select multiple categories), then click View Report.

   Your screen looks like this:

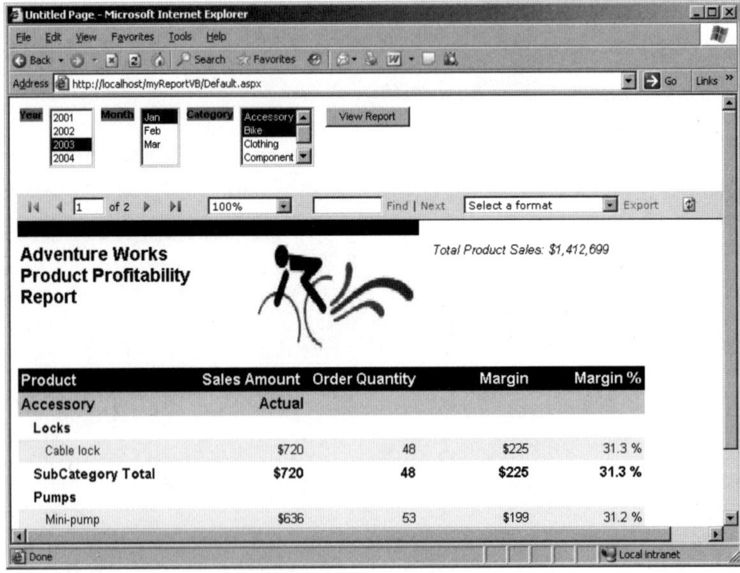

By clicking the Next Page button on the report viewer toolbar, you can verify that the Bike category is also included in this report.

You have successfully created an application that uses the *ReportViewer* control with a custom parameter interface to pass single or multiple values to a report parameter.

By completing the procedures outlined in this book, you have developed the skills you need to successfully implement and manage Reporting Services. You can now understand how the Reporting Services components work together to support the reporting life cycle as well as how to develop custom applications to integrate this functionality into your environment. With this foundation, you're ready to put what you've learned into practice by developing, deploying, and delivering your own reports!

Chapter 18 Quick Reference

To	Do this
Display a report by using URLs	Navigate the folder hierarchy starting from *http://localhost/ReportServer* to locate the report. *or* Type the URL of the report in your browser. For example: *http://localhost /ReportServer?/Custom+Reporting/Product+Profitability*.
Specify report parameter values in a URL	Create a string using the following syntax `&rc:ParameterName=ParameterValue` and append the string to the URL. For example: *http://localhost/ReportServer?/Custom+Reporting/Product+Profitability&rc:Category=Bike*.
Control the features of the HTML Viewer	Create a string using the following syntax: `&rc:URLAccessParameterName=URLAccessParameterValue` and append the string to the URL. For example, to hide the HTML Viewer toolbar, use: *http://localhost/ReportServer?/Custom+Reporting/Product+Profitability&rc:Toolbar=false*.
Control how Report Server retrieves items	Create a string using the following syntax `&rs:URLAccessParameterName=URLParameterValue` and append the string to the URL. For example: *http://localhost/ReportServer?/Custom+Reporting &rs:Format=PDF*.
Programmatically render a report	Use the Reporting Services *Render()* method or use the Visual Studio 2005 *ReportViewer* control.
Impersonate a user in an ASP.NET application	Add `<identity impersonate="true" />` to the Web.config file.
Create a parameter interface	Bind the results of the *ReportViewer1.ServerReport.GetParameters()* method to a *ListBox*, *DropDownList*, or *TextBox* control. Test each control for a selected value and pass that value as a *ReportParameter* object using the report viewer's *SetParameters()* method.
Allow the selection of multiple values for a single parameter	Create one report parameter to store values used to display options to the user and bind these values, using the *GetParameters()* method, to a *ListBox* control with the *SelectionMode* property set to Multiple. After requesting a new report (by pressing a button, for example), iterate through the items in the list box, add the selected item values to a ReportParameter object, and then refresh the report.

Glossary

action An interactive feature that is used to access information located in another place, whether in a separate section of the same report, in a completely different report, or in a Web page on an intranet or external Web site.

ad hoc reporting Reviewing, and possibly sharing, limited information with limited formatting requirements on an as-needed basis.

cached instance A temporary version of a report stored in the ReportServerTempDB to be used for rendering in response to multiple requests.

calculated field An expression added to a dataset that can be used in a data region as if it were part of the original dataset.

conditional formatting A change to the appearance of an item, such as a font size or background color, based on the result of evaluating a Boolean expression.

data region A report layout structure that contains data, such as a table or matrix.

data source view (DSV) An XML file used to describe the structures and relationships in a data source and to define logical tables, columns, or relationships that do not exist in the data source. The data source view is used as a source object for generating a report model.

data-driven subscription A subscription that uses a database query to set delivery options.

dataset Information used to retrieve data for a report, such as a query and a pointer to the data source, as well as information used when the query executes, such as a time-out value or a query parameter value.

declarative model A model that describes output rather than the series of instructions required to produce the output.

deploy Publish a report to the report server.

dynamic visibility An interactive feature that enables a user to click an item to toggle the state of an item between hidden and visible.

enterprise reporting Sharing of information on a regular basis across a wide audience.

enterprise reporting life cycle The process of authoring, managing, and accessing reports.

extensions Subcomponents of Report Server used to provide specific functionality, such as data processing, rendering, report processing, authentication, and delivery.

global variable A variable that is a member of the *Globals* collection used to access information unique to a report, such as the current page number or the total number of pages in a report.

group A set of detail rows that are organized by a common field.

intermediate format The result of merging data from a query with layout information from a report definition. The intermediate format is sent to a rendering extension to produce the final output, such as an HTML page or an Excel file.

item A report, image file, report model, folder, data source, or other file uploaded to the report server.

item role assignment An association between a security role and an item on the report server.

linked report A report that is based on a report definition and data source, but which has its own execution, parameter, subscription, and security properties. A linked report is often used to customize a single report for different users.

multidimensional expressions (MDX) An expression language used with Analysis Services to model database objects and to retrieve values from an Analysis Services cube.

Named Calculation A logical column added to the definition of a physical table, which is analogous to a derived column in a view defined in a relational database.

Named Query A logical table defined in a data source view, which is analogous to a view in a relational database.

perspective A subset of entities, attributes, and roles defined in a report model used to simplify the available ojects for building ad hoc reports.

rendering The process of converting a report definition and the report data into a specified output format.

report Information that is structured and formatted for print or online viewing.

report consumer An application used to transform a report definition and query results into a final report.

report definition A description of a report's data, layout, and properties.

Report Definition Language (RDL) An open XML schema used to create a report definition.

report item An item used to display text or graphical elements in a report, such as a textbox, table, chart, or image, to name a few.

report item expression An expression that performs operations after processing is complete, which makes it useful for situations in which a calculation can be performed only after the dataset is aggregated and the calculation cannot be derived directly from the dataset.

report model A logical view of a relational database used to build ad hoc reports. The report model describes the database's tables and columns as well as the relationships between them.

report producer An application used to create a report definition.

report snapshot A report that preserves a record of data at a point in time. A report snapshot is stored in the ReportServer database in its intermediate format and rendered only when a user requests the report.

scope A set of rows, or grouping, used to cacluate an aggregated value, or alternately, an entire data region or dataset.

source field A reference to a column defined in a data source view that is added to the report model after the report model is generated.

stored credentials A combination of user name and password that is encrypted and stored in the ReportServer database to allow unattended execution of reports. Stored credentials are required for snapshots and subscriptions.

subreport A report item used to display another report inside the current report.

system role assignment An association between a security role and a server-wide administrative task, such as schedule management.

table A collection of cells organized into a fixed number of columns. A table can have either detail rows or group rows, or both detail and group rows.

Index

C

D

E

F

G

L

M

N

O

P

T

U

V

W

X

Z

About the Authors

Stacia Misner manages Hitachi Consulting's education services practice, specializes in developing training and solutions for business intelligence (BI) and enterprise reporting, and delivers BI training world-wide. She has more than 20 years' experience as an IT consultant and educator, with experience in project management, life-cycle data warehouse design and development, and software development life-cycle management. Stacia is the author of both *Microsoft SQL Server 2000 Reporting Services Step by Step*, and *Microsoft SQL Server 2005 Reporting Services Step by Step*, and coauthor of *Business Intelligence: Making Better Decisions Faster*. She lives in Las Vegas, NV, with her husband, Gerry, and their seven parrots.

As Hitachi, Ltd.'s (NYSE: HIT) global consulting company, Hitachi Consulting is a recognized leader in delivering proven business and IT solutions to Global 2000 companies across many industries. We leverage decades of business process, vertical industry, and leading-edge technology experience to understand each company's unique business needs. From business strategy development through application deployment, our consultants are committed to helping clients quickly realize measurable business value and achieve sustainable return on investment. Hitachi Consulting is also a Microsoft Certified Gold Partner for Business Intelligence, an exclusive provider of curriculum and instructors for Microsoft's SQL Server 2005 Business Intelligence Ascend training program, and an experienced systems integrator with successful SQL Server 2005 BI implementations at companies participating in Microsoft's Technology Adoption Program (TAP). We offer a client-focused, collaborative approach and transfer knowledge throughout each engagement. For more information, visit *www.hitachiconsulting.com*. Hitachi Consulting – Inspiring your next success®.

Contributing Authors

Aaron Solomon, a Business Intelligence Architect at Hitachi Consulting, has been developing BI solutions for over six years. He has taught SQL Server 2000 and 2005 BI courses throughout the United States, and teaches courses for the University of Washington's Certificate Program in Database Management. He has engaged with a wide range of client business groups including accounting, mergers and acquisitions, data warehousing, IT, tax, and legal, and has worked on numerous projects that involved performing complex analysis on large data sets. He has a B.A. in Economics from the University of Washington. Aaron lives in the Seattle, WA, metro area with his wife, Darla, and their cats, Omar and Henry.

In addition, this book includes the contributions of many others who participated in the development or review of Hitachi Consulting's Reporting Services courseware: Elizabeth Vitt, Scot Reagin, David DuVarney, Steve Muise, Mark Dreessen, Shetu Yama, Pete Jevtic, and Susan O'Connell.

Additional Resources for Developers: Advanced Topics and Best Practices

Published and Forthcoming Titles from Microsoft Press

Code Complete, Second Edition

Steve McConnell • ISBN 0-7356-1967-0

For more than a decade, Steve McConnell, one of the premier authors and voices in the software community, has helped change the way developers write code—and produce better software. Now his classic book, *Code Complete*, has been fully updated and revised with best practices in the art and science of constructing software. Topics include design, applying good techniques to construction, eliminating errors, planning, managing construction activities, and relating personal character to superior software. This new edition features fully updated information on programming techniques, including the emergence of Web-style programming, and integrated coverage of object-oriented design. You'll also find new code examples—both good and bad—in C++, Microsoft® Visual Basic®, C#, and Java, although the focus is squarely on techniques and practices.

More About Software Requirements: Thorny Issues and Practical Advice

Karl E. Wiegers • ISBN 0-7356-2267-1

Have you ever delivered software that satisfied all of the project specifications, but failed to meet any of the customers expectations? Without formal, verifiable requirements—and a system for managing them—the result is often a gap between what developers think they're supposed to build and what customers think they're going to get. Too often, lessons about software requirements engineering processes are formal or academic, and not of value to real-world, professional development teams. In this follow-up guide to *Software Requirements*, Second Edition, you will discover even more practical techniques for gathering and managing software requirements that help you deliver software that meets project and customer specifications. Succinct and immediately useful, this book is a must-have for developers and architects.

Software Estimation: Demystifying the Black Art

Steve McConnell • ISBN 0-7356-0535-1

Often referred to as the "black art" because of its complexity and uncertainty, software estimation is not as hard or mysterious as people think. However, the art of how to create effective cost and schedule estimates has not been very well publicized. *Software Estimation* provides a proven set of procedures and heuristics that software developers, technical leads, and project managers can apply to their projects. Instead of arcane treatises and rigid modeling techniques, award-winning author Steve McConnell gives practical guidance to help organizations achieve basic estimation proficiency and lay the groundwork to continue improving project cost estimates. This book does not avoid the more complex mathematical estimation approaches, but the non-mathematical reader will find plenty of useful guidelines without getting bogged down in complex formulas.

Debugging, Tuning, and Testing Microsoft .NET 2.0 Applications

John Robbins • ISBN 0-7356-2202-7

Making an application the best it can be has long been a time-consuming task best accomplished with specialized and costly tools. With Microsoft Visual Studio® 2005, developers have available a new range of built-in functionality that enables them to debug their code quickly and efficiently, tune it to optimum performance, and test applications to ensure compatibility and trouble-free operation. In this accessible and hands-on book, debugging expert John Robbins shows developers how to use the tools and functions in Visual Studio to their full advantage to ensure high-quality applications.

The Security Development Lifecycle

Michael Howard and Steve Lipner • ISBN 0-7356-2214-0

Adapted from Microsoft's standard development process, the Security Development Lifecycle (SDL) is a methodology that helps reduce the number of security defects in code at every stage of the development process, from design to release. This book details each stage of the SDL methodology and discusses its implementation across a range of Microsoft software, including Microsoft Windows Server™ 2003, Microsoft SQL Server™ 2000 Service Pack 3, and Microsoft Exchange Server 2003 Service Pack 1, to help measurably improve security features. You get direct access to insights from Microsoft's security team and lessons that are applicable to software development processes worldwide, whether on a small-scale or a large-scale. This book includes a CD featuring videos of developer training classes.

Software Requirements, Second Edition
Karl E. Wiegers • ISBN 0-7356-1879-8

Writing Secure Code, Second Edition
Michael Howard and David LeBlanc • ISBN 0-7356-1722-8

CLR via C#, Second Edition
Jeffrey Richter • ISBN 0-7356-2163-2

For more information about Microsoft Press® books and other learning products, visit: **www.microsoft.com/mspress** *and* **www.microsoft.com/learning**

Microsoft Press products are available worldwide wherever quality computer books are sold. For more information, contact your book or computer retailer, software reseller, or local Microsoft Sales Office, or visit our Web site at **www.microsoft.com/mspress**. To locate your nearest source for Microsoft Press products, or to order directly, call 1-800-MSPRESS in the United States. (In Canada, call **1-800-268-2222**.)

What do you think of this book? We want to hear from you!

Do you have a few minutes to participate in a brief online survey? Microsoft is interested in hearing your feedback about this publication so that we can continually improve our books and learning resources for you.

To participate in our survey, please visit:

www.microsoft.com/learning/booksurvey

And enter this book's ISBN, 0-7356-2250-7. As a thank-you to survey participants in the United States and Canada, each month we'll randomly select five respondents to win one of five $100 gift certificates from a leading online merchant.* At the conclusion of the survey, you can enter the drawing by providing your e-mail address, which will be used for prize notification *only*.

Thanks in advance for your input. Your opinion counts!

Sincerely,

Microsoft Learning

* No purchase necessary. Void where prohibited. Open only to residents of the 50 United States (includes District of Columbia) and Canada (void in Quebec). Sweepstakes ends 6/30/2007. For official rules, see: *www.microsoft.com/learning/booksurvey*